*a century of*
NORTH WEST
European
ferries

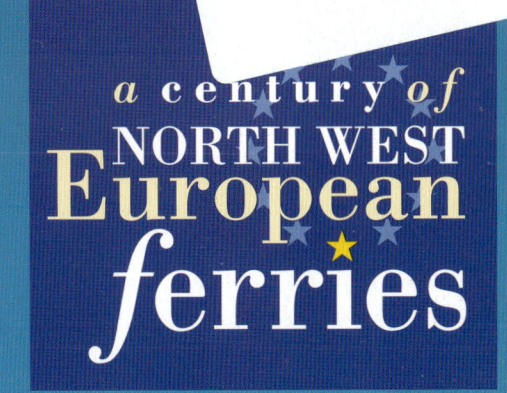

1900 – 2000

EARL GODWIN

Sealink

**Published by**
Ferry Publications,
PO Box 9, Narberth, Pembrokeshire, SA68 0YT
Tel: +44 (0) 1834 891460
Fax: +44 (0) 1834 891463

# CENTURY OF NORTH WEST EUROPEAN FERRIES 1900 - 2000

# Contents

Foreword ............................................................................................................................. 3
Introduction ....................................................................................................................... 4
The Future for the Ferry Trades ...................................................................................... 6
Marketing for the Millennium ......................................................................................... 8
**North Sea** ........................................................................................................................ 13
DFDS Group ................................................................................................................... 23
Dart Line ......................................................................................................................... 27
**Eastern Channel** ........................................................................................................... 28
Short Sea Freight ............................................................................................................ 52
Changing the Course of History - Cross-Channel Hovercraft ................................... 56
**Western Channel** .......................................................................................................... 62
Brittany Ferries into the 21st Century .......................................................................... 78
The Last Commercial British Passenger Ferry this Century ...................................... 84
**The Solent** ...................................................................................................................... 91
Wightlink ....................................................................................................................... 101
**Irish Sea** ....................................................................................................................... 104
Irish Ferries - Investing in Growth .............................................................................. 130
Stena Line - HSS 1500 .................................................................................................. 134
**Manx Waters** ............................................................................................................... 138
Sea Containers Irish Sea Operations .......................................................................... 148
**Scottish Scene** ............................................................................................................. 152
Caledonian MacBrayne's Millennium ........................................................................ 162
The Growth of Freight ................................................................................................. 166
The Train Ferry Era ...................................................................................................... 176
Fleet List ........................................................................................................................ 188

**Contributors** Graeme Dunlop, Richard Kirkman, John May; Ebbe Pedersen, Paul Hynds, Ian Carruthers, Kevin Le Scelleur, Mike Aiken, Garry O'Dea, Dick Clague, Hamish Ross, Colin Smith, Mike Blair, Matthew Punter, Alan de Burton, Brian Cork, Stephen Hepplewhite and Nick Widdows.

**Photography** DFDS, Dart Line, Stena Line, Paul Hynds; Hoverspeed, Brittany Ferries, Commodore Ferries, Wightlink; Irish Ferries, Sea Containers, Stan Basnett, Caledonian MacBrayne, FotoFlite, Dick Clague, Ambrose Greenway, Mike Louagie, John May, Dermot Walsh, Kevin Le Scelleur, Colin Smith, Henry Maxwell collection (held by John Hendy), John Bryant, Bill Mayes, Miles Cowsill and John Hendy.

**Acknowledgements** Bill Gibbons, Peter Kelly, Manx National Heritage, Andrew McNeill, Brian Mylchreest, Brendan O'Friel, John Pryce, Captain Jack Ronan, John Shepherd, Roger Sims, Lt Cdr Harold Thornber, Robin Boyd Aikman Smith Collection, the Clyde River Steamer Club, Alastair Cormack, Andrew Lowe (Haven Colourprint) and Pat Somner (Ferry Publications).

**Copyright** Ferry Publications 1999

Published by

Ferry Publications

# CENTURY OF NORTH WEST EUROPEAN FERRIES 1900 - 2000

# Foreword

I am delighted to have been asked to write the foreword to this book about passenger ferries by two very well known shipping authors, Miles Cowsill and John Hendy.

My experience with passenger ferries goes back to 1977, when I was Portsmouth manager for Sealink's new passenger service to the Channel Islands; with a second-hand vessel purchased from Townsend Thoresen renamed *Earl William*. At the same time Brittany Ferries, still in their infancy, started their new service from Portsmouth to St Malo in the teeth of opposition from the Southampton dockers; who rightly saw this service from the new ferry port of Portsmouth as the death knell of Southampton as a ferry port. I moved to Harwich where the Sealink port boasted nine British flag vessels in 1979, including two passenger ferries on the Harwich to Hook of Holland route.

It is amazing to recall that the two vessels then on the Hook route boasted first class cabins with no shower or lavatory and Duty Free shops were holes in the wall. The replacement of the *St. Edmund* and *St. George* with the jumbo ferry *St. Nicholas* in 1983 was a major step up in quality and economy of scale. I ended my time with Sealink in 1990, after three very enjoyable years as General Manager of the highly profitable Isle of Wight ferries (now Wightlink). For the last five years I have been very fortunate to be Director of the Passenger Shipping Association, the trade body for ferry and cruise companies.

Late 1999 is a significant time to be writing this foreword; since we have just lost the battle to gain a further extension for the sale of duty free goods. It was a good fight; we won the campaign in the UK and very nearly won it in Europe. The ferry companies stuck together and as a result the replacement regime, whilst complicated, does offer the possibility of substantially increased sales volume on ferry routes to low excise duty countries such as Belgium, France and Spain. Customers on these routes should not suffer; but the ferry companies face a substantial loss of profitability that can only be recouped by an increase in fares.

The last 25 years have seen the ferries transformed: from the image of lino and horsehair banquettes to the large cruise ferries and fast ferries of today. The wave-piercing catamaran was pioneered by Hoverspeed in 1990 and has since been joined by monohull wave piercers and the huge HSS. These craft are well suited to crossings formerly made by traditional ferries in 3-7 hours and can reduce times by nearly 50%. There are still weather and reliability problems; but the new technology has now been embraced by Condor, Hoverspeed, the Isle of Man Steam Packet, Irish Ferries, Stena and P&O. Reliability and the need to carry freight has also caused the emergence of the ro-pax concept as a back up for fast ferries. I feel confident that in five years time the fast ferry will predominate as the prime passenger carrier on all medium length routes; though not on the longer overnight crossings.

*Bill Gibbons*

The advent of Eurotunnel has been a challenge to the ferry sector, but has also spurred a huge increase in quality. In 1998 Eurotunnel carried 3.37 million cars against 3.46 million cars on the ferry routes out of Kent; giving the Tunnel a market share of nearly 50%. However, the market has continued to grow substantially and there is no doubt that Eurotunnel has been a major contributor. As a result of Eurotunnel, two quality companies on peripheral routes, Olau and Sally, have withdrawn.

The joint venture between P&O and Stena is a very positive step. Customers from Dover now have the choice between high quality British or French cruise ferries, fast catamarans and hovercraft. In the meantime, there has been huge investment on the Irish Sea by both Stena and Irish Ferries.

The *Herald of Free Enterprise* and *Estonia* disasters were major setbacks, but have led to major increases in safety, both in equipment and culture.

There is a huge further market to be tapped - only about 11% of UK registered cars cross to Europe or Ireland by ferry every year. With Duty Free behind us, we should concentrate on market growth and quality pricing. Investment in new tonnage will soon be required on major routes and P&O have already ordered two new cruise ferries for their Hull North Sea routes. The Industry looks forward with confidence.

*Bill Gibbons,*
*Director, Passenger Shipping Association*

# CENTURY OF NORTH WEST EUROPEAN FERRIES 1900 - 2000

# Introduction

The British Railways turbine steamer *Canterbury* about to leave Folkestone for Boulogne during the early 1950's. *(Henry Maxwell)*

The twentieth century was one of great change. In 1900 the Victorian era was at its end, Britain still rejoiced in her greatness and our transport systems were the envy of the civilised world. This publication attempts to summarise and capture those changes and to highlight just how the ferry industry in particular has progressed.

In 1900 the vast majority of sea routes were run by British-built ships and owned by an array of British-operated railway companies. The main role of what were then termed 'packet steamers' was to enable passengers to continue their rail journeys to distant destinations linking the express trains of their owners to those of the overseas railway companies.

Port selection had been relatively simple and usually involved the harbour at the closest point of any particular railway network to the foreign shore. The Great Eastern Railway chose Harwich, the London Chatham & Dover

# CENTURY OF NORTH WEST EUROPEAN FERRIES 1900 - 2000

Railway - Dover, the London & South Western Railway - Southampton, the Great Western Railway - Weymouth, the London & North Western Railway - Holyhead and so on. But what was seen as an ideal situation for the Victorian railway companies often posed something of a problem to modern day vehicle ferry operators. Road communications to such ports as Newhaven, Weymouth, Fishguard and Stranraer have been a positive hindrance to the development of the modern trades, and as traffic volumes increased in the last quarter of the century, a number of non-railway ports attracted new operators eg Portsmouth, Felixstowe, Pembroke Dock, Sheerness, Ramsgate and Cairnryan.

But not only have the ports and the nature of their being changed. In order to accommodate the growing traffic demands, the ships themselves have undergone a total design revolution.

The lift-on/lift-off era still survives on the Penzance - Isles of Scilly service. It is a time consuming business which not only uses valuable hold space but also depends for its success on the adeptness of the crane driver into whose skilful hands the valuable vehicles are entrusted.

Side loading drive-on/drive-off operations were provided by the Dover - Dunkerque train ferries in 1936 and by 1939 the stern loading *Princess Victoria* on the Stranraer - Larne route was showing the way. Sadly and tragically the new ferries provided unseen problems for their designers, and from the loss of the *Princess Victoria* (of 1946) in 1953 to that of the *Herald of Free Enterprise* in 1987 the lessons were slow to be learned. Legislation by the Government since the enquiry into the Zeebrugge disaster has been a great catalyst of change and there is no doubt that ferry travel in 1999 is safer than it has ever been.

The rise of roll-on/roll-off vehicle traffic from the late 1960s onwards has demanded greater vehicle deck headroom and the first generation of drive-on ferries, built primarily for summer tourist traffic, was soon outmoded. A series of conversions prolonged the useful careers of a number of vessels but with demand for freight space ever increasing, larger double-decked freight/ car/ passenger ferries were introduced from 1980.

The change from paddle to steam turbine propulsion after 1903 saw the tried and trusted side-wheelers hastily replaced by most operators. Early diesel-driven ships were slow to develop, their machinery being costly to install and both noisy and vibratory. There was justified concern that the comfort of passengers might be compromised. It will be remembered that the inventor Dr. Rudoph Diesel was lost overboard from the GER steam turbine vessel *Dresden* in 1913.

The pioneers of motor driven cross-Channel ships were DFDS in 1925, the Belfast Steamship Company in 1929 and Belgian Marine in 1934, but the final steam-driven car ferry to be withdrawn was the Isle of Man side loading car ferry *Ben-my-Chree* in 1985.

The railway fleets are now consigned to history and only the French through their SNCF subsidiary SeaFrance have any national interest in their ferry industry. Lack of investment was latterly a severe problem for the British railway-owned fleet (later Sealink) and coupled with the inability of its masters to construct vessels which reflected the changing non-railway based trends in traffic, was to have long lasting repercussions.

At Southampton in 1964 Otto Thoresen led the way for all operators by providing the first mixed traffic ferries (ie passengers, cars and freight) and succeeding on routes that had previously been abandoned as uneconomic. However from a marketing perspective it was Townsend some two years earlier that had provided the real first break with tradition by introducing a pale green-hulled ship. Thoresen's shocking orange provided the stimulus for change and even the staid British Rail adopted blue hulls for their vessels. Caledonian MacBrayne's fleet of Clyde and Western Isles ferries are today the only ships to retain the traditional black hull but even they now make use of the free advertising spaces that a large hull provides.

Influenced by the legislation introduced since the 'Herald' disaster, fast craft have, in recent years, made distinct inroads into many routes. They provide a cheaper but, we suspect, a short-term alternative to new ship building, although they have failed to provide the answer on longer routes. Erroneously referred to by their owners as 'wave piercers', fast craft have proved grossly uncomfortable on any crossing longer than 3 hours and are still very much fine weather vessels. They are unreliable in that they are plainly unable to provide a year-round service and experience has shown that they require the back-up of a conventional ferry. This intelligence has proved painful to some operators who unwisely believed that the introduction of such craft was the answer to all their prayers.

It is certainly true that on their day fast craft have reintroduced fast passages and it is pointed out later by Richard Kirkman that prior to their introduction, against the trend of all other types of passenger transport, the ferry industry had actually slowed down its crossing times during the twentieth century.

Regular readers of our quarterly journal 'European Ferry Scene' (now in its second successful decade) will recognise this celebratory book as an extension of the service which we provide for the followers of the ferry industry. The participating companies are warmly thanked for their timely input and support for the book which we hope will not only serve as a record of the development of the twentieth century's short sea ships and services but also as a statement of belief and support to all those who are continuing the proud and honourable tradition into the next millennium.

*Miles Cowsill,*
Narberth,
Pembrokeshire.

*John Hendy,*
Staplehurst,
Kent

# CENTURY OF NORTH WEST EUROPEAN FERRIES 1900 - 2000

# The future for the ferry trades

The next 10 years will see significant change in the ferry industry. The trend for Britain to become increasingly integrated into the European Union looks set to continue - at least industrially and commercially. As a consequence of this, the freight market has been growing at 6% per annum on average over the past 10 years: a rate of more than twice GDP growth. This trend is expected to continue. Year on year growth may fluctuate according to cyclical factors, but the trend, averaged, will be for 5% to 6% annual growth.

The freight ferry market is not affected by the abolition of tax and duty free sales and is relatively unexposed to the new SOLAS requirements. The fleet is however relatively elderly, and we envisage a series of new freight ferries appearing over the next decade. New vessels will be larger and faster than existing ships. They will be designed for ease and speed of turnround in port, and they will be more economically efficient and better able to deliver a profit.

Government and EU policy will affect the freight market, since there is a policy objective to get freight off roads and onto rail, or onto short sea shipping. How this will work in practice is unclear. However, the major points in favour of the continued strength of the Dover Straits routes are:-

a) the relatively uncongested road access to Calais from all of Europe

b) the frequency of crossings and speed of transit via the Dover Straits

c) these routes will always be the most economic to operate.

Whilst we expect to see growth in through rail movements via the Channel Tunnel, this will only slow the growth in the demand for freight on ferries, it will not reverse it. Through rail is not economic for even medium distance intermodal traffic.

*Graeme Dunlop*

The last decade has seen a boom in cross-Channel passenger movements. This has been driven by a combination of the growing attraction of day trips and short breaks to the residents of the south east of England for tax paid shopping in France and the falling cost of travel. The longer ferry routes across the North Sea and Western Channel grew more slowly and the number of passengers using Belgian ports has declined.

On 1st July 1999, tax and duty-free allowances were abolished for ferry travel within the EU. This is important because the profit made by the ferry companies from duty-free sales was used to reduce ticket prices for the travelling public. Now that tax and duty-free revenues have been lost, fares will rise. The dilemma is to what extent an increase in ferry fares

The *P&OSL Dover* and *P&OSL Kent* pass each other in mid-Channel during their daily routine on the Dover Strait. *(FotoFlite)*

will cut demand. Several passenger routes have closed in recent years and more may now be under pressure.

When the pound's value falls below eight French francs, then France becomes an expensive destination for British travellers and the main holiday market suffers. Conversely, at present exchange levels, the UK is relatively expensive for inbound tourists. Couple this with the point that non-EU holiday destinations are becoming increasingly competitive and this means that the main holiday market, which used to be the mainstay of ferry revenues, is less certain than it used to be. This market is price and product sensitive; and the weather in Brittany is less reliable than in the Caribbean. Ferry operators have offset this by growing the day trip and mini-break market especially during the shoulder and winter periods.

In addition the European ferry industry faces the challenge of modifying its fleet to comply with the new SOLAS regulations. The older ships will not comply with these regulations: the younger ships will. Whether we upgrade existing ships - or purchase newbuildings - the industry faces further capital expenditure. In a normal market this need not be a problem; it is part of ferry operating. The dilemma is if and when to switch from multi-purpose ferries to high speed craft.

High speed craft may be the craft of the future: they offer a speed of transit which the consumer prefers, especially on the medium distance routes like Portsmouth-Cherbourg. They offer the chance to grow the market by creating day-trip travel and enhancing a crossing that is seen by some potential travellers as too long on a conventional ferry. The issue is when can these craft deliver the necessary service, comfort and reliability, particularly in rough weather. The long term solution for some routes may be high speed craft running in parallel with ro-pax ships, with the ro-pax offering the bad weather backstop. However, on Dover-Calais the multi-purpose ship may remain as it is, since the 75 minute journey time is needed to allow passengers the time to eat, drink, shop and relax. Furthermore, they carry freight as well as passengers.

In terms of supply, the Channel Tunnel is arguably full of cars at crucial times of the day. It could increase the number of shuttles it operates, but this may involve enhancing the signalling system in the Tunnel and against any serious commercial criteria such investment should not happen in the near future. Indeed Eurotunnel should look to increase its yield per car. The ferry industry will continue to improve the quality of product available - where it is commercially sensible to do so.

We can therefore summarize as follows: Freight demand will continue to grow at a multiple of GDP growth. Assuming that the loss of tax and duty free income can at least partly be offset elsewhere, then passenger demand may stabilise and then grow at GDP growth. The quality of ship, and the relevance of the service it offers, will improve. Yield levels for both passengers and freight will improve, and with it profitability. Barriers to entry will however grow, with the established operators consolidating their positions on the prime routes.

Finally, the market will change as a result of the falling cost of air travel for passengers and an anti-road policy from both the EU and the British Government. As ever, survival will be for those who evolve with a changing market.

*Graeme Dunlop,*
*Chairman, P&O Ferries.*

P&O North Sea Ferries' *Norstar* leaving Zeebrugge for Hull. *(Mike Louagie)*

# CENTURY OF NORTH WEST EUROPEAN FERRIES 1900 - 2000

## Marketing for the Millennium

The twentieth century has seen dramatic changes in the style, quality and image of the ferry industry, matched by equally exciting developments in the way services have been marketed. The last twenty years have witnessed an information revolution, with developments in computer technology enabling operators to understand their customers intimately, and compete on a wider stage undreamed of a century ago.

For much of the century, ferry companies invariably served one of two simple purposes - providing a 'lifeline' service to outlying islands, or being part of an 'international' rail/sea link. The manner in which they approached promotion of the product was intrinsically linked to this core purpose. Thus the Isle of Man Steam Packet Company produced elaborate and highly detailed guides to holidays on the island, whereas the railway-owned cross-Channel operators focused more closely on the ferry being part of a through journey from, for example, London to Paris.

Railway companies utilised the selling opportunities created by their large station network. Yet most Island visitors also travelled by rail, and railway stations were also fertile ground for their advertisements, often in the form of artistic posters supplemented at key locations by accurately detailed ship models. Ships and rail/sea routes were promoted by extension of the classic railway poster, many of which are collectors' items today. These differing products were rarely in competition as the days of mass tourism were far off. Bookings were largely conducted by post or through railway station outlets. With high passenger certificates on ships and little control over numbers, advance reservations were rarely required.

In 1928 Capt. Stuart Townsend set out to challenge the railway monopoly on Channel crossings and the era of car based continental holidays began to take off. Early brochures focused on ships and cars, demonstrating the novelty and freedom of this new holiday proposition. The strange concept of craning cars aboard ships, and later driving them on, was presented visually for the uninitiated. Business growth was inhibited by the outbreak of war and the austere years that followed. Only during the 1950's did volumes really begin to expand, with rapid growth

*Richard Kirkman*

thereafter. The choice of routes and operators paralleled these developments in traffic.

Two distinct markets developed; the day-tripper - frequently on foot - and the tourist party travelling with a vehicle. The catchment for the former was very limited until short-sea operators grabbed the initiative by offering cheap day trip travel. Prices fell to as low as £1 return, promoted through national newspapers, with operators hoping to recover ticket price losses through sales of profitable duty free products. The strategy successfully generated off-peak volume, but at significant cost to the image of the industry - the 'booze cruise' tag took time to shake off. Hoverspeed eventually took this to its inevitable conclusion by paying passengers £1 to travel - surely unique in the transport business!

Cross-Channel Rail/Sea products survived until the opening of the Channel Tunnel, when the interests of the operating partners diverged. Promotion of long distance travel switched to the Eurostar services, but some of the new rail franchisees, notably Connex and South West Trains, have jointly promoted to localised catchments with ferry operators. Elsewhere, Irish routes have long been dependent

# CENTURY OF NORTH WEST EUROPEAN FERRIES 1900 - 2000

The *Pride of Portsmouth* (ex *Olau Britannia*) and *Pride of Le Havre* (ex *Olau Hollandia*) pass each other on their current daily routine between Portsmouth and Le Havre. *(FotoFlite)*

on rail connections, and these have been developed further post-privatisation.

The threat of the Channel Tunnel hung over the cross-Channel ferry industry for more than a century and the marketers had plenty of time in which to prepare their strategy. Brian Langford's famous 'Loo and a Lightbulb' condemnation of Eurotunnel's facilities emphasised the counter-positioning that the ferries had by then taken, with quality facilities backed by enhanced frequency. The merger of P&O and Stena ferry interests created strong competition for the tunnel, but it is noticeable that, once initially established, Eurotunnel did not identify a need to be 'more famous' through above the line advertising.

The classic image of a low quality - high discomfort cross-Channel ferry persisted through the 1980's, but the 90's delivered a revolution in quality and image. The cross-Channel ferry was the only method of transport that could boast journey times at the end of the century often slower than at its start. But the arrival of fast craft in Europe re-introduced speed, and delivered a sexy new product for the marketing teams to promote.

What was the exclusive preserve of the cruise liner of the 1970s and '80s is now commonplace aboard Cruiseferries. The modern vessel combines the attributes of a floating hotel, an entertainment complex, a high quality restaurant and a shopping centre as well as being a means of transport. The '5 star' graded vessels outmatch the facilities of many comparable shore establishments - the *Pride of*

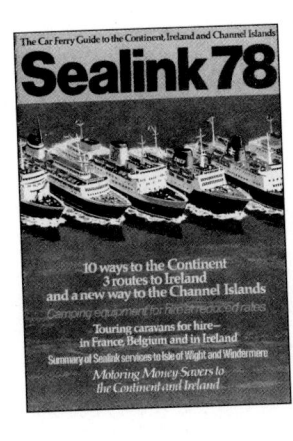

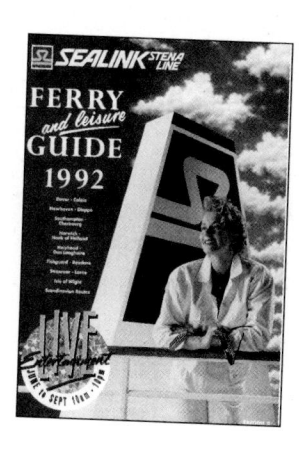

# CENTURY OF NORTH WEST EUROPEAN FERRIES 1900 - 2000

*Bilbao*, for example, has more beds than any hotel in Britain.

External threats to the industry from the Channel Tunnel and the loss of Duty Free revenues have catalysed major changes in its structure. Few of the major brands operating in 1999 have survived intact and unchanged for more than 15 years. Only Brittany Ferries can be said to fit into this category.

Changing ownership and consequent branding changes only create confusion in the minds of the consumer. In a little over a decade, the operator of the Newhaven-Dieppe service was variously branded as Sealink, Sealink British Ferries, Dieppe Ferries, Sealink Stena Line, Stena Sealink, Stena Line, P&O Stena Line and now Hoverspeed. This hardly contributes to customer confidence in continuity of the line! Investment in development of clear branding pays off. P&O European Ferries spent heavily after the take-over of Townsend Thoresen in brand advertising to create an image consistent with the core values of the company, which delivered clear consistency whilst its rivals metamorphosed from one identity to another. It's a salutary lesson that, unless the branding is carried through to the on board experience, customers often have little appreciation of which company they are sailing with.

The harsh realities of successful branding become apparent when you take a successful brand like P&O European Ferries and create new companies out of the old. Launching P&O Portsmouth in spring 1999 was an exciting task handed to London based tourism and leisure specialists Senior King. Following the creation of P&O Stena Line, the P&O operated cross-Channel services from Portsmouth still operated under the P&O European Ferries banner in a market place confused by changes in operator name. A new identity was needed to focus on the key attributes of the Portsmouth services and create a clear distinction from the legacy of the past. Hence P&O Portsmouth, and a new distinctive style. It will, however, take time to eradicate the old images.

These changes for P&O parallel a general move from big brands to smaller decentralised units, where individual operating companies project their own image. Hoverspeed have successfully retained the identity of individual brands within their corporate structure, with individual route brochure for different markets permitting new brands like the Argyll and Antrim Steamship Co to enter the arena.

On the High Street it is more difficult. The complexity of the ferry product and the constantly changing portfolio of routes and operators makes life extraordinarily difficult for the typical Travel Agent. As rates have fallen in real terms through the 1990's, so the commission payment to agents has reduced, resulting in less enthusiasm for promoting the product. Yet these outlets remain a prime distribution source for the ferry operator.

Internally, the old reservations department has become today's call centre. From the early days of manual records of passengers and sailings, to the highly complex computer systems employed today, the reservations function represents the heart of the business. From acting as an order-taking unit, the call centre has become a sophisticated extension to the sales force, capable of delivering a significant improvement to profitability.

As the quality and style of the ferry product has developed, so the operators have been faced with the dilemma of how to present their services. Each route and company has its own view on the appropriate attributes to promote, leading to a range of different approaches in different markets and media. In 1998, ferry companies spent around £19 million on 'above the line' advertising in the UK alone – down slightly from the

# CENTURY OF NORTH WEST EUROPEAN FERRIES 1900 - 2000

peak of £23 million in 1996 to counter the impact of the Channel Tunnel. The highest proportion (42%) of this total was spent on press advertising, with television spend (36%) accounting for the bulk of the remainder.

Historically the ship was the focus of attention in brochures and image advertising as the new concept of taking a car on a continental holiday grew. Today's operators have an almost bewildering range of selling opportunities and choose to promote themselves in a myriad of different ways. Some are listed below:

**Ships** - particularly those focusing on the Minicruise market
**Routes** - especially those with a wide route structure, or with significant geographical strengths
**Destination** - for those with a strong in-house holiday product or strong links with an island community
**Price** - particularly in the competitive short sea and Irish markets
**Duty Free and Onboard sales** - pioneered by Stena Line
**Entertainment** - built around Cruiseferry products
**Frequency** - for the short sea sector
**Crossing time** - in the fast craft business

Changes in booking pattern have altered the way in which operators plan their advertising campaigns. The travel industry as a whole has encouraged late booking, so the days when the family sat down, chose and booked their summer holiday immediately after Christmas have gone. There is still a strong early booking market, particularly on longer routes and for peak events such as the Isle of Man TT and the Le Mans 24 hour race, but the advent of greater cross-Channel capacity has generally encouraged a 'turn up and go' mentality. The implication of this for the ferry operator is that the period over which advertising needs to take place is much longer - arguably across the full season. Budgets can therefore be stretched quite thinly.

Having decided what to promote, there is then the question of how to promote it. The most expensive option by far is television. Available as an option only to the wealthiest operators, it is used regionally by some as a cost-effective means of hitting high audience levels in key catchment areas. Done well it can be highly memorable, done badly it becomes 'wallpaper'. Witness the effectiveness of P&O Stena Line's launch advert, whose musical accompaniment led to switchboards being jammed by viewers trying to identify the source. Digital television will massively expand the range of channels available to the viewer, and whilst making large audiences more inaccessible it will deliver the niche grouping.

Outdoor advertisements also hit large audiences in key locations, and high impact can be achieved by a high-density campaign over a short period of time. Many of the most creative images can be found in this medium. Long term holdings of sites at major 'chokepoints' on the road network can deliver huge viewership.

Radio has an increasing niche of the market, and it is increasingly popular to hit 'drivetime' travellers, for these are the natural car-borne target markets. Humour is used extensively and campaigns can be switched on at short notice.

The growth of travel supplements in weekend newspapers illustrates the general growth in the press advertising. An ongoing presence here provides relatively low cost exposure over a long period of time, particularly if a journal with a long 'shelf life' is chosen.

# CENTURY OF NORTH WEST EUROPEAN FERRIES 1900 - 2000

The above can all be wasteful mass media. Given that just 12% of the UK cars ever travel abroad, it is inevitable that television, radio, press and outdoor advertisements hit many people for whom they were not designed. More targeted delivery is therefore required. One of the most important assets of the Ferry Company of the future will be its database of customers and prospects. Ongoing communication with this group delivers a highly productive source of business. Profiling of the socio-demographic characteristics of this group defines further target prospects with similar lifestyles. The result is a sophisticated understanding of customers linked to their travel records to whom highly targeted communications can be addressed. This permits the development of loyalty schemes for regular customers, rewarding them for their custom.

For many, the clearest exposition of the individual company's offerings is found in the timetable and tariff brochures. They have been the primary source of communication with customers for many years, at a huge cost in production and distribution.

The style of brochures closely reflects their era, and there is no better social history of recent years than to look at the development of the ferry brochure through this period. The 1950's saw austere brochures with limited ship photography, reflecting the post war years. The optimism of the 1960's is seen in the introduction of bold colour, with stylised 'happy families' in their shining cars being pointed to gleaming ships by smiling staff. The 1970's were brasher, often using models on the cover. Ships came to the fore in the 1980's, whilst the 1990's saw more avant-garde approaches - particularly from P&O, who at one point included a free packet of sunflower seed on the cover.

The sheer complexity of scheduling and pricing of the ferry product has lead to many creative approaches to the layout of timetables and fares, with almost as many variants of design as there are operators. However the brochure has become an inflexible medium. Ferry fares, and indeed schedules, can change at a moment's notice, especially in the highly competitive cross-Channel arena. Finding a competitor's prices have undercut you as 200,000 brochures roll off the printing press can be highly wasteful. Brochures are now moving to the point where 'lead-in' prices are quoted, allowing the operator flexibility in pricing to respond to competitors and to demand for space.

A key recent innovation has been revenue management; the allocation of space to different 'bands' of customers at different rates, and the management of this allocation process by mechanical means, as in the airline industry. This creates a dynamic environment where space availability and price can vary by the hour. The days of publishing prices before Christmas and considering the task done for the year are long gone.

Future development of the Internet will allow accurate and dynamic on-line price quotations and bookings and will potentially supersede the traditional brochure. The Internet is rapidly opening up new opportunities, giving faster than ever customer access to pricing, product and punctuality information on a global scale. For the first time it is as easy to access information in Dubai as Douglas, in San Francisco as Scrabster. This brings new operator responsibilities to keep information fresh whilst creating new markets from hitherto largely untapped territory. As the technology develops, it has the potential to deliver a 'virtual brochure' anywhere, the ability to take a 3D tour of a vessel, and deliver seamless booking procedure with accurate pricing - a mouth-watering prospect. In summer 1999 on-line bookings have become a reality. With the explosion in e-commerce led by the United States, the possibilities of this medium are only just becoming apparent and the technology knows no bound for the future.

Change has become a way of life for the ferry industry, with the pace accelerating as the century developed. The only certainty about the new millennium is that the industry will have to compete even harder for business in the expanding leisure arena. The marketing and sales teams will play their part in ensuring the survival and prosperity of one of the most exciting and dynamic businesses in this sector.

*Richard Kirkman*

*Richard Kirkman joined Railtrack in September 1999 after a distinguished career in the ferry industry. His involvement in the ferry business extended over 15 years having worked for Sealink, BCIF, Isle of Man Steam Packet Co. Ltd and P&O Portsmouth.*

# CENTURY OF NORTH WEST EUROPEAN FERRIES 1900 - 2000

# North Sea

The wide and tempestuous seas between Duncansby Head and the Thames have seen vast changes in the ferry ships crossing them during the course of the 20th century. While providing some of the longest ferry crossings from the United Kingdom, they have continued to provide relatively few passenger services but an unending kaleidoscope of primarily freight routes provided by a range of vessels including the most advanced representatives of each generation.

Although ferry services have operated from almost all of the East Coast ports, it is from the five principal estuaries of Eastern England that the more significant services have operated.

## THE TYNE

At the beginning of the twentieth century the Bergen Line had almost half a century's experience of running its ships between Norway and the Tyne. Regular passenger and mail services had commenced more recently by the company and its long-standing rival in the Norwegian trade, Fred. Olsen Line in 1890, in their case running to the capital, Christiania (later renamed Oslo). Although Norwegian companies have remained in operation to the Tyne to the close of the millennium, they have never had a monopoly on services from Newcastle, but operation by British companies has been limited.

At the start of the century the Bergen Steamship Company stood as the leading shipping company in Norway with a fleet of 20 ships on 10 different services, including routes to Hamburg and Newcastle. The latter was served by the *Venus* and the *Vega*, both having been built in England and measuring only slightly over 1,000 tonnes each. By 1914, a daily service had been established, providing direct crossings in thirty-three hours, with certain sailings being diverted via Haugesund and Stavanger. Although regular services were provided throughout the year, even at the beginning of the century the Bergen Line employed several of their vessels on cruising through the fjords of the west coast of Norway and certain services from the Tyne were extended in summer to the northern city of Trondheim. In 1912, it was even proposed that the Norwegian Coastal Steamer Services, the Hurtigrute, should be extended to Newcastle but the proposal was rejected by the Norwegian Parliament, mainly due to the inadequacy of the steamers then in operation on the coast to maintain crossings of the North Sea in winter.

Service was continued during World War I until in November 1916 the *Vega* was stopped by a German U-boat and, her cargo having been declared to be contraband, was sunk by gunfire. This led to a suspension of services which were resumed in November 1918, only fifteen days after the Armistice. Modern anti-competitive restrictions had no place at the time and an agreement was shortly reached with Ellerman Wilson Line defining the sphere of influence of each company in the North Sea, which gave rise to the confidence which enabled further new vessels to be ordered in 1919 and 1920. The vessels used during the 1920s were modern and comfortable and the company prospered. In 1928 the new passenger terminal at Tyne Commissioners' Quay in North Shields was opened, improving direct railway communication to the site of the ship, including through carriages from London. However, the west coast of Norway had never been able to support a regular year-round

The fastest motor ship in the world when introduced by Bergen Line in 1931, the *Venus* survived for 37 years on North Sea services and cruising. (John May collection)

passenger trade without subsidy and the good communications between Gothenburg and Oslo and other parts of Scandinavia after the introduction of the new Swedish Lloyd service from Tilbury to Gothenburg in 1929 saw a gradual change in the business to year-round freight and summer holiday-makers. The change was emphasised by the delivery of the *Venus* in 1931, then the fastest motor ship in the world and capable of carrying 277 passengers - of whom as many as 201 were first class, joined in 1938 by a new *Vega*. The two large motor vessels provided some of the highest standards of service found on ferry routes anywhere until the outbreak of war in September 1939 forced them to be laid up. Subsequently taken over by the occupying Nazi forces, both were sunk by Allied bombing in 1945 and, whilst it proved possible for the *Venus* to be salvaged and rebuilt, her sister was irreparably damaged.

A regular service between Bergen and Newcastle was resumed in January 1946 and, with the return to service in early 1948 of the *Venus*, normal business was soon resumed. In the winter of 1948/49 she inaugurated what were to become regular winter cruises to Madeira and Tenerife, taking advantage of her splendid passenger accommodation and a capacity which continued to considerably exceed demand on North Sea services outside busy summer periods. She was joined on the ferry services in 1953 by the turbine-powered *Leda*, the last pure passenger ship to join the service. An elegant ship, built on the Tyne at Wallsend, she continued a three-times-weekly service until 1974 but, by the time of her withdrawal, the car ferry era and the explosion in fuel prices had made continued steamship operation uneconomic.

Fred. Olsen's services in the interim had followed a similar pattern. Until World War I, the company provided regular operations to Christiania (Oslo) via Arendal. Twice weekly sailings took passengers to Arendal in thirty two hours, a further ten hours being occupied with the splendid passage along the length of Oslofjord. Services were continued on a similar basis after the return of peace until a pair of beautiful motor ships were commissioned in 1938, the *Black Prince* and *Black Watch* - built in Oslo, they reduced the time on passage considerably and raised standards to the highest levels yet seen in North Sea Services. Unfortunately both were sunk by Allied bombing following seizure by the occupying Nazis but their replacements in 1951/2 were outstanding. The *Blenheim* and *Braemar* were built by Thornycrofts in Southampton and had their interiors completed in Norway. Motor vessels with high raked bows, eminently suitable for North Sea storms, they carried 100 first class passengers in total complements of 286. Slowly displaced by the arrival of car ferries, the *Blenheim* was badly damaged by fire when on passage in 1968 and her sister sailed on alone as the last

# CENTURY OF NORTH WEST EUROPEAN FERRIES 1900 - 2000

traditional North Sea passenger ship until August 1975.

The rival companies drew together with the introduction in 1966 of the large car ferries *Jupiter* and *Venus*, designed for joint operation with summer ferry duties under the Bergen Line flag and winter cruising under that of Fred. Olsen, using the alternate names of *Black Watch* and *Black Prince* respectively. During summers, the two vessels sailed from the Tyne to Bergen in the company of the increasingly outmoded *Leda*. In winter their admirable passenger accommodation carried passengers to the Canaries while their capacious vehicle decks were used for the transport of fruit to Northern Europe. Conversion between the two functions required little more than the repainting of the names and funnel designs. During the 1970s and 1980s, Bergen Line had been experiencing violent swings in its financial fortunes, finally becoming a subsidiary of the Kosmos Group in 1986. Services from the Tyne were never to be the same again, the *Venus* departed after the 1986 season for conversion to a full-time cruise ship under her alternate name of *Black Prince* and, whilst continuing to be a regular visitor to British and Norwegian ports during her cruise voyages, would not again serve as a ferry.

Her sister saw a change in her operating style in 1987, when the new owners of Bergen Line relaunched the service as Norway Line. Her place was taken in early 1990 by the former *Stena Scandinavica* (originally Sessan Line's *Prinsessan Birgitta*), yet again under the name *Venus*. The *Jupiter*, meanwhile, was sold to the Mediterranean for service with Marlines with whom she survived until the late 1990s.

The Tyne to Bergen service during the final decade of the century has seen continuing change, the route being subsumed into Color Line and the *Venus* was exchanged with DFDS for the former *King of Scandinavia* which assumed the name *Color Viking*. In early 1999 the route and vessel were sold to Fjord Line, with the ship changing her name once again to the familiar one of *Jupiter*.

Throughout the century DFDS, the Danish shipping conglomerate, had commenced operations to Newcastle in the 1880s and have maintained them continuously since, other than the interruption of the two World Wars. Until recently, the operation has been seen as subsidiary to the operations to Harwich, with vessels being moved to run to the Tyne when replaced by newer tonnage on other routes. The ships employed are considered later - the routes to Denmark and, in particular, to Esbjerg having dominated the company's operations from the Tyne and have been joined by routes to Gothenburg in Sweden, Hamburg and most recently to Ijmuiden in Holland. At the end of the century operations from the Tyne have taken over in importance from those at Harwich and the company provides the principal business of the ferry terminal at North Shields. With the abolition of Duty Free sales on journeys with the European Community the Harwich to Gothenburg service was trasferred to sail from the Tyne with an intermediate call at Kristiansand in Norway from 1999, taking advantage of calls at a neutral port.

Swedish Lloyd also provided regular services from the Tyne until the opening of their Tilbury service in 1929, also described later.

## THE TEES

Although a major export centre for coal from the early 19th century, the Tees did not come to prominence as a ferry port until the last quarter of the century. The installation of a ro-ro berth at Tees Dock in Middlesborough saw the introduction in 1978 of a new service to Sweden provided by P&O Ferrymasters, sailing twice weekly to Gothenburg, with one journey continued to Helsingborg. The vessel used, the *Elk*, provided comfortable accommodation for twelve passengers but more importantly accommodation for 80 trailers. Her services were interrupted by being requisitioned for service with the Falklands Task Force in 1982, after which she resumed her service from Middlesborough and was lengthened in 1986 to accommodate 140 trailers. Her very comfortable passenger accommodation was marketed from time to time for passengers prepared to travel on an unusual style of ferry, but pressure on crewing costs saw this end in 1998.

Although the Ferrymasters' service to Sweden has occasionally supported a second vessel, the majority of ferry traffic from the Tees has been provided by North Sea Ferries, who began operations only in 1988 with a freight service to Zeebrugge. In 1991, a series of short-term charterings were ended when the Finnish registered *Bore King* and *Bore Queen* were introduced on charter. Impressive freighters, with capacity for twelve drivers and 114 trailers, they were subsequently lengthened in 1996 to provide accommodation for 155 trailers.

1995 saw the introduction by North Sea Ferries of a new freight service to Rotterdam's Europoort, and after four years of growth in the service, the vessels from the Zeebrugge service were placed on the route, being replaced by a pair of newly-built vessels, again chartered from Bore Line, providing accommodation for 210 trailers.

Although not always recognised as a significant ferry port, due to the lack of passenger services, at the close of the century the Tees provides one of the principal focuses for freight in the North Sea.

## THE HUMBER

The century began with ferry services provided by Wilson Line, which would briefly become the world's largest shipping enterprise, and an assortment of railway companies which in time amalgamated to form Associated Humber Lines (AHL). Railway involvement included the Lancashire and Yorkshire Railway from Goole, while the Great Central Railway operated from Grimsby and its new port of Immingham. Neither AHL nor Ellerman Wilson lines - into which Wilson's was absorbed - would be able to survive the transition to roll-on/roll-off vehicle ferries and their places have been largely taken by North Sea Ferries and DFDS.

Wilsons, founded and firmly based in Hull, provided a network of services throughout Scandinavia and Northern Europe - as well as operating on routes outside the scope of this current survey across the North Atlantic and into the Mediterranean. The vessels used were among the largest ferries of their era - the *Calypso* of 1904 measured 2,962 gross tonnes and was able to carry 964 passengers, but in contrast to operations from Newcastle, no fewer than 863 of these were third class. However, the more typical steamer measured little more than 1,000 tonnes and might carry only four passengers along with a great mass of cargo which required several days to load and stow

Fred. Olsen's ***Blenheim*** of 1952, a wonderful example of streamlining in ferry design in the middle of the century. *(John May collection)*

# CENTURY OF NORTH WEST EUROPEAN FERRIES 1900 - 2000

aboard. Despite the dense network and large fleet employed, many services operated at intervals of a week or even greater.

Having started successful steamship operations in 1902 on the Irish Sea, the Lancashire and Yorkshire Railway began similar operations from its eastern port of Goole on the Humber in January 1905 with the take-over of the Goole Steam Shipping Company Ltd, with a network of services to Amsterdam, Antwerp, Bruges, Copenhagen, Dunkerque, Ghent, Hamburg and Rotterdam. Operating 19 steamers, the railway fleet sailing from unromantic Goole was considerably smaller than the competing vessels of Wilson Line but the solid freight business supplied through the railway and the enterprising switching of tonnage between Irish and North Seas to match demand at different seasons gave the services considerable prosperity. However, the railway grouping of 1923 led to a gradual co-ordination of railway services from the Humber and, from 1935, the Goole steamers of the LMS were managed by AHL. At railway nationalisation in 1948 there were nine ships in the AHL fleet at Goole, all steamers most of which were able to carry only 8 or 10 passengers. A lack of investment was partly arrested by the arrival of new vessels named *Byland Abbey* and *Kirkham Abbey* in 1957, but by the end of the 1960s ferry services had ceased at Goole.

The third railway company to provide shipping from the Humber ports was the Great Central. Their progressive and determined management not only introduced passenger sailings from Grimsby, provided by a large fleet of vessels, but also opened the new port of Immingham in 1912. In contrast to Goole, the port was close to the sea and a wide channel 70 feet deep was dredged from the entrance to the dock and continued in a straight line past Spurn Point out into the North Sea. Access to the port has consequently always been far easier and the ability to enter and leave the port at any state of the tide made the timetabling regular ferry services far easier than at other points on the Humber, but the isolated location of Immingham did not encourage the development of sophisticated passenger services. The ships provided by the railway were little more than coasters of about 1,600 tons gross. Specified with speeds of only 13 knots, the vessels often required 24 hours to complete their North Sea passages - scarcely ideal for passengers crossing the stormy North Sea in winter. The steamers were absorbed into AHL in 1935 and continued in a generally similar fashion but were depleted by war losses during World War II, when four of the five ships served as convoy rescue ships and, although only one was lost in this hazardous service, the other three were then transferred to Hull and Harwich. It would take many years before ferry services to Grimsby and Immingham would resume and they would be in a very different form when they did.

Wilsons had continued to operate their network of services from Hull, although the family had sold out to Ellermans in 1917. The ships continued to operate with their distinctive green hulls and red funnels with black tops as an effectively independent part of the giant Ellerman empire. The size of the fleet slowly dwindled during the 1960s and in 1966 the company joined with a consortium of Swedish Lloyd and Svea Line to form the England-Sweden Line which was to provide frequent and regular sailings for passengers, cars and containerised cargoes between Hull, London and Gothenburg. The vessel ordered for the service, the *Spero*, was built by Cammell Laird in Birkenhead to accommodate 408 passengers and 100 cars. Despite the luxury and comfort of the ship, her facilities did not match demand in the service which saw little scope for passenger carrying outside the summer season, particularly with the development of reliable airline services which took most passenger traffic at other times of the year. The continental terminal was transferred in 1972 to Zeebrugge while the Gothenburg route was taken over by new ro-ro freighters. However, the *Spero* never fulfilled the high hopes of a profitable trade and was sold in January 1973 to NEL Lines, the Maritime Company of Lesbos in Greece, with whom she remained in service until the close of the century.

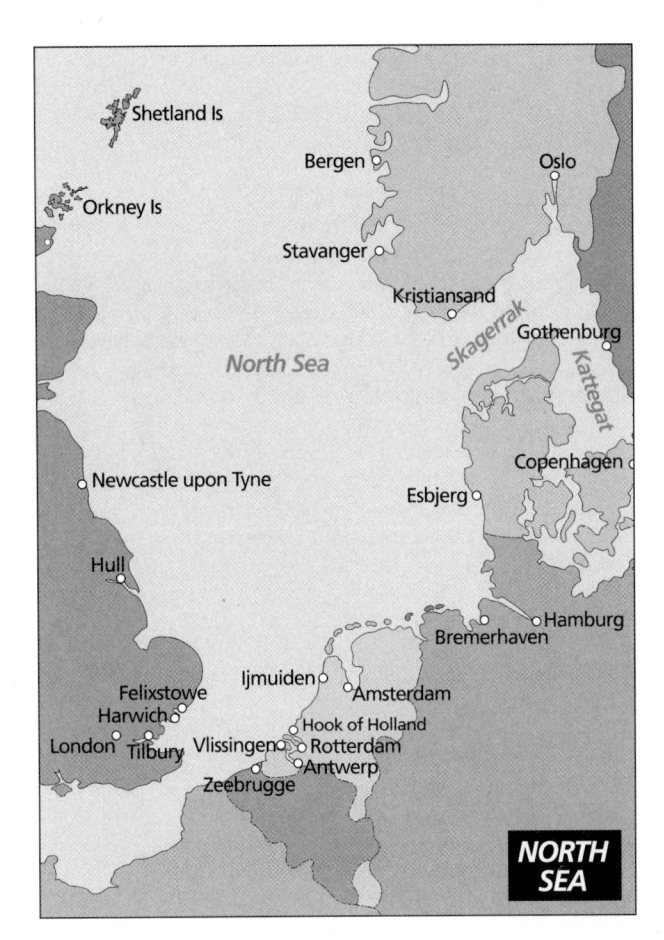

Ellerman's final ferry services were provided by freight vessels, including the *Hero* which was jointly owned with DFDS but was lost in a storm on passage to Esbjerg in 1977. With her sinking, the spirit of the company appeared to flag and, by 1980, it had completely abandoned shipping and the company finally closed.

The decline of the traditional British operators from the Humber had seen further growth by DFDS, primarily on services from Denmark to Grimsby and to Immingham. Although the company has never operated regular passenger service to the Humber, it has always been one of the principal delivery points for Danish farm produce and a succession of early ro-ro vessels were used during the 1960s and 1970s to develop the trade. Particularly notable was the *Dana Maxima* of 1978, built in Japan to exploit to the extreme the dimensions of the locks giving access to the dock system at Grimsby. As trade continued to grow, it became impossible to continue to use the facilities there and operations have transferred to an enlarged complex at Immingham, where DFDS have become one of the principal ro-ro operators. Freed from the constraints of the locks, the *Dana Maxima* has been lengthened and joined in service by a succession of ever larger freighters including the three *Tor Selandia* class vessels - scarcely imaginable at 24,196 tonnes and with capacity for 230 trailers when compared with the Great Central ship *Accrington* of 1910, measuring just 1,629 tonnes and carrying but a fraction of the loads of the ships that would ultimately take her place.

Immingham had in the interim become a passenger ferry port for a decade following the opening by the Tor Line consortium of a triangular service linking the port with Amsterdam and Gothenburg. The 22 knot *Tor Anglia* opened the route in March 1966 and with her sister *Tor Hollandia* and maintained it until

# CENTURY OF NORTH WEST EUROPEAN FERRIES 1900 - 2000

A line of steamers at Hull's riverside berths in the 1920s, the nearest being the **Duke of Clarence** on the LNER's service to Zeebrugge. *(John May collection)*

A North Sea ferry of the early years of the century, Lancashire & Yorkshire Railway's **Mellifont** operated from Goole to Antwerp until being transferred in 1912 to the company's services in the Irish Sea. *(John May collection)*

replaced a decade later by the large sister ships described below which joined the service (now omitting the leg to Amsterdam) at the time of its transfer to Felixstowe.

Meanwhile, back in Hull, despite the constraints of the lock system, ferry services had been revolutionised in December 1965 by the commencement of services by North Sea Ferries. The company initially shared facilities in Hull's King George Dock with Ellerman Wilson's *Spero* and the final gasps of Associated Humber Lines operations which were being gradually subsumed into the German Argo group.

Successive generations of roll-on/roll-off ferries have seen a steady development in the company's operations. The original pair of *Norwind* and *Norwave* initially operated to Rotterdam's Europoort. Measuring exactly 4,000 gross tons, and with capacity for 249 passengers, their principal business was carried on their vehicle decks which could accommodate 47 trailers and 70 cars. Rapidly achieving an enviable degree of reliability, they quickly saw off the last remnants of the AHL services and revolutionised ferry operations from the Humber. Sailing nightly and with an innovative fares structure which included the cost of meals within the passage ticket, they rapidly built up trade.

By 1974, they were unequal to the traffic that was then on offer and were replaced by the elegant *Norland* and *Norstar*, vastly bigger at 12,988 tons and with capacity for 1,243 passengers - again the vehicle capacity of 134 trailers and 72 cars was the source of their financial success. The *Norland* saw distinguished service as part of the British Task Force in the recapture of the Falkland Islands in 1982 but returned safely to port. The two ships were lengthened in 1987 when replaced on the Rotterdam service by the newly built *Norsun* and *Norsea*. They then took the place of the first pair on the service that the latter had inaugurated to Zeebrugge in 1974 and on which they had again been rendered obsolete by the growth of traffic.

The new pair of vessels, built to almost identical designs but in the very different surroundings of Glasgow and Yokohama, presented a further enlargement, measuring 31,598 tons and providing accommodation for 1,250 passengers and 180 trailers (or a combination of trailers and cars). They now measure 25.36 metres in breadth, giving less than one foot of clearance on each side of the vessel as it enters and leaves the 25.9 metre wide lock into the King George dock in Hull. Continuing to sail nightly at 18:30 from each port, they provide an extremely comfortable passage, making the 197 nautical mile crossing in 13½ hours.

The ownership of the company, initially based on a consortium of British and Dutch businesses but from 1981 equally owned by P&O and Royal Nedlloyd, was further changed in September 1996 when P&O finally purchased their Dutch partner's share. With effect from 1997, the company has traded as P&O North Sea Ferries and has continued to prosper. The century has closed with P&O having placed orders for two 60,000 tonnes superferries, ordered from Italy's Fincantieri yards for delivery in 2001.

Wilson Line's **Aaro** of 1909 was used on the company's services until being torpedoed and sunk by a U-boat in 1916. The illustration is from a series of paintings commissioned by the company at the height of its prosperity in the first decade of the century. *(John May collection)*

Launched in 1940 but not completed until after World War II, the DFDS mailship **Kronprins Frederik** sailed between Esbjerg and Harwich until replaced by the car ferry *England* in 1964. She was sold for further operation in the Red Sea during 1976. *(John May collection)*

16

# CENTURY OF NORTH WEST EUROPEAN FERRIES 1900 - 2000

North Sea Ferries' first generation of vessel demonstrated by the **Norwind** berthed at Zeebrugge in 1986. *(John May)*

### THE HAVEN PORTS

The long sweep of Eastern England past The Wash and around East Anglia presents few opportunities for ports capable of sustaining a ferry service. Although primarily noted for its fishing fleet, Great Yarmouth has always seen a regular coasting trade and in 1961 the Dutch Norfolk Line commenced regular operations with coasting vessels to the Dutch port of Scheveningen, the port of the capital The Hague. In 1969 this became a regular ferry service with the introduction of the ro-ro ship *Duke of Holland*. Although primarily a freight service, it briefly carried passengers in the mid 1970s. As the service prospered and the size of vessels employed had to grow the constraints of the port of Great Yarmouth became more apparent and the company transferred its operations to Felixstowe.

The Haven Ports of Felixstowe, Ipswich and Harwich together constitute one of the best natural harbours on the east coast of England and have long seen intensive ferry services for both freight and passengers.

The departure point of continental ferries since Tudor times, at the start of the 20th century Harwich rejoiced in some of the best facilities for passengers and freight to be found anywhere around the coasts of the United Kingdom. The opening of Parkeston Quay in 1893 had prepared the way for the development of services from the Essex port which has continued throughout the century.

At the start of the century services ran from Harwich to Gothenburg, Esbjerg, Hamburg, the Hook of Holland, Rotterdam and Antwerp. Although a railway-owned port until denationalisation in the mid-1980s, Harwich has always provided a hub for both passenger and freight operations in the North Sea for many companies.

Although freight operations from Harwich have spread throughout the length of the Baltic with services extending to Finland's icy Gulf of Bothnia, the most distant port to enjoy a regular passenger service has been Gothenburg. Initially provided by Swedish Lloyd as a seasonal call for passengers to save the sometimes noxious experience of a summer voyage along the Thames, the ships still required 36 hours to make the passage. The passenger service ended with the outbreak of World War II and did not revive until the transfer of the Tor Line vessels (after their acquisition by DFDS) from Felixstowe in 1983. These immensely powerful ships with a machinery design derived from the German pocket battleships of World War II provided a 23 hour crossing to Gothenburg until the last year of the century while carrying substantial quantities of freight and a passenger capacity which has grown from an original 1,350 to over 1,700 with successive rebuildings during the 1980s and '90s. While two sisters - originally named *Tor Britannia* and *Tor Scandinavia* but later the *Prince of Scandinavia* and the *Princess of Scandinavia* respectively, have served on the route, it was the latter which tended to monopolise the operation in later years, while her sistership operated on the Esbjerg and more recently on the Hamburg service. Despite their narrow hulls and massively tall funnels, the height of which more than doubles the overall distance from waterline to bridge, they are elegant vessels and their style has not been diminished by rebuilding in 1997/98 with new stability sponsons to meet the latest requirements of the Safety Of Life At Sea Regulations.

Although only intermittently enjoying ferry connections from Harwich, Norway has seen occasional services by Fred. Olsen Lines to the southern port of Kristiansand and to Oslo. While providing freight services on the North Sea for almost the entire century, Fred. Olsen's passenger services from Harwich did not begin until the delivery in 1971 of a new vessel, the *Blenheim* built by Upper Clyde Shipbuilders in Glasgow, which was an enlarged but less successful sister of Bergen Line's sisters *Jupiter* and *Venus*. The *Blenheim* spent increasing amounts of time sailing with them on the northern route until withdrawal in 1981 followed by conversion for cruising and later gambling voyages from Florida. The route was revived in 1984 using the elegant *Bolero* but was transformed in 1985 by the arrival of the superb *Braemar*, originally built for Viking Line service between Stockholm and Helsinki. Although only a weekly service fitted in between more prosaic sailings between Kristiansand and Hirtshals in Northern Denmark, the route established a niche in the market and became relatively successful. The recession of the late 1980s led to the withdrawal of the route in 1989 and direct passenger sailings to Norway have not been revived.

Although the longer services to Scandinavia have enjoyed mixed fortunes, the DFDS mail boat service from Denmark has continued its operations between Harwich and Esbjerg throughout the century, interrupted only by the two World Wars.

At the start of the century the service had already been running from Harwich for 20 years and it was still possible for the traveller to experience the joys of crossing the North Sea by paddle steamer on the *Koldinghuus*, which was not withdrawn until January 1903. Her 70 or so passengers enjoyed the customary experience of travel in the final days of Queen

# CENTURY OF NORTH WEST EUROPEAN FERRIES 1900 - 2000

Victoria's long reign with a large and splendidly equipped saloon contrasting with primitive cabins and far from luxurious bathrooms.

The company has always tended to obtain a long life from its vessels and the result has been a comparatively modest number of ships which have served on the route through the century. Among the longest lived was the *A.P. Bernstorff*, built at Helsingor in 1913, which saw service on North Sea routes until withdrawal in 1957. Her hull design was closely followed 12 years later when DFDS introduced the *Parkeston*, the world's first short sea passenger motor ship. While the inevitable vibration of her diesel engines was not always popular with her passengers, she provided considerable economic fuel consumption for a single crossing of the North Sea dropped from 55 tons of coal with the *A.P. Bernstorff* to 18 tons of oil with the new vessel and a significant reduction in the engine room crew. It was unsurprising that the *Parkeston* and her three sisters were popular vessels with the company and, despite an interruption for war service, the vessel was not withdrawn until September 1964.

Post-war services were provided by the sleek sisters *Kronprins Frederik* and *Kronprinsesse Ingrid*, both having been built at the Helsingor shipyard - the former in 1940 but laid up throughout World War II, while her sister was launched in 1949. Steady and comfortable vessels of almost 4,000 tons they had eventful lives. In April, 1953 the elder of the pair was at her berth at Parkeston Quay when an electrical fire broke out. The ministrations of the Fire Brigade put out the blaze but so filled the vessel with water that she capsized and she remained on her side at the quay until being refloated and towed to Helsingor for repair in August. Returning some 8 months later the vessel remained in service until being replaced on the route in 1964 by the similarly styled car ferry *England*, after which her career took her to the Newcastle service and then to the DFDS route to the Faroes before being sold in 1976 to a Red Sea operator. Her sister remained in service until the end of 1966 and after two years on the Newcastle service was sold to Greece, where she remained in operation until October 1983.

The car ferry era on the Danish service was introduced in 1964 with the *England*, another elegant vessel from the slipways of Helsingor. Although her unique side-loading system was very effective as a way of conveying cars in an era before the universal introduction of linkspans, the system had the considerable failing that even domestic caravans were a tight fit through the side doors of the vessel and the carriage of substantial commercial vehicles was impossible. Her consort which emerged in 1967 was the *Winston Churchill*, the first drive-through car ferry in the DFDS North Sea fleet and an ornament to the company until withdrawal at the end of the 1995 season. Her tonnage of 8,657, double that of the post-war mail ships, was comfortably overtaken by the *Dana Regina* of 1974 at 12,192 tons and finally by the *Dana Anglia* of 1978 measuring 14,399 tons. It was, however, in their vehicle capacity that the three ferries best demonstrated the progress in North Sea ship design. The *Winston Churchill* carried 180 cars and very limited commercial traffic, the *Dana Regina* carried 300 cars and 45 lorries while the final vessel accommodates 470 cars and a combination of up to 470 cars and 45 lorries. Whereas the mail ships of the 1960s carried substantial cargo loaded loose in the ship's holds, requiring the services of large gangs of dockers and considerable turnround times in port, the car ferries are able to convey far more cargo as well as passenger traffic and require only 3 hours or so in port to discharge and load.

Throughout the century DFDS have also provided regular cargo sailings with their varied fleet sailing the length and breadth of the North and Baltic Seas from Harwich and London. The modest cargo vessels of the start of the century have been replaced progressively by ro-ro freighters. In the mid-1970s the company was prompted by its growing dominance in the trade and the apparent availability of finance at economic rates to order the *Dana Futura* and *Dana Gloria* from the Helsingor shipyard. Most impressive vessels for their time, both for their large capacity accommodating 1,417 lane metres of freight and also for their high service speed of 22.5 knots. Demand for the ships was insufficient to fill them and, after several periods on charter, escalating fuel costs saw them relegated to lay up and subsequent sale.

In their place far more basic and slower tonnage was provided by DFDS. The size and complexity of the vessels has grown rapidly and the company has gradually taken over many of the formerly competing businesses on the North Sea, in early 1999 acquiring even the freight operations of Fred. Olsen Line. As elsewhere in the North Sea, the efficiency of DFDS operations during the course of the century has grown and has led to an explosion in freight traffic.

At the start of the century services to Hamburg were provided by the General Steam Navigation Company. At the turn of the century it operated a cat's cradle of passenger and freight services around Europe, including weekly operation between Parkeston Quay and Hamburg. Inevitably interrupted by the outbreak of World War I, the company's future operations were to be conducted from its quays on the Thames and regular ferry services to the Elbe were not resumed until May 1966 when the Prinz Line introduced the impressive car ferry *Prinz Hamlet* on a summer-only service from Bremerhaven. Although rapidly replaced by a smaller vessel with the same name, the operations of the company continued on a regular basis until taken over by DFDS in 1981, since when they have continued to operate on

Contrasting styles of vessel at the mouth of the River Maas in 1997, the **European Freeway** arriving from Felixstowe meets the **Norsea** sailing for Hull. *(John May)*

The British registered **Norsea** leaves the berth at Hull for the lock entrance at the port on her evening sailing to Holland in July 1995. *(Miles Cowsill)*

# CENTURY OF NORTH WEST EUROPEAN FERRIES 1900 - 2000

Soon after being absorbed by DFDS, the powerful *Tor Britannia* seen arriving in the Stour in 1984. *(John May)*

alternate days for many years using the eponymous *Hamburg*, subsequently re-engined, redeveloped to the Tyne and re-named the *Admiral of Scandinavia*. The century has closed with the *Prince of Scandinavia* finally able to demonstrate the power and sea-keeping necessary for regular fast crossing of the North Sea throughout the year.

The principal focus of ferry operations at Harwich has remained throughout the century that of the service to the Hook of Holland. The port is situated at the mouth of the New Waterway through which the River Maas (part of the delta of the River Rhine) - had opened in 1893 to replace the long and winding passage to Rotterdam. Equipped with comprehensive railway facilities, it provided a principal terminal for trains from Northern Europe and continued to support a daily sleeping car train to Moscow until the last decade of the century.

The ferry route was originally opened by the Great Eastern Railway Company, subsequently grouped into the larger London and North Eastern Railway and in 1948 subsumed into the nationalised British Railways. The route remained under railway control until denationalisation in 1984 brought the former railway shipping businesses firstly under the control of the Sea Containers Group and subsequently into Swedish ownership with the purchase by the business Stena Line.

The last paddle steamers had left the Hook service shortly before the beginning of the 20th century but the newest ships were a series of nine screw steamers built by Earle's on Humberside, each measuring no more than 1,800 tons. Accommodating around 200 First Class passengers and about half their number in Second Class, they were comfortable ships for their era and capable of the impressive speed of 18 knots, a factor in the railway company's bid for the mail contract held by the Zeeland Steamship Company. Although soundly built and generally successful, two of the class achieved notoriety. In February 1907 the *Berlin* was swept across the northern mole at the entrance to the New Waterway off the Hook during a violent winter gale. The ship snapped in two and the bow section sank while the stern remained locked fast on the breakwater. Despite heroic rescue attempts and in sight of horrified on-lookers 128 passengers and crew were swept to their deaths in the worst peace time disaster in the history of North Sea ferry travel. War contributed its own hazards to those of tempest and in 1915 the last ship in the series, the *Brussels*, was under the command of the courageous Captain Charles Fryatt. The Netherlands retained its neutrality throughout World War I and the mail service continued maintained by the Great Eastern ships whose speed enabled them to escape the attentions of the German U-boats. However, the *Brussels* was eventually caught by U33 and ordered to stop. Fryatt's response was to attempt to ram the submarine as it dived and, whilst elevating him to a national hero in England, it made him a marked man to the Germans and his ship was finally stopped in June 1916 by torpedo boats who escorted her in Zeebrugge. While her crew was imprisoned, Captain Fryatt was subjected to a show trial and shot by firing squad, an atrocity which was milked to its fullest extent by the war time newspapers.

The next development in the ships for the route had however taken place before the war with the introduction of three fine turbine steamers built by John Brown of Clydebank. Capable of 20 knots and accommodating 320 First Class Passengers and 130 Second Class they had become the principal steamers on the route before the war. Although the *Copenhagen* was sunk whilst serving as a hospital ship, her sisters *Archangel* and *St. Denis* survived the war and peace only to be sunk during World War II.

After the armistice the Great Eastern managed to obtain one of the Great Western's 1906 series of turbine steamers from the Fishguard Route, the *St. George* which had previously been sold to the Canadian Pacific Railway to operate on the Atlantic Coast of Canada but had returned to England for service as a hospital ship during the war. She filled the gap in the Great Eastern's fleet until replaced by the 1929 triplets. By the time of their delivery the Great Eastern had been absorbed into the London and North Eastern Railway and carrying the names *Vienna*, *Prague* and *Amsterdam* they provided greatly improved accommodation for 444 First Class Passengers and 104 Second Class in immensely comfortable cabins. Between them they maintained the Harwich to Hook service without incident until the outbreak of World War II but, while the *Prague* survived the war to reopen the Hook service in 1945, the *Amsterdam* had been sunk by enemy action off the Normandy coast in August 1944 and the *Vienna* was taken over by the government and remained on full time trooping

19

# CENTURY OF NORTH WEST EUROPEAN FERRIES 1900 - 2000

*The impressive **Prinz Hamlet** which inaugurated car ferry services between Hamburg and Harwich in 1966. (John May collection)*

service until sale for scrap in 1960.

The next major advance was the delivery in 1947 and 1950 of the new *Arnhem* and *Amsterdam*, again built by John Brown from Clydebank and measuring almost 5,000 tons. While continuing to provide extensive cargo accommodation, they were able to provide 321 First Class berths and 236 in Second Class. Following the transfer of Zeeland Line's service to Harwich the railway vessels had settled on to the night service with the days being occupied with the loading and unloading of freight. The two ships were joined in 1963 by the largest classic passenger ship delivered to British Railways, who had taken over the route on nationalisation in 1948. The *Avalon* was able to accommodate 750 passengers and both provided relief capacity to her older running mates as well as spring and autumn cruises taking her as far afield as Tangier and Leningrad (St. Petersburg).

The Dutch Zeeland Line had started the century running from the almost forgotten port of Queenborough near Sheerness to Flushing (now known as Vlissingen). At the turn of the century the company was operating a fleet of six large paddle steamers built by Fairfields on Clydeside, the last as recently as 1896 and capable of the impressive speed of 21 knots. The *Koningin Wilhelmina* carried 244 passengers and provided the fastest route from London to Amsterdam with direct boat trains from each port.

Before the end of the first decade of the century the company had returned to Fairfields for three new ships of 2,885 tons and capable of accommodating 246 First Class passengers and 110 Second Class. Their arrival soon revealed the inadequacy of the Medway port and in May 1911 the night service transferred to Folkestone. The loss of two of these vessels during World War 1 and the increasing unsuitability of the paddle steamers required the company to order new vessels again in 1920 when the *Prinses Juliana* and the *Mecklenburg* were built at the De Schelde yard in Flushing. It was therefore with these two ships and the *Oranje Nassau*, the survivor of the 1909 trio, that Zeeland Line transferred its service to run from Harwich in January 1927. Thus was established the pattern that would continue until the start of the car ferry era with the British ships operating on the night crossings and the Dutch vessels making day sailings from both ports.

Shortly before the outbreak of World War II the Zeeland company took delivery of two admirable motor vessels, again from the De Schelde Shipyard. The *Koningin Emma* and *Prinses Beatrix* which were the first vessels capable of accommodating large numbers of passengers, 1,800 each, due to the ability to avoid the need to provide many cabins on ships that could now be dedicated to an exclusively day service. Both served with distinction in the Royal Navy during World War II, the *Koningin Emma* ending the war in the Far East repatriating civilians to the then Dutch colony of Java. Rebuilt and renovated, the ships resumed in 1948 the service that they had only briefly served upon before the war and on which they would continue to serve regularly and reliably until replaced by car ferries. The last passenger ship to be provided for the company was the *Koningin Wilhelmina* which joined the service in 1960. Of streamlined appearance and with a remarkably stunted funnel, she survived the introduction of the car ferries in 1968 and remained as a relief vessel until sold in 1978 to Greece. She has remained in service until the close of the century, latterly running cruises from Crete.

The Hook service underwent a revolution in 1968 with the commissioning of the British *St. George* and the Dutch *Koningin Juliana*, each replacing the older pair of vessels in their respective fleets, not only exploiting their increased size (7,356 tons and 6,682 respectively - both accommodating 1,200 passengers on the day service and 750 on the night service) but also the inherent speed of loading of vehicle ferries enabling them to make a round voyage in 24 hours and so doubling the efficiency if not the style of the service.

The 1970s brought still larger ships - the British *St. Edmund* and the Dutch *Prinses Beatrix* but the next decade saw the greatest leap in size and standards of accommodation. One of the last acts of Sealink (as the British Railways shipping division had then chosen to describe itself) was the charter of the two year old *Prinsessan Birgitta* which had become available following the merger of Stena Line and its rivals Sessan Line on the Gothenburg to Frederikshaven route. Renamed *St. Nicholas* she brought about the demise of first class accommodation on the route which only a generation before had represented 2/3rds of its capacity and rather more of its profits. However, while her passenger capacity of 2,100 represented a further increase on anything that the route had seen previously, it was her vehicle capacity of 480 cars and 52 lorries that represented the greatest enhancement to the service. When the Zeeland company commissioned their last and largest vessel in 1986 it was possible for the four earlier car ferries to be withdrawn. The *Koningin Beatrix* matched the passenger capacity of her English running mate and accommodated 500 cars and 75 lorries while still providing adequate cabin accommodation for her overnight passengers - albeit without the luxury of the pre-war vessels. The earlier ships were rapidly disposed of, the *St. George* going first to the Adriatic and then to operate gambling cruises from Florida; the *St. Edmund* initially to the Ministry of Defence, then to British Channel Island Ferries and subsequently to Cenargo to

# CENTURY OF NORTH WEST EUROPEAN FERRIES 1900 - 2000

One of three large ferries introduced to the Harwich-Hook night service in 1930, the **Amsterdam** introduced luxury to the southern North Sea. World War II brought her career to an end when she was mined in 1944 while serving as a hospital ship. (John May collection)

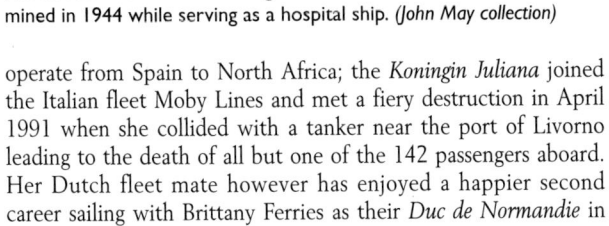

The impressive **Stena Britannica** served briefly on the Harwich-Hook service between 1991 and 1994 since when she has returned to Scandinavia. (John May)

operate from Spain to North Africa; the *Koningin Juliana* joined the Italian fleet Moby Lines and met a fiery destruction in April 1991 when she collided with a tanker near the port of Livorno leading to the death of all but one of the 142 passengers aboard. Her Dutch fleet mate however has enjoyed a happier second career sailing with Brittany Ferries as their *Duc de Normandie* in which guise she has seen the century to its end.

The Harwich-Hook service, however, had scarcely settled down with its two large ships before the instruments of so much change in North West European ferries in the last part of the 20th century arrived in the shape of Stena Line. When the Dutch Government decided to emulate the denationalisation of the British Railways fleet five years earlier, Stena Line promptly offered to acquire the company and their purchase was completed in June 1989. Change rapidly followed, as so often after Stena Line's arrival elsewhere. The final decade of the century saw radical change with the acquisition of the British Sealink ships by Stena being completed in December 1990. British management ceased in the following year and the British ship was soon replaced by the large and impressive *Stena Britannica*. Vehicle traffic continued to increase and Stena drafted in two freight ro-ro vessels to join the route and the fleet provided the most impressive service since the start of the car ferry era. However, the Stena revolution continued firstly by the replacement of the *Stena Britannica* with the smaller *Stena Europe* (sister ship to the former *St. Nicholas*) and then more spectacularly in early 1997 by the displacement of both conventional passenger vessels with the arrival of the HSS *Stena Discovery*. Plagued by controversy from its introduction both for its sea keeping qualities and its reputedly dangerous wash, the enormous catamaran - capable of accommodating 1,500 passengers and 375 cars/50 lorries - is able to provide two round trips per day in most weather conditions and, with the continuing use of the two ro-ro freighters. The route has ended the century in a radically different shape from that which could have been foreseen at its beginning.

However, if the ferry service to Holland has prospered, those to Belgium have not enjoyed similar success. Routes at the beginning of the century to Ghent and Antwerp which had almost matched the Dutch route in importance before World War II gradually declined to carry freight only and the routes finally closed in 1968. They were, however, replaced by a new route to Zeebrugge operated by two vessels which just qualify for inclusion within this review - the first purpose-built cellular-container ships to enter service from British yards - the *Seafreightliner I* and 'II'. Providing a regular service from Parkeston Quay, they represented the extension to Europe of the container revolution which had then begun the transformation of ocean freight and which British Railways hoped (not entirely successfully) would achieve similar results with their rail freight services. Although surviving into the privatisation era, both were withdrawn in 1987 and scrapped - their route becoming the province of coasters rather than ferries.

Belgian Marine briefly operated a car ferry service from Ostend to Harwich between 1968 and 1973 but failed to capture a significant slice of the market at which it had been aimed. The other Belgian service, however, enjoyed a far longer life. During World War 1 the British Government had sponsored the introduction of a train ferry service between Richborough, near Ramsgate in Kent, and the French ports of Dunkerque and Calais. A similar service operated between Southampton and Dieppe but all services ended in 1919 and the equipment was laid up. However, in 1924 it attracted the attention of the London and North Eastern Railway and a joint Anglo-Belgian venture was set up to operate three of the vessels between Harwich and Zeebrugge. Capital expenditure was kept to a minimum and even the linkspan at Harwich was a reconstruction of the Southampton berth. The route settled down to provide a regular service for freight wagons using the outstandingly ugly and prosaically named *Train Ferry No. 1*, '2' and '3'. During World War II the vessels served as transport vessels and landing ships and only No. 1 survived. Rebuilt and radically improved, she returned as the *Essex Ferry* in 1946 and was to remain in service until 1957 by when she had been joined by other more modern but still very basic ships. The 'Suffolk', 'Essex', 'Norfolk' and finally *Cambridge Ferry* provided four rail tracks and capacity for approximately 35 rail wagons. Although they carried heavy traffic in the 1960s and early 1970s, the popularity of the route declined and by 1980 were losing money heavily. The four older vessels were replaced by a single and more modern ship, the *Speedlink Vanguard* which was chartered from Stena and was capable of accommodating 56 railway wagons. She achieved some notoriety in December 1982 when she collided with Townsend Thoresen's *European Gateway* and sunk her in the approaches to Felixstowe. However, the decline in British Railway freight operations during the 1980s finally led to the withdrawal of the route in 1989. The ship however enjoyed a further spell in British waters as Brittany Ferries' *Normandie Shipper*.

Ipswich, a dozen miles from the sea along the winding River Orwell, did not see continental ferry services until 1977 when they were introduced by North Sea Ferries running to Europoort. Although enjoying considerable success with two sailings per day by the early 1980s, a reorganisation of business within the P&O group in early 1995 led to the closure of the service after 18

21

# CENTURY OF NORTH WEST EUROPEAN FERRIES 1900 - 2000

The Swedish Lloyd ferry *Suecia* appeared in 1929 on the long route from Gothenburg to Tilbury. Remaining in service until 1966 she spent four further years in Greek waters and was not finally sold for scrap until 1972. *(John May collection)*

years.

The third of the Haven ports, Felixstowe had remained a modest port during the first six decades of the century but exploded into life in the 1960s and has grown to become the busiest container port in the country. Although a ferry across the estuary from Harwich operated from the early years of the century, the first Continental ferry from the port was provided by Atlantic Steam Navigation's Transport Ferry Service which opened in 1965 when the service was transferred from Tilbury. Routes were developed to both Rotterdam and Antwerp, the former effectively paralleling the Harwich to Hook ferry but aimed at a very different market and providing a very different style of accommodation. The largest and fastest ship built for ASN, the *Europic Ferry* joined the service in 1967 and set a standard of accommodation which was probably unmatched by any of the competing vessels. The company had come under state control in 1954 and in 1971 was one of the few enterprises denationalised by Edward Heath's Conservative government when it was acquired by the European Ferries Group. Restyled as part of Townsend Thoresen, the route gradually acquired new tonnage and in 1975 the route was joined by the newly constructed car ferries *Viking Viscount* and *Viking Voyager* which provided comfortable sailings three times daily to Zeebrugge with accommodation for 1,200 passengers and 275 cars. ASN's fleet continued in operation in the new company's orange livery until replaced in 1981 by the *Baltic Ferry* and *Nordic Ferry*, two large freighters chartered from Stena Line. With the transfer of the "Super-Vikings" to Portsmouth in 1986, the Zeebrugge route was taken by the Stena freighters, which had passenger accommodation added on their previously open upper vehicle decks, while their places on the Rotterdam service were in turn taken by two lengthened sisters, initially named *Cerdic Ferry* and *Doric Ferry*. Following P&O's take-over of Townsend Thoresen they have been renamed *European Freeway* and *European Tideway* respectively and have remained in service on the Rotterdam route at the end of the century, while the longer serving sister vessels rejoined the route in 1995 following the withdrawal of passenger facilities on the Zeebrugge service and the removal of the passenger accommodation which has restored their upper decks for the carriage of vehicles.

Felixstowe has seen an assortment of other ferry services during the last 30 years of the century, particularly on the long freight routes to Scandinavia. However, the gradual take-over of many of these operations by DFDS has seen the routes migrate to Parkeston Quay, although Norfolk Line which had begun life at Great Yarmouth has grown and developed to provide four daily departures to the Dutch capital. The port of Felixstowe has continued to prosper and develop and, while it is not possible at the close of the 20th century to sail by passenger ferry from the port, it has a thriving freight business.

## THE THAMES

While the Port of London is not automatically associated with ferry services, it has seen a large and complex range of operations throughout the century.

The impact of the opening of the Swedish Lloyd service from Tilbury to Gothenburg in 1929 has been noted above in connection with services from Tyne. Operated by a splendid pair of turbine steamers built by Swan Hunters, the *Suecia* and *Britannia* measured 4,216 tons and carried 220 First Class passengers and 45 Second Class. They operated three times weekly in summer and weekly in winter, landing their passengers at Tilbury and continuing to Millwall Dock to unload their freight. Laid up throughout World War II, they reopened the service in February 1946. Joined later that year by the *Saga* and in 1951 by the *Patricia*, the earlier pair outlasted their younger and larger partners and remained in operation until 1966 when they were replaced by the most elegant car ferries of their generation - the *Saga* and *Svea*. Large car ferries for their time, measuring over 7,000 tons and capable of carrying 1,500 passengers and 300 cars, they failed to find a niche in the market of the late 1960s. While passenger traffic was increasingly taken by airliner, their vehicle decks were unable to cope with the explosion in lorry traffic and by 1971 the service closed.

Vehicle services to the Continent had started as early as September 1946 when the Atlantic Steam Navigation Company introduced converted tank landing craft on a route to Rotterdam. The service gradually developed with the introduction of purpose-built ferry ships and, by 1962, they had achieved a daily frequency to both Rotterdam and Antwerp. However, increasing industrial action at Tilbury and the long time taken for navigation of the Thames Estuary gradually led to the transfer of services to Felixstowe.

There remains one final aspect of North Sea ferry operations to note, the much lamented coastal ferry services between the capitals of England and Scotland provided from Victorian times until World War II by the London and Edinburgh Shipping Company. A very old Leith-based firm, founded in 1809, it provided three passenger sailings a week in each direction. Looking back from the end of the century it seems remarkable that such a service could continue in the face of competition from the railway companies but as late as 1928 the 2,187 ton *Royal Archer* was delivered to the company with accommodation for 100 first class and 120 second class passengers. The service did not survive World War II, but what a journey it would have offered at any time of the century and what a range of vessels it would have met!

Swedish Lloyd's first car ferry, the immensely elegant *Saga* of 1966. *(John May collection)*

*John May*

# CENTURY OF NORTH WEST EUROPEAN FERRIES 1900 - 2000

## The DFDS Group

DFDS, which was formed in 1866, has been active in freight and passenger shipping between Denmark and the UK since 1874, and also operated many services in the Baltic and Western Europe, the Mediterranean, South and North America. The main route to the UK was between Esbjerg and Harwich.

In the mid sixties DFDS started converting from conventional vessels to ro-ro freight vessels, as well as combined passenger and freight ro-ro vessels. In the early eighties the North Sea routes were expanded through the takeover of Tor Line of Sweden and also Prins Ferries, which operated from Hamburg and Bremerhaven to Harwich. The latest acquisition was at the beginning of 1999 when DFDS acquired Fred. Olsen's North Sea Line, including 3 freight ro-ro vessels operating between Norway and the UK, Germany, Holland and Belgium. The services were restructured in June 1999 and now operate as Norbridge.

Today the passenger routes are operated in the name of DFDS Seaways and the freight routes as DFDS Tor Line. Seven overnight passenger ferries are operated in the North Sea, and the Baltic led by the flag ship m.s. *Crown of Scandinavia*, of 35,498 gross tons, which was built in 1994, and has a cabin capacity for 2,136 passengers. The standard of the vessels is similar to 4-star cruise vessels. In fact, five of the vessels have AA 5-star rating, and the other two 4-star. The total berth capacity of the fleet is 10,760 berths. The routes are:

Harwich/Esbjerg
Harwich/Hamburg
Newcastle/Amsterdam
Newcastle/Kristiansand/Gothenburg
Copenhagen/Helsingborg/Oslo

The two latter services are retaining duty free status, following the abolition of duty and tax free sales between EC ports on 1st July 1999. In 1998, about 1.5 million overnight passengers were carried.

DFDS Seaways' target groups are transportation passengers with or without cars, mini cruises, group travel and sea conferences. DFDS Seaways operates a city-to-city concept.

The DFDS Group also has about 25 ro-ro freight vessels in the range of 1,500-2,875 lane metres including three 2,800 lane metre newbuildings being delivered in 1999 for the Immingham/Gothenburg service. The first newbuilding, *Tor Selandia*, entered service in March, 1999. She and her sisters have a very high service speed of 22 knots, which will reduce the sailing time from 34 to 24 hours.

In September 1999 DFDS merged its two ro-ro freight shipping divisions, DFDS Liner Division and DFDS Tor Line AB, into one new shipping division DFDS Tor Line Group A/S with headquarters in Copenhagen. DFDS Tor Line

*Ebbe Pedersen*

The *Princess of Scandinavia* inward bound from Gothenburg. *(DFDS)*

# CENTURY OF NORTH WEST EUROPEAN FERRIES 1900 - 2000

The elegant **Winston Churchill** pictured at North Shields during her last season on the North Sea with the company. *(Miles Cowsill)*

Group is responsible for the freight carryings on all the passenger vessels and in addition operates about 25 owned and chartered ro-ro vessels on the following routes:

Esbjerg/Harwich
Esbjerg/Immingham
Hamburg/Harwich
Cuxhaven/Immingham
Newcastle/Amsterdam
Immingham/Rotterdam
Immingham/Gothenburg
Harwich/Gothenburg
Immingham/Oslo-Brevik-Kristiansand
Felixstowe/Oslo-Brevik-Kristiansand
Rotterdam-Oslo-Brevik-Kristiansand
Hamburg/Oslo-Kristiansand-Oslo Fjord ports
Gothenburg/Ghent
Copenhagen-Fredericia/Klaipeda
Copenhagen/Helsingborg/Oslo
Newcastle/Kristiansand/Gothenburg

The main target traffic carried by the DFDS Tor Line Group is trailers, containers, tanks, cars and other automobile products, as well as forest products, steel and chemicals on cassettes and Mafi trailers. In 1998, well over five million lane metres were carried. Some driver-accompanied traffic is also carried - mainly on the passenger vessels, but the volume is relatively low, as the DFDS Group specialises in long overnight routes ranging from a transit time of 15-34 hours.

The DFDS Tor Line Group places great importance on controlling all parts of its service and, in most of the main ports, it operates its own terminals which include Immingham, Newcastle, Rotterdam, Hamburg, Esbjerg and Oslo. The largest is Nordic Terminal in Immingham which opened in 1994, making it possible to concentrate all the Group's services on the Humber through one terminal compared to three previously. Nordic Terminal has seen a massive growth from about 2 million lane metres in the first year to an expected 4 million in 2000. The terminal can discharge and load four ro-ro vessels simultaneously, and the

The **Crown of Scandinavia** maintains the Copenhagen-Oslo service with the **Queen of Scandinavia**. *(DFDS)*

DFDS freight vessel **Dana Futura** is seen arriving at Harwich from Esbjerg. *(DFDS)*

24

# Ferry RELIABLE

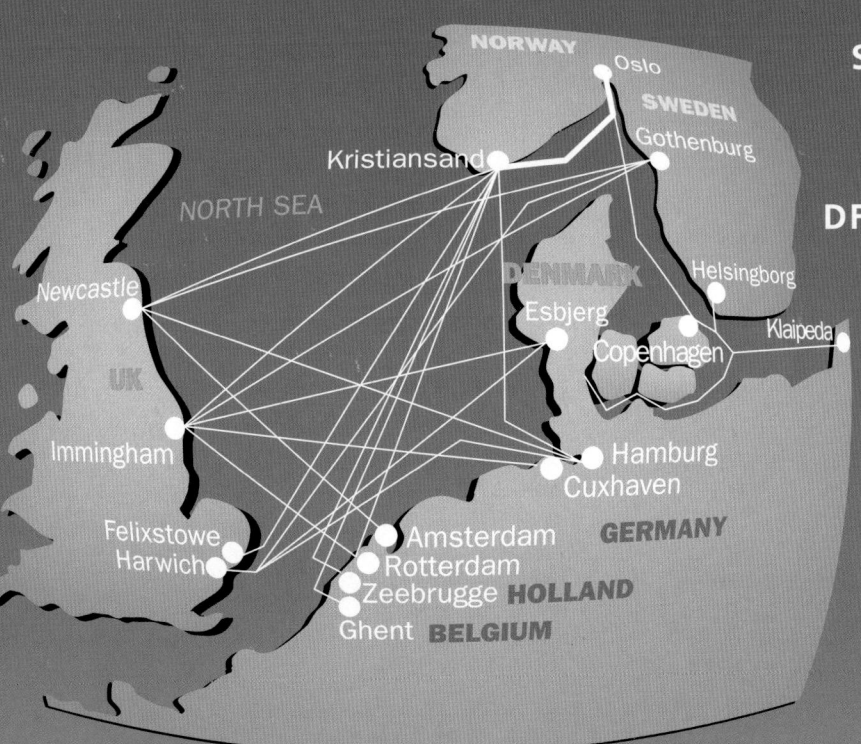

For RoRo services to Scandinavia and the Continent call DFDS Tor Line Limited on 01469 578899 or fax on 01469 552690 and get the reliable North Sea Solution

**DFDS TOR LINE**
THE NORTH SEA CARRIER

# CENTURY OF NORTH WEST EUROPEAN FERRIES 1900 - 2000

*In 1997 the DFDS group ordered a series of new freight vessels from Fincantieri for their vital operations on their North Sea freight services. (Mike Louagie)*

terminal area has already been expanded from 40 to 80 acres (320,000 sq.m.). It includes about 200,000 sq.ft. of warehousing for forest products, steel and other bulk cargoes. It the autumn of 1999 a new 50,000 sq.ft. steel warehouse will be opened with its own internal rail track for the handling and storage of sensitive steel strip products in coils. The warehouse will be insulated and heated in the winter, and will have two overhead 40 ton gantry cranes for the transfer between the warehouse and both rail and road transport. Since 1996, new direct rail services have been developed from Nordic Terminal, and in 1998 about 1.3 million tons of steel and forest products were moved by rail to and from the vessels at Nordic Terminal.

DFDS places great importance on safety and quality and in 1996 all the passenger vessels were certified in accordance with the ISM code (International Safety Management Systems), and most of the freight vessels have also been certified with the remaining ships due to be certified before IMO's deadline in 2001.

At the end of 1998 DFDS had about 7,600 employees in Northern Europe, the UK and Ireland. Apart from its shipping activities DFDS has extensive interactional and domestic transport and logistics operations and logistic operations including road haulage, warehousing and cold storage. About 5,000 personnel are employed in these activities operating under the name of DFDS Transport. During the middle of 1999 DFDS agreed to acquire one of the largest Danish forwarding companies, Dan Transport A/S, with about 4,000 employees in Europe, as well as North America and the Far East. The takeover was completed during the autumn of 1999 following EC approval.

DFDS is a public company quoted on the Copenhagen Stock exchange. Its main shareholder is the Danish shipping and industrial group J. Lauritzen Holdings, which owns 52.8% of the shares.

Following the acquisition of Dan Transport the DFDS Group restructured with three main operating subsidiaries as direct subsidiaries of the parent company DFDS A/S:

DFDS Dan Transport A/S (transport and logistics), DFDS Tor Line (freight shipping) and DFDS Seaways (passenger shipping). The enlarged Group has about 12,000 employees and will have a turnover of about £1.6 billion in 2000.

*Ebbe Pedersen*
*Managing Director,*
*DFDS PLC*

*The **Dana Anglia** has maintained the Esbjerg-Harwich service since 1978. (Miles Cowsill)*

# CENTURY OF NORTH WEST EUROPEAN FERRIES 1900 - 2000

# Dart Line

In 1986 a new double linkspan berth called Dartford International Ferry Terminal was opened on the River Thames near Dartford, only 16 miles (25 kilometres) from central London and a few minutes away from the Dartford Tunnel on the then newly opened M25 motorway. Services were established to Zeebrugge in Belgium and Esbjerg in Denmark by Kent Line, a company which later passed into the hands of the Danish Maersk group. However, the service was rather suddenly withdrawn in 1992 and the Dartford Ferry Terminal lay idle for over two years.

However, in 1994, the closure of Olau Line's Sheerness - Vlissingen passenger and freight service prompted Sally Line to open a Ramsgate - Vlissingen freight service. In September the service was transferred to Dartford and the port was again in operation.

Some of the senior management at Sally Line were convinced that the future for cross-Channel ferry operations, other than Dover - Calais, lay in unaccompanied freight - both for containers and trailers - and they saw Dartford as having better potential than Ramsgate for this.

In September 1994, Jacobs Holdings plc, headed by former Sally Line boss Michael Kingshott, acquired a lease of the Dartford International Ferry Terminal - which they renamed Thames Europort. The subsequently purchased the port in 1997. Sally Line's Scandinavian owners remained committed to Ramsgate and it was logical therefore for the Dartford operation, which was 50 miles away from Ramsgate, to be run separately. It was agreed that the service should, from the start of 1996, be taken over by a new company called Dart Line, which would be owned by Jacobs Holdings.

The new company decided that the vessels Sally Line was operating - the *Sally Euroway* and the *Purbeck* - two freight vessels designed for routes with a higher level of driver accompanied traffic, were not best suited to the route. A more attractive option would be vessels of the same type as Sally was employing on its Ramsgate - Oostende freight service, the *Sally Euroroute* and the *Sally Eurolink*. These Romanian-built vessels were part of a class of eight built for the Norwegian Balder group in the 1980s. Following the liquidation of the group, they passed into Romanian ownership and were renamed *Bazias 1* to *Bazias 8*. They had two large unobstructed vehicle decks, with separate loading ramps through the stern of the vessel, and could be turned round quickly and up to 12 passengers carried. The two vessels operated by Sally Line were still required so the new team had to find two more of the class for their service.

The *Bazias 2* was quickly chartered and arrived at Dartford in the late autumn of 1995. She entered service on 12th November, replacing the *Purbeck* - initially sub-chartered to Sally Line as they were still operating the service. She was renamed the *Dart 2*.

On 1st January 1996, Dart Line took over the service using the *Dart 2* and the *Sally Euroway*, sub-chartered from Sally Line. The second vessel did not arrive until February. Named the *Perseus* during a previous charter, she had previously been the *Bazias 5* and thus became the *Dart 5*.

Her arrival should have seen the departure of the *Sally Euroway*, however, this plan had to be postponed when the *Dart 2* was 'arrested' because of a charge against the ship's owners, Romline, in respect of a previous charter of the vessel. The *Dart 2* was out of commission for 14 weeks and the dispute was only settled when Jacobs purchased the ship from Romline, settling the outstanding claim.

By summer 1996, Dart Line bade farewell to the *Sally Euroway*. The decision to opt for more basic vessels was vindicated as the traffic of unaccompanied trailers and containers continued to grow but a small number of drivers could still be accommodated. A twice-daily service was offered, requiring some rapid handling at the two terminals. Containers were loaded on low trailers, known as Mafis, and with the excellent headroom of the Bazias vessels, it was found possible to 'double stack' - which further speeded up loading and unloading.

Dart Line soon began to look for possibilities for expansion and felt that re-opening the Dartford - Zeebrugge service had greatest potential. Zeebrugge is the largest freight ferry port in Belgium, as well as being a major container port - containers being a type of traffic Dart Line were developing. The Zeebrugge had constructed a new two berth ro-ro terminal on reclaimed land and a decision was therefore taken to lease this installation and start a Zeebrugge service in 1997.

The company decided that the ideal ships for the route would be two additional Bazias class vessels - although initially only one was available. The *Sally Eurolink*, no longer suitable for the Ramsgate service which now required more driver accommodation, moved to Dart Line and became the *Dart 4*.

The Zeebrugge service was launched on 10th April, started by the chartered *Merchant Victor* as the *Dart 4* was not initially available. The *Dart 4* entered service two weeks later, enabling a twice daily service to be operated. A number of other vessels were chartered until November when it was possible to acquire yet another Bazias vessel - the former *Bazias 1* owned by Octogon Shipping, a Romanian private sector company.

Commercially, the Zeebrugge service was highly successful and traffic soon exceeded that on the Vlissingen route. It was not long before consideration was being given as to how capacity could be increased on the new route.

The Vlissingen route continued to perform well commercially but the 16 knot Bazias ships often found difficulty in keeping to the exacting schedule over the rather longer distance, especially when performing slightly under specification. The short-term answer to these two problems was to charter two faster vessels for the Vlissingen service and operate three of the Bazias vessels on the Zeebrugge service. The two chartered vessels were the brand new Estonian Shipping Company (ESCO) *Varbola* and *Lembitu*. In early 1999 they were renamed the *Dart 6* and the *Dart 7* respectively.

Two knots faster than the 'Bazias' vessels, they found keeping to the schedule much easier, although their capacity was rather lower and their design rather less efficient in terms of cargo handling and loading. Their charter ended in September 1999 and they were replaced by two Bazias vessels, fitted with sophisticated engine monitoring devices to ensure optimum performance at all times.

Meanwhile, the search was on for a long-term solution to the Zeebrugge capacity problems continued. As well as lengthening two or more of the existing ships, building two new vessels was also considered. However, in 1999 Jacobs Holdings purchased three Japanese built deep sea ro-ro/container ships from COSCO of the People's Republic of China - the 22,748 gross tons *Xi Feng Kou*, *Gu Bei Kou* and *Zhang Jia Kou*. They had been built by Kawasaki Heavy Industries in Sakaide, Japan in 1980 and used on cross-Pacific services, mainly carrying containers.

The purchase price included all the necessary modification work, which was to be undertaken by the Nantung Ocean Ship Engineering Company (in which COSCO had a share) at Nantong.

# CENTURY OF NORTH WEST EUROPEAN FERRIES 1900 - 2000

The former Chinese deep sea ro-ro *Dart 8* an hour off Zeebrugge in August 1999. *(John Hendy)*

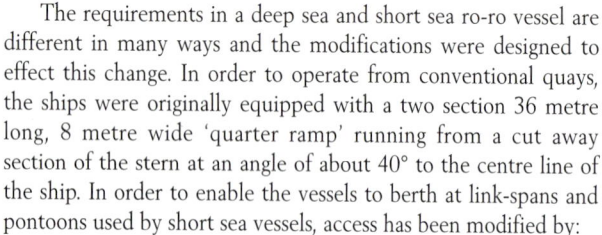

An aerial view of Dart Line's terminal at Dartford. This picture richly illustrates the easy access to the M25 and the Dartford Crossing. *(FotoFlite)*

The requirements in a deep sea and short sea ro-ro vessel are different in many ways and the modifications were designed to effect this change. In order to operate from conventional quays, the ships were originally equipped with a two section 36 metre long, 8 metre wide 'quarter ramp' running from a cut away section of the stern at an angle of about 40° to the centre line of the ship. In order to enable the vessels to berth at link-spans and pontoons used by short sea vessels, access has been modified by:

1. building a triangular platform to 'fill in' the cut-away part of the stern
2. shortening the ramp by discarding the outer section
3. widening the ramp to 10m to allow two-way traffic to pass over it
4. fitting the ramp onto the rear edge of the platform so that it now projects straight from the stern
5. building new masts to house the modified rigging that raises and lowers the ramp.

In order to ensure that the vessels can manoeuvre when berthing easily within the confines of the River Thames and the harbour at Zeebrugge, additional equipment has been fitted. A second bow thruster has been added and at the stern an 'Azimuth' propeller - which can be rotated through 360° - has been fitted on the port side. Each unit is powered by its own Caterpillar diesel engine.

The lower of the two principal internal vehicle decks was built to a clear height of 3.8m - OK for 2.9m containers but too low for many road trailers currently in use. Conversely, the bottom vehicle deck known as the 'Tanktop' was 3.6m high - more than enough for the trade cars which Dart Line would wish to convey there. It was decided therefore to lower the deck by about 1 metre to give heights of 4.89m and 2.65m respectively. This was a massive job and involved carefully cutting out sections of the deck, slowly lowering them by chain block until they were at the right height and re-welding them into position. In all the deck covered an area of about 1500 square metres and was broken down into sections for the lowering operation. As a result, the vessels can now accommodate 155 x 13.6m trailers or the equivalent in containers on 'Mafi' trailers - almost a 60% increase over their predecessors. The open upper deck and the main deck will cope with containers which have been double stacked - ie two containers on one trailer, which can be as high as 6.2m.

Previous use of these vessels had generated little demand for driver accompanied traffic and consequently no passenger accommodation was provided. On Dart Line service, this traffic - although only a small proportion of the total - is a vital part of the total service offered. Fortunately, crew accommodation was much larger than was required for short sea operation and one deck in the accommodation block at the rear of the ship was completely gutted and 12 luxury driver cabins provided, plus a lounge, bar and dining area and even a small gymnasium. Furnishing has been to full cruise-ferry standard, designed by Norman Lingwood of ship's architects 'Opus 2'. Each cabin is equipped with a TV set which gives drivers the choice of terrestrial TV or up to four feature films using the latest video disk system. Private facilities are provided in each cabin and some cabins are twin or double bedded - although a maximum of 12 passengers is carried at any one time.

Little modification has been necessary to the vessels' bridges. The bridge wings have been extended to make it easier to see the full length of the ship when berthing and controls fitted for the new manoeuvring equipment. The ships were built to operate at a service speed of 18 knots, although their previous owners generally ran them at between 12 and 14 knots to conserve fuel. Although the 'Bazias' vessels run at 15 knots, because the new, larger ships need a longer turn round time, a shorter crossing time is required. Consequently they are now required to operate at nearer their design speed. The engines have been given a thorough overall, with a large number of components replaced and have been fitted with the latest computer monitoring equipment to enable the Chief Engineer to keep them in tip-top condition. In the event of failure, the 'Azimuth' propeller can be brought into use.

The hull of each ship has been blasted to bare metal and repainted in Dart Line's blue with red boot topping colours. It is not anticipated that they will need to be dry-docked for another five years. The *Dart 8* entered service in early August and the *Dart 9* in early September. The *Dart 10* went direct to a charter in the Mediterranean. The new ships are already proving their worth in attracting more traffic and, with the lavish passenger facilities, more driver-accompanied business is being attracted.

The Dart Line story is one of success in a congested market, by tailoring a service carefully and providing good quality but without unnecessary frills. As Britain enters the 21st Century, there will be an increasing emphasis on environmentally friendly transport. By taking traffic from the crowded roads of Kent, Dart Line will be making its contribution.

*Stephen Hepplewhite*
Managing Director, Dart Line.

# Our new ships have DOUBLE the capacity

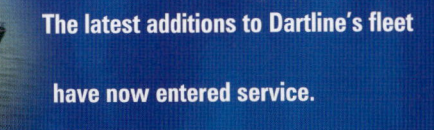

The latest additions to Dartline's fleet have now entered service.

This takes Dartline into a new era in customer service and driver comfort.

The new ships, Dart 8 and Dart 9, can carry up to 155 trailers and accompanied loads on our busy Dartford to Zeebrugge route - doubling the capacity of our previous ships.

Equipped with the latest technology, the vessels have been fitted out to cruise ferry standards, with even a gymnasium on board.

So, for the last word in efficiency, luxury and safety, have a word with us.

## Dart Line

Thames Europort Crossways
Dartford Kent DA2 6QB

tel +44 (0)1322 281122
fax: +44 (0)1322 281133
email: sales@dartline.co.uk
website: www.dartline.co.uk

**For more information call us on 01322 281122**

# Eastern Channel

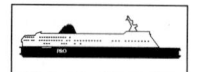

## DOVER AND FOLKESTONE
### The Passenger Ships

With the English Channel narrowing towards the Dover Strait beyond which the North Sea progressively widens, the sea crossings in this area have always been the most-favoured and intensively operated. The unique geographical positioning of both Dover and Calais serves them as well in the year 2000 as it did following the Roman invasion in 43 AD. The 22 miles separating the two towns are today crossed in as little as 35 minutes by hovercraft and between 75-90 minutes by conventional ferry, and it is interesting to note that in spite of the many technical advances that have been made during the twentieth century, the speed of passage by conventional vessels today rarely betters that achieved in the century's first decade.

On New Year's Day 1899, a working agreement was signed to end what was known as the forty years railway war between the South Eastern Railway (operators of the Folkestone - Boulogne link) and the London, Chatham and Dover Railway (whose vessels plied between Dover and Calais). The working union formed the South Eastern & Chatham Railways Joint Management Committee (SE&CR) and under their auspices the short-sea routes both blossomed and prospered.

The first major advance was the introduction of the world's first cross-Channel passenger turbine steamer, the 1,676 gross tons *The Queen* in June 1903. So successful was the five-screwed vessel that four more of the class were ordered from the fabled Dumbarton yard of William Denny & Bros. - the *Onward* and *Invicta* in April and July 1905 and the *Empress* and *Victoria* in April and June 1907. Their appearance saw the inevitable withdrawal of the remainder of the paddle steamer fleet and thus the SER's *Mabel Grace* of 1899 lasted just ten years before passing for scrap while the LC&DR's final paddlers, the *Dover, Calais* and *Lord Warden* of 1896 were all disposed of with the entry into service of two more turbine steamers - the *Riviera* and *Engadine* - in 1911. It was the SE&CR's practice to place its newest ships on the Dover - Calais link whilst switching the older units to the 26 mile Folkestone - Boulogne crossing.

The 1911 pair of vessels were improved versions of the original quintet with geared turbines and strengthened after decks for the carriage of motor cars which had already begun to make an impression on all Channel crossings.

The operation and style of service was quite different to that experienced by the traveller of today. In the days before the advent of aeroplane travel the only way to cross the Channel was by ship and the fact that the routes across the Dover Strait were the shortest and quickest meant that there was less time in which to be ill. Heads of State, royalty, prime ministers, the aristocracy, stars of the London theatre *et al* all arrived at Dover Pier by Continental Boat Express and were duly escorted to their private cabins on board the steamer before rejoining the awaiting continental expresses lined up on the quay at Calais Maritime. Should the Channel look at all unpleasant then the opulent Lord Warden Hotel at Dover and the Gare Maritime Hotel at Calais could accommodate passengers until such time as the gale abated. The steamers boasted first class accommodation for about 1,000 while second class (mainly for manservants, maids etc) was for some 400.

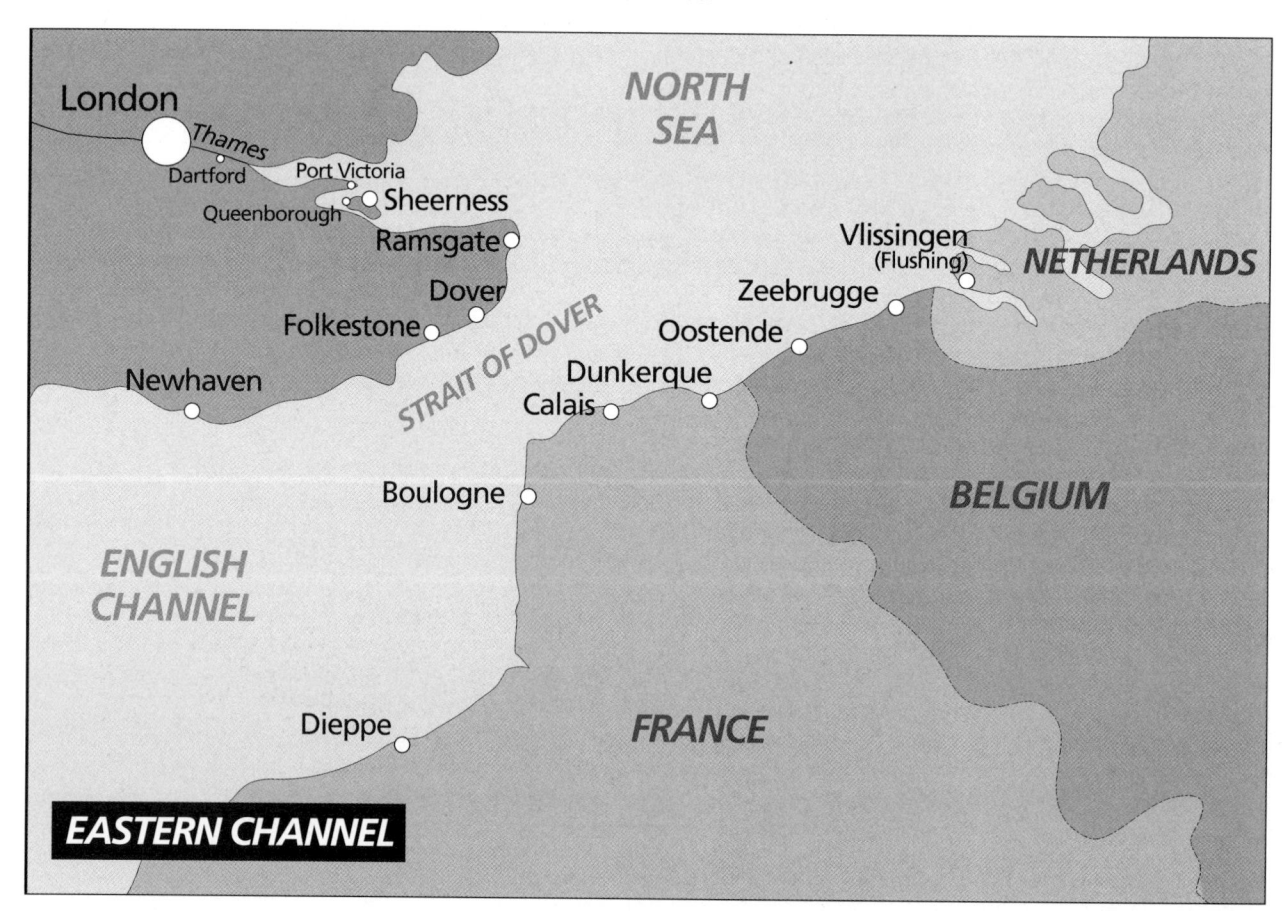

# CENTURY OF NORTH WEST EUROPEAN FERRIES 1900 - 2000

The original cross-Channel turbine steamer **The Queen** of 1903 alongside the Admiralty Pier waiting to sail to Calais. The Continental Boat Express has recently arrived from London. *(John Hendy collection)*

Infilling at Dover's Admiralty Pier in about 1910. The original steamer berths were on the right of this view, the Marine Station was constructed on the reclaimed area whilst the new berths were built to the left of the gantry. *(John Hendy collection)*

Very few passengers would join the steamers at the Channel ports and if any sailing looked like being uncomfortably full, then the reserve steamer would be called upon to operate a supplementary crossing. Ships sailed with one crew who slept and ate at home. It was unusual for any vessel to be required to operate more than one round sailing each day and refits were taken every three to four months. It was little wonder that the short-sea ships of the Edwardian era were beautifully kept by their crews who enjoyed an intense rivalry with those in the rest of the fleet.

The final pair of SE&CR turbine steamers, the *Biarritz* and *Maid of Orleans* (2,495 gross tons) were both launched during the First World War and entered service for the Admiralty but their design showed the final flowering of the original 1903 steamer.

The *Empress*, *Riviera* and *Engadine* all become seaplane carriers, the *Empress* taking part in the Cuxhaven raid in December 1914 while one of the *Engadine*'s planes sighted the German High Seas Fleet prior to the Battle of Jutland in May-June 1916. The *Biarritz* became a mine-layer and her mines were responsible for the loss of the German cruiser *Breslau* and for damaging the battle-cruiser *Goeben* in the eastern Mediterranean.

Sadly the first two turbines were both lost. *The Queen* was intercepted and scuttled by a German raiding party whilst on passage between Boulogne and Folkestone in August 1916 while the *Onward* caught fire and was scuttled whilst alongside at Folkestone Harbour in September 1918. She was subsequently raised, sold to the Isle of Man Steam Packet Company and as the *Mona's Isle* remained in service until 1948.

The resumption of services following the Armistice saw the SE&CR fleet operating from the new Marine Station at Dover which had been completed during the war. As an austerity measure, the ships now adopted black funnel colours in place of the previous white while the delayed *Maid of Orleans* took up the Dover - Calais passage in 1920 to be followed in 1921 by her sister ship *Biarritz*.

The mail-sharing agreement of 1896 had seen the French Chemin de Fer du Nord charter the former LC&DR paddle

The paddle steamer **Dover** was built at Denny of Dumbarton for the London, Chatham & Dover Railway's Dover - Calais service but was a casualty of the turbine revolution and was scrapped in 1911. *(John Hendy collection)*

# CENTURY OF NORTH WEST EUROPEAN FERRIES 1900 - 2000

The South Eastern & Chatham Railway's turbine steamer *Riviera* of 1911 leaving Folkestone for Boulogne in about 1922 with the post-war black funnels of her owners. For those who never witnessed it, the intense smoke of the coal-burning age was a sight to behold. *(Henry Maxwell collection)*

steamers *Invicta* (1882) and *Victoria* (1886) until such time that their own vessels were ready for service. The *Le Nord* and *Pas de Calais* (2,004 gross tons) were the largest paddle steamers ever built for the Channel passage and entered service in 1898. The French always operated the morning mail runs whilst the LC&DR and later the SE&CR ran the midday and night sailings. Both French twins were responsible for sinking submarines - the *Pas de Calais* accidentally rammed the French *Pluviose* in May 1910 while during the war the *Le Nord* purposely sank a German U boat near Dunkerque.

With the railway grouping of 1923, the South Eastern & Chatham Railway became part of the greater Southern Railway Company and funnels were painted buff with black tops. In June of that year the *Empress* and *Invicta* were sold to the Societe Anonyme de Gerance et d'Armament (SAGA) and they continued to operate for another ten years on the Calais link.

The Southern Railway lost no time in ordering two new vessels for their Dover Strait services. The 2,664 gross tons *Isle of Thanet* and *Maid of Kent* took up station in July and November 1925.

Then in 1927 the Southern Railway and the Nord Railway of France introduced a prestigious new train service linking London (Victoria) and Paris (Gare de Nord). What was to become the 'Golden Arrow' demanded a First Class steamer to provide the link across the Dover Strait and Denny's provided

A wonderful view of the turbine steamer *Biarritz* in Southern Railway livery before she was converted to oil burning in 1926. Her clean lines and perfectly raked funnels and masts showed the Denny design to perfection. *(National Maritime Museum)*

# CENTURY OF NORTH WEST EUROPEAN FERRIES 1900 - 2000

Left: On board the first **Maid of Orleans** in Dover Harbour in about 1922. The first class passengers on the ship's boat deck are enjoying the sea breezes in those timeless wooden deck chairs which were so much a feature of cross-Channel passenger ships until the 1980s. *(Henry Maxwell collection)*

the one and only *Canterbury*. She entered service in May 1929 carrying a maximum of just 300 passengers in opulent surroundings that included the most luxurious accommodation on any short-sea route around the British Isles.

The Depression saw the *Canterbury* became a two class vessel during the winter of 1931-32 at which time her palm court became a casualty. The French were the next operators to add new tonnage for the Dover - Calais link. In 1930 and 1932 they introduced the *Cote d'Azur* and *Cote d'Argent* which replaced the *Empress* and *Invicta*.

The Southern Railway disposed of the 1907 *Victoria* (the 'Old Vic' as she was popularly known) to the Isle of Man Steam Packet Company in 1928. After a remarkable career, the ship was not broken up until her fiftieth year.

In 1932 the *Riviera* and *Engadine* were also sold, the former becoming Burns & Laird Line's *Laird's Isle* on the daylight Ardrossan - Belfast route and remaining in service until 1957, whilst the *Engadine* was eventually purchased for further service in the Philippines where she hit a Japanese mine and sank in 1941.

The final SE&CR pair, the *Biarritz* and *Maid of Orleans* were converted to oil burners in 1925-26 thereafter becoming the inter-war Folkestone - Boulogne steamers.

The Second World War saw the loss of both 'Maids.' The hospital ship *Maid of Kent* was bombed at Dieppe in May 1940 whilst the *Maid of Orleans* was mined while returning from the Normandy beaches in June 1944. Both SAGA steamers were also 'lost' but were repaired by the Germans for use as minelayers. Luck was not on their side, however, and the Allies eventually caught up with them late in the war.

A replacement for the 'Golden Arrow' steamer *Canterbury* was under construction at Denny's when war broke out in 1939. This was the *Invicta* (4,178 gross tons) which finally took up the service for which she had been built in October 1946 and continued on the Dover - Calais route until her withdrawal in August 1972. She was the only local British cross-Channel steamer to continue on a single route throughout her career and the first to be built with an extra deck which always gave her a heavy and imposing appearance.

Nationalisation of the 'Big Four' British railway companies took place in 1948 and in June 1949 the second *Maid of Orleans* entered service on the Folkestone - Boulogne route. Although often seen at Dover during the annual refit of the *Invicta*, she became the seasonal Dover - Calais steamer in August 1972 following the withdrawal of the *Invicta* and her own replacement by the vehicle ferry *Horsa* at Folkestone. It was the *Maid of Orleans* that finally closed the 'Golden Arrow' at the end of September that year and after three more Easter-September seasons, she was withdrawn and scrapped after the close of her 1975 service.

French input into the short-sea services was restored in 1950 with the introduction of the second *Cote d'Azur* in August. The steamer was associated with the new post-war Folkestone - Calais service on which she continued until her withdrawal in September 1972 by which time Folkestone had become a car ferry port.

The **Cote d'Azur** of 1930 was the French reply to the Southern's **Canterbury**. Both she and her later sister ship **Cote d'Argent** were lost during the war. *(Henry Maxwell collection)*

·33·

# CENTURY OF NORTH WEST EUROPEAN FERRIES 1900 - 2000

The *Canterbury* arriving at Calais on the post-war 'Golden Arrow' in about 1946. Notice the two cars on her poop deck. *(Henry Maxwell collection)*

With the *Isle of Thanet* finally withdrawn at the close of her 1963 season, the Weymouth steamer *St. Patrick* moved eastwards. The *Canterbury* finished in September 1964 while the *St. Patrick* and *Maid of Orleans* worked the seasonal Folkestone - Boulogne route until the former's sale to Greece at the end of the 1971 season.

The final British Rail (Sealink) turbine passenger steamer was the *Caesarea* which departs from Dover for Boulogne in September 1979. *(John Hendy)*

With the withdrawal of the *Maid of Orleans*, the final turbine passenger-only steamer to be built for the Dover Strait, in 1975 the Weymouth turbine steamer *Caesarea* was transferred to the short-sea routes. Hers was again an Easter - September service operating from Dover, Folkestone, Boulogne and Calais until her final crossing from Folkestone to Boulogne and return on an RNLI charter in October 1980. The 1981 season saw the transfer from Weymouth of the area's final turbine steamer. The *Caledonian Princess* was Denny's last such vessel for UK use and she had entered service between Stranraer and Larne in December 1961. At the close of September 1981, the steamer was withdrawn from service and eventually sold for static use on the Tyne.

The Belgian Government's Ostend - Dover Line had been established as long ago as 1846, and at the turn of the century they were operating the largest and fastest fleet of side wheeled paddle steamers that the world had ever seen. The Denny-built *Princesse Josephine*, *Princesse Henriette* and *Leopold II* with the Cockerill-built *Marie-Henriette*, *Rapide* and *Princesse Clementine* were all fliers - the *Marie-Henriette* being the fastest of them all.

In 1905, Belgian Marine turned to turbine steamers in the form of the Cockerill-built *Princesse Elizabeth* which held the world record for the fastest such vessel until the advent of the Cunarder *Lusitania* in 1909. The sisters *Jan Breydel* and *Pieter*

The new 'Golden Arrow' steamer *Invicta* was built in 1940 but did not take over the service for which she was built until 1946. She is seen in October of that year coming astern into Dover Harbour with the wing cabs that her master, Captain Len Payne so detested. *(Henry Maxwell collection)*

# CENTURY OF NORTH WEST EUROPEAN FERRIES 1900 - 2000

Almost at the end of the passenger vessel era. The Belgian mail vessel *Reine Astrid* pulling away from Dover on her lunch time sailing to Ostend in September 1979. *(John Hendy)*

*de Coninck* joined the fleet in 1909 while the *Stad Antwerpen* and *Ville de Liege* entered service in 1913. Crossings on the 62 mile route were timed at 3 hours which even the shallow-draughted paddle steamers could achieve on favourable tides when they would cross over the numerous sandbanks rather than pass around them and thus sail directly between Ostend and Dover.

The Belgian steamers of this period offered a 25 knot service (only Newhaven - Dieppe and Holyhead - Dun Laoghaire were able to compete with such speeds) and in order to do so burned tons of poor quality Belgian coal. It was said that you could see the 'Ostenders' coming a long time before they appeared over the horizon simply by the tell-tale clouds of dun-coloured smoke in the direction of the South Goodwins.

Two of Belgian Marine's paddle steamers were sunk by the Germans as block ships during the First World War while the world record holder *Marie-Henriette* hit rocks off Cap Barfleur and was lost in December 1914. Her rival the *Leopold II* was retained by the British Admiralty after the war while the *Princesse Henriette* and *Rapide* were soon broken up. The final survivor was the *Princesse Clementine* which did not go to the breakers until 1928 by which time she had become the English Channel's last such vessel. A sixth turbine steamer, the *Princesse Marie-Jose* entered service in 1923 to be followed in 1930-31 by the route's final steam-powered ships, the 3,088 gross ton vessels *Prinses Astrid, Prince Leopold, Prince Charles* and *Prinses Josephine Charlotte*.

The first diesel-powered ferry in the English Channel was the *Prince Baudouin* of 1934. Attaining 25.5 knots on trials she became the world's fastest diesel ship until eclipsed by her sister *Prins Albert* in 1937. With the Ostend ships being involved in a longer and more costly crossing than the short-sea services, the Belgian Marine Administration saw from an early time that in order to remain competitive and yet not compromise on speed, the introduction of diesel propulsion would allow them to compete on an equal footing. The third ship of the class was the *Prince Philippe* which was still under construction when the Germans invaded the Low Countries in May 1940. She managed to escape to England before being accidentally rammed and sunk off the west coast of Scotland in July 1941 - the only Belgian cross-Channel vessel never to have entered commercial service.

With the *Prince Leopold* also lost whilst returning to Southampton after the D-Day Landings in June 1944, Belgian Marine now built the *Koning Albert* and *Prince Philippe* of 1947/1948. The first vessel was Belgian Marine's centenary ship and work on her had commenced towards the end of the German occupation.

The *Princesse Marie-Jose* was not returned to work and the *Prinses Josephine-Charlotte* was mechanically the worse for wear after a hard war and was withdrawn in 1950. Tragedy struck when in June 1949 the *Prinses Astrid* hit an old mine off Dunkerque and sank in shallow water with the loss of five of her engine room staff. An attempt was made to refloat her but the weather deteriorated in the following month when the steamer broke her back. The *Prince Charles* was therefore the last Belgian turbine steamer to remain in service until she was broken up in 1960.

Such were the passenger numbers using the Ostend route that in readiness for the Brussels Universal Exhibition of 1958 three more sisters were built at the Cockerill yard at Hoboken. The *Roi Leopold III, Koningin Elizabeth* and the *Reine Astrid* entered service in 1956, 1957 and 1958 after which just one more passenger-only vessel was constructed. This was the splendid *Prinses Paola* (4,356 gross tons) of 1966 which was the very last of her type to be built for service to any UK port and certainly the last to remain in commission, not being laid aside until as late as September 1987. The 'Paola' was a wonderful final example of the classic cross-Channel vessel, a type which dominated all short-sea passenger ports until inevitably replaced by the car ferry.

With as many as 33% of all passengers using the service classified as foot passengers, during 1981 the Ostend - Dover service introduced twin Boeing jetfoil, 316 (later 273) passenger craft, the *Princesse Clementine* and *Prinses Stephanie*, which crossed in just 100 minutes. They were very expensive craft to operate and without heavy Government subsidies it is doubtful whether they could have continued in service. Their British terminal at berth 1 on Dover's Admiralty Pier was the converted remains of the *Reine Astrid* of 1958.

P&O Ferries had briefly attempted a twelve month trial jetfoil service from London to Zeebrugge with the *Flying Princess* from June 1977 and later to Ostend with their larger *Jetferry One* and *Jetferry Two* but this was abandoned in September 1980.

Jetlink Ferries (operating as Seajet) also operated a Boeing jetfoil from Brighton - Dieppe from April 1979 with the *Normandy Princess*. P&O Ferries later chartered them their *Flying Princess* but after a promising start the service was suspended in August 1980.

## DOVER AND FOLKESTONE
### The Car Ferries

We have seen that the carriage of motor cars across the English Channel commenced during the early years of the century. The advancement of the internal combustion engine saw the European ferry industry undertake a slow yet unstoppable evolutionary change which gathered pace during the century's last quarter when roll on - roll off traffic demanded specialist ships.

Although the established operators at Dover welcomed the extra revenue that car carrying generated, traditional traffic and motor cars were never an altogether satisfactory mix. The steamers were designed to carry large numbers of passengers and their luggage in addition to the Royal Mail. They were the

# CENTURY OF NORTH WEST EUROPEAN FERRIES 1900 - 2000

sea-link between railway networks and their timing was such that their waiting trains would arrive in London, Paris, Brussels etc. according to tight schedules. The loading and unloading of an occasional motor car by crane (lift on - lift off) would not jeopardise the strict timetables but as more and more vehicles presented themselves for cross-Channel shipment, so problems began to occur.

Following the First World War, increasing numbers of motorists undertook cross-Channel voyages in order to inspect or revisit the battle sites many of which were but a few miles from the ports of Ostend, Calais and Boulogne.

Reasoning that the carriage of a motor car would reduce the numbers of passengers and cargo traffic on any particular sailing and that if their customers were rich enough to own a vehicle then they could afford to pay high rates of carriage, the Southern Railway's near monopoly of trade enabled them to charge whatever they wished.

It was against this background that Captain Stuart M. Townsend commenced a special motorists' service between Dover and Calais in July 1928. Townsend was an experienced continental motorist whose family were involved in the shipping industry. He chartered the 386 gross ton collier *Artificer* for an initial period of one month undercutting the Southern's rates. Townsend's aim was to force the Southern to bring down their own fares and then withdraw to the benefit of himself and his fellow motorists. From the start Townsend enjoyed an excellent relationship with Dover Harbour Board and its Chairman Sir William Crundall had an ongoing feud with the Southern Railway's Sir Herbert Walker. The Townsend service was welcomed with open arms and a part of the little-used Eastern Dockyard was leased for the embryo service. After an £80 profit had been made in the first year, a second season was offered using the collier *Royal Firth*. Then the redundant Royal Naval minesweeper *Ford* was purchased from the local scrapyard for just £5,000 and converted for civilian use. Carrying as many as 28 cars and 168 passengers, the renamed *Forde* entered service in April 1930.

By now the Southern Railway had moved to counter Townsend's actions. During the summer of 1929 they had chartered the coasters *Abington* and *Dublin* to operate a competing service from Dover Admiralty Pier to Calais while the new Southern cargo steamer *Whitstable* offered a similar service linking Folkestone and Boulogne. In March 1931 they introduced their own motorists' service between Dover and Calais using the first specially constructed cross-Channel vehicle ferry the *Autocarrier*.

Belgian Marine entered the car carrying arena in July 1936 using their converted passenger steamer *Ville de Liege* which became the *London-Istanbul* which was named after the new system of European roads which linked the two cities via the Dover - Ostend route. Using an internal system of spiralling ramps linked to strategically placed 'bridges' in her starboard side, the 23 year old ship offered a side-loading drive on service for the first time.

In the early 1930s, the Southern Railway drew up plans for a cross-Channel train ferry service between England and France. Dover was the natural choice for the English base and after much debate, Dunkerque, with its extensive dock system in which the water level remained constant, was selected as the French terminal. Dover, with its spring tide range of 5.9 metres, presented more of a problem and after many delays the new service was finally introduced during October 1936. Not only did the new link carry rail freight but also the famous 'Night Ferry' sleeping car train which enabled passengers from

*The Southern Railway's **Autocarrier** was the first purpose-built cross-Channel car ferry and entered service in 1931. After the war she served Folkestone before being withdrawn in 1954. (Henry Maxwell collection)*

London and Paris to board the Wagon Lits cars in their respective capitals and to wake from their slumbers, refreshed after a night's sleep, in the other city.

Three specially constructed train ferries were provided by Swan Hunter and Wigham Richardson of Wallsend-on-Tyne and were named after famous crossing places on the upper Thames. The *Twickenham Ferry* was followed by the *Hampton Ferry* and *Shepperton Ferry* in 1934/35 and, due to the problems experienced at Dover's Ferry Berth, all were ready for service long before the route commenced. Apart from the stern loading of railway wagons or the twelve 'Night Ferry' carriages, each ferry could also accommodate up to 25 cars in a garage on their upper decks. Vehicles were side loaded via inclined ramps fitted with small linkspans.

Prior to the service opening the *Twickenham Ferry* was sold to the French concern Angleterre Lorraine Alsace Societe Anonyme de Navigation (ALA) - a partnership between the Southern Railway and the French company SAGA - for £150,000.

The Southern were grateful for the extra revenue that the night crossing provided following the loss of the Flushing (Vlissingen) - Folkestone service to the London & North Eastern Railway's (LNER) port of Harwich (Parkeston Quay) in January 1927.

*The Belgian car ferry **London Istanbul** at Folkestone in March 1946. As the passenger steamer **Ville de Leige** she reopened the cross-Channel links from Ostend after the Great War and in her converted form did the same in October 1945 after World War II. (Henry Maxwell collection)*

# CENTURY OF NORTH WEST EUROPEAN FERRIES 1900 - 2000

Previous to the delayed opening of the Dover - Dunkerque train ferry service in October 1936 the three ferries were laid-up at Southampton. Here is the *Twickenham Ferry* at the port's Western Docks in the company of the Cunard White Star Liner *Majestic*. (Arthur Russell collection)

World War Two saw the three train ferries serving as mine layers before becoming transports on the North Channel route linking Stranraer with Larne.

At the war's end, the *London-Istanbul* earned the distinction of reopening the port of Ostend to commercial cross-Channel traffic thereby completing a remarkable double. As the *Ville de Liege*, she had recommenced sailings from Ostend at the close of the Great War. The ship was now past her useful life and following a disastrous summer season running from Folkestone to Boulogne in 1949 she was laid up and soon passed for scrap. By then she was spare as in June 1949 Belgian Marine had introduced their first purpose-built stern loading vehicle vessel, the *Car Ferry* which was renamed *Prinses Josephine Charlotte* in 1952. Capable of carrying 100 post-war cars, the new ship sailed three times a week in each direction serving from Dover Admiralty Pier in a lift on capacity until Dover's new car ferry terminal at the Eastern Docks was opened in June 1953.

Townsend Bros. Car Ferries introduced the converted frigate *Halladale* onto their Dover - Calais link in April 1950 and drive on facilities in the French port were made available in July 1951. With the Southern Railway's *Autocarrier* serving Folkestone - Boulogne until her demise in 1954, the former Southampton - St. Malo overnight steamer *Dinard* was converted for car ferry use and entered service between Dover Admiralty Pier and Boulogne (Bassin Loubet) in July 1947. The 23 year old vessel was subsequently converted to drive-on in 1952 while such was the increase in traffic that the train ferries were regularly used as summer supplementary car ferries to Boulogne throughout summer periods in the 1950s. They were joined by the Danish-built SNCF train ferry *Saint-Germain* in July 1951. Boulogne remained the principle vehicle ferry port until 1970 after which the main thrust of the operations were switched to Calais in direct competition with Townsend Car Ferries.

On New Year's Day 1948, the British Transport Commission was formed with the nationalisation of the 'Big Four' railway companies. For the railway fleet at Dover and Folkestone, they were now part of British Railways (Southern Region).

In June 1952, the car ferry *Lord Warden* (3,333 gross tons) entered service from Dover to Boulogne. A product of the Denny yard at Dumbarton the new ship carried 120 cars and was eventually joined by the *Maid of Kent* (with her twin vehicle decks) in May 1959 at which time the *Dinard* was withdrawn before sailing for a further 11 years in the Baltic as Viking Line's *Viking*.

The year 1958 finally saw SNCF enter the car ferry trade from Calais to Dover with their motor vessel *Compiegne*. She

The Southern Railway steamer *Dinard* was built for the Southampton - St. Malo service in 1924 but was converted to a car ferry for the Dover - Boulogne route in 1947. She is leaving the Admiralty Pier prior to receiving full conversion to drive on status. (Henry Maxwell collection)

37

## CENTURY OF NORTH WEST EUROPEAN FERRIES 1900 - 2000

was in many ways something of a trend-setter being built with all-welded construction, a stern docking bridge, bow-thrust units and controllable-pitched propellers. Although the stern bridge briefly gained favour, this feature was soon disregarded although the other technical developments were soon adopted by competing concerns. A modified running mate *Chantilly* joined her at Calais in June 1966.

In April 1962 Townsend Car Ferries introduced their *Free Enterprise* on the Dover - Calais link. Painted with a pale green hull (inspired by the Cunard cruise liner *Caronia*) the new ferry presented a rather garish sight and was the first to move from the traditional black hull. The stern-loading vessel also boasted higher headroom than usual on her main vehicle deck in anticipation of a perceived increase in commercial vehicle traffic. Townsend (since 1956 owned by George Nott Industries of Coventry) had anticipated a boom in commercial vehicles as early as 1959 when they introduced a chartered tank landing-ship *Empire Shearwater* onto the Dover - Calais route. This bold venture had ended in failure after just six months but all operators looked for off-season use for their ships which at this time provided summer tourist links with the continent and little else. Even in the early 1960's both Townsend and SNCF provided a single ship between them to work their winter schedules.

May 1965 saw the introduction of the *Free Enterprise II* which was the first British registered drive-through car ferry in operation. Although in principle this was a tremendous advance, in practice the 'FE II' was less than satisfactory as her low vehicle deck headroom did not favour the carriage of heavy goods vehicles and within five years she had been offered for sale.

In March 1966 the *Free Enterprise II* opened Townsend's route from Dover to Zeebrugge and the *Free Enterprise III* came on station in July 1966.

Dover Eastern Dock's Car Ferry Terminal was opened in June 1953 and it is seen shortly afterwards with the Belgian motor vessel **Prinses Josephine Charlotte** in berth 1 with the **Dinard** unloading from Boulogne in berth 2. *(John Hendy collection)*

Belgian Marine's car ferry operations also expanded when in anticipation for the increased traffic generated by the Brussels Universal Exhibition of 1958, the 160 car *Artevelde* entered service. A similar ship, the *Koningin Fabiola*, joined the fleet in June 1962 whilst the modified *Roi Baudouin* and *Prinses Astrid* came on station in June 1965 and August 1968. The latter ship boasted higher headroom than usual for the Belgian fleet but while the five vessels then in operation looked sleek, fast and beautiful, developments in vehicle ferry design were already overtaking them and they were to prove totally inept for the roll on - roll off boom. It can be argued that the seeds for the eventual demise of the Belgian Marine Administration (which joined the Sealink consortium in 1970 and the following year changed its name to Regie voor

The car ferry **Lord Warden** of 1952 en route from Dover to Boulogne early in her career. She could carry 120 cars with enough headroom at her after end for a lorry or a double-decker bus. *(FotoFlite)*

# CENTURY OF NORTH WEST EUROPEAN FERRIES 1900 - 2000

The *Normannia* was built for the Southampton - Le Havre link but was converted to became a Dover - Boulogne car ferry in 1963-64. She is seen in berth 13 at the French port during July 1971. *(John Hendy)*

The SNCF car ferry *Chantilly* of 1966 alongside the Gare Maritime at Calais in 1981. *(John Hendy)*

Maritiem Transport - RMT) lay in their inability to build ships which would cope with the changing traffic trends.

Meanwhile Townsend introduced five more almost identical 'Free Enterprise' ('FE IV'- 'FE VIII') class ships between 1969 and 1974 and operated the converted General Steam Navigation Co's day cruise ship *Royal Sovereign*, now renamed *Autocarrier*, in 1967 for their blossoming freight operation to Zeebrugge with the chartered *Stena Danica*.

The ability of the Townsend board (led by the energetic Roland Wickenden who following his untimely death was succeeded by his brother Keith) to anticipate market trends and to provide suitable tonnage to meet them was a salutary lesson to the entrenched attitudes then present amongst those who ran the nationalised ferry fleets in Britain, France and Belgium.

With the never-ending debate concerning whether or not to build a Channel Tunnel then stifling investment in ferry construction in the three countries, Townsend simply made hay while the sun shone but finally increased traffic saw the British Railways' Southampton - Le Havre passenger steamer *Normannia* converted for car carrying before switching to Dover - Boulogne in April 1964. Then came the *Dover*, the first ship to be delivered in the new red, white and blue British Rail livery, in April 1965 but this was all too little, too late. Her half sister the *Holyhead Ferry I* was first transferred to the port in 1967 and in 1976 and 1977 they were converted to drive-through operations with strengthened decks for 26 lorries. As such they became the *Earl Leofric* (ex *Holyhead Ferry I*) and *Earl Siward* (ex *Dover*). SNCF's *Chantilly* also received similar treatment during the winter of 1975-76, but these conversions were purely stop-gap measures.

With the three pre-war train ferries becoming increasingly outdated and costly to operate, British Rail introduced the multi-purpose ferry *Vortigern* in July 1969. She was the first diesel powered railway-owned vessel to work from Dover and was intended to operate as a car ferry from Dover to Boulogne during the summer months whilst switching to the Dover - Dunkerque train ferry links each winter. She was the most versatile vessel in the fleet and was the first local ship to adopt the name of a character from the Dark Ages.

Twin ferries for the introduction of the Folkestone - Boulogne car ferry link entered service in 1972 as the Brest-built *Hengist* and *Horsa*. Initial problems with the new Folkestone linkspan saw a month's delay and the revamped year-round service did not commence until July. The new ships were also involved in crossings from Folkestone to Calais and following the acquisition of a 15% stake in the Belgian route, which was then desperately short of roll on - roll off capacity, two overnight sailings to Ostend.

With the *Vortigern* replacing the *Hampton Ferry* in 1969, another three years were to pass before the withdrawal of the *Shepperton Ferry*. In her place came the *Anderida* - a purely freight ship being built for Stena Line in Norway and converted for train ferry use on the stocks.

SNCF's response to the *Vortigern* was the *Chartres*. Her hull was almost identical (to fit the confines of Dover's Ferry Dock) and she fulfiled a multi-purpose role of passengers, cars, commercial vehicles or trains. The final member of the 1934/35 trio of train ferries was the *Twickenham Ferry* which was finally withdrawn in May 1974. Her ALA replacement was the Italian-built *Saint Eloi* (named after the patron Saint of Dunkerque) which was seized by her yard's creditors shortly after being launched. She finally entered service some 39 months late in March 1975. Again her hull line was identical to that of the *Vortigern* but she was purely a train ferry with no drive-through facilities.

RMT's response to their partnership with the British Rail Shipping and International Services Division (since 1970 trading as Sealink) was to order twin drive-through ro-ro passenger vessels in the form of the *Prins Philippe* (1973) and *Prince Laurent* (1974). The former vessel's vehicle deck configuration, although ideal for the carriage of cars, gave

Townsend's *Free Enterprise III* entered service in 1966 and is seen berthing at Calais in 1982. *(John Hendy)*

39

# CENTURY OF NORTH WEST EUROPEAN FERRIES 1900 - 2000

Normandy Ferries made an impact with the former Ardrossan - Belfast car ferry *Lion* after she took up the Dover - Boulogne link in 1976. (John Hendy)

headroom for only 13 lorries and she was never a success. The 'Laurent' with a flexible mezzanine deck, which enabled her to carry 24 lorries, was always a far more flexible vessel and on her entry into service in June 1974 she opened the vehicle ferry berth at Dover Western Docks thereby allowing vehicle ferries to also convey train-connected passengers from the adjacent Dover Marine Station. In 1972, RMT still boasted a fleet of six passenger ships but ten years later there was just one.

Three new European class freighters, the *European Trader*, *European Clearway* and *European Enterprise*, entered service for Townsend-Thoresen between 1975 - 78 and were an immediate success on the Zeebrugge link.

The Southampton-based P&O Normandy Ferries introduced the eleven year old car ferry *Lion* onto the Dover - Boulogne link in April 1976. Her success was immediate and was built on the lack of interest in the service then being shown by Sealink who were busy consolidating the Calais route. Danish sisters *nf Tiger* and *nf Panther* joined the route in June 1978 and February 1980 by which time the route was carrying in excess of 2 million passengers a year. But the new generation of ferries which entered service on the Calais route in 1980-1 simply drew attention to the shortcomings of the small P&O vessels and in spite of a 'Raising the Standard' exercise the company struggled to compete. At one time a Zeebrugge link looked a distinct possibility but in January 1985 Normandy Ferries and its ships were purchased by the European Ferries Group for £12.5 million and the Boulogne operation was absorbed into the Townsend-Thoresen empire.

RMT continued to build and in May1975 introduced the first of three similar vessels, the *Prinses Maria-Esmeralda*, which was followed by the *Princesse Marie-Christine* in December 1976 and the modified *Prins Albert* in March 1978. The five smaller car ferries were all in turn sold to Greek owners, the last to go being the *Koningin Fabiola* in 1983 which was retained longer than the others due to a major modification in 1976/77 which converted her upper car deck into passenger space thus making her ideal for the still busy Dover Western Docks train-connected services whilst carrying as many as 88 cars.

July 1976 saw the opening of the new port at Dunkerque West which reduced crossing times from 3 hours 45 minutes to just 2 hours 20 minutes. It gave the train ferries far greater flexibility in their scheduling but a ro-ro service from Dover Eastern Docks failed to make any impression.

Still in need of additional freight space, RMT chartered the former Stena Line vessel *Stena Nautica* in April 1982 before purchasing the ship in the following February when she was renamed the *Reine Astrid*. A second charter from Stena Line involved the *Stena Nordica* (ex *Stena Danica*) which was duly renamed *Stena Nautica* before passing to Dieppe Ferries as their *Versailles* in 1986.

The need for additional lorry space saw the stretching of the 1975-78 trio during 1985-86 at which time they were given sufficient headroom for twin lorry decks.

The next generation of cross-Channel vehicle ferry boasted sufficient headroom for twin lorry decks and five such vessels - three for Townsend-Thoresen's (the *Spirit of Free Enterprise*, *Herald of Free Enterprise* and *Pride of Free Enterprise*) and two for Sealink (the *St. Anselm* and *St. Christopher*) were due in service for the summer season 1980 while Sealink partners SNCF were building their *Cote d'Azur* which would at last give a degree of parity between the rival fleets. As it happened, the 'Saint' class were both late in service but the summer of 1981 perhaps saw both Townsend with their 'Blue Riband service' and Sealink with their 'Flagship service' on as near an equal footing on the Dover - Calais link as since the mid-sixties.

In October 1984 SNCF introduced the *Champs Elysees* giving Sealink a fourth new generation ship but with the Armament Naval in Paris constructing a new double-deck linkspan at Boulogne for the reopening the secondary link from Dover, their British partners reacted with a degree of dismay. All their efforts had been directed at the principal Calais link and to dilute this with what could only be a loss-making diversion was indeed fool-hardy. The revived route finally succumbed in the New Year 1986.

Townsend-Thoresen's 'Spirit' class were all capable of operating an unprecedented daily five return sailings as each vessel in turn captured the pier to pier Dover - Calais speed record which is still held by the 'Pride.' Here for the first time since the days of the SE&CR and their under-the-hour turbine steamers was a return to speed. In the intervening period, passage times had actually become slower, both in order to conserve fuel and to a lesser extent to allow passengers to make full use of all facilities and therefore to maximise their on-board spending capability. As if to emphasise this last point, the 'Spirit' class were constructed with minimal outside deck space in order to keep the passengers within the accommodation areas.

With the ever-present shadow of a Channel Tunnel continuing to exercise extreme caution on the part of Sealink's masters, the pending de-nationalisation of the ferry company in July 1984 promised greater investment, new ships and a bright future. An impressive new livery was introduced to herald the freedom which this historic event would bring and much was promised by the board of Sea Containers when the company (37 ships, 24 routes, 10 ports) was purchased for just £66 million. Little wonder that Keith Wickenden, the Chairman of the European Ferries Group, called it "the sale of the century."

For the newly styled Sealink British Ferries, much was promised but little was actually delivered and the badly needed investment in new ships failed to materialise. Whilst it is true that much needed refurbishment was carried out (and in the case of the *Hengist* and *Horsa* crossing as they did on the route of the 'Orient Express' it was refurbishment of a very high standard), no purpose-built ships were added and when in 1985 Townsend-Thoresen announced the order for two more vessels which they claimed would be 'Chunnel Beaters'

# CENTURY OF NORTH WEST EUROPEAN FERRIES 1900 – 2000

Dover Eastern Docks Car Ferry Terminal in September 1967 with the Belgian Marine vessel *Artevelde* in berth 1 (15.30 to Ostend) and the British Rail steamer *Dover* in berth 2 (16.00 to Boulogne). On the right the *Free Enterprise II* is coming astern into berth 4 after which she will work the 16.30 service to Calais. *(John Hendy)*

The Belgian ferry *Princesse Marie-Christine* leaving Dover Eastern Docks for Ostend (via Dover Western Docks) during July 1991. As the *Primrose*, she today operates from Ramsgate to Ostend. *(John Hendy)*

there was no practical response. Plans were drawn up for the stretching of the twin 'Saint' class but the finance was not forthcoming and once again Sealink found themselves firmly in the back seat.

Not long after Sea Containers took over Sealink, the new board made it known that it was far from satisfied with its 15% share in RMT and would make every effort to increase this to 50%. As a first move in this direction, the *St. David* was transferred from the Irish Sea to operate the Dover - Ostend link in March 1985 at which time the overnight link from Folkestone was terminated. This horrified the Belgians who now did the unthinkable and entered into a trading partnership with the old enemy - Townsend-Thoresen at Zeebrugge. The Belgian ships were duly repainted with orange hulls and as from New Year's Day 1986 barred Sealink from the port of Ostend. The port of Zeebrugge also banned Sealink who retaliated by preventing Belgian car ferries from using their Western Docks linkspan thereby causing chaos. Belgian vessels would arrive at Dover, discharge cars at the Eastern Docks, cross to the Western Docks and discharge passengers, load passengers, cross to the Eastern Docks, load cars and sail back to Ostend. After questions had been asked in Parliament, sense finally prevailed and Sealink were allowed to use the Britannia Dock at Zeebrugge. In order to operate this service the company had acquired two quite unsuitable Italian-built deep sea ro-ro vessels - the *Seafreight Freeway*, with which they had commenced a service to Dunkerque West in July 1986, and the *Seafreight Highway*. The service to Zeebrugge was added in June 1987 but proved to be a disaster. The ships were too slow on passage and their turn-round times did not permit them to carry full loads of traffic. They were subsequently withdrawn in September 1988 after which they were part-exchanged for further service in Bulgaria.

The *Free Enterprise VI* and *Free Enterprise VII* were rebuilt

P&O European Ferries *Pride of Canterbury* (ex *Free Enterprise VIII*) leaving Boulogne for Dover in September 1992. The loss-making route was closed in the following January. *(John Hendy)*

41

# CENTURY OF NORTH WEST EUROPEAN FERRIES 1900 - 2000

at Bremerhaven during 1985/86. In a massive operation their superstructures were removed by crane and an extra freight decks were added. This was an immediate response to the growing need of the freight industry for extra capacity on the Zeebrugge service.

The *Pride of Dover* and *Pride of Calais* entered service in June and December 1987 but by that time the company for which they were built no longer existed. Townsend-Thoresen's parent company (the European Ferries Group) had invested badly in the United States where the dramatic drop in oil prices in 1986 had brought them to their knees. Both Wickenden brothers had died in tragic circumstances and without their guiding hand at the company wheel, the EFG were obliged to ask the P&O Group to bale them out. P&O Chairman Sir Jeffrey Sterling had previously joined the EFG board and in January 1987 the P&O shareholders approved the company's bid.

Whether or not P&O would have eventually felt obliged to remove the household name of Townsend-Thoresen is a matter of conjecture, but in March 1987 the disaster off the port of Zeebrugge left them with no alternative. Covering for winter refits on the Belgian service, the *Herald of Free Enterprise* was five days from leaving for her own annual refit at which time she was due to receive extra cabins for a permanent move to the Zeebrugge link.

The 'Spirit' class were the first to be fitted with 'clam' bow doors which slid open and close in a horizontal plain around the ships' stems rather than the usual bow-visor which lifted up and over. Tragically the 'Herald' left Zeebrugge with her bow doors wide open and as she had picked-up speed for Dover outside the port's outer mole, the sea poured in on her main vehicle deck causing instability and subsequent capsize. The disaster claimed the lives of 193 passengers and crew - the worst ferry disaster in British waters and most certainly the bleakest event in the one hundred years under review.

At the public inquiry the company was accused of 'the disease of sloppiness' and of placing profit before safety. Within weeks the entire Townsend-Thoresen fleet had received new funnel colourings and the company trading name was painted out from along the orange hulls. In October P&O European Ferries was launched, the sober dark blue livery was introduced and the fleet was renamed.

Sea Containers' purchase of twin deep-sea Bulgarian ro-ro vessels in 1988 was to be their answer to the P&O European Ferries' *Pride of Dover* and *Pride of Calais*. In the following year one was named *Channel Seaway* and operated a freight service between Dover and Calais before that winter retiring to Bremerhaven where her sister had previously arrived for conversion. The twins were completely rebuilt and refurbished and reappeared as the *Fantasia* and *Fiesta* in March and July 1990. The second vessel was transferred to the ownership of French route partners Sealink SNAT after which the *Champs Elysees* was switched to the Dieppe station while the *St. Anselm* moved across to the Folkestone - Boulogne route to become its largest ever ship.

P&O European Ferries immediately made an impact by ordering four super-freighters for the Zeebrugge route from SUAG, Bremerhaven. The *European Seaway*, *European Pathway* and *European Highway* entered service in October 1991, January 1992 and June 1992 but the fourth (originally to be called *European Causeway*) was converted on the stocks to become the *Pride of Burgundy*. The new ship entered service in April 1993.

The next major work was the conversion of the *Spirit of Free Enterprise*, which had been renamed *Pride of Kent*. The work was carried out in Sicily during the winter of 1991/92 and in order to increase her capacity the ship had a 31.5 metre section inserted. The result was not as successful as had been hoped for and the planned conversion of the former *Pride of Free Enterprise* (by now *Pride of Bruges*) was put aside.

In April 1990 a 13 month hostile take-over bid was concluded when Stena Line of Gothenburg in Sweden purchased Sealink British Ferries for £259 million, a price which industry analysts considered to be grossly in excess of the company's book value. With a further £178 million invested in new ships, a new route opened between Southampton and Cherbourg and £200 million of Sealink's existing debt, Stena faced an immediate crisis and launched Operation Benchmark in which one thousand staff were lost at all levels.

As part of their re-evaluation of all ships and routes, in February 1991 the *St. Christopher* was renamed *Stena Antrim* and transferred to the Stranraer station two months later, whilst after a short spell on the Folkestone - Boulogne service, the *St. Anselm* was renamed *Stena Cambria* in December 1990 and later switched to the Holyhead - Dun Laoghaire link.

Replacing the 'Saints' at Dover, Stena introduced the six year old former Danish State Railways' (DSB) ferry *Peder Paars* which was duly renamed *Stena Invicta* in July along with their new £35 million deep-sea ro-pax ferry *Stena Challenger* which entered service in the previous month. The ro-pax provided much needed freight space on the Dover - Calais route for although the new 'Invicta' boasted passenger accommodation for as many as 1,850 she was built was just a single freight deck and was therefore unsuitable for the crossing.

Although Stena's primary aim was naturally to generate profits for its shareholders, their long term fleet strategy was basically unsound and it appeared as if the company were prepared to place any sizeable unit on their Dover Strait routes without any due consideration of fleet cohesion. On the other hand Townsend-Thoresen and later P&O European Ferries had always sought to optimise new ship designs around discernible patterns of traffic and provided a purpose-built fleet. The last ships that Sealink built for the Dover - Calais link were the 1980/81 'Saint' class twins. Free of nationalisation matters should have improved and armed with new investment the private enterprise companies would enable Sealink to compete on an equal footing. This was far from the truth as neither Sea Containers nor Stena Line were to build a single ship for the Dover Strait. Instead of allowing Sealink to prosper and flourish, denationalisation was to prove a dreadful anticlimax.

As part of Stena's Operation Benchmark, the closure of the Folkestone - Boulogne route occurred on the final day of the year. The *Stena Horsa* duly completed the last day's roster after which both she and her sister *Stena Hengist* were both sold to Greek owners.

More changes were in hand when in 1992 Sealink Stena Line became Stena Sealink Line and after less than six months in service it was planned to remove the *Stena Challenger*. In the event she was transferred to operate the Dover - Dunkerque West route alongside the Sealink SNAT train ferry the *Nord Pas-de-Calais*.

The final ferry built for RMT, the impressive *Prins Filip* finally entered service seven months late on the Ostend - Dover link in May 1992. Excessive vibration on trials had seen RMT refuse to accept the ship until the problems had been

# CENTURY OF NORTH WEST EUROPEAN FERRIES 1900 - 2000

Following the purchase of Sealink by the Swedish Stena Line in 1990, the **Stena Invicta** (ex *Peder Paars*) was introduced to the Dover - Calais route but was always hampered by her insufficient freight space. *(John Hendy)*

rectified but this superbly finished vessel simply served to highlight the shortcomings of her fleet companions. After an eighteen month period of service on the link, the vessel was switched to Ramsgate after the Sally-RMT agreement commenced in January 1994.

The final passenger sailings from Dover Western Docks to Calais Maritime were operated by the *Chartres* on charter to ALA in September 1993.

The following year saw the *Stena Challenger* transferred back to the Calais link thereby allowing Stena Sealink to operate a five ship service in opposition to that of rivals P&O European Ferries.

The final day of 1995 saw the termination of the long-established century trading partnership stretching back to 1896 between the modern day successors of the old railway companies. While Stena fumed at SNAT's reluctance to do things their way, the French simply objected to Stena's methods of doing business and refused to convert their ships' interiors to mirror the much-vaunted but highly controversial 'service concept' of the Swedish group. They created SeaFrance - a new company with a modern identity and their ships were duly restyled and renamed after French artists with 'SeaFrance' prefixes. At the end of the year, Stena Sealink Line abandoned the popular Sealink name and image and henceforth branded themselves Stena Line.

Three days before Christmas the 59 year old train ferry service to Dunkerque West was withdrawn after which the *Nord Pas-de-Calais* was transferred to Calais - Dover freight operations.

With the end of the Stena - SNAT partnership, both operators sought to enlarge their respective fleets and in January 1996 the *Stena Cambria* (ex *St. Anselm*) returned to the Dover station whilst in the following month Stena introduced their own high speed service from the Eastern Docks to Calais with the *Stena Lynx II*. Her stay lasted just three months before she was called away to Gothenburg but in July the new *Stena Lynx III* reinstated the fast link, not that she made much difference to timings on a short 22 mile route. Whilst it was true that pier to pier crossing times were as little as 45 minutes, berthing procedures added another 10 minutes and the company met with a degree of resistance from their customers who saw little to be gained by saving 30 minutes in a craft which offered very few on board facilities.

The following month saw the introduction of the former *Stena Jutlandica* (28,727 gross tons) which after an £8 million refit commenced operations as the largest ferry ever to run across the Dover Strait. The *Stena Empereur* had accommodation for 2,300 passengers, 500 cars or 85 freight units and finally replaced the *Stena Challenger* which was transferred to Holyhead - Dublin.

In response, SeaFrance reclaimed both their Newhaven - Dieppe vessels *Stena Londoner* and *Stena Parisien* (ex *Champs Elysees*) which became the *SeaFrance Monet* and *SeaFrance Manet*.

Both P&O European Ferries and Stena Line had approached the Government on no fewer than three separate occasions with regard to the operation of a joint service to fight the Channel Tunnel and in July 1996 the 'amber light' was given for them to proceed. The joint venture would include both Dover - Calais and Dover - Zeebrugge links with the addition of that from Newhaven to Dieppe. P&O would supply eight ferries while Stena's share would be five with the addition of the fast craft *Stena Lynx III*. Voting rights in the new company were 60 - 40 in favour of P&O although each company would supply four members to the board. After further deliberations, P&O Stena Line was finally unveiled in March 1998. The Stena ships, which had catered for the bottom end of the market, were duly uprated and brought into line with P&O fittings, livery and standards of service. In the following year the Dover - Calais fleet was renamed with P&O units losing their "Pride of" prefixes in favour of the rather unwieldy 'P&OSL.' Former Stena Line ships the *Stena*

43

# CENTURY OF NORTH WEST EUROPEAN FERRIES 1900 - 2000

The **Spirit of Free Enterprise** was renamed **Pride of Kent** in 1987. She is seen arriving at Calais at speed in July 1991, months before her stretching in Italy. (John Hendy)

*Empereur* and *Stena Fantasia* were renamed *P&OSL Provence* and *P&OSL Canterbury*. It appeared to be less than a merger and more of a take-over.

The charter of the idle *Stena Royal* (ex *Prins Filip*) for ro-ro duties on the Zeebrugge link in November 1998 showed the P&O Stena fleet department what a splendid vessel she indeed was. Built to the highest standards with every top-of-the-range fitting that the Belgian tax-payer could buy, this was a vessel that the new cross-Channel company could ill-afford to slip through their fingers. Subsequently, in May the vessel was taken on a six and a half year charter with an option to purchase after two years. She was renamed *P&OSL Aquitaine* and after a major overhaul and refit at Falmouth in October 1999, commenced sailings on the Calais route in the following month.

Her acquisition saw the end of the the previous generation ferry *P&OSL Picardy* (ex *Pride of Free Enterprise*, ex *Pride of Bruges*) which was duly withdrawn and offered for sale in January 2000.

## FOLKESTONE SINCE 1991

Folkestone Harbour was duly purchased by Sea Containers Ports and in April 1992 the 74 metre SeaCat *Hoverspeed Boulogne* took up what has been a largely seasonal service to Boulogne.

The freight link has certainly seen its ups and downs in the years that followed Stena's withdrawal. It was started in June by the French concern Opale Ferries with the chartered *Marine Evangeline* which had seen previously seen charter work at both Newhaven and Pembroke Dock. All appeared to be going well until a fire on board produced cash flow problems and liquidation in April 1983. The service was smartly resurrected by the British-backed Meridian Ferries who renamed the ship *Spirit of Boulogne* before relaunching the service in July.

Folkestone - Boulogne Ferries had at this time all but chartered, amongst others, the Isle of Man vessel *Mona's Queen* which they planned to convert to stern loading but Sea Containers refused to allow them to operate until they had constructed their own berth.

Meridian's *Spirit of Boulogne* was fitted with stability sponsons during her winter 1994/95 refit and a long awaited second ship came on service in February 1995. This was the *Spirit of Independence* (ex *Innisfallen* of 1969, ex *Corsica Viva*) with which Meridian hoped to start a passenger service. Sadly this fell foul of their Folkestone landlords while the Polish crews earned the scorn of the French transport unions. Riots started at Boulogne and quickly lost Meridian 50% of their customers, the vessel even having rockets fired at her and being set alight by the protesting Frenchmen who finally

The **SeaFrance Renoir** (ex **Cote d'Azur**) leaving Calais for Dover. (John Hendy)

# CENTURY OF NORTH WEST EUROPEAN FERRIES 1900 - 2000

succeeded in liquidating the unfortunate company during March.

The present freight service commenced in November 1996 as a joint Hoverspeed/ Falcon Seafreight operation using Sea Containers's *Picasso* but in early 1998 Sea Containers left Falcon to operate the service alone. In April 1998 the well-known *Purbeck* took up the route and noises have been made concerning a second ship.

## OLAU AND EUROLINK AT SHEERNESS

The Danish ship owner Ole Lauritzen gave his name to Olau Line which after an unsuccessful attempt to operate a ro-ro service from a too shallow Ramsgate to Vlissingen (Flushing) in 1973 turned its attentions on the port of Sheerness.

The charter of the Norwegian flagged ferry *Basto V* was secured and in November 1974 the 1,877 gross ton vessel completed her maiden overnight voyage. Immediate indications showed that the service would operate at a profit and Lauritzen lost no time in purchasing twin Danish ferries which could not only offer daily sailings in each direction but could also offer passenger facilities for the first time. The eleven year old *Olau West* (ex *Grenaa*) took up station in January 1975 while the *Olau East* (ex *Hundested*) followed in March. It was originally intended that the second ship should offer sailings to Boulogne while Dunkerque was also interested in attracting the extra trade. Whichever port secured the French link, Lauritzen was determined that future Olau operations would involve twin Dutch/ French services.

The *Olau East* was mechanically the better of the twins and in November she was sold to Venezuela, at a price that Lauritzen could not refuse, and in her place came the chartered DFDS ferry *Dana Sirena* which was duly renamed *Olau Dana*. She was far from ideal having low headroom for freight and being an expensive vessel to operate.

In April 1976 the *Olau Kent* (ex *Apollo*) was introduced, soon after which the *Olau Dana* was returned to Denmark. A further vessel the *Olau Finn* (ex *Saga* of the Tilbury - Gothenburg route) was added to the fleet in May 1976 and now being the spare ship the *Olau West* enjoyed charters to Brittany Ferries and in the Baltic.

The new Dunkerque link finally opened in February 1977 with the *Olau Kent* making the first runs, calling at the French port during her day sailing to Vlissingen. The increased passage time caused severe operational problems and so a new direct service commenced in April. The French unions made no secret of their opposition to a Danish ship with a Danish crew operating to a French port and the link was abandoned until which time the *Olau West* had acquired a French catering crew. In early September the loss making route closed for the final time.

In order to re-coup some of the losses, the *Olau West* was sold to Corsica Ferries and in February 1978 the company was eventually thrown a lifeline by German company TT Line which was offered a 50% holding in Olau. TT immediately proposed the building of two new ferries with each partner financing the cost of one ship but Lauritzen sold his share in Olau Line in order to raise capital for his new French venture, Dunkerque - Ramsgate Ferries.

With Olau now under total West German ownership, the first *Olau Hollandia* and *Olau Britannia* (14,990 gross tons) entered service from the AG Weser yard at Bremerhaven in March 1981 and May 1982. They were very fine vessels and provided a standard of excellence which was difficult to beat on any of the routes operating across the southern North Sea. The route became a tremendous success and often demand outstripped capacity forcing the company to take on a number of short-term ro-ro charters to accommodate the extra freight on offer.

Such was the success of the new ships that in 1988 two more ferries were ordered with 80% more freight capacity than the earlier sisters. The new *Olau Hollandia* and *Olau Britannia* were even more spacious and luxurious than the first named ships. In order to accommodate them, 5 acres of land were reclaimed at Garrison Point, Sheerness where a new linkspan was constructed. The new 35,000 gross ton ships entered service in October 1989 and May 1990. They were easily the best ships on any of the Dutch routes and the rags to riches story of the route appeared to be one of the successes of the century.

The end of Olau Line came in a sudden and quite dramatic manner. The company put it down to the power of their on-board German workers' unions who demanded more pay for less work, undercut cost-savings by gross over-manning and eroded the very fabric of Olau Line UK Ltd. In an attempt to increase traffic and improve its road communications the company sought to switch its operations to Dartford and in January 1994 it was agreed to exchange ships with parent company TT Line. The *Peter Pan* and *Nils Holgersson* carried 500 fewer passengers than the Olau twins and the seamen's union duly went on strike.

With P&O European Ferries wanting to take the ships for their Portsmouth - Le Havre link, the Olau shareholders saw a quick way out of their manning dilemma and agreed to accept the lucrative charter offer. The Sheerness - Vlissingen service was subsequently terminated in May 1994.

In July 1994 the Mersey Docks & Harbour Company, owners of the port of Sheerness, restarted the Vlissingen route with their Ferrylink Ferries taking on charter twin Egyptian ro-ro vessels the *Al Hussein* and *Nuwayba*. If the route was to regain its popularity then it was vital that the operator offered some sort of continuity and although the ships were far from ideal, with the route reopened they looked to capture some of the previous traffic. Ferrylink gave way to Eurolink Ferries when the MD&HC chartered the AK Ventouris vessels *Euromantique* (ex *Union Hobart*) and *Euromagique* (ex *Attika*) which had been built as freight vessels in 1976 and 1977. As the *Agia Methodia* the former ship took up sailings in March 1995 and was joined by the latter in the following month. In spite of their absurd names, there was nothing 'romantique' or

The second ***Olau Britannia*** leaving Vlissingen for Sheerness during her final few weeks in service in 1994. She serves today as P&O Portsmouth's ***Pride of Portsmouth***. *(John Hendy)*

service was the new *Stena Nordica*, one of a pair of vessels built at La Trait for the Gothenburg - Frederikshavn service which, after poor early bookings was not required for service in Scandinavia. The ferry operated as 'The Londoner' which was written in large letters along her hull. In order to occupy passengers on the 5 hour service, gambling (roulette and bingo) was introduced as well as dancing and the now-familiar Swedish smorgasbord. Poor time keeping meant a 45 minute turn-round in Calais and day trips were soon advertised as day cruises.

The first season lasted from July until October after which the ship was offered for sale. Surprisingly Stena decided to offer a service for the 1966 season and chartered the smaller *Prinsessan Christina* from Sessan Line. The service was again advertised for 1967 using the tiny *Stena Baltica*, after which it closed, Stena claiming that the reason was due to "the financial situation of Great Britain."

## RAMSGATE

Following his split with Olau Line in 1978, Danish ship owner Ole Lauritzen was determined to make a success of a link to Dunkerque and he returned to Ramsgate from where he commenced his short-lived Dunkerque - Ramsgate Ferries in summer 1980. The ship which he had secured for the route was the former Mediterranean ferry *Fred Scamaroni* which was renamed *Nuits St. Georges* during her short and inglorious association with Ramsgate. Without a bow-thrust unit, with no weather protection at the Ramsgate berth and dredging not completed the service accumulated debts and the ship was arrested.

Early in 1981 Rederi AB Sally announced their participation in the link and under the leadership of Michael Kingshott, placed 'Sally Viking Line' onto the bright red hull of the seven year old ferry *The Viking* (ex *Viking 5*). Mechanical problems during August saw the charter of the former Sessan Line ferry *Safe Christina* which continued until the end of the season in October. Autumn gales had created havoc with the schedules and it was seen from the start that a new breakwater was necessary to afford the linkspan some protection from the prevailing south westerlies.

The service restarted in May 1992 when much traffic was generated by undercutting the ferry companies at Dover. The much-travelled *Viking 6* (ex *Stena Britannica*) was added to the schedules before taking up the Hull - Rotterdam service for North Sea Ferries but as the season had been advertised as a two ship operation, the *Prinsessan Desiree* (sister to the *Safe Christina*) was acquired being unofficially named 'Viking 2.'

The service was again seasonal and the autumn gales caused serious disruption to the schedules. The *Viking 3* (a sister to *The Viking*) commenced 1983 sailings and was later joined by the Danish ferry *Kalle III* which, following a £3 million refit, was duly renamed *The Viking* in place of the previous ship which was sold to Fred. Olsen Line.

In October of that year the freight operator Schiaffino Line and Port Ramsgate came to an agreement to operate the Schiaffino vessels to Ostend in the following March when a second linkspan had been opened. The French company had initially provided a freight service from Dieppe to Shoreham, and in June 1978 to Dover, but Ostend had been substituted for the Dieppe link in July 1979.

Land reclamation and the construction of twin breakwaters commenced in July 1984 and to operate the Dunkerque service with *The Viking* came the similar vessel, the Yugoslavian *Njegos* (ex *Travemunde*) which duly passed to Brittany Ferries as their *Tregastel* at the close of the season.

The 'Viking Line' part of the company name was dropped in 1985 as the *Viking 6* returned to the service but her lack of headroom was to prove her undoing and the next ship on station was the *Gedser* which the company took on a five year charter as from April 1986. The vessel was renamed *Viking 2* and that summer the Ramsgate breakwater was completed thereby allowing successful year-round operations.

The company was taken over by Effjohn in February 1987 (Effoa : Finland Steamship Co., and Johnson Line AB - later Silja AB) while a new terminal was opened at Dunkerque in July.

Continued growth saw the replacement of *The Viking* by the 9,210 gross tons *Sally Star* (ex *Travemunde*) in December 1988 and during her refit that year the *Viking 2* was renamed *Sally Sky*. A fire in the new ship shortly after entering service saw the charter of the *Botnia Express* (ex *Diana* - another of the first *The Viking* class of ferry). In order to make her compatible with the *Star Star*, in a major refit in early 1990 the *Sally Sky* was cut in two and stretched by 20.8 metres and during this period the second *The Viking* - by now renamed *Wasa Prince* - was called back to deputise.

At the close of 1993 P&O European Ferries' partners RMT closed their 147 year old Dover - Ostend route and on New Year's Day 1994 commenced operation from Ostend to Ramsgate. They had for some time been dissatisfied with their trading arrangements with P&O and knew that when the Channel Tunnel opened their superior share in passenger revenue would drastically decline. Statements were also made in the Belgian press concerning a move from Ostend to Zeebrugge which were emphatically denied by P&O but the final decision to switch UK terminals to Ramsgate was made at ministerial level in Brussels. The company briefly traded as Oostende Lines but the move to Ramsgate was the final nail in RMT's coffin and their historic service finally closed in February 1997.

All routes were hit hard by the opening of the Channel Tunnel in 1994 but especially those within Dover's influence. With new motorways being opened from Calais port to Dunkerque and Ostend, much traffic was funnelled into the shortest sea route to the detriment of Ramsgate which was still without its vital port approach road and a decent road communication via the Thanet Way. The close of 1995 saw the company trading as Sally Ferries but the intense competition in the Eastern Channel caused terminal problems for the company.

Continuing losses on the Dunkerque route saw its closure and the departure of the *Sally Star* in April 1997 by which time Sally's Scandinavian owners had sold 66% of their passenger/ car ferry operations to Australian fast craft operators Holyman.

The *Sally Sky* meanwhile was refurbished for the new Sally Freight ro-ro service linking Ramsgate with Ostend and renamed *Eurotraveller* took up service in a freight mode during March 1997. The route was also worked by the *Eurostar* (ex *Rosebay* and later renamed *Eurocruiser*) and *Euroway* (ex *Argo*).

A seasonal Holyman Sally operation linked Dunkerque East using the 74 metre SeaCat *Condor 10* but this ended in failure and was not repeated. Holyman Sally had taken over the loss-making Ramsgate - Ostend link in March 1997 with their 81 metre SeaCats *Holyman Diamant* and *Holyman Rapide* but continuing losses saw Holyman form an alliance

# CENTURY OF NORTH WEST EUROPEAN FERRIES 1900 - 2000

The second named *The Viking* with the town of Ramsgate and the Napoleonic harbour beyond. The new breakwater, to shelter the linkspans from the weather, is seen in the foreground and enabled a reliable year-round service to be offered. *(John Hendy)*

The *Viking 2* joined the fleet in April 1986 later being renamed *Sally Sky*. Following the closure of the Dunkerque route in April 1997 she was switched to the Sally Freight service to Ostend and was renamed *Eurotraveller*. *(John Hendy)*

with Hoverspeed at Dover and the removal of the Ostend service back to Dover as from March 1998. With the service quickly in the black and Holyman under threat at home, their participation in the English Channel ended in summer 1999.

In an attempt to make one more effort to generate traffic, Sally Direct was formed and duly introduced the *Eurotraveller* in a passenger mode, after initial problems from Belgian authorities had been overcome, in July 1998. This gesture also failed and owners Silja finally disposed of its loss-making asset in November.

Two of the three redundant former Oostende Lines vessels had been purchased by the Slovenian company Transeuropa Shipping Lines (TSL) and the *Prins Albert* had been taken on charter by Sally Freight and had been renamed *Eurovoyager*. Following the last sailing of the Sally Freight service, TSL continued its operation and later introduced the *Primrose* (ex *Princesse Marie-Christine*).

During November 1999 it looked as if a passenger service would be reintroduced between Ramsgate and Ostend.

## NEWHAVEN - DIEPPE

The Newhaven - Dieppe crossing is the most direct route between London and Paris and the respective shares in the famous Joint Service between successive British and French railway companies were based on the length of rail journeys from each port to its respective capital city. The British share was approximately 33% while the French owned the majority holding.

In 1900 the London Brighton & South Coast Railway (LB&SCR) operated the paddle steamers *Brittany* and *Normandy* (1882), the *Rouen* and *Paris* (1888) and the screw driven *Sussex* of 1896. The first pair of vessels were withdrawn and sold for service to the Isle of Man in 1902 and in the following year the *Rouen* too saw service to Douglas.

The Ouest Railway of France produced the Le Havre-built screw steamers *Seine* (1891), *Tamise* (1893), *Manche* (1897) followed by the *France* in 1899.

Following the success of the *Sussex*, Denny of Dumbarton produced the LB&SCR's *Arundel* in 1900 and in August 1903 they followed the South Eastern & Chatham Railway's precedent by introducing their first turbine steamer the *Brighton* which crossed to Dieppe when new in 3 hours 3 minutes.

In 1905 the *Brighton* was followed by the *Dieppe* and it is of interest that after their withdrawal from service in 1930 and 1933 they both passed to Lord Moyne and were converted into private yachts, the second vessel to replace the ex *Brighton* which had previously been wrecked off the coast of Galway.

In 1909 the Chemins de Fer de l'Etat took over the operation of the French service and the nation's first cross-Channel turbine steamers were the *Newhaven* and *Rouen* in May 1911 and September 1912. They were followed by the *Versailles* which was expected in service in 1914 but due to the outbreak of war was not completed until July 1921.

In 1913 the geared-turbine steamer *Paris* entered service for the LB&SCR. This 25 knot steamer was the first local vessel to be built with a cruiser stern and at the outbreak of war became a minelayer. After the war she was refitted and in 1934 took over the Brighton Palace Pier day excursions to Dieppe from the elderly *Arundel*.

The Southern Railway's first new ships for the route were the *Worthing*, which was delivered in August 1928, and the *Brighton* - delivered in March 1933 - which were smaller and faster versions of Dover's *Isle of Thanet* and *Maid of Kent*.

The *Paris* was lost at Dunkerque in June 1940 while the *Brighton* was bombed at Dieppe (together with Dover's *Maid of Kent*) in the previous month.

At the outbreak of war the French partners in the Joint Service were in the course of building twin vessels to replace the *Newhaven* and *Rouen*. The *Londres* was on the stocks in Le Havre at the time of the French surrender and she was completed by the Germans who used her as a minelayer. Returned to her builders in 1945 the ship finally entered service in April 1947 and was followed by her sister *Arromanches*.

The *Worthing* returned to service in March 1945 and was joined in April 1950 by the sixth-named *Brighton* which was a smaller version of the Folkestone - Boulogne steamer *Maid of Orleans*. The final and fastest passenger-only turbine steamer for the route was the French vessel *Lisieux* (based on the Calais-based *Cote d'Azur*) which entered service in 1953.

The increase in post-war motor car traffic had seen the French introduce a trio of lift on - lift off car ferries in 1946 - 50. The *Nantes*, *Rennes* and *Brest* also carried cargo but during the summer period up to 60 cars could be shipped in these vessels while their drivers crossed by passenger steamer.

The withdrawal of the *Worthing* in 1955 saw the transfer of

# CENTURY OF NORTH WEST EUROPEAN FERRIES 1900 - 2000

The French turbine steamer *Rouen* leaving Newhaven for Dieppe. (Henry Maxwell collection)

A post-war view of Dieppe with the *Londres* departing, the *Brighton* tucked up in the harbour and the cargo vessel *Brest* at lay-by. (Henry Maxwell collection)

the *Londres* to British control so that both British and French partners each operated two vessels, although in 1958 poor winter traffic saw the route become a seasonal March to October operation.

Newhaven's saviour was undoubtedly the introduction of the car ferry *Falaise* in June 1964. The steamer had been built at Denny's in 1947 and served principally on the overnight Southampton - St. Malo route but its closure had made her available for conversion to a car ferry at Vickers Armstrong's Hebburn yard. As such she could carry 100 cars and 700 passengers.

The *Londres* duly was withdrawn at the close of the 1963 season while the *Arromanches* followed her into Greek waters in the following year. The *Lisieux* and the *Brighton* continued in service throughout 1964 but the *Lisieux* finished in June 1965 (thereafter operating day cruises from St. Malo - Channel Islands, Torquay and Weymouth) before her sale to Greek owners. The *Brighton* completed her final sailing in September 1966 and was sold to Jersey Lines but by then two French car ferries had joined the service in May and July 1965. The diesel engined *Villandry* and *Valencay* were the first Dieppe ferries fitted with controllable pitch propellers and twin rudders thereby giving them far more manoeuvrability in the narrow confines of each port. For reasons of economy the crossings were slowed to 3 hours 45 minutes and each ship sailed twice daily.

During their 1967-68 refits the three Newhaven - Dieppe car ferries adopted the Joint Service houseflag on their buff funnels and did not follow the identity change as seen in the railway vessels elsewhere around the British Isles.

With traffic booming on the route a new vessel to replace the *Falaise* was ordered from the Naval Dockyard at Brest. The *Senlac* followed Folkestone's *Hengist* and *Horsa* and was to all intents and purposes a repeat ship entering service in May 1973. The ro-ro vessel *Capitaine Le Goff* had entered service in August 1972 but was never particularly successful being too slow to complete double daily round sailings. The stretching of the *Villandry* and *Valencay* during 1977 and 1978 raised their vehicle decks by 56 cm. and doubled their lorry space whilst giving them a drive-through capacity but at the close of 1978 the route had lost a reported £3 million.

In 1981 Sealink UK Ltd. announced their intention of withdrawing from the Joint Agreement and looked for a 50 - 50 partnership from which they could at last begin making money on the link. Negotiations continued for some time until in January 1982, following the inability of the partners to renegotiate the 1862 agreement, Sealink UK Ltd. announced that they were withdrawing from the service and leaving it to the French to operate alone. This plan involved the sale of the *Senlac* whose crew immediately responded by blocking the Newhaven linkspan. Further discussions were subsequently held and a new agreement made whereby the French would withdraw the *Villandry* and retain the *Valencay* for relief purposes. Furthermore the Calais-based *Chartres* would be introduced prior to a Stena Line vessel coming on station. The *Chartres* arrived in May 1982 while in January 1984 the spare Brittany Ferries vessel *Cornouailles* was taken on a year's charter.

Following the purchase of Sealink UK Ltd. by Sea Containers in July 1984, a lengthy evaluation of all routes was undertaken. It was announced that the *Senlac* would be withdrawn from the route in March 1985 but in the event this occurred on the final day of January after which the vessel came under SNCF control.

In spring 1986 SNCF formed a subsidiary company Dieppe Ferries to manage the Newhaven service. Dieppe Ferries were given four years to turn around the fortunes of the link or face the threat of closure. At the same time the redundant Calais ferry *Chantilly* was given £600,000 refit and duly joined the Dieppe fleet as their third ship.

The promised Stena Line vessel was the former *Stena Nautica* (ex *Stena Danica* - built in 1974) which became Dieppe Ferries' *Versailles* when she entered service in April 1987. With capacity for as many as 1,800 passengers and 425 cars (almost double that of the *Chartres*) the route's largest ever ship required £1 million dredging and widening of the harbour entrance at Newhaven.

The arrival of the *Fiesta* at Calais in June 1990 released the *Champs Elysees* for the Dieppe - Newhaven service in July and with the departure of the *Senlac* for Greek waters in 1987, both she and the Versailles now maintained the link together. The new livery of the French ships now reflected their reorganised ownership of Sealink SNAT.

Strikes and poor labour relationships had been a feature of the French service for many years. Strikes during June and July 1991 brought matters to a head. During December the route was given a final ultimatum - just six months to resolve its problems. In March 1992 Sealink SNAT announced that the link would close in the following month and this it duly did with one final strike pre-empting the advertised date of

# CENTURY OF NORTH WEST EUROPEAN FERRIES 1900 - 2000

closure.

The service was put up for sale and purchased by Sealink Stena Line (the Swedish company Stena Line had previously acquired Sealink from Sea Containers in 1990) and restarted the service in May after just 24 hours notice. The idle *Versailles* had been renamed *Stena Londoner* and she was later joined by the *Stena Parisien* (ex *Champs Elysees*). Both ships were chartered from the French.

July 1994 saw the opening of Dieppe's new ferry terminal but the rift between Stena Line and their French counterparts as from New Year's Day 1996 led to the termination of the ship charters and Stena Line had to find new vessels as both ferries were required to work the new SeaFrance link between Calais and Dover. The 'Londoner' completed her stint in April 1996 while the 'Parisien' was retained until January 1997.

In the event the *Stena Antrim* (ex *St. Christopher*) was transferred from Stranraer while the fast ferry *Stena Lynx III* was switched from Dover - Calais as from March 1997. The Dieppe fast ferry service was inaugurated by the *Stena Lynx I* in April 1996 and she was followed by the monohulled *Stena Pegasus* which proved to be something of a disaster. The 'Antrim' was replaced by sister ship *Stena Cambria* (ex *St. Anselm*) although until the arrival of the 'Lynx III' the former Dover-based sisters enjoyed a brief period in operation together.

With the P&O Stena Line Joint Venture getting underway in March 1998, the *Stena Antrim* was almost immediately withdrawn and replaced by the *Stena Cambria* in the following month. The *Stena Lynx III* was renamed *Elite* but became increasingly unreliable and was withdrawn from service in October. It was reported that passengers on the route were down by 62%, freight by 33% and that the revenue had dropped by £16 million in the previous five years. The *Stena*

The **Champs Elysees** strike-bound at the Dieppe linkspan in April 1992 (notice the 'body' swinging from the main mast!). *(John Hendy)*

*Cambria* continued until the end of January 1999 when she closed the link to traditional ferries.

Yet again there was a company willing to purchase the loss making service. Hoverspeed (a subsidiary of Sea Containers) recommenced the route in April 1999 with their fast craft *SuperSeaCat Two* and such was their success that what was intended to be a seasonal service continued until Christmas. During July she crossed from pier to pier in just 96 minutes.

*John Hendy*

The **Stena Cambria** (ex **St. Anselm** of 1980) closed the Newhaven - Dieppe service in January 1999. *(John Hendy)*

51

# CENTURY OF NORTH WEST EUROPEAN FERRIES 1900 - 2000

## Short sea freight

*P&O Stena Line's Freight Director Brian Cork charts the growth of the short sea freight market and the rise to market dominance by P&O Stena Line.*

Within the extensive sphere of operations undertaken by P&O Stena line, freight traffic contributes a significant proportion of our overall revenue. As must be obvious to anyone travelling between Dover and Calais the short sea freight market is very healthy indeed. It must be remembered though, that revenue yield, although rising, has yet to recover to the level enjoyed prior to the opening of the fixed link. In consequence the winner in the market place will be the operator offering the best mix of efficiency and economy - in short value for money.

Some readers may be surprised to know that, in response to intense competition from the other surface operators and the Channel Tunnel, P&O Stena Line is now carrying a record volume of freight traffic amounting to more than 1 million vehicles per year. At peak times this can mean handling nearly 5000 units in a single day, or more than 200 trucks per hour. In terms of market share this equates to P&O Stena Line capturing around 50% of the short sea market.

The pessimists who forecast a severe downturn for the Dover - Calais surface route in the wake of the tunnel achieving full operations could not have been more wrong. The combined freight volume of the short sea ferry operators is now more than double that passing through the tunnel. If it were possible to line up, bumper to bumper, all the trucks carried by P&O Stena Line last year the traffic jam would stretch from the White Cliffs of Dover to Sydney Opera House.

If this makes impressive reading it also poses two important questions: How do we manage the sheer volume of traffic? And how did it all start?

The answer to the first question is teamwork. From our European sales force, independent agents, shore side handling staff, behind the scenes administrative staff to the sea-going crews. And not least our valued freight clients themselves. Added to this of course is the P&O Stena Line fleet now comprises on the Dover - Calais route, and three dedicated freight vessels trading between Dover and Zeebrugge. That adds up to a total gross tonnage of 265,983, the largest single company fleet operating in British waters.

You may be interested to know that our European sales force comprises a team of just three people at head office, including myself, and twelve representatives throughout Europe including the United Kingdom. If you think about it, that works out at annual business worth 66,000 trucks per man! And the remarkable thing is that we achieve this with virtually no advertising at all.

Modern technology plays its part as well. With more than 4500 account clients and over 1 million individual vehicle movements each year the paperwork problems could be overwhelming. Technology allows our account clients to issue their drivers with smart cards that simply have to be swiped when they check in and all the paperwork, right through to invoicing is handled automatically. We are now developing Internet based

*Brian Cork*

system to further improve the efficiency of our service.

Fifteen years ago P&O Ferries abandoned the concept of advance booking for freight traffic. At the time this was considered somewhat radical and caused more than a little consternation, both within P&O and our customers. However the combination of cross-Channel capacity and frequency that we were able to offer meant that freight drivers could simply just turn up and go. The reduction in administrative procedures also allowed cost savings to be passed on to the freight companies who soon realised the advantages of this approach and were delighted at the efficiency and pricing benefits.

The second question can be just about answered: "by accident".

To be strictly accurate the first records of road freight passing through Dover date back to the late 1950s but the tonnage was low, vehicles small and movements infrequent. By the early 1960s more freight vehicles were being seen but the policy of the Dover Harbour Board at that time was for all freight vehicles to use the Western Docks, travelling to Dunkerque on the train ferry. The Eastern Docks was reserved for passenger and car traffic only. It so happened that a naïve young clerk working for Townsend Car Ferries was blissfully ignorant of this protocol and accepted a booking for a freight vehicle through the Eastern Docks (yes, it was yours truly). The Terminal Manager was less than pleased and had to be placated with a half bottle of whisky "smuggled" ashore from the *Free Enterprise I*. A trend however had been started. By the following year Townsend Car Ferries were carrying between ten and twenty freight vehicles each day through Dover's Eastern Docks and it was realised that a useful market existed.

One problem that restrained the potential of this market sector during the late 1960s was the design of the ships. The Townsend fleet comprised *Free Enterprise I* that could accommodate up to 10 trucks; *Free Enterprise II* that had a vehicle deck clear height of just 11'11"; and *Free Enterprise III* that featured a constrained car deck layout that hampered the manoeuvres of any vehicle longer than

# CENTURY OF NORTH WEST EUROPEAN FERRIES 1900 - 2000

The port of Dover with the **P&OSL Canterbury** at the berth, prior to another busy departure to Calais. *(P&O Stena Line)*

an average car.

As for the freight sales force of those days, the main method of winning new business was to send someone along Dover sea front to coerce truck drivers parked up and waiting for the Western Docks service to Dunkerque.

In March 1966 a new route was inaugurated between Dover and Zeebrugge in Belgium. This was set up in competition with British Railways and the Belgian state owned RMT operating out of Ostend. The "opposition" was then carrying large numbers of British Forces personnel and equipment but a market for general freight was growing.

At that time almost all commercial goods were being imported and exported by conventional cargo vessels using ports such as Tilbury and Southampton. When industrial action by port workers caused a series of dock strikes throughout the late 1960s and early 1970s, traders turned to road freight as an alternative mode of transporting goods between the UK mainland and continental Europe. Dover offering the shortest Channel crossing was well placed to take advantage of this and freight volumes began to rise significantly.

With continually rising freight traffic, ship owners began to realise that new investment was necessary but that new vessel designs would have to reflect the growth in demand for freight traffic and the increasing size of the freight vehicles themselves. The consequent introduction of new tonnage by all operators incorporated both raised vehicle deck clear heights and drive-through capability and signalled the beginning of Dover's ro-ro freight boom - a trend that has continued almost uninterrupted ever since.

Although freight traffic through Dover had become well established by the late 1970s the administration associated with conveying commercial goods across borders made life difficult for everyone involved. For the haulier the complexity of the paperwork and the general bureaucracy was at the least very frustrating and often daunting. This gave rise to the freight forwarding industry where specialised companies were set up specifically to handle the burgeoning administration for the hauliers. So valuable did these services become that individual freight forwarding clerks built strong relationships with their haulage clients. In many cases it did not take long for these enterprising clerks to realise that they could earn more money by establishing their own businesses than they could working for an employer. This they frequently did, taking large volumes of business with them. But these heady days were not to last. The introduction of the European Single Market in 1993 brought with it a

The **P&OSL Aquitaine** joined the fleet on the Dover-Calais route in November 1999. *(Mike Louagie)*

53

# SOME THINGS YOU WAIT FOR

## SOME THINGS YOU DON'T

With more channel crossings per day than any other ferry operator, and daytime departures every 30 minutes between Dover and Calais at peak times, P&O Stena Line leaves all others in its wake. Providing the most exciting range of on-board facilities designed to make your crossing even more enjoyable, it is the ferry service you've been waiting for without, of course, the wait. For more details or to book, please phone **087 0600 0600** or contact your local travel agent.

**P&O Stena**
LINE

*where time sails by*

# CENTURY OF NORTH WEST EUROPEAN FERRIES 1900 - 2000

The **P&OSL Provence** (ex **Stena Jutlandica**, ex **Stena Empereur**) makes a fine sight off Calais in August 1999. (John Hendy)

The **Stena Fantasia** (ex **Fantasia**) arriving at Calais in the P&O Stena Line livery in August 1998. She was later renamed **P&OSL Canterbury**. (John Hendy)

relaxation of cross border controls and an end to this dynamic era of freight forwarding. Prior to 1993 over 200 separate freight forwarding businesses were operating in Dover alone. Now the figure is less than 30.

Today more than 75% of commercial goods imported into Britain pass through the Dover-Calais route and it is highly likely that every household in the country contains at least one article that has been on the vehicle deck of a P&O Stena Line ferry. We maintain this strong market position by offering quality, competitive pricing, capacity, frequency and flexibility. It is this capability that attracts road haulage operators from all over Europe. Did you know for example that on its Dover-Calais service P&O Stena Line carries more than 6000 trucks per month originating in Spain?

Flexibility is very important: it is our ability to tailor schedules and capacity to the changing demands of the market. An example of this is the recent transfer of the dedicated freight ship *European Highway* from the Dover-Zeebrugge route to meet increased demand on Dover-Calais services. By doing this we were able to provide substantial additional freight capacity and relieve pressure on the peak sailings of the mixed traffic vessels serving Dover-Calais, where vehicle deck space is in great demand from short stay excursion motorists. The *Stena Royal* (ex *Prins Filip*) which has been on temporary charter to P&O Stena Line has been renamed *P&OSL Aquitaine* and, with the charter period extended, has replaced *European Highway* on the Dover-Calais route.

In the modern world of short sea freight market vessel design is critical, scheduling is a science and efficiency is paramount. For the future there is speculation regarding the potential of high speed freight vessels. While we would never say never, we believe that our vessels are fast enough. With 40 sailings every day in each direction and departures every 45 minutes we think we have got it right, offering the short sea freight market exactly what it wants - 1 million happy customers can't be wrong!

Double vision? Former sisters **P&OSL Kent** and **P&OSL Picardy** at Dover Eastern Docks in August 1999. (John Hendy)

# CENTURY OF NORTH WEST EUROPEAN FERRIES 1900 - 2000

## Changing the course of history – Cross Channel Hovercraft

The introduction of the vehicle carrying cross-Channel hovercraft services in 1968 met with a somewhat mixed reaction. On the one hand there was considerable media speculation that surface travel at sea was to be changed forever. Some even went as far as to forecast that conventional ferries would disappear completely to be replaced by the new breed of air cushion vehicles. The futuristic concept with its inherent aviation technology that was so different to the ferry tonnage of the day attracted global attention and was the cause of much excitement. On the other hand there was no shortage of detractors and critics who saw the concept as excessively complex and expensive. On balance it was not considered to have much of a future.

With hindsight the reality has fallen some way between the two views and it may be that, despite a decline in the number of cross-Channel hovercraft services now operated, as alternative fast ferry technology can provide a more cost effective option, hovercraft may still one day become a more common sight on the ferry routes of the world. That may seem a little too idealistic and the chances of it happening are not immediately favourable, but the fact remains that in fast ferry terms the amphibious hovercraft remains unchallenged in terms of performance. The 60 knots or more attainable in full load conditions is still a target milestone for the fast ferry industry of today over thirty years behind the hovercraft.

Aviation-style controls in the hovercraft. *(Paul Hynds)*

This performance advantage created by operating above the water and therefore avoiding the resistance of passing through it is still acknowledged. The major problem preventing any expansion of large scale hovercraft is simply that no one is building them, or to be more precise no one is investing in the research and development necessary to take the concept forward into the next century. The fact remains though that the only way to transport an economic payload at seriously high speeds is by employing some form of air cushion - be that generated mechanically as in the hovercraft or by exploiting aerodynamics as in ground effect craft concepts. If speed is to continue to be an increasingly important factor in the future air cushion technology cannot be discounted. Additionally the cost of providing shore side

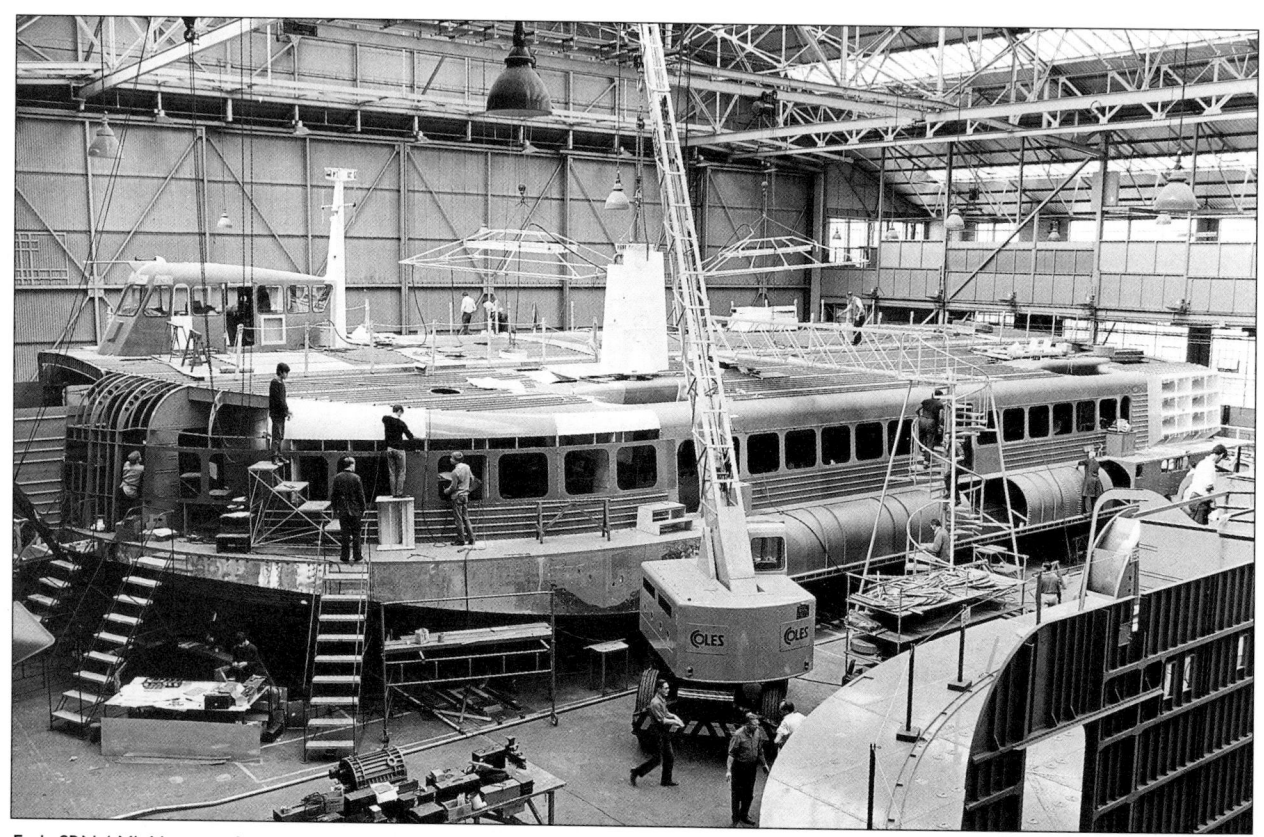

Early SRN.4 Mk I hovercraft under construction at Cowes. *(Paul Hynds collection)*

infrastructure for conventional vessels in the form of quays and berths is becoming increasingly expensive

Of course what is holding such developments back is the associated costs, both in terms of development and operation. That was as true in the 1960s as it is now. What made the difference then was that there existed a national optimism following the depressed atmosphere of the preceding decades and the fact that the hovercraft was a concept so revolutionary that it attracted development funding as the Government could see potential military applications and export sales. These days it will need a very far sighted commercial investor indeed to stimulate a resurgence of development.

Revolutionary as it was in the 1960s the idea of the hovercraft was not new. Using some form or air lubrication to reduce the frictional drag had been seen before but without any real measure of success. Theory was one thing, practicality is another. It was not until 1953 when inventor Christopher Cockerell modified a small river boat by applying pressurised air beneath the hull that any validity for the concept was apparent. Following these early experiments Cockerell began to investigate the possibility of developing a hull form that could be completely supported on a cushion of air. This, he correctly surmised, would have enormous performance benefits.

Two years later he was able to test a small wooden model of the first definitive hovercraft. At this point, however, his plans were to be frustrated. He was unable to attract any significant interest in the concept and was unsuccessful in trying to secure the necessary financial backing from industry. The Government did keep an eye on his developments and realising the military potential declared the hovercraft concept to be classified information. This had the effect of further frustrating development as study after study and committee after committee had to evaluate and pronounce on the subject. Cockerell's own calculations had to be checked, re-checked and verified, and there were interminable periods when nothing happened at all. It was during this time that Cockerell concluded that to make the concept workable in any practical operational sense the hovercraft would benefit greatly from having flexible air cushion seals or a "skirt". This was a feature not so far seen on any test models and the development was dismissed by the experts appointed to oversee the development of the hovercraft.

In 1958 responsibility for hovercraft development passed to the National Research Development Corporation and by the end of the year the concept was taken off the secret list. A manned craft was commissioned from Saunders Roe resulting in the construction of the skirtless SRN-1, the designation providing the direct lineage to the SRN-4 Hovercraft of today. On the 25th July 1959 SRN-1 was successfully piloted from Calais to Dover and demonstrated to the world that the hovercraft was a feasible transport proposition.

The passing of Sir Christopher Cockerell on 1st June 1999 signalled the departure of one of the greatest and most imaginative inventors of all time. Without his immense contribution to transport technology the shape of the contemporary fast ferry industry would arguably be very different. He died forty years to the day after the very first flight of the SRN-1.

In 1965 hovertravel started the world's longest running hovercraft service with the introduction of a type SRN-6 passenger-only craft operating between Portsmouth Southsea and Ryde on the Isle of Wight, a service that is still operating today deploying more advanced AP1-88 Hovercraft. In the same year Swedish Lloyd and Swedish

The first purpose-made hoverport at Dover's Eastern Docks in 1968. *(Paul Hynds collection)*

CENTURY OF NORTH WEST EUROPEAN FERRIES 1900 - 2000

# When you're crossing the water, you could just follow the herd...

**or you could try a more civilised approach.**

Sea Containers ferry services offer a relaxing and enjoyable alternative to the average ferry crossing. Forget the horrors of being herded in and out of ports, jostling for space and never being sure of a seat. We never compromise on customer service, comfort or safety, no matter how many people are travelling with us. All Sea Containers ferry services operate from their own dedicated port and terminal facilities to speed loading and unloading. And with fast SeaCats or SuperSeaCats on most routes there's no quicker way across the water. So why follow the herd when you can journey in style?

**superseacat**

**seacat**

DOVER-CALAIS • DOVER-OSTEND • FOLKESTONE-BOULOGNE • NEWHAVEN-DIEPPE
GOTHENBURG-FREDERIKSHAVN • BELFAST-STRANRAER • BELFAST-TROON
LIVERPOOL-DUBLIN • HEYSHAM-BELFAST • HEYSHAM-DOUGLAS • DOUGLAS-LIVERPOOL
DOUGLAS-BELFAST • DOUGLAS-DUBLIN • CAMPBELTOWN-BALLYCASTLE

Sea Containers Passenger Transportation Division, Sea Containers House, 20 Upper Ground, London SE1 9PF
Telephone: 0171- 805 5000  Fax: 0171-805 5900  http://www.seacontainers.com

# CENTURY OF NORTH WEST EUROPEAN FERRIES 1900 - 2000

SRN.4 Mk I departing Dover for Boulogne in 1969. *(Paul Hynds)*

America Lines announced a joint venture to set up a new company named Hoverlloyd to operate hovercraft across the English Channel. The following year saw a rush of activity as the Government of the United Kingdom encouraged the state owned British Railways to set up British Railways Hovercraft to operate another cross Solent service from Southampton to Cowes trading under the Seaspeed banner. Hoverlloyd commenced operations in April 1966 with a pair of SRN-6 craft operating out of Ramsgate Royal Harbour to Calais. Also on the English Channel during the same year Townsend Car Ferries started hovercraft operations between Dover and Calais with a single SRN-6, but the service was short lived.

In February 1968 the first SRN-4 Mountbatten class vehicle carrying hovercraft was launched by the British Hovercraft Corporation at Cowes. During trials the craft exceeded 50 knots and apparently performed encouragingly in strong winds and choppy sea conditions. The first cross-Channel flight for the prototype hovercraft car ferry took place in June of the same year but it did not enter commercial service until August. Named *The Princess Margaret* the SRN-4 operated between Dover and Boulogne but that inaugural season was beset with technical problems. Considering the complex technology of the craft this was not at all surprising. Four gas turbine engines were linked via a system of gearboxes and shafts to four fans which provided lift and the four air propellers which generated thrust. Each propeller was mounted on a pylon which could be moved through an arc to aid steering. The propellers themselves were fitted with adjustable pitch to vary thrust and could also be reversed. Aft of the propellers a pair of fins contributed further to manoeuvrability.

While the electrical and hydraulic systems needed to enable the hovercraft to function properly were problematic, it was the skirt that gave real cause for concern. On the prototype craft the skirt was arranged as a parallel bag round the periphery of the hull into which the lift fans forced air. This air was then bled into the fingers beneath the skirt bag which channelled the pressurised air beneath the hull and also acted as erosion strips. The wear rate of the skirt was considerably higher than predicted and the method of securing the skirt to the hull which employed a combination of bolts, hinges and chains was less than satisfactory. Furthermore the skirt itself was prone to damage in rough conditions and a number of failures were recorded.

In December of 1968 Hoverlloyd's first SRN-4 was launched with a revised skirt designed that now featured a deeper chord bag at the bow. The *Swift* entered service in April 1969 from Pegwell Bay, near Ramsgate to Calais. Later that year Seaspeed introduced its second SRN-4 The *Princess Anne* and Hoverlloyd accepted delivery of its second craft the *Sure*. In 1970 Seaspeed started a new service linking Dover to Calais sharing facilities in France with Hoverlloyd.

By the summer of 1972 Hoverlloyd had a third craft, the *Sir Christopher*, imminent and announced that all three craft were to be uprated to Mark II specification which increased capacity from the original 252 passengers and 28 cars to 278 passengers and 37 cars. Seaspeed continued with their two craft in Mark I specification although the skirts had been modified to incorporate the latest developments to improve reliability, sea keeping and passenger comfort. In 1976 Seaspeed decided to stretch their two existing Mark I hovercraft to Mark III

# CENTURY OF NORTH WEST EUROPEAN FERRIES 1900 - 2000

SRN.4 Mk III discharging at Western Docks Hoverport, Dover. *(Paul Hynds)*

Seaspeed's two SRN.4 Mk I hovercraft at Dover Eastern Docks. *(Paul Hynds)*

specification which involved cutting the craft in two and inserting a 55 feet section to increasing capacity to 424 passengers and 54 cars. To maintain performance the engines were to be uprated. The first of the Mark III hovercraft was due to enter service in the summer of 1978 operating from a new hoverport located at Dover's Western Docks which was opened in the same year replacing the smaller facility used by Seaspeed's Mk I craft at the Eastern Docks in the same port. Hoverlloyd had added a fourth Mk II craft, *The Prince of Wales*, in 1977.

The design for the stretched SRN-4 Mk III Hovercraft also included a considerably revised skirt featuring a tapered bag with a deeper chord at the bow reducing toward the stern. This development returned many advantages including better fuel efficiency, higher speed, improved wear, and greatly enhanced passenger comfort.

The hovercraft industry suffered a setback at this point when the first of two French designed and built SEDAM N500 hovercraft intended to operate in alongside the Seaspeed craft was destroyed by fire during its pre-delivery trials programme in May 1997. The intention had been to introduce this craft, the *Cote d'Argent*, during the summer of 1977. The second French hovercraft *Ingenieur Jean Bertin* entered service on the English Channel in 1978.

Throughout this period of cross-Channel hovercraft growth neither of the two operating companies had ever managed to record any significant profits. On the contrary, in most years significant losses were endured. Despite a combined market share approaching 20% of the short sea traffic, this latest spell of expansion, allied to rising fuel

SEDAM N500 Hovercraft entered service in 1978. *(Paul Hynds)*

# CENTURY OF NORTH WEST EUROPEAN FERRIES 1900 - 2000

*The Princess Margaret* on passage to Calais. *(FotoFlite)*

costs, increased competition and escalating overheads, did not signal an economically comfortable future for either company. As the decade of the 1970s closed there was considerable speculation concerning a merger of the two companies.

In 1981 permission was granted for the merger and a new company was formed under the name of Hoverspeed. Initially the company continued operations out of both UK ports to Calais and Boulogne deploying the combined fleet of four SRN-4 Mk II craft and two SRN-4 Mk III craft supported by the single SEDAM N500 operated by SNCF under the Hoverspeed corporate identity. The French hovercraft however suffered from lack of development and schedules were persistently disrupted by its non-availability.

The following year Hoverspeed closed its hoverport at Ramsgate and concentrated its operations out of Dover. The SEDAM N500 missed much of the year after being withdrawn for extensive modifications to improve reliability and poor weather performance. In 1983 Hoverspeed terminated their operating relationship with SNCF and the SEDAM N500 was withdrawn from service permanently after the modifications proved unsuccessful. Rationalisation, which included the scrapping of the SRN-4 Mk II Hovercraft *Sure*, had done little to improve the long term financial prospects of the company and in early 1984 Hoverspeed was sold by its joint owners British Railways and the Swedish shipping group Brostroms to a management consortium for a nominal sum.

Two years later, with the company now profitable, Hoverspeed was sold to Sea Containers, owners of the recently privatised Sealink British Ferries. Sea Containers also owned and operated the luxury Orient Express railway service and the acquisition of the cross-Channel hovercraft service was seen by the company as a complementary, up-market addition to its corporate portfolio.

Under the Sealink British Ferries umbrella Sea Containers also operated ferry services linking the mainland to the Isle of Wight, and it was on the Solent that the company first introduced two high speed passenger catamarans. The builders of these craft, International Catamarans of Tasmania, were to feature strongly in the development of fast ferries. It was to the Australian yard that Sea Containers turned in the search for a suitable replacement for the now ageing hovercraft fleet.

In 1990 Sea Containers sold the shipping division of Sealink British Ferries but retained among other assets Hoverspeed. The hovercraft operator was to form the backbone of a new global group of fast ferry services operating the latest fast ferry technology. The replacement of the remain five amphibious hovercraft on cross-Channel services by catamaran car ferries was planned to be phased in by 1994 but the popularity of the hovercraft with the travelling public combined with the opportunity to set up new routes with the catamarans persuaded Sea Containers to retain the hovercraft as its first choice vessels on the Dover - Calais service.

Now, ten years after Hoverspeed took delivery of its first catamaran, the *Hoverspeed Great Britain*, the two SRN-4 Mk III Hovercraft *The Princess Margaret* and *The Princess Anne* remain in regular service from Dover Hoverport. In the interim period Hoverspeed, together with its associate companies, has grown into a major force in the world ferry industry. Sea Containers now numbers the original two hovercraft, seven InCat catamarans and four Fincantieri monohull fast ferries in its fleet of high speed car ferries with operations on the English Channel, Irish Sea, Scandinavia and South America. Additionally, high speed commuter services are also operated in New York harbour. Without the cross-Channel hovercraft would any of this been possible?

*Paul Hynds*

# CENTURY OF NORTH WEST EUROPEAN FERRIES 1900 - 2000

# Western Channel

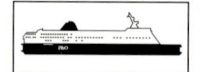

The Western Channel operations have radically changed during the hundred years from the established railway operated services to a privately operated fleet of jumbo and fast ferries offering limited services across the Channel.

The Channel Tunnel has had a greater effect on the area than originally envisaged. To add to the problems of the Western Channel operations, it is now possible to drive from either Le Havre or Caen to Calais in just under three hours on the new motorway which serves both the Channel Tunnel and the port of Calais. These new links have put pressure on both Brittany Ferries and P&O Portsmouth in recent years as they have had to fight to retain their traffic levels from the fierce competition on the Dover-Calais services of P&O Stena Line, SeaFrance and Eurotunnel.

The routes which British Railways abandoned as being non-profitable in the sixties have seen their fortunes change. The St. Malo link is now considered one of the best routes to France whilst today the Le Havre service is operated by two large luxury jumbo ferries.

Routes to Spain were established in the sixties, perhaps a little ahead of their time, as it was not until Brittany Ferries opened their Spanish service from Plymouth to Santander that traffic levels began to increase.

Following the withdrawal of Sealink from the Channel Islands in 1986, Jersey and Guernsey were both faced until 1999 with a period of erratic operations which inevitably led to the downturn in holiday traffic to the islands.

With limited space within this publication it has not been possible to cover all the ferry operations of the Western Channel this century, so therefore the text is concentrated on the Le Havre, Caen, Cherbourg, St. Malo, Roscoff, Santander, Bilbao and Channel Island services.

## PORTSMOUTH - CAEN (OUISTREHAM)

During the summer of 1985, in the space of less than a month, Brittany Ferries announced that they had purchased the Dutch ferry, the *Prinses Beatrix* from SMZ for a new service between Portsmouth and Lower Normandy. This announcement was followed by the news that they had also acquired the successful freight shipping company Truckline at Poole.

The company had been investigating for some time a new link from Portsmouth to Normandy, following the decision by their rivals at Portsmouth, Townsend Thoresen, not to open a new ferry service to the port of Ouistreham (north of Caen). Brittany Ferries were offered the new French port instead. They could see the new French terminal offered great potential and would enable them to rival the operations of Townsend Thoresen at both Cherbourg and Le Havre.

The *Prinses Beatrix* would not only be the biggest ship of the fleet, but also the largest ferry ever to operate out of Portsmouth. The *Prinses Beatrix* underwent a major refit in the Netherlands, was renamed the *Duc de Normandie* and entered service in June 1986. Her extremely well appointed accommodation brought a new style and taste for ferry travel, which was to set new standards on the Channel which in turn was to offer a real challenge to the other rival ferry operators. Overnight the Caen operation was to prove to be a great success achieving traffic levels far ahead of expectations.

The *Normannia* is seen leaving St. Helier for Weymouth during her period on the Channel Islands services as a car ferry in the seventies. *(Kevin Le Scelleur)*

# CENTURY OF NORTH WEST EUROPEAN FERRIES 1900 - 2000

*The **Armorique** passes the **Normandie** off Portsmouth Harbour prior to the entry into service of the new giant superferry on the Caen-Portsmouth route. (Brittany Ferries)*

Just before the end of 1987, Brittany Ferries announced that they planned to introduce a second ship on the Caen service during the following season. The company took a one year bareboat charter of the Yugoslav built *Gotland*.

During 1989 Brittany Ferries put in hand a re-organisation of their fleet. On the Caen–Portsmouth service the *Duc de Normandie* was joined by the former *Prince of Brittany*, which for her new role was renamed *Reine Mathilde*. In addition to the extra passenger sailings offered for 1989, further freight capacity was provided by the newly chartered Truckline vessel *Normandie Shipper*.

In May 1990 Brittany Ferries announced plans to build two new vessels to replace some of the older tonnage in the fleet and to expand the Caen–Portsmouth operations. The contract for the first ferry, a new jumbo ship for the Caen service, was awarded to the Masa Yard, at Helsinki in Finland. A second ship for the Truckline passenger operation was also later secured with Masa at Turku: both orders were worth some £130 million. The company also announced that the *Duc de Normandie* would undergo an extensive £3 million refit and upgrading of her passenger accommodation, prior to the new vessel the *Normandie* entering service. The new ship was a far cry from the early days of the company, boasting 220 luxury cabins, and a capacity for 2,120 passengers and space for 630 cars on two decks. The elegant interior of the superferry was designed to cruise-like standards, with the main accommodation situated over four decks.

In May 1992, under the command of Captain Bertrand Apperry, the *Normandie* entered commercial operations between Caen and Portsmouth on the 08.00 sailing to Britain. Her entry into service increased the capacity on the route by some 40% overnight.

Prior to the arrival of the *Normandie*, the *Reine Mathilde* was transferred to the British Channel Islands Ferries (BCIF) fleet and the ever faithful *Armorique* filled her slot on the link until the new superferry arrived from Finland. Both the *Duc de Normandie* and her new operating partner the *Normandie* soon settled into a routine of three sailings a day from each port; this pattern is still maintained today, with only the larger tonnage *Val de Loire* operating the route in the winter instead of the *Duc de Normandie*.

The *Normandie* has proved an overwhelming success on the Caen route and the standard of service and accommodation has yet to be rivalled by other competitors on the Western Channel. The 24 year old *Duc de Normandie*, which has supported the *Normandie* on the link, will have to be replaced by the company during the early part of the next century.

## PORTSMOUTH - ST. MALO

In September 1964, the B.R. steamer *St. Patrick* made her final crossing from Southampton to St. Malo following the railway company claiming they could not make the operation pay.

Brittany Ferries began to investigate starting another route from Brittany to England, following the success of their new Roscoff link. As an experiment during the late summer of 1975, they operated three sailings a week from St Malo to Plymouth. The trial operation proved to be a great success, and it was decided to open a St. Malo link with the UK as from 1976, using the newly established ferryport at Portsmouth. The ship chosen to operate the new service was the French-built *Terje Vigen*. The newly acquired vessel was renamed *Armorique* and was to become the most faithful and widely travelled ship of the company during the next two decades.

The *Armorique* opened the St. Malo–Portsmouth service in June. With two ferry links from Brittany to England and three ships (two vessels on the Roscoff service), the company now

# CENTURY OF NORTH WEST EUROPEAN FERRIES 1900 - 2000

The *Falaise* and *Brittany* on the Mole des Noires at St. Malo in the early fifties. *(John Hendy collection)*

Brittany Ferries purchased the *Prince of Brittany* for their St. Malo-Portsmouth route in 1980. *(FotoFlite)*

looked set to break new records. Such was the confidence of the company that it ordered a new ship from a Norwegian yard. Sadly, operations did not go as planned for the 1976 season as in July the *Armorique* ran aground as she approached St. Malo and had to be withdrawn from service. The *Bonanza*, which had been chartered for the Roscoff service for the summer, was switched to the St. Malo route as a temporary measure but, with only a few cabins, she was not ideal for the 9 hour link.

In August, the Danish ship *Olau West* was chartered to replace the *Armorique*, whilst she was still under repair. Again the new vessel was not ideal for the route, running aground herself, and as a result the link was closed in October to enable the port authorities to carry out a further programme of improvements to the approaches. Even with the problems of the season at St. Malo, the route attracted some 75,000 passengers and 18,000 cars in the four months of operation.

The *Armorique* was replaced by the chartered Swedish vessel *Prince of Fundy* on the St. Malo service in 1978, as she was required on the new Spanish link. The newly chartered ship was named *Prince of Brittany* and operated the St. Malo service, with the support of the *Penn-ar-Bed* in 1978.

Three new vessels entered service with Brittany Ferries in 1980. Firstly, the company decided to charter the Italian freight ship *Faraday* to cover the St. Malo route. The summer passenger schedules from St. Malo to Portsmouth were

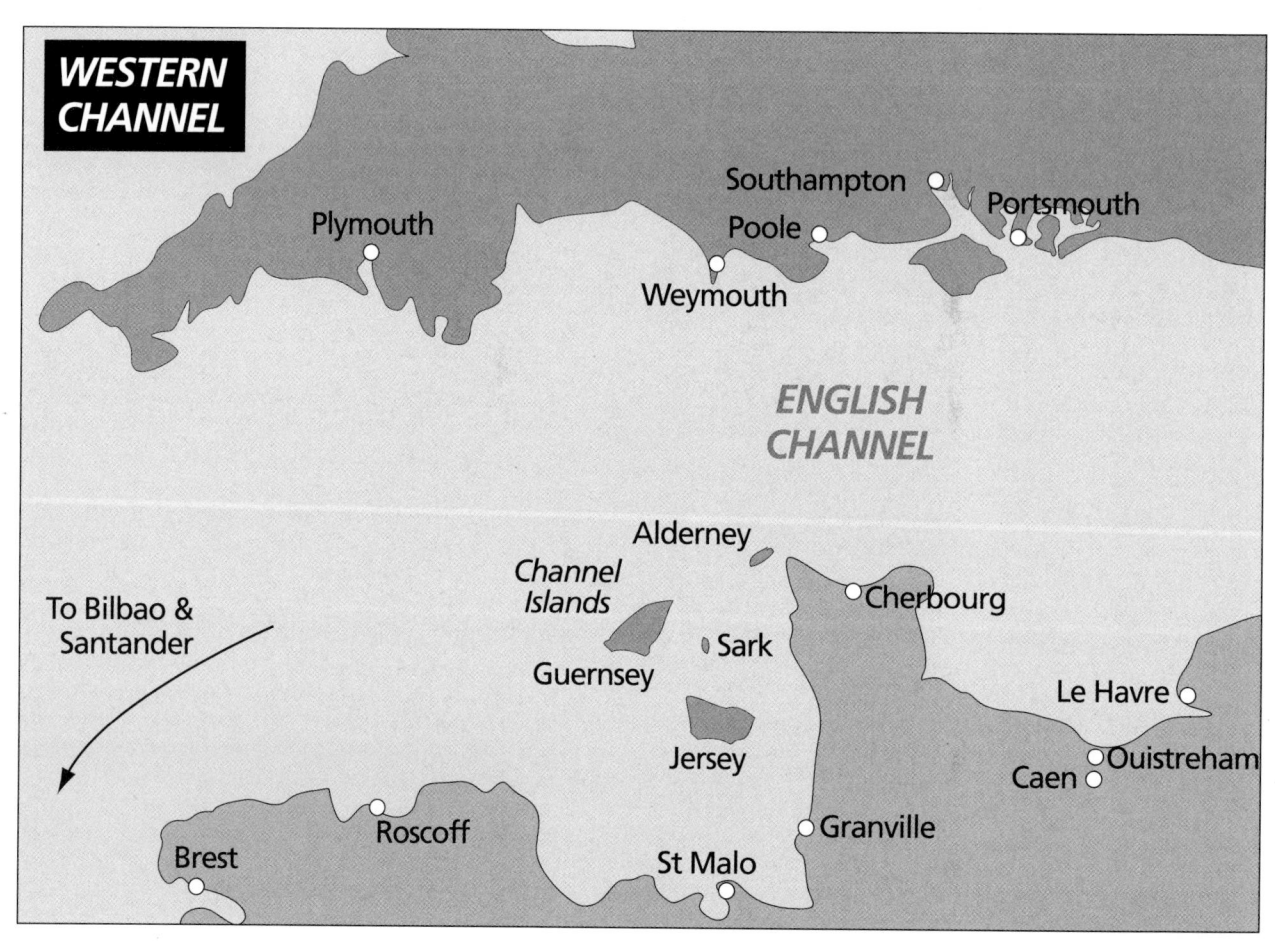

64

# CENTURY OF NORTH WEST EUROPEAN FERRIES 1900 - 2000

The **Bretagne** initially entered service with Brittany Ferries between Plymouth and Santander and Roscoff-Cork. She was later transferred to the St. Malo-Portsmouth route in place of the **Armorique** and the **Duchesse Anne**. She is seen here arriving at Plymouth. *(Mike Louagie)*

extended in the light of a good level of bookings for the route and to meet the increased demand they chartered the *Viking 6* to cover the service with the *Prince of Brittany*. The newly chartered ship was renamed the *Goelo* and proved an excellent operating partner for the *Prince of Brittany* for the next two years. Meanwhile, the *Prince of Brittany* was purchased from her Swedish owners in 1980.

On the entry into service of the *Quiberon*, the *Armorique* returned to the St. Malo route following the end of the charter of the *Goelo*. For the next five years both the *Prince of Brittany* and *Armorique* were to be the mainstay of the link.

In June 1988 Brittany Ferries announced that they had purchased the Irish ferry *Connacht*, which had been built originally for B&I in 1978 for their now defunct Cork–Pembroke Dock route. It was disclosed by Brittany Ferries that she would undergo a £2 million refit prior to her becoming the principal ship on the St. Malo route for 1989, in place of the *Prince of Brittany*. In mid-December the former *Connacht* completed her refit in Germany and emerged as the *Duchesse Anne* for her new role.

It was decided that as from 1989 the St. Malo route would be a seasonal service instead of an all the year round operation. The *Duchesse Anne*, the largest vessel to date to serve on the link, opened the new seasonal service in February, and was joined in May by the faithful *Armorique*.

In March 1992 the company announced that they had purchased the German ferry *Nils Holgersson* for their Spanish operations. The new vessel would replace the *Bretagne* on the Spanish link, this would then allow the *Bretagne* to transfer to the St. Malo–Portsmouth route, in place of both the *Armorique* and the *Duchesse Anne*. The *Armorique* was later sold for service in the Far East following the introduction of the *Bretagne*.

On the introduction of the *Val de Loire* on the Spanish and Irish services, the *Bretagne* was duly transferred to the Portsmouth-St Malo route. Her success on the nine-hour link was to be overwhelming. In an effort to offer additional capacity during the winters of 1998/1999, the *Quiberon* has supported the *Bretagne*. It is likely that further expansion and improvements to the St. Malo service will take place in the foreseeable future, in the light of demand from the travelling public for this route.

## POOLE - CHERBOURG

Truckline was established in 1972 and two small ro-ro vessels were immediately ordered from a French yard. Exclusive rights for the use of the terminal at Poole were negotiated and the equivalent exclusive rights were obtained at Cherbourg. Three basic principles were agreed at the start of Truckline and as far as possible they have been adhered to and still hold good today under the management of Brittany Ferries. The three principles were firstly, that the operation should be Anglo-French; secondly, it should be a freight-only service; and finally, that it should provide a service which would be second-to-none, operating from unemcumbered port to unemcumbered port.

The first vessel to enter service was the British registered

Truckline's purpose-built freight vessel **Coutances** is seen here leaving Cherbourg for Poole. Her sister the **Purbeck** was withdrawn from operations on the entry into service of the **Barfleur**. *(Miles Cowsill)*

65

# CENTURY OF NORTH WEST EUROPEAN FERRIES 1900 - 2000

*Poole Antelope*, at the end of June 1973, The French registered sister, *Dauphine de Cherbourg*, was to follow later in the year. Soon after the first ship entered service, it became obvious that both were going to be far too small. At the beginning of 1975 the two premier ships were replaced by two charter vessels, the *Cotentin* and *Dorset*, both of which had a capacity for 25 x 12 metre trailers, plus space for 50 production cars and accommodation for lorry drivers.

Following the initial error in failing to build the right tonnage for the service, it was necessary for Truckline to set up a new financial package to save its operations and meet the heavy losses incurred to date. It became necessary to involve two other French shipping companies in Truckline. As a result of their involvement, substantial financial grants were made available for building new ships in France.

After the re-organisation of Truckline, two new vessels were ordered from a French yard to replace the chartered ships. The new tonnage doubled the carrying capacity of the company and raised the standard to that never before obtained from a freight-only service on the Channel. The new sister ships, the *Purbeck* and *Coutances*, measured some 109.7m overall and offered four decks for cargo. Both vessels offered good passenger accommodation, which included a cafeteria, TV room and cabins for up to 50 drivers. The new ships operated at a service speed on 16 knots, taking some four and a half hours to cross the Channel. A third vessel, the *Tourlaville*, was later purchased for the operations following the success of the two new ships on the route. From the modest carryings of 2,324 lorries in 1973, some ten years later Truckline was carrying almost 65,000 units a year.

In 1985 Truckline was purchased by Brittany Ferries, as part of an expansion plan by the Breton company. Brittany Ferries injected £3.5 million into Truckline shortly after the takeover, to expand and improve the service. As part of the expansion plans for Truckline, it was decided to jumboise the *Coutances* and *Purbeck*. Ateliers et Chantiers, La Rochelle were given the contract to enlarge the freight ships within a five month period starting in January 1986. Whilst both vessels were absent from service, the *Cornouailles* and *Breizh-Izel* from Brittany Ferries covered the freight operations. Following the extension of both ferries from 109.7 metres to 125.17 metres, their freight capacity was increased from 46 to 63 trailers.

During December 1985, Brittany Ferries announced that they planned to open a new passenger ferry service between Cherbourg and Poole from 1986, under the banner of Truckline operations. The new route would be integrated into the existing freight services and marketed under the banner of 'Les Routiers' which would be based on offering a no-frills, value-for-money approach. Up to two return sailings a day between June and September would be offered by the Brittany Ferries' ship *Cornouailles*, which would be limited to 300 passengers. The new route proved a great success during its first season of operation and was repeated in 1987.

In the autumn, Brittany Ferries announced that a larger ship the *Tregastel* from the Roscoff route would be placed on the passenger route for the following summer. In the event the former BCIF vessel *Corbiere* had to be used, as the *Tregastel* could not be released from her operations at Roscoff, with the late delivery of the new superferry *Bretagne*. Meanwhile, the *Coutances* completed its 10,000th crossing on the Cherbourg freight service on 18th October 1988.

In May 1989 Truckline chartered the Swedish freight ship *Stena Shipper* to maintain the Cherbourg and Caen freight services. The new ship, renamed *Normandie Shipper*, was to be

The ***Barfleur*** at her berth in Poole. The vessel has operated the Cherbourg route since she entered service in 1996. *(Brittany Ferries)*

the largest freight ship on the English Channel operations at the time, with a capacity for up to 140 x 12 metre trailers and accommodation for 120 drivers.

The following year, the *Tregastel* and *Corbiere* operated the service together with up to four sailings a day in each direction. A similar timetable was offered the next year, prior to the arrival of the new ro-pax ferry *Barfleur*. The introduction of the new superferry increased the capacity on the route and also brought new standards to the link.

During 1993 the *Purbeck* was withdrawn from service and laid up, while the *Coutances* continued to operate with the multi-purpose passenger vessel on the Poole-Cherbourg link.

The following year the *Duchesse Anne* opened a new St. Malo-Poole service, operating four times a week between her Cork service from St. Malo; however, the route was only to last two seasons.

In 1999 the *Barfleur* appeared in Brittany Ferries livery, following the parent company deciding to market the route with their other operations.

## SOUTHAMPTON - CHERBOURG/ LE HAVRE/ ST MALO

The Le Havre service prior to the Second World War was operated as a night operation by the former London & South Western Railway steamers *Hantonia* and *Normannia*, which were built in 1911 to replace the *Alma* and *Columbia*.

Meanwhile, the St. Malo service was in the hands of the *Hilda* at the turn of century but after she was lost outside the French port in 1905, she was replaced by the *Princess Ena*. After the First World War the *Lorina* took up the route and rejoined later by the *Princess Ena*. In 1924 the Southern Railway introduced the new sisters *Dinard* and *St. Briac* on the route.

Following the end of the war the Le Havre operation was opened again by the *Hantonia* (her sister having being lost at Dunkerque) and it was not until 1947 that the St. Malo link was reopened by the new steamer *Falaise*. The *Falaise* operated the link on a seasonal basis (July to September) and this short period allowed her to carry out a series of cruises, just as the *St. Briac* (sunk by a mine off Arbroath in March 1942) had done before the war.

A new *Normannia* replaced the *Hantonia* on the Le Havre route in 1952. Her normal roster was usually to operate three weekly sailings each way in the summer and two in the winter and she continued on this link until late 1963 when, shortly before its closure, she was converted into a car ferry for the

66

# CENTURY OF NORTH WEST EUROPEAN FERRIES 1900 - 2000

The *Hantonia*, photographed when new in 1911, maintained the Southampton-Le Havre service until 1952. The vessel is seen here leaving Le Havre for England. *(Ambrose Greenway collection)*

Dover station.

In the early sixties at Southampton, British Railways withdrew their long-established Channel Islands passenger service from the port and decided to concentrate all traffic at Weymouth on the former rival route established by the old Great Western Railway. It was also known at the time that British Railways wished to terminate their overnight service to Le Havre which had been losing money for years. The St. Malo night crossing was also under scrutiny and there were those who even foresaw the complete abandonment of Southampton as a railway port.

In the light of these moves by BR, the Norwegian businessman Otto Thoresen decided to start his own operation. British Railways Board finally declared their intentions to close the one hundred and twenty year old Le Havre service as from May 1964. It was claimed by British Railways that the Le Havre service had lost £1 million since the previous attempt to close it.

In May 1964, the British Railways steamer *St. Patrick* left Le Havre on the last voyage of a railway steamer between the French port and Southampton. The St. Malo service also closed at the end of the summer season in 1964 but was to re-open again twelve years later with Brittany Ferries from Portsmouth. The company were to turn its fortunes around into possibly one of the most sought after routes on the western Channel.

During the last quarter of 1963, plans for the new Southampton – Cherbourg route gathered further pace and in September a second ship was ordered, while negotiations for an additional service to Le Havre were underway.

Each vessel would carry 180 cars on two decks and the *Viking I* was delivered in May while the *Viking II* followed in July when the Le Havre link was opened. As a safety measure, their hulls were coloured bright orange, deck houses were an anti-glare green and the rest of the superstructure was white.

Fares were fixed at £2.17s.6d. (£2.87) adult single while children under 14 were priced at £1.10s.0p. (£1.50). Single car rates were £4.10s.0p. (£4.50) for vehicles up to 11 ft. long and a pound extra for vehicles up to 12ft.6inches. Fares were considerably cheaper than those of British Railways.

During their first three operating weeks, Thoresen Car Ferries carried 13,000 passengers and 3,500 cars. Bookings already showed that a profit would be made, yet British Railways had claimed that their service lost them £173,116 a year.

As far as passenger services were concerned, the Thoresen 'Vikings' offered the guarantee of a seat for each person. The interiors were very Scandinavian, making use of teak facings, plastics, aluminium fittings and bright upholstery fabrics throughout. From the start, Thoresen set out to offer a friendly service making a Channel crossing a pleasant experience instead of just another tiresome journey.

In early July 1964, the decision was make to order the *Viking III* for the following season – this after just two months of operation. The ship was built at Lubeck, West Germany, and Otto Thoresen stated that the third ship would give the company greater flexibility and enable them to cope with the anticipated increase in traffic.

In 1964, Thoresen Car Ferries carried 192,274 passengers and 55,139 cars, although Southern Region experts believed that the Norwegians would eventually abandon the Le Havre route. Thoresen's success was put down to four reasons:
1. the attractiveness of the new ships
2. the frequency of the service
3. cheaper fares than previously
4. the reluctance of motorists from the Midlands and the west to pass through London to Dover.

The *Viking III* entered service in June 1965 and in November 1966, Thoresen Car Ferries announced the order of the freight only roll-on/roll off vessel *Viking IV* at a cost of £650,000.

Following the B.R. withdrawal from Le Havre, the P&O subsidiary, the General Steam Navigation Company (GSNC), had operated a limited cargo service on the route. However, the success of the Thoresen venture prompted them to enter into a partnership with the French company, Societe Anonyme de Gerance et d'Armement (SAGA) and two similar vessels were ordered from Ateliers et Chantiers of Nantes for delivery in spring and winter 1967 to rival the new operation. The joint company was to be known as Normandy Ferries.

The ships cost just under £2 million each and boasted excellent accommodation for 850 passengers, while their stern loading garages could hold some 250 cars. The *Dragon* was launched in January 1967 and entered service in June. Looking forward to the *Leopard*'s arrival, Normandy Ferries planned a weekly crossing from Le Havre to the Irish port of Cork but

An aerial view of the *Viking I* shows her modern lines on her maiden voyage from Southampton to Cherbourg in 1964. *(Miles Cowsill collection)*

# CENTURY OF NORTH WEST EUROPEAN FERRIES 1900 - 2000

These two views onboard the **Viking Venturer** show the vessel's modern accommodation. The left-hand picture shows her dining room, at the aft end, and the right-hand view shows the bar amidships. The internal areas of the ship have changed little since her entry into service in 1975. *(Miles Cowsill collection)*

this was later modified to Rosslare. The *Leopard* entered service the following May and duly opened the new Rosslare link the following month.

Both Thoresen at Southampton and Townsend at Dover used Hambro's Bank and both companies had been the only private enterprise operators in the Channel. During July 1968, agreement was reached in principle for a merger of Thoresen Car Ferries by Townsend's parent company, George Nott Industries Ltd. of Coventry. The merger of the two fleets created a much stronger operation and in due course was to provide considerable scope for improvements in operational efficiency. As far as the general public were concerned, things at Southampton were the same as usual. The ships remained the same and there were not even any livery changes. The first example of co-operation between the Townsend and Thoresen partnership was seen during November 1968 when the *Viking II* left Southampton for Dover to operate the Zeebrugge route for six weeks. In the summer of 1970, Dover's *Free Enterprise II* started her first season of the Cherbourg sailings.

During December 1970, Europe's largest, private car ferry company, Townsend Thoresen, announced a further five year expansion programme for five new ships, costing some £20 million. Two new 'Free Enterprise' class ships were ordered for Dover, while Southampton would have three 'Super Vikings' built at Aalborg Vaerft A/S in Denmark. The new ships ordered for Southampton were to be modelled on the original ferries but with the influence of the 'Free Enterprise' class ships. This was seen in the internal layout of the passenger accommodation with the introduction of open-plan lounges first adopted in the *Free Enterprise* back in 1962.

By the end of 1970, Southampton was handling in the region of 130,500 vehicles and 475,000 passengers per year; and with further demand for more passenger and car space on the Le Havre and Cherbourg routes, the new 'Super Vikings' were designed to carry 1,200 passengers and 275 cars.

In early October 1974 the *Viking II* left Southampton for the company's new passenger service linking Felixstowe and Zeebrugge.

The first 'Super Viking' class ship was not named *Viking V*, as originally assumed, but *Viking Venturer*. The external appearance of the new 'Viking' and her Danish sisters, which were to follow over the next seventeen months, included twin-funnels, similar to the early 'Vikings', with accommodation for passengers on four deck levels.

The *Viking Venturer* left Denmark under the command of Captain Tony Shopland. The 'Venturer' entered service in January 1975 on the Le Havre run, operating with the *Viking III*, thus releasing the *Viking I* for charter work and, later in the year, for the Felixstowe – Zeebrugge service, until the arrival of the second 'Super Viking'.

Meanwhile, the *Viking Valiant* was launched during October 1974. TTF decided to introduce her on the newly opened Felixstowe–Zeebrugge service to boost both passenger and freight space. The *Viking Valiant*, which had originally been destined for Southampton, arrived at the Suffolk port in May 1975 to join *Viking II* on service. The third 'Super Viking', the *Viking Voyager*, entered service in January 1976, which then released the 'Valiant' for her originally intended station at Southampton. The *Viking Viscount* completed the last of the quartet during May 1976, and the 'Viscount' sailed to Suffolk to join her sister, instead of Southampton as originally planned.

The year 1976 was the beginning of the end for the Southampton ferry port at the Princess Alexandra Dock when Portsmouth opened its doors to ro-ro traffic. Not only was Portsmouth an hour's saving on sailing times but it also provided excellent road communications with a spur of the M27 leading right to its door. More importantly perhaps, Portsmouth lacked the fierce and militant trade union practices

The **Viking III** was chartered out to other ferry operators following the introduction of the 'Super Vikings'. She is seen here on charter to Sealink on their Channel Islands operations. *(Kevin Le Scelleur)*

68

# CENTURY OF NORTH WEST EUROPEAN FERRIES 1900 - 2000

*This view shows the **Viking Venturer** at the lay-by berth at Southampton following her arrival from the builders in Denmark. The vessel was jumboised in 1986 and still remains in service on the English Channel at the end of the century as the **Pride of Hampshire**. (Miles Cowsill collection)*

which had all but strangled Southampton.

The 'Super Vikings' did not go to Portsmouth in its first year as a ferryport; however in 1977 they did commence limited sailings there. One of the 'Super Vikings' was transferred at peak weekends to operate to and from Le Havre as an experiment. The pattern of these new sailings meant better utilisation of the ships for the company with the shorter crossing time to Portsmouth. The experiment proved a great success and from 1978 the company gradually scaled down their operations at Southampton in favour of the new port.

Townsend Thoresen decided to withdraw their passenger/car ferry operations from Southampton as from January 1984 in favour of Portsmouth, leaving only the freight sailings of the *Viking Trader* behind. All freight sailings would have been moved at the same time, but there was not enough storage for freight at Portsmouth. Some 12 months later all services were withdrawn from Southampton.

January 1980 saw yet another change when, for marketing purposes, the P&O Normandy Ferries title was dropped in favour of P&O Ferries. The *Dragon* and *Leopard* continued to operate as before, the British ship sailing to Le Havre by day and the French vessel by night. They really were two very reliable work-horses for their owners, and in all their years gave them very little trouble.

In December 1984 P&O Ferries had transferred their services from Southampton to Portsmouth; a move which was prompted by yet another period of dockers' industrial unrest

During 1990, Sealink Stena Line announced their plans to open a new service between Southampton and Cherbourg using the former Harwich-based *St. Nicholas*. Renamed the *Stena Normandy*, she took up service in June 1991, with an operation planned to rival those of Brittany Ferries and P&O.

Following a successful inaugural season, additional capacity was introduced in 1992 with the ro-pax vessel *Stena Traveller* for the peak season. By the end of the 1992 season, Sealink Stena Line claimed that they had captured 23% share of the western sector traffic with their Newhaven - Dieppe and Southampton - Cherbourg routes. Whilst the company at the time had to be congratulated for its efforts, the share of the market had only been achieved in many cases by bargain fare offers and special vouchers in the tabloid press. The more discerning motorist and seasoned traveller appeared not to be influenced by their cheap fare campaign and continued to support the existing operators Brittany Ferries and P&O European Ferries. The company continued its aggressive price war against the Portsmouth operators for a further four seasons ,but in the light of a demise in traffic, as a result of increased competition on the Dover Strait from the ferry operators and the Channel Tunnel, the service eventually closed at the end of 1996.

## SOUTHAMPTON - SPAIN - PORTUGAL & AFRICAN SERVICES

Swedish Lloyd opened their service to Bilbao in April 1967 with their *Patricia* . Initially the service was a great success and prompted the introduction of the similar vessel *Hispania* (ex *Svea*) which had been withdrawn from the Hull - Gothenburg

*In 1965 Normandy Ferries ordered two vessels to start a rival service to that of Thoresen Car Ferries between Southampton and Le Havre. The British registered vessel **Dragon** is seen here outward bound from Southampton. (FotoFlite)*

# CENTURY OF NORTH WEST EUROPEAN FERRIES 1900 - 2000

The former **St. Nicholas** was transferred from the Harwich-Hook of Holland service in 1990 to open a new ferry route between Southampton and Le Havre. The vessel is seen here as the **Stena Normandy** during her period on the English Channel. *(FotoFlite)*

The **Pride of Winchester** turns off the berth at Cherbourg during her last season in service with P&O. Today she currently operates between mainland Greece and Crete. *(Miles Cowsill)*

link but two years later she was switched to Swedish Lloyd's other route from Tilbury to Gothenburg and renamed *Saga*.

This was followed by a second Spanish service to Santander by Anzar Line with their *Monte Toledo*. Meanwhile, P&O had acquired the *Peter Pan* in order to start yet another rival service from Southampton to San Sebastian. There was now far too much competition on the Spanish links and none of the three routes lasted. The P&O operation closed in 1976, Anzar Line and Swedish Lloyd operations closed in 1977 while a year later Brittany Ferries opened their link to Spain from Plymouth.

Another service of interest from this port started during the winter of 1968/69, with the *Leopard* offering sailings from Rouen – Southampton – Lisbon – Casablanca. In light of the early success of the link, P&O ordered a large new cruise ferry, the *Eagle*. Until her delivery, the *Dragon* and the *Leopard* continued the off-peak service operating every eleven days during the winter of 1970.

The *Eagle* entered service in April 1971 offering three trips each fortnight to Lisbon and Casablanca, with one sailing extended to Tangier. However, the climate was not then right for such an operation and she was withdrawn from service in October 1975.

## PORTSMOUTH - CHERBOURG/LE HAVRE

At a special ceremony at Portsmouth prior to the inaugural crossing in June 1976, the *Viking I* was renamed *Viking Victory* after H.M.S. *Victory*, Nelson's famous flagship. Chairman Keith Wickenden said that the decision to rename the ship had been as a gesture to the people of Portsmouth "who have welcomed us so warmly into their city."

The 'Super Vikings' did not go to Portsmouth in its first year as a ferryport; however in 1977 they did commence sailings there. One of the 'Super Vikings' was transferred at peak weekends to operate to and from Le Havre as an experiment. The pattern of these new sailings meant better utilisation of the ships for the company with the shorter crossing time to Portsmouth. The experiment proved a great success and from 1978 the company gradually scaled down their operations at Southampton in favour of the new port.

The *Viking II* had spent the whole of the summer of 1976 on charter in Scandinavia. Now surplus to requirements, she was purchased by Lloyd's Leasing Ltd. on behalf of British Rail (Sealink). The *Viking II* was converted for a new year-round service between the Islands and Portsmouth, for which purpose she was renamed *Earl William*.

Summer 1981 saw the sale of the diminutive *Viking IV* which was converted into a livestock carrier for the Middle East trade and was renamed *Guernsey Express*. Her place at Southampton was taken by the older but larger *Europic Ferry*. The *Viking III* was sold during 1982 to the Da-No Linjen for use on their Frederikshavn–Fredrikstad route across the Kattegat, trading as the *Terje Vigen*. In the spring of 1983, the *Viking Victory* was sold to the Euphoria Navigation Co. of Limassol, Cyprus, being renamed *Sun Boat* for a service linking Cyprus with Greece.

In early spring 1982, the Falklands War broke out, causing major problems for European Ferries with three ships being requisitioned for the Task Force. The *Europic Ferry* eventually returned unscathed from the Falklands in July. After an extensive refit at Avonmouth, the war hero entered service once again on the Le Havre freight service in August.

Townsend Thoresen decided to withdraw their passenger/car ferry operations from Southampton as from January 1984 in favour of Portsmouth, leaving only the freight sailings of the *Viking Trader* for a further year.

During December 1984 the company announced that the *Viking Venturer* and *Viking Valiant*, together with two of the 'Free Enterprise' class ships, would be enlarged to meet the increasing demand for freight space on the Le Havre and Zeebrugge routes. The two 'Super Vikings', like the *Free Enterprise VI* and *Free Enterprise VII*, would be fitted with larger forward sections, as well as being horizontally cut in two with an additional full length vehicle deck inserted, enabling, in the case of 'Venturer' and 'Valiant', up to 60 lorries to be carried after jumboisation.

In December 1984 P&O Ferries had transferred their services from Southampton to Portsmouth; a move which was prompted by yet another period of dockers' industrial unrest. Meanwhile, in January 1985, P&O announced that they had sold their interests on the English Channel (Dover–Boulogne and Portsmouth–Le Havre) to European Ferries for £12.5 million. The P&O sister ships, the *Dragon* and the French registered *Leopard*, were quickly brought under European Ferries' management and were included in the schedules of the company at Portsmouth for the forthcoming season.

In October 1985, Townsend Thoresen decided to convert the freight ships *Baltic Ferry* and *Nordic Ferry* to multi-purpose

# CENTURY OF NORTH WEST EUROPEAN FERRIES 1900 - 2000

passenger/ freight ships for the Felixstowe–Zeebrugge service. The conversion of these ships would release the *Viking Voyager* and *Viking Viscount* from the Zeebrugge link so they could be transferred to Portsmouth to operate the Cherbourg route.

Jumboisation work started on the *Viking Venturer* in December 1985. Meanwhile during March, Townsend Thoresen announced that the *Leopard* would be withdrawn from service with the loss of 140 jobs. The linkspan at Le Havre was immediately blocked by the French crew of the *Leopard* and as a result services from Portsmouth were diverted to Cherbourg. Eventually the company agreed that the *Leopard's* crew would be transferred to the *Viking Viscount* until the end of September 1986. It was agreed that the 'Viscount' should be transferred to the French flag, but due to pressure from the British crews at Portsmouth to allow the first 'Super Viking' from Suffolk to remain under the British flag, it was the 'Voyager' which was re-registered at Le Havre. The *Viking Viscount* entered service at Portsmouth on the Le Havre run in May and was joined later in the month by the *Viking Voyager* on the Cherbourg link.

While the industrial unrest was going on at Le Havre, work also stopped on the new double-deck ramp and building work at the Portsmouth end also fell behind.

Following her conversion, the *Viking Venturer* sailed to Portsmouth in May, now looking a very different ship and rather dwarfing her newly-arrived sisters from Felixstowe. The new linkspans at Portsmouth and Le Havre were not completed until early July, so the *Viking Venturer* was put on the Cherbourg link in early July until the arrival of the *Viking Valiant* from Germany. The 'Valiant' entered service on the Le Havre route in July, joining her jumboised sister, the *Viking Venturer*, which had been transferred a week earlier. The smaller 'Super Vikings' were then transferred to the Cherbourg route.

Meanwhile, in the same month, the *Dragon*, following a refit in Scotland, entered service on the Cairnryan–Larne link and was renamed *Ionic Ferry*. The *Leopard* was sold for further service in Greece and was later to be joined by the *Ionic Ferry* after she was withdrawn from service

In December 1986 European Ferries was taken over by the P&O Group. Following this event the household name of Townsend Thoresen was to disappear the following October in favour of the new brand name for the company, P&O European Ferries. The bright orange livery introduced by Otto Thoresen was replaced by dark blue hulls and funnels. During 1986 all four 'Super Vikings' were renamed in line with the rest of the former Townsend Thoresen fleet. Portsmouth ships were renamed as follows:

| | |
|---|---|
| Viking Venturer | Pride of Hampshire |
| Viking Valiant | Pride of Le Havre |
| Viking Voyager | Pride of Cherbourg |
| Viking Viscount | Pride of Winchester |

In a further effort to replace their ageing fleet, P&O European Ferries looked for further charters to replace the existing tonnage on their Cherbourg and Le Havre services. During August 1993 there were high hopes that they had acquired the Viking Line vessels, the *Athena* and *Calypso*, but at the eleventh hour, the company were outbid by another shipping operation.

In March the following year the company secured a five year charter of the twin sisters of Olau Line, following the demise of the Sheerness-Vlissingen route. The charter of these vessels enabled P&O to offer larger and more luxurious tonnage against their rivals Brittany Ferries. The 'Olau twins' replaced the jumboised 'Super Vikings' on the Le Havre service, both ships underwent a short refit and were renamed *Pride of Portsmouth* (ex *Olau Britannia*) and *Pride of Le Havre* (ex *Olau Hollandia*). The new ships in turn allowed the jumboised 'Super Vikings' to transfer to the Cherbourg service to offer

This view shows the **Pride of Hampshire** (ex **Viking Venturer**) following her jumboisation. *(FotoFlite)*

These two views show part of the jumboisation works of the 'Super Vikings'. The left-hand view shows the new hull sections of the **Viking Venturer** and **Viking Valiant** being launched. The right-hand view shows the original accommodation of the **Viking Venturer** being raised from her original hull. *(Miles Cowsill collection)*

# CENTURY OF NORTH WEST EUROPEAN FERRIES 1900 - 2000

Following the demise of Olau Line, P&O were successful in chartering the two purpose-built ships for their Portsmouth-Le Havre route in 1994. The **Pride of Portsmouth** (ex *Olau Britannia*) is seen here leaving Portsmouth for Le Havre. *(Miles Cowsill)*

increased capacity. The former *Pride of Le Havre* (ex *Viking Valiant*) was renamed *Pride of Cherbourg*, the original *Pride of Cherbourg* received the suffix 'II' during her brief remainder of service that summer. The *Pride of Winchester* and *Pride of Cherbourg II* were both sold for further trading that summer and still remain in service today in Greece and the Canary Islands.

Following the disastrous trading season for Hoverspeed with their fast ferry, the *Hoverspeed Great Britain*, between Portsmouth and Cherbourg in 1990, P&O began evaluating possibilities of starting their own fast ferry service between Portsmouth and Cherbourg with the now better designed fast craft. In May 1998, they were successful in chartering the Australian-built 82 metre catamaran *Superstar Express* from a Malaysian company. The 38.5 knot craft had originally been earmarked to operate between Langkawi and Butterworth but with the economic downturn in the Far East she was not required by Star Cruises. The new fast ferry service commenced in May, offering three round trips a day between Portsmouth and Cherbourg, with additional sailings at peak weekends. The *Pride of Hampshire* and *Pride of Cherbourg* remained on the route with the new fast craft. This pattern of three vessels on the Cherbourg service was repeated in 1999 after a very successful initial season with the *Superstar Express*.

The Le Havre route still remains in the hands of the *Pride of Portsmouth* and *Pride of Le Havre*. In the short-term the 1975 built 'Super Vikings' will have to be replaced on the Cherbourg route. Their replacement will probably be with a ro-pax vessel, with either one or two fast craft operating alongside the traditionally-operated service.

## PLYMOUTH - ROSCOFF

In the early months of 1972 a group of vegetable farmers surprised the shipping world with the news that they planned to operate a ferry service between the port of Roscoff to Plymouth in Devon. Breton farmers for many years had been considering a quicker way of transporting their goods to Britain, following the closure by British Rail of the Southampton - St. Malo service in 1964. With the closure of the St. Malo service, farmers were forced to use the other services to England from Le Havre and Cherbourg.

The new operation was the brain-child of Alexis Gourvennec and his fellow associates of the SICA group (an organisation set up to protect the interests of vegetable producers). Prior to the operation being opened, major construction work had to be undertaken on both sides of the English Channel, as neither port was suitable for a ferry operation.

Alexis Gourvennec's initial plans envisaged a freight-only service, and the ro-ro ship *Lilac* (2,293 gross tons) was

In 1998 P&O European Ferries introduced a fast ferry service between Portsmouth and Cherbourg using the **SuperStar Express**. The Australian-built fast craft is seen arriving at Portsmouth. *(Miles Cowsill)*

# CENTURY OF NORTH WEST EUROPEAN FERRIES 1900 - 2000

Brittany Ferries chartered the German-built **Nils Dacke** in 1982 to replace the **Armorique** on their Spanish and Irish routes. The vessel is seen here at Cork pending her afternoon departure to Roscoff. *(Miles Cowsill)*

purchased for the new operation. She could accommodate 45 commercial lorries and was renamed the *Kerisnel*, after a village in Brittany.

On New Year's Day 1973, Brittany Ferries was officially born. Nearly 3,000 people attended the official opening of the terminal at Roscoff on a bleak New Year's Day. A spokesman for Brittany Ferries announced at the opening that the company hoped to convey in the region of 150,000 tons of cargo during its first year. The operation opened the next day and the *Kerisnel* arrived at Plymouth for the first time on the morning of 3rd January. During the first three months, Brittany Ferries were to carry only 17,000 tons of traffic and not the 40,000 tons originally planned.

Following the introduction of the new freight-only service

The **Kerisnel** was the vessel that launched Brittany Ferries in 1972. She is seen here leaving Roscoff during her first season in operation for the Breton company. *(Miles Cowsill collection)*

it quickly became evident that there was a demand for a passenger service to and from Brittany. As a result of this demand Brittany Ferries decided to operate a passenger-only service using a former Baltic vessel the *Poseidon*. At first the service was rather erratic but eventually settled down and during July the *Poseidon* was to average some 120 passengers a day before she finished her summer season.

Whilst the trial passenger service was operating, the company announced it had placed an order with a yard at La Rochelle to build a new ferry for the link. The new ship, named *Penn-ar-Bed*, entered service in January 1974. The following year the company chartered the *Falster* which was renamed *Prince de Bretagne*.

Another new ferry was ordered for the link and in May 1977 the newly built *Cornouailles* entered service when sailings were increased between Roscoff and Plymouth with up to three sailings a day being offered at weekends. In addition to the increased service on the Roscoff route, the *Penn-ar-Bed* also operated between Plymouth – St Malo.

Brittany Ferries celebrated its tenth birthday with a fleet of six ships and four ferry services. The next ten years of the growth of the company were to be even more dramatic.

The Roscoff service continued to attract good loadings over the next couple of years, and with the introduction of the new Spanish and Irish services additional sailings were slotted in the Plymouth-Roscoff route as a result. Three new vessels entered service with Brittany Ferries in 1985. One of the vessels purchased was a Greek freight ship for use on the Roscoff service to back up the *Cornouailles*. The ship was renamed the *Breizh-Izel* for her new role with the company, which was to last until 1989.

The summer schedules for 1983 were similar to those of the previous year, however the company chartered the Danish

# CENTURY OF NORTH WEST EUROPEAN FERRIES 1900 - 2000

The **Val de Loire** makes an impressive view as she leaves Santander for Plymouth in June 1999. The vessel originally was built for TT Line for their service between Germany and Sweden. *(Miles Cowsill)*

registered *Gelting Nord* for the Roscoff–Plymouth service in place of the *Cornouailles*. The new ship was renamed *Benodet* for her new role. However she was only to have one season on the route as she had to be switched to a new Channel Islands operation in which Brittany Ferries took an interest.

With the *Benodet* now required on the new Channel Islands link, Brittany Ferries took out a three year bareboat charter of the Yugoslav ferry *Njegos*. The chartered vessel entered service on the Roscoff–Plymouth service in May 1985 as the *Tregastel*.

With the *Breizh-Izel* and new passenger tonnage on the link, the *Cornouailles* became surplus within the fleet and as a result she was chartered to SNCF in 1984 for two years. This in turn allowed the *Penn-ar-Bed* to return to operations for her final season following a long lay-up, before she was sold at the end of the season. She remains in service today in the Middle-East.

It was planned that the *Quiberon* would maintain the Spanish and Irish services until the delivery of the *Bretagne*. On the arrival of the new vessel, the *Tregastel* would then transfer to the Truckline passenger route between Cherbourg and Poole, and the *Quiberon* would then become the main vessel on the premier route. After further frustrating delays, the new flagship *Bretagne* slipped into Plymouth Sound in mid-July 1989, entering commercial service two days later. The *Val de Loire* replaced the *Bretagne* in 1993.

The *Quiberon* is due for replacement by the year 2002. She has proved to be an extremely valuable asset to the company during her 18 years of service.

## PLYMOUTH/ PORTSMOUTH - SANTANDER & ROSCOFF - CORK

In autumn 1977, Brittany Ferries announced further expansion plans for 1978, which were to include links to Spain from England and a new ferry service from Roscoff to Cork.

Brittany Ferries took the bold step of reopening the link, not from Southampton, as they believed that the time at sea was too long for passengers, but instead they decided to resume the operation from Plymouth. By providing a service from Plymouth, the company were able to offer a 23 hour link, thereby cutting out the two nights on the ship, which had been the downfall of the previous operations. The *Armorique* was chosen to operate the twice-weekly service on Mondays and Wednesdays from Plymouth. On her return from Spain on a Friday, she would then provide an extra sailing on the Roscoff route, to enable her to be in a position ready for a round trip to Cork at the weekends.

The *Armorique* opened the new Plymouth-Santander route during April 1978. The new Spanish service was to grow very rapidly over the next ten years and gradually larger tonnage had to be introduced to meet the increased demand. The new seasonal Irish service operated very successfully and like the Spanish operation grew. In 1979 the Spanish service was extended to an all the year round basis.

In the light of the increased demand on all the company's routes, especially on the Santander service, Brittany Ferries now chartered the *Nils Dacke*. The German-built ship of 1975 could operate at 22.5 knots, enabling her to reduce the crossing time to Spain by some two hours during the peak season if required. The ship was renamed *Quiberon* and she was sent for an extensive refit before entering service. Following these works she was able to carry 1,040 passengers and 252 cars. She entered service in May, allowing the *Armorique* to return to the St. Malo–Portsmouth link. The *Quiberon*, like the *Armorique*, covered the Cork service at weekends.

Brittany Ferries invited tenders to build a new purpose-built ferry for their Santander route in 1986, to meet the growing summer demand on this ferry link, which was now 10 years old. Following many months of speculation as to which

# CENTURY OF NORTH WEST EUROPEAN FERRIES 1900 - 2000

yard would be awarded the work, Brittany Ferries finally signed contracts with the French yard of Chantiers de L'Atlantique at St. Nazaire. The new superferry would be named *Bretagne* and would offer cruise-liner standards for 2,000 passengers with berths for just over half the passengers in two and four berth cabins and space for 600 cars.

It was planned that the *Quiberon* would maintain the Santander, Roscoff and Cork services until the delivery of the new *Bretagne*. Following the new flagship entering service, the *Tregastel* would then transfer to the Truckline passenger route between Cherbourg and Poole, and the *Quiberon* would become the main vessel of the premier route.

The £55 million *Bretagne* entered service in mid-July on the Santander, Cork and Roscoff services.

In March 1992 the company announced that they had purchased the German ferry *Nils Holgersson* from TT Line for £70 million for their Spanish operations. She would undergo a major building programme and overhaul to make her more suitable for the Spanish route. On her entry into service in 1993, the *Bretagne* would then be transferred to the St. Malo – Portsmouth route, in place of the *Armorique* and the *Duchesse Anne*.

Further expansion plans were announced by the company in autumn 1993, with increased sailings between Roscoff and Plymouth, and additional sailings between Roscoff and Cork would be introduced to meet the growing demand on the route. In addition to the increased sailings to Ireland the *Duchesse Anne* would open a new 18 hour route between St. Malo and Cork from mid-June.

On January 1993, Brittany Ferries took delivery of the *Nils Holgersson* and she then sailed from Lubeck under her new name *Val de Loire* for Italy, for a major refit and rebuilding programme. In late May, the company took delivery of their new flagship *Val de Loire*. The new giant cruise ferry, with a capacity for 2,120 passengers and 570 cars, or 100 freight vehicles, heralded the climax of the three year £350 million investment plan, which now put the company in the position of operating the youngest fleet on the Channel.

In June 1993 the new flagship of the company entered commercial operations between Plymouth and Santander. Some four days later she reached the Irish port of Cork making shipping history as the biggest ferry ever to operate from Ireland. Meanwhile the *Duchesse Anne* opened the new Cork – St. Malo service. The service was only to last three years before the former Irish Sea vessel was sold as the giant *Val de Loire* was able to cope with the then traffic levels from Ireland.

## PORTSMOUTH – BILBAO

Following the success and expansion of Brittany Ferries' operations to Spain, P&O European Ferries looked into developing their own service to the Iberian Peninsular. P&O were successful in chartering the Swedish superferry *Olympia* in order to operate their new service linking Portsmouth with the Basque city of Bilbao in Spain. The chartered vessel *Olympia*, which had originally been built for Viking Line, was at the time one of the largest ferries in the world with accommodation for up to 600 cars and 2,447 passengers. She was renamed *Pride of Bilbao* and entered service in April 1993, offering two round trips a week to Spain. To offer additional capacity on the Portsmouth-Cherbourg service at weekends, she was rostered to undertake a special round trip on a Friday night to Cherbourg with a Saturday return prior to her evening departure again to Bilbao. This pattern of service for the *Pride of Bilbao* has continued since the inaugural sailing.

The **Pride of Bilbao** is currently the largest ferry operating out of the UK to Europe. During 2001 the new North Sea Ferries' vessels will become the largest ferries operating out of the UK. The 'Bilbao' is seen here arriving at Portsmouth from Spain. *(Miles Cowsill)*

# CENTURY OF NORTH WEST EUROPEAN FERRIES 1900 - 2000

## CHANNEL ISLANDS

An agreement was reached between the London & South Western Railway (L & SWR) and the Great Western Railway (GWR) for the operation of a joint service to the Channel Islands from October 1899. This resulted in the GWR using the *Roebuck* and *Reindeer* during the summer periods, with the back-up of the *Ibex*, but within a few months of the agreement trouble struck the new operation with the sinking of the *Ibex*, when en-route from Weymouth to Guernsey in January 1900 she struck rocks off the north-east coast of the Island. The ship was later raised and towed to Birkenhead for repairs and returned to service in 1901.

In June 1900 the L&SWR's *Alberta* entered service on the Channel Islands services and brought new standards of service to the route. In 1910, the turbine steamer *Caesarea* replaced the *Frederica*. She was followed by a sister vessel, the *Sarnia*, which replaced the *Lydia*, which was sold at the end of the First World War.

Following the Great War, it was not until 1919 that services returned to normal operations. Amalgation came into being in January 1923, which saw the London & South-Western Railway becoming part of the newly formed Southern Railway (S.R.). The newly formed S.R. ordered two ships for the St. Malo route, which resulted in the *Lorina* replacing the *Caesarea* on the Channel Islands service. In 1928 the *St. Julien* and *St. Helier* were built for the GWR to replace the *Ibex* and *Reindeer*, while two years later the *Isle of Jersey* and *Isle of Guernsey* were built for the Southampton route, followed later by a third sister, the *Isle of Sark* - the first vessel in the world to be fitted with Denny-Brown fin stabilisers.

Prior to the Second World War, there were no fewer than three cargo vessels running to the Channel Islands while passenger services were covered by the *Isle of Jersey*, *Isle of Guernsey* and *Isle of Sark*. The *Brittany* also ran to the Islands and to St. Malo, Granville and Cherbourg. After war had been declared, there was a sharp decline in the numbers of civilians travelling. U-boats continued to menace shipping in the Channel prior to the German Army taking occupation of the Islands.

Following the liberation of the Channel Islands in May 1945, a month later the *Isle of Guernsey* arrived in the Islands, she was later joined by the *Isle of Jersey* and *Isle of Sark*. The *Brittany* returned to Jersey in June 1946 and soon took up the service to St. Malo, which she operated once a week, while at weekends she helped out on the cross-Channel services. The GWR also re-opened the Weymouth – Channel Islands service in June 1946 using the *St. Helier*. S.R.'s new flagship the *Falaise* entered service in July 1947, and for her first two seasons operated once a week to the Islands, before the service was taken over by the *Isle of Thanet*.

On New Year's Day 1948 all the assets of the railway companies were taken over by the British Transport Commission (BTC) which traded under the title of British Railways. British Railways was only a month old when their first new ship, the *St. Patrick*, was delivered and placed on the Channel Islands route.

During the early fifties the tourist trade to the Channel Islands had increased considerably. The major increase occurred in 1952 when a new runway opened at Jersey allowing larger aircraft to operate, and within four years the air-passenger arrival figures had overtaken the figures for those arriving by boat.

The comfort offered by the aeroplane caused complaints to be voiced about the facilities on the boats, as the *St. Patrick* was the only modern ship on the Channel Islands service.

By 1955 the ever increasing number of passengers travelling to the islands was causing distress to many of those using the cramped overnight sailings by sea. In November 1956 came the announcement that the BTC had agreed to the building of four new ships (two passenger and two cargo). This decision to build new ships was followed by the States of Jersey agreeing to spend £280,000 on the deepening of St. Helier Harbour

In 1955 'No Passport' day-excursions were again allowed, after agreement between the French and British Governments. Despite this opening of the market, the winter passenger figures were even worse, and in August 1958 came the news that both the Southampton – Le Havre and Southampton – Channel Islands routes were to be reduced by one sailing each week. This would allow the *Falaise* and *Normannia* to cover both routes for the winter. The Jersey – St Malo sailing would be covered by the *Normannia*. The Weymouth – Channel Islands route was also reduced by one trip per week.

With new ships on order, 1959 saw the withdrawals of the coal burning cargo steamers *Whitstable* and *Haslemere*. The new *Elk* made her maiden voyage in August, which allowed the old *Ringwood* to make her last voyage, while in October 1959 the *Isle of Jersey* made her last call at St. Helier

The 1959–1960 winter service from Southampton to the islands was further reduced to only one round-trip each week – nearly all the passenger traffic was forced to use Weymouth. Part of the plan to upgrade the Channel Islands services saw the *St. Patrick* become a permanent member of the fleet at Weymouth.

It was revealed in June 1960 that BR wished to concentrate all shipping operations on the shortest sea route from Weymouth, and furthermore they planned to introduce a one class service to the Islands. With the proposals only a month

The *St. Helier* is seen here arriving at Weymouth from the Channel Islands in her original condiiton. *(Ambrose Greenway collection)*

The Southampton-based vessel *Isle of Sark* with her two sisters maintained the Channel Islands operations until the early sixties from Southampton. *(Ambrose Greenway)*

# CENTURY OF NORTH WEST EUROPEAN FERRIES 1900 - 2000

The distinctive looking **Brittany** is seen here off Jersey. The vessel was sold in 1963 for further service in Finland and renamed the **Alandsfarjan**. *(Kevin Le Scelleur)*

The rather fully loaded **St Julian** seen here leaving Weymouth for the Channel Islands. *(Ambrose Greenway collection)*

old, the shipping services were dealt a further blow in July, when it was announced that to improve the mail services to the Islands, all mail except printed material and parcels would from July be transported to the Islands by air.

At the end of the 1960 summer service, three more of the older ships were withdrawn; the *St. Helier, St. Julien* and the *Isle of Sark*. The new *Caesarea* was delivered to her owners in November 1960. The entry into service of the new ship allowed the *St. Patrick* to be converted into a one-class ship while the *Isle of Guernsey* closed the Southampton service in May allowing BR to concentrate on the shorter Weymouth link. The last sailing arrived in the Islands in mid-May 1961, when the new one-class service was inaugurated from Weymouth by the *Caesarea* and *St. Patrick*. In June the *Sarnia* entered service, which allowed the *St. Patrick* to become the relief ship within the fleet. The *Brittany* being stationed in Jersey no longer fitted into the new thinking and she made her last voyage from St. Malo to Jersey in November 1962. The service was only to continue for a further two years.

Although passenger figures were still in decline, the number of people wishing to take their cars with them on holiday was increasing sharply and, to cater for this, a special lift-on/lift-off cargo boat service was operated between July and September 1966 to coincide with the operation of the passenger ships. The success of the lift-on/lift-off car ferry service in 1966 caused BR to step up the operation for the

A wonderful summer's scene at Southampton as the **Isle of Guernsey** prepares to leave for the Channel Islands. *(Henry Maxwell)*

77

# CENTURY OF NORTH WEST EUROPEAN FERRIES 1900 - 2000

*The imposing BCIF vessel **Rozel** leaves St. Helier for Guernsey in June 1989. The **Rozel** was the biggest ferry ever to operate to the Channel Islands during her period of charter to BCIF. (Miles Cowsill)*

undertook not to offer any services to the Islands for twelve months.

Following the joint venture falling through, BCIF quickly had to charter two vessels, to maintain a credible service for the forthcoming summer season. British Channel Island Ferries looked to Brittany Ferries for a freight ship and the *Briezh-Izel* was chartered to run opposite the *Corbiere* between Portsmouth and the Channel Islands. Eventually a suitable ferry was found to operate the Weymouth route for the forthcoming season from Marlines of Greece. The chartered Greek ship *Baroness M* was no stranger to British waters, for as the *Lion* she had originally been built for the Burns and Laird service between Ardrossan and Belfast and later operated from Dover to Boulogne. The ship was renamed *Portelet*.

Both the Weymouth and Portsmouth links settled down into a regular pattern for the summer on the arrival of the *Portelet*. The *Corbiere* covered the morning sailing from Portsmouth to Jersey and then on to Guernsey. Meanwhile the *Portelet* offered a daylight service to Weymouth from the Islands and a nightly run from the UK.

During August 1988, British Channel Island Ferries announced that as from the following January they would be moving both their passenger and freight services from Portsmouth and Weymouth to Poole. The new mainline terminal would offer faster crossings of up to two hours on some sailings.

A month later BCIF secured the long-term charter of the *Scirocco* from Cenargo Navigation Limited. The new vessel would replace the *Corbiere* in the New Year and would be the largest-ever ship to operate between Britain and the Channel Islands. The new ship would be renamed the *Rozel*, after the north east bay in Jersey, and would be able to carry about 300 cars and 1,300 passengers. Meanwhile BCIF entered into negotiations with Brittany Ferries for the long-term charter of the *Cornouailles* to replace the freight ship *Breizh-Izel*. The *Scirocco*, like the *Portelet*, was no stranger to British waters, as she had been built for Sealink UK Limited in 1973 for their Harwich–Hook of Holland service, as the *St .Edmund*.

In December 1988, BCIF secured the charter of the *Cornouailles*, in place of the *Briezh-Izel*, the newly chartered ship was to be renamed *Havelet*. The *Corbiere* undertook her last sailing from Portsmouth to the Channel Islands on the last day of 1988. Two days later she then departed on her inaugural sailing from the Dorset port to the Channel Islands.

The *Scirocco* arrived from the Mediterranean in early January 1989 for a £1 million refit and emerged from refit the next month as the *Rozel*.

Following the successful introduction of the *Rozel* on the Poole-Channel Islands service, the company was to consolidate its operations and win back some of the lost traffic over the recent years from air travel and the demise of the ferry operations in recent years. Despite their successes with passenger operations the freight market was slow to grow for them, as Commodore Ferries and MMD decided to commence their own rival freight service from Portsmouth in competition to BCIF. Commodore were later to take control of MMD. Meanwhile at Weymouth, Condor's passenger-only operation began to gain an ever-inceasing share of the passenger market from BCIF. In 1990 they introduced the *Condor 9* to cater for further passenger capacity.

In a surprise move in late summer 1991, BCIF announced that they were not going to renew the charter of the *Rozel*. Instead they had decided to charter the former Brittany Ferries' vessel *Reine Mathilde* (ex *Prince of Brittany*, ex *Prince of Fundy*) from her new American owners for two years. The company claimed at the time that the vessel was only a stopgap. However, it was to be a major turning point in BCIF's fortunes and ultimately was to see the demise of the company. The

# CENTURY OF NORTH WEST EUROPEAN FERRIES 1900 - 2000

The *Condor Vitesse* at her berth at Poole. The fast ferry service of Condor operates from both Poole and Weymouth to the Channel Islands. *(Philippe Holtof)*

*Rozel* completed her final passenger sailings to the Islands in January 1992.

The newly acquired vessel, renamed *Beauport*, underwent a £1 million refit before entering service on the Channel Islands operations in February.

In August 1992, Condor announced that they would be introducing a rival operation to that of BCIF with two new car-carrying catamarans from Weymouth to the Channel Islands. In the event only one craft was introduced. In the light of this announcement and another downturn in the market, BCIF announced that they would operate a reduced service for 1993.

In March 1993, Condor's new rival service to that of BCIF opened with their fast craft the *Condor 10*. Despite BCIF's earlier announcement the previous year, the company did operate for the 1993 season a two vessel operation with a twice-daily passenger service to and from the Islands until the middle of September. During the summer BCIF and Condor were involved in an intensive price war on fares.

At the end of the season the charter of the *Beauport* was not extended by BCIF, instead the company decided that the *Havelet* would become the mainstay of their passenger operations. To offer additional freight capacity, BCIF chartered the *Purbeck* for eight years. In January 1994, in a surprise announcement, it was disclosed that BCIF had been bought out by Commodore Shipping for an unknown figure following major losses of the company during 1993. The passenger operations of the former company were passed to Condor, while the freight business was moved to Commodore at Portsmouth.

Condor and Commodore immediately announced that the *Havelet* would continue to maintain the traditional passenger service and that the newly acquired *Purbeck* would support their freight operation from Portsmouth. With the reduced passenger capacity to the Islands with only the fast craft *Condor 10* and the traditional ferry the *Havelet*, there was an immediate reaction from the travel trade on the Islands.

Meanwhile in October 1993, Commodore had ordered a purpose-built freight vessel to replace their then current chartered tonnage; in the light of the takeover of BCIF a second sister vessel was ordered. The first section of the hull to the *Island Commodore* was laid in July 1994 and she duly entered service the following May. Her sister, the *Commodore Goodwill*, entered service the following year. Meanwhile Condor replaced the *Condor 10* with a larger InCat craft, the *Condor 11*, in 1995 and an even larger craft, the *Condor 12*, in 1996. The following year the *Condor Express* entered service.

During the next couple of years an erratic passenger service was offered to the Islands with a series of fast craft with the back-up of the *Havelet*. With continued pressure from the travel trade on both Jersey and Guernsey and residents themselves, following periods of cancelled operations during the height of the season and a non-reliable service during the winter period, the States of Jersey and Guernsey invited tenders for the licence to operate the mainland UK services to the Channel Islands.

There were three main contenders for the licence. Condor's proposals allowed for their existing vessels *Condor Express* and *Condor Vitesse* to operate the service from both Weymouth and Poole, which would also link St. Malo. A new ro-pax vessel would be built by Commodore for service by the year 2000. Hoverspeed meanwhile proposed that they would operate a year-round SuperSeaCat service from Weymouth and support the operation with either the *Lady of Mann* or *King Orry* during the summer. Either of these vessels would also support the operation during the winter when the SuperSeaCat might not be able to operate due to weather conditions. P&O European Ferries planned to introduce a conventional ferry, believed at the time to be the *Pride of Bruges*, with two new fast craft which would be scheduled to run between Portsmouth - Guernsey - Jersey - St. Malo.

The outcome of the three tenders was to favour Condor continuing the service to the Islands with their proposals. Following Condor being successful in securing the licence to operate from mainland UK to the Channel Islands, the company purchased the *Havelet* from Channel Island Ferry Ship Managment to ensure at least that their operations could be maintained during bad weather conditions when the fast craft might not be able to operate. The company immediately ordered with their parent Commodore Ferries a new vessel for the route from Van der Giessen based on a similar design to that of the Isle of Man Steam Packet's vessel *Ben-my-Chree*. The new ro-pax vessel, the *Commodore Clipper*, entered service commercially in October from Portsmouth to the Channel Islands, which in turn displaced the *Island Commodore*.

In the future Condor will offer a conventional service to the Islands during the winter months for reliability for the travelling public from Portsmouth with a limited fast craft operation from Weymouth. During the summer the service will be increased with two fast ferries operating between Poole/ Weymouth -Guernsey - Jersey and St. Malo, with the back-up of the *Commodore Clipper*.

The *Island Commodore* arriving at Jersey during her first season in service. *(Kevin Le Scelleur)*

*Miles Cowsill*

CENTURY OF NORTH WEST EUROPEAN FERRIES 1900 - 2000

# Brittany Ferries into the 21st Century

As the Chinese say, we live in interesting times and as we enter the new millennium, perhaps it would be relevant to look back from whence we came before looking in the crystal ball as to where we might be in another 20 odd years.

We have always viewed the world of ferries and, specifically, the UK market to France and Spain, from a slightly differing perspective than our competitors have or, indeed, still do. It started with a view that we should create links directly to the main holiday areas of France - in effect, taking people to where they would wish to be rather than where, historically, it was commercially preferable to drop them off. It was not an easy task, as all the existing ports at that time with ferry links were either large deep water ports or had been evolved as rail links. To provide for a new generation of motorists and offer different options, we had to create the ports. All of the nine ports that we serve, with the exception of one - namely Cherbourg - had no UK or French ferry links when we started.

The formula quickly became a winning one, but not without the difficulties associated with starting a business with ships not specifically designed with the routes in mind. I recall our advertising at that time used to be based upon the simple philosophy of "Only Brittany Ferries goes direct to Brittany" and finding some wag had written on our poster "Ah - but when?"

However, originating as we do from a large farming co-operative in Brittany, with management and mariners largely scoured from outside the traditional "ferry" industry, we built our own technical experience, allied to a certain operating and marketing flair that gave us our own clear identity in what was a fairly crowded but traditionalist market. We attracted a growing, loyal and faithful clientele that eventually allowed us

*Ian A. Carruthers*

to invest in the type of ships that we had only previously dreamed of building. When first introduced nearly 10 years ago, they were the pace-setters of standards on the Channel to France and Spain.

The test of people, as of a business, is the ability to handle adversity. We have had our share of that. A combination of events in the mid 90s that would have been dismissed as not credible in any business school scenario combined to almost overwhelm us. Imagine the scenario - sterling devalues by 20% overnight and both your own and destination costs increase accordingly, the tunnel opens with enormous capacity and then direct competitors increase dramatically their capacity, in

The *Barfleur* arrives at Poole from Cherbourg in August 1999. *(Mike Louagie)*

82

Shouldn't getting there
be as relaxing as being there?

It's been our philosophy since our maiden voyage in 1973. It's one shared by our passengers. Which is why that single route has grown to six today. And three of our six ships have been awarded the AA's coveted 5-star award for on-board facilities and services. Nor do things stop when we dock. For more and more of our passengers, sailing is just the first part of a complete Brittany Ferries' holiday. So if you haven't yet, it's time to come aboard and enjoy the philosophy.

**Brittany Ferries**
*as relaxing as being there*

www.brittany-ferries.com   08705 360 360

The *Normandie* has proved to be an overwhelming success on the Caen-Portsmouth route. She is seen here leaving for France. *(Miles Cowsill)*

# CENTURY OF NORTH WEST EUROPEAN FERRIES 1900 - 2000

The *Duc de Normandie* outward bound from Portsmouth. *(John Bryant)*

reaction. The tunnel then halves prices and loses £1000m in one year alone (more than the total turnover of all the ferry companies operating on the Channel at that time). Prepare your business plan!

Well, we did. Apart from the obvious cost-cutting, where possible and appropriate, we concentrated even more on the destination and the reasons for our clients to travel. Our services are not the reason, but rather the means, to travel and whilst we cannot be more popular than the destination, we had to increase the range and reasons to do so. We also had to develop all of our systems such that we could both provide for and react to changes as they occurred in the market place. We needed management information about everything at our fingertips, to develop elegant reservation systems, yield management systems, etc. It worked.

Having just completed the most financially successful year since inception, with our finances now in robust health, one of the largest holiday businesses to France developed without acquisition, the largest property owners' club to France, a good strong respected brand and most fortunately loyalty from our valued clients we can now, once again, turn our attention to creating more blue water between ourselves and our competition.

How can we do this? By concentrating even more on the things we do well and at the same time working hard at reducing the weaknesses.

Our name must be synonymous with efficient service, good food, clean ships, good people and general value for money.

We will use the benefits of technology to provide for the increasing trends to give personal service, treating individuals as that, not as a "market".

We shall address the necessity to provide even more homogeny and modernity across our fleet by building and acquisition.

Let me stay for the moment on the question of ships. What type, size, etc., for the future?

Firstly, regarding fast craft, I think it is true to say that the jury is still out on the whole question of the economics of these craft. For the moment, we cannot make the figures fit for what should, on the face of it, be the ideal solution for additional summer capacity. Unfortunately, "me-too" is not an adequate strategy for acquiring capacity, although we remain optimistic that the economics could improve one day.

For ships in the future, we still believe in the philosophy of the holiday starting on board and that the experience should be "as relaxing as being there".

We shall have to ensure that the mix of facilities and general experience is, again, ahead of expectations. Who would have believed an ice rink would be on a Caribbean cruise ship. We too have to think differently for our market.

Moving on. We will continue down our own path of increasing our vertical integration rather than the outsourcing of our competitors.

From food to holidays to maintenance to computer systems, it is all our own people. Everyone works for us and we cannot blame anyone else if we do not provide quality and value. Taken to extremes, maybe we shall be able to say we are a truly vertically integrated business when even all the vegetables on our ships are grown by our shareholders!

The foregoing is not intended to sound like a mission statement, rather the sense of pride, identity and direction that has and will set us apart from others.

Finally, I hope that we shall achieve my own personal vision that Brittany Ferries will grow from being not just the leader in the West, but the only real alternative to the tunnel or any sea shuttle to Calais; two clear alternatives: fast and furious routing to the heart of industrial France, with clients making their own holiday arrangements; or a range of relaxing routes direct to holiday France with a full range of holidays provided.

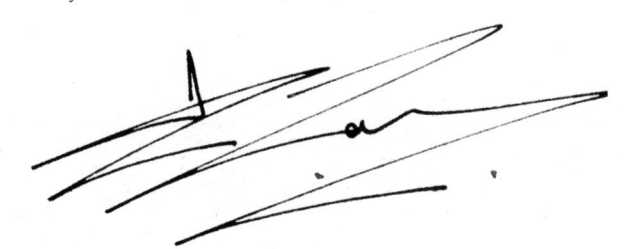

*Ian A. Carruthers*
Managing Director (UK & Ireland)

# CENTURY OF NORTH WEST EUROPEAN FERRIES 1900 - 2000

## The last conventional British passenger ferry this Century

As we reach the end of the twentieth century it will fall to a Channel Island company, Commodore Ferries (C.I.) Ltd. to take delivery of the last conventional passenger ferry to be delivered to a U.K. company this century - the *Commodore Clipper*; a century which has seen great changes in ships and the methods of transporting cargo.

Commodore Ferries (C.I.) Ltd. is a subsidiary of the Commodore Shipping Group whose history in the Channel Islands spans over fifty years. The company maintains the roll-on/roll-off (ro-ro) cargo service to the Islands, and in this day and age for a shipping service to continue to achieve a more than 96 % punctuality record when maintaining a triangular service from Portsmouth to the Channel Islands of Guernsey and Jersey with the large rise and fall of tide and the notoriously dangerous waters is something of which Managing Director Mr. Jeff Vidamore of Commodore Ferries (C.I.) Ltd. is very proud.

The figure has been achieved since the introduction of their two ro-ro freight vessels, *Island Commodore* in 1995, and *Commodore Goodwill* a year later, and it is a testament to the design of the vessels and the skill and seamanship of the masters and crew. It is even more noteworthy as it is a twice daily service, and the ships are by far the largest freighters to have operated to the islands.

It is only ten years since Commodore Shipping first became involved in ro-ro transportation, but the origins of the company date back to 1947 when one of its vessels commenced on the route between the Channel Islands of Guernsey and Sark. Later Commodore won the contract to operate from Guernsey to Sark and Alderney, and from these beginnings the company grew into a cross-Channel freight operator in 1962, and later stretched its legs to Portugal and Spain.

Along with the development of Commodore Shipping, one of its principles Mr. Jack Norman became involved with Mr. Peter Dorey (of Onesimus Dorey (Shipowners) Ltd.) in the formation of Condor Ltd, a company which with a hydrofoil *Condor I* introduced a high speed passenger service in the Channel Islands in 1964. The company was not a subsidiary of Commodore Shipping but the latter held some shares, and following the tragic death of Peter Dorey, Commodore purchased the remaining shares in August 1983.

The drive which saw the development of Commodore was

*Club Class Lounge - **Commodore Clipper** (Commodore Ferries)*

*The **Commodore Clipper** inward bound from Guernsey to Jersey. (Kevin Le Scelleur)*

Commodore Ferries has now introduced a new RoPax vessel "Commodore Clipper" on their well established and efficient twice daily Roll-on Roll-off service between Portsmouth and the Channel Islands.

This new vessel not only maintains the present freight carrying capacity but in addition, in partnership with **Condor Ferries,** offers a new all weather route connecting Portsmouth to Jersey and Guernsey.

Commodore Clipper has quality facilities for 500 passengers and their cars.

## Services tailored to the needs of our customers

**Commodore Ferries**

**FREIGHT RESERVATIONS**
UK          TEL: +44(0)23 9287 1538
Jersey      TEL: +44(0)1534 872509
Guernsey TEL: +44(0)1481 728620

**CONDOR Ferries**

**PASSENGER RESERVATIONS**
UK          TEL: +44(0)1305 761551
Jersey      TEL: +44(0)1534 601000
Guernsey TEL: +44(0)1481 729666

Members of the Commodore Shipping Group of Companies

Commodore Shipping Company Limited, P.O. Box 10, Les Banques, St.Peter Port, Guernsey, GY1 3AF **TEL: +44(0)1481 729101 FAX: +44(0)1481 716732**

# CENTURY OF NORTH WEST EUROPEAN FERRIES 1900 - 2000

Quiet Lounge - **Commodore Clipper** (Commodore Ferries)

Brasserie Lounge - **Commodore Clipper** (Commodore Ferries)

applied to Condor, and following the provision of an emergency passenger service from the Islands to Poole in October 1986 to cover the chaos caused by the abortive merger of Sealink and Channel Islands Ferries, it was decided to enter the cross-Channel trade using two hydrofoils. The service to Weymouth commenced in May 1987, and the traffic grew steadily with a revolutionary passenger wavepiercer being built for the company in 1990.

The roll-on/roll-off revolution in the Channel Islands commenced to Jersey in 1973 and Guernsey the following year, and although initially seen for the transport of holiday-makers cars, commercial traffic soon started to be carried, mainly for perishable items, but gradually all types of freight were transported by this method.

Commodore Shipping had continued to maintain a lift-on /lift-off container service on the Channel Islands route, and by taking over other services the company had become the main carrier. Its entry into the roll-on/roll-off trade took place when British Channel Islands Ferries (BCIF), the company then providing a passenger / freight service to the Islands decided to move their U.K. terminal from Portsmouth to Poole as from January 1989. One of its main customers Mainland Market Deliveries Ltd. (MMD), being based in Portsmouth wished to continue using the port, and consequently teamed up with Commodore Shipping to launch a daily freight only service under the banner of C & M Shipping Ltd., which commenced operating in January 1989, with the chartered freight vessel *Pride of Portsmouth* coming on line in March.

The joint service led to talks between the two companies resulting in Commodore Shipping acquiring the MMD Group in August 1989. MMD not only operated road transport services but also a stevedoring, warehousing and fruit handling business based at the Flathouse Quay in Portsmouth which adjoined Commodore's Albert Johnson Quay.

With Commodore Shipping Co. Ltd. having grown substantially, it was seen that there was a need for a management restructure, and this took place in 1990. Commodore Ferries (C.I.) Ltd., was established to provide the ship owning services, which includes the day to day operation of the ships, and the selling of the freight space on board the vessels, while Commodore Express Ltd. provides the groupage services and MMD continues the stevedoring, fruit handling and road transport business at Portsmouth.

The ro-ro traffic quickly grew, carrying 70,000 metres of units in the first year, resulting in Commodore deciding to add a second vessel to provide a twice daily service as from 1st August 1990, and to discontinue the container service as from that time.

The enhanced service caused an even sharper rise in traffic, which for the year 1993 saw 450,000 metres of units having been carried. With such growth it was decided to build a vessel tailor-made for the route. Ordered in October 1993 the vessel would be able to carry 94 x 12m units, and was to replace the smaller of the two ships in service when delivered in March 1995, but other events overtook these plans.

At Weymouth, Condor had continued with their summer only passenger service to the Islands, and with the wavepiercer concept being developed into a car ferry, the company ordered one of the 74 metre craft following the Australian transport company T.N.T. taking a 50% share in Condor.

The vessel, *Condor 10*, entered service in April 1993, and such was its success, that this coupled with the growth of Commodore's ro-ro service from Portsmouth, forced their competitors BCIF into deciding to stop trading in January 1994. The passenger business was sold to Condor, while the freight traffic passed to Commodore together with the charter of a freight vessel.

This caused Commodore to have an immediate rethink of their fleet requirements, with the result that a second vessel was ordered from the same builders. The two vessels would be able to offer 2,500 metres of space each day compared to 1,720 metres of the three ships then in service, and this additional space would be needed as the enhanced business had seen 650,000 metres of units carried in 1994.

The first new ro-ro freight ship *Island Commodore* duly entered service in June 1995 and in December that year the *Norman Commodore* (ex *Pride of Portsmouth*) went off charter and this allowed an accelerated service to be introduced. The new ship was not only faster and larger than the smaller vessel, but instead of a lift to take trailers to the upper deck she had a permanent ramp which substantially reduced loading / discharge time.

The schedule called for a departure from Portsmouth at 09:30 and 20:30 each day to reach Guernsey at 03:00 and 16:00, and Jersey at 06:00 and 19:00 . This is altered at the weekends to allow for a voyage from Jersey to St. Malo to

# CENTURY OF NORTH WEST EUROPEAN FERRIES 1900 - 2000

Food Service Area - **Commodore Clipper**. *(Commodore Ferries)*

Bridge - **Commodore Clipper**. *(Commodore Ferries)*

meet the charter requirements of the French company Morvan & Fils. This schedule varies at times to take into account the tide times in the islands. The second new ship the *Commodore Goodwill* entered service in March 1996.

It is a tribute to the management of Commodore Shipping Co. Ltd, a company which has just celebrated its first half century, that it has successfully made the transition from inter-island services, to containers, to ro-ro, and also encompassed passenger services. To show how they have always moved with the market it is interesting that in 1977 it took seven ships to carry the Jersey potato export crop of 34,000 tons; in 1987 it took five ships to transport 36,000 tons; while in 1997 the two freight ships carried 57,000 tons in addition to all the other ro-ro cargo!

Condor Ferries as the company was now titled, had chartered larger wavepiercers for the 1995 and 1996 seasons to maintain their cross channel service, until in February 1997 the purpose built *Condor Express* was introduced. The craft initially operated from Weymouth but moved to Poole in March when Condor transferred their U.K. terminal in the hope that it would eliminate the road bottlenecks which were experienced during the summer months on the approaches to Weymouth.

After the first few months in service *Condor Express* began to experience engine problems and despite huge efforts by the engine manufactures these continued through the summer. The company came in for some severe criticism for the way in which it handled the problems, resulting in the States of both

The **Commodore Clipper** on sea trials off the Dutch coast in September 1999. *(Commodore Ferries)*

# CENTURY OF NORTH WEST EUROPEAN FERRIES 1900 - 2000

Built for the 'Joint Company' (London & South Western and London Brighton & Coast Coast Railways), the **Duchess of Albany** entered service on the Portsmouth - Ryde route in 1890. She carried 479 passengers in two classes until both she and her sister **Princess Margaret** were replaced by the **Merstone** and **Portsdown** in 1928. *(John Hendy collection)*

The western Solent vessel **Lymington** loading at Lymington Pier slipway in July 1971. She was built by Denny of Dumbarton in 1938 and was the UK's first Voith-Schneider propelled ferry. *(John Hendy collection)*

side, into half-barges which where towed by the service vessels. All cargo to the island had been carried thus since the early days and the barges were popularly known as 'horse boats.' As their name suggests, prior to the advent of mechanised road transport, horses and their carriages, general cargo and livestock were all carried this way and when motor cars began to make themselves available for shipment, they too were handled in the time-honoured manner.

During these early years of motoring, the Lymington - Yarmouth link was the most popular and convenient passage and in order to free the steamers for their scheduled timetables, a special tug was acquired to tow the car carrying barges.

The year 1913 saw 700 cars landed at Yarmouth Quay, a rise of 400 since 1907 but during the Great War services to Totland were severely curtailed before their final abandonment in 1927. The formation of the Southern Railway on New Year's Day 1923 saw continued growth and in June 1927 the largest and final paddle steamer was introduced on the route. Built at the famous East Cowes yard of J. Samuel White, the

The final traditional Isle of Wight passenger ferry in service was the **Southsea** of 1948 which was not withdrawn from service until the end of her fortieth season. *(John Hendy)*

# CENTURY OF NORTH WEST EUROPEAN FERRIES 1900 - 2000

An early morning scene at the entrance to Portsmouth Harbour in May 1990 as Sealink British Ferries' *St. Helen* nears the end of her passage from Fishbourne. *(John Hendy)*

*Freshwater* (264 gross tons) boasted accommodation for 500 passengers and proved to be a handsome addition to the route. By 1930, vehicle numbers had risen to 1,650 and this in spite of a new car carrying service at Portsmouth.

There was much discussion and deliberation concerning a specially constructed car ferry for Lymington which was complicated by the intervention of a new company, the Isle of Wight Ferry Co. who announced that they were to start a service from Keyhaven (at the shore end of Hurst Spit) to Fort Victoria (at the closest part of the island to the mainland). The plan was to utilise two redundant Mersey ferries which were then surplus to requirements following the opening of the Mersey Tunnel. The Southern entered into negotiations with the new company, but no money was forthcoming to purchase the twin vessels and much time and energy was wasted before the announcement was made concerning the Southern's own car ferry. It is interesting to speculate that if a service from Keyhaven to Fort Victoria had materialised with the Southern Railway's assistance, then the severe restrictions placed on Wightlink for the replacement for the present three ships would most certainly not apply.

The revolutionary car ferry *Lymington* was built at Denny's Dumbarton yard and entered service in May 1938. With capacity for 400 passengers and 16 cars, the double-ended ship was able to work up to seven round crossings each day and by the end of 1938, some 4,000 cars has been carried as opposed to just 2,500 in the previous year. She was in every way an immediate success and operated from new slipways while the paddle steamers *Freshwater* and *Solent* ran from Lymington Pier to Yarmouth Pier.

The *Lymington* was not just revolutionary in her looks or performance but also in her propulsion. She was the first British ferry to be powered by the now ubiquitous Voith-Schneider propellers which enabled her to move in any direction without the aid of rudders.

The diesel electric paddle vessel *Farringford* (also a Denny product) joined the link in March 1948 by which time the 'Big Four' railway companies were nationalised and had become British Railways. The new ship was the largest yet carrying 320 passengers and 32 cars or as many as 800 passengers and no vehicles.

By 1955, 42,000 cars were carried on the Lymington - Yarmouth route and a third car ferry, a new *Freshwater*, entered service from the Ailsa yard at Troon in September 1959. The three car ferries continued in operation until 1973 and towards the end of this period were barely able to cope with the traffic on offer. With cars on offer rising to 107,000 by 1967, in the late sixties the shore facilities were enlarged to increase the car standage areas on both sides and then in 1971, to make it possible to increase the frequency of sailings, the Lymington River was dredged to allow two ships to pass each other within its confines.

The next major step to improve the western Solent crossing came with the order of three identical sisterships from the Robb Caledon yard at Dundee. The first was the *Caedmon* which entered service on the Portsmouth station to be followed by Lymington's *Cenwulf* in October 1973 (replacing the *Lymington*) and then the *Cenred* in January 1974 which replaced the *Farringford*. The new ships could accommodate 750 passengers and 52 cars while the *Freshwater* was kept as a

# CENTURY OF NORTH WEST EUROPEAN FERRIES 1900 - 2000

In September 1994 Wightlink's *St. Helen* is viewed on passage to Fishbourne and in the process of being passed by the Ryde-bound catamaran *Our Lady Patricia*. (John Hendy)

summer relief vessel until her withdrawal at the close of the 1983 season after which time the *Caedmon* was transferred to the western Solent.

The new ferries at Lymington soon generated their own traffic and by the end of their first year in service they had shipped 179,000 cars and, for the first time, over one million passengers.

During 1977-78 mezzanine decks were fitted to enable the ferries to accommodate 70 cars while the construction of linkspans at Lymington in 1976 and Yarmouth in 1983 enabled speedier turn-rounds and easier embarkation for the increasing flow of heavy goods vehicles using the link.

Plans have been drawn-up for many years to provide the Lymington - Yarmouth route with larger, modern, ferries with low wash but local and environmental concerns particularly on the mainland side have so far prevented this from occurring. Whilst the present 'C' class continue to provide excellent service they are now approaching thirty years of age and matters may well come to a head early in the new millennium when replacements will be required. At stake is the continuance of the current western Solent ferry service.

## PORTSMOUTH - FISHBOURNE

Although today the busiest of all routes to the Isle of Wight and therefore its number one gateway, the Portsmouth - Fishbourne service is one of the youngest and is a product of the increase in vehicle traffic.

For many years the main entry into the island for goods, livestock and, later, motor cars was the George Street slipway to the east of Ryde Pier. As at Lymington, the time-honoured 'horse boats' were used but matters were far from ideal as at low tide, the sea went out almost as far as the pier. Thus sailings from Portsmouth's Broad Street slipway were usually about two hours before high water and from Ryde about 30 minutes before high water. What was required was a sheltered deep water harbour in the area of Ryde which could handle specialist traffic at all states of the tide. Two miles west of the town is Wootton Creek and it was here in 1925 that the Southern Railway purchased some 2 acres of ground and prepared for their improved service.

After some delays, the new service opened in March 1926. A tug would pull up to three tow-boats across before grounding them on the new slipway while loading boards would be laid-out to ease the angle between barge and shore. Using this method, nine cars could be shipped at one time and although some passengers would choose to cross on the steamer from Portsmouth to Ryde and rejoin their cars later, some hardy motorists remained in their cars throughout the spray-swept passage while they were likely to be in the company of nearby livestock which could certainly be an unpleasant experience.

To begin with, two round trips were given each day but with almost 2,000 cars being carried in that first year, the new service was barely able to cope with the traffic on offer.

The solution was the construction at Denny's Dumbarton yard of the motor car ferry *Fishbourne* which entered service in August 1927. Two return crossings were given each day, the 8 knot vessel completing the crossing in 55 minutes with as many as 16 cars on board. The manually operated fold-down bow was a tremendous improvement on the old loading boards and the provision of ladies' and gentlemen's saloons with the availability of light refreshments meant that all motorists would now cross with their cars. Cattle meanwhile continued to be carried in the 'horse boats' - segregation that was welcomed by all. The success of the pioneer car ferry saw the

# CENTURY OF NORTH WEST EUROPEAN FERRIES 1900 - 2000

entry into service of the larger *Wootton* (in June 1928) and two years later by the *Hilsea*. By 1929, almost 29,000 cars were crossing on the new Fishbourne route.

On the outbreak of war in 1939 one car ferry was kept in service while the other two found limited war work available to them. Both the *Fishbourne* and the *Wootton* were involved in the evacuation of Dunkerque in 1940 but by the late fifties the trio of car ferries were becoming increasingly outdated and unable to cope with the traffic on offer. They were therefore replaced by twin ferries which were built by Philip & Son of Dartmouth and very much modelled on the lines of the Lymington-based vessel *Freshwater*. The second named *Fishbourne* entered service in July 1961 and her sister in the following month. Interestingly the second ship was originally to be named *Wootton* but in order to keep people happy in Hampshire, she was instead given a mainland name. She was strangely named *Camber Queen* after the new slipway which was in the commercial dock in Old Portsmouth known as the Camber.

The new ships carried 34 cars and 168 passengers. At that time all foot passengers were expected to cross on the Portsmouth - Ryde ferry; and as car passenger space was severely restricted on the new ships, motorists were expected to remain in their cars during the passage while the deck crew made extra pocket money by offering to wash cars!

In preparation for the entry into service of the twin ships, there was a general £1 million revamp of facilities at both Portsmouth and Fishbourne. New wider slipways were built with new terminal buildings and car parks. With larger ferries in service, commercial vehicle traffic began to grow and a new £275,000 consort was added in June 1969. This was the *Cuthred* which was provided by Richards' of Lowestoft and was the first vessel to provide passenger accommodation right across the vehicle deck. Her high freeboard and low power made her rather an unwieldy vessel, a matter which was corrected in the construction of a fourth vessel, the 750 passenger, 52 car *Caedmon* in July 1973.

By the close of the 1970s the Broad Street terminal was proving to be inadequate and its severe capacity problems were eventually solved with the purchase of the redundant Gunwharf site at which coal for the city's power station had been unloaded. A £2 million loan was arranged and today's fine terminal building and car park was constructed, opening in February 1982. The old slipway method of loading was replaced by linkspans both at Portsmouth and at Fishbourne where a new terminal for the island was opened in June 1983.

By this time an order had been made for for first of the route's fourth generation ferries, the £5 million *St. Catherine*, at Henry Robb's Leith yard. The ship completed her maiden voyage in July 1983 and boasted accommodation for as many as 1,000 passengers and 142 cars. For the first time ever, passengers were asked to vacate their cars during the passage and from ample and spacious accommodation high above the vehicle decks, the Solent can be viewed through large panoramic windows. The *Fishbourne* was immediately retired and her sister followed before the second new ship, the *St. Helen*, arrived at Portsmouth during November. The *St. Helen's* arrival also saw the transfer of the *Caedmon* to join her sisters at Lymington while the *Cuthred* was retained for extra summer duties until the pending arrival of the third of the class, the *St. Cecilia* in March 1987.

Sealink UK Ltd. (as the shipping division of the British Railways Board had become) was privatised in July 1984 when it was purchased by Sea Containers of Bermuda. The *St. Cecilia* was built by Cochrane's of Selby and was the first vessel to be constructed for the new company carrying a number of internal modifications in the light of operation with the first two ships. She was carpeted throughout and offered her passengers a degree of comfort previously unknown on the Solent routes.

The spring of 1990 saw Sealink taken-over by the Swedish ferry company Stena Line although the Isle of Wight services were not included in the sale and continued to be owned and operated by Sea Containers. The fourth and final ship of the series was the £7 million *St. Faith* which entered service in July 1990. That November the new livery and brand name of Wightlink were launched although after its further sale to CinVen Ltd. (one of Europe's largest venture capital companies) for £107 million five years later, the livery was slightly modified.

## PORTSMOUTH - RYDE

The history of the Portsmouth - Ryde passage is as long and as fascinating as any of the routes which operate from our shores. The route is particularly interesting as its ownership involved a joint service between the London & South Western Railway and its neighbour the London Brighton & South Coast Railway. In October 1876 their alliance had seen the construction of the line from Portsmouth Town to Portsmouth Harbour stations and they immediately sought to operate their own steamers. After some final acts of defiance (including an attempt to enter a trading union with the Southampton Co., owners of the Southampton - Cowes link), an Act of Parliament of 1879 empowered The Joint Railway Companies Steampacket Service to purchase the seven vessels then in service for £38,000. They were immediately rewarded by the opening of the new Ryde Pier which for the first time allowed trains to bring their passengers to the new Pier Head station where they terminated their journeys within a short walking distance of the steamers.

By the turn of the century therefore, the Joint Company was operating its own fleet of steamers from the twin railway piers which are so important for the success of today's services. The fleet was comprised of the following vessels the second, third and fourth of which were double-ended for speed of turn-round: *Alexandra* (1879), *Victoria* (1881), *Duchess of Edinburgh* and *Duchess of Connaught* (1884), *Duchess of Albany* (1890) and *Princess Margaret* (1893), *Duchess of Kent* (1897), *Duchess of Fife* (1899). The final two vessels were much larger than the previous paddle steamers built for the route, the "Fife" in particular being used for the excursion trade around the Isle of Wight and elsewhere. In this Edwardian heyday of the British excursion steamer, all resorts had piers alongside which a variety of steamers would daily sail to a number of destinations which included Cherbourg. It is difficult to appreciate just how popular were these excursions or the rivalry which existed between the different companies and Captains that operated their ships.

The *Duchess of Richmond* and *Duchess of Norfolk* arrived on station in 1910 - 11, the 'Richmond' being lost in mine-sweeping operations in the Mediterranean during 1919. Most of the larger and more modern steamers were used in a similar role leaving the Ryde passage to the elderly *Duchess of Albany* and *Princess Margaret* which during the winter before war broke out had been fitted with electric lighting in order for them to operate the winter service.

With the formation of the Southern Railway in January

# CENTURY OF NORTH WEST EUROPEAN FERRIES 1900 - 2000

1923, a new vessel was hastily constructed to replace the lost *Duchess of Richmond*. This was the *Shanklin* which revived the practice of naming ships after local places and which entered service in the summer of 1924. Similar steamers *Merstone* and *Portsdown*, which replaced the 'Albany' and 'Margaret' in 1927, each had passenger certificates for 723 against the 479 of the ships they replaced.

Twin steamers to be primarily used for excursions entered service in 1930 in the form of the *Southsea* and *Whippingham* which replaced the 'Fife' in the fleet. Superbly fitted-out in mahogany and oak, their ample shelter made certain that excursionists would enjoy their trip even in unkind weather. The 36 years young *Duchess of Kent* was sold in 1933 and was replaced in the following June by the *Sandown*. She was followed in July 1937 by the final paddle steamer the *Ryde* which saw off the last of the old Joint Company steamers, the *Duchess of Norfolk*. Amazingly, as the *Embassy*, the 'Norfolk' continued in service for Cosens of Weymouth until 1967 - a wonderful career of 57 years.

The newer units of the Southern Railway's Isle of Wight fleet were all requisitioned on the outbreak of war in 1939 leaving the Ryde route in the hands of the oldest three ships, *Shanklin*, *Merstone* and *Portsdown*. Sadly on an early morning mail run to Ryde during September 1941, the *Portsdown* hit a mine off the entrance of Portsmouth Harbour and sank immediately with her bows blown away. The ancient *Solent* (1902) was transferred from Lymington for the remainder of the war but worse was to come when after striking a mine in February 1941, the *Southsea* was run ashore near the mouth of the Tyne and was subsequently declared a total loss.

With peace restored, the *Ryde* was the first back on station in July 1945 followed by the *Sandown* and lastly the *Whippingham* in 1946. Although a tremendous people-mover and very useful for Saturday morning ferry duties, her pre-war excursions were confined to the sheltered waters of the Solent.

A pair of revolutionary motor vessels joined the link in November and December 1948. The Denny-built *Southsea* and *Brading* were an immediate success and carried 1,331 passengers in two classes. They were given the 'magic-eye' of radar and for the first time in the island's history, services were operated in fog. They were joined in June 1951 by the similar *Shanklin* when the service became one class.

As the price of fuel became more expensive, one by one the paddle steamers were withdrawn: the *Shanklin* passing to Cosens in 1951, the *Merstone*, *Whippingham* and *Sandown* being sold in 1952, 1962 and 1966. With the withdrawal of the *Ryde* at the close of the 1969 season came the end of year round steam navigation in the Solent. She was sold for static use to a marina near Newport on the Isle of Wight and remains there as a hulk to this day. It is sobering to realise that the last of the paddle steamers has lain in her present berth for almost longer than she plied the Portsmouth - Ryde route.

Experiments by Seaspeed (a British Rail subsidiary) were tried with SRN 4 hovercraft in 1966 when a service linking Southampton to Cowes was commenced followed in 1967 by a further link from Portsmouth to Cowes and finally from Portsmouth - Ryde with the side-walled Hovermarine HM2 in 1968. The Portsmouth - Cowes link closed in 1969, Portsmouth - Ryde finished in September 1972 while the Southampton - Cowes route ended in May 1976.

With the *Ryde's* passing, the Ryde link was left in the hands of the trio of post-war diesels which received extra passenger decks in 1967 and were given £100,000 modernisations during 1973/74 after which time electric passenger ramps on both sides of the Solent greatly sped up passenger embarkation. Recurring engine problems saw the retirement of the *Shanklin* in March 1980 before her sale to supporters of the Glasgow-based paddle steamer *Waverley* for just £25,000. The following August she was wrecked in Port Eynon Bay.

Hovertravel's AP1-88 hovercraft **Freedom 90** approaching her Southsea terminus from Ryde during August 1990. *(John Hendy)*

# CENTURY OF NORTH WEST EUROPEAN FERRIES 1900 - 2000

British Rail made several attempts to replace the remaining vessels *Southsea* and *Brading* with fast craft but they soldiered on and were returned to private owners when Sealink was denationalised in July 1984. New owners Sea Containers lost little time in ordering twin catamarans from InCat, Tasmania and the first, *Our Lady Patricia*, took up service in March 1986 directly replacing the *Brading* which had been withdrawn in the previous month following a number of breakdowns. The second 'cat' *Our Lady Pamela* arrived on station in August 1986 when the *Southsea* became the relief vessel. She continued to prove her worth during the heavy Saturday passenger sailings in the holiday season and continued to run these during the following two summers by which time she had become the final excursion vessel of any size to grace the Solent's shores. Sailings from Southsea (Clarence Pier), Ryde, Sandown, Cowes, Southampton and Yarmouth were offered but poor weather, linked with a degree of indifference on the part of some local managers, saw the scheme to keep the *Southsea* end in failure and the forty year old veteran was finally withdrawn in September 1988.

After laying-up firstly in Falmouth and then Newhaven, the vessel was sold to Brasspatch Ltd. in early in 1997 with a promise that she would be returned to service in the following season. This totally ill-conceived plan ended with dismal failure and after further sales, the forlorn and historic *Southsea* presently lies in the dock at Newport, Gwent.

Meanwhile the £1.9 million catamarans continue to cross to Ryde in just 15 minutes carrying 470 (later reduced to 448) passengers. During refits local excursion vessels are used and calls are made by car ferries if inclement weather cancels 'cat' sailings. With the Fishbourne route now carrying the bulk of Wightlink's passengers, the traditional Ryde service continues to provide the valuable train-connected through services to Ryde, Sandown and Shanklin and with the additional possibility of Ventnor being rejoined to the Island Line network, such an occurrence can only act in Wightlink's favour.

## HOVERTRAVEL

We have seen that prior to the opening of Fishbourne in March 1926, the Isle of Wight cargo services were based on the George Street slipway to the east of Ryde Pier. Historians searching for the site today will find the hoverpad of the newest of the Isle of Wight operators and their passenger hovercraft service linking Ryde Esplanade with Southsea.

Hovertravel have maintained the world's first year-round hovercraft service since July 1965. The four mile service (originally marketed under the name, Solent Seaspeed) commenced with two SRN 6 hovercraft named the *Sea Hawk* and *Sea Eagle* which were chartered from the British Hovercraft Corporation and previously employed on the British Rail (Seaspeed) link between Southampton and Cowes.

During the early years of the link, the SRN6 craft were expensive to operate using both aviation fuel and a design based upon aeronautical engineering which meant that the fare structure was about twice that of the competing British Rail ferries. The turning point came with the naming, by hovercraft inventor Sir Christopher Cockerell, and immediate introduction of the £750,000, 84 passenger, diesel-powered AP1-88 craft *Tenacity* in March1983 followed by her sister *Resolution* in June.

The new design was jointly developed by the British Hovercraft Corporation and Hovertravel to both greatly

A century old post card showing an impression of the Southampton Company's paddle steamer **Lorna Doone**. (Henry Maxwell collection)

reduce noise levels and also to improve sea keeping qualities in order to raise the 98.5% reliability of the SRN6 craft. Passenger comfort was greatly improved and in order to speed up turn round times, the AP1-88 was able to simultaneously load and unload. The *Perseverance* entered service in May 1985 when she replaced the *Resolution* which was chartered to Florida.

With more competitive rates now being charged, during the company's first thirty years of operation some 14 million passengers were carried. New and improved AP1-88 craft later appeared in the form of the *Courier* (1986), and the 98 passenger *Double O Seven* (1989) and *Freedom 90* (1990) which replaced the older units. The acquisition of three more craft - the 98 passenger *Idun Viking* (built 1983) and the smaller capacity *Liv Viking* and *Regja Viking* (both built in 1985), which were built to the order of Scandinavian Air Services (SAS), gave Hovertravel added flexibility. At the time of writing only the *Idun Viking* had operated across the Solent while the other two remained laid-up at Fishbourne. Recent AP1-88 craft have been constructed at Hovertravel's yard at St. Helens, Isle of Wight, in conjunction with Westland Aircraft Ltd.

## RED FUNNEL

Red Funnel today claims that theirs are the 'original' Isle of Wight ferries and with its formation as long ago as 1861, this is certainly a proud boast. The Isle of Wight Royal Mail Steam Packet Company and the Isle of Wight Steam Packet Company had been joined in 1860 with a third operator, the Southampton, Isle of Wight & Portsmouth Improved Steam Boat Company. Sense eventually prevailed and the three joined forces under the title of the Southampton, Isle of Wight and South of England Royal Mail Steam Packet Company Ltd. which is today abbreviated to Red Funnel.

At the turn of the century, the company owned and operated the following ten vessels: *Southampton* (1872), *Carisbrooke* (1876), *Prince Leopold* (1876), *Princess Beatrice* (1880), *Princess Helena* (1883), *Her Majesty* (1885), *Solent Queen* (1889), *Prince of Wales* (1891), *Duchess of York* (1896 - renamed *Duchess of Cornwall* in 1928) and the *Lorna Doone* (1891 - acquired in 1898).

The fleet operated services which until the early 1920s linked Southampton with Cowes, Ryde, Southsea and Portsmouth Harbour after which time the winter service was withdrawn east of Cowes. The calls at Portsmouth were

# CENTURY OF NORTH WEST EUROPEAN FERRIES 1900 - 2000

Red Funnel's *Cowes Castle* approaching Cowes in August 1990 in the company's recently introduced red hulled livery. The 'Cowes' with fleet companions *Norris Castle* and *Netley Castle* were all sold for further service in Croatia. *(John Hendy)*

discontinued in 1937 followed by those at Southsea in the following year. Ryde services were also run down and were not reintroduced after World War II. However, in May 1902 a new twice daily service was introduced to Portsmouth (Victoria Pier), Southsea (Clarence Pier), Southsea (South Parade Pier), Sandown, Shanklin and Ventnor and three years later it was extended to call at Ryde before closure in 1909. Although a ferry service, many of the passengers could certainly have been excursionists and this lucrative business was a second major string to Red Funnel's bow.

We have seen with the railway fleets at Portsmouth, the fondness of the British public for long day excursions to sea, and Red Funnel were most certainly amongst the leaders in this field. During her remarkable career (she was not scrapped until 1948) the famous *Lorna Doone* was known all around the Isle of Wight, eastwards to Bognor Regis and Brighton and westwards to Bournemouth, Swanage and Weymouth. The arrival of the 19 knot, first named *Balmoral* in 1900 helped to increase the company's sphere of influence to Torquay, Dartmouth, Eastbourne, Boulogne and Cherbourg. These two ships were the first purely excursion ships to be owned by the company and a third, the *Bournemouth Queen*, was added in 1908. Prior to that time, excursions were normally operated by the most modern vessels in the fleet (latterly the *Solent Queen*) while the ferry services were left in the hands of the oldest steamers although in theory they were all dual purpose vessels - suitable for both ferry work and excursions.

Some of the longer excursions were terminated before the Second World War but the damage caused to many of the piers during the period of hostilities saw the post-war excursion programme severely curtailed. Then when the fleet was gradually replaced by car ferries, the excursions gradually ceased until in September 1968, the motor vessel *Balmoral* (1949) completed the final regular sailings.

A third major role for the Red Funnel fleet was to provide a tender service to liners which were at anchor in the Solent, usually in Cowes Roads, while since 1885 a fourth has been the provision and operation of tugs.

Following the arrival of the *Balmoral* in 1900, two years later the *Queen* was delivered primarily (but not exclusively) for excursion services. She was followed by the locally built *Princess Royal* in 1906 which sadly failed to meet the stipulated contract speed and after the shortest of careers was duly returned to the builders. Two years later she was purchased by Cosens of Weymouth who ran her as the excursion steamer *Emperor of India* until 1957. The gap in the fleet left by the non-appearance of the *Princess Royal* coupled with the disposal of elderly units in 1905, saw the company purchase the eight year old *Stirling Castle* in 1907. She had been built for service on the Firth of Forth and even boasted a telescopic funnel to enable her to pass under the bridges on her way to Stirling. Most of the vessel's subsequent career was spent on the Bournemouth - Swanage service until her loss in the Mediterranean in September 1916.

In 1908 the purchase of the Bournemouth & South Coast Steam Packets Ltd. strengthened the company's position at the popular holiday resort and during the same year, the excursion steamer *Bournemouth Queen* was put into service at her namesake resort. The year 1908 also saw Red Funnel acquire the 32 year old steamer *Lord Elgin* from Bournemouth & South Coast Steam Packets Ltd. and like the *Stirling Castle*, she too had originally been built for service on the Firth of Forth but came south in 1881.

It was never Red Funnel's intention to return her to passenger service but instead they converted her for cargo duties. As such she was the last paddle cargo steamer in

# CENTURY OF NORTH WEST EUROPEAN FERRIES 1900 - 2000

operation around our shores, not passing to the breakers until the age of 79 in 1955. During summer seasons in the 1930s, her consignments of livestock gave way to motor vehicles when she was pressed into service as a relief lift on - lift off car ferry.

The final pre-war steamer was the *Princess Mary* of 1911 which enjoyed only a brief career, being sunk in the Dardanelles in August 1919.

A modified *Princess Mary* entered service in August 1927 in the form of the famous *Princess Elizabeth* - a vessel still afloat at Dunkerque. Although at first employed in her capacity of ferry steamer, she was soon switched to excursion work, making four trips to evacuate soldiers from the beaches of Dunkerque in 1940 before returning to operate excursions from Ryde and then Bournemouth until 1952 when she became the final Red Funnel vessel to operate from the resort. She was withdrawn from stand-by duties at Southampton early in 1959.

There now came a revolutionary ship when in February 1931, the *Medina*, the company's first diesel propelled ferry was introduced. She was mainly intended for winter work and remained with the fleet until March 1962 after which she was sold for further work in Gibraltar.

The final paddle steamer entered service in June 1936 and was unusually named after a popular actress and singer of that period. The *Gracie Fields* was built with a bow rudder for going astern out of Cowes and like her earlier half-sister *Princess Elizabeth* carried a number of cars on her foredeck. Excursion duties were also performed as in summer 1936 when she was sent to Bournemouth to support her sponsor who was also appearing daily at the end of the pier. Her career ended during the evacuation of Dunkerque in May 1940 when she was sunk by a bomb.

Just prior to the outbreak of World War Two (in March 1939), the company introduced their second motor ship, *Vecta*. She was a quite unusual vessel as she was the first Southampton ferry to be fitted with the Voith-Schneider method of propulsion which was also being used by the Southern Railway's *Lymington* at Lymington. She was a smart-looking vessel with her car deck under cover forward of the bridge but the problems of obtaining spare parts for her German engines saw her spend much of the war laid-up and she was subsequently re-engined with normal diesels and propeller shafts, lasting in the fleet until September 1965.

In 1946, Red Funnel acquired 70% of the shares of the renowned excursion ship company, Cosens of Weymouth. To provide cover for the war-losses *Gracie Fields* and *Her Majesty* (sunk during an air raid on Southampton in 1940) and the post war scrapping of the *Lorna Doone* and the *Balmoral*, the company hastily purchased a number of vessels, all of which proved to be less than adequate.

The *Upton* was a former Mersey ferry purchased to replace the *Gracie Fields* but was withdrawn after four slow seasons. The *Robina* lasted for just one season while the larger paddle excursion steamers *Lorna Doone* and *Solent Queen* were intended to revive the pre-war excursion trade in memory of the steamers whose proud names they bore. By 1952 they had also passed to the breakers. The only post-war second-hand tonnage to remain in service for an appreciable period was the former tank landing craft *Norris Castle* which was built in 1942 and acquired by Red Funnel in 1947. She was purchased in order to block a proposed new motor car service by a rival company linking Calshot with Cowes. From October 1952 she replaced the *Lord Elgin* on the cargo run after which, with more car traffic on offer, she became the company's first roll on vehicle ferry and as such carried about 30 cars. She sided loaded at Southampton and West Cowes but was soon using her bow ramp at East Cowes when during 1950 a concrete slipway was provided. The vessel continued in service until replaced by the *Osborne Castle* in March 1962.

The final passenger vessel entered service in November 1949. Named *Balmoral* after her illustrious predecessor, the motor vessel's vehicle deck was at her after end and for most of her career she additionally acted as a summer excursion vessel from Southampton. Withdrawn in September 1968, she continued her excursion work on the Bristol Channel until after a period of inactivity laid-up at Dundee, in 1985 she was acquired as a consort for the preserved paddle steamer *Waverley* and continues to operate in that role.

With increasing numbers of motorists wishing to take their cars to the Isle of Wight, change was inevitable and in May 1959 the first purpose-built ro-ro car ferry, the *Carisbrooke Castle* (45 cars) entered service. She was followed by a modified *Osborne Castle* in March 1962 and the *Cowes Castle* in December 1965. A fourth 'Castle' was added in December 1968. The *Norris Castle* was built with a smaller passenger capacity than her consorts but with a greater capacity for carrying freight vehicles. Such was the increase in traffic that a larger, double-ended ferry was ordered in January 1972 for delivery in the following June. However the *Netley Castle's* builders, Ryton Marine of Wallsend-on-Tyne, went into liquidation and the hull was eventually towed to Southampton in February 1974 not being ready to enter service until June that year. The *Carisbrooke Castle* was duly retired from service that September and sold to Italy.

A linkspan was installed at Southampton in 1976 and the *Netley Castle's* 'north end' was thus modified to use it giving her an odd appearance as she continued to require the ramp at her 'south end' at East Cowes. In order to create extra capacity, the 'Cowes' and the 'Norris' were stretched in Rotterdam during late 1975 and early 1976 and given higher vehicle deck headroom, mezzanine decks and drive-through capabilities. The *Osborne Castle* was retained for the 1977 season after which she was sold to Canadian interests.

Into the 1980s, the fleet of three vehicle ferries continued to ply the familiar route up and down Southampton Water without any long-term prospect of replacements. At Fishbourne Sealink/ Wightlink introduced their four state-of-the art 'Saint' class ferries and by the mid-80s were carrying some 82% of all cross-Solent traffic. Red Funnel's 'Castle' class became increasingly outmoded and a large injection of capital was badly needed to replace the elderly tonnage. In October 1989, when facing a hostile take-over bid by Sally Line, the Red Funnel Group was absorbed by Associated British Ports (ABP), owners of the Port of Southampton, and orders for new vessels were soon forthcoming. The £8 million 'Raptor' class ferries, *Red Falcon* and *Red Osprey* entered service in March and October 1994 followed in April 1996 by a modified *Red Eagle*. The three 'Castle' class were duly replaced in order of age and were soon sold for coastal service in Croatia.

The 'Raptors' have led Red Funnel's fight to recapture their lost trade and ABP's £24 million investment has enabled them to make inroads in the coach and heavy vehicle trade that was so restricted with the older generation of ferries. New terminals at Southampton Town Quay (for ferries and the 'Hi-Speed' service), and at both East and West Cowes have greatly improved the company profile, although the lack of standage area at both Southampton and East Cowes may well inhibit

# CENTURY OF NORTH WEST EUROPEAN FERRIES 1900 - 2000

further growth and is something that the company will need to examine closely early in the next millennium.

Finally, mention must be made of the tremendously popular 'Hi-Speed' service from Southampton to West Cowes. Between the years 1933 - 38, the 11 seater 'Sea Coach' *Island Enterprise* was engaged on the Southampton - Cowes crossing after which the 30 knot vessel was disposed of.

Then following the successful SRN6 hovercraft service operated by British Rail (Seaspeed) in 1966, Red Funnel replied with their own high speed link. The service was ready to commence in 1968 with a Hovermarine side-walled hovercraft, chartered from and operated by Hovertravel however it was cancelled at short notice and the craft (in Red Funnel livery) ran for a while on Hovertravel's own service between Southsea and Ryde. The following year however the Italian hydrofoil *Shearwater* appeared followed by *Shearwater 2* (1970), *Shearwater 3* (1972), *Shearwater 4* (1973), *Shearwater 5* (1980) and *Shearwater 6* (1982). The month after their acquisition of the Red Funnel Group in 1989, ABP ordered twin catamarans from FBM Marine of Cowes and the *Red Jet 1* and *Red Jet 2* entered service in April and July 1991. With the entry into service of the larger and modified *Red Jet 3* in July 1998, the final two 'Shearwater' hydrofoils were laidaside although during summer 1999, one was on stand-by at Town Quay. An unsuccessful service between the Gosport ferry landing stage in Portsmouth Harbour and West Cowes was tried from August 1991 in an attempt to utilise hydrofoils made redundant by the entry into service of the 'Red Jets.'

During the twentieth century, the company also ran the East Cowes - West Cowes ferry service with the steam launches *Princess Louise* (1891-1944), *Medina* (1884 - 1931) and the *Precursor* (later converted to diesel) which operated from 1898 until 1939. She was joined by a similar sized *Norris Castle* in 1938. In addition to the launches the Cowes Floating Bridge was also operated by Red Funnel from 1868 until 1901

The second of the 'Raptor' class ferries **Red Osprey** approaching the River Medina at Cowes shortly after entering service in October 1994. (John Hendy)

when it was taken over by the joint committee of East and West Cowes councils.

## COWES EXPRESS

There was one more attempt at high speed rivalry between Southampton (Town Quay) and Cowes (Thetis Wharf) and this was from a company called Cowes Express who introduced their chartered Norwegian craft *Sant Agata* (later renamed *Wight King*) in May 1990 and started a price war. In July 1991 they introduced the *Wight Queen* (ex *Virgin Butterfly*) followed by the smaller *Wight Prince* (ex *Royal Schelde*). For a while things went well but breakdowns and a failure to come to terms with ABP at Southampton saw the service close in February 1992.

*John Hendy*

Red Funnel's motor ship **Balmoral** approaching Cowes in July 1967. The vessel was built in 1949 and remains in service for Waverley Excursions. (John Hendy)

100

# CENTURY OF NORTH WEST EUROPEAN FERRIES 1900 - 2000

# Wight*link*

*"Wightlink, everyday operations and the importance of maintaining a regular ferry service to the island".*

Operating three ferry routes across what is one of the busiest shipping lanes in the world is part of the everyday activities for Wightlink, the UK's largest independent ferry and ports operator. Being the principal custodian of ferry services between the Isle of Wight and the English mainland is a heavy responsibility and Wightlink takes its role providing a lifeline to the island's 127,000 residents extremely seriously. Not only are they supplying the means by which islanders get to work and obtain all their goods and services, they also bring the Island's beauty, varied activities and unique charm to over 5 million travellers each year.

Behind the scenes of this unique ferry company is a well oiled machine that ensures that it continues to service the needs of island residents, tourists, commerce and industry in a friendly, efficient and punctual manner, 365 days a year.

Wightlink owns and operates 9 vessels on its three routes which run between Portsmouth Harbour and Ryde Pier Head, Portsmouth Gunwharf and Fishbourne, plus Lymington and Yarmouth. Wightlink is the largest single user of the Port of Portsmouth with over 40,000 movements of vessels in a year, over four times more than all continental ferry movements combined. Running a faultless timetable is therefore key to Wightlink's customers and the efficient running of the Port of Portsmouth. In the past four years Wightlink has increased the number of sailings it offers by almost 25% with over 63,000 scheduled for 1999.

There are an enormous number of activities that ensure that the ships keep running, most of which are unseen and unsung. It is testament to the smooth running of the business, that last year less than 1% of all sailings were cancelled. Wightlink has had to accommodate a considerable increase in traffic over the past three years without the benefit of additional ships but by better utilisation of its current capacity and timetabling more frequent sailings. In the last three years Wightlink has increased its number of cars carried to over 1 million per annum, passengers to over 5 million, coaches to 20,000 and freight vehicles to 130,000. The company now employs over 615 staff, although those who work as crew or terminal staff are the only ones on view

*Mike Aiken*

In 1999 Wightlink introduced a new livery for their fast craft operation between Portsmouth and Ryde. The Australian-built ***Our Lady Pamela*** is seen arriving at Portsmouth. *(Miles Cowsill)*

to the public. There are many behind the scenes that ensure the company runs a safe and successful operation.

Wightlink takes considerable care in the selection of all of its employees. Key positions are manned by professionals with proven track records, whether they are shore-based managers or Ship's Masters on the bridge of the vessel. They are supported by experienced staff or qualified officers and crew. There are numerous skills required to maintain a fleet, care for passengers, utilise technology, provide transportation, book holidays and manage a company. Wightlink survives and flourishes through employing a flexible, multi-skilled workforce, which enables it to run a seamless service ensuring customer satisfaction.

One of the invisible procedures that is key in running a ferry operation is adhering to the most stringent safety rules and Wightlink prides itself on operating its ships to the highest possible safety standards. Safety checks are made daily, weekly or monthly, depending on the area concerned. Wightlink was the first cross Solent operator to achieve the accreditation to the International Safety Management Code which applies to all passenger ships and ro-ro ferries.

To maintain an effective operation it is key that Wightlink operates an efficient crewing operation. Not only is the passengers' comfort and safety a key concern but the whole process of embarkation, disembarkation and navigation has to be enacted with the utmost precision. Every year seasonal/temporary staff go through a comprehensive training programme covering safe working practices on board, including customer care.

The amount of crew on a vessel depends on the actual passenger count and, while this can be estimated in advance, the management have to allow for last minute fluctuations and be able to provide additional crew should the need arise. In all cases the number of crew allows for all emergency procedures to be enacted whatever the passenger load.

The maintenance of its fleet is a key function for Wightlink, not only is it important for passenger comfort, but it is also necessary for the seamless running of the service

# CENTURY OF NORTH WEST EUROPEAN FERRIES 1900 - 2000

*Wightline's **St. Faith** was the last of the 'Saint' class vessels to be built for their Portsmouth-Fishbourne service in 1990. She is seen here leaving at Portsmouth in June 1999. (Miles Cowsill)*

and the long term reliability of the ships. All the ships go into dry dock annually in order to establish the condition of the hull and the underwater fittings. As is necessary, all the machinery that is due for survey is inspected by the registered authority, The Marine and Coastguard Agency. At each refit all the safety equipment is thoroughly inspected and overhauled. In addition, the main and auxiliary machine is worked on under the ongoing maintenance plan ensuring that all vessels maintain their reliability. The maintenance team at Wightlink consists of the chief marine superintendent, 4 superintendents, 3 support staff and 14 workshop workers. The majority of maintenance activity takes place between January and Easter when the marine workshop staff are increased to 28.

The majority of people think of ferry companies transporting just commuters and holidaymakers and forget that they also carry all the supplies to and from the mainland. The timely delivery of freight is an important part of the everyday activity of a ferry business. Wightlink works in partnership with the freight industry to ensure punctuality and cost effectiveness through bulk booking. The goods carried on the ferries include post office mail, petrol, food, clothes, dairy and farm products, gas and HM Prison vehicles. Wightlink prides itself on recent honour of being voted sea carrier of the year by Coach and Bus Weekly. Coach operators can bulk book, which guarantees them a place on their chosen ferry sailings. In addition they carry feeder coaches which enable coaches to meet up from different destinations to swap passengers, which is critical if delay occurs and coach operators have deadlines to meet.

While all this activity goes on behind the scenes, the 5 million passengers carried across the Solent every year by Wightlink can enjoy in comfort the journey across one of the busiest stretches of water in the UK between Island and mainland. Wightlink spends over £2.5 million annually refurbishing its ships, ensuring that customers enjoy a clean and fresh environment. Each ship has an annual refurbishment, which takes 3 weeks including refitting and survey. Every 3 to 4 years the company conducts a major refit of the passenger lounges on the ships.

Behind the scenes and at the end of a phone line Wightlink runs a dedicated reservations division which employs the most up to date systems to ensure the timely and efficient booking and ticket issuing procedures. There are numerous ingredients to running an efficient and effective ferry service. There is an enormous amount of activity that passengers never see and cargo travels at times when most people are totally unaware of exactly how the milk will appear on their doorstep in the morning.

In 3 years the cross Solent market has increased by almost 17% thanks to Wightlink as the dominant market leader ensuring it runs its everyday operations with the maximum ease and providing a 24 hour link between the mainland and the Isle of Wight.

*Mike Aiken*
Chairman
Wightlink Isle of Wight Ferries

# Your Solent partner

With three routes between the Isle of Wight and the English mainland, the largest choice of sailing times and a round-the-clock service, Wightlink is far and away the most popular ferry operator across the Solent. For information and enquiries, call us on 0870 582 7744 or visit us at www.wightlink.co.uk

**WIGHT*link***
*Isle of Wight Ferries*

# CENTURY OF NORTH WEST EUROPEAN FERRIES 1900 - 2000

# Irish Sea

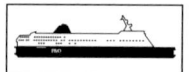

Operations on the Irish Sea this century have seen radical changes, especially during the last twenty years since the Irish Republic joined the EU. The large number of foot passengers which were an integral part of the market up to the fifties have substantially declined with the advent of cheap air travel. It is now possible to travel from London to Dublin for as little as £29, a fare which both the railways and shipping companies are unable to match for customers for time and convenience.

Freight traffic has exploded beyond all expectations during the last ten years. Sealink, who dominated the Irish Sea up until the early nineties, are no longer the major ferry or freight operator. New ferry companies, like Merchant Ferries, Seatruck and Norse Irish Ferries, have come on the scene to fill the void left by Sealink and Stena Line. The company which has made the greatest impact on the Irish Sea during the last ten years is Irish Ferries, who have turned the loss-making operations of B & I round to possibly one of the best ferry operations in the British Isles.

New, larger and luxurious ferries are currently on order for the Irish Sea services. In two years' time, Irish Ferries will introduce the largest ferry ever to come into service on the Irish Sea. The new vessel has been introduced to compete with Stena Line's HSS operations on the central corridor. Meanwhile, P&O European Ferries have currently ordered two large ro-pax vessels, the first of which is due to enter service next year on the Cairnryan-Larne route.

Ireland's ties with mainland Europe are becoming more important each year. Brittany Ferries and Irish Ferries' established passenger operations continue to see growth and possibly in the next ten years there will be further expansion on these vital services, as a bypass to Britain.

## SWANSEA/ PEMBROKE DOCK - CORK

By 1896, the City of Cork Steam Packet Co. were operating the link and the first vessel to carry the name *Innisfallen* had been built. By 1903, the *Inniscoma* was operating the service, following the *Innisfallen* being transferred to the Cork - Liverpool route.

In 1906 the Cork route moved to Fishguard where it was to stay until 1968. The *Innisfallen* was lost during the First World War and the Coast Line's vessel *Kenmare* was used to maintain the link until the second *Innisfallen* was introduced. The *Kenmare* took over the route again in 1940 and was eventually replaced by the newly built *Innisfallen* (III) in 1948. She remained on the Cork service until 1968, prior to the service moving to Swansea.

During the late sixties, B&I decided that they wanted a port of their own, and they also considered that Swansea would in the long term be a better port than Fishguard for Cork, once the M4 motorway reached the city from London. A new purpose-built vessel and a new terminal at Swansea were built for the nine hour link between Wales and Ireland. The modern looking *Innisfallen* (IV) built in Cork was modelled on the earlier *Munster* design built for the company's Dublin - Liverpool service. She was built with a service speed of 21 knots so the vessel could maintain crossing schedules, especially during bad weather. The new *Innisfallen* was in stark contrast to the vessel she replaced on the Fishguard service, with very modern lines and drive-on facilities for 245 cars.

The Cork service continued to operate from Swansea for the next eleven years, until B&I decided to transfer their operations back to Pembrokeshire in an effort to save fuel costs and to offer passengers a shorter sea crossing.

Work for the new service started in 1978 on a new terminal at the former naval dockyard of Pembroke Dock. Meanwhile a new vessel was ordered at Verolme Dockyard, Cork which was to be the largest vessel ever built for the company. The *Connacht* was launched in June 1978, boasting a capacity for 1,500 passengers and 350 cars. She was built also in mind to operate on the Dublin - Liverpool service, having a sufficient beam for the locks on the Mersey. The *Connacht*

The **Innisfallen** is seen here at City of Cork terminal pending her evening departure to Swansea. This terminal was used by both B&I and Brittany Ferries until the new terminal was opened down river to Ringaskiddy. *(Dermot Walsh)*

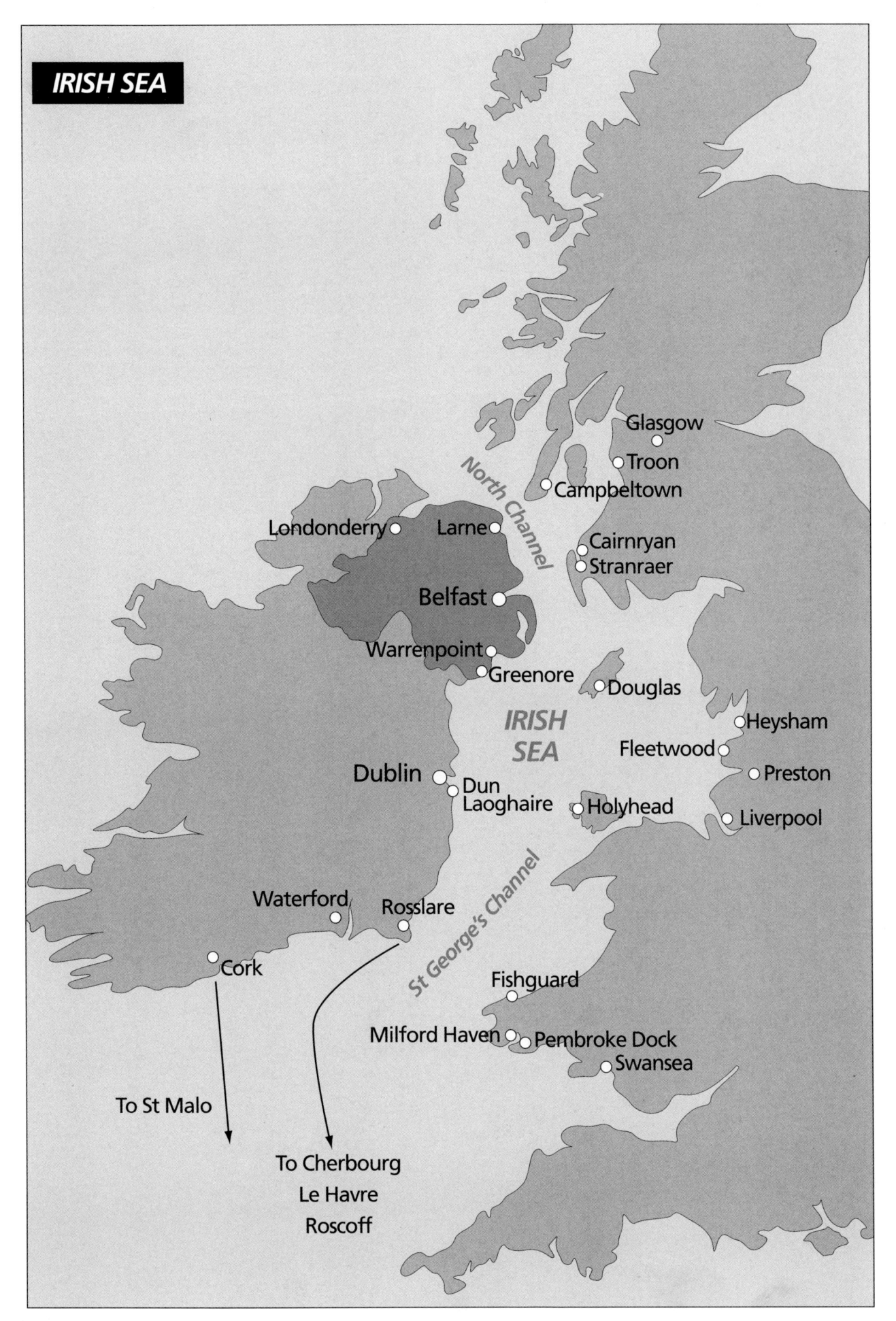

# CENTURY OF NORTH WEST EUROPEAN FERRIES 1900 - 2000

## IRISH SEA

# CENTURY OF NORTH WEST EUROPEAN FERRIES 1900 - 2000

made her maiden voyage on the Swansea - Cork link, and remained on the longer route until the new terminal at Pembroke Dock was completed in May of the next year.

B&I operations from Liverpool in early 1980 were covered by the *Leinster* (1969), *Innisfallen* (1969) and *Munster* (1968). The *Innisfallen* was sold during the early part of the year to Mediterranean interests and her departure meant that the *Connacht* had to be switched to the Dublin service to cover for the refits on the central corridor vessels. So that the Cork service could be maintained, B&I chartered the *Espresso Olbia* (ex *Tor Anglia*). The Italian registered vessel maintained the Cork service until the *Connacht* returned just before Easter.

By the end of September, the Irish company was facing financial problems and was faced with making reductions within the fleet. As part of this reorganisation, the *Connacht* was transferred to the Dublin – Liverpool service, with the smaller and older *Leinster* making reduced sailings on the Cork link. The *Leinster* arrived at Pembroke Dock for the first time in late September, offering a very sad and backward step for the now 16-month operation. The former Liverpool vessel was renamed *Innisfallen* (V), a name long-associated with the Cork service.

B&I were faced with further financial losses at the end of summer season 1981, which resulted in more cutbacks in the Cork operation. The future of the Cork link was now very much in doubt, following these further losses. In the event the link was maintained, but using the same ship to operate both the Cork and Rosslare operations. The challenge of operating a two route service on some of the roughest seas in Northern Europe was to result in sailings being cancelled or delayed with new schedules.

The tourist industry and business in the Cork district claimed that B&I were now no longer interested in operating to Cork and that they wished to concentrate their operations between Rosslare and Pembroke Dock instead. Further evidence that B&I wanted to pull out of the nine hour service came during May, when the new ferry terminal at Ringaskiddy was opened (down river from the City of Cork); B&I refused to transfer their operations to the new terminal as they did not want to enter into a long term agreement to use the new port.

Just before Christmas, B&I announced that they planned to close the Cork service as from January 1983 as they could no longer afford to operate the loss-making route.

Immediately, two concerns announced that they were interested in starting their own operations from Cork to the UK, Avonmouth and Barry being listed as possible ports. In the event B&I announced, just before their planned closure date, that they would carry on the service for the time being. However, a month later, following their contrary announcement, the route was suddenly closed overnight.

In late March, B&I announced that they were going to recommence sailings once again from Cork to Pembroke Dock, from June to September, using a chartered vessel from the new port to Ringsakiddy at Cork. The new operation of B&I was doomed at the outset to make a considerable loss, as the announcement came too late to catch the majority of bookings in the travel trade for the year. Meanwhile, the Irish Government gave a large subsidy to B&I to operate it. The company chartered the Finnish registered ferry *Fennia*. To support the seasonal link, British Rail laid on a special Inter-City service between London and Pembroke Dock, which did attract good loadings.

The Cork service was not reopened until 1987, when Swansea Cork Ferries established the route again, with the aid

*Swansea Cork Ferries'* **Superferry** *arrives at Swansea in May 1997. The former Greek registered vessel is due for replacement on the nine hour link during the early part of the next decade. (Miles Cowsill)*

and backing of the Irish Government and the local Councils of Cork and Swansea. Swansea Cork Ferries opened their new link using the Polish registered vessel *Rogalin*, which was renamed *Celtic Pride* for the new summer only operation. Substantial savings were made by the company by using Polish crews on the vessel. The link was to run for two seasons with the *Celtic Pride* and in the second year of operation began to make a small profit. The operation failed to get off the ground in 1989 but in the following year the service was resumed using the former B&I vessel *Leinster* (renamed *Innisfallen* (IV)) in 1980 for the Cork–Pembroke Dock service). The former Irish ship, now the *Ionian Sun* in the ownership of Strintzis Lines, was chartered to Swansea Cork Ferries with a Greek crew. The third year of operation of SCF proved to be very erratic on all fronts. The next two seasons proved very successful with the *Celtic Pride*. However, she was now becoming too small for the service and also had insufficient room to carry any freight.

At the end of 1992, Swansea Cork Ferries was sold to the Greek shipping company Strintzis Lines, who introduced a slightly larger vessel by the name of *Superferry*. The Japanese-built ferry has operated the route since that date with a Greek crew and Polish catering staff, but during 1999 Strintzis Lines resold the company. The *Superferry* is now becoming too small for the route and new larger tonnage will have to be introduced in the future, if it is to compete with the rival operations at Fishguard and Pembroke Dock.

## PEMBROKE DOCK - ROSSLARE

Following B&I's decision to transfer their Cork service to the new ferry terminal at Pembroke Dock in 1979, the Irish company decided to open a new service between there and Rosslare in direct competition to Sealink's established operation at Fishguard.

B&I had originally decided to use the *Munster* to open the link in 1980 but in the event she had to be retained on the Liverpool run and so instead they chartered the smart looking *Viking III* from Townsend Thoresen. The Norwegian vessel offered very comfortable accommodation for 940 passengers and space for 180 cars. She was also fast and ideal to maintain 22 round sailings a week on the four-hour route.

The *Viking III* opened the service in May and was to prove very successful on the link, maintaining the service on most days to schedule. The company sadly failed to take up a

# CENTURY OF NORTH WEST EUROPEAN FERRIES 1900 - 2000

The distinctive-looking **Innisfallen** (ex *Leinster*) arrives at Pembroke Dock from Rosslare on a bleak November morning. *(Miles Cowsill)*

further charter of the vessel and the service closed in September on the termination of her charter, and no suitable replacement was found until mid-October.

A new vessel by the name of *Stena Nordica*, a sister ship to the *Stena Normandica* operated by Sealink at Fishguard, was chartered for the route from Stena Line. There were delays with getting her into operation, as her crew went on strike before she could be put into service. Some weeks later she was to suffer engine problems, which again brought the Rosslare operations to a halt.

Over the Christmas and early New Year, period B&I were able to charter the Irish Continental Line's (ICL) *Saint Patrick* and the service then closed again in January 1981, until the following month when the *Stena Nordica* returned to the link. The reliability of B&I's Rosslare service was now very much in doubt with the travelling public and freight operators.

It was announced in the early spring that the *Munster* would replace the 'Nordica' in May, but operational staff at Rosslare were very unhappy over her transfer from the Dublin service, as her accommodation was not suitable and her headroom was far too low for most freight lorries of the day. Their concerns were dismissed by management in Dublin. However, with delays with the completion of the new *Leinster*, sister to the *Connacht*, the *Munster* was unable to transfer in May as planned.

As a stop-gap for the *Munster*, the *Prinsessan Desiree* was chartered for 40 days for the Rosslare service on the completion of the charter of the *Stena Nordica*. The Baltic-built vessel proved to be a very erratic time-keeper, and she was to receive some very bad press reports on both sides of the Irish Sea.

The *Munster* made her inaugural passage on the link in July and was to remain on the route until November, when she was withdrawn from service as a result of a strike. B&I decided to use the *Innisfallen* to maintain both the Cork and Rosslare services for the next season, as a result the Rosslare service was reduced from twenty-two to eight round sailings per week.

During 1983, sailings on the Rosslare service were increased as the *Innisfallen* was no longer required on the Cork service. During the overhaul of the *Innisfallen* in 1984, the new *Leinster* was transferred to maintain the link. The flagship proved a most impressive time-keeper and was able to cope with all freight-carryings on the link, which only went to show that what the service needed to compete with Sealink was a modern purpose-built vessel.

The *Innisfallen* returned to the link between April and October, when it became evident that B&I had sold her to an Italian company. Her place was taken by the *Saint Patrick II* from ICL, and in the event the deal to sell the *Innisfallen* fell through.

In January 1985, B&I and Sealink announced that they would pool their operations. All traffic was transferred from Pembroke Dock to Fishguard until April, when the *Innisfallen* returned making only night sailings on the Pembroke Dock-Rosslare service until July. Two round sailings a day were introduced to support the joint operation during the peak season. At the end of the year, the agreement between both companies was extended for a further two years. As a result of this new package it was agreed that operations at Pembroke Dock would be closed in January 1986.

For the 1986 season, it was agreed by both companies that Sealink would operate the *St. Brendan* on an all the year round basis and B&I would offer extra sailings between Rosslare and Fishguard during the peak season with the *Innisfallen*. Following the *Innisfallen's* short spell at Fishguard in July and August, she was sold to Strintzis Lines. The next year B&I chartered the spare Belgian ferry *Prins Phillipe* and then Newhaven - Dieppe's *Senlac* to support the *St. Brendan*.

The following year B&I re-established their operation at Pembroke Dock, without Sealink as partners. The *Saint Colum*

# CENTURY OF NORTH WEST EUROPEAN FERRIES 1900 - 2000

*Following the transfer of the **Connacht** back to the southern corridor the vessel maintained the Rosslare-Pembroke Dock route prior to her sale to Brittany Ferries. She is seen here outward-bound to Ireland off Angle. (Miles Cowsill)*

I (ex *Saint Patrick*) re-opened the service until the *Connacht* was able to take up the route following the closure of the Liverpool link. Later in the year the *Connacht* was sold to Brittany Ferries and the 10 year old ship was replaced by the *Saint Patrick II* in the short term again

Following the withdrawal of Sealink from the Channel Islands operations, the *Earl Harold* became available. She was duly chartered by B&I until the end of the year from their rivals on the Irish Sea and underwent a major overhaul and repainting programme in the new B&I livery for her role on the Irish Sea. The 'Harold' took over the link from the *Saint Patrick II* in April 1989 but, sadly, the former Channel Islands vessel was to prove far too small for the service.

The Company replaced the *Earl Harold* on the Rosslare service in the autumn with the passenger ferry *Norrona* from Smyril Line. Meanwhile, in late December B&I announced that they had been able secure the charter of the ferry *Cruise Muhibah* from a Singapore shipping company. The vessel was no stranger to British waters having operated for more than a decade between Harwich and Bremerhaven as the *Prins Oberon*. The newly acquired ferry, renamed *Munster*, underwent a major refit costing some IR£3.5 million, prior to her entering service in April 1990. She was to prove popular on the route and managed to maintain the link at most times on schedule.

During the early part of 1991, the Irish Government opened negotiations to sell off their interests in B&I to Irish Ferries. These talks were to take all year before the privately owned company were able to secure the right terms for their purchase of the ailing state-owned shipping company. As part of the take-over terms, Irish Ferries agreed to invest some IR£30 million into B&I.

As the first part of their investment, the new company chartered the *Stena Nautica* (ex *Niels Klim*) from Stena Line to replace the *Munster* on the Rosslare link. She offered passenger accommodation for 2,000 and probably by far the best freight capacity the link had seen since it was established in 1980, with capacity for 411 cars or 40 x 15 metre lorries. The only drawback to the former Danish State Railways' vessel was her service speed of only 17 knots, which was far too slow for the route, especially during bad weather conditions. The new vessel was re-named *Isle of Innisfree*.

During early January 1993, the Irish management were considering transferring the *Isle of Innisfree* to the Dublin - Holyhead route and replacing her with the *Leinster*. The Company were fully aware that the introduction of the smaller vessel would be another backward step for the Rosslare route, but with the increased competition at Holyhead from Stena Sealink her transfer was necessary. In March it was announced that the *Leinster* would be transferred to the route, as from the end of April, to allow the 'Innisfree' to go north.

The *Leinster* underwent a major overhaul in Dublin for her new role on the Rosslare link, including a change of name to the *Isle of Inishmore*. The *Isle of Innisfree* completed her final sailing on the Rosslare service in May and the former *Leinster* took up her southern corridor duties on the same day.

Following the transfer of the *Isle of Innisfree* from the Rosslare-Pembroke Dock service to the central corridor, the new parent company announced in 1994 that a new purpose-built vessel for the Dublin-Holyhead route. would be built. She was to be the turning point in the company's fortunes as she quickly established herself as a comfortable and reliable ship on the route, so much so that Irish Ferries ordered a second and larger vessel to replace her in 1995. The new larger vessel, *Isle of Inishmore*, duly entered service in 1997, which allowed the *Isle of Innisfree* to be transferred to the Rosslare - Pembroke Dock service to replace the smaller vessel *Leinster*, which had been on the route since 1994 and latterly renamed *Isle of Inishturk*. The *Isle of Innisfree* was to make an immediate impact on the route, just as she had done at Holyhead, which had been plagued with a series of unsuitable vessels since the inaugural sailing of the *Viking III* in 1981.

# CENTURY OF NORTH WEST EUROPEAN FERRIES 1900 - 2000

The *Isle of Innisfree* has operated the link since 1997 with great success, so much so that Stena Line have seen a drop in their passenger and freight traffic at Fishguard to the Irish Ferries operations at Pembroke Dock.

## FISHGUARD – ROSSLARE

In 1895 the Great Western Railway (GWR) put forward proposals for a major modernisation programme at New Milford from where their southern Irish service was operated. These proposals were only to be short-lived, as far as New Milford was concerned, as the GWR were now considering a move to Fishguard and opening a new terminal at Rosslare in Ireland – only 54 nautical miles apart.

The construction of Fishguard Harbour was authorised by the Fishguard and Rosslare Railways and Harbours Act of 1899. During the next few years no expense was to be spared in making Fishguard the port for Irish traffic, with the possible advantage of being used also as a trans-Atlantic terminal. Meanwhile, two new ships were ordered for the route: the *St. Patrick* and *St. David*, and later a third ship, the *St. George*; this was followed by a fourth ship, the *St Andrew* in 1908. On the other side of the St. George's Channel, the Great Southern Railway of Ireland had to construct a new railway line from Waterford to the port of Rosslare. The official opening of the Fishguard-Rosslare service was to take place in August 1906.

Recovery from the First World War was to be slow, as far as the Fishguard – Rosslare service was concerned, and the uncertain political situation in Ireland was to have an adverse effect on the route, and it was not until January 1920 that all the three 'Saints' returned to the Rosslare service.

The early Fishguard 'Saint' class were replaced in the early thirties by the *St. Patrick* (II) in 1930. She was followed by the *St. Andrew* (II) and *St. David* (II). On the outbreak of the Second World War, the *St. Andrew* and *St. David* were

The ***St. Andrew*** (1908-1933) at full speed as she approaches Fishguard harbour during her career on the Rosslare service. *(Ambrose Greenway collection)*

commandeered by the Crown and following the *St. Patrick* running for a short spell as a troopship in October 1939, she returned to Fishguard to maintain the route. The Rosslare service was cut back to three days a week during the war years.

During the war the *St. Andrew* and *St. David* were to see much active service. In June 1941, the *St. Patrick*, en route from Rosslare, was hit by several bombs off Fishguard when thirty lives were lost, including her Master, Captain Faraday. Following the loss of the *St. Patrick* the route was closed until 1947.

Two new ships, bearing the names of their predecessors, were ordered to replace the war losses and the new *St. David* entered service in July 1948, followed by the *St. Patrick*. Early in the following year the *St. Patrick* was transferred to the Weymouth station, where she was to remain until 1964.

The *St. David* and *St. Andrew* were to remain the mainstays of the Fishguard – Rosslare service until the early

The G.W.R. ***St. David*** makes an impressive view as she arrives at Rosslare. The vessel was lost during the Second World War during the Anzio landings. *(Ambrose Greenway collection)*

# CENTURY OF NORTH WEST EUROPEAN FERRIES 1900 - 2000

The *Caledonian Princess* was transferred to the Fishguard-Rosslare route in 1969. The vessel is seen here during her later career on the Channel Islands routes. *(Kevin Le Scelleur)*

sixties and it was not until 1961 that daylight sailings were introduced twice a week as an experiment. All cars on both sides of the St. George's Channel had to be crane-loaded until 1964. It was therefore decided that the *St. David* would be converted to enable cars to be driven on at the side at both ports. In late autumn 1966, British Rail announced that the Heysham - Belfast steamer *Duke of Rothesay* would be converted to a side-loading ferry for the route.

The port of Fishguard still remained rather old fashioned, compared with Holyhead and Stranraer, with side-loading facilities only available. In early 1969 it was announced that the *Caledonian Princess* would be transferred from Stranraer to join the *Duke of Rothesay* for the summer when the ageing *St. David* would be withdrawn from Fishguard.

In July 1971, British Rail decided to spend £624,000 on providing a linkspan for the port of Fishguard, together with major modernisation of the port facilities. The new linkspan would for the first time enable lorries, coaches and caravans to use the route. Meanwhile a linkspan had already been built at Rosslare in 1967 for the new service operated by Normandy Ferries from Le Havre.

On 6th July 1972, the new port facilities were opened after which the *Caledonian Princess* continued to enjoy popularity on the route, especially as she could now carry freight and coach traffic on the link.

Two years' later, Sealink announced that the Harwich - Hook passenger steamer *Avalon* would be converted to a car ferry for the Fishguard – Rosslare service at a cost of £1 million. The vessel was one of Sealink's most luxurious ships at the time and when converted could provide accommodation for 1,200 passengers and 210 cars. The *Caledonian Princess* made her final farewell from the Fishguard service in June 1975.

The *Avalon* was to prove to be a great success and remained on the Pembrokeshire link until January 1976, when she was transferred to Holyhead. In late 1978, Sealink announced further expansion plans for Fishguard which would involve transferring the *Lord Warden* from Dover. For an eight week period during the summer the *Lord Warden* would provide an extra round sailing between Fishguard and Rosslare and in addition to this a new peak season link from Fishguard to Dun Laoghaire. The service was not repeated the following year.

With the threat of a new rival service between Rosslare and Pembroke Dock operated by B&I, Stena Line's *Stena Nordica* underwent berthing trials at Fishguard in September 1978. Following the successful berthing trials of the 'Nordica', Sealink announced that they were ordering from Harland & Wolff at Belfast a new ship (*St. David* (IV)) for the port, its first new tonnage since 1947. The new £16 million ferry would allow the *Avalon* to be switched to Holyhead and the freighter *Anderida* to return to Dover.

In March 1979, Sealink announced that the sister to the *Stena Nordica*, the *Stena Normandica*, would be chartered for a 19 month period until the arrival of the new ship from Belfast. The arrival of the *Stena Normandica* in April brought a sudden significant change to the link and by the early summer, the company was claiming that the passenger and freight figures were up by some 10%. In December 1980 the charter of the *Stena Normandica* was extended, to enable the new ship *St. David* to be utilised on the Holyhead route instead.

With the forthcoming sale of Sealink by the Government in July 1984, the *Stena Normandica* sailed to Falmouth for her refit and reappeared in the company's new livery and image for privatisation. During early 1985, Sealink British Ferries and B&I Line announced that they had concluded discussions aimed at solving the now over-capacity on the Irish Sea. Talks had started in December against a background of achieving

# CENTURY OF NORTH WEST EUROPEAN FERRIES 1900 - 2000

The **Stena Normandica** is seen here in the new Sealink livery of the company prior to privatisation. *(Miles Cowsill)*

The giant **Felicity** towers over Rosslare harbour following her arrival from Fishguard. She was replaced in 1997 by the **Koningin Beatrix**. *(Miles Cowsill)*

savings for both rival companies and bringing frequency of service more in line with demand.

In April, Sealink British Ferries acquired the *Stena Normandica* from Stena Line and shortly afterwards she was renamed *St. Brendan*.

During October, Sealink British Ferries announced that they had revised their agreement with B&I Line. The major change as far as the St. George's Channel services were concerned, was the closure of the Rosslare – Pembroke Dock route with a loss of 535 jobs.

At Fishguard, Sealink British Ferries agreed to introduce 'a new jumbo ferry' which was rumoured at the time to be the *Peter Pan* from TT Line of Germany. Sealink British Ferries made worldwide enquiries for their new jumbo ship to replace the *St. Brendan*, but the company were admitting by the early summer that they were finding it difficult to find such a ship for the service. As a result of this it was decided under the pooling arrangement that the *Innisfallen* would undertake extra sailings to meet the demand on the southern corridor following the closure of the Pembroke service. During 1987, as in the previous year, a second ship was required for the peak season and B&I chartered the French ferry *Senlac* from Sealink Dieppe Ferries. The *Senlac* commenced her summer season on the Irish Sea in June. At the end of 1987 B&I withdrew from the pooling agreement with Sealink.

By the late autumn the level of freight on the link had increased to such an extent that Sealink decided that an additional vessel would have to be brought in on the link to support the *St. Brendan*. The veteran train ferry *Cambridge Ferry* was brought up from the Fal to support the service until Christmas. It was decided that the 'Cambridge' would be an ideal support vessel for the following peak season as the company had still not found a suitable jumbo ferry to replace the *St. Brendan* and she continued on the link until early

A serene May afternoon sees the **Koningin Beatrix** leaving Fishguard for Rosslare. The former Harwich-Hook of Holland ship is the largest ferry operating on the Irish Sea at the turn of the century. *(Miles Cowsill)*

# CENTURY OF NORTH WEST EUROPEAN FERRIES 1900 - 2000

January 1990.

In September 1989, plans were unveiled by Sealink British Ferries to introduce the largest and most luxurious ferry ever seen on the Irish Sea services. Following extensive negotiations with Gotland Line, the company secured a five year charter of the *Visby* to replace the *St. Brendan*. The *Visby* (15,001 gross tons) had originally been built for Gotland Line for a service between Nynashamm (south of Stockholm) and Visby, capital of the Island of Gotland. The Swedish ship would have a capacity for 2,000 passengers, 517 cars or 54 freight units.

The renamed ship *Felicity* completed her maiden voyage during March, when the *St. Brendan* sailed from Fishguard for Italy as the *Moby Vincent*.

In April 1990, Sealink British Ferries' operations were acquired by Stena Line of Sweden, heralding a new chapter of management for the port of Fishguard.

Following the announcement of Irish Ferries that they would introduce the *Isle of Innisfree* on the southern corridor, Stena Line announced in November 1996 that the *Koningin Beatrix* would be transferred to the Fishguard - Rosslare service as from July 1997 in place of the *Stena Felicity*.

On the entry of the third HSS craft at Harwich, the *Koningin Beatrix* was duly transferred from Harwich to Fishguard in late June 1997 and following some inclement weather replaced the *Stena Felicity* on the route in the following month. The 'Felicity' meanwhile was returned to her owners and currently operates between mainland Sweden and the island of Gotland.

The *Koningin Beatrix* has been a successful replacement to the 'Felicity', despite a number of drawbacks with the Dutch-built ship, one of which is that she has too many cabins for the 3½ hour link. The fast craft *Stena Lynx*, which was introduced on the Fishguard - Rosslare service to support the conventional passenger service in 1994, was replaced in April 1999 by the *Stena Lynx III*, the larger InCat craft offered additional capacity for both cars and passengers on her 90 minute crossing between Pembrokeshire and Southern Ireland.

If Stena Line are to compete with their rivals on the southern corridor, a more suitable vessel must be found for the link, like the *Stena Jutlandica* (currently operating in the Baltic) with a faster service speed, more freight capacity and far more suitable accommodation for the route. The fast ferry service on the other hand has been an overwhelming success for Stena since its introduction eight years ago.

## FISHGUARD – WATERFORD

This link opened originally in 1850 from Milford. Some years later the little single-funnelled ship *Great Western* (I) operated this service. She had no great speed, only boasting 16 knots, but this was quite sufficient for the route with its long turn rounds. In 1906 the service moved to Fishguard.

In 1933, the *Great Western* was replaced by a new vessel of the same name, with passenger accommodation for 450 passengers in two classes, but in the main she was principally a cargo and cattle vessel. The service until the war was a night-only service, carrying only small numbers of passengers compared to the Fishguard - Rosslare link. After the war, the service continued its pre-war pattern until June 1959, when it was announced that passengers would no longer be carried on the route. Following the decision not to take passengers on the service any longer, the *Great Western* was refitted to carry more livestock and cargo.

The gradual run down of the Waterford service in the early sixties was of real concern amongst the townspeople of the Irish port. The *Great Western* was withdrawn from service at the end of 1966, and was replaced by the chartered container vessel *Eden Fisher*. Two years' later, the *Harrogate* was transferred to the route in place of the chartered cargo vessel. In 1971, the *Container Enterprise* was moved from Heysham to operate the link three times a week in each direction, and some two years later she too was replaced by the longer *Isle of Ely*, which could carry 62 tons more than the previous vessel.

In 1976, the *Container Venturer* replaced the *Isle of Ely* on the link. During the same year British Rail claimed that the Waterford service was now losing something in the region of £300,000 per year and that they would like to close the route. The operation could not close overnight, as British Rail were under a statutory obligation to keep it open. By the end of the year the Labour Party were claiming that the route had been mismanaged and that it could be made to pay.

A Committee of Enquiry was set up in 1977 to look into the future of the service. It was announced in October that the Waterford service should be closed, as it was unprofitable with the Fishguard-Rosslare route so close at hand. On the same day, British Rail applied for the closure of the route as from March of the following year. The service closed in March 1978, ending nearly 100 years of traffic between Pembrokeshire and Waterford.

## HOLYHEAD – DUN LAOGHAIRE/ DUBLIN

The new railway line to Holyhead was opened in 1848 and a subsidiary company of the Chester and Holyhead Railway was formed to provide a link to Ireland. Four paddle steamers were commissioned for this service - the *Hibernia*, *Scotia*, *Anglia* and the *Cambria*. By August 1948 the Admiralty Packets had been transferred from Liverpool to the newly-established route. The service from Holyhead was established to Kingstown, which was renamed Dun Laoghaire during the 1920s.

By the end of the 19th century the London & North Western Railway (L&NWR) was operating a service with four new ships, which had been built in the light of fierce competition from the rival company which operated out of Holyhead. The City of Dublin Company and the new quartet of Denny-built ships were to maintain the service until the First World War.

The *Hibernia* and the *Anglia* were lost during the Great War, but the *Cambria* and *Scotia* were returned to the Railway company in 1918. Following the war, the L&NWR went back to Denny's at Dumbarton for four new ships.

At the 'grouping' in 1923 the service was taken over by London Midland and Scottish Railway Company (LMS) and the new concern took a good look at operations at Holyhead and its ships on the passenger and mail runs to Ireland. It was decided for reasons, most probably of economy, that only three ships were required on the route and the *Anglia* was withdrawn.

During the Second World War the Holyhead route was maintained as far as possible by the *Hibernia*, while the *Cambria* was transferred to Heysham to cover the Belfast service. The *Scotia* was lost during the evacuation at Dunkerque.

In 1946 the LMS placed a long-overdue order with Harland & Wolff for two 4,900 ton motor ships. Meanwhile, the *Princess Maud* (in place of the *Scotia*) was transferred from Stranraer to Holyhead to assist the older ships before the new

# CENTURY OF NORTH WEST EUROPEAN FERRIES 1900 - 2000

This impressive view shows the *Scotia* leaving the Welsh coast for Dun Laoghaire. The vessel was lost during enemy action at Dunkerque in May 1940. *(Ambrose Greenway collection)*

tonnage arrived. The new *Hibernia* entered service in April 1949 followed by the *Cambria* a month later.

Both vessels were designed to carry some 2,360 passengers in two classes, with sleeping accommodation consisting of two-berth cabins-de-luxe, one and two-berth cabins for the first-class passengers and two, four and six-berth cabins and open berths for the second-class passengers. They could maintain a speed of 21 knots and when built they had the distinction of being the largest of the British cross-Channel ships. During the winter of 1964/65 the *Hibernia* and *Cambria* underwent a modernisation programme, which included renewal of their passenger accommodation.

To meet the growing demand for passengers to take their cars with them during the early sixties, British Rail decided to

In 1949 LMS ordered two replacement vessels for the Holyhead-Dun Laoghaire route, the *Hibernia* and *Cambria*. The latter is seen here arriving at Dun Laoghaire. *(Ambrose Greenway)*

order the first vehicle-carrying ship in 1964, with drive-on/drive-off facilities for the Holyhead-Dun Laoghaire route. Hawthorn-Leslie (Shipbuilders) Limited were appointed to build the new ship, which would be able to carry 1,000 passengers and 160 cars. Meanwhile work was to be put in hand for a new berth at Holyhead with a ramp for stern loading at the site of the inner harbour side of the Old Admiralty Pier at Salt Island, while similar arrangements were put in hand at Carlisle Pier at Dun Laoghaire. The new ship for the car ferry service, the *Holyhead Ferry I* was late entering service and the *Normannia* from Dover opened the new Holyhead-Dun Laoghaire service in July 1965 and maintained the service until the *Holyhead Ferry I* was able to make her maiden voyage. She operated only as a one-class ship, as opposed to the two passenger ships which operated both first and second class travel. With a gross tonnage of 3,879 and two sets of oil-fired turbines she was able to achieve 19.5 knots. By today's standards, she was a small car ferry with only a capacity for 160 cars. The passenger ships *Hibernia* and *Cambria* maintained the passenger-only and mail services to Ireland. During the winter period, while the car ferry service was not running, cars had to be crane-loaded onto the passenger ships.

The car ferry service continued to expand and for the peak season of 1969 it was decided to have two ferries operating the route. The *Dover* was earmarked from the Dover Strait to run with her near sister *Holyhead Ferry I*.

In 1974 British Rail announced that a new £650,000 linkspan would be built in the inner harbour close to the main line railway station at Holyhead, thereby allowing both rail and vehicle traffic to use the same vessel at off-peak periods.

In March 1975, British Rail Sealink placed an order with Aalborg Vaerft A/S of Aalborg, Denmark for a new passenger

113

# CENTURY OF NORTH WEST EUROPEAN FERRIES 1900 - 2000

The **Hibernia** is seen here leaving Dun Laoghaire in July 1974 for Wales with a backdrop of the Wicklow Mountains. *(Ambrose Greenway)*

car ferry to be specially designed for service between the ports. Meanwhile in 1976, the *Holyhead Ferry I* was sent to Swan Hunter's for conversion to a drive-through ship to meet the ever-increasing demand on the Dover Strait's operations. On completion of this work, she emerged as the *Earl Leofric*, with increased capacity to 205 cars but with a reduced passenger accommodation of 725.

The new vehicle ferry *St. Columba* arrived at Holyhead from the builders in April 1977. She was built as a two-class multi-purpose ship and offered a higher standard of comfort and facilities than ever before on Sealink's Irish Sea routes. Her original capacity was for 1,600 passengers – augmented to 2,400 in the peak season – with comfortable under-cover seats for all passengers. The vehicle deck was designed with bow and stern access and her car deck could take 335 cars or 36 x 40 ft. road haulage vehicles or a mixture of the two. Little more than a year after entering service for Sealink between Holyhead and Dun Laoghaire, the *St. Columba* carried her millionth passenger.

In September 1981, the new £16 million *St. David*, the last of the quartet of ferries ordered at Harland & Wolff, was duly launched at Belfast. Already some four months behind schedule, it was still uncertain whether or not the vessel would be employed on the Fishguard - Rosslare service as originally planned. However, in the event she was placed on the Holyhead route. Within a very short period of time, it became clear that the new vessel would be a more economic unit for the winter schedules and the *St. Columba* was laid up.

With continued losses from B&I Line on their Irish services, the company looked for better utilisation of their tonnage on the central corridor. Sealink Holyhead were approached by B&I to start a new ferry service from Dublin to Holyhead using the Dublin vessels *Leinster* and *Connacht*. The planned new service would allow the Dublin ship to sail by daylight to Anglesey and return before sailing overnight on the established Dublin-Liverpool service. This would allow the company better utilisation of their vessels. The announcement of the service was greeted with hostility by Sealink staff at Holyhead. The first sailings of B&I to Holyhead were to be delayed with a series of opposition tactics at the Anglesey port and then later off Dun Laoghaire by the Irish company against Sealink's operations at the port.

Following extensive talks between management and unions on both sides of the Irish Sea, the Irish were finally able to start their new daylight service from Dublin to Holyhead in early April, using the *Leinster*.

Despite the fears of those at Holyhead that the new B&I service would see traffic being taken from the established service of Sealink, the two ship operation using the *St. David* as a one-class vessel and the *St. Columba* as a first and second class ship was extended due to increased trade on the link.

In early 1987, the Irish Government approved a restructuring plan for B&I Line agreeing to the closure of the Dublin-Liverpool service and to allow them to concentrate their sailings on the central corridor to Holyhead. Following this announcement, Sealink confirmed that they were considering establishing their own service from Liverpool to Dun Laoghaire. The feasibility study continued despite B&I claiming that they might possibly run a summer service, but Sealink duly started their own service in April 1988. Sadly, the route was suspended in August after the *Earl William* developed problems with both her variable pitch propellers and it was becoming evident by the early autumn that the Liverpool - Dun Laoghaire route was not attracting the anticipated business. It finally closed in January 1990.

Sealink closed the dedicated container service to Dublin as from December 1989. The two container vessels *Brian Boroime* and *Rhodri Mawr* were disposed of as part of the financial package against the Stena/Tiphook takeover bid.

During April 1990 the hostile take-over battle for the control of Sea Containers was finally resolved. Most of the company's container business went to Tiphook for £321

# CENTURY OF NORTH WEST EUROPEAN FERRIES 1900 - 2000

million while Sealink British Ferries was acquired by Stena Line of Sweden for £259 million.

The new owners announced that the *St. Columba* would undergo a major £6 million refit which would include a complete rebuilding programme of all her passenger accommodation for the following season. The twelve year old ship would also be renamed *Stena Hibernia* following these works. To increase freight capacity on the link, the *St. Anselm*, renamed the *Stena Cambria*, would be transferred from Folkestone to Holyhead to offer two additional round sailings a day.

After a disastrous first year's trading, during which time Stena made a pre-tax loss of £28.2 million, it was accepted within the industry that Stena's desire to acquire the ferry operations of Sea Containers had resulted in an offer in excess of the company's market value and that severe retrenchments were now necessary. The company received a £60 million cash injection from Sweden and immediately launched its Operation Benchmark which looked for restructuring and economies. Meanwhile in March the *Stena Hibernia* re-entered service following her extensive refit.

Stena Sealink introduced a new fast ferry service between Holyhead and Dun Laoghaire using the new 74 metre wavepiercer catamaran *Stena Sea Lynx* in June 1993. The new service took 1 hour and 50 minutes on passage instead of the conventional ferry timing of 3 hours 30 minutes.

The company then announced that they had placed an order for two massive high-speed ferries from Finnyards, Rauma, Finland for delivery in 1995. One of the revolutionary craft would be placed on the Holyhead - Dun Laoghaire service within two years. Stena Line AB claimed they would be a technological breakthrough, with both cars and freight being able to be carried on the 40 knot craft. The new HSS (high speed sea service) would boast a length of some 124 metres and a beam of 40 metres and would be able to carry 1,500 passengers and 375 cars or 50 trucks and 100 cars. The craft would be powered by water jets via four gas turbines, which would be able to operate in most weather conditions. Loading and unloading would be via a special stern ramp and anticipated turnrounds would be some 30 minutes at each end. Over the next three years the fast craft was developed in great secrecy and eventually made her debut on 20th February 1996.

Following the transfer and success of the *Isle of Innisfree* from Rosslare to the Dublin - Holyhead route, B&I's new parent company Irish Ferries, announced that they would build a new vessel for their route to Dublin, which would triple their freight capacity and provide an 81% increase in car capacity on the central corridor service. The new four engined vessel built in Holland would have an operating speed of 21.5 knots, with a car capacity for 600 and accommodation for 1,700 passengers. With the forthcoming introduction of the HSS, the company had no alternative but to order new tonnage. Later the B&I trade name was dropped in favour of Irish Ferries.

The *Stena Sea Lynx II* arrived at Holyhead from Tasmania in June which allowed the renamed *Stena Sea Lynx I* to sail south to take up service between Fishguard and Rosslare. Meanwhile a new Holyhead-Dublin freight ferry service started in November 1995 using the *Stena Traveller*.

The new *Isle of Innisfree* was to be the turning point in Irish Ferries' fortunes as she quickly established herself as a comfortable and reliable ship on the route, so much so that Irish Ferries ordered a second and larger vessel to replace her in 1997. The larger vessel, *Isle of Inishmore*, duly entered service in 1997, which allowed the *Isle of Innisfree* to be transferred to the Rosslare - Pembroke Dock service.

The *Stena Hibernia*, which had played an important role at Holyhead for over eighteen years, was renamed *Stena Adventurer* in anticipation of her transfer to Dover from the Irish Sea on the arrival of the HSS. In the event, the vessel was not put on the Dover Strait but was to remain at Holyhead in a supportive role to the HSS during her first season.

The HSS *Stena Explorer* entered service in April on a low-

The *Dover* was originally built for the Dover-Boulogne service. She is seen here whilst on the Holyhead-Dun Laoghaire route prior to her conversion to a drive-through vessel. *(Ambrose Greenway)*

# CENTURY OF NORTH WEST EUROPEAN FERRIES 1900 - 2000

The *Horsa* makes a strange sight as she leaves Dun Laoghaire for Holyhead in June 1990. *(Miles Cowsill)*

The *Stena Sea Lynx II* is seen here leaving Holyhead with the *Stena Cambria* at the Salt Island berth in 1995. *(Miles Cowsill)*

key basis following an imposition of a 2.6 metre wave height operating restriction by the Department of Transport, pending a bad weather testing of the marine evaluation system of new craft. The craft achieved a speed of 47.8 knots in April, with the fastest recorded crossing between Wales and Ireland at 94 minutes later in the month. Meanwhile, the *Stena Adventurer* was withdrawn from service in September and was put on the disposal list.

In the same month the *Stena Challenger* was transferred from Dover and entered service on the Holyhead - Dublin route with a passenger certificate for 500 passengers, in place of a sister ship the 'Traveller'.

In an effort to offer additional capacity between Dublin and Holyhead, Irish Ferries ordered in 1998 a fast craft from the Australian builders Austal on a similar design to that of the *Superstar Express* operated by P&O Portsmouth. Following a frustrating industrial period with the Officers Union, Irish Ferries eventually introduced their fast craft the *Jonathan Swift* on the route in July 1999. During the same month, the company announced that they would build the world's largest car ferry for the Dublin - Holyhead route. The new vessel to be built in Finland would be capable of carrying 1,300 cars or 206 articulated lorries and 2,000 passengers. The new vessel is due for launch in autumn 2000 and will enter into service in spring 2001. Operationally the new ship will have a speed of 22 knots.

The introduction of further new tonnage by Irish Ferries posed an immediate threat to Stena Line's operations between Dublin/Dun Laoghaire and Holyhead. As a temporary measure, the company announced in autumn 1999 that the *Stena Invicta* would be chartered short-term to operate in tandem with the *Stena Challenger* between Holyhead and Dublin. Meanwhile the *Stena Explorer* continues to operate to Dun Laoghaire but it seems likely that Stena Line will have to introduce further new tonnage if they are to continue to hold their current market share on the central corridor.

The *Isle of Inishmore* replaced her smaller sister, the *Isle of Innisfree*, in 1997. The 'Innisfree' is seen here leaving Rosslare for Pembrokeshire on her four hour crossing. *(Miles Cowsill)*

116

# CENTURY OF NORTH WEST EUROPEAN FERRIES 1900 - 2000

*Originally built as the **St. Columba**, the former Sealink vessel is seen here during her last season on the Irish Sea as the **Stena Adventurer**. Stena Line had planned to use the ship on the Dover Strait for the lucrative day-trip market following the entry into service of the **Stena Explorer**; Nothing came of these plans and the vessel was sold for further service in Greece. (Miles Cowsill)*

## LIVERPOOL - DUBLIN

This route can be traced back to 1820, when the link was opened by the *Waterloo*. Some seventy years later the operation was in the hands of the City of Dublin Steam Packet Co., employing six ships on the eight-hour link. Following the end of the First World War, three new steamers, the *Lady Louth*, *Lady Limerick* and *Lady Longford*, were ordered for the new operator of the link, the British & Irish Steam Packet Co. These vessels established the popularity of the overnight service between the cities, which connected with the same trains as the overnight steamers from Belfast at Liverpool. The three steamers were displaced in 1929 by the *Heroic*, *Patriotic* and *Graphic* from the Belfast Steamship Co. and all three ships were renamed for their new role, the *Lady Connacht*, *Lady Leinster* and *Lady Munster*.

These vessels were to maintain the route until 1938, when they were displaced by *Munster* and *Leinster*, which had been built for the Belfast route. Two years' later the *Munster* was lost off the Mersey Bar after hitting a mine. During the Second World War the *Leinster* was used as a hospital ship and after the war was transferred to the Belfast Steamship Co.

*The **Lady Leinster** was originally built as the **Patriotic** for service between Belfast and Liverpool. In 1930 after an extensive refit a second funnel was added to her profile and she was transferrred to the ownership of the British & Irish SP Company for use on their Dublin-Liverpool route as the **Lady Leinster**. (Henry Maxwell collection)*

117

# CENTURY OF NORTH WEST EUROPEAN FERRIES 1900 - 2000

Atlantic Steam Navigation Company's *Bardic Ferry* is seen here on trials in the Clyde prior to her delivery to the company. *(Miles Cowsill collection)*

In April 1954, ASN was taken over by the British Transport Commission (BTC) as part of the Labour Government's policy for nationalisation. During 1957, ASN were to acquire their first two purpose-built vessels. They were especially designed for the Company for the carriage of lorries, trailers, cars and passengers. The first ship, the *Bardic Ferry*, was to make her maiden voyage in September 1957 between Preston and Larne. The 'Bardic's' sister entered service from Preston in October when the *Bardic Ferry* was transferred to the Antwerp operation from Tilbury.

This picture richly illustrates a sixties' view of ro-ro traffic with the comparatively small lorry moving its load off the *Bardic Ferry* at Preston. *(Miles Cowsill collection)*

The two further ships were ordered from Ailsa Shipbuilding Company Limited, Troon, and were to be of a very similar design and appearance to the 'Bardic' and 'Ionic', but they were to be slightly larger than the earlier twins. With the arrival of a further new vessel, the *Europic Ferry*, the *Doric Ferry* was then transferred to the Preston–Belfast service in November 1968.

The year before ASN was sold out to private enterprise, the Company began to implement plans for the repair of its Cairnryan Pier, which was to be repaired for a new passenger and freight service to Larne. The development of Cairnryan was eventually to see the closure of Preston, in the light of labour problems at the port and the difficult navigation of the River Ribble.

## HEYSHAM - BELFAST

The Midland Railway's *Antrim* and *Donegal* were built to open the route in 1904 and both ships were to be the first ferries on the Irish Sea to offer single-berth cabins for passengers. They were to maintain the link until displaced by the new 'Dukes' of 1928. The new ships for the route were built by Denny of Dumbarton and when the three ships entered service they were to be the largest employed on the Irish cross-Channel trade at the time. They had twin funnels and passenger accommodation for 400 saloon and 100 steerage passengers.

The *Duke of Argyll* and *Duke of Rothesay* led quiet and uneventful careers, in comparison to that of the *Duke of Lancaster*. During her first month in service, she ran into a fishing boat off the Isle of Man; in the same year she had a minor collision with the *Duke of Rothesay*; in 1931 she caught fire and sank and was later salvaged; the following year she ran ashore at Copeland Island in fog; she also ran aground near the Point of Ayre in the Isle of Man in 1937; finally, three years'

120

# CENTURY OF NORTH WEST EUROPEAN FERRIES 1900 - 2000

*The **Duke of Argyll** leaves Heysham on her final departure to Belfast. (D. I. Harmsworth)*

later she collided with and sank a coaster.

Prior to the outbreak of the war, the *Duke of Argyll*, *Duke of Lancaster* and *Duke of Rothesay* were the mainstay of the service, with the support of two other passenger ships during the summer peak periods. Following the outbreak of the war the 'Dukes' maintained the route until 1942, when the link was left in the hands of the *Cambria* and the turn of the century built vessel *Louth*. The *Duke of Lancaster* was first to return to the route after the war, followed by the 'Argyll' and 'Rothesay', and later the *Duke of York* for a short period.

The 1928 'Dukes' were still maintaining the link in the mid-fifties, when they were replaced with new tonnage of the same names. The new vessels operated at a speed of 21 knots and offered two class accommodation for 1,800 passengers. The *Duke of Lancaster* was the first of the three new 'Dukes' and was designed to undertake special cruises in addition to operating the Heysham night ferry link. In 1967 the *Duke of Rothesay* was converted to a side-loading car ferry and transferred to the Fishguard-Rosslare route.

With increased competition from the shorter links at Stranraer and Cairnryan, plus increased competition from air travel between London and Belfast, Sealink were forced to close the route in April 1975 in the light of huge losses.

The history of the passenger service did not end here; in a

*In 1928 three sister vessels were ordered from Wm. Denny & Bros. Ltd. of Dumbarton for the Heysham-Belfast service. This postcard painting shows the **Duke of Lancaster** which remained in service until 1956. (Henry Maxwell collection)*

121

# CENTURY OF NORTH WEST EUROPEAN FERRIES 1900 - 2000

*This view shows the **Ibex** following her jumboisation in 1996. The following year she was renamed **European Envoy** and currently serves on the Liverpool-Dublin route. (Miles Cowsill)*

surprise move in 1999 Sea Containers announced that they planned to reopen the service, using their 74 metre fast craft *SeaCat Danmark*. The fast craft would operate the link in four hours each way for an initial period of six months as an experiment. With good traffic levels to the route during its first few months of operation, the service was extended, and it seems likely the route will remain part of the Irish Sea operations for the next century.

## HEYSHAM - BELFAST/ DUBLIN/ WARRENPOINT (Freight Operations)

Merchant Ferries, part of the Cenargo group, was possibly to see the most radical growth during the nineties out of all the freight shipping companies; initially starting their operations between Heysham and Warrenpoint. Following the restructuring of Merchant Ferries' operations in 1997 and their decision to withdraw from Warrenpoint in favour of Dublin, the company took a major hold of the traffic in the central part of the Irish Sea. By the end of the century they were operating services from Liverpool to Dublin, Heysham to Dublin and Belfast, following their takeover of Norse Irish Ferries in 1999 and Belfast Freight Ferries in 1998.

Seatruck Ferries took over the service to Warrenpoint from Heysham following Merchant Ferries withdrawal from the port. They too have been successful with their operations, so much so that during the latter part of 1999 they opened a new freight ferry service on the English Channel between Newhaven and Dieppe.

## FLEETWOOD - LARNE/ DUBLIN

The former operating company of Pandoro, which is now part of P&O European Ferries (Irish Sea), can be traced back to 1974, when it was merged with Ferrymasters (Ireland) Ltd. to operate a new freight-only service between Fleetwood and Larne. Later in the same year the British Transport Docks Board started work on a new terminal at the Lancashire port and in 1974 P&O purchased the *Bison* and *Buffalo* for the new link. In addition to the new service to Larne, one of the vessels also served Dublin in a new joint venture with B&I. The *Bison* was first in service in February 1975, while the *Buffalo* followed in March.

The company then chartered, and later purchased, the *Union Melbourne* which was later stretched and became the *Puma*. This work proved so successful that both the *Bison* and *Buffalo* were to receive similar work. Further increases in freight in the nineties saw extension works on both the *Bison* and *Buffalo*.

The *Viking Trader* was transferred from Portsmouth to Pandoro in 1989 and eventually renamed the *Leopard* for the Fleetwood–Dublin route. During late 1997 and early 1998, in preparation of the formation of the new operating company P&O European Ferries (Irish Sea), the entire Pandoro fleet was renamed.

Today the company operates a fleet of eleven ships, including the passenger ship *Pride of Rathin* and the fast craft *Jetliner*.

The operation at Fleetwood is very much limited by the Lune estuary and also by poor road communications from the M6. How long the port will survive, with larger tonnage coming on stream, is unknown but it is likely to become less important if and when the new river berths at Liverpool are built.

## ARDROSSAN - BELFAST

The steamer service from the Scottish port of Ardrossan can be traced back to 1841 when the *Ayrshire Lassie* started a rather erratic operation. By 1879, the route was in the hands of G. & J. Burns. The service from its very early years was very dependent upon the railways and the close liaison was maintained until the night service closed in 1936. Daylight sailings were introduced by the *Eclipse* in 1821, however it was not until 1889 that a regular service was provided.

During 1906, the *Viper* replaced the *Adder* on the daylight

# CENTURY OF NORTH WEST EUROPEAN FERRIES 1900 - 2000

Built for L&NWR (LMS from 1923) the **Curraghmore** was originally built for the Greenore-Holyhead route in 1919. When the vessel was transferred to the Heysham-Belfast route in 1930 she was renamed **Duke of Abercorn**. *(Ambrose Greenway collection)*

service until the outbreak of the First World War. After the War, the daylight operation remained erratic and it was not until the mid-twenties that the service settled down once again. A series of vessels were to operate the route until 1932 when the former Southern Railway steamer *Laird's Isle* (ex *Riviera*) was assigned to the link. She was to maintain the route until 1957, when the *Irish Coast* or the *Scottish Coast* covered.

In 1968, the Ardrossan - Belfast car ferry service opened with the *Lion*, which was built at a cost of £2.6 million. The new drive-through ferry could carry 1,200 passengers and 200 cars. The opening of the car ferry service allowed the frequency of the overnight Belfast - Glasgow service to be reduced to three sailings a week but the 'troubles' saw the route closed in 1975 when the *Lion* was transferred to the Normandy Ferries' fleet to open a new service between Dover and Boulogne. The service was continued as a freight operation, eventually using the *Belard* (built 1979) which, following a period of charter for their ill-fated Great Yarmouth - IJmuiden route, was sold by Pandoro to the Isle of Man Steam Packet Co. in 1994.

Originally built for the Stranraer-Larne service in 1934, the **Princess Maud** is seen here outward-bound late in her career from Holyhead. *(Ambrose Greenway collection)*

Today a P&O European Ferries freight-only service is operated from Ardrossan with the *European Highlander* (ex *Lion*, ex *Merchant Valiant*), which serves the modern port of Larne, not Belfast. P&O plan to move to Troon in favour of Ardrossan in the near future.

## BELFAST - GLASGOW

The history of this link can be traced back to 1818, when a number of individual owners operated the service in fierce competition with each other. By 1830 there was a phase of consolidation when G. & J. Burns began to emerge as the strong operator and by 1851 they achieved a monopoly on the route. After the First World War the company was absorbed by Coast Lines Ltd, who in 1922 formed Burns and Laird Lines Ltd to operate their cross-Channel operations.

In 1906 the *Woodcock* and *Partridge* were employed on the route, which now included calls at Ardrossan. In 1929, the *Lady Limerick* and *Lady Louth* were transferred from the Dublin - Liverpool service and renamed *Lairdscastle* and *Lairdsburn* respectively. These vessels were the last steamers with reciprocating engines to be built for the Irish Sea services with almost vertical single funnels.

During 1936 both vessels were replaced by the *Royal Ulsterman* and the *Royal Scotsman*, which were built at Harland & Wolff. Both ships were about 330 feet in length with a service speed of some 18 knots. After the war both ships returned to their old haunts where they maintained the link until 1967, when both were sold. The route closed in favour of the Ardrossan - Belfast route which had introduced the newly-built car ferry *Lion*..

## STRANRAER – LARNE

The Portpatrick Railway was opened from Castle Douglas to Stranraer in 1861, shortly afterwards the Glasgow and Stranraer Steam Packet Company announced plans to operate a service to Belfast from Stranraer. In 1903 the link between

# CENTURY OF NORTH WEST EUROPEAN FERRIES 1900 - 2000

The **Ailsa Princess** was built in Italy after much controversy following the order not going to a British yard. She is seen here during a relief stint at Heysham leaving for Douglas. Today she operates in Greek waters. *(D. I. Harmsworth)*

Stranraer and Larne was operated by the *Princess Victoria* (1), *Princess May* and *Princess Beatrice*. Prior to the outbreak of the First World War a second *Princess Victoria* was ordered from Wm. Denny & Brothers of Dumbarton.

Continued growth in passenger numbers saw the LMS order new tonnage in 1930. The first of these vessels, the *Princess Margaret*, entered service in April 1931 while the second ship, the *Princess Maud*, entered operations on the Stranraer service in March 1934.

Further growth on the link was to see Britain's first purpose-built drive-on/drive-off ferry, the stern-loading *Princess Victoria* (III), being ordered for the Stranraer - Larne service. The new ship was small compared to that of the ferries of today, but nevertheless was revolutionary at the time and could carry up to 80 cars, with a restricted headroom of 12 feet 6 inches! When she entered service in July 1939, she was described by the local press as a "floating garage".

After only five months in service, the *Princess Victoria*, with her operating partner on the route the *Princess Maud*, were requisitioned by the Admiralty for the Second World War, during which the *Princess Victoria* was lost when she became a victim of an enemy mine off the Humber in May 1940.

Following the end of the war, LMS approved the building of a repeat replacement for the lost *Princess Victoria*.

During the great storms at the end of January 1953, the *Princess Victoria*, under the command of Captain James Ferguson, left Stranraer with 127 passengers and 49 crew in addition to 44 tons of cargo which had been stowed on trays in the car deck. Storm force winds on the day had prevented the loading of any cars and the loading of cargo had to be by hand.

Some time after leaving the shelter of Loch Ryan, a cargo man working on the car deck became aware of a quantity of water coming from the ship's after end. On investigating, he found the stern doors open and buckled. Following an unsuccessful attempt to close the stern doors, she was turned into the seas, which caused the 44 tons of cargo to shift to starboard, thus aggravating the situation even further. She continued to take on water and because of the growing list, of her six lifeboats, only one was to be of any use. Out of the 176 on board the *Princess Victoria* when she left Stranraer, only 42, all men, survived.

The inquiry into the loss of the *Princess Victoria* opened on March 1952. The report of the formal inquiry was issued and

The evening sun catches the **Darnia** as she arrives at Larne from Stranraer in May 1987. The vessel was withdrawn from the Sealink fleet in 1991 and currently remains in service in the Baltic. *(Miles Cowsill)*

# CENTURY OF NORTH WEST EUROPEAN FERRIES 1900 - 2000

Originally built for the Fishguard-Rosslare service, the **St. David** is seen here arriving at Larne following her transfer from the Holyhead-Dun Laoghaire route were she entered service orginially. She currently remains in service for Stena Line as the **Stena Caledonia**. (Miles Cowsill)

stated that the loss of the *Princess Victoria* was due to her unseaworthy condition arising from two circumstances:

(1) the inadequacy of the stern doors which gave to the stress of the seas, allowing the influx of water onto the car deck.

(2) the inadequacy of clearing arrangements for the water which accumulated on the freeboard deck causing an increasing list to the starboard, culminating in the ship eventually capsizing and foundering.

The court also found fault with the management of the ship in the two earlier incidents.

The *Hampton Ferry* was transferred from Dover to Stranraer in early June 1953 to assist the *Princess Margaret* each summer season until 1961, following the loss of the 'Victoria'.

In January 1957 it was announced that the British Transport Commission had approved the provision of a new ship for the service. The new ferry was ordered in the shadow of the route losing money and increased competition from air-travel to and from London - Belfast. British Transport Commission warned that if the route was unable to make a reasonable return on the new investment for the service, she would be transferred elsewhere in the fleet. The new vessel, the *Caledonian Princess* , entered service in December 1961.

By late 1965, a second ship was ordered for the route. The plans for the new ferry were very different from the *Caledonian Princess*, as the new ship would be the company's first drive-through purpose-built vessel. The *Antrim Princess* took up service in December 1967. In July 1969, a another new vessel was ordered with Cantiere Navale Breda of Venice. There was an outcry at a nationalised concern spending British taxpayers' money outside Britain, but the BRB stuck to its decision on the grounds of delivery date and price for the new ship, the *Ailsa Princess*.

The *Ailsa Princess* joined the service in July 1970. She was nearly a twin sister of the *Antrim Princess* differing to only a small extent in the positioning of the public rooms.

Some seven years later, Sealink announced that another new ship would be built for the route designed to carry 600 passengers and 300 cars. The new vessel, the *Galloway Princess* made her maiden voyage as a 'one class ship' on May Day.

In 1981 it was decided to transfer the *Ailsa Princess* to the seasonal Weymouth link as from the following summer.

The ro-ro vessel *Darnia* went to Immingham to have additional passenger accommodation built, during the early summer, and while she was away the Brittany Ferries' freighter *Breizh Izel* was chartered. Sealink therefore decided to charter another French ship, the SNCF *Villandry* for six weeks from June 1982, until the return of the *Darnia*.

Following Sealink's withdrawal from the Ostend route, which the *St. David* had been operating, she then transferred to Stranraer in place of the 'Antrim'. Following the arrival of the *St. David* on the route in early 1986 the service of the North Channel continued a regular pattern with the *Galloway Princess* and *St. David* as the mainstay of the route, with the *Darnia* as the back-up ship.

Major changes were to take place at Stranraer in 1990 and, following the takeover of the company by Stena Line, it was announced that the *St. Christopher* would be transferred from Dover and renamed *Stena Antrim* as from 1991. She would operate with the renamed *Stena Galloway* (ex *Galloway Princess*) and *Stena Caledonia* (ex *St. David*). The transfer of

# CENTURY OF NORTH WEST EUROPEAN FERRIES 1900 - 2000

*In 1993 SeaCat Scotland started a rival service from Stranraer to Belfast against Sealink Stena Line's operations to Larne. Their InCat craft **SeaCat Scotland** is pictured here arriving at the Scottish port. (Miles Cowsill)*

*Both the **Stena Caledonia** and **Stena Galloway** are due to have sponsons put on them to extend their career on the North Channel. The 'Caledonia' is seen here leaving Loch Ryan. (Miles Cowsill)*

the *St. Christopher* to the Scottish port allowed the *Darnia* to be sold.

Sea Containers started a new high-speed rival ferry service between Stranraer and Belfast on 1st June 1992 using their new InCat craft *SeaCat Scotland*. A new terminal was built at Stranraer at a cost of some £3 million to handle the SeaCat and the existing terminal at Belfast was upgraded for the new link. This new operation went into direct competition to Sealink's operations and that of P&O European Ferries at Cairnryan.

Mounting speculation continued throughout 1995 that Stena Sealink Line would withdraw their operations from Larne in favour of Belfast. Meanwhile Stena Line confirmed that they planned to introduce their second new HSS craft on the North Channel, which further fuelled the view that they would transfer them to Belfast. In the event the move was made and in November the *Stena Antrim* completed the last sailing from Larne, ending an era of over 123 years. Some six weeks' later, at midnight on the last day of 1995, Stena Sealink Line adopted the trading name of Stena Line.

The *Stena Voyager* (the second HSS) commenced service in July 1996, which allowed the *Stena Antrim* to lay-up at Belfast. Meanwhile the *Stena Caledonia* and *Stena Galloway* were retained on the route, operating both as passenger and freight. The *Stena Antrim* was then transferred to the Newhaven-Dieppe service and later sold for service between Spain and Morocco.

Whilst the ferry terminal at Belfast has already been completed, major work still needs to done at Stranraer, which has put the Scottish port's future in doubt. In the future we may well see the fast ferry service (HSS) operating between Belfast and Holyhead, while the traditional operation might use Cairnryan with P&O; both operators can then invest in the deep water port's future, being that much nearer to the North Channel than Stranraer.

## CAIRNRYAN - LARNE

As part of the Conservative Government's policy of transferring back into private enterprise those nationalised companies which were viable, ASN and its subsidiaries, the Transport Ferry Service became part of the European Ferries Group during November 1971. Following the take-over, the new management quickly took over the decision to move their Northern Ireland operations from Preston to Cairnryan. A new terminal and linkspan had to be built to handle the new service at the small Scottish village of Cairnryan on the edge of Loch Ryan.

In July 1973, the *Ionic Ferry* opened the new service under the command of Captain William Close. Initially the *Ionic Ferry* sailed twice a day from Larne but following the closure of the Preston – Larne service, the Preston – Belfast link was increased to a daily service each way with the *Bardic Ferry* and *Doric Ferry*. The Belfast route was to be abandoned a year later in favour of the by now well-established Larne – Cairnryan service.

During 1974 the trading name of Townsend Thoresen was introduced to market the services. Meanwhile in the spring the news came from Dover that the *Free Enterprise III* would be transferred to the Irish service as from July for the summer season and would join the *Ionic Ferry*. The *Free Enterprise III*, with a capacity for 250 cars and 1,200 passengers, was to make a sudden and dramatic change to the link. In 1975 the smaller *Free Enterprise I* was transferred to the route for the summer operations.

The following year *Free Enterprise IV* was switched from Dover to the service as from May 1976. She was to become a great success and firm favourite on the link for the next ten years. During the next couple of years the *Doric Ferry* and *Cerdic Ferry* were to become the operating partners with the *Free Enterprise IV* on the Ulster service.

During March 1980, the *European Gateway* was transferred from Felixstowe to cover the dry-docking period of

*The **Ionic Ferry** opened the new Cairnryan service in in July 1973. (Miles Cowsill collection)*

**126**

# CENTURY OF NORTH WEST EUROPEAN FERRIES 1900 - 2000

The **Ionic Ferry** was transferred to the Larne-Cairnryan route in 1986. The vessel, originally named **Dragon**, operated the Southampton-Le Havre service from 1965 until 1985 when P&O Normandy Ferries was taken over by Townsend Thoresen. *(Miles Cowsill)*

*Free Enterprise IV*. Meanwhile, in September 1980 the *European Gateway* was sent to Amsterdam Dry-Dock Company for lengthening before returning to the Ulster link again in 1981 for nearly a year with the *Free Enterprise IV*. The *Free Enterprise IV* and the *European Gateway* were to enjoy a very good reputation, both with freight operators and passengers. Sadly, during mid-December, the *European Gateway* was lost off Felixstowe in a collision with the Sealink train ferry *Speedlink Vanguard*, whilst covering for the refits of the vessels at Felixstowe.

During October 1985, European Ferries decided upon a major redevelopment of their fleet at Portsmouth, Felixstowe, Larne and Dover. At Cairnryan, the *Free Enterprise IV* was transferred back to Dover to operate with the *Free Enterprise V* on the Boulogne route and her place would be taken by the *Dragon*. In July 1986 the *Ionic Ferry* (ex *Dragon*) arrived at Cairnryan following her month's refit at Glasgow. The *Ionic Ferry*, with her operating partner the *Europic Ferry* then settled down into a regular pattern of sailings on the link.

Following the takeover of European Ferries Group by the P&O in December 1986, operations at Larne remained very much the same.

The operating name of the European Ferries Group, Townsend Thoresen, disappeared in October 1987, as part of a reorganisation of the Company, and the new P&O European Ferries Group was launched.

P&O European Ferries introduced their own fast ferry service on the North Channel in 1995 with the chartered mono-hulled craft *Jetliner*. The vessel is seen here getting underway from Cairnryan for Larne. *(Miles Cowsill)*

The last of the famous ASN ships **Europic Ferry** finished her distinguished career on the Cairnryan-Larne route. She is seen here sporting the Townsend Thoresen livery. *(Miles Cowsill)*

**127**

# CENTURY OF NORTH WEST EUROPEAN FERRIES 1900 - 2000

The last of the 'Free Enterprise' class ships to remain in service in British waters at the end of the century was the **Pride of Rathlin** (ex **Free Enterprise VII**). The former Dover ship is seen leaving Larne for Cairnryan in May 1996. *(Miles Cowsill)*

In 1992, P&O European Ferries replaced the *Ionic Ferry* and *Europic Ferry* on their Larne - Cairnryan service in favour of the former 'Free Enterprise' twins from the Dover-Zeebrugge service. The new tonnage for the route the *Pride of Rathlin* (ex *Pride of Walmer*) and *Pride of Ailsa* (ex *Pride of Sandwich*) came into operation as from March 1992. This allowed the company to offer for the first time a full passenger operation on their 2½ hour service and to the rival operations of that of Sealink and the new SeaCat service of Sea Containers at Stranraer. The *Europic Ferry* and *Ionic Ferry* were later sold by the company for further service in Greece.

P&O European Ferries' operations at Larne were restructured following the withdrawal of Stena Line from the Antrim port in favour of Belfast in 1995. The freight vessels *European Endeavour* and later the *European Trader* were transferred to the Cairnryan-Larne service in 1995/96 to increase capacity on their link, following the withdrawal of Stena Line. On the introduction of Stena Line's fast ferry service between Stranraer and Belfast with their *Stena Voyager*, P&O were successful in chartering the mono-hulled craft *Jetliner* for their Larne-Cairnryan route in June 1996. In spite of some fairly erratic operation during her first season, the fast craft has proved extremely successful running in tandem with the *Pride of Rathlin*. The introduction of the *Jetliner* saw the demise of the *Pride of Ailsa*, which was sold for further service in the Red Sea.

The *Pride of Rathlin*, now 27 years old and the last of the series of 'Free Enterprise' class ships still currently operating in the British Isles, is due to be withdrawn in September 2000 and replaced by a modern ro-pax vessel which is currently under construction in Japan. A further vessel of a similar design was ordered by P&O in mid 1999 for their Liverpool - Dublin service for delivery in the year 2001.

## GLASGOW - LONDONDERRY

The oldest and most important of the four passenger routes between Londonderry and Great Britain was always that to Glasgow, which opened in the early 1820s. The route for many years was dominated by the emigrant and reaper trade. The former travelled to Great Britain either to seek work or board a liner for a new life in America. The other rival services from Londonderry included links with Morecambe/Heysham, Fleetwood and Liverpool.

At the turn of the century the *Rose* was operating the route with the *Maple* and the *Olive*. The *Rose* offered berths for only 100 saloon passengers but offered a large steerage accommodation. From 1944 until 1966 the passenger and cargo route was operated by the *Laird's Loch* with accommodation for 44 passengers on the twelve hour passage. In the summer she would make three crossings in each direction, while the winter operation was reduced to two round sailings. The service closed in the mid-sixties with the change of thinking of travel and transport.

## IRISH - FRENCH SERVICES

Following B.R.'s withdrawal from Southampton - Le Havre service and the success of the Thoresen Car Ferries at Southampton, P&O entered into a partnership with the French company, Societe Anonyme de Gerance et d'Armement (SAGA) and two similar vessels were ordered for their new operation. The joint company was to be known as Normandy Ferries. The *Dragon* took up the new service in June 1967 and prior to the *Leopard's* arrival, Normandy Ferries announced plans to open a weekly crossing from Le Havre to the Irish port of Cork, but this was later modified to Rosslare.

# CENTURY OF NORTH WEST EUROPEAN FERRIES 1900 - 2000

This view shows the *Saint Killian* following her jumboisation leaving Rosslare for Le Havre in August 1982. *(Miles Cowsill)*

She duly opened the new Rosslare link in June 1968, leaving Le Havre at 12.15 on Saturdays, arriving at Rosslare at 10.15 the following day. The Irish service was to prove very successful, however it was later announced in 1971 that they planned to withdraw as from October 1971. It was stated that the route was profitable but the decision had been made to keep the twin ships in service on the route for which they were built.

There was no service in 1972 between Ireland and France, however the following year Irish Shipping found a suitable ship from Lion Ferry for the route. In June 1973, the *Saint Patrick* reopened the route to Le Havre from Rosslare. As the route grew over the next couple of years new and larger tonnage was introduced. In 1978 the larger *Saint Killian* was put on the route with the *Saint Patrick* but traffic had increased so much by the early eighties that the 'Killian' was lengthened and became the *Saint Killian II*. In the same year the Irish Continental Line acquired the *Aurella* from Viking Line and renamed her the *Saint Patrick II*. This in turn released the *Saint Patrick* for the new Belfast - Liverpool service.

In 1998 Irish Ferries introduced the chartered *Normandy* for their continental operations, in place of the 'Killian' and 'Patrick'. The company purchased the vessel during 1999. At the same time the Le Havre route was closed in favour of Cherbourg and Roscoff.

Brittany Ferries started the Irish/French service in 1978 with the *Armorique*, this was followed by a series of larger vessels over the next twenty years. Today the route is operated by the *Val de Loire*, and *Quiberon* out of season.

P&O opened a new freight-only service in 1993 between Rosslare and Cherbourg, using the former Dover freight ship *European Clearway*; which was later renamed *Panther* and today currently operates as the *European Pathfinder*.

During 1999, Swansea Cork Ferries opened a new ferry freight and limited passenger service between Cork and St Malo, using the chartered Greek ferry *Venus*.

The next century will lead to further growth of services between Ireland and France, and possibly a link to Spain will be opened in the not too distant future.

*Miles Cowsill*

*Like the Western Channel chapter in this publication, it has not been possible to cover the entire history of all the services on the Irish Sea this century. There has been a complicated web of operations during the last 100 years on the Irish Sea, so only the main ferry services are covered in this title.*

The *European Pathfinder* arrives at Cherbourg from Rosslare in October 1999. *(Miles Cowsill)*

129

## CENTURY OF NORTH WEST EUROPEAN FERRIES 1900 - 2000

# Irish Ferries -
# Investing in Growth

Irish Ferries, which operates passenger/ro-ro services between Ireland, Britain and Continental Europe, came into public focus in 1992. This followed the coming together of Ireland - France ferry operators Irish Continental Line and the long-established state-owned B&I Line.

After an initial period of post-marriage rationalisation and restructuring - a new enlarged Irish Ferries emerged fighting fit and ready to benefit from a programme of investment that lay ahead. Little wonder therefore that, in the intervening years, Irish Ferries has grown to become one of Europe's leading passenger ferry companies and operators of Europe's most modern passenger ferry fleet.

### CONFIDENCE

The new sense of confidence that has taken hold of Irish Ferries is reflected across every aspect of its operations.

To the man on the street, the company's status as a modern, progressive ferry company is reflected in a new television commercial currently playing to audiences on both sides of the Irish Sea.

In the film - in which scenes are acted by crew members of their Dublin - Holyhead vessel *Isle of Inishmore* - senior Captain, Peter Ferguson introduces viewers to the vessel. After a fast moving tour of the features which it has to offer, the sequence closes with a shot of Captain Ferguson advising viewers as to how they might substantiate claims made in the film regarding the quality of services that customers may find on board. Confidently, he advises: '*Ask any of our passengers*'.

This filmed statement - which includes impressive footage of the vessel at sea with delightful interior views and voice-overs from crew - projects the strong sense of confidence that now exists within the Irish passenger and ro-ro ferry company.

Created to promote the quality services that passengers may expect travelling on their Dublin - Holyhead and Rosslare - Pembroke routes, it is doubly significant for the fact that it is the first occasion on which Irish Ferries has appealed to customers on British television screens.

### SIGNIFICANT INVESTMENT

The very significant investment which Irish Ferries has made over recent years towards improving its services at all levels has been the engine room which has helped the company turn up the heat in its drive to win an even larger share of the UK - Ireland passenger market.

Over the past five year, Irish Ferries has invested more than £230 million in new ships and shore facilities. This level of investment contrasts with the promise made to the Irish Government when B&I Line came under Irish Ferries' ownership in 1992. Then an undertaking to invest £30 million over the following five years was given.

The first major investment made in bringing their Irish Sea services up to 21st century standards came about in 1994 when a decision was taken to purchase new tonnage.

This led to the building of Irish Ferries' first new cruise ferry - the £50 million *Isle of Innisfree* which was built in Rotterdam by Van der Giessen-de Noord.

Weighing in at 23,000 tons, it has space for 1760 passengers, 600 cars and 108 freight units. Its superior levels of appointments transformed the quality of service which Irish Ferries was able to offer. This had a major marketing impact, re-positioning the company as a leading, modern, passenger ferry operator.

### ISLE OF INISHMORE

So successful was the *Isle of Innisfree*, Irish Ferries lost little time in deciding to proceed with the construction of another new vessel along similar lines.

Soon, the go-ahead was given to build a second new ferry - an even larger vessel with space for 2,200 passengers, 855 cars and 122 freight units.

This turned out to be the *Isle of Inishmore*. Launched in 1996,

The *Isle of Innisfree* is pictured here prior to her launch at the Dutch yard of Van der Giessen-de-Noord. *(Irish Ferries)*

# FOR THE BEST OPTIONS TO IRELAND...

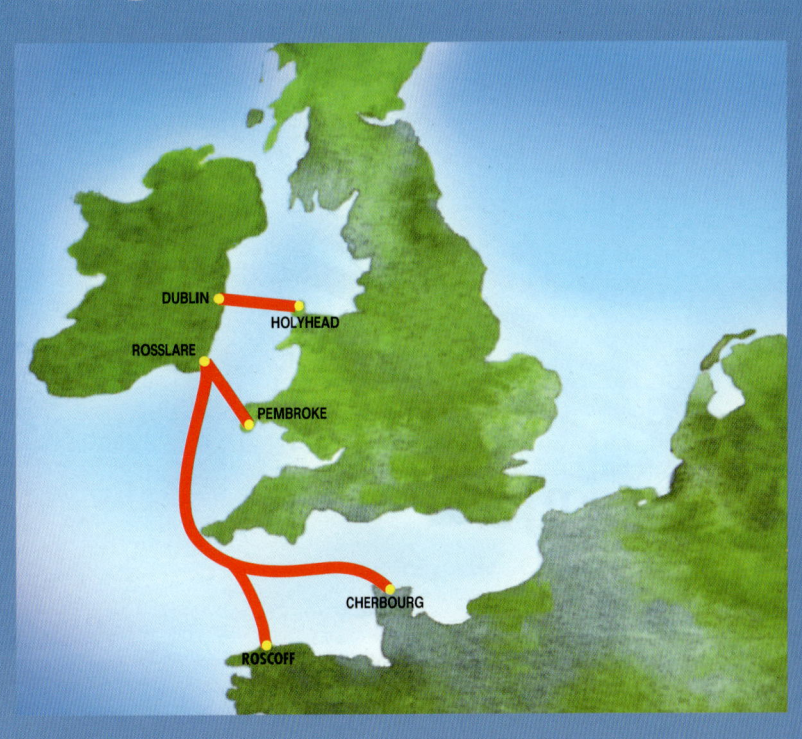

## ...ASK IRISH FERRIES FIRST

### IRISH FERRIES
*Ask Irish Ferries first*
Call 08705 17 17 17.
or see your travel agent.
Bookings: www.irishferries.ie

## CENTURY OF NORTH WEST EUROPEAN FERRIES 1900 - 2000

manoeuvrability which is supported by bow thrusters.

The advanced technology of the HSS 1500 extends to bridge operations and docking procedures. The navigation station is occupied by the captain and navigating officer positioned in an aircraft style cockpit fitted with the very latest technology. During passage and even during berthing manoeuvres there is no need for the officers to leave their seats. Wing bridge stations are not required as positioning of the vessel in port is controlled by a network of local GPS beacons linking into the vessel's own navigation system and control system. Data fed into this system is evaluated by the computer system which in turn sends command signals to the engine and propulsion management system to adjust engine speed and nozzle angles to manoeuvre the vessel and at the same time to compensate for variances in tidal movements and wind conditions. The system can position the vessel to an accuracy of one metre.

HSS stands for High-speed Sea Service and the whole concept is based on an integrated package combining the efficiencies of the vessel itself with the shore side logistics. To achieve this Stena Line has invested in dedicated berths in each of the ports serviced by the three HSS 1500 vessels. The berths incorporate plug-in linkages for fuel and water, passenger walkways and four lane vehicle routing. Additionally all of the ship's stores are replenished by a container system that is hoisted above the stern by on-board winches and then run along a track on top of the vessel's superstructure to a lift which delivers the container internally to the correct deck level.

Delivered in 1996 by Finnyards facility located a

The *Stena Explorer* seen before entering service on the Irish Sea. *(Stena Line)*

Rauma in Finland, the *Stena Explorer* and *Stena Voyager* entered service on the Holyhead - Dun Laoghoire and the Stranraer- Belfast routes on the Irish Sea. The third vessel in class, *Stena Discovery*, was delivered the following year for the North Sea route linking Harwich - Hoek van Holland. Up to five sailings per day are operated on both Irish Sea routes with passage times reduced to approximately 1 hour 45 minutes on both services. Between Harwich and Hoek van Holland the crossing is scheduled at 3 hours 40 minutes with two services per day.

*Paul Hynds*

### IRELAND • HOLLAND

## Your No.1 Ferry Partner to Ireland and Holland

Holyhead - Dun Laoghaire/Dublin Port • Fishguard - Rosslare • Stranraer - Belfast • Harwich - Hook of Holland

**For reservations call**
**08705 70 70 70**

*www.stenaline.co.uk*

**Stena Line**

*The world's leading ferry company*

The delivery of the **Stena Explorer** from Finland had to be achieved before the ice season closed in. *(Stena Line)*

# CENTURY OF NORTH WEST EUROPEAN FERRIES 1900 - 2000

# Manx Waters

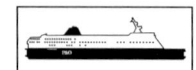

## THE BOOM YEARS UP TO 1914

The holiday trade, which provided the main demand for travel to the Isle of Man, was expanding fast in the opening years of the century. In 1900 five main companies operated services to the Island:

• The Isle of Man Steam Packet Company, which was already 70 years old, operated a fleet of 11 ships of which 8 were paddle steamers.

• Liverpool and Douglas Steamers - formed in 1899 - operated 5 paddle steamers - (not all employed on IOM routes) adding a sixth in December 1900 before going out of business at the end of 1902.

• The Liverpool and North Wales Steamship Company (L&NWSSCo) provided a limited IOM summer service from Llandudno using their paddle steamer the *St Elvies*.

• The railway controlled Barrow Steam Navigation Company also ran services to IOM using the two paddle steamers *Manxman* (ex *Antrim*) and *Duchess of Buccleuch* (ex *Rouen*), plus the two screw steamers the *City of Belfast*, and the *Duchess of Devonshire*. With the opening of the port of Heysham in 1904 the main railway service to the Isle of Man switched to that port in 1905 with the main Barrow ships being transferred to the Midland Railway in 1906, although some services continued to Barrow until 1914.

• The other service which operated at this time was twice weekly between Dublin and Silloth, calling at Douglas en route. This was operated by Dublin, Silloth and IOM Steamers from 1893 until March 1929 using the *Yarrow* which carried both cattle and passengers. The service was then offered to the Steam Packet who declined to take it on "as the profit would be small and uncertain". The outcome was the formation of a new company - the Dublin and Silloth SSCo - who continued the service until the Second World War using the same ship but renamed the *Assaroe*.

Barrow Steam Navigation Company's paddle steamer **Manxman** (ex *Antrim*, built 1873) which was withdrawn in 1903, seen leaving Douglas. *(Peter Kelly collection)*

By 1903 the Steam Packet were without competition on the Liverpool route and carried over 700,000 passengers a year - having more than doubled in the previous 20 years - and by 1913 this had increased to 1.15 million. The business was highly seasonal with most of the fleet active only between late May and early September - a pattern which was to be substantially maintained until the mid 1980s.

Apart from the year round Liverpool route, Steam Packet seasonal services operated to Fleetwood, Ardrossan, Workington, Belfast and Dublin. Douglas - Belfast services called at Ramsey and there were also direct sailings between Belfast and Peel. Ramsey also enjoyed direct services to Liverpool and Whitehaven for a number of years before the First World War. Services from Glasgow and Kingstown (Dun Laoghaire) were soon to be phased out in favour of those from Ardrossan and Dublin respectively.

The Fleetwood service was worked in close co-operation with the Lancashire and Yorkshire (L&Y) and London and North Western (LNWR) Railways who conveyed most of the passengers to Fleetwood to join either their own steamers to Ireland or the Steam Packet services to Douglas. The railways had been pressing for a new ship to be built for the Isle of Man route but following the collapse of Dumbell's Bank the Manx company were strapped for cash and tried - without success - to persuade the railways to put up some of the capital. The railways were also anxious that day excursions - for which they saw a great potential - should be operated on Sundays but this was strongly resisted on the Island as it would "destroy the quiet and orderly conduct of people resident in Douglas on Sundays." In 1904 the L&NWSSCo proposed to offer Fleetwood - Douglas services but backed down under the weight of protest from the Steam Packet's directors! It was not until 1939 - in the face of falling revenue - that the Steam Packet initiated its own Sunday sailings.

By the outbreak of the First World War the Steam Packet fleet had increased to 15 passenger ships. Four new builds and four purchased second hand had replaced five ships all of which were sold for breaking, except for the ill fated *Ellan Vannin* which was lost with all hands in the Mersey approaches in December 1909 whilst on passage from Ramsey. The only major route not under Steam Packet control was that from Heysham, operated by the Midland Railway's *Manxman* (built 1904).

The 1908 built **Ben-my-Chree** (3) and the **Viking** at the Victoria Pier before the First World War. Lying ahead of the 'Viking' is one of the Midland Railway Heysham fleet and in the foreground the double-ended Douglas Head quadruple screwed ferry **Shamrock**. *(Peter Kelly collection)*

# CENTURY OF NORTH WEST EUROPEAN FERRIES 1900 - 2000

The Armstrong Whitworth built **Viking** (1905-1954) makes a fine sight leaving Fleetwood. (*Ambrose Greenway collection*)

## THE FIRST WORLD WAR

All the Steam Packet fleet were in operation when war broke out at the peak of the tourist season. There was a dramatic fall off in traffic which led to the lay-up the *Ben-my-Chree*, the *Empress Queen* and the *Viking* in mid-August and the withdrawal of minor services. In October the *King Orry*, *The Ramsey* and the *Peel Castle* were requisitioned. By February 1915 six ships had been taken up for war service and by the end of the year eleven ships had either been chartered or purchased by the UK Government, of which only four, plus the Midland Railway's *Manxman*, were to see further Steam Packet service.

The four smallest ships were retained for the wartime Liverpool service - the *Tynwald* (3), the *Fenella* (1), the *Douglas* (3) and the coaster the *Tyrconnel*. Whilst it is unclear what level of potential business might have been available to the company at this time, there were those who thought the size of the fleet was inadequate and initially wanted to blame the Board for sacrificing the interests of the island to obtain profitable charters. In June 1915 Ramsey Commissioners "respectfully urged" the Steam Packet "to open up steam communication with Whitehaven during the season, as it is the shortest and safest sea passage between the Island and the mainland". The company were unable to oblige "owing to the smallness of our fleet and the requirements of our present services". In practice the threat - rather than the reality - of U-boat attack was enough to discourage many would be travellers. (Legend has it that U-boat commanders did not attack IOM steamers as they were regularly carrying German nationals who were to be imprisoned on the Island). In July 1915 Douglas Town Council were expressing concern at the Admiralty restrictions on traffic as well as having been asked to call a public meeting with reference to "steam boat services and fares between Liverpool and Douglas". In October 1915 Tynwald (the Manx Parliament) appointed a committee to "consider the best means of providing an adequate service of steamers between this island and the mainland", but the Admiralty would not allow their restrictions to be divulged to this committee.

Most of the ships taken up for war service underwent substantial conversions to act as armed boarding vessels, seaplane carriers or net layers and some served in distant waters. *The Ramsey* was sunk in August 1915 by the German raider the *Meteor*. The *Empress Queen* and the *Mona's Queen* were employed for troop carrying, both being based in Southampton under the command of Steam Packet masters. The *Empress Queen* went ashore in thick fog on the Ring Rocks off Bembridge, Isle of Wight on 1st February 1916 whilst proceeding at full speed without lights under Admiralty orders. Attempts to refloat her failed and Captain Tanner was suspended for two months - although the company declined to re-employ him at the end of the War. The *Ben-my-Chree* (3) served in the Mediterranean and Middle East and was sunk by Turkish shore batteries off the island of Castellorizo in January 1917. Although she was raised in 1920 the company declined to re-purchase her and she was scrapped in Venice in 1923. The final war casualty was the *Snaefell* which was torpedoed in June 1918 whilst proceeding from Alexandria to Malta. The *Mona's Isle* (3) survived the war as a net layer but the cost of re-conditioning her for further service was prohibitive and she was scrapped in 1919.

# CENTURY OF NORTH WEST EUROPEAN FERRIES 1900 - 2000

These two pictures show the difference 25 years of technological progress can make. On the left is the stokehold of the coal fired *Viking* - note the officer in full uniform supervising. In contrast the oil fired *Lady of Mann*'s firing aisle performs the same function. *(Peter Kelly collection/ IOM Steam Packet)*

## BETWEEN THE WARS

By the end of the War the Steam Packet fleet was down to six ships with a capacity of 6,300 passengers, barely a third of their pre-war capability. As a result of compensation for vessels lost, charter fees received and proceeds of ships purchased by the Admiralty the company was cash-rich and early in 1919 attempts were made to break up the Company and share out the cash amongst the shareholders. In 1903 a similar effort within the board failed by three votes to four, but this attempt was much more serious. A shareholders meeting passed three resolutions:

- opposing any policy which involves the realisation of the company's present investments (est. value £800,000) for the purchase of new steamers
- in favour of nationalising the Steam Packet
- proposing a dividend of 20%.

A month later at the company AGM - which lasted two days - there was a narrow majority for continuing the business and paying a 20% dividend. The company looked to refurbishment and the second hand market to rebuild its fleet, and within two years was so short of cash it had to raise a new £300,000 issue of debenture stock. It was not until 1927 that it was to build another new ship.

By January 1919 Douglas Town Council were asking for assurances that "an adequate passenger service would be provided for the coming season" to which the company replied that it was "doing everything possible to obtain the release of our steamers and to secure other vessels to replace those which had been lost or appropriated by the government". In March it seemed likely that the *King Orry*, *Peel Castle* and *Mona's Queen* would be released between April and June but would require refurbishment before being brought back into service. To provide immediate extra capacity Laird Line's *Hazel* (built 1907) was purchased for £65,000 and re-named the *Mona* (4) and L&NWSSCo's *La Marguerite* was chartered for the 1919 season.

The L&NWSS chairman visited the Steam Packet board on 22nd January 1920 to explore the possible amalgamation of the two businesses but by April the company decided they were "not disposed to proceed further in the matter". A few months previously they had also declined to purchase the Blackpool Passenger Steamboat Co Ltd with its two ships - the 25 year old *Greyhound* and the *Bickerstaffe* which was already 40 years old. That service still operated in competition on the Fleetwood route in 1921.

By December 1919 the Steam Packet had finally agreed to purchase three ships from the Admiralty for a total of £425,000. These were their own *Viking*, the *Manxman* (ex Midland Railway) and the Denny-built *Onward* (ex South Eastern & Chatham Railway) which was renamed the *Mona's Isle* (4). All three were available for the 1920 season, plus the *Viper* purchased from Burns Line and renamed the *Snaefell* (4).

The re-establishment of normal winter services was hampered in 1919 by restrictions on daylight working imposed by the Liverpool transport workers and in order to maintain the flow of essential imports and exports through the port, only alternate day and night sailings could be operated to the IOM, to the annoyance of Island residents from the Governor downwards. By 1920 the Post Office were insisting under the terms of the mail contract that there were daily day sailings in winter and two a day in summer. For this service level the Steam Packet were to be paid £8,000 a year. The extra revenue was of great importance to the cash strapped company at this stage.

The Midland Railway Heysham - Douglas service restarted

This picture of the Dining Room on the *Ben-my-Chree* (3) shows the high quality of accommodation provided for first class passengers. *(Peter Kelly Collection)*

**140**

# CENTURY OF NORTH WEST EUROPEAN FERRIES 1900 - 2000

The first **Lady of Mann** (1930-1971) resplendent in her pre-war white livery going astern from Fleetwood. *(John Shepherd collection)*

early in 1920, using the ex Barrow SNCo ships *Duchess of Devonshire* and the *City of Belfast*. Following railway re-organisation the route was taken over by the LMS who put the *Menevia* (ex *Scotia*) and the *Duke of Cornwall* on the service in June 1923. The *Menevia* was chartered to the Steam Packet for 5 weeks in the summer of 1925 and operated the last railway sailing from Heysham on 12th September 1927 and the 'Duke' was then purchased by the Steam Packet.

The question of oil firing was first discussed by the Steam Packet Board in September 1919. Oil supplies were still under Government price control but prices were expected to fall when this was lifted. The *Manxman* was the first to be converted in 1921. The supply contract for 1921/22 was placed with Shell and it is believed that the Steam Packet would go on to become Shell Marine's oldest customer. The timing of her entry into service coincided with a three month long coal strike which required a curtailment of services and the importation of Belgian coal.

The Steam Packet were both slow and reluctant to install wireless telegraphy on their ships. Although a trial Marconi installation had been put on the *Empress Queen* in 1903, by 1909 the board could not "see our way to incur any expense on the installation of wireless on the company's vessels". In 1919 the Board of Trade indicated that IOMSPCo steamers should be equipped with Wireless Telegraphy apparatus but the company replied that "nothing in the Merchant Shipping (Wireless Telegraphy) Act 1919 requires our steamers now in service to be provided with wireless" and pointed out that the Island was without a wireless station. The Statutory Rules and Orders 1920 required "every seagoing passenger steamer to be equipped with W.T. from and after 1st September". This ruling was to cost the company £2,000 per year.

The 1920s were a period of consolidation. The 1921 season suffered a 3 month coal strike and a rail strike prevented coal deliveries in early 1924. The *Caesarea* was purchased from the Southern Railway in November 1923 and after conversion to oil firing entered service in June 1924 as the *Manx Maid*. She replaced the *Douglas* which had sunk after a collision in August 1923. During the General Strike of 1926 - and the coal strike which continued for longer - services were disrupted for seven months, the Liverpool service being maintained by the company's two oil-fired ships - the *Manxman* and the *Manx Maid* which were also required to carry food to the island.

In 1926 tenders were invited for the building of the first new ship since before World War 1. The keel of *Ben-my-Chree* (4) was laid on 17th November at Cammell Laird's Birkenhead shipyard. In the aftermath of the General Strike and in order for her to be completed in time for the 1927 season some of the materials for her construction had to be purchased from the continent. She entered service on 29th June 1927 and was reported to be "a magnificent ship in every

**141**

# CENTURY OF NORTH WEST EUROPEAN FERRIES 1900 - 2000

This photo of Douglas Harbour was taken sometime between 1937 and 1939. It shows no fewer than twelve Steam Packet ships in port at the same time. The white ship with the high bow in the centre is the **Mona's Queen** (3) lying across the pier from the **Tynwald** (4) from which the post-war "King Orry" series of ships was developed. *(E W Fargher)*

way, and an excellent sea boat". Her first season was a short one, as, following a collision with the *Snaefell* in Douglas Bay on 20th August she had to be withdrawn for repairs and her captain was offered no winter employment.

Until now fleet replacement policy seemed to have been dealt with on a very ad-hoc basis, but in November 1927 it was decided that three new ships were required. The first was met by the purchase of the 1907 built *Victoria*, the second by the building of the company's first new cargo ship *Peveril (2)* and finally by the construction of the *Lady of Mann* at Barrow in 1930 for service on the Fleetwood route. The LMS decided to discontinue their Heysham - Douglas service at the end of the 1927 season and the route was taken over by the Steam Packet the following year, using two of the existing ships renamed the *Ramsey Town* and the *Duke of Cornwall* which became the *Rushen Castle*. In order to meet peak demand the *Duke of Connaught* was chartered for Saturday service in August 1928 and the *Curraghmore* the following August.

The same year the company ran excursions from Blackpool North Pier but as these were not profitable enough to continue in subsequent years. The Douglas - Ramsey - Workington service was also withdrawn after the 1929 season.

The *Lady of Mann* entered service on 28th June 1930 and on arrival in Douglas fell heavily onto the Victoria Pier damaging the fore end of her main belting. Although from a different yard she was very similar in appearance to the *Ben-my Chree* (4) except for the bridge being one deck higher. A third - but slightly smaller and slower - near sister *Mona's Queen* (3) was built at Birkenhead, entering service in 1934. The 'Queen's' distinguishing characteristic was a high bow under which the dining room was built - but this had an adverse effect on her manoeuvrability.

In 1932 the *Ben-my Chree* was painted white at cost of £63 "such a colour scheme being deemed to have a definite advertising value when the vessel was in the River Mersey". The *Victoria* was converted to oil firing and the IOM Publicity Board wanted the company to provide better facilities for conveying motor cars - of which 112 had been carried to Douglas the previous year. The company responded that as the ships were already crowded at weekends there was no space for cars.

Despite increasing numbers of travellers during the 1930s a resolution was passed in the IOM Government in December 1934 "that a commission with power to summon and examine witnesses on oath, be appointed to consider, investigate and report on the present transport facilities to the Island, and means whereby more people can be encouraged and persuaded to travel to the Island". Although the outcome of this commission is unknown the increase in passenger arrivals the next season was minimal. In 1935 the Wednesday afternoon Douglas - Heysham steamer called at Fleetwood en route.

In November 1935 the Board, apparently for the first time in their history, were presented with a report on the life expectancy of the fleet. The boilers of the *Ramsey Town* would be life expired by the end of the 1936 season and between 1939 and 1942 a further 7 ships were expected to need replacement. It was therefore proposed to build two new ships of 1,700/1,800 passenger capacity to replace the *Ramsey Town* and the *Peel Castle*, to sell the *Manxman* and the *Rushen Castle* at the end of the 1938 season and replace both with one ship to carry 2,600 passengers, and thereafter to build a new ship every two years. The first two ships in this programme - the *Fenella* (2) and the *Tynwald* (4) were built by Vickers at Barrow, launched on the same day in December 1936, and entered service in April and June 1937 respectively. Both had trim problems, being 4' down at the stern instead of the planned 1'6" which rendered them too deep to be used on the Fleetwood service at low water on spring tides.

By the end of 1937 the prospect of war seemed real, a re-armament programme was in progress and shipbuilding costs were escalating so by April 1938 the decision was taken to defer further orders for new ships, although an outline specification for a longer version of *Tynwald/Fenella* to carry 2,000 passengers at a speed of 20 or 21 knots and for delivery

# CENTURY OF NORTH WEST EUROPEAN FERRIES 1900 - 2000

in 1939/40 had been drawn up. In October 1938 it was agreed to convert the 25 year old *King Orry* (3) to oil firing at a cost of £12,570 which was expected to reduce running costs by £100 per week and extend the life of the ship by 5 years.

The 1939 season brought the first Steam Packet Sunday sailings (from Liverpool, Fleetwood and Heysham) despite protests led by the Mayor of Douglas. The end of season report to the Board indicated that "the type of person patronising the new services was above the average and there was not the slightest indication of drunkenness or unseemly behaviour".

## WORLD WAR TWO

The *King Orry*, the *Mona's Isle* and the *Manx Maid* were requisitioned four days before the outbreak of war and a further seven ships followed in the opening weeks of September 1939 although two were to be returned temporarily in November and December. Dual purpose guns were fitted to all the company's passenger ships early in 1940.

In June 1940 the *Mona's Queen*, the *Fenella* and the *King Orry* were all lost at Dunkerque. The *Lady of Mann*, *Ben-my-Chree*, *Tynwald* and *Manxman* were also heavily involved in the Dunkerque operation. Despite nearly 25,000 troops - one in 14 of those saved - being evacuated by Steam Packet ships there was some controversy over "officers and men who refused to volunteer" to take their ships back on subsequent trips.

On the 30th December 1940 it was decided to transfer the passenger service from Liverpool to Fleetwood with winter sailings from Douglas at 10.00 and Fleetwood at 13.00 (although timings were subsequently brought forward by 15 minutes). The ships maintaining the war time service were mainly the *Snaefell* and the *Rushen Castle*, although from time to time service was reduced to alternate days to enable repairs to be carried out. Occasionally other vessels were released back to the company for short spells of relief service. In mid November 1942 the entire fleet was requisitioned, which gave the UK Government the right to determine which ships were used on Manx services, and all passenger revenue was for the account of the Ministry of War Transport. During the summer of 1943 weekend capacity was inadequate and passengers were regularly being left behind - despite which no additional ships could be introduced and the military authorities were unwilling to reduce weekend leave. Early in 1944 the Island's Governor expressed the view that "having regard to the national interest it is desirable to discourage excessive passenger traffic to the Island this summer". Despite this passengers were still being left behind and the company was asked to introduce a pre-booking system.

As early as February 1942 consideration began of new tonnage "for delivery at the conclusion of hostilities" and later that year it was reported that the war Committee of Tynwald (the Manx parliament) had been asked to look at the "restoration of the visiting industry" after the war and to "consider the question of transport facilities". In mid 1943 the company indicated a preparedness to order two ships "somewhat similar to the *Tynwald* and the *Fenella*" and at the end of the year negotiations were opened with Vickers and Cammell Laird. Firm prices could not be quoted although it was apparent that costs had doubled since 1937. Two 21 knot ships (the *King Orry* and the *Mona's Queen*) were ordered in September 1944 for delivery in Spring 1946 on a cost plus agreed profit of £32,000 per ship. The final costs being £399,000 and £411,000 respectively.

The Steam Packet's 1955 **Manxman** (2) was going astern out of Douglas into a winter gale. She was the sixth post-war and last pure passenger steamer built for the company. *(John Shepherd collection)*

# CENTURY OF NORTH WEST EUROPEAN FERRIES 1900 - 2000

The **Manx Viking** in her original 1978 Manx Line livery when re-opening the Heysham route. She was later to run in Sealink livery after Manx Line had been baled out and finished her Irish Sea service on charter to and in the livery of the Steam Packet. *(Manx Line)*

### 1945 - 1984

Despite the protests of Fleetwood and Blackpool Councils, the year round service was switched back to Liverpool from 8th April 1946. For the 1946 peak season 9 passenger ships were available, including the two new builds which joined the fleet in April and June. Almost 442,00 passenger arrivals were reported (over 80% of the 1939 level) despite no Irish sailings being operated.

Four further ships of the 'King Orry' class were to be built by Cammell Laird in the 10 years after the war. The *Tynwald* (5), *Snaefell* (5), *Mona's Isle* (5) and the *Manxman* (2). The possibilities of building the *Snaefell* as a larger 2,500 passenger ship similar in design to the 1934 *Mona's Queen* and fitting diesel engines in the *Manxman* were also considered but in neither case were these ideas pursued. The *Manxman* differed mechanically from her predecessors in having double reduction geared turbines and superheated steam boilers. There appears to have been no discussion of the possibility of the *Manxman* being built as a car ferry, despite the fact that incentives were being offered to induce customers to ship their cars on the cargo service "and so relieve congestion on the passenger vessels". The handling of cars on passenger vessels involved the removal of passenger seating and at Douglas it was necessary, at most states of the tide, to crane cars on and off the ships.

In 1947 Belfast sailings were resumed, with a call at Ramsey but the Ardrossan ship did not make this call until the year after. Despite pleas from Ramsey Commissioners direct sailings to Liverpool did not resume after the war. Ramsey calls ceased in September 1970 when the berthing head on the pier was beyond economic repair. Peel Commissioners also tried to persuade the Steam Packet to resume direct sailings between Peel and Belfast and occasional excursions were operated between 1950 and 1956. The first post-war day excursion from Douglas to Dublin operated on 19th July 1950 followed by two in September and a regular service resumed the following summer. Seven profitable Heysham services operated in 1953 which led to a regular limited summer service in the following years until 1974.

By 1957 it became apparent that the berths at Fleetwood were nearing the end of their life. Replacement cost was estimated at £627,000 against dues paid by the company of £15,000 annually - showing British Transport Docks (the port owners) a loss of £12,000 a year. No progress was made and by 1959 it was uncertain that the berths would be usable beyond the end of that season - with replacement costs now estimated at £700 - 750K. Despite the involvement of the Manx Government it was apparent that no money could be found to finance this work, although offers of doubling the passenger tax paid and making do with one berth (at a cost of £500k) instead of two were made. The service therefore closed at the end of the 1961 season.

The loss of the Fleetwood service was offset by the introduction of extra sailings on the Heysham and Liverpool routes in 1962 and also the take-over of the Llandudno - Douglas route from which L&NWSSCo withdrew the *St. Seiriol* at the end of the 1961 season. Despite these new services the 1962 summer season passenger arrivals at 282,659 were down by over 69,000. In 1962 L&NWSS closed completely enabling the Steam Packet to operate limited services on the Liverpool - Llandudno route in place of the *St. Tudno* from 1963.

This was not the end of the Fleetwood story. Having lost

**144**

# CENTURY OF NORTH WEST EUROPEAN FERRIES 1900 - 2000

Over the years a wide range of vessels have served for short periods on IOM routes. During June 1983 the SNCF car ferry **Villandry** was brought in to cover for the **Manx Viking** on the Douglas - Heysham service. *(Manx Line)*

After the Steam Packet/Sealink merger **Tynwald** (6) (ex **Antrim Princess**) took over the Heysham route from 1985 to 1990. She had first visited the Island in 1969 and had covered for the **Manx Viking** during the winter 1980/81. *(Miles Cowsill)*

the passenger berths ABP decided in 1962 that they needed to berth their dredger outside the Wyre Dock and dolphins were built for this purpose. These dolphins were to provide the basis for a new small passenger berth from which Norwest Hovercraft Limited operated to Douglas with the chartered *Stella Marina* in summer 1969 and the unsuitable *Norwest Laird* (ex *Lochiel*) the following season. The Steam Packet were offered the agency for this service but turned it down as they regarded it as opposition. Following the failure of this service further modifications were made to the berth which enabled the Steam Packet vessels again to use the port from August 1971 and in summer 1972 sailings operated 5 days a week.

At the end of 1966 the owners of the Llandudno Pier reported major structural problems the repair of which they were unable to fund. Again the company was asked to provide the money or lose its berth. Just as the Fleetwood problem appeared to be solved the Liverpool Landing Stage fell into a serious state of disrepair in the early 70s. The provision of a replacement was readily agreed on a 'cost-plus' basis but ran into severe technical problems and cost over-runs before finally being commissioned in July 1976. On this occasion funding was provided by the IOM Government (£2.75 million against the original estimate of £750k) which the Steam Packet had to repay with interest over a 25 year period. There appears to have been no consideration at the time of providing berths capable of handling anything other than side loading vessels - a decision which was to dog the company's handling of vehicles at Liverpool for the rest of the century.

It was not until 1960 that the Steam Packet decided that the time had come to build a car ferry although the *Manx Maid* (2) did not enter service until 23rd May 1962. Built by Cammell Laird in Birkenhead - who had built all the company's post-war passenger steamers - her steam turbine engines were similar to those of the *Manxman* (2), but she was the first vessel in the fleet to have stabilisers. She was followed in May 1966 by the almost identical *Ben-my-Chree* (5) - the last two-class ship built for the company. Both were designed to carry cars and light vans which could be side loaded from the ship's spiral ramps at any state of the tide. The car decks were also fitted with side doors forward which could be used alongside Liverpool Landing Stage.

The issue of fast craft first came up in the mid 60s. Manx Sea Transport was formed as a Steam Packet subsidiary and late in 1966 was offered an option on one of the four SRN4 Hovercraft then being built. This was beyond the resources of the Steam Packet alone but early the next year the remit of a Transport Committee of Tynwald included a joint working group to evaluate air cushion vehicle development. The same committee also investigated the possibility of the Manx Government taking financial control of the Steam Packet.

Another pair of car ferries, the *Mona's Queen* (5) and the *Lady of Mann* (2) joined the fleet in 1972 and 1976. Whilst being of similar size and layout to the 'Maid' and the 'Ben', they were the first diesel passenger ships operated by the company and were built at Troon by the Ailsa Shipbuilding Company.

In 1978 the limitations of the Steam Packet vehicle carrying capacity were recognised by others but not by the company itself, and the newly formed Manx Line put the *Manx Viking* into service between Heysham and Douglas. This ro-ro ship was capable of carrying commercial vehicles, including coaches, as well as cars and operated from a newly installed £1.3 million linkspan in Douglas harbour - the approach viaduct for which had been provided by the IOM Government. This operation faced a baptism by storm - with the newly installed linkspan, on which its livelihood depended, being severely damaged - and the economic prospects consequently ruined. Instead of the operation going bankrupt it was supported by Sealink who took a major share in the operation and ultimately became part of the Sea Containers Group.

The Steam Packet were slow to take this competition seriously - seeing it as something they hoped would go away if they ignored it. Reluctantly they decided to convert their containerised cargo operation to ro-ro in 1981 and at their own expense installed a second linkspan in Douglas harbour at a cost of £1.5 million. In Liverpool the service had to use the enclosed dock system - as had previous freight services to IOM. The ship that was to become *Peveril* (4) entered service as the *NF Jaguar* initially chartered from P&O and for freight operations only.

Late in 1984 the competition had not gone away and was taking valuable freight business from the Steam Packet who finally realised that the cost of running separate freight and passenger operations was a luxury it could no longer afford. This led to the purchase of the *Tamira*, (ex *Free Enterprise III*) which was re-named the *Mona's Isle* (6) and after extensive

145

# CENTURY OF NORTH WEST EUROPEAN FERRIES 1900 - 2000

The TT races have always brought huge traffic peaks - this picture taken in the 1970s shows motor-cyclists queuing on the Victoria Pier to board the **Mona's Queen** (5) for their journey home. *(W S Basnett)*

The **Peveril** arrives at Douglas during her last few days in service, prior to the **Ben-my-Chree** replacing her role on the daily freight runs from Heysham. *(Miles Cowsill)*

conversion entered service in April 1985. The ship was unable to use the Landing Stage at Liverpool and, although never publicly announced, it appears to have been the company's intention to switch their service to compete head on with Manx Line on the Heysham route, to dispose of the older two car ferries and charter out the *Peveril*. Before that plan could be implemented a merger between the Steam Packet and Manx Line was announced, with Sea Containers taking a 40% share in the "new" IOM Steam Packet Company.

### 1985 - 1999

For the period from 1985 until the spring of 1996 Sea Containers, although the largest shareholder in the Steam Packet, maintained a generally low public profile in the running of the company. The first task was to get the combined operation up, running and profitable. Decisions were taken which did more to help Sea Containers' bottom line than achieve these objectives. A two ship 3 sailing a day schedule was introduced between Douglas and Heysham (this port now being owned by Sea Containers) - the ships to carry both passengers and freight with the Liverpool passenger and high labour cost freight operations being closed down. Passenger traffic fell by nearly 14% over that carried through Liverpool and Heysham the previous year. The *Mona's Isle* proved quite unsuitable after her costly conversion and soon the Heysham service was in the hands of two Sealink (Sea Containers) chartered vessels the *Antrim Princess* - to be renamed the *Tynwald* (6) in April 1986 and the ex Manx Line *Manx Viking*. The *Mona's Queen* and the *Lady of Mann* were reduced to summer season and back-up vessels.

In 1986 the Ardrossan service was switched to Stranraer - at the time owned by Sea Containers Sealink subsidiary, and the Fleetwood route was closed. However during July and August charter sailings, marketed by Associated British Ports were operated twice a week from Fleetwood by the *Mona's Queen* and twice weekly peak season sailings to Liverpool were re-introduced. At the end of September the Heysham route was reduced to one round passenger trip a day, the *Manx Viking* returned to Sealink UK, and the *Peveril* brought back to provide a nightly freight service.

Rationalisation to restore profitability was the theme for the "merger years". Attempts to reduce labour costs led to strike action early in 1988 and there was some doubt whether the TT races could be run due to action in sympathy with striking P&O seamen at Dover. This led the Manx Government to charter the *Bolette* from Fred Olsen Lines to run an emergency service between Douglas and Holyhead although in the event the strike was called off in time. The year round passenger service was soon to be provided by the *King Orry* (5) (ex *Channel Entente* ex *Saint Eloi*) purchased early in 1990 and which replaced the *Tynwald*. The 'King' was given her Manx name after completing a major refit to increase her car capacity enabling the *Mona's Queen* to be withdrawn in September 1990.

The politics of the merger years were complex In 1988 the IOM Government commissioned a consultants' report which led to the decision to sell its 8.15% holding in the company and to take control of the linkspans in Douglas Harbour. In 1990 Sea Containers attempted to take complete control of the company but were blocked by action in the Manx Parliament. Clearly there was unease at the prospect of control of the company being taken away from Douglas - but how free a hand did the board in Douglas actually have with the different interests of Sea Containers, the IOM Government and its independent shareholders to satisfy - whilst still trying to run a service for its customers? Fares were perceived to be high, passenger traffic continued to fall until 1992. The only area of growth was freight. In the mid 90s new labour deals were struck which reduced the company's wage bill by about £1 million. The concept of monopoly was unpopular yet there was not enough business for competition to be viable. Instead of taking control of both Douglas linkspans, the IOM Government built a third - and then required the removal of the original Steam Packet one! It then negotiated a "user agreement" giving the company a virtually guaranteed monopoly for 10 years - in return for some control over fares, guaranteed numbers of sailings and investment in new vessels. Hardly was the ink dry on the agreement when Sea Containers launched a second bid which resulted in them taking full control of the company and its substantial positive cash flow early in 1996.

An important issue in the early 1990s was that of fast ferries. Sea Containers saw this as the way forward and had been one of the first investors in such craft for carrying vehicles as well as passengers. Whilst a fast passage time was attractive the economics and weather vulnerability of such craft on Manx routes was questionable. A late decision was made to introduce the *SeaCat Isle of Man* in June 1994 but, although popular with passengers, she was not a financial

# CENTURY OF NORTH WEST EUROPEAN FERRIES 1900 - 2000

*The **Lady of Mann** leaves Douglas for Liverpool during the height of the TT season in 1996. (Miles Cowsill)*

success and her charter was not renewed for the 1996 season. The Board were however convinced that fast ferries had a future and plans to order a mono-hull fast ferry were well advanced when the company was taken over.

With the take-over it was hardly surprising that fast craft were re-introduced in 1997 but more surprising was the range of promotional fares introduced which helped growth in passenger and car numbers. Autumn services from Fleetwood to Dublin and Douglas were tried during the Blackpool lights season in 1996 and the *Lady of Mann* went on to re-open the Liverpool - Dublin passenger link the next year. In 1998 this route was taken over by Sea Containers' monohull fast ferry the *SuperSeaCat Two* which also provided a Liverpool - IOM weekend service in the autumn and spring whilst the smaller SeaCat was withdrawn. In summer 1998 the new build ro-pax *Ben-my-Chree* (6) was introduced on the Heysham run replacing both the *King Orry* and the *Peveril*. The vessel proved controversial, the Manx public being taken by surprise at the ship's limited passenger accommodation. Had the ship been built with greater and more spacious passenger capacity, and perhaps a slightly greater speed, public reaction might have been more favourable.

The combination of weather vulnerability of both the fast craft and the 'Ben' led to yet another Manx Government Select Committee being formed in Autumn 1998 to look into the adequacy of services being provided. Whilst the outcome of this enquiry was unknown at the time of writing, there is no doubt that fast ferry services combined with some promotional pricing have increased the market for travel to and from the Isle of Man at a time when there has also been growth in air travel. The benefits of a faster sea journey are widely welcomed despite the fact that the craft are more vulnerable to the weather conditions than the conventional ferries they replace.

*Dick Clague*

*The **King Orry** arrives at Douglas during her last season on the Irish Sea. (Miles Cowsill)*

# CENTURY OF NORTH WEST EUROPEAN FERRIES 1900 - 2000

## Sea Containers
## Irish Sea Operations

Sea Containers now has an extensive route network on the Irish Sea and the rapidity of their build-up owes much to the development of fast ferries and Sea Containers' commitment to them.

In 1991 whilst working as Director of Ports and Marketing for Clyde Port Authority I was asked by Sea Containers to rejoin them to head up and establish a fast ferry service between Northern Ireland and Scotland. Having been General Manager of Sealink Scotland when Sealink was owned by British Rail and having remained so whilst Sealink was owned by Sea Containers following the privatisation of the company in 1984, this challenge appealed to me. It was also attractive to me of course because Sea Containers had very much pioneered the introduction of car carrying fast catamarans. I believed that fast ferries would revolutionise ferry travel despite the scepticism we then faced. The Stranraer-Belfast SeaCat route was launched in 1992 and was the first car carrying fast ferry service on the Irish Sea. Today all the major ferry operators on the Irish Sea run fast ferries, whether catamarans, monohulls or semi-swaths.

*Hamish Ross*

### STEAM PACKET

Soon after rejoining Sea Containers I was appointed a non-Executive Director of the Isle of Man Steam Packet Company, in which Sea Containers was a major shareholder. In 1996, following the takeover of the Steam Packet by Sea Containers, I was appointed Managing Director of the Isle of Man Steam Packet Company. To me, having a sea going background, this was a great honour as I was very aware of the Steam Packet's history on the Irish Sea. The company had been formed in 1830 following local dissatisfaction with the quality of shipping services to the Island. To the best of our knowledge it is the oldest passenger shipping company in the world still trading under its original name.

Ever since its formation, the Company has played a vital role in the Island's development. Transport communications are of such importance to any island that it is not surprising that the Steam Packet has always had a high profile and has often stirred up strong emotions. Throughout the years it has been the subject of much debate and comments, not all of them complimentary. This remains so today. Everyone who works for the company however, whether ashore or afloat, is aware of the need to provide a good, frequent and reliable service to serve the Island efficiently. The Company in its long and proud history has come through many tough and turbulent times, not least during the wars when the Steam Packet's ships and people served with such distinction. It is also true to say that the Company was sometimes loath to move quickly and to accept new developments. An example of this was its failure to embrace the ro-ro concept for

*The SeaCat Isle of Man arrives at Douglas from Liverpool. The introduction of the InCat craft to the Isle of Man has reduced sea crossing times from the UK in recent years. (Dick Clague)*

148

# CENTURY OF NORTH WEST EUROPEAN FERRIES 1900 - 2000

The *Ben-my-Chree* operates twice a day to and from Heysham to the Isle of Man. *(Miles Cowsill)*

freight until long after it had been well proven elsewhere. Indeed it was not until under heavy pressure from a competitor that this step was finally taken in 1981.

## MODERNISATION

The Company today is here to serve a modern and very different Island. To do that the Steam Packet fleet has been modernised, operating a mix of conventional and fast ferry tonnage to meet the needs of both the freight and passenger market. The large ro-pax vessel *Ben-my-Chree*, built at the Van der Giessen Shipyard near Rotterdam, was delivered in 1998. At an overall length of just under one hundred and twenty five metres she is near the optimal size for the Douglas-Heysham operation. She has 1,200 lane metres of vehicle capacity and can carry up to 500 passengers. Her primary role is to provide a fast regular freight service with enough capacity to meet the Island's needs well into the new century. It is essential that the Isle of Man's economic development is in no way constrained by lack of shipping capacity. The freight side of our business is perhaps not as 'sexy' as the passenger side, but it impacts strongly on the day to day quality of life on the Island. Since her introduction the *Ben-my-Chree* has given a first class service to our freight customers in addition to providing vital secondary roles in the passenger side of our business. She is there to provide back up to our fast ferry service and to carry out a car and passenger carrying role at certain 'off peak' and 'shoulder' periods.

The fast ferry services which now operate the Steam Packet's English and Irish routes are there to carry out the core passenger and car carrying duties especially at times of peak demand. They have transformed the passenger business, reversing the decline of a few years ago. Our customers now want speed, especially the tourist sector, and the SeaCat and SuperSeaCat certainly provide just that. Liverpool, Belfast and Dublin are just over two and a half hours from Douglas by SeaCat, and only two hours from Heysham. Fast ferries bring countries closer together and create new reasons for travel. They are a fast, modern, exciting means of transport, allowing excellent craft utilisation and thus frequency of service. Amazingly enough there are now more sailings throughout the year to and from Douglas than ever before, even in the days of mass tourism to the Island.

## CHANGING TRENDS

The numbers of tourists and type of tourism which made the Isle of Man such a popular destination have gone forever, as with other British tourist resorts such as Bangor in Northern Ireland and Rothesay in Scotland. As exchange controls were loosened, and cheap holiday packages to Spain, Portugal and other sunny climes became widely available, people chose to holiday in what were then and are now seen as more exotic destinations. The Isle of Man today, however, offers a very different but excellent visitor product which can be sold virtually year-round. With strong destination marketing by the Tourism Department backed up by powerful marketing and sales campaigns by the air and surface carriers, visitor numbers to the Island are again on the increase. This has been helped by the Steam Packet's aggressive promotional fares which have stimulated travel throughout the year, especially at 'off peak' and 'shoulder' periods, developing the potential of the short break market. The introduction of fast ferries pulls the Island closer to its major tourism markets and allows a regular and frequent sailing schedule which is attractive to our customers.

The needs of special events on the Isle of Man, especially the TT, creates real difficulty in meeting the short sharp demand. The population of the Island increases by virtually 50% for this festival. In recent years vessels from Sea Containers' other Irish routes have been drafted in to ensure sufficient capacity. Again, in 1999, seven vessels were

149

# CENTURY OF NORTH WEST EUROPEAN FERRIES 1900 - 2000

The classic passenger ferry, the **Lady of Mann** is pictured sporting the company's new livery intoduced in 1999, as she arrives at Douglas from Heysham in August. *(Miles Cowsill)*

involved in Isle of Man services during the TT period. The *Lady of Mann*, a car carrying side loader built in 1976 and still going strong, plays an especially important role during the TT as she can carry upwards of 500 motor cycles. She remains a very fine and popular vessel and will be retained in the fleet for seasonal and TT work and also as fast ferry back up.

## FAST FERRIES

Fast ferries will play an increasingly important role in building-up passenger numbers to the Island. These craft have come a very long way in a very short time and are revolutionising ferry travel in the Irish Sea. Including the Isle of Man services, Sea Containers now has an extensive network of fast ferry routes on the Irish Sea. In 1999 SeaCo had three SeaCats and one SuperSeaCat serving its Irish Sea routes. These fast, exciting craft have enabled us to look again at possible new routes or indeed the restoration of old historic links which had been discontinued. In 1998 we re-established a city centre to city centre Liverpool-Dublin service with a SuperSeaCat, and in 1999 the Belfast-Heysham route was restarted by a SeaCat. A new SeaCat service between Belfast and Troon was launched in 1999.

Fast ferry design and technology is still at a relatively youthful age. Lively debate continues as to the best type of designs; the most suitable construction materials – aluminium, high tensile steel, composites etc; and the best type of propulsion – diesel, gas turbine, a mix of both.

As fast ferries become more efficient, robust, comfortable, reliable and economical, we will be able to consider a much wider range of route options. We in Sea Containers are proud of the pioneering role we have played in the development of fast ferries. The speed of improvements in fast ferry technology allows us to have an exciting vision of the future of ferry travel around this coast.

*Hamish Ross*
Managing Director
Sea Containers Irish Sea Operations

The **SuperSeaCat Three** currently maintains the Liverpool-Dublin high-speed service. *(Miles Cowsill)*

150

# man's lifeline
## FOR THE PAST 170 YEARS

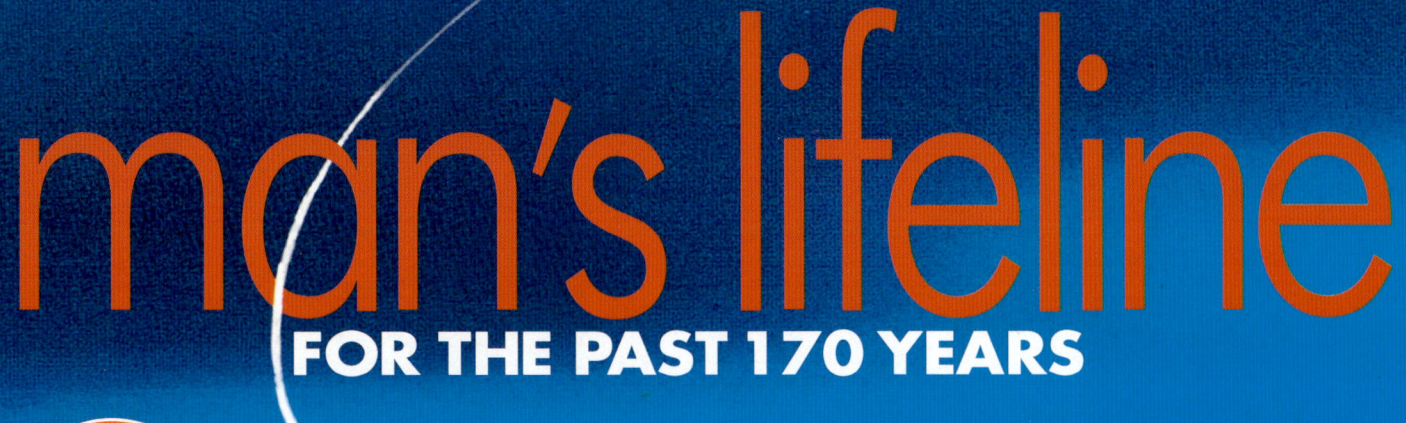

The Isle of Man Steam Packet Company is one of the oldest registered shipping lines in the world, with a proud history spanning 170 years of continuous operation.

The company was founded in 1830 on the principles of providing a first class, reliable and value for money passenger and freight service to the Isle of Man. The company's current owners, Sea Containers, are continuing to build on this sound foundation by investing in the company's fleet. This investment means that todays passengers enjoy the speed and comforts of the sleekest fastcraft, whilst a new multi-purpose ro-pax vessel reflects the company's ongoing commitment to provide an efficient passenger and freight service for the new Millennium.

For further details of the Steam Packet Company's passenger services, please call Central Reservations,   Tel 08705 523 523.
For details of the company's freight services,   Tel 01624 645 6210.

ISLE OF MAN STEAM PACKET COMPANY   IMPERIAL BUILDINGS   DOUGLAS   ISLE OF MAN   IM1 2BY

# CENTURY OF NORTH WEST EUROPEAN FERRIES 1900 - 2000

# Scottish Waters

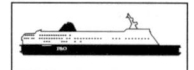

A land surrounded on three sides by water, with a myriad of offshore islands, Scotland is a proud maritime nation. Today, these islands are served by fleets of modern roll on – roll off ferries, which provide essential lifeline services throughout the year and in all weathers. Their story is a fascinating one, which has its roots in the very origins of steam navigation itself.

The paddle steamer *Waverley* underway on the Clyde in 1999. *(Colin J. Smith)*

## LET GLASGOW FLOURISH

With over 30 shipyards along its length and with ferries, coastal steamers, cargo ships and ocean liners departing for all parts of the world, the River Clyde and the City of Glasgow were at the height of their Victorian power at the dawning of the 20th century. Added to their maritime industries, the nearby locomotive works, steelworks, foundries and coalfields meant that Glasgow and the West of Scotland were rightly known as the Workshop of the British Empire.

Glasgow's populace demanded respite from their daily tasks and the coasts of the Firth of Clyde provided it. The wealthy built mansions at Highland clachans such as Tighnabruaich, Kirn, Innellan, Port Bannatyne and Craigmore, turning them into genteel watering holes, whilst the working classes took lodgings in towns such as Rothesay, Dunoon and Millport, transforming them into bustling holiday resorts. Day-trippers discovered the Coast and a sail "Doon the Watter" became a favourite excursion for West of Scotland families in summer months. It had all started in 1812 when Henry Bell's paddle steamer *Comet*, the world's first commercial steamboat, threaded its way from Glasgow to Helensburgh. In the early 19th Century sailing "all the way" from the heart of Glasgow was the most convenient way to reach one's intended resort. But the River Clyde was little more than an open sewer, whilst the reckless exploits of steamship owner/captains who raced each other for piers led to trippers avoiding such practices as railways began to snake out from the city to the coastal resorts via new railheads. Throughout the late 19th century, the passenger traffic moved from the long and unhygienic steamer sailings from the Broomielaw, to services linking the steamer journey with a train connection through a railhead. The multitude of private steamer companies gave way to the railway owned fleets and the final two decades of the 19th Century witnessed the three deadly Scottish railway rivals build their own comfortable and fast steamers, giving passengers vastly improved conditions compared with those provided by the small operators. Only the railways, with their huge financial resources, could provide the quantum leap in comfort and service provision that took place in those years.

## THE FAMOUS CLYDE STEAMERS

The North British Railway (NB) served the towns of Dumbarton, Balloch and Helensburgh from Glasgow's Queen Street Station. Since 1866, they had provided steamer services of sorts from Helensburgh Pier but in 1882, the company opened an impressive two-armed pier, nicknamed "the station in the sea", at nearby Craigendoran, from where its new steamers with their red and black funnels with narrow white band sailed for the coastal towns and villages. With names drawn from the works of Sir Walter Scott, the *Guy Mannering*, ex *Sheila* of 1877, *Jeanie Deans* (1884), *Diana Vernon* (1885), *Lucy Ashton* (1888), *Talisman* (1896), *Kenilworth* (1898), the magnificent *Waverley* (1899), and their fleet mates served the Upper Firth of Clyde well into the 20th century. In 1899, the NB and its Caledonian rival entered into joint operation of the Dumbarton – Balloch railway and together the two companies operated the Loch Lomond paddlers *Princess May* and *Prince George* of 1898.

Until 1889, the NB's rival, the Caledonian Railway, had made arrangements with private steamer companies to serve Greenock's Custom House Quay in connection with train services from Glasgow. Spurred on by the North British push to the coast, the Caley established a steamship subsidiary in 1889 and its railway pushed westwards to an impressive new steamer terminal at Gourock Pier. From here, train services connected with the steamers of the new Caledonian Steam Packet Company with their first ships *Meg Merrilies* (1883) and *Madge Wildfire* (1886) soon being joined by the *Caledonia*, and *Galatea* of 1889 and the *Marchioness of Breadalbane*, and *Marchioness of Bute* in 1890. Others followed, including the *Marchioness of Lorne* of 1891 and the "Duchesses" of "Rothesay" (1895), "Montrose" (1902) and "Fife" (1903). In 1865, the Caledonian Railway had begun rail services to Wemyss Bay, connecting with the steamers of the Wemyss Bay Steamboat Company but the CSP took over the

The pioneer turbine steamer *King Edward* at speed in the Firth of Clyde. *(Clyde River Steamer Club)*

152

# CENTURY OF NORTH WEST EUROPEAN FERRIES 1900 - 2000

The MacBrayne flagship *Columba* of 1878 arriving at Dunoon. *(Clyde River Steamer Club)*

sailings in 1890, placing the new "Marchionesses" on the Millport and Rothesay routes. Also in 1890, the Caledonian Railway opened a new route to Ardrossan (Montgomerie Pier) placing the Denny built paddler *Duchess of Hamilton* on the Arran sailing in competition to the outdated *Scotia*. The *Ivanhoe*, introduced by the Firth of Clyde Steam Packet Company in 1880 to offer respite from the habit of excessive on board liquor consumption through operating "on teetotal lines", joined the CSP fleet in 1897 and suffered the ignominy of having bars installed. The dominance of the Caley was complete.

The third railway giant soon responded. In 1891, the Glasgow & South Western Railway began to operate steamers from their Princes Pier terminal at Greenock, linking with trains to the coast originating at St. Enoch Station in Glasgow. Initially, the GSWR acquired several ships from other owners, placing the *Chancellor* (1880), the *Viceroy* (1875) and the *Marquis of Bute* (1868) on routes from Princes Pier and Fairlie whilst taking over operation of the *Scotia* on the Arran run from Ardrossan (Winton Pier). But a new fleet of crack paddle steamers soon arrived, including a worthy competitor to the CSP in the shape of the great *Glen Sannox* of 1892, which challenged the *Duchess of Hamilton* for supremacy on the Arran services. The other new ships bore the names of Roman deities – *Neptune* (1892), *Mercury* (1892), *Minerva* (1893), and the exception, the *Glen Rosa* of 1893 whilst the *Jupiter* (1896), the mighty *Juno* (1898) the little *Mars* of 1902 and the second hand *Vulcan*, formerly the *Kylemore* of 1897, completed the line-up. The scene was set for many years of glorious competition on the Firth of Clyde.

Other operators competed strongly. David MacBrayne had operated his steamers since 1879. The successor to the Hutcheson Company of 1851, David MacBrayne Ltd. was established in 1907 when control passed to his sons. They operated on the "Royal Route" from Glasgow to Tarbert (Loch Fyne) and Ardrishaig, so called because of a passage made by Queen Victoria in 1847. At the turn of the century, this illustrious route, the privilege of the landed gentry, was in the hands of the great *Columba* of 1878 and *Iona* (1864) in summer, or the *Grenadier* (1885) at other times of the year. Overshadowed only by the *Columba* in prestige, the second *Lord of the Isles* (1891) performed the long trip from Glasgow to Inveraray every day. Captain John Williamson continued to run his fleet, including the ancient *Benmore* of 1876 and the *Strathmore* (1897), whilst Buchanan Steamers operated the *Isle of Arran* (1892), *Isle of Bute* (1877) and *Vivid* (1864), with her steeple engine. The *Isle of Cumbrae*, formerly the NB *Jeanie Deans*, joined Buchanan's fleet in 1904 and from 1908, the *Kylemore*, complete with her cattle ramp, joined the Williamson company. Finally, the Campbeltown and Glasgow Company Joint Stock Company linked the city with the furthest flung town on the Clyde, using the passenger and goods steamers *Davaar* (1885), *Kintyre* (1868) and *Kinloch* (1878). The steamers carried Glaswegians from all walks of life and a class-ridden society was reflected in the hierarchy of the ships themselves. The "Tourist Steamers", designed and built for Victorian aristocracy, served the burgeoning demand from Highland estate owners to welcome their well-heeled guests in style. At the other end of the spectrum, the Glasgow boats retained a reputation for raucous crowds on day trips. These cheaper, slower ships were attractive to those who still desired to sail from the heart of Glasgow, whilst the more genteel railway steamers carried well-behaved middle class families to their destinations.

At the turn of the century, there were 43 passenger steamers in service on the Firth of Clyde. In winter months, the population of the islands of Bute and Cumbrae was 18,700 whilst in summer it rocketed to over 80,000. The Sabbath remained sacrosanct even though the late 19th century had seen the occasional "Sunday breaker" seek to beat the tranquillity of the day by landing crowds of intoxicated passengers at various piers with the resulting fracas often meriting press coverage in national newspapers. Racing between steamers was still common, but the habit had become

# CENTURY OF NORTH WEST EUROPEAN FERRIES 1900 - 2000

The elegant **Queen Mary II** proceeds past Port Glasgow on a summer evening in 1967 *(Colin J. Smith Collection)*

less widespread than in the 1860s, although the stakes remained high. Duplication of services was the norm and the sight of the "five o' clock racers" ploughing the waters of the Firth as one steamer from each of the railheads thundered towards Dunoon was a sight to behold. Oh yes, the Clyde was a wonderful place to be at the turn of the century.

In 1901, having produced the *Comet* almost a century earlier, the Clyde gave the world another technological leap. A syndicate comprised of Captain John Williamson, Denny Shipbuilders of Dumbarton and Parsons Marine Steam Turbine Co. of Wallsend, placed a revolutionary vessel into service on the Greenock - Fairlie - Campbeltown route. The *King Edward* was the first commercial ship in the world to be powered by steam turbines and she was an instant success. Followed in 1902 by the larger *Queen Alexandra*, the two ships, owned by Turbine Steamers Limited, were prototypes for all subsequent turbine powered passenger ships built anywhere in the world. In 1906 the Caledonian Steam Packet placed a third turbine steamer, the *Duchess of Argyll* into service, but the G&SWR offering, the *Atalanta*, also of 1906, was a little disappointing, although she was a test bed for the Cunarder *Carmania*, then under construction at Clydebank. The new NB steamer of the first decade was not a turbine steamer, but a smart little paddle steamer, the *Marmion* of 1906.

Throughout the first decade of the 20th century, the companies competed wastefully. It was clear that extravagant competition could no longer be sustained and in 1907, the CSP and the GSWR established a pooling arrangement which would last for twenty years. To avoid mounting costs and wasteful competition, duplication on services was eliminated and the two companies shared service provision throughout the Firth. Some ships left the joint fleet, whilst others were laid up. Two new steamers appeared for private owners, the *Eagle III* in 1910 for Buchanan Steamers and the *Queen-Empress* for Williamson in 1912. The NB's *Prince Edward* arrived on Loch Lomond in 1911 and Turbine Steamers Ltd. built a new *Queen Alexandra* in 1912 to replace her namesake, which was sold to the Canadian Pacific Railway. The "Queen" was the last newbuild of the golden age of the Clyde steamers.

In 1914, the clouds of the Great War rolled over the Firth of Clyde. When they cleared, the zenith of the Clyde steamers had passed and it was a tired and ageing fleet which revived sailings in 1919. The CSP had lost the mighty *Duchess of Hamilton* and the *Duchess of Montrose* whilst the GSWR lost the *Neptune*, *Minerva* and *Mars*. The *Glen Sannox* had been returned to the Clyde in 1915, deemed to be unsuitable for use as a minesweeper. The NB lost the new *Fair Maid*, requisitioned in 1916 and destined never to see peacetime service, whilst the Turbine Steamers fleet returned unscathed, as did those of the Williamson and Buchanan companies, which merged in 1919.

Four years later, the CSP and GSWR fleets merged under the auspices of the London. Midland and Scottish Railway Company and red, yellow and black funnels appeared, giving way only two years later to the familiar yellow and black top of recent years. The *Glen Sannox* was replaced by a turbine steamer of the same name in 1925 and the remaining GSWR steamers disappeared by 1939. Meanwhile the *Lord of the Isles* was broken up in 1928 and MacBraynes' *Columba* bade farewell in 1935, whilst 1926 saw the arrival of a new ship for the C&G, the *Dalriada*, replacing the graceful *Kinloch*. Williamson Buchanan and Turbine Steamers Ltd. were acquired by the LMS in 1935 although their ships, by now joined by the turbine steamer *Queen Mary II* of 1933, remained in their distinctive white funneled livery. The *King George V* and the *Queen Alexandra* transferred to MacBraynes,

# CENTURY OF NORTH WEST EUROPEAN FERRIES 1900 - 2000

whilst new railway steamers appeared, including the turbine steamers *Duchess of Montrose* (1930), her quasi-sister ship, the *Duchess of Hamilton* (1932), the four CSP/LMS ferry paddlers *Caledonia* and *Mercury* (1934) and *Jupiter* and *Juno* (1937). The London and North Eastern Railway Company, successors to the NBR in 1923, placed into service the much loved paddler *Jeanie Deans* in 1931 and followed up with the diesel electric paddler *Talisman* in 1935. In the same year, the CSP added the Holy Loch steamer *Marchioness of Lorne* and 1936 saw the turbine powered, but paddle steamer profiled *Marchioness of Graham* join the CSP fleet. Old favourites remained, with the *Duchess of Fife*, *Duchess of Rothesay*, *Kenilworth*, and *Lucy Ashton* plodding onwards. However, wartime loomed again. Further casualties ensued, with the loss, amongst others, of two of the four 1930s paddlers, the *Mercury* and the *Juno*, and the *Waverley* of 1899 whilst the *Duchess of Rothesay*, *Queen-Empress* and *Eagle III* were scrapped in 1946. A new *Waverley*, the last Clyde paddle steamer, was built in 1947 and the following year witnessed the absorption of the LNER fleet into that of British Railways. The post-war era would see the end of the remaining old favourites and even of most of their younger consorts.

## THE DECLINE OF THE STEAMERS

The world emerged from War in 1945 a changed place. On the Clyde, the steamers were soon at work again but change was at hand. Although the *Maid of the Loch* appeared on Loch Lomond in 1953, she was the last large paddle steamer to be built in Britain. The era of the steamship was now drawing to a close and the nineteen fifties saw the introduction of seven new diesel powered ferries - four passenger vessels, the *Maid of Ashton*, "Argyll", "Skelmorlie" and "Cumbrae" and three car ferries, the *Arran*, *Bute* and *Cowal*, - to service the anticipated future demand for passenger and car carrying. But the growth in car traffic had been underestimated and 1957 saw the arrival of a fourth and larger car ferry, the third *Glen Sannox*, to serve the Arran route. The arrival of these new ships heralded the end for the *Duchess of Fife*, *Jupiter* and others and also for smaller piers around the coast, as the motor car began to offer more convenient access to outlying communities.

The sixties saw further reduction in the steamer fleet, with the departure of the *Jeanie Deans* and the *Duchess of Montrose* in 1964 whilst 1969 and 1970 saw the *Caledonia* and the *Duchess of Hamilton* leave the fleet, with the *Queen Mary II* and the *Waverley* remaining as the last Clyde excursion steamers. Only the former Thames ferry *Keppel* (ex *Rose*), a small Voith Schneider powered passenger ferry, entered Clyde service, replacing the Millport paddler *Talisman* in 1967. The Scottish Transport Group was established in 1969, taking over all of the ferry and shipping services on the West Coast. Their influence was to prove fundamental in sweeping Scottish ferry services into a new era in which the steamship had no place and car ferries reigned supreme, whilst the Clyde and West Highland shipping services would now share a common story. STG intentions were apparent when a new *Caledonia*, formerly the *Stena Baltica*, took up service on the Arran route in 1970, becoming the Clyde's first drive through ferry.

## THE MACBRAYNE STORY

West of the Kintyre peninsula, which separates the Firth of Clyde from the Atlantic Ocean, lie the Hebrides, dominion of David MacBrayne Ltd. In 1851, David Hutcheson & Co. took

The paddle steamer **Caledonia** (1934) arriving at Rothesay. *(Clyde River Steamer Club)*

155

# CENTURY OF NORTH WEST EUROPEAN FERRIES 1900 - 2000

over the trade of Messrs Burns, with David MacBrayne as a partner and owner from 1879. The first steamer to appear in the Highlands had been the *Comet* in 1819, which operated from Glasgow to Fort William via the Crinan Canal. In 1847 Queen Victoria visited the Highlands and started the tourism boom. With the opening of railways to Oban, Fort William, Kyle of Lochalsh and Mallaig, MacBraynes provided links to the islands with their fleet of steamers. Vessels such as the *Columba* (1878), *Iona* (1864), *Chevalier* (1866), *Grenadier* (1885) and *Fusilier* (1888) provided the mainline passenger services, linking the major ports of call all the way from Glasgow to Inverness via the Caledonian Canal and offering excursion sailings to Iona and other destinations from Oban. Mail services were provided from railheads to Islay, Mull, Lewis, Skye and the Outer Isles by vessels such as the *Lochness* (1853), *Lovedale* (1867), *Staffa* (1861), *Fingal* (1877) and the veteran *Glencoe* of 1846, whilst the *Glengarry* (1844), *Lochness* (1853) and the *Gondolier* (1866) operated on the Caledonian Canal. In addition, the crack "all the way" steamers such as the *Clansman* (1870), and *Claymore* (1881), and smaller cargo ships such as the *Cavalier* (1883), *Handa* (1878) and *Ethel* (1880) sailed from Glasgow to Stornoway, Inverness, Islay and remote mainland communities. Early in the 20th century, new ships appeared, including the neat little *Lapwing* (1903), the *Plover* and *Cygnet* of 1904 and the *Sheila*, also of 1904, which became the much-loved Stornoway mailboat. In 1907, the magnificent *Chieftain* joined the fleet although her career was short and, as we shall find out, her future lay elsewhere. In 1908, the utilitarian *Lochinvar* arrived whilst two attractive paddlers, the *Pioneer* and the *Mountaineer* appeared in 1905 and 1910 respectively. The Great War saw many MacBrayne ships requisitioned or operate on the Clyde under charter. Losses included the *Dirk* (1909) and the *Lochiel* (1908) whilst 1927 saw the loss of the *Grenadier*, *Chevalier* and *Sheila*, in unhappy circumstances. In 1928, the LMS and Coast Lines acquired the ailing Company and new ships soon appeared. The imposing *Lochness* took up service on the Stornoway route in 1929, followed by the *Lochearn* and *Lochmor* of 1930, *Lochfyne* (1931), *Lochnevis* (1934), and the Islay mailboat *Lochiel* (1939). In 1935, the Clyde turbine steamers *King George V* and *Queen Alexandra* joined the fleet; the latter becoming the three funneled *Saint Columba*, successor to the great *Columba*. World War 2 saw only one loss, namely the sumptuous *Lochgarry*, formerly Burns' *Vulture* (1898), which joined the fleet in 1937. Post War, the fleet expanded again with the arrival of the *Loch Seaforth* in 1947, the second *Claymore* in 1955 and further cargo ships, although the *Saint Columba* was scrapped in 1958.

From 1960 the *Loch Arkaig* operated from Mallaig, but the focus was now moving towards the provision of car ferries to service burgeoning demand. The construction of the *Hebrides*, *Clansman* and *Columba* in 1964 heralded the dawn of the new age in the West Highlands. Further car ferry provision was slow, allowing a private sector competitor, Western Ferries Ltd to provide the first drive-through service in the West

Caledonian MacBrayne ferry ***Caledonia*** approaching Ardrossan Harbour. *(Roy Pedersen)*

The CSP car ferry ***Glen Sannox*** of 1957 arriving at Brodick. *(Aikman Smith Collection)*

# CENTURY OF NORTH WEST EUROPEAN FERRIES 1900 - 2000

Caledonian MacBrayne ferry *Isle of Arran* of 1984 departs from Oban in 1997. *(Colin J. Smith)*

Highlands with the *Sound of Islay* (1968) and the larger *Sound of Jura* (1969) based at Kennacraig. In 1969 MacBraynes came under the auspices of the Scottish Transport Group and their new ship, the *Iona* of 1970, took up service on the Clyde, rather than in the West Highlands as had been originally planned. The emergence of the STG also witnessed the end of many of the older vessels and soon the famous "Lochs" of the 1930s sailed for the breakers yards.

Another company, McCallum Orme operated a West Highland fleet which had been brought together under one flag in 1929 through amalgamation and included the *Hebrides* of 1898 and the *Dunara Castle* of 1875. It was the latter, which introduced tourists to remote St., Kilda in 1877 and assisted HMS *Harebell* in evacuating the remaining residents of the island, at their own request, in August 1930. McCallum Orme did not last much beyond the Second World War, the company being subsumed into MacBraynes in 1948, adding the *Hebrides* and *Dunara Castle* to their fleet.

## MODERNISATION AND AMALGAMATION

The continuing trend towards car ferries and shorter crossings stepped up a gear with the formation of Caledonian MacBrayne in January 1973. Effectively the CSP renamed, the new organisation took over all Clyde and West Highland sailings with the exception of routes dependant upon subsidy. A new livery was introduced and applied to all of the company's vessels. 1974 was a momentous year for the joint fleet with the twin car ferries *Jupiter* and *Juno* appearing on the Clyde whilst the *Pioneer* and the *Suilven*, the company's largest

The *Maid of Cumbrae* berthed at Tighnabruaich Pier in the Kyles of Bute. *(Harold Sinclair)*

MacBrayne's *Claymore* of 1955 arriving at Lochboisdale. *(Aikman Smith collection)*

157

# CENTURY OF NORTH WEST EUROPEAN FERRIES 1900 - 2000

The *Iona* in her last season approches Armadale in blustery weather from Mallaig. *(Miles Cowsill)*

vessel at that time, entered service on the Islay and Stornoway routes respectively. Old favourites left the fleet, with the departure of the *King George V* in 1974, and the *Queen Mary* in 1977, whilst the Paddle Steamer Preservation Society returned the *Waverley*, by now the world's last seagoing paddle steamer, to active service in 1975, following the gifting of the ship by Caledonian MacBrayne.

In 1973, Western Ferries opened a new Clyde car ferry service between McInroy's Point and Hunter's Quay, using former Swedish vessels renamed *Sound of Shuna* (1962) and *Sound of Scarba* (1960). The *Sound of Sanda* was added in 1974 followed by the catamaran *Highland Seabird* on the Clyde in 1976. However, the vessel was uneconomic and following a further year of Clyde service, she found various tasks in West Highland waters, sailing out of Oban in summer until 1981. On the Islay routes, the arrival of new Caledonian MacBrayne ships led to Western Ferries withdrawing from Kennacraig in September 1981. Their performance on the Clyde, by contrast, was encouraging and Western Ferries (Clyde) Ltd introduced a succession of second hand vessels, namely the *Sound of Sleat* (1988), *Sound of Seil* (1986), *Sound of Scalpay* (1995) and a second *Sound of Sanda* (1996).

Caledonian MacBrayne introduced eight small bow loading ferries, the *Kilbrannan*, *Morvern*, *Eigg*, *Rhum*, *Canna*, *Raasay*, *Coll* and *Bruernish*, on short crossings throughout the west coast, between 1972 and 1976. They rapidly developed traffic on these new routes and their success merited their replacement by a new class of double ended "Loch" ferries, the first to arrive being the *Loch Striven*, *Loch Riddon*, *Loch Ranza* and *Loch Linnhe* in 1986. This class has been modified and developed for further short routes, with the most recent being the *Loch Alainn* in 1997. Only four of the "Island Class", as the bow loaders became known, remained in service as the century drew to its close, these being the *Canna*, *Eigg*, *Raasay* and *Bruernish*.

1978 saw the introduction of the *Saturn* on the Clyde, whilst 1979 saw the appearance of the new Small Isles passenger ferry *Lochmor*. The third *Claymore* was introduced on the Outer Isles sailings from Oban in 1979 and it was this ship, which opened the Campbeltown – Ballycastle service in 1997, being operated by the Argyll & Antrim Steam Packet Co. On Loch Lomond, the last Caledonian MacBrayne steamship, the *Maid of the Loch* was sold in 1981. By this time, the original Clyde car ferries had been replaced although the *Glen Sannox* continued to operate year round on Clyde and West Highland services. 1984 saw the introduction of the new Arran ferry *Isle of Arran* replacing the *Clansman*, which had been converted to drive through configuration in 1973. New vessels introduced high standards of passenger comfort and increased vehicular capacity throughout the fleet as the *Hebridean Isles* (1986), the *Isle of Mull* (1987), and the *Lord of the Isles* (1989), replaced the *Caledonia*, *Hebrides* and *Columba*, which became the cruise ship *Hebridean Princess*. The nineties have continued in that vein, with the *Caledonian Isles* the largest ferry ever to sail on the Clyde, arriving in 1993, whilst the *Isle of Lewis*, the largest ship currently in the fleet, took up the Stornoway sailings in 1995. Further "Loch" class vessels have taken up service on shorter routes whilst introducing new short crossings. The Kyleakin – Kyle of Lochalsh Skye ferry crossing, an outpost of the CSP network for many years, was inherited by Caledonian MacBrayne in 1973 and 1981 saw the placing into service of the *Loch Fyne* and the *Loch Dunvegan*, the last car ferries to operate on the crossing prior to opening of the Skye Bridge in 1995. The most recent addition to the fleet, the *Clansman* of 1998, sets the pattern for the future, with a near sister, the *Hebrides*, due for delivery in Autumn of 2000 whilst a new *Lochnevis*, replacement for the *Lochmor*, will be the first new ship of the 21st century.

Meanwhile, the paddle steamer lives on. The habits of the

# CENTURY OF NORTH WEST EUROPEAN FERRIES 1900 - 2000

travelling public have come a long way since paddlers raced each other on summer excursions or maintained essential services throughout the year. Yet the *Waverley* continues to offer something of the romance of that more spacious era, whilst great strides are now being made to secure the future of that other old favourite, the *Maid of the Loch* on Loch Lomond.

## EASTERN ECHOES

Scotland's capital city also has a proud maritime past. As a haven for the legal and financial wizards who frequented the elegant New Town of Edinburgh, the breezy coasts of Fife and East Lothian offered relaxation and bracing air. Several companies operated pleasure sailings to the resorts of the Firth of Forth including North Berwick, Aberdour and Anstruther. Foremost amongst these was the Galloway Saloon Steam Packet Company, established in 1856. The company operated from the Isle of May and North Berwick in the East, all the way up the "Windings" to Stirling and Alloa in the west. By the turn of the century, Galloway operated the paddlers *Wemyss Castle* (1891), and the *Stirling Castle* and *Tantallon Castle*, both built in 1899, although they departed in 1907 and 1901 respectively. From 1906, for two short years the company operated the screw steamer *Roslin Castle*, replacing her with the former Clyde paddler *Redgauntlet*. In 1892 the company had come under the control of the NBR, who ensured that it did not compete with their railway services, and indeed, the excursion business did not continue beyond 1914 when the outbreak of war forced them to cease operations. Thanks to the development of rail and motor coach services, the Forth excursion trade was declining and although the twenties and thirties saw the arrival of the NBR Clyde paddler *Fair Maid*, (ex *Madge Wildfire*), and MacBrayne's *Fusilier*, only small vessels such as *The Second Snark* and the *Royal Forth Lady* continued to provide excursions following World War 2, a tradition continued today by the *Maid of the Forth* and the *May Princess*.

A ferry service had operated between Granton and Burntisland since 1844, offering train connections and employing a sizeable fleet of vessels including the *Auld Reekie*, *Thane of Fife*, *Forth* and *Express*, in addition to five cargo boats. They were joined in 1879 by the *William Muir*, which had the dubious honour of carrying passengers across the Forth who were destined to meet their end in the Tay Bridge disaster of 1879. The opening of the Forth Bridge in 1890 reduced the Burntisland service to only one ship, the *William Muir*.

The **Clansman** leaving Oban for the Outer Isles. *(Colin J. Smith)*

Another *Thane of Fife* replaced her in 1937 and in spite of attempts to develop a car ferry service, the crossing closed in December 1952. Attempts to revive the route in 1991 employed a catamaran named *Spirit of Fife*, but the service lasted less than two years. Since ancient times, the villages of North and South Queensferry were linked by the "Queensferry Passage", and in 1913, the NBR took over the crossing. In 1934, the operation of the service was leased to Denny of Dumbarton who built two new double-ended paddle ferries, the *Queen Margaret* and the *Robert the Bruce* each capable of carrying 28 cars. A third ship, the *Mary Queen of Scots* joined them in 1950 and a fourth, the *Sir William Wallace* arrived in 1956. Together, they operated the service until the Forth Road Bridge was opened in September 1964. Today, the cruise vessel *Maid of the Forth* has revived the ferry crossing in summer months.

On the Firth of Tay, "Juteopolis", namely the City of Dundee, was a thriving industrial centre linked to the dormitory towns of North East Fife by passenger and vehicle ferries, forever remembered as the "Fifies". They operated from Craig Harbour in Dundee to Newport-on-Tay and with motor vehicle traffic increasing rapidly, the main incumbents of the route became the paddler *Sir William High* of 1924 and the *B.L. Nairn* of 1929. In 1939, Dundee Harbour Trust added the Voith-Schneider powered *Abercraig* and in 1951, a near sister, the *Scotscraig* was introduced. However, upon the opening of the Tay Road Bridge in August 1966, the "Craigs" sailed for Malta whilst the *B.L. Nairn* was scrapped. Their landing place at Craig Harbour is now home to another famous ship, Captain Scott's *RRS Discovery*.

## NORTHWARDS BY SEA

The North of Scotland, Orkney and Shetland Steam Packet Company will be forever known as the "North Company". Their black funneled ships were based at Aberdeen and Leith and operated the main services to the Orkney and Shetland Islands. Steamship services to Kirkwall and Lerwick commenced in 1833, with the *Velocity* serving Kirkwall and the *Sovereign* opening the Lerwick service in 1836. The Scrabster – Stromness route was inaugurated in 1856 by the *Royal Mail*, and from 1865, a screw steamer, the *Express* served the route. She was replaced in 1877 by the *John o' Groats*, whilst in 1882 the North Company took over the route and introduced the first *St. Ola* in 1892. In addition to serving Orkney and Shetland, the North Company operated to Caithness, Fraserburgh, Loch Eriboll and as far west as Stornoway. But as new roads linked mainland communities to the major population centres, the North Company gradually withdrew the coastal routes until by 1956, the Northern Isles were the sole recipients of calls. The early years of the century saw the company construct several new ships, including the *St. Giles* (1903) and the *St. Rognvald* (1901) and by the outbreak of World War 1, the fleet was comprised of eight vessels. Three were lost during wartime, namely the *St. Margaret* of 1913, which was torpedoed in 1917 whilst on passage from Lerwick to the Faroe Islands, the *Express* (1869) and the *St. Magnus* (II) of 1912. The acquisition of replacement ships saw the North Company return to peacetime with nine steamers including the *St. Sunniva* (1887), which stranded on Mousa in 1930. The *St. Catherine*, formerly the *Olive* of 1893, replaced her. Four of these ships were mainline steamers although their elderly status necessitated the building of further new ships. The first was the *St. Magnus* (III) of 1924. The *St. Clement* (I)

# CENTURY OF NORTH WEST EUROPEAN FERRIES 1900 - 2000

P&O Scottish Ferries' vessel **St. Clair** leaving Aberdeen in August 1999. *(Colin J. Smith)*

arrived in 1928 and the second *St. Sunniva*, a steamer of clipper like appearance, was built in 1931, whilst the veteran *St. Clair* of 1868 remained as a reminder of the Victorian era until 1937 when the second ship of the name replaced her. Of similar appearance to the *St. Sunniva*, the *St. Margaret* was formerly MacBraynes' *Chieftain* and served the North Company from 1919 until 1925. Another MacBrayne vessel, the *Cavalier* (1883), was also acquired in 1919, becoming the *Fetlar* for a short time.

Black funnels gave way to yellow around 1937 and World War 2 proved costly. The *St. Sunniva* was lost during convoy duties in 1943 and other losses were the *St. Clement* and the cargo vessel *St. Fergus* of 1913. Only the *St. Magnus*, the first *St. Ninian* (1895) and the *St. Rognvald* (1901) of the pre-war fleet remained. Post World War 2, the North Company built a fleet of new ships including the *St. Ninian* of 1950 and their largest ever passenger vessel, the *St. Clair* of 1960. Upon the arrival of the latter, the second *St. Clair* became the *St. Magnus* (IV), the previous ship of that name being broken up in 1960. New cargo ships arrived in the shape of another *St. Clement* and a third *St. Rognvald* whilst the last of the North Company passenger steamships, the *St. Magnus* (IV), departed for the breakers in 1967. But changes were in the air. In 1961, the North Company became a subsidiary of Coast Lines and, in turn, of P&O Ferries in 1971. Yellow funnels gave way to blue in 1975 and car ferries replaced passenger ships as the third *St. Ola* and the fourth *St. Clair* appeared on the Orkney and Shetland services respectively. In 1971, the last scheduled passenger and cargo sailing was made from Leith and the company concentrated services on Scrabster and Aberdeen. But with the North Sea oil boom, there arrived the need to provide improved roll on-roll off freight services. The company provided a dedicated freight operation using the *rof Beaver*, followed by the freight ferry *St. Magnus* and subsequently a new *St. Rognvald*, formerly *Marino Torre*, which took up service in 1989. From 1975, the company again used Leith, serving Sullom Voe in addition to Lerwick, but the link was severed for a second time in 1990. Meanwhile, the third *St. Sunniva*, a passenger and car ferry, formerly Normandy Ferries *nf Panther*, joined them in 1986 and reintroduced the indirect link with Shetland, sailing from Aberdeen via Stromness to Lerwick. The company name was changed to "P&O Scottish Ferries" in 1989 and in 1992 a new *St. Ola* (IV) and a larger *St. Clair* (V) joined the fleet. Today, four passenger and cargo ships serve Stromness, Kirkwall and Lerwick from the mainland ports of Scrabster and Aberdeen.

The second *Orcadia* operated inter-island services in Orkney at the turn of the century, but she was superseded upon the arrival of two new steamers, the *Earl Thorfinn* (1928) and the *Earl Sigurd* (1931). Like the *Orcadia*, they were owned by the Orkney Steam Navigation Co. 1961 saw the introduction of a new diesel powered passenger and cargo ship, the third *Orcadia* and a cargo ship, the *Islander*, appeared in 1969. With their introduction, the Orkney Islands Shipping Company was born to replace its predecessor and, in the seventies and eighties, this company introduced roll on-roll off ferries on inter island crossings. These services were introduced in 1983 in the South Isles, by the *Lyrawa Bay* (1976), and developed by the third *Hoy Head* in 1986 and the fourth in 1994, whilst 1987 saw roll on-roll off services arrive at the North Isles and at Shapinsay, being introduced by the *Eynhallow* (1987) and the *Shapinsay* (1989). In 1991, the *Thorsvoe* introduced an improved service to the South Isles and the same year saw the commencement of a programme of roll on - roll off development on the Outer North Isles of Westray, Papa Westray, Sanday and North Ronaldsay accompanied by the arrival of two new ferries, the *Earl Thorfinn* and the *Earl Sigurd* in 1990. A third vessel, the *Varagen*, built in 1989 for

# CENTURY OF NORTH WEST EUROPEAN FERRIES 1900 - 2000

The **Thora** is one of Shetland's first generation ferries, originally built for the Toft-Ulsta link. *(Miles Cowsill)*

an ill-fated service between Gill's Bay in Caithness and Burwick, joined them in 1991. Together, the three vessels replaced the *Orcadia* and the *Islander*, whilst the OISC changed its name to become Orkney Ferries in 1995.

In Shetland, the *Earl of Zetland*, built in 1877 for the Shetland Islands Steam Navigation Company and acquired by the North Company in 1890, fulfilled the same role as the *Orcadia* had done in Orkney. A new *Earl of Zetland* took over the role in 1946 and maintained services to the islands until the advent of the first roll on – roll off ferries in 1975. The first batch of these ferries was built in the Faroe Islands and followed Norwegian design. Named *Fivla*, *Grima*, *Geira*, *Fylga* and *Thora*, they were joined by the second hand *Kjella* in 1980. More ferries have arrived since, such as the *Hendra* and the *Filla* (both 1983) the *Fivla* (1985) and the *Geira* (1988). But the first batch of ferries is now giving way to new vessels such as the *Bigga* (1991) and the *Leirna* of 1992, the largest roll on-roll off ferry to sail within the Shetland Islands. Meanwhile, the outlying islands of Foula and Fair Isle are served by the *New Advance* (1996) and the *Good Shepherd IV* of 1986.

## FERRIES OF THE FUTURE

Scotland's ferry scene is ever changing. Steam has given way to diesel and car ferries have replaced passenger ships. The romance may have departed yet again, but the interest most certainly has not. The ferries remain essential lifelines for the islands as well as being deliverers of that necessary summer commodity, tourists, who also find much interest in the various ships. Scots have always held an affection for their ships, but one wonders if future generations will mourn the passing of the *Hebridean Isles*, the *Isle of Mull* and the *St. Sunniva* as the ferries of the future take their place, or will the car ferry never command the same affection as the old steamers of the past have so rightly deserved? Only time will tell.

*Colin J. Smith*

The **Earl Sigurd** rests at Kirkwall between sailings to the North Isles on 16th April 1992. *(Colin J. Smith)*

## CENTURY OF NORTH WEST EUROPEAN FERRIES 1900 - 2000

# Caledonian MacBrayne
# Millennium

Caledonian MacBrayne is the name synonymous with sea travel to the islands off Scotland's west coast: the Inner and Outer Hebrides and the Islands of the Firth of Clyde. The world famous shipping company with its head office in Gourock, operates a fleet of 30 modern roll-on/roll-off car and passenger ferries to islands from Arran in the south to Lewis in the north.

In total, they operate to 22 Scottish islands and use 52 different ports or terminals.

The Company's origins go back many, many years with the present company being formed in 1973 following the amalgamation of David MacBrayne, who operated the shipping services to the Western Isles, combining with Caledonian Steam Packet Company, who operated the shipping services in and around the Firth of Clyde.

The David MacBrayne 'empire' has been in existence around the west coast and Hebridean Islands since 1851. The Caledonian Steam Packet Company was formed in 1889. David MacBrayne was 50% owned by former railway companies and 50% by Coastlines Ltd. The Caledonian Steam Packet Company was totally owned by railway companies. Originally the Caledonian Railway Company and latterly the London, Midland and Scottish Railways were its owners. Both companies were taken over by the Scottish Transport Group in 1969. The Scottish Transport Group was also responsible for public bus companies in Scotland.

In 1990 Caledonian MacBrayne ceased to be part of the Scottish Transport Group, when the Company became owned by and directly responsible to the Secretary of State for Scotland. With the advent of devolution in Scotland, the Company is now responsible to the Scottish Executive and, in particular, the Transport Secretary.

Caledonian MacBrayne operate an amazing range of routes - from the five minute 'shuttle' service across the Kyles of Bute from Colintrave (Cowal) to Rhubodach to the seven and a quarter hour voyage from Oban in Argyll, via Barra, to Lochboisdale in South Uist.

The vessels, too, are equally varied, from the small 'Island' class ferries which can carry 44 passengers and 6 cars to vessels capable of carrying up the 1,000 passengers and 120 cars, the largest of which is the *Isle of Lewis* currently operating between Ullapool and Stornoway. The larger ships have self-service restaurants, fully licensed bars and shops.

Whether travelling on foot, bicycle, by car or towing a mobile home, sea barriers present no problems, thanks to CalMac, as the Company are affectionately known throughout Scotland.

CalMac operate regular crossings all year round with frequency depending on the distance involved.

In addition to sailing to 22 Scottish islands, CalMac also operate the Gourock-Dunoon ferry service with another couple of routes linking two mainland areas - Tarbert (Loch Fyne) and Portavadie on the Cowal Peninsula, and the popular route from Kilchoan on the Ardnamurchan Peninsula to Tobermory on the Island of Mull is also operated by the Company.

The introduction of several new vessels, and the

The *Clansman* is currently the company's most modern ship in the fleet. *(CalMac)*

redeployment or "cascade effect" of others in recent years, has resulted in a considerable growth in traffic. Over five million passengers and almost one million cars are carried each year. This is more than the entire population of Scotland and gives an idea in practical terms of the tremendous number of passengers carried annually. Another good record for the Company is that more than 95% of sailings are completed on time.

In addition to sailing to the Scottish Islands, in April 1997 Caledonian MacBrayne started a new car and passenger ferry service between Ballycastle on the Northern Ireland mainland and Rathlin Island just off the coast.

Rathlin Island nestles just 6 miles northwards of the Antrim Coast and measures four and three quarter miles long. Its Scottish connections go beyond Caledonian MacBrayne to the Scottish hero Robert the Bruce who is believed to have hidden in one of the caves on the island's limestone cliffs.

Besides being the lifeline to the islands for essential supplies, and passengers with or without vehicles, Caledonian MacBrayne's ferries also carry the produce of the islands to the markets on the mainland. The conveyance of livestock is another important task done by these ferries.

Amongst the deals available for tourists are 'Island Hopscotch' tickets which are attractive fares for cars and accompanying passengers on a selection (there are 20 to choose from!) of pre-planned routes on island hopping holidays. 'Island Rover' runabout tickets for passengers, with or without cars allow flexibility over an 8 or 15 day period and for those less adventurous souls there are a number of attractive 'Day Saver' tickets and joint tickets with visitor attractions and other transport modes.

One way in which these various attractive propositions are promoted is by the Company's Exhibition Roadshow which can be seen touring throughout the UK for 5 weeks every spring and in early summer. The Company also take part in holiday exhibitions in the UK and also Europe.

All you ever wanted to know about holidaying in the Scottish Isles can be found inside the Roadshow Vehicle from Tourist Information brochures to ferry timetables and even detailed descriptions of CalMac's fleet. There is something to appeal to everyone with more than just a passing interest. Figures for the past 2 years show that more than 14,000 people turned up to quiz the Roadshow crew.

The Roadshow is only one of the many ways in which

# Caledonian MacBrayne

## Scotland's Enchanted Isles

Caledonian MacBrayne is the name synonymous with sea travel to the islands off the West Coast of Scotland. The company operates services on the Firth of Clyde and the Hebrides.
In total, we sail to 22 Scottish Islands, using 52 different ports or terminals.

"Island Hopscotch®" and "Island Rover" tickets are available for tourists who wish to visit several islands in their holiday programme.
Go for a full holiday, a short break or even just a day trip, to explore some of the finest scenic locations in Europe.

Why not try one of our Evening Dinner Cruises from Ardrossan or Oban enjoying the delights of a Hebridean sunset, while sitting down to a three course meal served at your table.

For a holiday brochure giving details of times and fares, contact:

### Caledonian MacBrayne

The Ferry Terminal, Gourock, PA19 1QP
Tel: 01475 650100 Fax: 01475 637607
Vehicle Reservations : (0990) 650000
Brochure Line: (01475) 650288
www.calmac.co.uk

# CENTURY OF NORTH WEST EUROPEAN FERRIES 1900 - 2000

the Company promote the islands of the Clyde and the Western Isles. Tourists enjoy visiting these islands to escape the hustle and bustle of urban life, to admire the beautiful scenery, to meet the friendly people of the islands and to listen to the lilt of the Gaelic.

Many of the islands have beautiful unspoilt beaches and offer some of the best sporting facilities in the British Isles.

Whether your passion is golf, sailing, cycling, scuba diving, hill-walking or climbing, the terrain, mountains, lush green pastures and wild seas offer magnificent natural facilities.

The Clyde Coast of Ayrshire is already world renowned for its first class golf courses, and many of the islands and peninsulas also offer golf courses with superb facilities and magnificent views, but for those who prefer their sports slightly more demanding, the Highlands and Islands offer superb opportunities aplenty for the hillwalker and climber.

Cyclists are guaranteed a fantastic and inexpensive trip with the islands already made for tourists of the two wheeled variety, and for those with a nautical outlook there are modern marinas to cater for the serious enthusiast and the novice paddler, with easy access slipways for family vessels and wide choice of hired boats or charters.

Off many an island seals can be seen, and for ornithologists there is the opportunity to study various species of rare bird. Other islands have special geographical features and are of interest to people studying geology and archaeology. Many of these are interpreted on the Wands available on board the Ardrossan-Brodick ship.

There are old castles to be seen and ancient monuments to be visited with opportunities for many other activities.

Glorious sunsets are of almost breathtaking beauty; while the longer hours of daylight in the mid summer months never fail to delight tourists from less favoured places in the south where the shades of night fall much more early.

As the Company approaches the opportunity of the millennium, clear objectives have been set out to meet the challenge continuing to serve the islands. These are:

* Improvement of customer services
* Devolution of responsibility and accountability to the local offices and ships
* Development and improvement of staff training
* Revitalisation of the working environment
* Control of costs.

These objectives make it clear the Company's awareness of the importance of its services to the communities served by it.

Exciting new developments for the Millennium are the introduction of two new vessels. The *Hebrides* will go into service on the triangular route from Skye to Tarbert in Harris and Lochmaddy in North Uist. She will replace the ever popular *Hebridean Isles*. The *Hebrides* will be a sister to the *Clansman* but with several differences. The most obvious will be to her life-saving equipment which will

# CENTURY OF NORTH WEST EUROPEAN FERRIES 1900 - 2000

result in a much more photogenic vessel than the *Clansman*.

The *Loch Nevis* will enter service on the Mallaig to the Small Isles route. With new infrastructure being currently provided on the islands of Muck, Eigg, Rum and Canna, the *Loch Nevis* will have the facility to carry 6 cars thus allowing much greater access to the Small Isles than before. Her propulsion is of an extremely sophisticated nature. The *Loch Nevis* will also allow the provision of a limited vehicle service in the winter time between Mallaig and Armadale on Skye to complement the full vehicle service offered in the summer season.

Although Caledonian MacBrayne's routes are steeped in history, the Company is ever mindful of the need to embrace new technology. Its vessels in recent years have used new technology to its best advantage allowing specialised ships to be built for specific routes. The prime example of this technology is used by the *Loch Bhrusda* on the Otternish to Leverburgh route which is an extremely hazardous crossing, particularly at low tide. Her advanced jet propulsion allows her to operate in extremely shallow water without damage to her propulsion units.

Ashore, as well as afloat, the Company utilises cutting edge technology. The Company website at www.calmac.co.uk allows an infinite number of messages to be conveyed via the worldwide web to people all over the world. These messages range from the promotion of the area as an attractive venue to holiday in to the provision of bad weather disruption information. The Company is in the vanguard of transport operators as it has enabled direct booking by e.commerce via the internet and its website. There is much to interest the net surfer. There are pages of archive information about the Company and its ships and also up to date information about the existing fleet.

It used to be said that there is no Gaelic word to equate with the urgency of the Spanish word "manana" but, with the advent of new technology, this is definitely no longer the case, and many of the businesses operating in the islands now use new technology, but still remain dependent on the Company's services to get their goods to the Market Place.

It is, therefore, still very appropriate to remember the old saying of Scotland

*The earth belongs unto the Lord,*
*and all that it contains:*
*except for the Clyde and Western Isles,*
*because they're Caledonian MacBrayne's.*

*Mike Blair*

*Further information: tel: 01475 650100, fax: 01475 650262, e.mail: mike.blair@calmac.co.uk.*
*Reservations: 0870 5 650000, www.calmac.co.uk*

The *Isle of Lewis* at Stornoway during the Tall Ships visit in August 1999. *(CalMac)*

# CENTURY OF NORTH WEST EUROPEAN FERRIES 1900 - 2000

# Freight Ferries

## INTRODUCTION

A map of the current North West European ferry scene displays a wide range of routes, and for many sectors, it is the freight ferry services that are responsible for most of the movement between the various parts of the continent. In some sectors, freight ferries far outnumber their more glamorous passenger counterparts and freight is now the backbone of the vast majority of ferry operators, regardless of whether they are known as a passenger or freight carrier. For example, at the time of writing, May 1999, there are 21 services between Ireland and Scotland, England, Wales and France of which, seven are freight only. The story on the North Sea is even more biased in favour of freight services with no fewer than twelve operators providing services between Scandinavia, Germany, the Low Countries and the UK compared to four passenger lines.

It has not always been like this however: at the turn of the century, when the term 'ferry' implied little more than a wooden barge hauled across a river. It was the 'steam packets' that carried passengers, and more importantly, the mail across the sea routes of the continent. These vessels accommodated the cargo that they could, but most freight movement was in the hands of completely different classes of vessels. However, the same processes that have seen the development of the modern car ferry have also been responsible for creating its near cousin, the ro-ro freighter.

Attempts such as these, however, to classify the vast collection of roll on, roll off vessels now in service around Europe are somewhat futile and to a certain extent, becoming even harder, as many a follower of the ferry industry would be able to testify. Whilst no-one would be in doubt, when sailing on the likes of *Cinderella*, *Color Festival* or *Val de Loire* as to their passenger-carrying, cruiseferry credentials, further along the spectrum, the classification becomes less clear. At the opposite extreme are the ro-ro vessels that cross the continent carrying paper produce as seen in the likes of Transforest's *Obbola* which most would not consider a true freight ferry and the more conventional freighters of established ferry companies such as Transfennica and Finncarriers. However, in between lie hundreds of ferries, all capable of carrying freight and at least a few passengers. Precisely what sorts the *Barfleur*s from the *Clementine*s of the industry is a task that would probably take this entire book. However, this chapter will attempt to provide a review of the development of North West European freight ferries since the turn of the century and to chart the rise of this important component of the ferry industry to the current day.

## EARLY DEVELOPMENT

The twentieth century has seen rapid and vast changes across the transport industry. Societal shifts have resulted in a number of revolutions that have seen the main thrust of transport move from the railways, to the roads and now increasingly to the skies. One hundred years ago, steam locomotives were the workhorses of Europe, transporting passengers and cargo from one end of the continent to the other. Geographically, the fragmented nature of much of Europe necessitated ships to provide linkages between the main railway networks. At the purest level, this took the form of the train ferries, documented in the final chapter of this book but the passenger steam packets also played a significant part.

One of the earliest freight-only vessels on the English Channel was Thoresen's *Viking IV*. (Miles Cowsill collection)

# CENTURY OF NORTH WEST EUROPEAN FERRIES 1900 - 2000

The Atlantic Steam Navigation Company were pioneers in the freight ferry industry, their final ship being the **Europic Ferry**. *(Miles Cowsill collection)*

By the mid-1970s, the next generation of freighters was entering service, such as the **European Trader** for Townsend Thoresen. *(Miles Cowsill)*

However, during the inter-war years, the development of the motor car suddenly became a particularly important element of social change. With its growing popularity, the extensive road network was also gradually upgraded, reaching its pinnacle in the construction of the motorways, autoroutes and autobahns. By the early 1960s, not only had the passengers deserted the railways but freight too was finding it increasingly convenient to travel by road.

As soon as the first car ferries entered service, most notably in the form of Captain Townsend's *Forde*, there was the opportunity for road freight to be conveyed as well. However, this was not a priority of the ferry pioneers of the early decades of the century as operations were slow, relatively expensive and the national railway companies provided perfectly adequate services utilising their own freight ships.

It was during the Second World War that the idea of the freight ferry was germinated. Not long after hostilities ceased, and as trade between the countries of North West Europe increased due to the new *entente* that was now growing, one of the first such services was inaugurated in order to provide a connection between Britain and the Netherlands. The Atlantic Steam Navigation Company utilised three former tank landing craft, chartered from the UK Admiralty, to provide daily sailings between Tilbury and Rotterdam. From swords into ploughshares, the *Empire Baltic*, *Empire Cedric* and *Empire Celtic* each provided the ability to carry not tanks and other weapons of war but trucks and trade, thereby acting as the first threads of peace that were to unite a continent.

However, the memories of war were never far during the early years of freight ferry services across the North Sea. Not only did the success of the ASN's Rotterdam and later Hamburg services depend on the carriage of military vehicles to the growing bases in Germany but the ships had to sail a course between thousands of mines left by the German forces along a cleared channel. Indeed, the connections between the ASN and the UK military were eventually to see them awarded the contract for the management of 12 similar vessels.

The success of the ASN's services out of Tilbury encouraged the establishment of a similar route across the Irish Sea, this time linking Preston, Lancashire and Larne, Northern Ireland in 1948, thanks to the introduction of a fourth ship, the *Empire Doric*.

The design of these craft was crucial to the success of the new services. Their ability to rapidly discharge personnel and vehicles ashore to join military campaigns wherever needed was a concept that could easily be applied to battle on the new front: commerce and trade. With their bow doors, the unique ships could offload a full complement of two decks of 80 lorries in addition to tanks and other cargo. Their shallow draft and design for off loading onto beaches meant that no expensive port installations had to be constructed and in the early years, trucks and vans drove up the sand in the same way that tanks had in previous years.

So successful were the early years of these routes that within a decade, the company had ordered a series of purpose built vessels to replace the pioneer LSTs on their routes. First out of the shipyard were the *Bardic Ferry* and *Ionic Ferry* in 1957-8 and by 1967, four other similar vessels were to arrive on the growing network of routes. At around 2,500 gross tons, the first of the new ships, the *Cerdic Ferry* and *Doric Ferry*, could accommodate 55 passengers in two classes and had the capacity for 70 trailers. The later pair, the *Gaelic Ferry* and *Europic Ferry* incorporated further design advances with the ability to carry even greater numbers of passengers and freight.

Elsewhere however, development of freight ferry services progressed in a different direction. Most cargo was accommodated on either traditional lift-on lift-off ships or road freight sailed with passengers on the multi-purpose ferries. As demonstrated in many of the other chapters in this book, freight was the key factor in the rapid and continuous development of this type of ship in the 1960s and 1970s. However, by the end of the 1960s, two unstoppable processes were to revolutionise the ferry industry and create the diversity of freight services we now see today.

## ALL CHANGE

On the technological side, a major factor in this change was the development of containerisation. Now convenient and popular the world over, this new concept saw freight boxed, conveniently loaded onto a lorry and taken to whatever port the customer required. Whilst it was sensible enough for the long distance trans-global services to stack containers on the decks of a purpose built ship, the voyage of a few hours across the relatively narrow waterways of North West Europe hardly warranted such a time consuming task. The most obvious solution was to keep the containers on the lorry and, as passengers had been doing for a number of years, drive on board.

On the wider social front, however, the growing importance

# CENTURY OF NORTH WEST EUROPEAN FERRIES 1900 - 2000

of the European Economic Community in the everyday life of European citizens was to have a dramatic effect on the seaways of the continent. The original Gang of Six – France, Germany, Italy and the Benelux countries – had no obvious impact on sea routes, but it was in 1973 when the community was extended (after years of wrangling) to include Denmark, Ireland and the UK that a fresh era was begun for sea transport. Firstly, any restrictions on the amount of freight that could be carried were lifted and secondly, a vast new market and potential trading area was opened up.

This process had been steadily building during the 1960s as the importance of the new EEC and other similar organisations such as the UK and Scandinavian European Free Trade Area grew in strength. Many traditional liner services were converted to ro-ro and commercial traffic began to boom. In many cases, pioneer ro-ro ferries were soon joined by dedicated freight vessels in order to increase both passenger and freight capacity.

One such example was Tor Line, sailing between Sweden, Holland and the UK, which added the Norwegian built 1,600 gross tons *Tor Mercia* and *Tor Scandia* in 1969 to their services. By 1971, the company was in the process of commissioning a large fleet of even bigger vessels from the Fremnaes Yard in Norway beginning with the *Tor Gothia*. Six 4,000 gross tons freighters were commissioned by 1976 with a further four vessels completed for other owners. The highly successful design could carry 1,550 metres of freight and enabled a vast expansion in services. Five of the ten are still in service in North West Europe today, the *Tor Hollandia*, *Tor Caledonia*, *Tor Gothia* and *Stena Gothica* for Tor Line and the *Seahawk* on charter to P&O.

As the EEC increased, not only in size but also in importance, so did the ferry companies see it as an opportunity to expand their operations in anticipation of the new freight market. One of the first off the mark was Townsend Car Ferries who purchased the old coastal steamer *Royal Sovereign* which underwent a major conversion, emerging in 1967 as the 24 lorry freighter *Autocarrier* for their Dover – Zeebrugge route. At the other end of the channel, Thoresen Car Ferries introduced the purpose built freighter *Viking IV* to their multi-purpose services from Southampton to Normandy in June of the same year with the ability to carry 40 lorries in addition to 130 cars. By the early 1970s, Thoresen's somewhat modest freight operation was facing a challenge from the newly formed Truckline who commenced services between Poole and Cherbourg (a Thoresen port) in 1973 utilising the purpose built *Poole Antelope* and *Dauphin de Cherbourg*. These small ships were replaced by 1975 with the larger *Contentin* and *Dorset*, which had space for 25 trailers and 50 cars. The Truckline route was a pioneer in that freight could be accompanied for the first time unlike so many other operations which did not allow this facility.

At the other end of the English Channel, Townsend Thoresen introduced three freighters in 1975 from a German shipyard onto their Zeebrugge services. The *European Gateway* was the first to arrive operating out of Felixstowe whilst the second and third of the class (*European Trader* and *European Clearway*) were based at Dover. These vessels offered 1,000 metres of freight space and like the Truckline vessels could carry a number of passengers. A fourth – the *European Enterprise* (now *European Endeavour*) - arrived in 1978. Whilst the *European Gateway* (following her sinking off Felixstowe in 1982) was sold to Greece for conversion to a passenger carrier, the surviving sisters are now in regular service for P&O across the Irish Sea.

The new status of Britain and Denmark within the EEC also had an impact on the North Sea. During the 1960s, DFDS introduced three freighters on their routes connecting the UK with Esbjerg called the *Stafford*, *Somerset* and *Surrey* with the capability of carrying 113 trailers. Such was the pace of traffic growth over the forthcoming decade that by 1975 DFDS introduced the large and innovative freighters *Dana Gloria* and *Dana Futura* to replace the original trio. With a service speed of 23 knots, the pair could carry (in addition to a limited number of passengers) three decks of freight and were amongst the first freighters to be built as such. However, the Achilles heel of the pair was their speed, requiring vast quantities of fuel which inevitably made them uneconomical when the oil crisis hit in the late 1970s. In 1977 they were replaced by the slower 17-knot Japanese built *Dana Maxima* and were then periodically chartered out until the mid 1980s. The *Dana Gloria*, by then named *Dana Hafnia*, was sold to GT-Link for conversion to a passenger vessel, operating between Gedser and Travemunde as *Gedser Link*, whilst the latter was lengthened and resumed service between the UK, Sweden and Denmark until her later sale to Nordo Link.

Across the Irish Sea, it was P&O who decided the time was now right to launch this revolutionary new type of service. By 1975, a new terminal had been completed at Fleetwood and two new ships of Stena origin were built at Hamburg. The *Buffalo* and *Bison* entered service in February and April of that year providing sailings to Larne and Dublin. This service was unique in that not only did P&O offer seabourne freight sailings but also operated a distribution network providing 'door to door' facilities for its customers. Together, the sea and road operations were marketed as Pandoro – P and O Ro. A third vessel, a sister to the original pair, the *Union Melbourne* (later renamed the *Puma*) was added in 1978 and the following year, two newly built ferries, the *Ibex* and *Tipperary* arrived heralding the involvement of the Irish B&I Line in the operation.

## STENA – THE WORLD'S LEADING FREIGHT FERRY DESIGNER

The use by P&O of the *Buffalo*, *Bison* and *Puma* and the success of the Fremnaes/Tor series of freighters illustrates a growing trend during the late 1960s and early 1970s. Whilst passenger vessels were almost always constructed to the precise specification of the operators, freight ships were built in classes, often by companies not involved in their daily operation and then released onto the charter or sale market. At this time, there was a wide range of designs coming onto the market, including a number from the Stena stable of which the P&O triplets were but a small part. Indeed, it could be argued that if any single company revolutionised freight ferry operation, it was the giant Swedish concern.

Now renowned for their cruiseferry and high speed operations, Stena's heritage as a design house for some of the most significant freight ferries of the century is often forgotten despite the fact that they are still commissioning some of the most advanced freighters at the end of the 1990s. However, during the 1970s, the company commissioned a large number of different freight ferry classes that were to serve a wide range of routes throughout Northern Europe.

One of the first and the most prolific of these designs was a class of small freight ferries which began with the *Stena Carrier* and *Stena Trailer* in 1971. Constructed by a number of Norwegian shipbuilders, the vessels were immediately snapped up by the British Railways Board and introduced as the *Ulidia* and *Dalriada* on their Irish Sea services. They had capacity for 20 and 12 passengers respectively and could accommodate 540

# CENTURY OF NORTH WEST EUROPEAN FERRIES 1900 - 2000

One of the many Mercandia built ships to serve northwest Europe became DFDS's **Dana Cimbria**. *(Miles Cowsill)*

One of the more recent designs of freighters is P&O North Sea Ferries' **Norbank.** *(Miles Cowsill collection)*

metres of freight. Not only did British Rail order a third and fourth in the class (as the *Anderida* and *Penda*) but Silja Line also built a pair for service across the Baltic Sea, the *Holmia* and *Silvia* entering service out of Stockholm at the same time as their British sisters. Another of the class went to Deutsche Reichsbahn as the *Stubbenkammer* whilst at least four others have done the charter rounds of Northern Europe including the much travelled *Transbaltica*, which joined the Estonian Shipping Company in 1998 for service from Kiel. In the past this vessel has operated for Finnfranline, Brittany Ferries, Transfennica and Commodore Ferries demonstrating the versatility of the design to suit a wide range of operators and types of service. Indeed, the *Grey Master*, originally completed in 1972 saw military service in the early 1980s as *Sir Caradoc* for the UK Royal Fleet Auxiliary. This latter ship was briefly reunited with sister *Stena Carrier* when both were acquired by Norwegian operator Rogaland Kystferger, converted to carry 500 passengers and renamed the *Fjordveien* and *Stamveien* for service between Randaberg and Skudeneshavn. This class must now be one of the most recognisable freight ferries in the world with members operating out of numerous ports. The reluctance of many owners to divest themselves of the ships (such as Sea Containers and the *Peveril*) demonstrates their usefulness.

Not long after this design, Stena began work on the next, developing with the Dutch Scheepswerven yard three similar vessels which entered service in 1973 as the *Stena Sailer*, *Stena Seatrader* and *Stena Shipper*. Whilst showing a superficially similar profile to their earlier cousins, the new 2,600 gross tons trio offered freight space for 86 trailers, more than double that of the Norwegian class. Each has enjoyed a widely varied life: the first two were taken on demise charter by Adelphi Vergottis of Cyprus and whilst the *Stena Sailer* never returned, the *Stena Seatrader* was back with her owners by 1981 and spent a number of years on the charter market before taking up regular service between Gothenburg and Frederikshavn as the train ferry *Stena Scanrail* - a role which she is still in. The *Stena Shipper* also spent her early years on charter including stints in New Zealand and Greece before she too was converted to a train ferry and chartered to British Rail as the *Speedlink Vanguard*. On completion of this, she joined the Brittany Ferries fleet operating between Portsmouth and Caen as the *Normandie Shipper* until 1997.

Stena's next series was developed in two phases. The first of these were the already mentioned German 'Stena Seaporter' class which were taken by P&O for Irish Sea service. At 3,500 gross tons, each vessel could carry around 90 trailers and the three were all lengthened at different times, the most recent being the *Buffalo* in 1998 when she underwent the operation for the second time which saw her gross tonnage increase to 12,800. The second phase of this development saw the emergence of a further three ships in 1976-77 with more than a passing resemblance to the *Buffalo* and company from an Austrian yard. The first of this class, *Stena Tender* was purchased and immediately lengthened by the United Baltic Corporation for whom she operated as the *Goya*. By 1983, having spent a number of years on charter in the Caribbean and Canada, she was acquired by Townsend Thoresen and renamed *Viking Trader*, replacing the earlier ship of that name (which was originally *Stena Trailer/Dalriada*) on their service between Southampton and Le Havre, a route originally operated, it will be remembered, by the *Viking IV*. In 1989 the *Viking Trader* transferred to P&O for Irish Sea service joining the Pandoro fleet eventually becoming *European Navigator*. The second ferry *Stena Timer* went on short term Irish Sea operation firstly for Sealink and then as *Jaguar* for P&O before heading out to the Government of Mexico as the *Loreto*. The third in the class – *Stena Topper* - was immediately chartered by British Rail to replace the *Dalriada* between Stranraer and Larne, taking the name *Darnia*. She saw unusually long service on this route lasting until 1991 when she was sold to Nordstrom & Thulin operating to Gotland as *Nord Neptunus* and later for Estline between Stockholm and Tallinn as *Neptunia*.

The final Stena design of the 1970s however was amongst the largest class of ferries ever built, with 11 vessels completed for a number of operators worldwide. Christened the 'Stena Searunner' class, the 5,500 gross tons design offered 1,650 metres of freight laneage and each ship also featured a full container deck. The ships were intended as deep sea ro-ros but such was their versatility, they were all to be operated by short sea operators, at least for part of their lives. The first vessel arrived in 1977 and spent a number of years on the charter market as *Stena Freighter* before entering regular service between Gothenburg and Travemunde in 1988 for Stena. Subsequent vessels went to North Sea Ferries, Merzario Line, P&O and Atlantic Container Line, demonstrating the extent to which the class has assisted in services worldwide with the Irish Sea, North Sea, Baltic, Mediterranean, Canadian and global container operations all benefiting from their far reaching design.

The arrival of the *Stena Transporter* for Finnlines service as

# CENTURY OF NORTH WEST EUROPEAN FERRIES 1900 - 2000

Cobelfret's **Loverval** is seen passing **Dart 4**, one of the most successful of freight ferry designs of the 1980s. *(Mike Louagie)*

the *Finnrose* in 1978 was the final freight ferry commissioning by Stena Line during this period, and the 1980s and 1990s were barren decades for the company in this field as they concentrated on cruiseferries and high speed craft. However, the late 1990s saw Stena return to their roots with the launch of two major designs of ship. The first was the 'Stena Seapacer' ro-pax class of which four were built, the first two purchased by Finnlines as the *Finnclipper* and *Finneagle*, whilst the second class called 'Stena 4-Runner' saw five ships ordered, the first two chartered to the British Ministry of Defence as the *Sea Centurion* and *Sea Crusader*.

### OTHER CLASSES OF THE 1970s

It was not only Stena, however, who were responsible for introducing a large number of freight ferries into service during the 1970s, a number of other shipowners and shipbuilders were also leaders in this field. One such company is the German Reinecke who have been instrumental in a large number of charters. Indeed, it has been owners such as this who have kept many a ferry service going during periods of refit, breakdown or even war with their fleets of freighters that have been chartered by almost every operator in North Western Europe. One of the most well known classes of ships built by Reinecke is the Hamburg built class between 1973 and 1977. Four ships were built for the charter market taking the names *Fuldatal*, *Wupertal*, *Wesertal* and *Travetal*. These ships have had an ever more varied existence than the Stena family of ships: the *Wesertal* has seen service for North Sea Ferries, TT/Olau, Stena and DFDS, whilst the *Wupertal* has operated for North Sea Ferries, DFDS/Tor Line, Truckline and more recently in the service of Falcon Seafreight as the *Picasso*.

In addition to these has been the five-strong class best known in the *Gabriele Wehr* and *Thomas Wehr*, built for Oskar Wehr Transport but having spent much of their recent lives working for P&O. Prior to this, the pair also operated for Tor Line for a number of years as the *Tor Anglia* and *Tor Neerlandia*, during which time they were lengthened. The class has varying carrying capacities due to a number of lengthenings over the years but in their original form carried around 70 trailers with a gross tonnage of approximately 3,000. Much travelled during their early years, notching up service for Tor Line, North Sea Ferries, Kent Line, Brittany Ferries, DFDS, Cobelfret and TT-Line between them, the pair seemed to have found a niche with P&O at Felixstowe in recent years until their recent replacement by *Rodona* and *Sapphire*. A third member of the class is also now operating within the P&O group as *European Highlander* on the Irish Sea. The final two sisters are also in the area owned by Seatruck since 1997 as the *Moondance* and *Riverdance* and operating between Heysham and Warrenpoint. The Seatruck pair and *European Highlander* all saw early service with Gilnavi of Italy before heading north. Cenargo owned *European Highlander* and *Moondance* for a period during the 1990s whilst the *Riverdance* spent much of the 1980s with Schiaffino and later Sally operating out of Ramsgate.

Another class of workhorses dating from this era is a Norwegian quartet comprising the *Anu*, *Starmark*, *Leila* and *Ilkka* of 1971-2. A development of the original Tor Line freight ferries *Tor Mercia* and *Tor Scandia*, the ships have had a wide and varied service, although they have not been such a regular feature of European ports as others mentioned above. The *Anu* and *Ilkka* in 1980 joined the 'Stena Carrier' quartet with British Rail on the service between Heysham and Belfast as the *Lune Bridge* and *Lagan Bridge* respectively but this was not a success. The latter ended her ferry days as a Canadian research vessel whilst the *Lune Bridge* went on to serve B&I, the British Ministry of Defence, Merchant Ferries, Mols Line and Commodore Ferries.

Of course, another company which has long been synonymous with freight ferry construction is that of Mercandia. Established by the Danish entrepreneur Per Henriksen in 1966, through an agreement with the Frederikshavn Værft shipyard, the company has constructed 84 vessels and a further 53 at other yards. These have happened in series of between seven and 10. However, Mercandia's vessels have never become as common a currency in the world of Northern European freight ferry operation as have other designs and their main sphere of operations has been deep sea services. One design that has been adapted to serve on ferry services is that of the 1982 built *Mercandian President*, *Mercandian Governor* and *Mercandian Admiral II*. These were acquired by DSB in 1988-90 and converted to carry up to 600 passengers, taking the names *Kraka*, *Lodbrog* and *Heimdal* respectively, operating between Knudshoved and Halsskov until 1998.

# CENTURY OF NORTH WEST EUROPEAN FERRIES 1900 - 2000

The **Pride of Flanders** is seen here after her conversion from a freight vessel to a passenger ship for the Felixstowe-Zeebrugge route. *(FotoFlite)*

Another well known Mercandia design now serving in Northern Europe is that of the 1986 built *Dana Cimbria*, originally the *Mercandian Express II* and sold to DFDS for service between Immingham and Esbjerg.

## THE 1980s AND CONSOLIDATION

Many established freight operators rely on ships such as these from the charter market. Their abundance means that services can be increased in line with market fluctuations. Companies can charter in and out tonnage according to the season and sometimes according to how much traffic is waiting on the quayside – or so it seems ! However, by the beginning of the 1980s, many operators were beginning to consolidate and the flow of freight ferry designs onto the market began to run dry.

This process was for a number of reasons. Firstly many of the multi-purpose operators were by now commissioning their second generation ro-ro ferries which incorporated enough freight space to see the end of the previously chartered in tonnage. One such example is that of Sealink on the Irish Sea who replaced 1960s tonnage and a wide number of freight ferries at Fishguard, Holyhead and Stranraer with *Stena Normandica*, *St. Columba*, *St. David* and *Galloway Princess* which obviated the need for *Ulidia* and her consorts. A second reason was that many freight operations which began in the early 1970s were now coming of age and were demanding ships built to their own specification. In addition, patterns of service were becoming more like passenger operations with more reliable, regular arrival and departure times.

It is important to note the diverging patterns that developed across Northern Europe for freight ferry operations during the 1970s and 1980s. In the West of the continent, the relatively short stretches of water comprising the Irish Sea, English

The **Stena Traveller** pictured shortly after entering service on the Southampton-Cherbourg route. *(FotoFlite)*

171

# CENTURY OF NORTH WEST EUROPEAN FERRIES 1900 - 2000

Channel and Southern North Sea have resulted in short sea freight routes being operated in much the same way as the passenger services. However, across the rest of the North Sea and between the Scandinavian countries, services have developed more along the lines of the deep sea operators with services often comprising round trips lasting up to two weeks and calling at many ports. On the short sea services, drivers would have the opportunity to rest during the voyage and as this aspect was becoming increasingly regulated, the driver-accompanied services became more popular. On the longer routes however, even direct services would have taken the best part of a day on many routes and it would have been uneconomical to have drivers wasting time in this way. Therefore, unaccompanied services became the norm and with no pressure of time, could be extended to incorporate a number of ports of call. At the forefront of this type of service has been Finnlines, who with their numerous partners, have developed a fleet of vessels serving Finland, Sweden, Germany and the UK. Fred. Olsen Lines have also been a name closely associated with this type of service although at the end of 1998 this historic company's ferry services were absorbed into DFDS Tor Line.

These longer services at this time were to see the introduction of a number of important classes of vessels. It is no surprise that for much of the 1980s, the 'Stena Searunner' class provided valuable support to numerous operators. Having completed their initial period of service with Atlantic Container Line, the *Atlantic Prosper* and *Atlantic Project* were utilised by firstly Kotka Line between Finland and the UK and later Stena Portlink linking Sweden and Britain. 1988 saw the pair with Bore Line and today they are in the service of Finnlines as the *Finnforest* and *Finnbirch* between Hull, Felixstowe, Hamina and Helsinki.

Another notable pair of vessels of the same era as the 'Searunner' class is the *Inowroclaw* and *Baltic Eagle* constructed for service between the UK and Poland for Polish Ocean Lines and the United Baltic Corporation. Finnlines and its associates have also taken delivery of a wide range of tonnage during the last 20 years such as the *Finnrose* and *Finnhawk* of 1980 which were eventually sold to Nordo-Link for conversion to passenger carriers as *Malmo Link* and *Lubeck Link*.

On the short sea services the process of consolidation increased throughout the 1980s. Whilst the multitude of small 1970s built freighters were still being called upon to provide seasonal and relief support on established services, there was also a move towards new generations of both passenger and freight ferries that could cope with these fluctuations in demand. Across Europe, the pioneer freight ferries were gradually being replaced by more modern and suitable vessels. For example, the decade saw the end of the historic former Atlantic Steam Navigation Company ships. Now under Townsend Thoresen control, the company also opted for four 'Stena Searunner' ships for their next generation of ferries, two of which (the *Baltic Ferry* and *Nordic Ferry*) were converted to passenger operation between Felixstowe and Zeebrugge. Most operators however, concentrated their efforts on developing true multi-purpose vessels that could incorporate sufficient amounts of both passengers and freight. The 1980s therefore became one of the quietest periods of development for freight ferries.

A notable exception to this however, was the development of the Norwegian 'Balder' class of ferries constructed in Romania during 1983 to 1986. Although such an order was an undoubted boost to the Romanian state's economy, events unfolded rather unexpectedly when Balder went bankrupt early on in the construction programme and the 8 vessels passed into the ownership of state run Romanian companies, taking the names *Bazias 1* to *Bazias 8*. Their early years were spent in Romania and it was not until the late 1980s when they started to appear onto the charter market, a process aided by Stena who purchased the final three naming them *Stena Tender*, *Stena Topper* and *Stena Timer* respectively. It was the burgeoning freight market between South East England and the Low Countries that was to be the main beneficiary of the class with both Olau and Kent Line taking up short term charter options before Sally acquired the *Bazias 3* and *Bazias 4* in 1991 for their Ramsgate – Ostend service, renaming them the *Sally Euroroute* and *Sally Eurolink*. The end of Olau Line's cruiseferry service between Sheerness and Vlissingen eventually resulted in the establishment of a new route out of Dartford to the Dutch port by Dart Line and a further two Balder vessels – the *Bazias 2* and *Bazias 5* - were chartered with the names *Dart 2* and *Dart 5* adopted. The *Bazias 1* also arrived at Dart Line in 1997 as did the *Sally Eurolink* becoming *Dart 1* and *Dart 4*. The Irish Sea also received a selection of the class with Belfast Freight Ferries using the seventh ship as the *River Lune* and subsequently acquiring the *Sally Euroroute* as the *Merle* in 1996.

The Communist connections of the 'Balder' class was also to see the design re-appear in the late 1980s when a Chinese shipyard produced four similar vessels for the Belgian freight operator Cobelfret. The *Symphorine* was the first to arrive on the services linking Zeebrugge with Immingham and Harwich (now Purfleet) in 1988 and by 1992 had been joined by sisters *Undine*, *Cymbeline* and *Elgantine*. The ancestry of the Balder/Cobelfret ships can also be seen in the Norwegian built *Norwegian Crusader* and *Norwegian Challenger*, originally constructed for Steineger & Wilk but now owned by Cenargo as *Merchant Bravery* and *Merchant Brilliant*.

## THE RISE OF RO-PAX

The change of decade from the 1980s to the 1990s was also to witness important changes in the ferry industry. On the one hand, it was a time when operators were upgrading second generation multi-purpose ferries into third generation vessels such as Olau's *Olau Hollandia* and *Olau Britannia* and Silja's *Silja Serenade* and *Silja Symphony*. This meant that once again, the capacities of routes were increased and there was less of a need for additional freight tonnage. However, acting as a counterpoint to this, was the increasing threat of fixed links in a number of important sectors and a growing trend to concentrate passenger services on a selection of core routes. It was not always possible, however, to serve the passenger and freight sectors on the same routes and therefore in many areas, the two began to develop once again in different ways.

One important example of this is the Dover Straits; threatened by the impending opening of the Channel Tunnel, ferry companies were cutting costs by rationalising services. In the case of P&O, this meant the construction of new generation car ferries in the *Pride of Dover*, *Pride of Calais* and *Pride of Burgundy*, the concentration of passenger services on Dover to Calais (with Boulogne and Zeebrugge closed as passenger terminals) but with the upgrading of the freight service into Zeebrugge through the construction of three large 'superfreighters' – the *European Seaway*, *European Pathway* and *European Highway* in 1991-2. These new ships replaced the earlier German built 'European' trio and not only offered capacity for 120 lorries but had driver accommodation for 200 people.

This was to become an increasingly important feature

# CENTURY OF NORTH WEST EUROPEAN FERRIES 1900 - 2000

By the end of the 1990s, the increasing trend in freight ferry operations was to include facilities for several hundred passengers. These ro-pax vessels are exemplified in the **Mersey Viking**. *(Miles Cowsill)*

during the 1990s as growing numbers of large freight ships were arriving with the ability to carry ever more passengers. Stena commissioned a pair of ships with capacity for up to 500 passengers. The first, *Stena Challenger*, served at Dover between 1991 and 1996 prior to moving to Holyhead whilst the second, *Stena Traveller* had a more nomadic existence before finding a niche with TT-Line between Travemunde and Trelleborg as the *TT Traveller*. TT-Line themselves had developed the *Nils Dacke* and *Robin Hood* in 1988 as 'combi-carriers' with capacity for several hundred people to support their cruiseferry operations. A further two ships of the same names arriving in 1995 once the first had been converted to full multi-purpose mode, and two far larger cruiseferry ro-pax ships are now under construction for arrival in 2001.

This concept was now known as 'ro-pax' denoting full ro-ro (freight) and passenger capability. A growing number of passenger operators were realising the benefits of this type of ship and commissioning similar vessels although with a full passenger complement, as seen in Brittany Ferries' *Barfleur* and Irish Ferries' *Isle of Innisfree* of 1992 and 1995.

Once again it seemed that freight ferry construction was entering a golden age. Early classes of the decade included a five-strong series by the Dutch yard Van der Giessen - de Noord for the Italian Finmare Group and this design reappeared within a few years, in this instance as the *Norbank* and *Norbay* for North Sea Ferries but now with facilities for over 100 drivers. Likewise, another Italian design seen in sisters *Linda* (currently with Cobelfret), *Norse Mersey* (originally operated by Norse Irish but now with DFDS) and *Dana Futura* of DFDS were soon upgraded to provide the ro-pax *Mersey Viking* and *Lagan Viking* for Norse Irish service between Liverpool and Belfast in 1997.

The Irish Sea became something of a feeding frenzy by the late 1990s as the previously sleepy operations of P&O and Cenargo suddenly changed into the far more dynamic services we see today. The advent of Norse Irish Ferries' ro-pax services in 1991 provided the catalyst of competition that resulted in significantly upgraded tonnage. First to respond was P&O who chose to reconstruct two of their elderly 1970s built vessels the *Ibex* and *Buffalo*, emerging as *European Envoy* and *European Leader* with capacities for 107 and 50 passengers respectively with the services advertised to the general public as 'value routes' in 1999. Cenargo, however, opted for the far more powerful response of ordering four impressive 250 passenger ro-pax vessels, the first of which opened a new fully advertised service between Liverpool and Dublin in 1999 as *Dawn Merchant* and *Brave Merchant*. P&O was to order two similar ro-pax vessels for service out of Liverpool and Cairnryan in 2000 and 2001.

North Sea services, however, have developed differently; the passenger market has experienced something of a downturn in recent years due to the effect of the Channel Tunnel, and whilst freight movements have increased, the latest generation of ships have not featured the ro-pax concept. Maersk was amongst the earliest to develop a new generation of ships for their Norfolk Line service connecting Felixstowe and Scheveningen with the commissioning in 1996 of the Japanese built *Maersk Exporter* and *Maersk Importer* with two additional vessels scheduled for the year 2000. These ships displaced the diminutive *Maersk Flanders* and a selection of chartered ships into secondary roles, but whilst the new ferries offered increased capacities of 122 trucks each, these were modest in comparison with competitor development at this time.

Having successfully upgraded their fleet with the Chinese *Symphorine* class by 1992, Cobelfret turned again to the Far East for their next generation of freighters. These new ships were to be substantially larger again, having capacity for 188 trucks and a gross tonnage of nearly 24,000. As with the earlier class, and in common with Maersk and Dart Line, the new ships offered little if any facilities for drivers to accompany their vehicles. The first in the series was named *Celestine* but was chartered to the British Ministry of Defence as the *Sea Crusader*. The second – *Clementine* – was introduced onto Cobelfret services and orders were placed for a further four in the class for delivery by the end of the decade. P&O too opted for traditional freight ferry tonnage in updating their former North Sea Ferries fleet by returning to Bore Line to provide two new generation freighters (the *Norsky* and *Norstream*) for service out of Middlesborough in 1999 as they had done with the 1980s built *Norking* and *Norqueen*.

Within Scandinavia, both of these trends can be seen. Tor Line, having maintained their fleet using second-hand tonnage

# CENTURY OF NORTH WEST EUROPEAN FERRIES 1900 - 2000

during the 1980s and early 1990s also placed an order for three new vessels arriving in 1999 as *Tor Selandia*, *Tor Suecia* and *Tor Britannia*. These are designed as traditional freighters, carrying 230 trucks and only 12 passenger. They will operate between Gothenburg and Immingham and may finally see the end of the remaining Fremnaes ships. On the other hand, Finnlines and their partners have developed an impressive series of ro-pax vessels that have seen their services opened up to passengers. The 1994-5 Polish built series comprised the *Finnhansa*, *Finntrader*, *Finnpartner* and *TransEuropa*, each with a gross tonnage of 32,531 and with the ability to carry 250 trucks and 112 passengers. Finally, Stena have returned to the fray with two classes of vessels for the charter market, the traditional freighter 'Stena 4-Runner' design and the 'Stena Seapacer' ro-pax.

## TOWARDS A NEW CENTURY

The story of European freight ferries can provide a fascinating, if not a little bewildering antidote to the development of passenger vessels. Their origins lie in the development of containerisation rather than that of the mail carrying packet boats that are so often viewed as synonymous with ferry service histories. However, as demonstrated at the start of this chapter, the world of the freight ferry is wide and varied. It incorporates not only the long voyages around Scandinavia and the North Sea where passengers of any sort are seldom welcome, through to the regular express freight services offered across the southern Baltic and English Channel and even the growing merger between freight and passenger operations on the Irish Sea.

Readers of this story may, however, be struck as to how the success of most modern freight ferry services has been achieved through the construction of a large number of different vessels during the early decades. The credit for this must surely go to Stena Line with their never-ending succession of freighter designs that have become so common a sight in ports around Europe. The most versatile of these ships must be the original 'Stena Carrier' class which was copied by so many other operators, but the role played by the 'Stena Searunner' workhorses must also be acknowledged.

During recent years it has sometimes seemed as though the paths of freight and passenger operation were becoming increasingly distant due to the use of ever larger multi purpose ships. However, the new ro-pax trend has lately provided a counterbalance to this. The final year of the century sees one of the largest orderbooks for freight and ro-pax ferries yet seen and the next decade and those beyond will undoubtedly see further development including freight carrying high speed ferries.

By the time this book is in print, some of the largest freight ferries that are currently under construction will be in service: Finnlines will have taken delivery of *Finnclipper* and *Finneagle* from Stena, Tor Line of their *Tor Selandia* trio whilst *Dawn Merchant* and *Brave Merchant* will have made their impression on the Irish Sea. As this unfolds, so the builders will be working on their next projects: P&O's new Irish Sea ferries and further ships for Cenargo and Cobelfret to name but a few. When one considers the new Europe, a continent largely at peace and united through commerce and trade, it is worth remembering the role played in this by the generations of freight ferries that have seen not only the birth of the European Economic Community but the development of the Single Market and the European Union. What would have happened were the LSTs to have continued in their original role is perhaps unimaginable but their descendants, towering over ports everywhere, have achieved immeasurable success in trade throughout Europe.

*Matthew Punter*

The **European Seaway** leaving Zeebrugge for Dover. The **Norland** can be seen at the berth awaiting her evening sailing to Hull. *(Mike Louagie)*

# CENTURY OF NORTH WEST EUROPEAN FERRIES 1900 - 2000

# Significant Freight Ferries

| Name | Operator & Route | GRT | Freight | Pax | Built | Notes |
|---|---|---|---|---|---|---|
| Empire Baltic | ASN: Tilbury-Antwerp | 4157* | 70L | 0 | Montreal, CA, 1945 | Broken up. |
| Bardic Ferry | ASN:Tilbury-Antwerp | 2550* | 70T | 55 | Dumbarton, UK, 1957 | Sold as *Nasim II*. |
| Viking IV | Thoresen:So'ton-Le Havre | 1152* | 40L | 0 | Brevik, NO, 1967 | Became livestock carrier *Guernsey Express*. Sank 1997. |
| Stafford | DFDS:Grimsby-Esbjerg. | 2602* | 113T | 12 | Helsingor, DK, 1967 | To Tzamar as *Voyager* for Brindisi-Patras. |
| Tor Mercia | Tor Line:Imm'ham-Halmstad | 1599* | 650m | 0 | Floro, NO, 1969 | To Ignazia Merssina in 1975 as *Jolly Marone*. |
| Tor Gothia | Tor Line:Imm'ham-G'burg | 4128* | 94T | 12P | Sandefjord, NO, 1972 | Lengthened 1977. Still in service. |
| Ulidia | Sealink:Stranraer-Larne | 1599* | 40T | 20 | Kristiansand, NO, 1970 | 1988: Converted to passenger carrier *Fjordveien*. |
| Stena Seatrader | Stena:Charter Market. | 2572* | 62T | 65 | Kreppel, NL, 1973 | Lengthened 1976. Now *Stena Scanrail* trainferry G'burg-F'shavn for Stena Line. |
| Contentin | Truckline:Poole-Cherbourg. | 1206* | 25T | 12 | Bremerhaven, GE 1970 | Became P&O's *St Magnus* for Shetland service and then to Mediterranean. |
| European Gateway | Townsend:F'xstowe-Rott'dam. | 3953* | 76T | 132 | Bremerhaven, GE 1975 | Lengthened 1980. |
| Dana Gloria | DFDS:Harwich-Esbjerg. | 5990* | 100T | 12 | Helsingor, DK, 1976 | To GT Link as *Gedser*, then Mediterranean service. |
| Coutances | Truckline:Poole-Cherbourg. | 2736* | 46L | 58 | Le Havre, FR, 1978 | Lengthened 1986. |
| Bison | P&O:Fleetwood-Dublin. | 3453* | 90T | 12 | Hamburg, GE, 1975 | Lengthened 1981. Now *European Pioneer* Liverpool-Dublin for P&O. |
| Stena Tender | Stena:Charter Market. | 2905* | 70T | 12 | Korneuburg, AU, 1976 | Lengthened and launched as *Goya* for United Baltic Corp. Now *European Navigator* for P&O |
| Wupertal | Reinecke:Charter Market. | 1599* | 64T | 12 | Hamburg, GE, 1977 | Sold to Sea Containers as *Picasso* |
| Stena Runner | Stena:Charter Market. | 5724* | 81L | 12 | Ulsan, SK, 1977 | Now *European Tideway* for P&O Felixstowe-Rotterdam. |
| Thomas Wehr | Wehr Transport:Charter Market. | 2184* | 71T | 12 | Bremerhaven, GE, 1977 | Now with Ferryways Ostend-Ipswich. |
| Ibex | P&O: Fleetwood-Dublin. | 6310* | 138T | 12 | Tamano, JA, 1980 | Rebuilt 1996 as *European Envoy* for Liverpool-Dublin. |
| Inowroclaw | POL: UK-Gdynia. | 14786 | 116T | 12 | Rauma, FI, 1980 | Still in service. |
| Balder Fjord | Balder: Charter Market. | 9071 | 100T | 12 | Galatz, RO, 1984 | Now *Dart 1* for Dart Line Dartford-Zeebrugge. |
| Dana Cimbria | Mercandia: For sale to DFDS. | 12189 | 150T | 12 | Frederikshavn, DK, 1986 | Immingham-Esbjerg as *Dana Cimbria*. |
| Symphorine | Cobelfret: UK-Zeebrugge. | 10030 | 130T | 10 | Dalian, CH, 1988 | Still in service. |
| Nils Dacke | TT Line:T'munde-Trellb'g. | 24000 | 160L | 300 | Bremerhaven, GE, 1988 | Converted to cruiseferry 1993. Now *Peter Pan* for TT Line. Same route. |
| European Seaway | P&O:Dover-Zeebrugge. | 22986 | 120L | 200 | Bremerhaven, GE, 1991 | Transferred to P&O Stena Line in 1998. |
| Stena Challenger | Sealink Stena Line:Dover-Calais. | 18523 | 100T | 500 | Rissa, NO, 1991 | Now Holyhead-Dublin for Stena Line. |
| Norbank | NSF:Hull-Rotterdam. | 17464 | 156T | 114 | Krimpen, NL, 1993 | Now with P&O. To Felixstowe-Rotterdam in 2001. |
| Finnhansa | Finnlines:Helsinki-Germany. | 32531 | 250T | 112 | Gdansk, PO, 1994 | Still in service. |
| Norse Mersey | Norse Irish:Liverpool-Belfast. | 13500 | 160T | 61 | Donanda, IT, 1995 | Now with DFDS for Immingham-Rotterdam. |
| Island Commodore | Commodore:Portsmouth-Chan. Is. | 11166 | 95T | 12 | Vlissingen, NL, 1995 | Sold 1999 for conversion to cablelayer |
| Maersk Exporter | Norfolk Line: Felixstowe-Schev'n. | 13017 | 122T | 12 | Shimizu, JA, 1996 | Still in service. |
| Bayard | Fred.Olsen: UK-Norway. | 20198 | 216T | 0 | Ancona, IT, 1997 | To Trasmediterranea in 1998 as *Superfast Andalucia*. |
| Mersey Viking | Norse Irish: Liverpool-Dublin. | 17000 | 164T | 340 | Donanda, IT, 1997 | Still in service. |
| Clementine | Cobelfret: UK-Zeebrugge. | 23986 | 156T | 24 | Sakaide, JA, 1997 | Still in service. |
| Dawn Merchant | Merchant Ferries: Liverpool-Dublin | 22152 | 175T | 250 | Seville, SP, 1999 | Still in service. |
| Tor Selandia | Tor Line: Imm'ham-G'burg. | 21700 | 230T | 12 | Ancona, IT, 1999 | Still in service. |
| Finnclipper | Finnlines: Helsinki-Lubeck. | 30500 | 206T | 440 | Puerto Real, SP, 1999 | Still in service. |
| Stena 4-Runner class | Stena: For charter market. | 21000 | 2715m | 12 | La Spezia, IT, 1998 | First two to British MOD. |

\* Denotes tonnage measured under pre-1982 rules.

## CENTURY OF NORTH WEST EUROPEAN FERRIES 1900 - 2000

# The Train Ferry Era

## OVERVIEW

The purpose of this chapter is to provide a summary history of the larger North West European rail ferries in the twentieth century. As readers will see, a high proportion were, and still are to be found in Germany and Scandinavia.

Train ferries have been largely a twentieth century phenomenon. Although their origins stretch back into mid-nineteenth century Scotland, there was a great expansion of interest in the early years of the twentieth century, notably in Scandinavia, although the number of routes has recently contracted through replacement by tunnels and bridges. On the other hand, there has been an expansion of long distance freight only ferry routes in the Baltic.

The design of train ferries and their related port facilities demanded a number of major advances in the design of both ships and port facilities, as follows:
* Vessels with flat decks not divided into separate watertight compartments
* Vessels with either (or both) bow and stern doors
* Healing tanks to maintain the equilibrium of the vessel while it is being loaded with often uneven point loads
* Link spans to cater for tidal range, a particular problem in Britain with its wide tidal range of 8 metres in many places. When handling rail wagons, especially bogie vehicles, the maximum acceptable incline on a link span is + or - 3.5%, shallower than acceptable to road vehicles
* The shape of the end of the vessel where loading takes place must be specifically tailored to the berth and linkspan and in consequence, many train ferries have been tied for their working lives to the single route for which they were built.

These design requirements are so similar to those of road

The *Shepperton Ferrry* with her two sister vessels maintained the Dover-Dunkerque train ferry service until the seventies. *(FotoFlite)*

vehicle ferries that train ferries provided the first vehicle ferries on many routes by carrying cars on their train decks. Many train ferries after disposal from their original use have served out their last years as vehicle ferries.

The broad assumption can be made in the descriptions following that unless otherwise specified, all train ferry services described below have been operated by the national railway administration of the relevant countries. In the 1990s, this has begun to break down, partly because of the reorganisation of the shipping sections of national railway administrations into separate autonomous units and partly because of the entry into the train ferry business of private sector shipping lines.

## BRITISH ISLES
## FREIGHT FERRIES ACROSS THE FORTH AND TAY (1849 - 1890)

Europe's first train ferries were in Scotland. The Edinburgh and Northern Railway, later known as the Edinburgh, Perth and Dundee Railway and from 1862 as the North British Railway, was faced with the problem of connecting its system in Fife both southwards across the Firth of Forth towards Edinburgh, and northwards across the Firth of Tay towards Dundee. To cross the Forth, the railway's engineer Thomas Bouch designed both the first train ferry, the *Leviathan*, (399 gross tons) built by Robert Napier and Sons at Govan in 1849, and linkspans at the harbours at Granton, north of Edinburgh, and at Burntisland in Fife. Service for freight began in February 1850 while in 1851, this was followed by a service across the Tay between Tayport and Broughty Ferry provided by the *Robert Napier* (234 gross tons), built in the same yard.

The service over the Tay never required more than one vessel. The *Robert Napier* was displaced from the service over the Tay by the opening of the first Tay Bridge in May 1878, but was hastily recalled in December of that year following the partial collapse of the bridge (also designed by Thomas Bouch). The service was withdrawn again when the second Tay Bridge opened in 1887, and the vessel was scrapped in the following year.

The service over the Forth required further vessels over the years, the *Carrier* of 1858, the *Balbirnie* of 1861, the *Kinloch* of 1865, and the *Midlothian* of 1881, built in a variety of British yards. The *Midlothian* was the largest at 920 gross tons, but the service was withdrawn when the Forth Bridge opened in 1890 and all the vessels were scrapped before the turn of the century.

The last British train ferry to be built was the *Cambridge Ferry* which came from the Tyne in 1963. After finishing on the Harwich-Zeebrugge link in late 1986 she was switched to Dover-Dunkerque West before eventual transfer as a ro-ro vessel for the Fishguard-Rosslare service late in 1987. She was sold for further service in the Adriatic in 1992. *(Miles Cowsill)*

**176**

# CENTURY OF NORTH WEST EUROPEAN FERRIES 1900 - 2000

*A product of the Helsingor shipyard in 1951, the SNCF train ferry **Saint-Germain** maintained the Dunkerque-Dover link until her withdrawal in May 1988. (Miles Cowsill)*

## FIRST WORLD WAR FREIGHT FERRIES BETWEEN ENGLAND AND FRANCE

During the First World War, the British army was faced with enormous logistic problems in supplying the forces in northern France. All munitions had to be transhipped from train to ship at a British port and transhipped again back to a train in France. The solution was seen to be a train ferry service. This was implemented from Southampton to Dieppe in December 1917 and from a new port at Richborough near Sandwich in Kent to Calais in February 1918 and to Dunkerque later in the year. Services ceased after the War, the port at Richborough was decommissioned and the ferries laid up.

Three ferries were built for the service: the *Train Ferry 1* and *Train Ferry 2* by Armstrong Whitworth on the Tyne and the *Train Ferry 3* by Fairfield of Govan. In 1918 the fleet was supplemented by the *Train Ferry 4*, second-hand from the St. Lawrence River in Canada. This had originally been built in Britain by Cammell Laird as the *Leonard* and was conceptually very different, not requiring linkspans since the entire train deck was capable of being lifted to match the level of rail tracks on shore.

## FREIGHT OPERATIONS FROM HARWICH (1924 - 1987)

After the War, the Great Eastern Railway (and its successor from 1923 the London & North Eastern Railway) saw the possibilities of a civilian freight operation between Britain and the European mainland, but in conjunction with Belgium rather than France. They purchased the three conventional wartime train ferries, and the linkspans from Southampton and Richborough. These were installed in Harwich and Zeebrugge and service commenced in 1924. Operations ceased in 1939, and the *Train Ferry 2* and *Train Ferry 3* were lost in the war.

After the war the *Train Ferry 1* was restored to civilian use, renamed the *Essex Ferry* and took up the Zeebrugge service once again in 1946. The lost tonnage was replaced by the *Suffolk Ferry* of 1947 and the *Norfolk Ferry* of 1951. Meantime, the London & North Eastern Railway had become British Railways (BR) in 1948. The original *Essex Ferry* was replaced by a new *Essex Ferry* in 1957. All three post-war vessels were built by John Brown's at Clydebank and in 1964, this fleet was supplemented by the *Cambridge Ferry*, 3,294 gross tons, built by Hawthorn Leslie. This enabled an additional route from Harwich to Dunkerque to be added in 1967 and from 1970 BR's shipping services traded as 'Sealink'.

*The Italian-built **Saint Eloi** entered service on the Dunkerque-Dover route in 1975 remaining on that link until withdrawn in April 1988. She was then used as a car ferry between Calais and Dover and then sold to the Isle of Man Steam Packet Company for use to the Isle of Man. She currently operates for Moby Lines. (FotoFlite)*

**177**

# CENTURY OF NORTH WEST EUROPEAN FERRIES 1900 - 2000

The final product of the Normed yard at Dunkerque, the train ferry/ro-ro vessel **Nord Pas-de-Calais** entered service late in 1987 but did not commence operations as a train ferry until the following May. Following the opening of the Channel Tunnel this link was terminated in December 1995 since when she has served as a ro-ro vessel on the Calais-Dover route. *(Miles Cowsill)*

In their later years the Harwich routes were handicapped by the inability of the Harwich linkspan to handle the increasing numbers of bogie freight wagons. Nevertheless, in 1980 BR placed in service on the route the *Speedlink Vanguard*, 3,514 gross tons, a converted ro-ro vessel originally built as the *Stena Shipper* by Vuyk & Zonen in the Netherlands in 1973. The *Suffolk Ferry* was withdrawn in 1980, followed by the *Essex Ferry* and the *Norfolk Ferry* in 1983. The Harwich - Dunkerque route was withdrawn in 1982 and two years later BR sold Sealink to Sea Containers who now operated the route on contract to BR. The remaining Harwich - Zeebrugge route was closed in 1987 as part of the reorganisation of the Dover - Dunkerque service described below. The *Speedlink Vanguard* was returned to Stena and the *Cambridge Ferry* transferred to Dover.

### DOVER - DUNKERQUE (1936 - 1976) / DUNKERQUE WEST (1976-1995)

The Dover - Dunkerque ferry route was a by-product of the rejection by the British Parliament in 1930 of a scheme to build a cross-Channel rail tunnel. As an alternative, the Southern Railway decided on the operation of a train ferry from Dover to Dunkerque in conjunction with the French company Societe de Navigation Angleterre - Lorraine - Alsace, generally known as ALA.

To cope with the problem of extreme tidal ranges at Dover, the Southern Railway decided to build an enclosed dock for the train ferries within Dover Harbour. In the event, its construction proved rather difficult and delayed the start of ferry operation until October 1936. Meanwhile three train ferries had been delivered by Swan Hunter and Wigham Richardson of Wallsend-on-Tyne, the *Twickenham Ferry*, *Hampton Ferry* and the *Shepperton Ferry*. From the commencement of the service the *Twickenham Ferry* was operated by ALA under the French flag. A passenger service was provided on the route in the form of the 'Night Ferry' train, through Wagons-Lits sleeping cars operating overnight between London and Paris.

The route was suspended at the outbreak of the Second World War, when the vessels entered war service. None were lost, and service resumed in 1947. Increasing demand led to addition of a fourth vessel in 1951, the *Saint-Germain*, 3,084 tons, built at Helsingor in Denmark and operated by SNCF, the French railways. Thereafter, little changed for almost 20 years, apart from the addition of through London - Brussels sleeping cars to the 'Night Ferry' from 1957.

By the mid-1960s, the pre-war train ferries needed replacement, but the possibility of the construction of a Channel Tunnel cast a planning blight on replacement vessels. The pre-war ferries were finally withdrawn in 1969 - 1973, and replaced by three multi-purpose ferries, the BR *Vortigern*, 4,797 gross tons, built by Swan Hunter in 1969, the ALA *Saint Eloi*, 4,649 gross tons, built by Cantieri Navale in Italy in 1975, and the SNCF *Chartres*, 4,590 gross tons, built by Dubigeon Normandie at Nantes, France in 1974, as well as the freight only BR vessel, *Anderida*, 1,579 tons, built in Norway. The bulk of the train ferry service was provided by the *Saint-Germain* and the *Saint Eloi*, while the *Vortigern* and *Chartres* were normally used as conventional passenger and road vehicle ferries.

In 1976, the Dunkerque ferry terminal moved to a new facility at Dunkerque West, and in 1977 BR bought out ALA.

# CENTURY OF NORTH WEST EUROPEAN FERRIES 1900 - 2000

The 'Night Ferry' through passenger service ceased in 1980, and the *Anderida* was disposed of in 1981.

The operation of the service was transformed in its last years. Firstly, the old train ferry dock in Dover was replaced by a more conventional linkspan arrangement on the Admiralty Pier extension in 1988. Secondly, all four present train ferries were replaced in train ferry service by the new SNCF train ferry *Nord Pas-de-Calais*, 13,727 gross tons, built in Dunkerque in 1987. The *Saint-Germain* was disposed of while the *Vortigern*, *Saint Eloi* (briefly renamed *Channel Entente*) and *Chartres* continued in service as conventional car ferries.

Following the opening of Eurotunnel, train ferry services across the Channel eventually ceased in December 1995. The *Nord Pas-de-Calais* continues in service as the *SeaFrance Nord Pas-de-Calais* operating as a freight ro-ro vessel.

## GERMANY
### FEHMARN (1903 - 1963)

Off the Baltic coast of Schleswig-Holstein lies the island of Fehmarn. The local standard-gauge railway, the Kreis Oldenburger Eisenbahn (KOE), opened a local railway on Fehmarn in 1903 accessed for passengers and freight by train ferry service between Grossenbrode Fahre on the mainland over the 1,200 metre strait to Fehmarnsund on Fehmarn. Service commenced with the *Fehmarnsund*, built by W. Klawitter in Danzig in 1903, supplemented from 1928 by the *Fehmarn*, built by Nobiskrug of Rendsburg, Germany. In 1941, ownership of the undertaking passed to the national German railways. In 1949, the service was further supplemented by the second-hand *Schleswig-Holstein*, originally built as the *F11 / Frauke* for the Luftwaffe by Otto Kuscewski in Konigsberg (now Kaliningrad in Russia). None of these vessels exceeded 351 gross tons.

The train ferry service ceased in 1963 with the opening of a bridge to Fehmarn as part of the the Vogelfluglinie rail route to Puttgarden described later.

### STRALSUND (1883 - 1936)

Until the construction of a bridge and causeway in 1936, the Baltic island of Rugen had no fixed link to the German mainland.

Following the construction of railways on the island, in 1883 the Prussian State Railways opened train ferry service for freight and foot passengers over the 1 km. from Stralsund to Altefahr on Rugen. They used the single-ended vessels *Prinz Heinrich* and *Rugen (1)*, followed by the *Stralsund* of 1890.

To enhance capacity, the original vessels were replaced by the double-ended *Sassnitz*, *Putbus*, *Rugen (2)* and *Bergen* over the period 1897 - 1906. Ferries carried through passenger carriages from 1902. In 1920, the *Altefahr* was added to the fleet. All the ferries were built by Schichau of Elbing (now Elblag in Poland) and none exceeded 1,000 gross tons.

As described later, in 1909 the train ferry at Stralsund became a link in an international route when train ferry services began from the port of Sassnitz on the further end of Rugen to Trelleborg in Sweden. Following increasing congestion, a causeway replaced the Stralsund train ferries in 1936 and the vessels were dispersed, mainly to Swinemunde, as described below.

# CENTURY OF NORTH WEST EUROPEAN FERRIES 1900 - 2000

The **Prins Richard** (photographed) (and sistership **Prinsesse Benedikte**) were products of the Frederikshavn shipyard in 1997. They maintain the Danish Scandlines half of the service from Rodby to Puttgarden. *(Miles Cowsill)*

## WITTOW (1896 - 1971)

The most northerly part of the island of Rugen forms a peninsula separated from the rest of the island by a waterway. In the 1890s, the Rugensche Kleinbahn-Aktiengesellschaft constructed a 75 cm. gauge railway system to provide local transport on the island, from 1896 using a train ferry to cross this 630 m. wide waterway at Wittow,. The company used the small vessels *Wittow* and *Jasmund* built by Vulcan of Stettin. In 1911, the *Jasmund* was replaced by the *Jaspar v. Malzahn*, built by von Nuske of Stettin which was renamed *Bergen* in 1945.

In 1949, the railway system passed into the hands of the Deutsche Reichsbahn, the state owned East German railway system. When this part of the narrow gauge rail system and therefore the train ferry service were abandoned in 1971, the vessels passed into the hands of the East German Weisse Flotte fleet for use as car ferries. In the 1990s, the vessels were still in service, although the *Wittow* was now a century old!

## USEDOM AND SWINEMUNDE (NOW SWINOUJSCIE) (1901 - 1993)

Usedom is a further large island off the Baltic coast of Germany. At its eastern end is the town of Swinoujscie, formerly Swinemunde, which is partly located on the island, and partly on the other side of the River Oder. In 1901 the Prussian State Railways began freight train ferry services across the 700 metre wide Oder between their railways on the 2 banks, using the *Rugen* (renamed *Swinemunde*) brought over from the Stralsund service. The *Swinemunde* was assisted later by a number of the previous Stralsund train ferries operating as vehicle ferries. The service was abandoned in 1945 when the extreme eastern end of the island of Usedom including the town of Swinemunde was handed over to Poland.

The handover of Swinemunde to Poland also severed rail communication from the German mainland to the remaining railways on Usedom which included a key industrial line to the former rocket works at Peenemunde. To provide access to the island's railways for freight wagons and other rolling stock transfers, the Soviet forces installed linkspans in 1945 for a train ferry to Usedom at Wolgast, where the river Peene is only 600 metres wide. The former Stralsund train ferry *Stralsund*, used during the war by the rocket works, took up the service under Red Army control but in 1949 she was handed over to the civilian control of the East German Railways and continued in service until 1993, when the vessel was 103 years old. Since 1986, the *Stralsund* had worked as an unpowered barge and has now been preserved.

## INTERNATIONAL SERVICES BETWEEN GERMANY AND DENMARK
## WARNEMUNDE TO GEDSER (1903 - 1995)

The first international train ferry route across the Baltic was opened over the 42 km. between Warnemunde and Gedser in 1903 jointly by the Mecklenburgische Friedrich-Franz-Eisenbahn and the Danish Railways (Danske Statsbaner - DSB). Two double-ended vessels were provided by each party. The Germans provided the *Friedrich Franz IV* (a passenger paddler built by Schichau in Elbing) and the *Mecklenburg* (a freight screw vessel built by Schichau in Danzig). The Danes provided the *Prinsesse Alexandrine* (a sister paddler to the *Friedrich Franz IV* from the same yard) and the *Prins Christian* (a freight screw vessel built in Helsingor). Tonnages of all these vessels were in the range 1402 - 1824 gross. After the First World War, the Mecklenburg railways and their ferry interests passed into the hands of the new German national railway system.

Three of the four vessels were withdrawn in the inter-war period. The *Friedrich Franz IV* was scrapped in 1926, the *Prinsesse Alexandrine* withdrawn in 1930, and the *Prins Christian* transferred to internal Danish use in 1923. There were two somewhat larger replacement screw vessels, the Danish *Danmark* of 1922 (built at Helsingor), and the German *Schwerin* of 1926 (built by Schichau of Elbing). The *Mecklenburg* continued in service as a summer reserve ship. The service continued during the war until 1943. The *Schwerin* was destroyed in 1944, while the *Danmark* was sunk in 1945. After the war, the *Mecklenburg* was handed over by the Allies to the Soviet forces, who in turn passed the vessel to Poland for whom she sailed until 1958 under a number of names. As the *Kopernik*, she was briefly used again as a train ferry between Swinoujscie and Trelleborg.

The post-war political changes placed Warnemunde in East Germany, cutting off much of the route's potential traffic and sending the route into slow decline. The Danish *Danmark* was raised and resumed service in 1947. This remained the only vessel on the route until in 1963 the East German railways introduced the *Warnemunde*, 6,149 gross tons, built by VEB Neptun in Rostock, East Germany. In 1968, DSB finally replaced the 46-year old *Danmark* by the *Kong Frederik IX* built in 1954 and previously used elsewhere. The Danes also used other vessels on occasion. For some years only one vessel was needed and this was provided by the East German railways in the summer and by the Danes in the winter.

While there was a great expansion in road vehicle traffic after German reunification, the port of Warnemunde proved entirely unsuitable for this traffic. Train ferry services ceased in 1995 and road vehicle ferry services were diverted to nearby Rostock.

## GROSSENBRODE - GEDSER (1951 - 1963) AND VOGELFLUGLINIE (PUTTGARDEN TO RODBY) (1963 TO PRESENT)

Before the Second World War, both Germany and Denmark saw the need for a new direct route from western Germany towards Copenhagen and beyond towards Sweden. This would involve new ports and new connecting railways. A certain amount of work was done in 1941 - 43 until the war finally stopped

# CENTURY OF NORTH WEST EUROPEAN FERRIES 1900 - 2000

construction.

After the war and the division of Germany, which placed the port of Warnemunde in the East, through rail traffic from Sweden and Copenhagen to West Germany had to be routed circuitously over the Great Belt train ferry and through Fredericia in Denmark. This created serious capacity problems, resolved in the short term by opening a new train ferry port at Grossenbrode in Schleswig-Holstein in West Germany. From here it was 67 km. to the existing Danish port of Gedser.

Services between Grossenbrode and Gedser began in 1951, temporarily with the DSB *Danmark*, replaced shortly after by the new Danish *Dronning Ingrid*, built at Helsingor. After the war neither part of Germany had been left with any sea-going train ferries, so a West German contribution had to wait until the *Deutschland* (built by Howaldtswerke Deutsche Werft of Kiel, West Germany) entered service in 1953. In subsequent years the Danes added the *Kong Frederik IX*, built at Helsingor in 1954, after which the *Dronning Ingrid* was transferred to the Great Belt, and the Germans the *Theodor Heuss* (built by Howaldtswerke in 1957).

In 1958, the German and Danish governments agreed to a resumption of the pre-war concept of a more direct route, the so-called Vogelfluglinie (bird's flight route), although some variations were made to the original plans. This route involving new connecting railways in both countries, and new ports at Puttgarden in Germany and the 19 km. distant Rodby in Denmark opened in 1963 after which the Grossenbrode - Gedser route then closed. The ferry berths at the ports were designed so that DSB vessels could be interchanged between the Vogelfluglinie and the Great Belt, no doubt subject to the provision or deletion of the crucial duty free facilities! In the meantime, in 1961 the Danes had swapped the *Kong Frederik IX* for the new *Knudshoved*, again built at Helsingor.

Over the next 35 years, road traffic steadily grew at the expense of that by rail. During this period, new German vessels included a replacement *Deutschland* in 1972 (built by Nobiskrug at Rendsburg, West Germany), and the *Karl Carstens* (built by Howaldtswerke), replacing the *Theodor Heuss* in 1986. In 1968, DSB introduced a new *Danmark* (built at Helsingor), and in 1981 - 82, replaced the oldest vessels with the *Prins Henrik* and the *Dronning Margrethe II*, which had originally been introduced to the Great Belt service in 1973 - 74. The partners also added non-train ferry tonnage.

After these years of uneventful but steady growth, a fundamental reassessment took place in the 1990s. By this time, through day passenger train services were mainly operated by the Danish IC3 diesel multiple unit trains. The partners decided to route all through rail freight away from the route following electrification of the railway from Copenhagen to Germany via Fredericia and the opening of a Great Belt bridge-cum-tunnel. The partners would introduce a new generation of double-ended vessels of about 15,000 gross tons (larger than previous vessels), providing a higher frequency service for road users, but with no provision for rail freight.

The Germans introduced a new *Deutschland* (IV) and *Schleswig-Holstein*, both built by van der Giessen-de Noord in the Netherlands, and the Danes the *Prins Richard* and *Prinsesse Benedikte*, both built at Frederikshavn in Denmark. All four ships entered service in 1997 when the previous vessels were withdrawn or went into non-train ferry service. The two countries merged their ferry operations into a single organisation, Scandlines AG, in 1998.

The 1973-built **Dronning Margrethe II** was built for the Nyborg-Korsor route in 1973 but in 1981 she was switched to the Rodby-Puttgarden service receiving an extra vehicle deck in the following year. Withdrawn in 1997 she remains in the Scandlines fleet in a relief role. *(Miles Cowsill)*

181

# CENTURY OF NORTH WEST EUROPEAN FERRIES 1900 - 2000

The DSB paddle train ferry *Prinsesse Alexandrine* leaving Warnemünde. Built in 1903, she is seen after rebuilding in 1905 and lasted until 1935. *(John May collection)*

## DANISH INTERNAL SERVICES

The Kingdom of Denmark includes a large number of islands. When railways were built in the nineteenth century it was economically impractical to build railway bridges over the many waterways. The Danish State Railways, DSB, and other companies bridged the gaps with the train ferry services described below.

## LITTLE BELT (1872 - 1935)

The State Railways (DSB) opened the first Danish train ferry route in 1872. This crossed the Little Belt between Fredericia on Jutland and Strib on the island of Fyn, using the double-ended paddler *Lillebaelt* built in England by Wigham Richardson. Over the years, eleven vessels were used on the 3.8 km. route all of which grossed less than 1,000 tons, and were frequently interchanged with other short routes such as over the Oddesund and Oresund.

The route ceased when a bridge was opened in 1935 and most of the vessels scrapped. Until then, through passenger trains from Copenhagen to Jutland, for example to Esbjerg, had to use both the Great and Little Belt train ferry routes en route.

## GREAT BELT (1883 - 1997)

The route across the 26 km. of the Great Belt between the ports of Nyborg on Fyn and Korsor on Sjaelland was always the prime Danish State Railways internal train ferry route for passenger and freight trains and has generally been provided with the prime ships. Vessels have often been cascaded subsequently to other routes or operated as pure vehicle ferries on the parallel route between Halsskov and Knudshoved established in 1957.

The main vessels used over the 114 years of operation of the route are listed below.

Paddlers (up to 1,114 gross tons):
| | | |
|---|---|---|
| *Korsor* | 1883 | Kockums (Sweden) |
| *Nyborg* | 1883 | Do. |
| *Sjaelland* | 1887 | Burmeister & Wain |
| *Storebaelt* | 1900 | Do. |

Screw vessels (up to 1,581 gross tons):
| | | |
|---|---|---|
| *Jylland* | 1894 | Burmeister & Wain |
| *Christian IX* | 1908 | Do. |
| *Odin* | 1910 | Do. |

New generation of screw vessels requiring modified ferry berths (up to 2,942 tons):
| | | |
|---|---|---|
| *Korsor* | 1927 | Helsingor |
| *Nyborg* | 1931 | Do. |
| *Sjaelland* | 1933 | Do. |
| *Freia* | 1936 | Alborg (Denmark) |
| *Storebaelt* | 1939 | Helsingor |

The operational fleet at the time of the Second World War comprised the vessels from the *Christian IX* onwards.

Post war construction (up to 6,211 gross tons):
| | | |
|---|---|---|
| *Fyn* | 1947 | Burmeister & Wain |
| *Dronning Ingrid* | 1951 | Helsingor |
| *Prinsesse Benedikte* | 1959 | Do. |
| *Knudshoved* | 1961 | Do. |
| *Sprogo* | 1962 | Do. |
| *Asa-Thor* | 1965 | Nakskov (Denmark) |
| *Dronning Margrethe II* | 1973 | Do. |
| *Prins Henrik* | 1974 | Do. |

The final generation of train ferries of over 10,000 gross tons capable of crossing in one hour rather than 75 minutes but again requiring modified berths:
| | | |
|---|---|---|
| *Prins Joachim* | 1980 | Nakskov |
| *Dronning Ingrid* | 1980 | Do. |
| *Kronprins Frederik* | 1981 | Do. |

In this final phase, the Danish railways were carrying a through Inter-City train on the Great Belt train ferry service every hour. Freight crossings were additional and provided by older vessels.

In 1997, a through bridge-cum-tunnel was opened for rail traffic after which train ferry operation ceased and the fleet was dispersed or laid up. It has proved difficult to find suitable alternative uses for such specialised vessels.

## STORSTROMMEN (1884 - 1937)

The 3.8 km. route from Masnedo on Sjaelland to Orehoved on Falster formed part of the through passenger and freight route

Korsor was the eastern terminal of the Great Belt train ferry service in Denmark before it was replaced by the new bridge in 1997. *(Miles Cowsill)*

# CENTURY OF NORTH WEST EUROPEAN FERRIES 1900 - 2000

from Copenhagen to the train ferry port of Gedser on the way to Warnemunde in Germany. A State Railways train ferry service started in 1884 and most of the vessels on the route were transferred from the Little Belt. Three vessels were built specially for the Storstrommen route, the *Alexandra* of 1892, the *Thyra* of 1893 and the final *Orehoved* of 1916, before the route was replaced by a bridge in 1937.

## INTERNAL FREIGHT ROUTES

In the past the Danish State Railways (DSB) and private shipping and railway companies operated a number of short freight ferry routes with small vessels of less than 500 gross tons. In most cases there was no railway at the far end, just goods sidings to which the train ferry delivered wagons.

## INTERNATIONAL SERVICES OVER THE KATTEGAT AND SKAGERAK
### HIRTSHALS - KRISTIANSAND (1939 AND 1958 - 199?)

The Kristiansands D/S commenced freight train ferry service over the 71 sea miles from Hirtshals in the north of Jutland (Denmark) to Kristiansand in Norway with the *Skagerak I* in 1939, built at Alborg in Denmark. Service ceased in the war when the vessel was sunk and the link did not resume until the entry into service in 1958 of the *Skagen* built by Pusnes in Norway. In 1965, service was supplemented by the new Alborg built *Skagerak* which sank a year later in a storm.

In 1968 the line was taken over by Fred. Olsen, and the new Alborg-built *Christian IV* entered service. Further new tonnage included the *Buenavista* (Ulstein, Norway, 1971), *Bonanza* (Ulstein 1972) and the *Borgen* (Alborg 1975). Train ferry traffic subsequently faded, and had ceased by the mid-1990s. Vessels used had ranged in tonnage from 1,281 to 7,570 tons.

### FREDERIKSHAVN - GOTHENBURG (1988 - PRESENT)

A new service from northern Jutland started in about 1988, when Stena Line introduced the *Stena Scanrail* from Frederikshavn in Denmark to Gothenburg in Sweden. The *Stena Scanrail* has a complicated history. She was built by van der Giessen and Vuyk & Zonen in the Netherlands in 1973 as the ro-ro cargo ferry the *Stena Seatrader*. After being renamed on a number of occasions she was finally converted to a freight train ferry of 11,344 gross tons in 1987 and renamed the *Stena Scanrail* in the following year.

## SWEDEN
### HELSINGOR - HELSINGBORG (1892 - 2000)

For many years, the 5km. between Helsingor in Denmark and Helsingborg in Sweden supported the prime Danish State Railways operated train ferry route between Denmark and Sweden, carrying the bulk of through rail passenger and freight vehicles with a typical service frequency of a crossing every 20 minutes. The port arrangements permitted use of the same small double-ended vessels as the former route over the Little Belt and until that route closed in 1935 there was frequent interchange of vessels. Despite the short journey, recent vessels have included extensive restaurants and duty-free supermarkets.

Service commenced with the *Kronprinsesse Louise* from the Little Belt route in 1892 supplemented by the *Kronprins Frederik* from 1898. The *Helsingborg* of 1902 was the first screw vessel but no new vessels were built for the route in the inter-war period.

The earlier vessels had been of less than 1,000 gross tons. Post-war, larger vessels of between 1,000 and 2,000 gross tons were built, including the *Helsingor* of 1955, the *Helsingborg* of 1960, the *Najaden* of 1967, the *Karnan* of 1967, the *Kronborg* of 1973 and the *Holger Danske* of 1976. The volume of rail traffic greatly reduced when all freight was diverted in 1986 to the new service described later between Helsingborg and Copenhagen Frihavn.

In the 1990s, the operation fundamentally changed. The service became a joint Danish-Swedish operation trading as ScandLines. All previous vessels were replaced by three new and much larger vessels of over 10,000 gross tons, the *Tycho Brahe* of 1991, the *Aurora af Helsingborg* of 1992, and the similar non-train ferry *Hamlet*. The first two new vessels were built at Langsten in Norway, the *Hamlet* by Finnyards, Rauma, Finland, unlike their predecessors which came from a variety of Danish yards. The residual passenger train operation will cease when the new Oresund bridge-cum-tunnel between Malmo and Copenhagen opens in 2000.

### COPENHAGEN FRIHAVN - HELSINGBORG (1986 - 2000)

This new jointly Danish and Swedish operated route for rail freight only (Danlink) began in 1986 to provide improved facilities for rail freight between Sweden and West Germany and beyond. The Swedes introduced the *Oresund*, purpose built by Moss Rosenberg in Norway, while the Danish *Trekronor* was a conversion to a train ferry of the freighter originally built in 1979 as the *Milora* by Ankerlokken in Norway. Both vessels are of about 15,000 gross tons. This service will cease in July 2000 when the new Oresund bridge-cum-tunnel opens.

### COPENHAGEN FRIHAVN - MALMO (1895 - 1986)

From 1895, the Helsingor - Helsingborg ferry route over the Oresund was supplemented by a 30 km. passenger and freight route between Copenhagen and Malmo, jointly operated by the Danes and the Swedes. The first vessel was the 1,091 gross ton Danish *Kjobenhavn*, built by Burmeister & Wain, followed by the Swedish 1,588 ton *Malmo*, built by Kockums in 1900. In 1923, the old *Kjobenhavn* was replaced by the *Prins Christian* from the Gedser - Warnemunde route. In 1945, both vessels were replaced by the new Swedish 2,558 gross ton *Malmohus* built by Kockums, which operated the route until she was withdrawn in 1986 and replaced by the new Copenhagen Frihavn - Helsingborg freight route described above. Through services of passenger train vehicles had already been progressively withdrawn in the early 1970s.

### SASSNITZ - TRELLEBORG (1909 - PRESENT)

Ever since its inauguration as the Konigslinie (Royal Route) in 1909, the passenger and freight route between Trelleborg in Sweden and Sassnitz on the German island of Rugen has formed one of Europe's prime train ferry routes. It provides Sweden with a direct route to mainland Europe, especially for rail freight. While Sassnitz was in East Germany for most of the post-war period, traffic continued at high levels. With a route length of 107 km., the route has always required substantial sea-going vessels of 3,000 gross tons or more.

Initially, each international partner provided two vessels. Vulcan of Stettin provided the Germans with the *Deutschland* and the *Preussen*, while Swan Hunter & Wigham Richardson

# CENTURY OF NORTH WEST EUROPEAN FERRIES 1900 - 2000

The **Sassnitz** is engaged on the 3 hour 30 minutes service linking her namesake port in Germany and the Swedish port of Trelleborg. The ship was built in 1989. *(Bill Mayes)*

provided the *Koning Gustav V*, and Lindholmens in Sweden the *Drottning Victoria* for the Swedes.

Following a number of very bad winters in the 1920s, the Swedes added the icebreaker-cum-freight train ferry *Starke* in 1931, built by Deutsche Werft in Kiel, Germany. The service continued almost through the Second World War, ceasing only in 1944. In the meantime, the *Starke* had been sunk by a mine in 1942, but was raised, repaired and extended by Kockums.

The *Deutschland* and the *Preussen* were taken over by the Allies in 1945 and handed over to the Soviets who renamed them the *Aniva* and the *Krilyon* respectively, and transferred them to the Far East for use as non-train ferries. The *Aniva* was modernised in Vladivostock in 1950 - 51 but sank in 1959 while the *Krilyon* was at first used between Vladivostock and the Kamchatka peninsular, and was rebuilt at Dalien in China in 1957 - 59 for further use in the Far East as a passenger vessel. She was finally taken out of service in 1975.

After the war, the Swedes resumed the service in 1947, but for the first year had to use the German port of Warnemunde instead of Sassnitz because of war damage to the port. By the mid - 1950s, replacement and additional tonnage became necessary. In 1958 the Swedes introduced the new *Trelleborg*, built at Helsingor, and in 1959 the East Germans joined operation on the route with the *Sassnitz*, built by VEB Neptun in Rostock, East Germany. In 1967 - 68, the Swedes introduced two new vessels, the *Skana* and the *Drottningen*, both built at Uddevalla, Sweden, enabling the twin original Swedish vessels to be scrapped after a working life of almost 60 years. In 1971, the East Germans added the *Stubbenkammer*, built at Trosvik in Norway, followed in 1972 by the *Rugen*, built by VEB Neptun.

Up to this point, all ships on the route had a width of 18.8 metres, but now the partners agreed to provide berths for vessels 22.6 metres wide. The first wider vessels were the Swedish freighters *Gotaland* and *Svealand* built by Nakskov in Denmark in 1973, supplemented by the East German freighter *Rostock* built by Bergens in Norway in 1977. This vessel was subsequently rebuilt with a passenger capability in 1993. In 1977, the *Sassnitz*, *Trelleborg* and *Stubbenkammer* were all taken out of service and in 1982 the Swedes received a new passenger and freight *Trelleborg* from Oresundsvarvet, Sweden, and the East Germans another *Sassnitz*, from Danyard in Alborg in 1989.

In 1994, a proportion of the freight service was diverted to the German port of Rostock, as described below. The Sassnitz terminal was relocated in 1998 from the old Sassnitz Hafen to the nearby Sassnitz - Fahrhafen, a redevelopment of the 1980s port of Mukran also described later.

## ROSTOCK - TRELLEBORG (1994 - PRESENT)

After starting this new route in 1994 with the *Rostock* and *Gotaland* diverted from the Sassnitz service, each partner has now acquired a major new vessel for the route. The Germans have introduced the *Mecklenburg - Vorpommern* of 36,185 gross tons delivered by Schichau of Bremerhaven, Germany in 1996, and the Swedes the even larger *Skane* delivered by ASEA in Cadiz, Spain in 1998.

184

# CENTURY OF NORTH WEST EUROPEAN FERRIES 1900 - 2000

## SWEDEN TO POLAND (1946 - 1953 AND 1974 - PRESENT)

Train ferry services between Sweden and Poland are a post Second World War phenomenon. Service was started over the 225 sea miles between Trelleborg and Gdynia by the Swedes in 1946 using vessels from the Trelleborg - Sassnitz route, no doubt pending reinstatement after war damage of port facilities at Sassnitz. The service included through sleeping cars as far as Praha. In 1948 the route was shortened to 100 sea miles by changing the Polish port to Odra Port, part of Swinoujscie (formerly Swinemunde). From 1950, the Poles contributed tonnage in the shape of the *Kopernik*, formerly the German *Mecklenburg*. Traffic then declined, and the route ceased at the end of 1953.

The train ferry service was revived twenty years later when Polish Ocean Lines on behalf of the respective state railways commenced a freight service over the 90 sea miles between Swinoujscie in Poland and Ystad in Sweden, using the 2,898 gross tons *Mikolaj Kopernik* built at Trosvik in Norway. In 1977, the larger *Jan Heweliusz* from the same yard was added to the service (this vessel sank with loss of life in 1993), followed in 1988 by the *Jan Sniadecki*, 14,417 gross tons from Falkenburg, Sweden. The latest vessel is the 29,875 gross ton ro-pax *Polonia* of the (Polish) Unity Line, built by Langsten in Norway.

## MALMO - TRAVEMUNDE (1987 - PRESENT)

Since 1987, the shipping line Nordo-Link have operated ro-ro freighters with a rail wagon capability between Malmo in Sweden and Travemunde in Germany. They originally used the second-hand *Svealand* and *Scandinavia*, later the 1980-built but also second hand *Lubeck Link* and *Malmo Link*. These two vessels of over 33,000 gross tons were built at Oskarshamn in Sweden as the *Finnhawk* and *Finnrose*.

## STOCKHOLM - TURKU (1989 - PRESENT)

Since 1989, SeaWind Line have operated between Stockholm and Turku in Finland. While their route primarily serves road freight, their vessels also have standard gauge rail track for freight

The elegant Swedish Railways train ferry **Malmohus** of 1945. *(John May collection)*

wagons. Their first vessel was the 15,879 gross ton *Sea Wind*, originally built as the *Svealand* at Helsingor in 1971. From 1999, the *Sea Wind* has been supplemented by the *Star Wind*, 13,788 gross tons, formerly the *Rostock* from the Trelleborg - Sassnitz and Trelleborg - Rostock routes. As with other routes between western Europe and Finland, wagons need to be re-gauged in Finland for the 1524 mm. gauge railways of Finland and Russia.

## STOCKHOLM - NAANTALI (1967 - 1975)

Between 1967 and 1975, the Swedish Railways operated a similar but short lived route from Stockholm to Naantali in Finland using the *Starke* and the *Drottningen* from the Trelleborg - Sassnitz route.

## NORWAY
## LAKE TINNSJO (1909 - 1985)

The train ferry probably best known to the British public was the *Ammonia*, which as the *Hydro* was 'sunk' by the Rank Organisation in the film the 'Heroes of Telemark'.

Since the early years of the century, the chemical company

The 1998-built **Skane** was built in Spain for the 6 hour service between Trelleborg and Rostock. At 42,500 gross tons she is one of the largest train ferries to be built. *(Bill Mayes)*

185

**We're with you all the way…**

Suppliers of fine quality print and 100% commitment to Ferry Publications 1988 – 2000.

Pembroke Dock, West Wales   Tel: **01646 684976**

Haven COLOURPRINT

# CENTURY OF NORTH WEST EUROPEAN FERRIES 1900 - 2000

Stena Line run a train ferry service between Denmark and Sweden. The **Stena Scanrail** is seen here at Frederikshavn pending her departure to Gothenburg. *(Miles Cowsill)*

Norsk Hydro has manufactured fertiliser using hydro-electric power at the town of Rjukan, about 100 km. west of Oslo. However, until recent years the only practical access to Rjukan was by ferry along the 38 km. length of the lake of Tinnsjo.

Freight train ferry service began in 1909 with the wooden *Tinnsjo* built by Norsk Hydro, and the *Rjukanfoss* built by Fevig at Tinnoset on the lake. In 1915, the *Hydro* built by Akers was added. In 1929 the *Tinnsjo* was replaced by the new 929 gross tons *Ammonia* built by Moss in Norway.

During the Second World War, the German occupation forces adapted the chemical plant at Rjukan to make heavy water for a prospective German atomic bomb. In 1944 the *Hydro* was sunk by Norwegian saboteurs when carrying the first train of tank wagons carrying the precious cargo to Germany. The *Ammonia* was temporarily renamed as the *Hydro* when the film was made in 1964. Viewing the film is highly recommended!

In 1956, a replacement vessel, the 1,119 tons *Storegut* was built by Glommen at Tinnoset. Following road construction along the shores of the lake the train ferry service finally ceased in 1985.

## GERMANY TO FINLAND
### TRAVEMUNDE-FINLAND (1975 - PRESENT)

The use in Finland of the Russian 1524 mm. rail gauge has always been an impediment to through rail freight. However, in 1973, a consortium of German and Finnish companies formed the private sector company Railship GmbH to operate a train ferry service for standard gauge freight wagons between Travemunde in Germany and Hanko in Finland, a distance of 1,022 km.. The port of Hanko was equipped with gauge changing facilities for the freight wagons.

The first vessel was *Railship I*, originally 5,322 gross tons, built by Rickmers in Bremerhaven, Germany in 1975. The success of the route led to the building of two more vessels of just over 20,000 gross tons, the *Railship II* of 1984 by Seebeckwerft in Bremerhaven, and finally the *Railship III* at the same yard in 1990. More recently, Finnlines has taken ownership of the route, and in 1998 the Finnish port was moved from Hanko to Turku.

## FORMER SOVIET UNION
### SASSNITZ FAHRHAFEN (MUKRAN) - KLAIPEDA (1988 - PRESENT)

Following the success of a freight train ferry route inaugurated in 1978 parallel to the Black Sea coast between Varna in Bulgaria and Iljitchovsk in Ukraine (near Odessa), the East German and Soviet authorities agreed to operate a similar route avoiding politically unreliable Poland. This involved the construction of a new German port on the island of Rugen at Mukran, just south of Sassnitz Hafen used by train ferries to Sweden. This time, the ferries would have broad gauge tracks, and would tranship their loads to standard gauge wagons at a major transhipment facility at Mukran. Six ferries were intended to operate the service, but in the event only five were built. They were all originally of 22,404 gross tons, and came from the yard of VEB M. Thesen in Wismar, East Germany, in 1986 - 89. They were the *Mukran* and *Greifswald* (both German) and the Lithuanian vessels *Klaipeda*, *Vilnius* and *Kaunas*.

Service on the 506 km. route began in 1988, but with the dramatic changes in eastern Europe, 90% of the traffic was soon lost. The *Mukran* (renamed the *Petersburg* in 1995) and the *Greifswald* now belong to Scandlines AG subsidiary Euroseabridge GmbH. The *Kaunas* and *Vilnius* are now operated by Lisco (the Lithuanian Shipping Co.), and operate between Klaipeda and Kiel as non-train ferries, along with the *Greifswald*. The Lisco owned *Klaipeda*, the only vessel not to have had her passenger accommodation substantially increased, operates between Sassnitz and Klaipeda jointly with the *Petersburg*.

### OXELOSUND-KLAIPEDA (2000 -

The Swedish CombiTrans and Lithuanian company Lisco are planning a new route to commence in the year 2000 between Oxelosund in Sweden and Klaipeda, using Lisco's existing train ferries originally built for the Sassnitz Fahrhafen (Mukran) - Klaipeda route.

*Alan de Burton*

# FLY OR CRUISE FROM PORTSMOUTH.

Whether you choose to nip across to France or travel at a more leisurely pace, then choose P&O Portsmouth. The Fastcraft will whisk you in real style to Cherbourg in just 2 hours 45 minutes. On the other hand you could cruise to Cherbourg or Le Havre on the Channel's best-appointed Cruiseferries. Revel in the immaculate service and top-class amenities onboard; casinos, pools, discount shopping, bars, top entertainment, Club Class, and Les Routiers approved restaurants. Whichever way, you'll arrive perfectly placed to enjoy the delights of Normandy and Brittany, or to explore the rest of France. Alternatively, turn your journey into a MiniCruise to Spain onboard the luxurious Pride of Bilbao. With 3 days to make the most of our facilities, plus time ashore to explore, it's the ideal break for those in need of a break.

*For further details and to book call 0870 2424 999, or see your travel agent. For a full brochure call 0870 9000 212, quoting NW. Ships and facilities may vary between routes. Fastcraft does not operate during the winter.*

www.poportsmouth.com

Altogether more civilised.

**P&O PORTSMOUTH**

PORTSMOUTH TO BILBAO, CHERBOURG & LE HAVRE

# CENTURY OF NORTH WEST EUROPEAN FERRIES 1900 - 2000

# Vehicle/Passenger ferries in use from British Isles at end of 1999

*(INCLUDES FAST FERRIES WHICH MAY BE LAID UP OR AWAY ON CHARTER)*

| Name | Tonnage | Year | Speed | Pass | Cars | Lanes | Class | Built | Flag | Operator |
|---|---|---|---|---|---|---|---|---|---|---|
| ADMIRAL OF SCANDINAVIA | 18888t | 76 | 21k | 1132P | 400C | 45L | BA | Rendsburg, GY | BA | DFDS Seaways |
| ÁRAINN MHÓR | 64t | 72 | 8k | 138P | 4C | - | B | Port Glasgow, GB | GB | Arranmore Island Ferry Service |
| ATLANTIC II | 3012t | 90 | 35k | 350P | 80C | - | BA | Hobart, AL | BA | Sea Containers Ferries |
| BARFLEUR | 20133t | 92 | 19k | 1173P | 550C | 125T | BA | Helsinki, FI | FR | Brittany Ferries |
| BELNAHUA | 35t | 72 | 8k | 40P | 5C | 1L | BA | Campbeltown, GB | GB | Argyll & Bute Council |
| BEN-MY-CHREE | 12504t | 98 | 19k | 500P | - | 100T | A | Krimpen, NL | IM | Sea Containers Ferries |
| BIGGA | 274t | 91 | 11k | 96P | 21C | 4L | BA | St Monans, GB | GB | Shetland Islands Council |
| BRAVE MERCHANT | 22152t | 98 | 22.5k | 250P | - | 175T | IM | Sevilla, SP | GB | Merchant Ferries |
| BRETAGNE | 24534t | 89 | 21k | 2030P | 580C | 40L | BA | St Nazaire, FR | FR | Brittany Ferries |
| BRUERNISH | 69t | 73 | 8k | 164P | 6C | - | B | Port Glasgow, GB | GB | Caledonian MacBrayne |
| CAEDMON | 763t | 73 | 9.5k | 520P | 58C | 6L | BA | Dundee, GB | GB | Wightlink |
| CALEDONIAN ISLES | 5221t | 93 | 15k | 1000P | 120C | - | BA | Lowestoft, GB | GB | Caledonian MacBrayne |
| CANNA | 69t | 73 | 8k | 140P | 6C | - | B | Port Glasgow, GB | GB | Caledonian MacBrayne |
| CARRIGALOE | 225t | 70 | 8k | 200P | 27C | - | BA | Newport (Gwent), GB | IR | Cross River Ferries |
| CENRED | 761t | 73 | 9.5k | 520P | 58C | 6L | BA | Dundee, GB | GB | Wightlink |
| CENWULF | 761t | 73 | 9.5k | 520P | 58C | 6L | BA | Dundee, GB | GB | Wightlink |
| CLANSMAN | 5499t | 98 | 16.5k | 634P | 90C | - | BA | Appledore, GB | GB | Caledonian MacBrayne |
| CLAYMORE | 1871t | 78 | 14k | 300P | 50C | - | AS | Leith, GB | GB | Sea Containers Ferries |
| COLL | 69t | 74 | 8k | 152P | 6C | - | B | Port Glasgow, GB | GB | Arranmore Island Ferry Service |
| COMMODORE CLIPPER | 13460t | 99 | 19k | 500P | 250C | 105T | A | Krimpen, NL | BA | Commodore Shipping/Condor Ferries |
| CONDOR EXPRESS | 5005t | 96 | 39k | 774P | 185C | - | A2 | Hobart, AL | SI | Condor Ferries |
| CONDOR VITESSE | 5005t | 97 | 39k | 774P | 185C | - | A2 | Hobart, AL | BA | Condor Ferries |
| CROMARTY ROSE | 28t | 87 | 8k | 50P | 2C | - | B | Ardrossan, GB | GB | Seaboard Marine (Nigg) |
| DANA ANGLIA | 19321t | 78 | 21k | 1372P | 470C | 45L | BA | Aalborg, DK | DK | DFDS Seaways |
| DAWN MERCHANT | 22152t | 98 | 22.5k | 250P | - | 175T | IM | Sevilla, SP | GB | Merchant Ferries |
| DIAMANT | 4305t | 96 | 39k | 674P | 155C | - | A | Hobart, AL | LX | Sea Containers Ferries |
| DUC DE NORMANDIE | 13505t | 78 | 21k | 1500P | 350C | 44T | BA | Heusden, NL | FR | Brittany Ferries |
| EARL SIGURD | 771t | 90 | 12k | 190P | 26C | - | BA | Bromborough, GB | GB | Orkney Ferries |
| EARL THORFINN | 771t | 90 | 12k | 190P | 26C | - | BA | Bromborough, GB | GB | Orkney Ferries |
| EDMUND D | 300t | 68 | 9k | 250P | 30C | - | BA | Dartmouth, GB | IR | Passage East Ferry |
| EIGG | 69t | 75 | 8k | 75P | 6C | - | B | Port Glasgow, GB | GB | Caledonian MacBrayne |
| EILEAN BHEARNARAIGH | 67t | 83 | 7k | 35P | 4C | 1T | BA | Glasgow, GB | GB | Comhairle Nan Eilean Siar |
| EILEAN DHIURA | 86t | 98 | 9k | 50P | 13C | 1L | BA | Bromborough, GB | GB | Argyll & Bute Council |
| EILEAN NA H-OIGE | 69t | 80 | 7k | 35P | 4C | 1T | BA | Stornoway, GB | GB | Comhairle Nan Eilean Siar |
| ERNEST BEVIN | 1214t | 63 | 8k | 310P | 32C | 6L | BA | Dundee, GB | GB | Woolwich Free Ferry |
| EYNHALLOW | 79t | 87 | 9.5k | 95P | 8C | - | BA | Bristol, GB | GB | Orkney Ferries |
| F.B.D. DUNBRODY | 139t | 60 | 8k | 107P | 18C | - | BA | Hamburg, GY | IR | Bere Island Ferries |
| FILLA | 130t | 83 | 9k | 12P | 6C | 1T | A | Flekkefjord, NO | GB | Shetland Islands Council |
| FIVLA | 230t | 85 | 11k | 95P | 15C | 4L | BA | Troon, GB | GB | Shetland Islands Council |
| FYLGA | 147t | 75 | 8.5k | 93P | 10C | 2L | BA | Tórshavn, FA | GB | Shetland Islands Council |
| GEIRA | 226t | 88 | 10.8k | 95P | 15C | 4L | BA | Hessle, GB | GB | Shetland Islands Council |
| GLENACHULISH | 44t | 69 | 9k | 12P | 6C | - | BSt | Troon, GB | GB | Glenelg - Kylerhea Ferry |
| GLENBROOK | 225t | 71 | 8k | 200P | 27C | - | BA | Newport (Gwent), GB | IR | Cross River Ferries |
| GOD MET ONS III | 95t | 63 | - | 95P | 18C | - | BA | Millingen, NL | IR | Valentia Island Ferries |
| GOOD SHEPHERD IV | 76t | 86 | 10k | 12P | 1C | 0L | C | St Monans, GB | GB | Shetland Islands Council |
| GRAEMSAY | 82t | 96 | 10k | 73P | 1C | - | C | Troon, GB | GB | Orkney Ferries |
| GRIMA | 147t | 74 | 8.5k | 93P | 10C | 2L | BA | Bideford, GB | GB | Shetland Islands Council |
| GRY MARITHA | 550t | 81 | 10.5k | 12P | 5C | 1L | C | Kolvereid, NO | GB | Isles of Scilly Steamship Co. |
| HEBRIDEAN ISLES | 3040t | 85 | 15k | 507P | 68C | - | BAS | Selby, GB | GB | Caledonian MacBrayne |
| HENDRA | 225t | 82 | 11k | 100P | 18C | 4L | BA | Bromborough, GB | GB | Shetland Islands Council |
| HOVERSPEED GREAT BRITAIN | 3003t | 90 | 37k | 577P | 80C | - | BA | Hobart, AL | GB | Sea Containers Ferries |
| HOY HEAD | 358t | 94 | 9.8k | 125P | 18C | - | BA | Bideford, GB | GB | Orkney Ferries |
| ISLE OF ARRAN | 3296t | 84 | 15k | 659P | 68C | - | BA | Port Glasgow, GB | GB | Caledonian MacBrayne |
| ISLE OF CUMBRAE | 169t | 77 | 8.5k | 138P | 15C | - | BA | Troon, GB | GB | Caledonian MacBrayne |
| ISLE OF INISHMORE | 34031t | 97 | 21.3k | 2200P | 800C | 122L | BA2 | Krimpen, NL | IR | Irish Ferries |
| ISLE OF INNISFREE | 22365t | 95 | 21.5k | 1700P | 600C | 142T | BA | Krimpen, NL | IR | Irish Ferries |
| ISLE OF LEWIS | 6753t | 95 | 18k | 680P | 123C | - | BA | Port Glasgow, GB | GB | Caledonian MacBrayne |
| ISLE OF MULL | 4719t | 88 | 15k | 1000P | 80C | - | BA | Port Glasgow, GB | GB | Caledonian MacBrayne |
| JAMES NEWMAN | 1214t | 63 | 8k | 310P | 32C | 6L | BA | Dundee, GB | GB | Woolwich Free Ferry |
| JETLINER | 4563t | 96 | 31k | 600P | 160C | 12T | BA | Bergen, NO | BA | P&O European Ferries (Irish Sea) |

# CENTURY OF NORTH WEST EUROPEAN FERRIES 1900 - 2000

| Name | Tonnage | Year | Speed | Pax | Cars | Other | Type | Built | Flag | Operator |
|---|---|---|---|---|---|---|---|---|---|---|
| JOHN BURNS | 1214t | 63 | 8k | 310P | 32C | 6L | BA | Dundee, GB | GB | Woolwich Free Ferry |
| JONATHAN SWIFT | 5992t | 99 | 39.5k | 800P | 200C | - | A | Fremantle, AL | IR | Irish Ferries |
| JUNO | 902t | 74 | 14k | 531P | 40C | - | AS | Port Glasgow, GB | GB | Caledonian MacBrayne |
| JUPITER | 20581t | 75 | 19k | 1250P | 285C | 42T | BA | Nantes, FR | NO | Fjord Line |
| JUPITER | 898t | 74 | 14k | 531P | 40C | - | AS | Port Glasgow, GB | GB | Caledonian MacBrayne |
| KING OF SCANDINAVIA | 13336t | 74 | 22.5k | 1100P | 300C | 38L | BA | Turku, FI | DK | DFDS Seaways |
| KOADA | 35t | 69 | 8k | 12P | 1C | 0L | C | Bideford, GB | GB | Shetland Islands Council |
| KONINGIN BEATRIX | 31189t | 86 | 20k | 2100P | 500C | 75L | BA | Krimpen, NL | GB | Stena Line |
| LADY OF MANN | 4482t | 76 | 21k | 1000P | 130C | 0L | S | Troon, GB | IM | Sea Containers Ferries |
| LAGAN VIKING | 21500t | 97 | 22k | 340P | 100C | 164T | A | Donanda, IT | IT | Norse Irish Ferries |
| LEIRNA | 420t | 93 | 10k | 100P | 20C | 4L | BA | Greenock, GB | GB | Shetland Islands Council |
| LOCH ALAINN | 396t | 97 | 10k | 150P | 24C | - | BA | Buckie, GB | GB | Caledonian MacBrayne |
| LOCH BHRUSDA | 246t | 96 | 8k | 150P | 18C | - | BA | Bromborough, GB | GB | Caledonian MacBrayne |
| LOCH BUIE | 295t | 92 | 8k | 250P | 9C | - | BA | St Monans, GB | GB | Caledonian MacBrayne |
| LOCH DUNVEGAN | 550t | 91 | 9k | 150P | 36C | - | BA | Port Glasgow, GB | GB | Caledonian MacBrayne |
| LOCH FYNE | 550t | 91 | 9k | 150P | 36C | - | BA | Port Glasgow, GB | GB | Caledonian MacBrayne |
| LOCH LINNHE | 206t | 86 | 8k | 199P | 12C | - | BA | Hessle, GB | GB | Caledonian MacBrayne |
| LOCH RANZA | 206t | 87 | 8k | 199P | 12C | - | BA | Hessle, GB | GB | Caledonian MacBrayne |
| LOCH RIDDON | 206t | 86 | 8k | 199P | 12C | - | BA | Hessle, GB | GB | Caledonian MacBrayne |
| LOCH STRIVEN | 206t | 86 | 8k | 199P | 12C | - | BA | Hessle, GB | GB | Caledonian MacBrayne |
| LOCH TARBERT | 211t | 92 | 8k | 149P | 18C | - | BA | St Monans, GB | GB | Caledonian MacBrayne |
| LOCHMOR | 175t | 79 | 10k | 129P | - | - | C | Troon, GB | GB | Caledonian MacBrayne |
| LORD OF THE ISLES | 3504t | 89 | 16k | 506P | 56C | - | BAS | Port Glasgow, GB | GB | Caledonian MacBrayne |
| LYONESSE LADY | 50t | 91 | 9k | 12P | 1C | 0L | A | Fort William, GB | GB | Isles of Scilly Steamship Company |
| MAID OF GLENCOUL | 166t | 75 | 8k | 116P | 16C | - | BA | Ardrossan, GB | GB | The Highland Council |
| MERSEY VIKING | 21500t | 97 | 22k | 340P | 100C | 164T | A | Donanda, IT | IT | Norse Irish Ferries |
| MISNEACH | 30t | 78 | 7k | 80P | 4C | - | B | New Ross, IR | IR | Bere Island Ferries |
| MORVERN | 64t | 73 | 8k | 138P | 4C | - | B | Port Glasgow, GB | GB | Arranmore Island Ferry Service |
| NEW ADVANCE | 21t | 96 | 8.7k | 12P | 1C | - | C | Penryn, GB | GB | Shetland Islands Council |
| NORLAND | 26290t | 74 | 18.5k | 881P | 500C | 134T | A | Bremerhaven, GY | GB | P&O North Sea Ferries |
| NORMANDIE | 27541t | 92 | 20k | 2263P | 630C | 66T | BA | Turku, FI | FR | Brittany Ferries |
| NORMANDY | 24872t | 82 | 20.4k | 2100P | 480C | 52L | BA2 | Göteburg, SW | IR | Irish Ferries |
| NORRÖNA | 12000t | 73 | 19k | 1050P | 300C | 44L | BA2 | Rendsburg, GY | FA | Smyril Line |
| NORSEA | 31785t | 87 | 18.5k | 1250P | 850C | 180T | A | Glasgow, GB | GB | P&O North Sea Ferries |
| NORSTAR | 26919t | 74 | 18.5k | 881P | 500C | 134T | A | Bremerhaven, GY | NL | P&O North Sea Ferries |
| NORSUN | 31598t | 87 | 18.5k | 1250P | 850C | 180T | A | Tsurumi, JA | NL | P&O North Sea Ferries |
| P&OSL AQUITAINE | 28833t | 91 | 21k | 1350P | 710C | 145T | BAS | Temse, BE | GB | P&O Stena Line |
| P&OSL BURGUNDY | 28138t | 93 | 21k | 1420P | 600C | 148T | BA2 | Bremerhaven, GY | GB | P&O Stena Line |
| P&OSL CALAIS | 26433t | 87 | 22k | 2290P | 650C | 100L | BA2 | Bremen-Vegesack, GY | GB | P&O Stena Line |
| P&OSL CANTERBURY | 25122t | 80 | 19k | 1800P | 550C | 80T | BA2 | Malmö, SW | GB | P&O Stena Line |
| P&OSL DOVER | 26433t | 87 | 22k | 2290P | 650C | 100L | BA2 | Bremen-Vegesack, GY | GB | P&O Stena Line |
| P&OSL KENT | 20446t | 80 | 21k | 1825P | 460C | 64L | BA2 | Bremerhaven, GY | GB | P&O Stena Line |
| P&OSL PICARDY | 13061t | 80 | 23k | 1326P | 330C | 48L | BA2 | Bremerhaven, GY | GB | P&O Stena Line |
| P&OSL PROVENCE | 28559t | 83 | 19.5k | 2036P | 550C | 108T | BA2 | Dunkerque, FR | GB | P&O Stena Line |
| PENTALINA B | 1908t | 70 | 16k | 250P | 47C | - | BAS | Troon, GB | GB | Pentland Ferries |
| PIONEER | 1088t | 74 | 16k | 356P | 33C | - | AS | Leith, GB | GB | Caledonian MacBrayne |
| PORTAFERRY FERRY | 151t | 62 | 9k | 200P | 18C | - | BA | Pembroke, GB | GB | Strangford Lough Ferry Service |
| PRIDE OF BILBAO | 37583t | 86 | 22k | 2553P | 600C | 90T | BA | Turku, FI | GB | P&O Portsmouth |
| PRIDE OF CHERBOURG | 14760t | 75 | 18k | 1200P | 380C | 53L | BA2 | Aalborg, DK | GB | P&O Portsmouth |
| PRIDE OF HAMPSHIRE | 14760t | 75 | 18k | 1200P | 380C | 53L | BA2 | Aalborg, DK | GB | P&O Portsmouth |
| PRIDE OF LE HAVRE | 33336t | 89 | 21k | 1600P | 575C | 118T | BA | Bremerhaven, GY | GB | P&O Portsmouth |
| PRIDE OF PORTSMOUTH | 33336t | 89 | 21k | 1600P | 575C | 118T | BA | Bremerhaven, GY | GB | P&O Portsmouth |
| PRIDE OF RATHLIN | 12503t | 73 | 17k | 1041P | 340C | 52L | BA2 | Schiedam, NL | BD | P&O European Ferries (Irish Sea) |
| PRINCE OF SCANDINAVIA | 21545t | 75 | 23k | 1692P | 385C | 70T | AS | Lübeck, GY | DK | DFDS Seaways |
| PRINCESS OF SCANDINAVIA | 21545t | 76 | 23k | 1704P | 385C | 70T | AS | Lübeck, GY | DK | DFDS Seaways |
| QUIBERON | 11813t | 75 | 20k | 1302P | 300C | 35L | BA2 | Rendsburg, GY | FR | Brittany Ferries |
| RAASAY | 69t | 76 | 8k | 75P | 6C | - | B | Port Glasgow, GB | GB | Caledonian MacBrayne |
| RAPIDE | 4112t | 96 | 39k | 674P | 155C | - | A | Hobart, AL | LX | Sea Containers Ferries |
| RED EAGLE | 3028t | 96 | 13k | 900P | 140C | 16L | BA | Port Glasgow, GB | GB | Red Funnel Ferries |
| RED FALCON | 2881t | 94 | 13k | 900P | 140C | 16L | BA | Port Glasgow, GB | GB | Red Funnel Ferries |
| RED OSPREY | 2881t | 94 | 13k | 900P | 140C | 16L | BA | Port Glasgow, GB | GB | Red Funnel Ferries |
| RHUM | 69t | 73 | 8k | 164P | 6C | - | B | Port Glasgow, GB | GB | Arranmore Island Ferry Service |
| ROSEHAUGH | 150t | 67 | 8.5k | 150P | 18C | - | BA | Berwick on Tweed, GB | GB | The Highland Council |
| SATURN | 899t | 78 | 14k | 531P | 40C | - | AS | Troon, GB | GB | Caledonian MacBrayne |

## CENTURY OF NORTH WEST EUROPEAN FERRIES 1900 - 2000

| NAME | TONNAGE | YEAR | SPEED | PASS | CARS | LORRY | ACCESS | BUILT | FLAG | OPERATOR |
|---|---|---|---|---|---|---|---|---|---|---|
| SCILLONIAN III | 1256t | 77 | 15.5k | 600P | - | - | C | Appledore, GB | GB | Isles of Scilly Steamship Company |
| SEACAT DANMARK | 3003t | 91 | 37k | 432P | 80C | - | BA | Hobart, AL | GB | Sea Containers Ferries |
| SEACAT ISLE OF MAN | 3003t | 91 | 37k | 500P | 80C | - | BA | Hobart, AL | GB | Sea Containers Ferries |
| SEACAT SCOTLAND | 3003t | 91 | 37k | 450P | 80C | - | BA | Hobart, AL | GB | Sea Containers Ferries |
| SEAFRANCE CEZANNE | 25122t | 80 | 19.5k | 1800P | 600C | 150T | BA2 | Malmö, SW | FR | SeaFrance |
| SEAFRANCE MANET | 15093t | 84 | 18k | 1800P | 330C | 54T | BA2 | Nantes, FR | FR | SeaFrance |
| SEAFRANCE MONET | 12962t | 74 | 18k | 1800P | 425C | 51L | BA2 | Trogir, YU | BA | SeaFrance Laid Up |
| SEAFRANCE RENOIR | 15612t | 81 | 18k | 1600P | 330C | 54T | BA2 | Le Havre, FR | FR | SeaFrance |
| SHANNON DOLPHIN | 501t | 95 | 10k | 350P | 52C | - | BA | Appledore, GB | IR | Shannon Ferry |
| SHANNON WILLOW | 360t | 78 | 10k | 300P | 44C | - | BA | Bowling, GB | IR | Shannon Ferry |
| SHAPINSAY | 199t | 89 | 9.5k | 91P | 12C | - | BA | Hull, GB | GB | Orkney Ferries |
| SOLIDOR 3 | 2068t | 96 | 33k | 430P | 51C | - | A | Omastrand, NO | FR | Emeraude Lines |
| SOLIDOR 4 | 1064t | 87 | 30k | 302P | 40C | - | A | Mandal, NO | FR | Emeraude Lines |
| SOUND OF SANDA | 403t | 61 | 10k | 220P | 37C | - | BA | Arnhem, NL | GB | Western Ferries |
| SOUND OF SCALPAY | 403t | 61 | 10k | 220P | 37C | - | BA | Arnhem, NL | GB | Western Ferries |
| SOUND OF SCARBA | 175t | 60 | 7k | 200P | 22C | - | BA | Åmål, SW | GB | Western Ferries |
| SOUND OF SHUNA | 244t | 62 | 7k | 200P | 25C | - | BA | Åmål, SW | GB | Western Ferries |
| SOUND OF SLEAT | 466t | 61 | 10k | 296P | 30C | - | BAS | Hardinxveld, NL | GB | Western Ferries |
| ST CATHERINE | 2036t | 83 | 12.5k | 769P | 142C | 12L | BA | Leith, GB | GB | Wightlink |
| ST CECILIA | 2968t | 87 | 12.5k | 769P | 142C | 12L | BA | Selby, GB | GB | Wightlink |
| ST CLAIR | 8696t | 71 | 19k | 600P | 160C | 30L | A | Bremerhaven, GY | GB | P&O Scottish Ferries |
| ST FAITH | 3009t | 90 | 12.5k | 769P | 142C | 12L | BA | Selby, GB | GB | Wightlink |
| ST HELEN | 2983t | 83 | 12.5k | 769P | 142C | 12L | BA | Leith, GB | GB | Wightlink |
| ST OLA | 4833t | 71 | 16k | 500P | 140C | 12L | BA | Papenburg, GY | GB | P&O Scottish Ferries |
| ST SUNNIVA | 6350t | 71 | 16k | 400P | 199C | 28L | A | Helsingør, DK | GB | P&O Scottish Ferries |
| STENA CALEDONIA | 12619t | 81 | 19.5k | 1000P | 280C | 56T | BA2 | Belfast, GB | GB | Stena Line |
| STENA CHALLENGER | 18523t | 90 | 18k | 500P | 480C | 100T | BA2 | Rissa, NO | GB | Stena Line |
| STENA DISCOVERY | 19638t | 97 | 40k | 1500P | 375C | 50L | A | Rauma, FI | NL | Stena Line |
| STENA EXPLORER | 19638t | 96 | 40k | 1500P | 375C | 50L | A | Rauma, FI | GB | Stena Line |
| STENA GALLOWAY | 12175t | 80 | 19k | 1000P | 280C | 56T | BA2 | Belfast, GB | GB | Stena Line |
| STENA INVICTA | 19763t | 85 | 17.5k | 1750P | 320C | 42T | BA2 | Nakskov, DK | GB | Stena Line |
| STENA LYNX III | 4113t | 96 | 45k | 677P | 181C | - | A | Hobart, AL | BA | Stena Line |
| STENA VOYAGER | 19638t | 96 | 40k | 1500P | 375C | 50L | A | Rauma, FI | GB | Stena Line |
| STRANGFORD FERRY | 186t | 69 | 10k | 263P | 20C | - | BA | Cork, IR | GB | Strangford Lough Ferry Service |
| SUPERSEACAT TWO | 4463t | 97 | 37.8k | 800P | 175C | - | A | Riva Trigoso, IT | IT | Sea Containers Ferries |
| SUPERSEACAT THREE | 4463t | 99 | 37.8k | 800P | 175C | - | A | Muggiano, IT | IT | Sea Containers Ferries |
| SUPERSTAR EXPRESS | 5517t | 97 | 36k | 900P | 175C | - | A | Fremantle, AL | BA | P&O Portsmouth |
| THE PRINCESS ANNE | - | 69 | 50k | 360P | 55C | - | BA | Cowes, GB | GB | Sea Containers Ferries |
| THE PRINCESS MARGARET | - | 68 | 50k | 360P | 55C | - | BA | Cowes, GB | GB | Sea Containers Ferries |
| THORA | 147t | 75 | 8.5k | 93P | 10C | 2L | BA | Tórshavn, FA | GB | Shetland Islands Council |
| THORSVOE | 400t | 91 | 10.5k | 96P | 16C | - | BA | Campbeltown, GB | GB | Orkney Ferries |
| VAL DE LOIRE | 31395t | 87 | 21k | 1800P | 550C | 114T | BA | Bremerhaven, GY | FR | Brittany Ferries |
| VARAGEN | 950t | 89 | 12k | 144P | 33C | 5L | BA | Selby, GB | GB | Orkney Ferries |

## Key

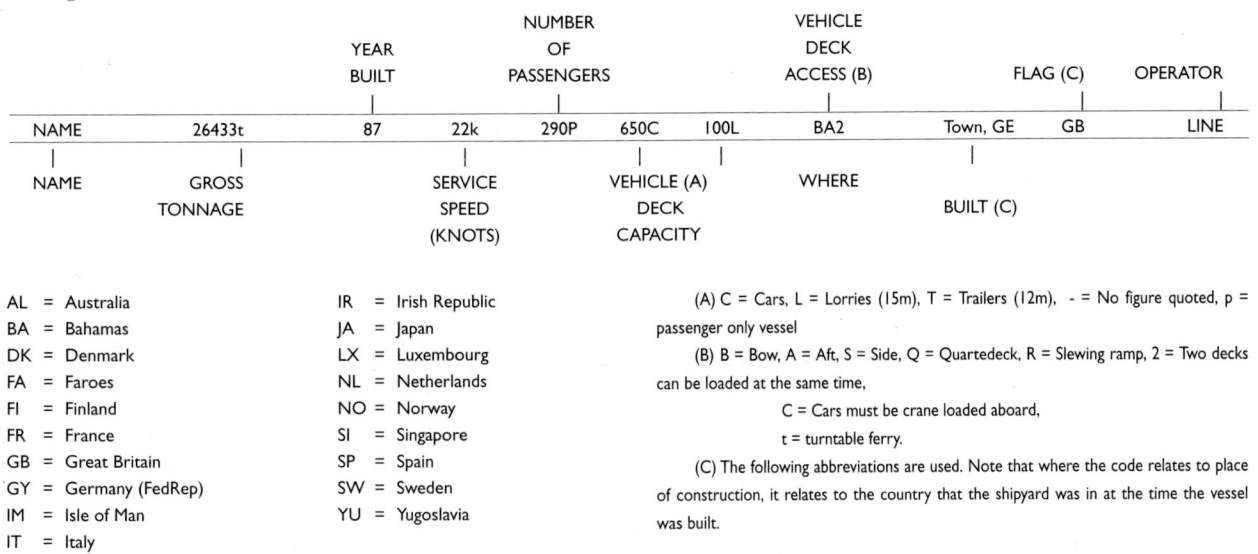

| NAME | GROSS TONNAGE | YEAR BUILT | SERVICE SPEED (KNOTS) | NUMBER OF PASSENGERS | VEHICLE DECK CAPACITY | VEHICLE (A) DECK | VEHICLE DECK ACCESS (B) | WHERE BUILT (C) | FLAG (C) | OPERATOR |
|---|---|---|---|---|---|---|---|---|---|---|
| NAME | 26433t | 87 | 22k | 290P | 650C | 100L | BA2 | Town, GE | GB | LINE |

AL = Australia
BA = Bahamas
DK = Denmark
FA = Faroes
FI = Finland
FR = France
GB = Great Britain
GY = Germany (FedRep)
IM = Isle of Man
IT = Italy

IR = Irish Republic
JA = Japan
LX = Luxembourg
NL = Netherlands
NO = Norway
SI = Singapore
SP = Spain
SW = Sweden
YU = Yugoslavia

(A) C = Cars, L = Lorries (15m), T = Trailers (12m), - = No figure quoted, p = passenger only vessel

(B) B = Bow, A = Aft, S = Side, Q = Quartedeck, R = Slewing ramp, 2 = Two decks can be loaded at the same time,
C = Cars must be crane loaded aboard,
t = turntable ferry.

(C) The following abbreviations are used. Note that where the code relates to place of construction, it relates to the country that the shipyard was in at the time the vessel was built.

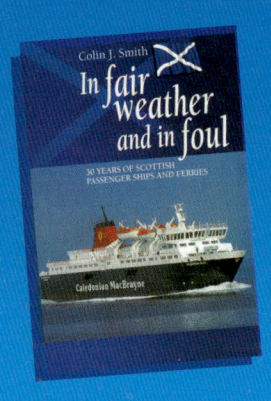

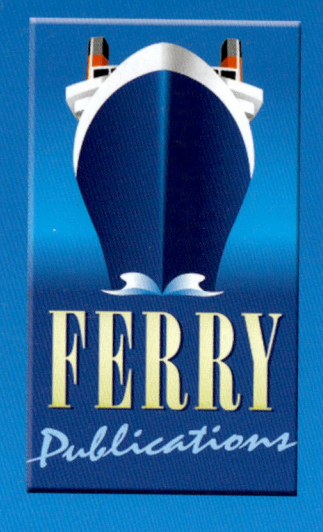

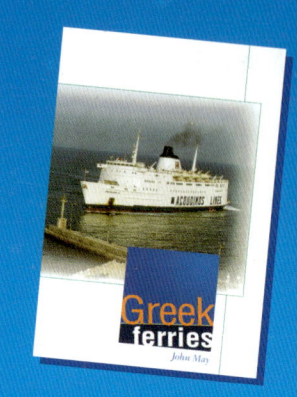

During the last twelve years we have produced over 50 books covering the history of ferry operations in the UK and Europe. Today we are the leading ferry industry publishing specialists. Ferry Publications also produce a quality ferry magazine **"European Ferry Scene"** which is accepted as Europe's leading ferry journal.

Our most recent titles include:

- **Caledonian MacBrayne - The Fleet**
- **Designing Ships for Sealink**
- **DFDS - The Fleet**
- **Ferries of the British Isles and Northern Europe 1999**
- **Ferry Port Dover**
- **Greek Ferries**
- **Holyhead-Dun Laoghaire - From Car Ferry to HSS**
- **In Fair Weather and in Foul**
- **Ferries of the English Channel - Past and Present**

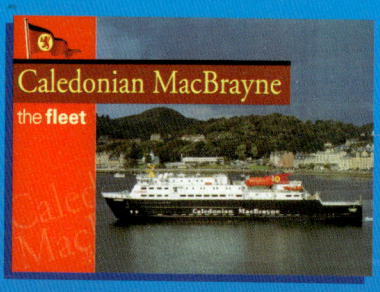

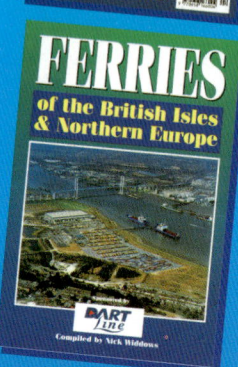

For more information or a copy of the current booklist please contact us at:

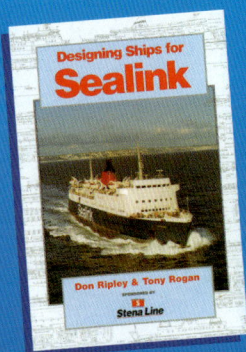

Ferry Publications
PO Box 9, Narberth,
Pembrokeshire, SA68 0YT
Tel: (01834) 891460
Fax: (01834) 891463
email: ferrypubs@aol.com

# OXFORD
UNIVERSITY PRESS

## ESSENTIAL
## MATHEMATICS STAGE 8
### FOR CAMBRIDGE SECONDARY 1

Patrick Kivlin, Sue Pemberton, Paul Winters

Oxford excellence for Cambridge Secondary 1

# OXFORD

#  OXFORD
UNIVERSITY PRESS

Great Clarendon Street, Oxford, OX2 6DP, United Kingdom

Oxford University Press is a department of the University of Oxford. It furthers the University's objective of excellence in research, scholarship, and education by publishing worldwide. Oxford is a registered trade mark of Oxford University Press in the UK and in certain other countries

Text © Patrick Kivlin, Sue Pemberton and Paul Winters 2014
Illustrations © Oxford University Press 2014

IGCSE® is the registered trademark of Cambridge International Examinations.

The moral rights of the authors have been asserted

First published in 2014

All rights reserved. No part of this publication may be reproduced, stored in a retrieval system, or transmitted, in any form or by any means, without the prior permission in writing of Oxford University Press, or as expressly permitted by law, by licence or under terms agreed with the appropriate reprographics rights organization. Enquiries concerning reproduction outside the scope of the above should be sent to the Rights Department, Oxford University Press, at the address above.

You must not circulate this work in any other form and you must impose this same condition on any acquirer

British Library Cataloguing in Publication Data
Data available

978-1-4085-1986-8

10 9 8 7 6 5

Printed and bound by CPI Group (UK) Ltd, Croydon, CR0 4YY

**Acknowledgements**

Page make-up: OKS Prepress, India
Illustrations: OKS Prepress, India

The publishers would like to thank the following for permissions to use their photographs:

**Cover:** ivanmateev/iStockphoto; **p1**: Mary Evans Picture Library/Alamy; **p18**: Julien Tromeur/Shutterstock; **p33**: ZU_09/iStockphoto; **p53**: sculpies/iStockphoto; **p64**: diane39/iStockphoto; **p78**: Christine Osborne Pictures/Alamy; **p91**: Detlev Van Ravenswaay/Science Photo Library; **p92 top**: ozgurdonmaz/iStockphoto; **p92 mid**: xxmmxx/iStockphoto; **p92 bottom**: FONG_KWONG_CHO/iStockphoto; **p93 top l**: Henrik5000/iStockphoto; **p93 top mid**: MarkSwallow/iStockphoto; **p93 top r**: Cameramannz/iStockphoto; **p93 bottom l**: Antagain/iStockphoto; **p93 bottom mid**: LuckyStrike/iStockphoto; **p93 bottom r**: jhorrocks/iStockphoto; **p94**: FineArtCraig/iStockphoto; **p95 top**: tibor5/iStockphoto; **p95 mid**: skhoward/iStockphoto; **p95 bottom**: Mike_Kiev/iStockphoto; **p96 l**: deepblue4you/iStockphoto; **p96 mid**: gerisima/iStockphoto; **p96 r**: JuSun/iStockphoto; **p97 l**: Krasyuk/iStockphoto; **p97 mid**: CarolinaSmith/iStockphoto; **p97 r**: narvikk/iStockphoto; **p100**: THEPALMER/iStockphoto; **p102 top l**: Bim/iStockphoto; **p102 top r**: kupicoo/iStockphoto; **p102 bottom**: claylib/iStockphoto; **p105**: zulufriend/iStockphoto; **p115**: mstay/iStockphoto; **p131**: Bettmann/CORBIS; **p147**: domin_domin/iStockphoto; **p167 top**: kcline/iStockphoto; **p167 bottom**: rzelich/iStockphoto; **p175 l**: Middle Temple Library/Science Photo Library; **p175 r**: roomauction/iStockphoto; **p193**: joingate/Shutterstock; **p205**: Alyssum/iStockphoto; **p218**: The Art Archive/Alamy; **p233 top l**: AndrewJohns/iStockphoto; **p233 top mid**: pepj/iStockphoto; **p233 top r**: GeorgeManga/iStockphoto; **p233 bottom**: ClarkandCompany/iStockphoto; **p239**: LuisaPizza/iStockphoto; **p244**: Science Museum/Science & Society Picture Library; **p256 l**: narvikk/iStockphoto; **p256 r**: filo/iStockphoto; **p265**: JacobH/iStockphoto; **page 273**: Alan Fersht, Gonville and Caius College, Cambridge; **p284**: Lionel Alvergnas/Shutterstock

We are grateful for permission to reproduce data from the following copyright sources:

**p138**: Data on age distributions for the populations of South Africa and Austria, Central Intelligence Agency; **p140**: Data on the average temperature for each month in Israel, Canty Media, Weatherbase; **p144**: Data on the 'all time best' times for the men's 400m sprint, IAAF; **p146**: Data on the average precipitation for each month in Greece, Canty Media, Weatherbase

Although we have made every effort to trace and contact all copyright holders before publication this has not been possible in all cases. If notified, the publisher will rectify any errors or omissions at the earliest opportunity.

Links to third party websites are provided by Oxford in good faith and for information only. Oxford disclaims any responsibility for the materials contained in any third party website referenced in this work.

# Contents

| | Introduction | iv |
|---|---|---|
| 1 | Integers, powers and roots | 1 |
| 2 | Expressions | 18 |
| 3 | Shapes and geometric reasoning 1 | 33 |
| 4 | Fractions | 53 |
| 5 | Decimals | 64 |
| 6 | Processing, interpreting and discussing data | 78 |
| 7 | Length, mass and capacity | 91 |
| 8 | Equations | 105 |
| 9 | Shapes and geometric reasoning 2 | 115 |
| 10 | Presenting, interpreting and discussing data | 131 |
| 11 | Area, perimeter and volume | 147 |
| 12 | Formulae | 167 |
| 13 | Position and movement | 175 |
| 14 | Sequences | 190 |
| 15 | Probability | 202 |
| 16 | Functions and graphs | 215 |
| 17 | Fractions, decimals and percentages | 230 |
| 18 | Planning and collecting data | 241 |
| 19 | Ratio and proportion | 253 |
| 20 | Time and rates of change | 262 |
| 21 | Sets (extension work) | 270 |
| 22 | Matrices (extension work) | 281 |
| | Glossary | 288 |
| | Index | 293 |

# Introduction

Welcome to **Mathematics for Cambridge Secondary 1**! This student book has been written for the Cambridge International Examinations Secondary 1 Mathematics Curriculum Framework and provides complete coverage of Stage 8. Created specifically for international students and teachers by a dedicated and experienced author team, this book covers all areas in the curriculum: number, algebra, geometry measure, handling data and problem solving.

The following features have been designed to guide you through the content of the book with ease:

> **Learning outcomes**
>
> The learning outcomes give you an idea of what you will be covering, and what you should understand by the end of the chapter.

> **Worked examples**
>
> Worked examples to illustrate and expand the content. Work through these yourself and then compare your answers with the solutions.

**Problem solving questions:** Help develop knowledge and skills by requiring creative or methodical approaches, often in a real life context.

**Extension questions:** Provide you with further challenge beyond the standard questions found in the book.

> **Hints:** Useful tips for you to remember whilst learning the maths.

**Key words:** The first time key words appear in the book, they are highlighted in **bold red** text. A definition of each key word can be found in the glossary at the back of the book.

**Extension Chapters:** Chapters 21 and 22 are included in the Cambridge IGCSE curriculum. This additional content is included to challenge more able students.

This book is part of a series of six books and three teacher-support CD-ROMs. There are three student textbooks covering stages 7, 8 and 9 and three workbooks written to closely match the textbooks, as well as a teacher's CD-ROM for each stage.

The accompanying **Workbooks** provide extensive opportunities for you to practise your skills and apply your knowledge, both for homework and in the classroom.

The **teacher's CD-ROMs** include a wealth of interactive activities and supplementary worksheets, as well as the answers to questions in the books.

# 1 Integers, powers and roots

> **Learning outcomes**
> - Add, subtract, multiply and divide integers.
> - Calculate squares, positive and negative square roots, cubes and cube roots; use the notation $\sqrt{49}$ and $\sqrt[3]{64}$ and index notation for positive integer powers.
> - Identify and use multiples, factors, common factors, highest common factors, lowest common multiples and primes; write a number in terms of its prime factors.

## In his prime

In the 17th century, a French monk and scholar, Marin Mersenne, found that some prime numbers are of the form $2^n - 1$

Since then mathematicians have searched for Mersenne primes.

In February 2013, newspapers announced that a new Mersenne prime number had been found.

It is the biggest prime number found so far.

It has more than 17 million digits.

## 1.1 Working with integers

### Review of addition and subtraction

In your Stage 7 Student Book, you learned how to add and subtract **positive** and **negative** numbers using a given set of rules.

The rules for combining the signs when adding or subtracting directed numbers are:

| | |
|---|---|
| Change + + to + | For example, $-4 + (+6)$ becomes $-4 + 6 = 2$ |
| Change + − to − | For example, $-4 + (-6)$ becomes $-4 - 6 = -10$ |
| Change − + to − | For example, $-4 - (+6)$ becomes $-4 - 6 = -10$ |
| Change − − to + | For example, $-4 - (-6)$ becomes $-4 + 6 = 2$ |

# Mathematics for Cambridge Secondary 1

## Multiplying integers

Multiplication is the same as repeated addition.

For example, $3 \times 9 = 9 + 9 + 9 = 27$

$7 \times 18 = 18 + 18 + 18 + 18 + 18 + 18 + 18 = 126$

You can use repeated addition if you multiply a positive number by a negative number.

For example, $4 \times (-6) = (-6) + (-6) + (-6) + (-6) = -24$

and $5 \times (-3) = (-3) + (-3) + (-3) + (-3) + (-3) = -15$

Notice that $4 \times 6 = 24$ and $4 \times (-6) = -24$ and that $5 \times 3 = 15$ and $5 \times (-3) = -15$

The digits are the same. It is only the signs that are different.

**When you multiply a positive number and a negative number together the answer is negative.**

### Worked example 1

Work out    **a** $5 \times (-12)$    **b** $9 \times (-34)$    **c** $(-15) \times 8$

**a** $5 \times 12 = 60$

$5 \times (-12) = -60$

You know this from your multiplication tables.
The same digits with a negative sign.

**b** $9 \times 34 = 306$

Write out in long hand multiplication like this.

Or work out $10 \times 34 = 340$ so
$9 \times 34 = 340 - 34 = 306$

$\begin{array}{r} 34 \\ \times\ 9 \\ \hline 306 \\ \scriptstyle 3 \end{array}$

$9 \times (-34) = -306$

**c** The order of the numbers in a multiplication does not matter.

$(-15) \times 8$ is the same as $8 \times (-15)$

$8 \times 15 = 120$

$8 \times (-15) = -120$

## Two negative numbers

What happens when you multiply two negative numbers?

For example, what is the value of $(-9) \times (-7)$?

You know that $9 \times 7 = 63$

You know that $9 \times (-7) = -63$

So $-(9 \times (-7)) = -(-63) = 63$

**When you multiply two negative numbers together the answer is positive.**

# 1 Integers, powers and roots

## Worked example 2

Work out          **a** $(-5) \times (-9)$          **b** $(-10) \times (-39)$

**a** $5 \times 9 = 45$                You know this from your multiplication tables.

$(-5) \times (-9) = 45$         The same digits and the answer stays positive.

**b** $10 \times 39 = 390$         You know how to multiply by 10.

$(-10) \times (-39) = 390$    The same digits and the answer stays positive.

## Rules for multiplying

The rules for multiplying directed numbers are:

$$\text{positive} \times \text{positive} = \text{positive}$$
$$\text{positive} \times \text{negative} = \text{negative}$$
$$\text{negative} \times \text{positive} = \text{negative}$$
$$\text{negative} \times \text{negative} = \text{positive}$$

This is often written as:

$+ \times + = +$

$+ \times - = -$         If the two signs are the same the answer will be positive.

$- \times + = -$         If the two signs are different the answer will be negative.

$- \times - = +$

## Exercise 1.1

**1** Work out

| | | | |
|---|---|---|---|
| **a** $(-5) + (+8)$ | **b** $2 + (-7)$ | **c** $(-4) - (+9)$ | **d** $2 - (-8)$ |
| **e** $(-3) + (-6)$ | **f** $(-1) + (+11)$ | **g** $(-6) - (-9)$ | **h** $0 + (+13)$ |
| **i** $(-17) + (+19)$ | **j** $(-12) + (-23)$ | **k** $7 - (+5)$ | **l** $0 - (+28)$ |
| **m** $27 + (-10)$ | **n** $(-13) - (+23)$ | **o** $(-19) - (-28)$ | **p** $(-8) + (-21)$ |
| **q** $(-13) - (-12)$ | **r** $(-5) - (-28)$ | **s** $(-1) + (-37)$ | **t** $(-43) + (+56)$ |

**2** Work out

| | | | |
|---|---|---|---|
| **a** $(-4) \times (+6)$ | **b** $(-8) \times (-6)$ | **c** $(+9) \times (-5)$ | **d** $(-7) \times (-8)$ |
| **e** $(+10) \times (+6)$ | **f** $(-11) \times (+4)$ | **g** $(+12) \times (-9)$ | **h** $(-7) \times (-20)$ |
| **i** $(+6) \times (-34)$ | **j** $(-8) \times (+56)$ | **k** $(-17) \times 0$ | **l** $21 \times (-4)$ |

3

**3** This is a multiplication grid.

It shows numbers between −3 and 3.

  **a** Copy the grid on to squared paper.

  **b** Fill in all of the answers.

Some are done for you.

  **c** How many answers are positive?

  **d** How many answers are negative?

  **e** How many answers are neither positive nor negative?

| × | −3 | −2 | −1 | 0 | 1 | 2 | 3 |
|---|---|---|---|---|---|---|---|
| 3 |  |  |  |  |  |  | 9 |
| 2 |  | −4 |  | 0 |  |  |  |
| 1 |  |  |  |  |  |  |  |
| 0 |  |  |  |  |  |  |  |
| −1 |  |  | 1 |  |  |  |  |
| −2 |  |  |  |  |  |  |  |
| −3 |  |  |  |  |  |  |  |

**4** Anna thinks that there are five integer multiplications with an answer of 36.

Rosa says that there are more than that.

Write down all the multiplications you can with an answer of 36.

Who is right, Anna or Rosa?

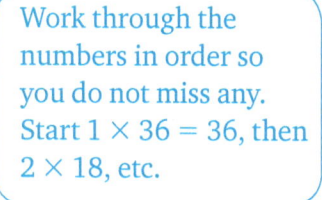

> Work through the numbers in order so you do not miss any. Start $1 \times 36 = 36$, then $2 \times 18$, etc.

**5** Work out

  **a** $2 \times (-4) \times (-5)$     **b** $(-6) \times 3 \times 10$

  **c** $(-2) \times (-3) \times (-5)$     **d** $4 \times 7 \times (-10)$

  **e** $4 \times 2 \times (-5) \times (-6)$     **f** $(-4) \times (-5) \times (-3) \times (-10)$

  **g** $(-2) \times (-2) \times (-2) \times (-2)$     **h** $(-7) \times 3 \times (-5) \times (-8)$

> Work from the left. For example, in part **a** work out $2 \times (-4) = -8$ then $(-8) \times (-5) = 40$

## 1.2 Division and mental strategies

Division is the **inverse** (or opposite) of multiplication.

If $6 \times 7 = 42$ then $42 \div 7 = 6$

You can use this fact when working with directed numbers.

For example:

$(+4) \times (+5) = +20$    so    $(+20) \div (+5) = +4$

$(-4) \times (-5) = +20$    so    $(+20) \div (-5) = -4$

$(-4) \times (+5) = -20$    so    $(-20) \div (+5) = -4$

$(+4) \times (-5) = -20$    so    $(-20) \div (-5) = +4$

These show the general rules for dividing directed numbers, which are:

positive ÷ positive = positive
positive ÷ negative = negative
negative ÷ positive = negative
negative ÷ negative = positive

# 1 Integers, powers and roots

This is often written as:

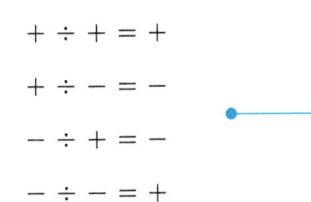

$+ \div + = +$
$+ \div - = -$
$- \div + = -$
$- \div - = +$

> The basic rule is the same as multiplication.
> If the two signs are the same the answer will be positive.
> If the two signs are different the answer will be negative.

## Worked example 1

If $6 \times 247 = 1482$ write down the answers to these calculations.

**a** $1482 \div 6$  **b** $1482 \div 247$  **c** $6 \times 248$  **d** $60 \times 2470$

**a** $6 \times 247 = 1482$ so $1482 \div 6 = 247$ — This is the inverse operation.

**b** $6 \times 247 = 1482$ so $1482 \div 247 = 6$ — This is the inverse operation.

**c** $6 \times 247 = 1482$
$6 \times 248 = 1482 + 6 = 1488$ — There is an extra 6 to be added on.

**d** $6 \times 247 = 1482$
$60 \times 2470 = 6 \times 10 \times 247 \times 10$ — Each number is 10 times bigger.
$\qquad\qquad = 6 \times 247 \times 10 \times 10$
$\qquad\qquad = 1482 \times 100 = 148\,200$

## Worked example 2

Work out

**a** $72 \div (-9)$  **b** $(-54) \div 6$  **c** $(-584) \div (-8)$

**a** $72 \div 9 = 8$ — From the multiplication tables.
$72 \div (-9) = -8$ — Because $+ \div - = -$

**b** $54 \div 6 = 9$ — From the multiplication tables.
$(-54) \div 6 = -9$ — Because $- \div + = -$

**c** $584 \div 8 = 73$ — Use a calculator for larger numbers.
$(-584) \div (-8) = 73$ — Because $- \div - = +$

5

# Mathematics for Cambridge Secondary 1

You can use other inverse operations to work things out in your head. These examples show you how.

> **Worked example 3**
>
> a When 32 is added to a number the answer is 57. What is the number?
> b If 950 ÷ 25 = 38, write down the answer to 38 × 25
>
> a The number is 57 − 32 = 25      *The inverse of addition is subtraction.*
> b 950 ÷ 25 = 38 so 38 × 25 = 950   *The inverse of division is multiplication.*

## Exercise 1.2

**1** Copy these calculations. Fill in the missing numbers.

  a  … × 8 = 56    b  9 × … = −45    c  … × (−7) = −49    d  (−10) × … = 80
  e  (−12) × … = −48    f  20 × … = −120    g  … × 9 = 81    h  … × (−9) = 81

**2** Work out

  a  32 ÷ 8    b  48 ÷ (−6)    c  (−36) ÷ 9    d  (−54) ÷ (−6)
  e  77 ÷ (−11)    f  (−150) ÷ 10    g  (−147) ÷ (−7)    h  (−255) ÷ 5
  i  (−320) ÷ 4    j  (−468) ÷ (−9)    k  1000 ÷ (−10)    l  (−602) ÷ (−7)

**3** If 15 × 24 = 360, write down the answers to these calculations.

  a  150 × 24    b  360 ÷ 15    c  16 × 24    d  150 × 240

**4** If 1620 ÷ 45 = 36, write down the answers to these calculations.

  a  1620 ÷ (−45)    b  16 200 ÷ 45    c  36 × 45    d  1620 ÷ 450

**5 a** When 12 is subtracted from a number the answer is 9. Work out the number.
  **b** When 15 is added to a number the answer is 46. Work out the number.

**6** Jonas finds a piece of paper with part of a multiplication on it.
  The first two numbers are covered with ink.

  **a** Jonas assumes that the first number is positive.
  Write down four possible multiplications with this answer.

  **b** Jonas now discovers that the first number is negative.
  Write down some more multiplications with this answer.
  Make sure your first number is negative.

  **c** Jonas then discovers that the two numbers are the same.
  What is the only possible multiplication that fits?

  *■ × ■ = 64*

  > If one number is negative then the other must also be negative if the answer is positive.

## 1.3 Order of operations

In some calculations there is more than one operation.

In these cases it is important to do the operations in the correct order.

This is the order to use:

  **1 Brackets**

  **2 Indices or powers**

  **3 Division**
  **4 Multiplication**

  **5 Addition**
  **6 Subtraction**

(The initial letters spell out the word **BIDMAS**, which helps you to remember the order.)

Note the spacing of the operations.

Division and multiplication have equal importance.

Addition and subtraction have equal importance.

> **Worked example 1**
> 
> Work out
> 
> **a** $(-4) \times (-3) + (-8)$  **b** $(-7) + (-12) \div (-3)$  **c** $8 + (-4) \times 5 - (-12)$
> 
> **a** $(-4) \times (-3) + (-8)$     Multiplication comes before addition.
>    $= (+12) + (-8)$     $- \times - = +$
>    $= +4$     This can be written as 4, the + sign is not needed.
> 
> **b** $(-7) + (-12) \div (-3)$     Division comes before addition.
>    $= (-7) + (+4)$     $- \div - = +$
>    $= -3$
> 
> **c** $8 + (-4) \times 5 - (-12)$     Multiplication comes before addition and subtraction.
>    $= 8 + (-20) - (-12)$     Addition and subtraction are equal so work from left to right.
>    $= (-12) - (-12)$
>    $= 0$

## Worked example 2

Put brackets in this calculation to make it correct:    $3 + 6 \times 8 - 4 = 27$

You need to try putting brackets in different places to find the correct place.

| With no brackets: | $3 + 48 - 4 = 51 - 4 = 47$ | This is not correct. |
| Try $(3 + 6) \times 8 - 4$ | $9 \times 8 - 4 = 72 - 4 = 68$ | This is not correct. |
| Try $3 + 6 \times (8 - 4)$ | $3 + 6 \times 4 = 3 + 24 = 27$ | This is the correct answer. |

So the calculation is:    $3 + 6 \times (8 - 4) = 27$

> You don't need to try $3 + (6 \times 8) - 4$ because multiplication comes first without the brackets.

## Exercise 1.3

**1** Work out

a  $6 \times 5 - 7$
b  $5 + 8 \times 3$
c  $10 \div 2 + 6$
d  $4 \times 5 + 12 \div 4$
e  $(-6) + (-3) \times 2$
f  $18 - 7 \times 2 + 6$
g  $(16 - 5) \times 3 + 2$
h  $(7 + 5) - 3 \times 4$
i  $(8 + 9) \times 2 - (-3)$
j  $((-5) \times (-8)) \div (3 + 7)$
k  $36 \div 9 - 6 \times 4$
l  $(-2) \times (-5) - 9 \times 3$
m  $6 + 5 \times (-7)$
n  $42 - (-8) \times (-7)$
o  $(6 - 8) \times (-4)$
p  $(-8) \times (-6) + (-6) \div (-2)$

**2** Put brackets in these calculations to make them correct.

a  $4 + 7 \times 2 + 3 = 25$
b  $3 \times 6 - 2 \times 4 = 48$
c  $5 \times 4 \div 2 + 3 = 4$
d  $2 \times 3 + 5 \times 6 = 66$
e  $9 - 6 \times 2 + 1 = 7$
f  $9 - 6 \times 2 + 1 = -9$

> You may need to try with brackets in several different places before you find the answer that works.

**3** Put brackets in both sides of these equations to make them correct.

a  $2 + 3 \times 4 = 5 + 1 \times 4 - 4$
b  $6 + 9 \div 3 = 3 \times 4 - 3 + 4$

**4** Put brackets in to make these calculations correct, where necessary.

a  $(-5) + (-2) \times (-7) = 9$
b  $(-6) - (-8) \div 2 + 4 = 5$
c  $(-8) \times (-6) - 9 \div (-3) = 24$

## 1.4 Powers

### Squares and cubes

These diagrams show some squares.

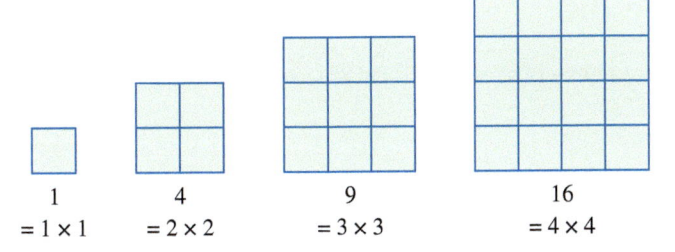

1
= 1 × 1

4
= 2 × 2

9
= 3 × 3

16
= 4 × 4

1, 4, 9 and 16 are examples of **square numbers**.

A square number is a number formed by multiplying any integer by itself.

25 is another square number because 25 = 5 × 5

144 is the 12th square number because 144 = 12 × 12

12 × 12 can also be written as $12^2$.

> You need to know the first 20 square numbers.

These diagrams show some cubes.

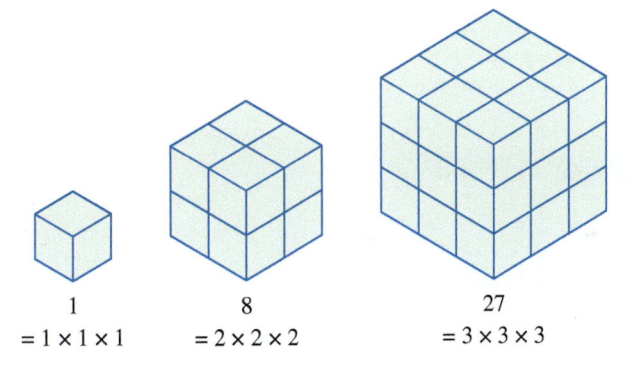

1
= 1 × 1 × 1

8
= 2 × 2 × 2

27
= 3 × 3 × 3

1, 8 and 27 are examples of **cube numbers**.

A cube number is formed by multiplying an integer by itself and then by itself again.

64 is the next cube number because 64 = 4 × 4 × 4

512 is the 8th cube number because 512 = 8 × 8 × 8

8 × 8 × 8 can also be written as $8^3$.

> You need to know the first five cube numbers.

### Index notation

The small raised numbers in $12^2$ and $8^3$ are called **index numbers** or powers.

Index numbers are used to simplify expressions.

Mathematics for Cambridge Secondary 1

They tell you how many times to multiply a number by itself.

$2 \times 2 \times 2 \times 2 \times 2$ can be written as $2^5$.

$10 \times 10 \times 10 \times 10 \times 10 \times 10 \times 10 \times 10 \times 10$ can be written as $10^9$.

> **Worked example**
>
> Work out which of these is greater, $4^3$ or $3^4$.   — 'Greater' means larger/bigger.
>
> $4^3 = 4 \times 4 \times 4 = 16 \times 4 = 64$
>
> $3^4 = 3 \times 3 \times 3 \times 3 = 9 \times 3 \times 3 = 27 \times 3 = 81$
>
> $3^4$ is larger than $4^3$.

## Exercise 1.4

1  Copy this sequence and continue up to $20^2$.

   $1^2 = 1 \times 1 = 1$

   $2^2 = 2 \times 2 = 4$

   $3^2 = 3 \times 3 = 9$

   $4^2 = 4 \times 4 = 16$

   ...

2  Copy this sequence and continue up to $5^3$.

   $1^3 = 1 \times 1 \times 1 = 1$

   $2^3 = 2 \times 2 \times 2 = 8$

   ...

3  Work out which is the greater of the following pairs of numbers.

   **a** $2^3$ or $3^2$    **b** $2^4$ or $4^2$    **c** $2^5$ or $5^2$

4  Write the following using index notation.

   **a** $4 \times 4 \times 4 \times 4$    **b** $9 \times 9 \times 9 \times 9 \times 9 \times 9$    **c** $2 \times 2 \times 2 \times 2 \times 2 \times 2 \times 2 \times 2$

5  Work out the value of:

   **a** $2^4$    **b** $3^4$    **c** $10^3$    **d** $2^6$

6  Find the area of squares with sides:

   **a** 8 cm    **b** 12 mm    **c** 15 m    **d** 20 cm    **e** 30 mm

7  Find the volume of cubes with sides:

   **a** 2 cm    **b** 3 mm    **c** 5 mm    **d** 10 cm    **e** 20 m

**8** 1 is a square number and also a cube number.

   **a** Find another number that is both a square number and a cube number.

   **b** Can you find another greater number that is both a square number and a cube number?

   > You will need to continue the lists from questions **1** and **2** to find another number.

## 1.5 Roots

### Square roots

**Square root** is the inverse of squaring a number.

The square root sign is $\sqrt{\phantom{x}}$

You know that $4^2 = 16$ so the inverse $\sqrt{16} = 4$

The square root of a number is usually given as a positive answer.

But note that $(-4)^2 = (-4) \times (-4) = 16$

So $-4$ is also a square root of 16.

You should use the positive square root unless the negative root is also asked for.

You can use the $\sqrt{\phantom{x}}$ button on your calculator to work out square roots.

The calculator only gives the positive value.

You may need to round your answer.

> You need to know the square roots of the first 20 square numbers.

### Worked example 1

**a** Without using a calculator, write down $\sqrt{144}$

**b** Write down both square roots of 225.

**c** Use your calculator to find $\sqrt{238}$ giving your answer to 2 decimal places.

**a** You should know that $12^2 = 144$ so $\sqrt{144} = 12$

**b** You should know that $15^2 = 225$ so $\sqrt{225} = 15$

  The two square roots are 15 and $-15$.

**c** The calculator gives $= \sqrt{238} = 15.42724862$

  $= \sqrt{238} = 15.43$    to 2 decimal places

# Mathematics for Cambridge Secondary 1

## Cube roots

**Cube root** is the inverse of cubing a number.

The cube root sign is $\sqrt[3]{\phantom{x}}$

$\sqrt[3]{8} = 2$      because $2^3 = 8$

$\sqrt[3]{125} = 5$      because $5^3 = 125$

$\sqrt[3]{1000} = 10$      because $10^3 = 1000$

> You need to know the cube roots of the first five cube numbers.

You can use your calculator to find cube roots.

You may have a button that looks like $\sqrt[3]{\phantom{x}}$ or $\sqrt[x]{\phantom{x}}$.

---

### Worked example 2

Use a calculator to find these roots.

Round your answers to 1 decimal place.

**a** $\sqrt{50}$      **b** $\sqrt[3]{75}$

**b** $\sqrt{50} = 7.071067812$ on a calculator

$\sqrt{50} = 7.1$ (or $-7.1$) to 1 decimal place

**c** $\sqrt[3]{75} = 4.217163327$ on a calculator

$\sqrt[3]{75} = 4.2$ to 1 decimal place

---

## Exercise 1.5

**1** Without using a calculator, write down the positive value of:

     **a** $\sqrt{9}$      **b** $\sqrt{36}$      **c** $\sqrt{81}$      **d** $\sqrt{324}$      **e** $\sqrt{121}$

**2** Use a calculator to find both square roots of these numbers.

     Round your answers to 2 decimal places.

     **a** 30      **b** 6      **c** 10      **d** 1000      **e** 320

**3** Without using a calculator, write down the value of:

     **a** $\sqrt[3]{8}$      **b** $\sqrt[3]{64}$      **c** $\sqrt[3]{1}$      **d** $\sqrt[3]{27}$      **e** $\sqrt[3]{125}$

**4** Use a calculator to find these cube roots.

     Round your answers to 2 decimal places.

     **a** $\sqrt[3]{20}$      **b** $\sqrt[3]{50}$      **c** $\sqrt[3]{250}$      **d** $\sqrt[3]{720}$      **e** $\sqrt[3]{1024}$

5 The areas of these squares are shown.

Write down the side length of each square.

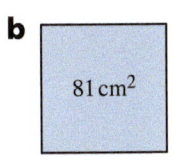

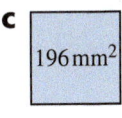

a  64 cm²     b  81 cm²     c  196 mm²

6 The volume of a cube is 64 cm³.

What is the length of each side?

7 Ramesh wants to construct a cube with a volume of 2000 cm³.

How long should he make each side?

Give your answer to the nearest millimetre.

> Remember that the volume of a cube with side $x$ is $x^3$.

8 a  Show that $(-2)^3 = -8$

> $(-2)^3 = -2 \times -2 \times -2$

b  Use your answer to part **a** to write down $\sqrt[3]{-8}$

c  You can see that the cube root of a negative number is also negative. Use this to work out:

   i  $\sqrt[3]{-1000}$     ii  $\sqrt[3]{-64}$     iii  $\sqrt[3]{-125}$

## 1.6 Prime factors

A **prime number** is a number with exactly two factors: 1 and itself.

The first six prime numbers are 2, 3, 5, 7, 11 and 13.

> Remember that 1 has only one factor so it is not a prime number.

In your Stage 7 Student Book you found all of the prime numbers between 1 and 100.

A **prime factor** is a factor of a number that is itself prime.

For example, the factors of 10 are 1, 2, 5 and 10.

1 is not prime and 10 is not prime.

The prime factors of 10 are 2 and 5.

10 is a product of its prime factors:   $10 = 2 \times 5$

A **composite number** is a number that is the product of two or more factors other than 1 and itself.

Every whole number greater than 1 is either a prime number or a composite number.

Each composite number can be written as a **product of prime factors**.

The method shown here for writing a number as a product of prime factors uses a **factor tree**.

## Worked example

Write the number 60 as a product of prime factors.

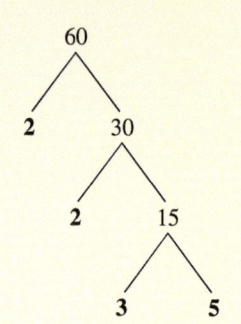

At each level choose two factors of the line above.

$60 = 2 \times 30$, stop at 2 as it is a prime number.

$30 = 2 \times 15$, stop at 2 as it is a prime number.

$15 = 3 \times 5$, both of these factors are prime numbers.

$60 = 2 \times 2 \times 3 \times 5$ — It is helpful if you write the prime factors in order, starting with the smallest.

$= 2^2 \times 3 \times 5$ — If a factor is repeated you can use powers to write it.

Note that it does not matter which factors you choose at each stage.

Here it is again in a different order:

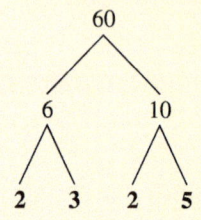

$60 = 6 \times 10$, neither factor is a prime number.

$6 = 2 \times 3$ and $10 = 2 \times 5$, all factors are prime numbers.

$60 = 2 \times 2 \times 3 \times 5 = 2^2 \times 3 \times 5$

The prime factors of 60 are 2, 3 and 5.

Written as a product of prime factors $60 = 2 \times 2 \times 3 \times 5$

## Exercise 1.6

**1** Which of the following numbers are prime numbers?

11, 21, 31, 41, 51, 23, 33, 43, 53, 91, 93

**2** Multiply these prime factors to find out what number is represented in each part.

**a** $2 \times 2 \times 3$    **b** $2 \times 5 \times 5$    **c** $2 \times 2 \times 2 \times 7$    **d** $3 \times 3 \times 5 \times 5$

**e** $2^2 \times 3^2$    **f** $2^3 \times 11$    **g** $2 \times 3^2 \times 5$    **h** $2^3 \times 3^2 \times 5$

**3** Write each of these numbers as a product of prime factors.

**a** 30    **b** 42    **c** 48    **d** 75    **e** 96    **f** 100

**g** 112    **h** 121    **i** 176    **j** 200    **k** 225    **l** 1000

**4 a** What is the smallest integer to have four different prime factors?

**b** What is the smallest integer to have five different prime factors?

> The smallest integer with three different prime factors is 30 because $30 = 2 \times 3 \times 5$

## 1.7 Highest common factors and lowest common multiples

You know how to find the **highest common factor (HCF)** of a set of numbers by listing all of their factors.

You also know how to find the **lowest common multiple (LCM)** of a set of numbers by listing their multiples.

You can use prime factors to find the HCF and LCM. This is very helpful with bigger numbers.

This worked example shows you how to do it.

### Worked example

Find, for the numbers 210 and 660:

**a** the highest common factor

**b** the lowest common multiple.

Firstly, write each number as a product of prime factors:

$210 = 2 \times 3 \times 5 \times 7$

$660 = 2 \times 2 \times 3 \times 5 \times 11$

Next, put the factors into a diagram like the ones you saw in Chapter 21 of your Stage 7 Student Book:

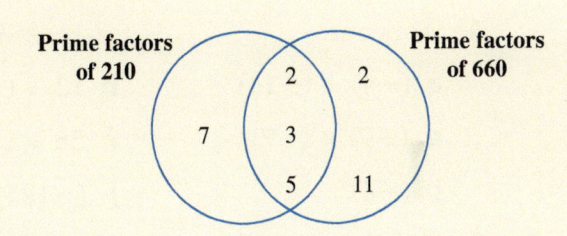

Prime factors of 210: 7 | 2, 3, 5 | 2, 11 : Prime factors of 660

The left-hand circle has the factors 2, 3, 5 and 7, which make up 210.

The right-hand circle has the factors 2, 2, 3, 5 and 11, which make up 660.

The factors 2, 3 and 5 are in the middle because they appear in both of the lists.

**a** The highest common factor is the product of the prime factors in the overlapping section in the middle of the diagram.

$2 \times 3 \times 5 = 30$

The highest common factor of 210 and 660 is 30.

**b** The lowest common multiple is the product of all of the prime factors in the diagram.

$2 \times 2 \times 3 \times 5 \times 7 \times 11 = 4620$

The lowest common multiple of 210 and 660 is 4620.

Mathematics for Cambridge Secondary 1

## Exercise 1.7

**1** Find the highest common factor of these pairs of numbers.
   **a** 36 and 81   **b** 120 and 72   **c** 75 and 140   **d** 132 and 176

**2** Find the lowest common multiple of these pairs of numbers.
   **a** 12 and 21   **b** 15 and 24   **c** 36 and 81   **d** 66 and 150

**3** Find the highest common factor and the lowest common multiple of these lists of numbers.
   **a** 25, 30 and 40   **b** 18, 45 and 72   **c** 48, 72 and 120   **d** 32, 80 and 192

**4 a** What is the highest common factor of two prime numbers?

   **b** How do you find the lowest common multiple of two prime numbers?

> Choose two prime numbers, for example 3 and 7, and find their lowest common multiple. Do this again with some other pairs of prime numbers.

**5** Two numbers are called co-prime if their highest common factor is 1.

   Which of the following pairs of numbers are co-prime?

   **a** 21 and 8   **b** 21 and 18
   **c** 35 and 33   **d** 20 and 42

> In each question, list the factors of each number to find the highest common factor.

## Review

**1** Work out
   **a** $(-4) + (-14)$   **b** $13 + (-21)$   **c** $(-15) - (-12)$   **d** $(-6) \times 8$
   **e** $(-9) \times (-7)$   **f** $56 \div (-8)$   **g** $(-81) \div (-9)$   **h** $(-7)^2$
   **i** $(-4)^3$   **j** $(-125) \div 5$

**2** Find the value of:
   **a** $5 + 6 \times 7$   **b** $18 - 32 \div 4$   **c** $12 \times 4 + 1$
   **d** $10 \times (16 - 9)$   **e** $(-5) - (-2) \times (-8)$   **f** $(4 + (-9)) \times 7$
   **g** $45 \div 9 - 36 \div 6$   **h** $65 - (-9) \times (-3)$   **i** $(-3) \times (-4) \times (-5)$

**3** Put brackets in to make these calculations correct, where necessary.
   **a** $3 + 4 \times 5 + 6 = 41$   **b** $3 + 4 \times 5 + 6 = 47$
   **c** $3 + 4 \times 5 + 6 = 77$   **d** $3 + 4 \times 5 + 6 = 29$

**4** Write down the value of:
   **a** $9^2$   **b** $13^2$   **c** $20^2$   **d** $3^3$   **e** $5^3$   **f** $7^2$
   **g** $15^2$   **h** $6^2$   **i** $4^3$   **j** $1^2$   **k** $12^2$   **l** $10^2$

**1 Integers, powers and roots**

**5** Write the following using index notation.

    **a** $6 \times 6 \times 6 \times 6$      **b** $4 \times 4 \times 4 \times 4 \times 4 \times 4$

    **c** $10 \times 10 \times 10 \times 10 \times 10 \times 10 \times 10 \times 10$

**6** Work out the value of:

    **a** $6^3$     **b** $10^3$     **c** $2^5$     **d** $1^5$     **e** $3^4$

**7** Here is a list of 15 numbers.

    1, 4, 7, 9, 10, 13, 25, 27, 29, 32, 67, 81, 125, 128, 256

    **a** Write down the numbers that are square numbers.

    **b** Write down the numbers that are cube numbers.

    **c** Write down the numbers that are prime numbers.

**8** Work out the lengths of the sides of squares with the following areas.

    **a** $121 \, cm^2$      **b** $324 \, mm^2$      **c** $81 \, m^2$

**9** Work out the length of each side of these cubes.

    **a** Volume = $27 \, cm^3$

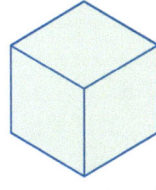

    **b** Volume = $125 \, cm^3$

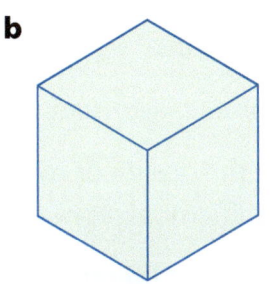

**10** **a** This sequence is made by adding an extra odd number each time.

        Add another six lines to the sequence, and then write out the ten answers.

        $1 = 1$

        $1 + 3 = 4$

        $1 + 3 + 5 = 9$

        $1 + 3 + 5 + 7 = 16$

    **b** What type of numbers are the answers?

**11** Without using a calculator, write down the value of:

    **a** $\sqrt{144}$     **b** $\sqrt{25}$     **c** $\sqrt[3]{64}$     **d** $\sqrt{196}$     **e** $\sqrt[3]{8}$     **f** $\sqrt{361}$

**12** Sort these into order of size, starting with the smallest.

    $3^3$      $\sqrt[3]{125}$      $5^2$      $\sqrt{225}$      $2^5$

**13** Write each number as a product of prime factors.

    **a** 45     **b** 64     **c** 84     **d** 132     **e** 175

**14** Find the highest common factor and the lowest common multiple of:

    **a** 45 and 105      **b** 63 and 84      **c** 25, 30 and 35      **d** 16, 24 and 40

# 2 Expressions

> **Learning outcomes**
> - Construct linear expressions.
> - Simplify or transform linear expressions with integer coefficients; collect like terms; multiply a single term over a bracket.
> - Know that algebraic operations, including brackets, follow the same order as arithmetic operations; use index notation for small positive integer powers.
> - Substitute positive and negative integers into linear expressions and expressions involving small powers.

## Robotics

Algebra is used by people in many interesting jobs.

These include engineers, architects, accountants, astronauts and animators.

Robotics is the study of technology used in the design of robots. It is an area of engineering that needs some very difficult algebra.

Robotics involves lots of moving parts that need different levels of energy to work. The engineers must work out how to make the robot parts move a certain distance in a certain direction and at a certain speed.

## 2.1 Using letters for unknown numbers

In your Stage 7 Student Book, you learnt how to use letters to represent unknown numbers.

When writing or simplifying algebraic **expressions** you must remember the following rules:

- $x + x = 2 \times x = 2x$
- $3 + 2x = 2x + 3$
- $x \div 4 = \frac{x}{4}$
- $3 \times (x + 8) = 3(x + 8) = 3x + 24$
- $x \times x = x^2$
- $x \times y = xy$
- $y \times 7 \times x = 7xy$
- $x \div y = \frac{x}{y}$

$2x$, $2x + 3$, $3(x + 8)$ and $\frac{x}{4}$ are called **linear expressions**.

$x^2$, $xy$, $7xy$ and $\frac{x}{y}$ are not linear expressions.

Can you explain the difference between a linear and a non-linear expression?

> **Worked example**
>
> Rafiu starts with the number $x$.
>
> Write an expression for the number Rafiu gets when he:
>
> **a** divides the number by 3 and then subtracts 2
>
> **b** adds 7 to his number and then multiplies by 4
>
> **c** multiplies the number by 4 and then subtracts the result from $y$.
>
> **a** $\frac{x}{3} - 2$
>
> **b** $4(x + 7)$ or $4x + 28$
>
> **c** $y - 4x$

## Exercise 2.1

**1** Write these sentences as expressions.

  **a** Start with the number $a$, multiply by 5 and then add 8.

  **b** Start with the number $b$, multiply by 4 and then subtract 7.

  **c** Start with the number $c$, multiply by 4 and then multiply by 8.

  **d** Start with the number $d$, multiply by 3 and then subtract from 6.

  **e** Start with the number $e$, add 4 and then multiply by 3.

  **f** Start with the number $f$, subtract 10 and then multiply by 4.

  **g** Start with the number $g$, multiply by 2 and then subtract from the number $x$.

  **h** Start with the number $h$, divide by 5 and then subtract 2.

  **i** Start with the number $i$, add 3 and then divide by 8.

  **j** Start with the number $j$, multiply by the number $x$ and then add 4.

  **k** Start with the number $k$, multiply by the number $x$ and then subtract from the number 10.

**2** The instructions for a question in Anna's homework are:

Start with the number $x$. Subtract 5 from the number and then multiply by 3.

She writes:

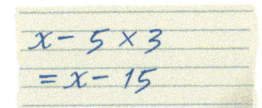

$$x - 5 \times 3$$
$$= x - 15$$

Explain why Anna is wrong.

**3** Match each statement with the correct expression.

The first one has been done for you.

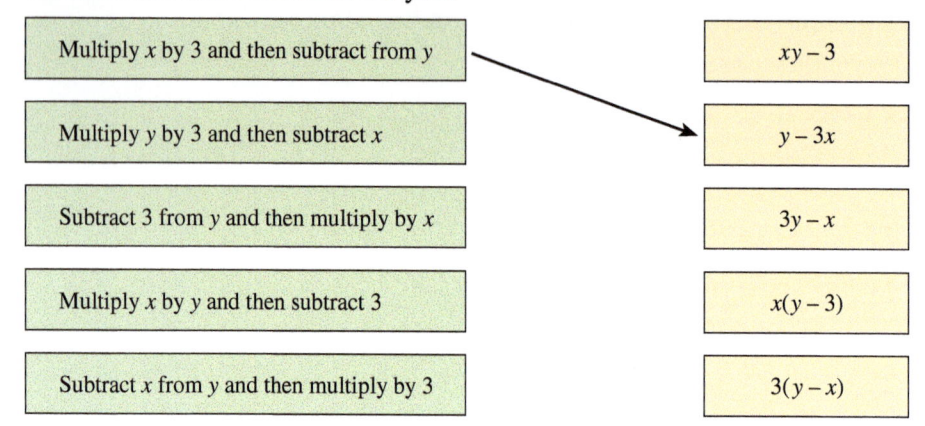

| Multiply $x$ by 3 and then subtract from $y$ | → | $xy - 3$ |
| Multiply $y$ by 3 and then subtract $x$ | | $y - 3x$ |
| Subtract 3 from $y$ and then multiply by $x$ | | $3y - x$ |
| Multiply $x$ by $y$ and then subtract 3 | | $x(y - 3)$ |
| Subtract $x$ from $y$ and then multiply by 3 | | $3(y - x)$ |

**4** Write an expression for the perimeter of each of these shapes.

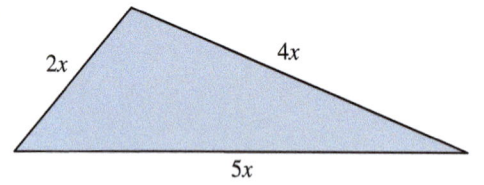

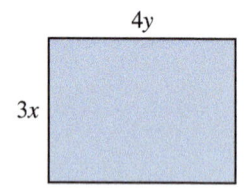

**a** Triangle with sides $2x$, $4x$, $5x$.

**b** Rectangle with sides $4y$ and $3x$.

**5** Write an expression for the length of:

**a** $BC$

**b** $CD$.

Shape with $AB = 3$, $AF = x$, $FE = y$, $DE = 2$.

**6** Richard is $x$ years old.

**a** How old was Richard $y$ years ago?

**b** How old will Richard be in $2x$ years' time?

**7** A box contains $m$ marbles.

**a** How many marbles are there in the box when:

**i** 3 marbles are taken out of the box

**ii** $x$ marbles are added to the box?

**b** The marbles are shared equally between 2 children.

How many marbles does each child receive?

**c** How many marbles are there in 5 identical boxes of marbles?

**8** A book costs $b$ dollars and a magazine costs $m$ dollars.

Write an expression for the total cost, in dollars, of 5 books and 3 magazines.

**9** A pencil costs $p$ cents, an eraser costs $e$ cents and a ruler costs $r$ cents.

Write an expression for the total cost, in cents, of 5 pencils, 7 erasers and 2 rulers.

**10** The rule to change a temperature in degrees Celsius (°C) to degrees Fahrenheit (°F) is:

**Multiply by 1.8 and then add 32.**

   **a** Change these temperatures to °F:    **i** 5°C    **ii** 20°C    **iii** 50°C

   **b** Change $x$°C to °F.

**11** Pusti changes $x$ British pounds (£) into US dollars ($) when £1 = $1.61.

Write an expression for the number of dollars that Pusti receives.

**12**

**BOAT HIRE CHARGES**
Fixed fee: $5
AND THEN
$4 per hour

   **a** Find the total cost of hiring a boat for 4 hours.

   **b** Write an expression for the total cost of hiring a boat for $n$ hours.

   **c** Write an expression for the total cost of hiring 3 boats for $n$ hours.

   **d** Ryta hires a boat for 2 hours. She pays with a $50 note.

      How much change does Ryta receive?

   **e** Karl hires a boat for $n$ hours. He pays with a $50 note.

      Write an expression for the amount of change that Karl receives.

**13** A packet of white paper costs $w$ dollars.

A packet of coloured paper costs $c$ dollars.

   **a** Match each statement with the correct expression.

| | |
|---|---|
| | $cy$ |
| The total cost, in dollars, of 3 packets of white paper and 5 packets of coloured paper | $3w + 5c$ |
| The change, in dollars, from $20 when Iman buys 3 packets of coloured paper | $20 - wx$ |
| The total cost, in dollars, of $y$ packets of coloured paper | $20 - 3c$ |
| The change, in dollars, from $20 when Mario buys $x$ packets of white paper | $20 - 5w$ |
| | $5c - 3w$ |

   **b** Write a statement for each of the two expressions that are left.

**14** A pencil costs 75 cents and a ruler costs 98 cents.

Write down an expression for the total cost, in dollars, for $x$ pencils and $y$ rulers.

## 2.2 Multiplying algebraic terms

It is important to remember when multiplying numbers that the order does not matter.

For example, $2 \times 3 \times 4$ is the same as $3 \times 2 \times 4$ or $4 \times 2 \times 3$

This idea can be used when multiplying algebraic terms.

$5x \times 7y$ is the same as $5 \times x \times 7 \times y = 5 \times 7 \times x \times y = 35xy$

You must also remember the following rules:

- $x \times x \times x = x^3$
- $x^2 \times x = x \times x^2 = x^3$

### Worked example

Simplify

**a** $4xy \times 3x$

**b** $4p^2 \times 2q \times 5p$

**c** $(2xy)^3$

**a** $4xy \times 3x = 4 \times x \times y \times 3 \times x = 12x^2y$

**b** $4p^2 \times 2q \times 5p = 4 \times p \times p \times 2 \times q \times 5 \times p = 40p^3q$

**c** $(2xy)^3 = 2 \times x \times y \times 2 \times x \times y \times 2 \times x \times y = 8x^3y^3$

## Exercise 2.2

**1** Simplify

    **a** $2x \times 3y$      **b** $5a \times 4b$      **c** $3y \times 7x$      **d** $x \times 2z \times 7y$

    **e** $3fg \times 2h$      **f** $5q \times 3p \times 7r$      **g** $6y \times x \times 2w$      **h** $7wy \times 9zx$

**2** Simplify

    **a** $h \times h$      **b** $5x \times x$      **c** $y \times 3y$      **d** $5c \times 8c$

    **e** $5y \times 3y \times 2$      **f** $4d \times 3 \times d$      **g** $g \times 2g \times 7$      **h** $6 \times y \times 2y$

**3** Simplify

    **a** $pq \times p$      **b** $7a \times ab$      **c** $5x \times 2xy$      **d** $4ab \times 3b$

    **e** $xy \times xy$      **f** $ab \times ba$      **g** $cd \times 5dc$      **h** $4pq \times 3pq$

    **i** $5hk \times 2kh$      **j** $8ab \times 7ba$      **k** $3abc \times 5ac$      **l** $2fh \times 5fgh$

**4** Simplify

    **a** $h \times h \times h$      **b** $d \times d \times d$      **c** $k \times k \times 2k$      **d** $7h \times 2h \times 4h$

    **e** $4m \times 5m \times 6m$      **f** $2x \times 3x \times 4x$      **g** $2h \times 5h \times h$      **h** $3x \times 2 \times 2x \times 5x$

**5** Simplify

a $x^2 \times x$  
b $5p \times p^2$  
c $3f^2 \times 5f$  
d $m \times 7m^2$  
e $fg \times g^2$  
f $3x^2 \times 5xy$  
g $5a^2b \times b$  
h $7p^2 \times 4pq^2$  
i $3xy \times 4xy^2$  
j $8x^2y \times 2xy^2$  
k $ab^2 \times 4a^2b$  
l $3a^2 \times 4b \times 2ab$  
m $5ab \times 3b^2c$  
n $2xy \times y^2 \times 4xz^2$  
o $2f \times 5fg \times 3g^2$  
p $2a \times 5ab^2 \times 3abc^2$  

**6** To find the expression in each block you **multiply** the expressions in the two blocks below it. Copy and complete the diagram.

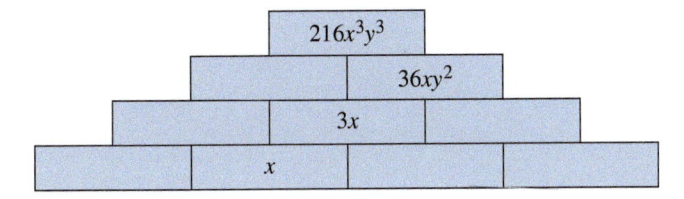

```
           216x³y³
        [     ][36xy²]
      [   ][3x ][      ]
    [   ][ x ][    ][    ]
```

**7** Robert is given the expression $(5x)^3$ and is asked to simplify it. He writes:

$(5x)^3 = 15x^3$

$(5x)^3$ means $5x \times 5x \times 5x$

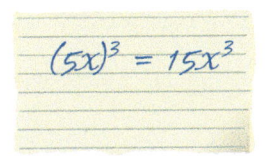

Explain why Robert is wrong.

**8** Simplify

a $(2x)^2$  
b $(3y)^2$  
c $(5a)^2$  
d $(3ab)^2$  
e $(2a)^3$  
f $(5f)^3$  
g $(xy)^3$  
h $(4fg)^3$  

**9** Copy and complete:

a $2x^2 \times \square = 8x^3$  
b $5xy \times \square = 15x^2y^2$  
c $3xy^2 \times \square = 21x^3y^3$  
d $6y^2 \times \square = 18x^2y^3$  
e $7ab \times \square = 28a^3b^2$  
f $5y \times \square = 30x^2y^3$  
g $(\square)^2 = 4x^2$  
h $(\square)^3 = 1000y^3$  
i $(\square)^2 = 49x^2y^2$  
j $(\square)^2 = 81f^2g^2$  
k $(\square)^3 = 27c^3d^3$  
l $(\square)^3 = 216a^3b^3c^3$  

**10** Simplify

a $x^2 \times x^3$  
b $3x^2 \times 5x^2$  
c $3ab^2c \times 4a^2b^2c^2$  
d $(2x)^5$  
e $8x^3 \times 2x \times 5x^2$  
f $(2x)^4$  
g $0.1pq^2r^3 \times 50p^2qr$  
h $8y \times 3y^2 \times 2y^3$  

2 Expressions

23

# 2.3 Collecting like terms

The expression $9x^2y + 5xy - 3xyx$ has three **terms**.

The term $3xyx$ can be written more simply as $3x^2y$. This means that the above expression can be simplified by collecting the **like terms** together.

$$9x^2y + 5xy - 3xyx = 9x^2y + 5xy - 3x^2y$$
$$= 9x^2y + 5xy - 3x^2y \qquad \text{Find the like terms.}$$
$$= 9x^2y - 3x^2y + 5xy \qquad \text{Put the like terms next to each other.}$$
$$= 6x^2y + 5xy$$

## Worked example 1

Simplify these expressions.

**a** $-8x + 3x$

**b** $5y^2 + y^2 - 2y^2$

**c** $(2xy)^3$

**a** $-8x + 3x = -5x$ $\qquad$ Because $-8 + 3 = -5$

**b** $5y^2 + y^2 - 2y^2 = 5y^2 + 1y^2 - 2y^2$ $\qquad$ Remember that $y^2$ means $1y^2$
$\qquad\qquad\qquad\qquad = 4y^2$ $\qquad$ Because $5 + 1 - 2 = 4$

**c** $(2xy)^3 = 2xy \times 2xy \times 2xy$
$\qquad\qquad = 8x^3y^3$

## Worked example 2

Simplify the expression $12xy + 5x^2 - 3y + 3x^2 - 7xy$

$$12xy + 5x^2 - 3y + 3x^2 - 7xy = 12xy + 5x^2 - 3y + 3x^2 - 7xy \qquad \text{Find the like terms.}$$
$$= 12xy - 7xy + 5x^2 + 3x^2 - 3y \qquad \text{Put the like terms next to each other.}$$
$$= 5xy + 8x^2 - 3y$$

## Exercise 2.3

**1** Simplify

**a** $2x + 5x$ $\qquad$ **b** $x + 8x$ $\qquad$ **c** $4y + 3y$ $\qquad$ **d** $9a - 3a$

**e** $2h - 4h$ $\qquad$ **f** $7p - 7p$ $\qquad$ **g** $-4x - 8x$ $\qquad$ **h** $-7x + 2x$

**i** $5x^2 + 3x^2$ $\qquad$ **j** $7t^2 + t^2$ $\qquad$ **k** $2y^2 + 3y^2$ $\qquad$ **l** $8x^2 - x^2$

**m** $6y^2 - 9y^2$ $\qquad$ **n** $h^2 - 9h^2$ $\qquad$ **o** $-4y^3 + y^3$ $\qquad$ **p** $-3q^3 - 2q^3$

2 Expressions

**2** Sort these terms into two groups of like terms.

$5p^2q$   $\frac{1}{2}qpq$   $8pq^2$   $-2qp^2$   $3pqp$   $0.3q^2p$

**3** Simplify

a  $8x + 2x + 3x$
b  $6x - 2x + x$
c  $8y - 2y - 3y$
d  $2a - 5a - 4a$
e  $3x^2 + 2x^2 + 5x^2$
f  $7x^2 - 3x^2 + 2x^2$
g  $9y^3 - 4y^3 - 5y^3$
h  $5p^3 - 9p^3 + 2p^3$
i  $3ab^2 + 4ab^2 + 2ab^2$
j  $8x^2y - 3yx^2 - 2x^2y$
k  $4a^3b^2 - 6b^2a^3 - 7a^3b^2$
l  $7aba - 2a^2b + 5ba^2$

**4** Simplify

a  $3x + 5 + 2x$
b  $5x^2 + 3x + x^2$
c  $2x + 5 + 5x + 8$
d  $7y + 8 - 3y$
e  $8 - 5x - 2 + 3x$
f  $2xy + y + 3xy + x$
g  $3y^3 + 5x^2 + 4x^2 - 8x$
h  $12x^2 + 3x - 8x + 5$

**5** Hayley has done her homework on simplifying expressions wrong.

Copy out each question and correct her mistakes.

a) $5x^2 + 8 - 2x^2$
  $= 5x^2 + 6x^2$
  $= 11x^2$

b) $5x^2 + 3x + 4x + 1$
  $= 5x^2 + 7x^2 + 1$
  $= 12x^2 + 1$

c) $7y + 3y + 2y^2$
  $= 21y^2 + 2y^2$
  $= 23y^2$

**6** Copy and complete:

a  $7x^2 + \square + 2x^2 + 9y = 9x^2 + 12y$
b  $8x - 2y + 5x - \square = 13x - 8y$
c  $6xy - 5x^2 - \square + 2x^2 = xy - 3x^2$
d  $8x^3 - \square - 8x^2 - 3x^3 = 5x^3 - 13x^2$

**7** The diagram shows some expressions that are equivalent to $2x^2 + 8y^2$.

Copy the diagram and add four more expressions that are equivalent to $2x^2 + 8y^2$.

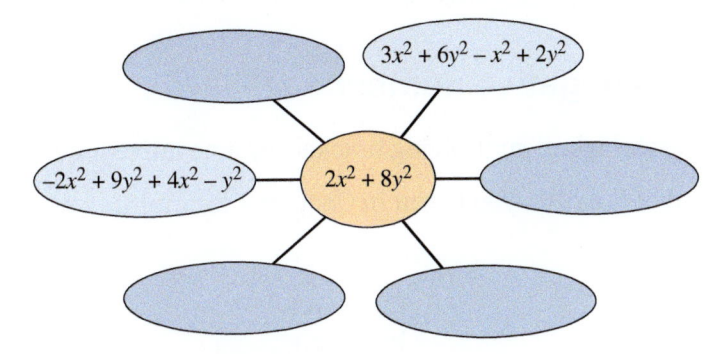

$3x^2 + 6y^2 - x^2 + 2y^2$

$-2x^2 + 9y^2 + 4x^2 - y^2$

$2x^2 + 8y^2$

**8** To find the expression in each block you **add** the expressions in the two blocks below it.

Copy and complete the diagram.

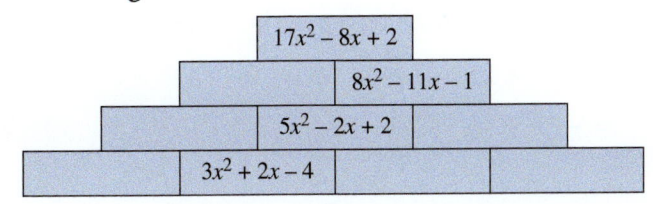

$17x^2 - 8x + 2$
$8x^2 - 11x - 1$
$5x^2 - 2x + 2$
$3x^2 + 2x - 4$

25

# Mathematics for Cambridge Secondary 1

9 Simplify

   a  $5x^4 + 3x^2 - 5x^3 + 7x^2 - 9x^4$    b  $(6ab)^2 + 9ab^2 - 2a^2b^2$    c  $(2xy)^3 - 8xy + 2x^3y^3$

## 2.4 Expanding brackets

### Multiplying by a positive number

In your Stage 7 Student Book, you learnt how to multiply out brackets by a positive number.

Multiplying out brackets is also called **expanding brackets**.

The next example is a reminder of the work that you did in Stage 7.

> **Worked example 1**
>
> a  Expand $5(2x + 9)$
>
> b  Expand and simplify $4(3x + 1) + 7(3 + 2x)$
>
> a  $5(2x + 9) = 5 \times 2x + 5 \times 9$        Multiply each term in the bracket by 5.
>           $= 10x + 45$
>
> b  $4(3x + 1) + 7(3 + 2x) = 4 \times 3x + 4 \times 1 + 7 \times 3 + 7 \times 2x$   Expand each set of brackets.
>
>                        $= 12x + 4 + 21 + 14x$
>
>                        $= 26x + 25$

### Multiplying by a negative number

You must be very careful when multiplying brackets by a negative number.

You need to remember the rules you learnt in Chapter 1 for multiplying positive and negative numbers:

$$+ \times + = +$$
$$+ \times - = -$$
$$- \times + = -$$
$$- \times - = +$$

To expand $-3(x - 5)$ you multiply both terms in the bracket by $-3$:

$$-3(x - 5) = (-3 \times x) + (-3 \times -5)$$
$$= -3x + 15$$

## 2 Expressions

### Worked example 2

**a** Expand $-8(5 + 4x)$

**b** Expand and simplify $4(7x - 2) - 2(3x - 2)$

**c** Expand and simplify $4x(3x + 1) - 2(3x + 5)$

**a** $-8(5 + 4x) = (-8 \times 5) + (-8 \times 4x)$
$= -40 - 32x$

**b** $4(7x - 2) = 28x - 8$ and $-2(3x - 2) = -6x + 4$    Expand each set of brackets.

$4(7x - 2) - 2(3x - 2) = 28x - 8 - 6x + 4$
$= 28x - 6x - 8 + 4$    Collect like terms.
$= 22x - 4$    $28x - 6x = 22x$ and $-8 + 4 = -4$

**c** $4x(3x + 1) = 12x^2 + 4x$ and $-2(3x + 5) = -6x - 10$    Expand each set of brackets.

$4x(3x + 1) - 2(3x + 5) = 12x^2 + 4x - 6x - 10$
$= 12x^2 - 2x - 10$    Collect like terms.

### Exercise 2.4

**1** Multiply out the brackets:

    **a** $3(x + 6)$      **b** $5(y - 4)$      **c** $7(2 - x)$      **d** $8(9 - x)$

    **e** $2(5x + 1)$      **f** $4(3 - 2x)$      **g** $8(3 - 4x)$      **h** $7(4x - 9)$

    **i** $x(x + 7)$      **j** $y(6 - y)$      **k** $x(3x + 5)$      **l** $p(2q + 3)$

    **m** $2x(3x - 4)$      **n** $6y(1 - 5y)$      **o** $3x(7 - 5x)$      **p** $2y(5 - 4x)$

**2** Write an expression for the area of each of these rectangles.

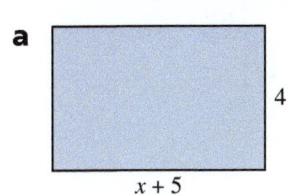

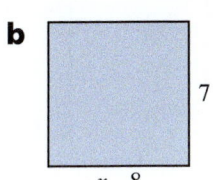

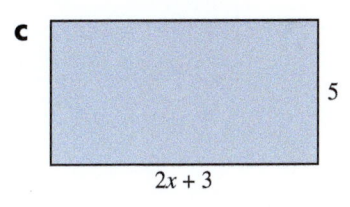

    **a** rectangle with sides $x + 5$ and $4$

    **b** rectangle with sides $x - 8$ and $7$

    **c** rectangle with sides $2x + 3$ and $5$

**3** Multiply out the brackets:

    **a** $-3(x + 2)$      **b** $-4(y + 5)$      **c** $-6(x + 7)$      **d** $-(2y + 9)$

    **e** $-5(y - 3)$      **f** $-4(x - 6)$      **g** $-7(2x - 4)$      **h** $-3(5 - 6x)$

    **i** $-x(x + 6)$      **j** $-y(8 - y)$      **k** $-3x(2x + 5)$      **l** $-4p(2q - 9)$

**4** Multiply out the brackets and simplify:

    **a** $5(x + 2) + 3(x + 8)$      **b** $7(x + 1) + 4(x + 6)$      **c** $2(x + 5) + 4(x + 7)$

    **d** $9(x + 3) + 6(x + 5)$      **e** $8(x + 1) + 3(x - 4)$      **f** $3(x + 6) + 2(x - 1)$

**g** $7(x-2) + 2(x+4)$  **h** $6(x-4) + 3(x+2)$  **i** $2(x-2) + 6(x-7)$
**j** $5(8-x) + 9(x-9)$  **k** $x(x-4) + 2x(x+8)$  **l** $5x(x+1) + 3x(x-7)$

**5** Write an expression for the **total area** of these two rectangles.

Simplify your expression.

Rectangle 1: 6 by $x-7$

Rectangle 2: 2 by $2x+8$

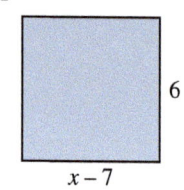

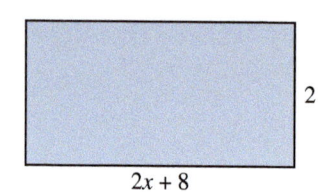

**6** Write an expression for the perimeter of each of these shapes.

Simplify your expressions.

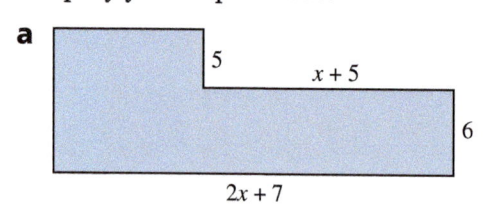

**a** Shape with dimensions: 5, $x+5$, 6, $2x+7$

**b** Shape with dimensions: 7, $3x+5$, 4, $3x+5$, $2x+1$

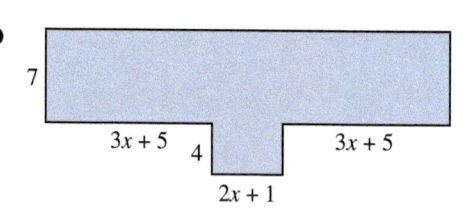

**7** Multiply out the brackets and simplify:

**a** $4(x+1) - 3(x+7)$  **b** $8(x+2) - 4(x+5)$  **c** $6(x+5) - 2(x+1)$
**d** $8(5+x) - 4(x+3)$  **e** $7(x+2) - 3(x-2)$  **f** $5(x+1) - 4(x-5)$
**g** $6(x-2) - 4(x-9)$  **h** $2(x-3) - 3(5-x)$  **i** $2(x-3) - 6(x-8)$
**j** $5(9-x) - 9(x-7)$  **k** $3x(x-4) - 5x(x+2)$  **l** $5x(x+1) - 3x(x-7)$

**8** Write an expression for the area of each of these shaded regions.

Simplify your expressions.

**a** Large rectangle 8 by $5x+2$, with inner rectangle 3 by $3x+5$ removed.

**b** Large rectangle 10 by $7x+3$, with two squares (3 by $2x$) and rectangle (2 by $3x+5$) removed.

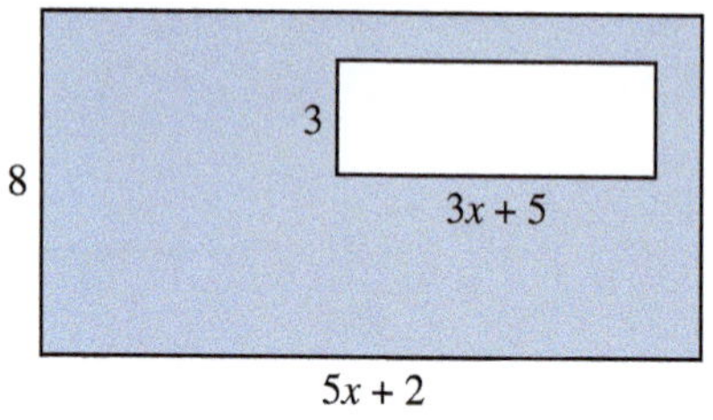

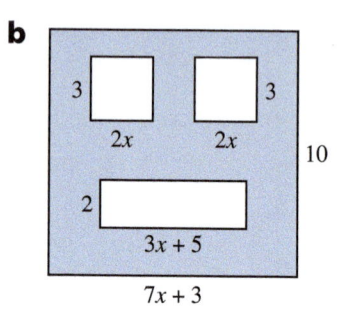

**9**  **A** $5x-3$   **B** $4-2x$   **C** $8x+7$

Expand and simplify:

**a** $2A + 3C$  **b** $2B - A$  **c** $2A + 3B + 4C$  **d** $3A + 4B - 2C + 1$

**10** Expand the brackets:

**a** $2x(3x + 2y - 5)$  **b** $y(4xy + x + 3)$  **c** $5a(2a + 3b - 7)$  **d** $3y(5 - 2x + 4y)$
**e** $7x(x^2 + 6x - 8)$  **f** $2xy(3x + 2y - 9)$  **g** $5ab(2a - b^2 + 5)$  **h** $6x^2y(8x + 2y + 1)$
**i** $-2(x + 3y - 2)$  **j** $-2(5x - 3y - 7)$  **k** $-4x(2x + 7y - 2)$  **l** $-2xy(x + 5 - 2y)$

**11** Multiply out the brackets and simplify:

    **a** $4x(2x + 3) + x(x - 5)$      **b** $5x(y + 8) + 3(x - 8)$

    **c** $5(6 - 5y) + y(2x + 7)$      **d** $3x(2 - 5y) + 2y(3x - 4)$

## 2.5 Substitution into an expression

**Substitution** into an expression means replacing the letters in the expression with given numbers.

As you learnt in chapter 1, when a calculation involves more than one operation it is important that you do the operations in the correct order.

1. Work out the **Brackets** first.
2. Work out the **Indices** (the power of a number) next.
3. Work out the **Division** and **Multiplication** next.
4. Work out the **Addition** and **Subtraction** last.

**Memory aid:**
**B I D M A S**
**B**rackets
**I**ndices
**D**ivision
**M**ultiplication
**A**ddition
**S**ubtraction

### Worked example

If $x = 2$ and $y = -3$ find the values of:

**a** $x^2 + 3y$      **b** $8 - xy$      **c** $3y^2 + 7x$      **d** $y + (3x)^2$

**a** $x^2 + 3y = 2^2 + (3 \times -3)$     Do the indices first and then the multiplication.

    $= 4 + -9$

    $= -5$

**b** $8 - xy = 8 - (2 \times -3)$     Do the multiplication first.

    $= 8 - -6$

    $= 14$

**c** $3y^2 + 7x = 3 \times (-3)^2 + 7 \times 2$     Do the indices first and then the multiplications.

    $= 3 \times 9 + 7 \times 2$

    $= 27 + 14$

    $= 41$

**d** $y + (3x)^2 = -3 + (3 \times 2)^2$     Do the brackets.

    $= -3 + 6^2$     Do the indices next.

    $= -3 + 36$

    $= 33$

# Mathematics for Cambridge Secondary 1

## Exercise 2.5

**1** Brendon has worked out a question wrong in his homework on substitution.

Copy out the question and correct his mistake.

> QUESTION: Find the value of $4y^2$ when $y = 2$
> ANSWER: $4y^2 = 4 \times 2^2$
> $= 8^2$
> $= 64$

**2** If $x = 3$ find the value of:

- **a** $2x + 5$
- **b** $8 + 5x$
- **c** $2 - 3x$
- **d** $14x$
- **e** $x^2$
- **f** $2x^2$
- **g** $7x^2 - 6$
- **h** $\dfrac{4x^2}{6}$
- **i** $x^3$
- **j** $2x^3 + 3$
- **k** $5x^3 + 4x$
- **l** $\dfrac{5x^3}{9}$
- **m** $(4x)^2$
- **n** $(2x)^3 + 5x$
- **o** $x^2 + 5x - 3$
- **p** $\dfrac{9x^2 - 4}{3x + 2}$

**3** If $a = 4$ and $b = 2$, find the value of:

- **a** $2a + 3b$
- **b** $5b - 7a$
- **c** $3ab$
- **d** $a^2 + b^2$
- **e** $2a^2b$
- **f** $5a^2 - b$
- **g** $4ab^3$
- **h** $\dfrac{4a^2b}{2a}$
- **i** $3ab^2 + 2a^2b$
- **j** $(ab)^2$
- **k** $\dfrac{a^2}{2} + \dfrac{b^3}{2}$
- **l** $\dfrac{5ab^2}{25a^2b}$

**4** Padmaja has worked out a question wrong in her homework on substitution.

Copy out the question and correct her mistake.

> QUESTION: Find the value of $4 - 2y^3$ when $y = -3$
> ANSWER: $4 - 2y^3 = 4 - 2 \times -3^3$
> $= 2 \times -3^3$
> $= (-6)^3$
> $= -6 \times -6 \times -6$
> $= 216$

**5** If $y = -2$, find the value of:

- **a** $8y$
- **b** $10 + 5y$
- **c** $8 - 3y$
- **d** $y^2$
- **e** $y^3$
- **f** $3y^2$
- **g** $y^2 + 7$
- **h** $4y^2 - 8$
- **i** $5y^2 + 4y$
- **j** $3y^2 + 2y - 5$
- **k** $(6y)^2 + 1$
- **l** $(2y)^3 - 2y^3$

**6** If $p = -3$, $q = 2$ and $r = -1$, find the value of:

- **a** $p + q + r$
- **b** $2p + 5q + 3r$
- **c** $3p + 8 - 2r$
- **d** $pqr$
- **e** $3p^2 + 4$
- **f** $2q^2 - 5$
- **g** $2p^2 + 3q^2$
- **h** $4p^3q^2$
- **i** $p^2 + 4qr$
- **j** $q^3 - 2r$
- **k** $2r^3 + 4q^2r$
- **l** $5pq^2r + 6$

7 Find the odd one out when $x = 3$

    A  $2x^2 - 3$       B  $x^3 - 13$       C  $3x^2 - 4x$

8 Find the value of $x$ that makes each of these expressions equal.

    $2x^2 + 12$       $3x^2 - 4$       $x^2 - 5x + 8$

## Review

1 Bruce starts with the number $x$.

Write an expression for the number Bruce gets when he:

    **a** multiplies the number by 5 and then adds 8

    **b** divides the number by 3 and then subtracts 1

    **c** adds 4 to the number and then divides by 10

    **d** subtracts 2 from the number and then multiplies by 9.

2 A paper clip costs 15 cents and a piece of paper costs 8 cents.

Write an expression for the total cost, in cents, of $c$ paper clips and $p$ pieces of paper.

3 Write an expression for the perimeter of the rectangle.

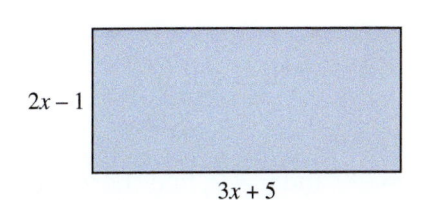

    $2x - 1$

    $3x + 5$

4 Simplify

    **a** $5x \times 3y$     **b** $3a \times 2b \times 5a$     **c** $5x \times 8x$     **d** $8xy \times 7y$

    **e** $5f \times 3 \times 4fg$     **f** $7x \times 2x \times 3x$     **g** $4xy \times 2x^2y$     **h** $6x^2 \times 4y \times 2xy$

    **i** $(4y)^2$     **j** $(2d)^3$     **k** $5(xy)^3$     **l** $(2x \times 3y)^2$

5 Find the cards that simplify to $6x^2y$

    A  $5x \times yx$       B  $3x \times 2yx$       C  $6x^2 + y$       D  $-3y \times -2x^2$

6 Simplify

    **a** $9y + 7y$     **b** $6x - 10x$     **c** $5x^2 - x^2$

    **d** $-6h^3 + 2h^3$     **e** $2x^2 + 7x + 2x - 3$     **f** $5y^2 + 2x^2 - 2y^2 + 4x^2$

    **g** $x^3 + 5x^2 + 4x - 8x^2$     **h** $7d^3 - 9d^3 + 6 + 2d^3$

7 Find the cards that simplify to $3x - 3$

    A  $x \times 3 - 3$       B  $-3x + 3$       C  $-3 + 3x$       D  $3 + x \times 3$

**8** To find the expression in each block you **add** the expressions in the two blocks below it.
Copy and complete the diagram.

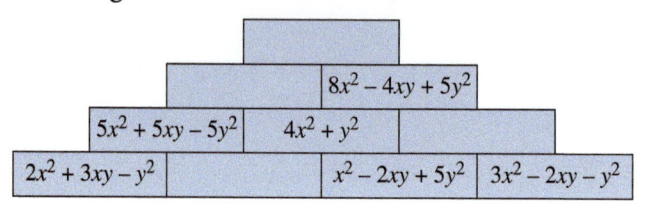

| | | $8x^2 - 4xy + 5y^2$ | | |
|---|---|---|---|---|
| | $5x^2 + 5xy - 5y^2$ | | $4x^2 + y^2$ | |
| $2x^2 + 3xy - y^2$ | | $x^2 - 2xy + 5y^2$ | | $3x^2 - 2xy - y^2$ |

**9** Multiply out the brackets:
   **a** $5(2x + 3)$   **b** $7(3x - 5)$   **c** $-4(5 - 2x)$   **d** $-3(6x + 7)$

**10** Multiply out the brackets and simplify:
   **a** $5(x + 3) + 2(3x + 4)$        **b** $4(2x - 5) + 3(5x - 1)$
   **c** $9(x + 4) - 3(x - 2)$         **d** $5(2x - 3) - 2(3x + 7)$

**11** Write an expression for the area of the shaded region.

Simplify your expression.

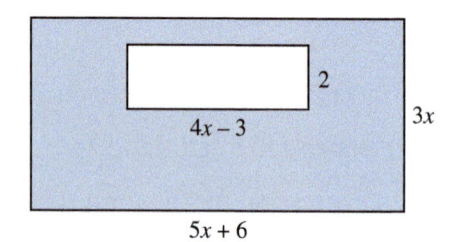

**12** If $x = 2$, find the value of:
   **a** $7 - 3x$   **b** $5x^2$   **c** $x^3 + 3x^2$   **d** $(3x)^2 + 2x - 9$

**13** If $x = -3$ and $y = 2$, find the value of:
   **a** $5x + 4y$   **b** $x^2 + xy$   **c** $4x^2y$   **d** $\dfrac{(5x)^2}{3} + 4y$

# 3 Shapes and geometric reasoning 1

## Learning outcomes

- Identify alternate angles and corresponding angles.
- Understand a proof that:
  – the angle sum of a triangle is 180° and that of a quadrilateral is 360°
  – the exterior angle of a triangle is equal to the sum of the two interior opposite angles.
- Solve geometrical problems using properties of angles, of parallel and intersecting lines, and of triangles and special quadrilaterals, explaining reasoning with diagrams and text.
- Know that the longest side of a right-angled triangle is called the hypotenuse.
- Know that if two 2D shapes are congruent, corresponding sides and angles are equal.
- Classify quadrilaterals according to their properties, including diagonal properties.
- Draw simple nets of solids.
- Identify all the symmetries of 2D shapes.

## Euclid's *Elements*

The branch of mathematics called geometry was largely developed by the Greek mathematician Euclid.

He lived about 2300 years ago and wrote 13 very important mathematics books called the *Elements*.

The mathematics in *Elements* is mainly concerned with angles, lines, circles and other geometric shapes, but there is also some work on number theory such as prime numbers and perfect numbers.

Euclid's *Elements* was used as a main teaching text in many schools until the late 20th century.

## 3.1 Parallel lines

### Alternate and corresponding angles

When two straight lines cross, four angles are created.

The angles opposite each other are equal.

They are called **vertically opposite** angles.

These diagrams show vertically opposite angles.

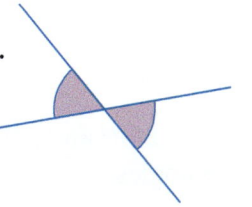

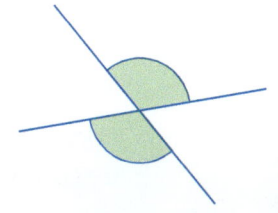

33

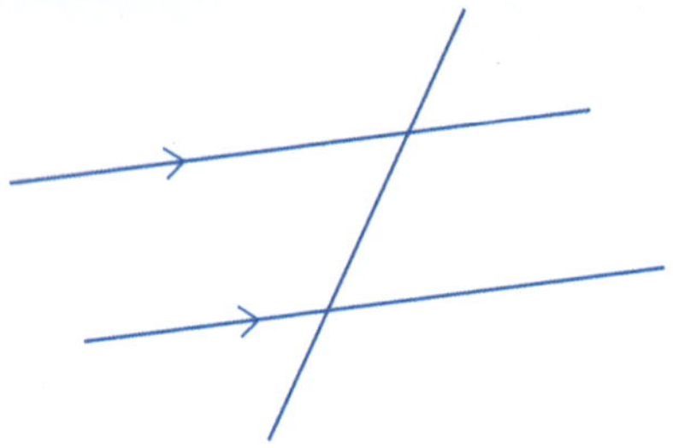

When a straight line crosses two **parallel** lines, there are two intersections or cross-over points.

At each point, there are vertically opposite angles.

**Corresponding angles** are in the same position at each intersection.

Here are four examples of pairs of corresponding angles.

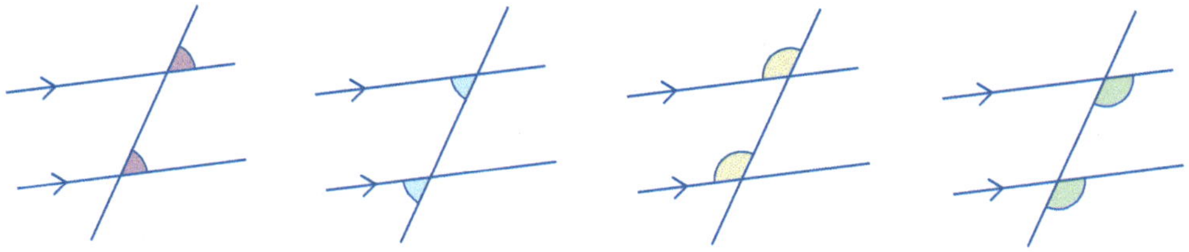

**Corresponding angles are equal.**

**Alternate angles** are in the opposite position at each intersection.

Here are four examples of pairs of alternate angles.

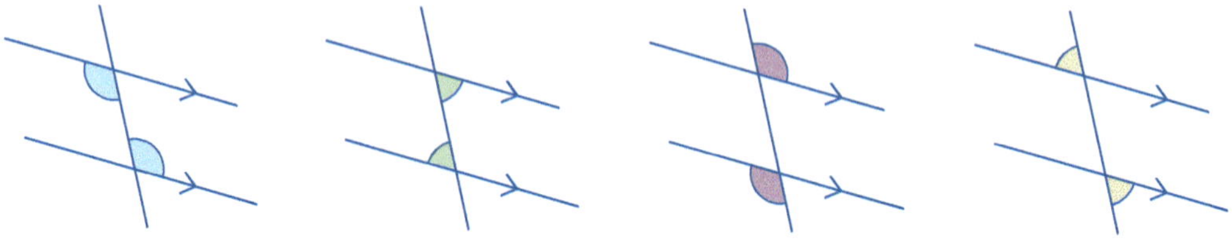

Alternate interior angles          Alternate exterior angles

**Alternate angles are equal.**

## Worked example 1

The diagram shows parallel lines *AB* and *CD*.

Line *EF* crosses them at *M* and *N*.

Angle *DNF* = 105°.

Find the size of these angles. Give reasons for your answers.

a  *BMN*          b  *CNM*          c  *AME*

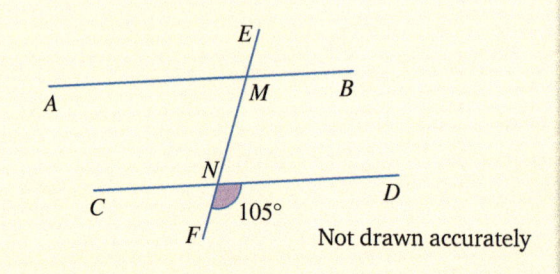

Not drawn accurately

a  The diagram shows the position of angles *DNF* and *BMN*.

They are both in the lower right-hand corner of the intersections.

*BMN* = 105° because *BMN* and *DNF* are corresponding angles.

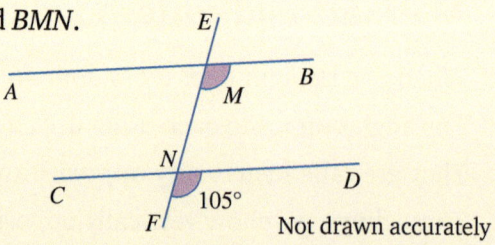

Not drawn accurately

34

**3** Shapes and geometric reasoning 1

**b** *CNM* and *DNF* are at the same intersection.

They are opposite one another.

*CNM* = 105° because *CNM* is vertically opposite angle *DNF*.

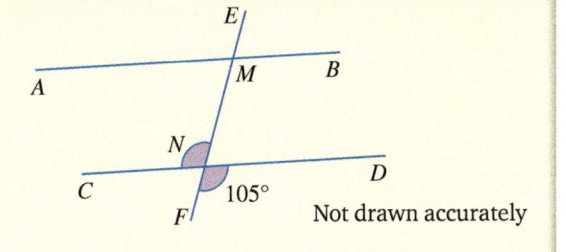

**c** *DNF* is in the lower right-hand corner of the intersection at *N*.

*AME* is in the upper left-hand corner of the intersection at *M*.

*AME* = 105° because *AME* and *DNF* are alternate angles.

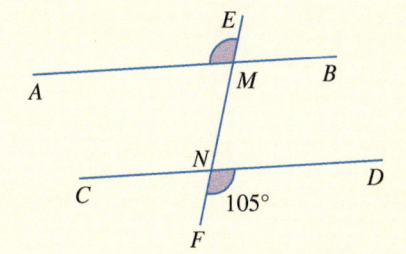

## Worked example 2

*AC* and *PR* are parallel lines.

A line joins them, meeting *AC* at *B* and *PR* at *Q*.

Angle *ABQ* = 47°.

Write the down the size of these angles.
Give reasons for your answers.

**a** *BQR*     **b** *QBC*

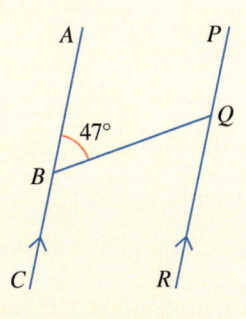

**a** *BQR* and *ABQ* are on opposite sides of the line.

*BQR* = 47° because *BQR* and *ABQ* are alternate angles.

**b** *ABQ* and *QBC* are on a straight line.

*QBC* = 180° − 47°

*QBC* = 133° because angles on a straight line add up to 180°.

## Exercise 3.1

The diagrams in this exercise are not drawn accurately.

For questions **1** to **6**, find the size of the angles marked with letters.

Give reasons for your answers.

**1** 54°, *a*, *b*

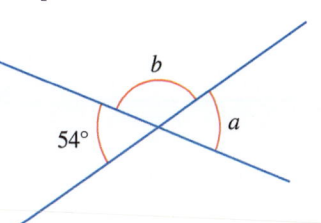

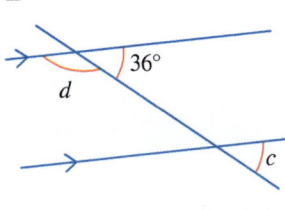

**2** 36°, *c*, *d*

**3** 59°, *e*, *f*

35

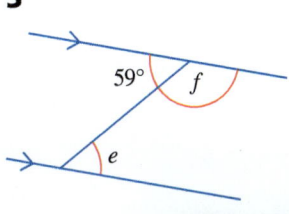

**4**

118°, g, h, i, k

**5**

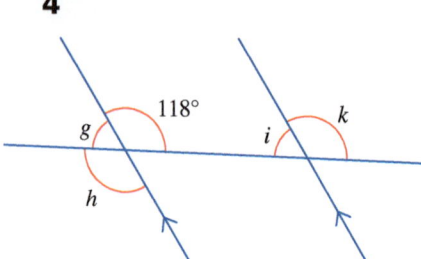

68°, l, m

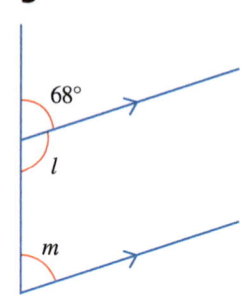

**6**

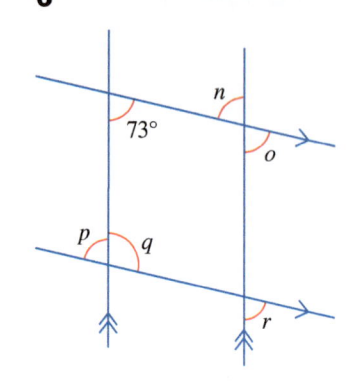

n, 73°, o, p, q, r

**7** AB and CD are parallel lines.

ST cuts the lines at the points X and Y.

Angle XYD = 80°.

Find these angles, in degrees. Give reasons for your answers.

**a** AXY

**b** SXB

**c** TYD

**8** ABCD represents the end of a shed with vertical sides.

ST represents the roof.

The roof lies at an angle of 12° to the horizontal.

Find the following angles. Give reasons for your answers.

**a** ABC

**b** TBC

**c** SAD

**d** DAB

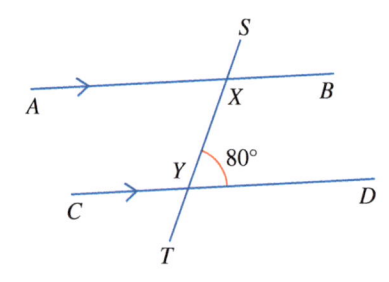

> It may help if you start by marking the parallel lines and right angles on the diagram.

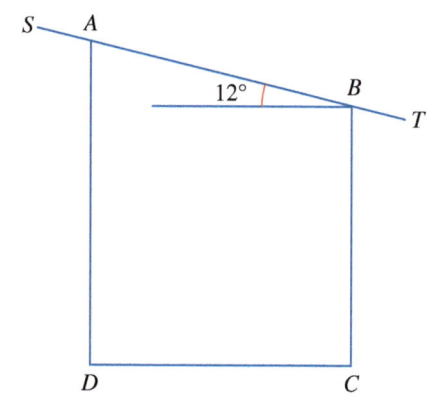

## 3.2 Angles and triangles

### Sum of the angles

You have been told that **the sum of the angles of a triangle is 180°**.

Here is a **proof** that this is always true.

Consider any triangle ABC.

Label the angles $a$, $b$ and $c$.

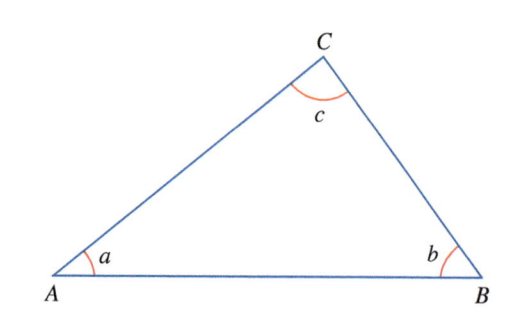

# 3 Shapes and geometric reasoning 1

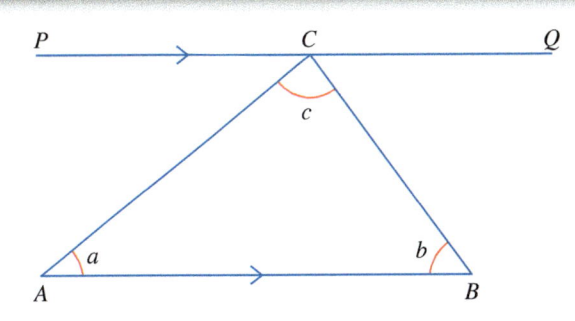

Draw a line parallel to AB that goes through C.

Label the line PQ.

Angle PCA = CAB as they are alternate angles.

So angle PCA = a.

Angle QCB = CBA as they are alternate angles.

So angle QCB = b.

The three angles shown at C are a, c and b.

They lie on a straight line.

The angles on a straight line add up to 180°.

Therefore $a + c + b = 180°$.

This shows that the angles in the triangle add up to 180°.

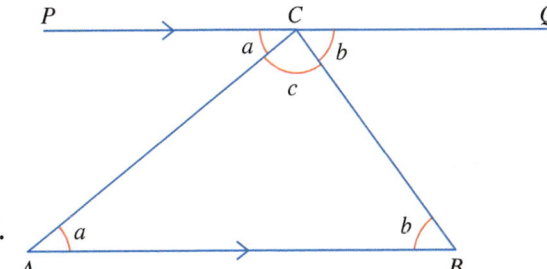

## Exterior angles

The diagram shows a triangle.

One side has been extended beyond the vertex.

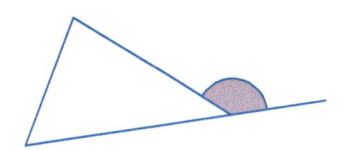

This makes an angle outside the triangle.

This is called an **exterior angle** of the triangle.

This diagram shows triangle ABC with an exterior angle shown at A.

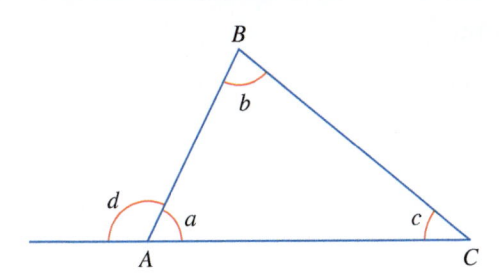

$a + d = 180°$     Angles on a straight line add up to 180°.

$d = 180° - a$     Subtract a from each side.

But also:

$a + b + c = 180°$     Angles in a triangle add up to 180°.

$b + c = 180° - a$     Subtract a from each side.

If $d = 180° - a$ and $b + c = 180° - a$ then $d = b + c$

> If two quantities both equal 180° − a then they must be equal to each other.

This shows that **the exterior angle of a triangle is equal to the sum of the two interior opposite angles.**

# Mathematics for Cambridge Secondary 1

## Worked example

In this diagram, PQR is an isosceles triangle with PR = QR.

PQS is a scalene triangle. SPR is a straight line.

**a** If angle QRP = 28° find angle QPR.

**b** If angle QSP = 36° find angle SQP.

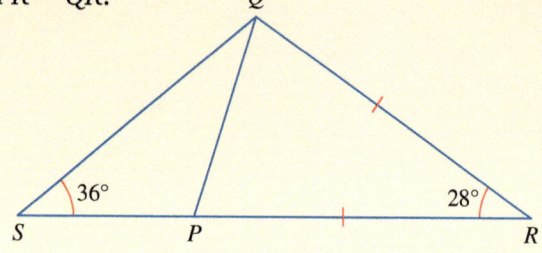

Not drawn accurately

**a** QPR = PQR          Triangle PQR is isosceles.

QPR + PQR = 180° − 28° = 152°     Angles in a triangle add to 180°.

QPR = 152° ÷ 2 = 76°

Angle QPR = 76°

**b** Angle QPR is an exterior angle of triangle PQS.

QPR = SQP + QSP     Exterior angle = sum of the two interior opposite angles.

76° = 36° + SQP

SQP = 76° − 36° = 40°

Angle SQP = 40°

## Exercise 3.2

The diagrams in this exercise are not drawn accurately.

For questions **1** to **8**, find the angles marked with letters.

**1** 62°, 58°, a

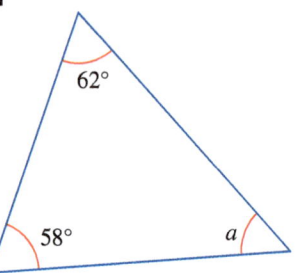

**2** b, b, b

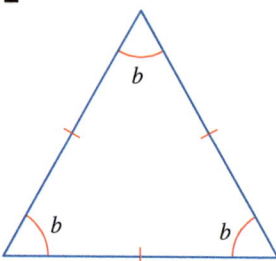

**3** d, 71°, c

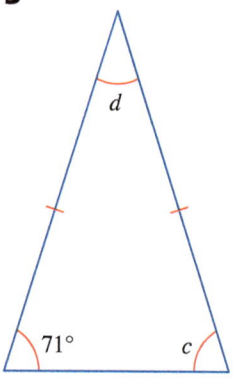

**4** 59°, 82°, e

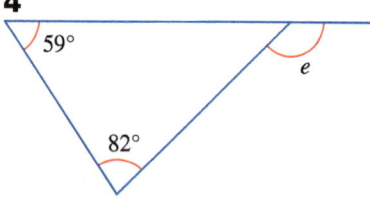

**5** 127°, f

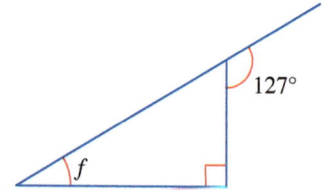

**6** i, h, g, 114°

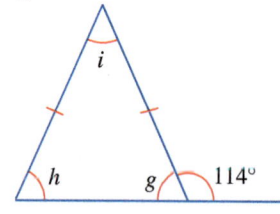

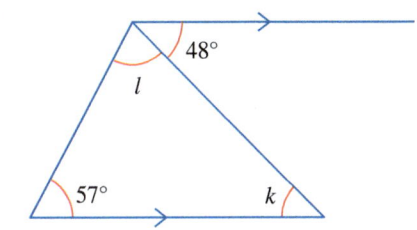

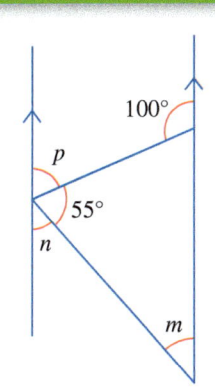

**7**  [diagram: triangle with angles 48°, 57°, k, and l, with parallel marks]

**8**  [diagram: angles 100°, 55°, p, n, m between parallel lines]

**9** *ABCD* is a straight line.

*EF* is a straight line cutting *AD* at *B*.

In triangle *AEB*, sides *AB* and *EB* are equal.

Angle *EAB* = 72°.

Angle *DCF* = 98°.

Find these angles. Give reasons for your answers.

   **a** *AEB*    **b** *EBA*

   **c** *CBF*    **d** *BFC*

**10 a** Find the value of *x* in this diagram. Give the reason for your answer.

   **b** Show that the triangle is isosceles, explaining your reasons.

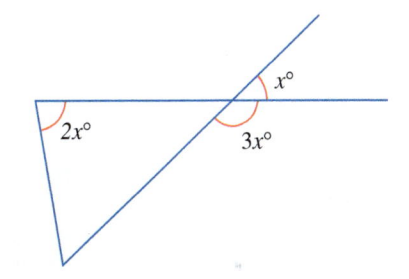

[diagram: triangle with angles $2x°$, $3x°$, and $x°$]

## 3.3 Congruent shapes

In your Stage 7 Student Book, you learnt about three transformations. These are **translation**, **reflection** and **rotation**.

The starting shape is called the **object**.

The final shape is called the **image**.

Here is a translation 3 squares to the right and 2 squares up.

The object is 3 squares high and 2 squares across.

The image is also 3 squares high and 2 squares across.

They both have right angles in the left-hand corner.

The **hypotenuse** of the object is the same length as the hypotenuse of the image.

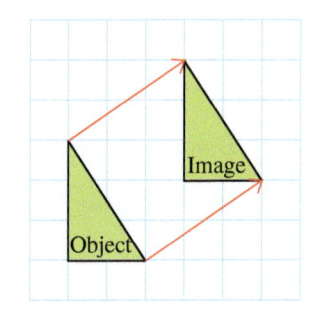

> The hypotenuse of a right-angled triangle is the longest side. It is the side opposite the right angle.

In fact, all of the corresponding sides are equal and all of the corresponding angles are equal. Shapes like this are said to be **congruent**.

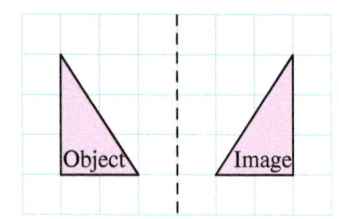

Here is a reflection of a triangle in a mirror line.

The triangles are not the same way round.

The triangles are congruent to one another.

The right side of the image corresponds to the left side of the object.

You need to be sure which are the corresponding sides and angles.

Here a quadrilateral is rotated 90° clockwise about point $O$.

The object is labelled $ABCD$.

The image is labelled $PQRS$.

Side $BC$ corresponds to side $QR$. They are equal.

Side $AD$ corresponds to side $PS$. They are equal.

Angle $BCD$ corresponds to angle $QRS$. They are equal.

All of the corresponding sides and angles are equal.

$ABCD$ is congruent to $PQRS$.

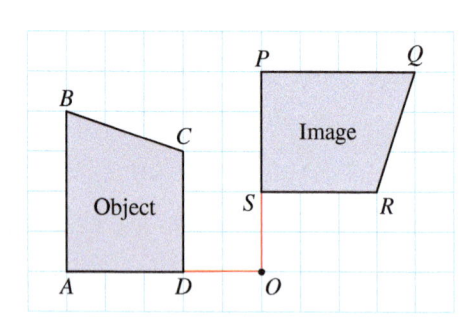

> When you describe congruent shapes try to match the vertices. $ABCD$ is congruent to $PQRS$ because $A$ corresponds to $P$, $B$ corresponds to $Q$, $C$ corresponds to $R$ and $D$ corresponds to $S$.

### Worked example

Write down which of these shapes are congruent to shape A.

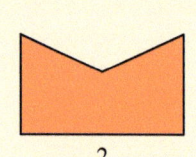

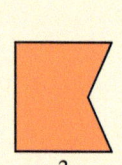

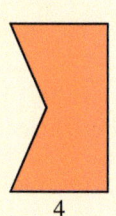

Shape 1 is the same shape as A, but a different size.

Shape 2 is the same shape and size as A. It has been rotated through 90° anticlockwise.

Shape 3 is the same width as A, but not as tall.

Shape 4 is the same shape and size as A. It has been rotated through 180°.

Therefore, the shapes numbered 2 and 4 are congruent to shape A.

# 3 Shapes and geometric reasoning 1

## Exercise 3.3

**1** In each part, write down the numbers of the shapes that are congruent to shape A.

a

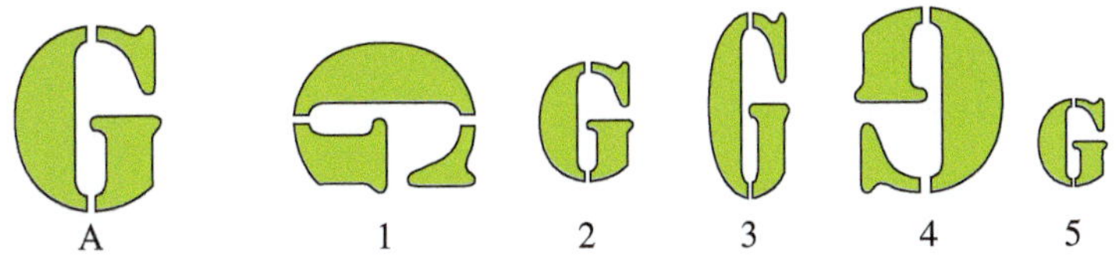

b

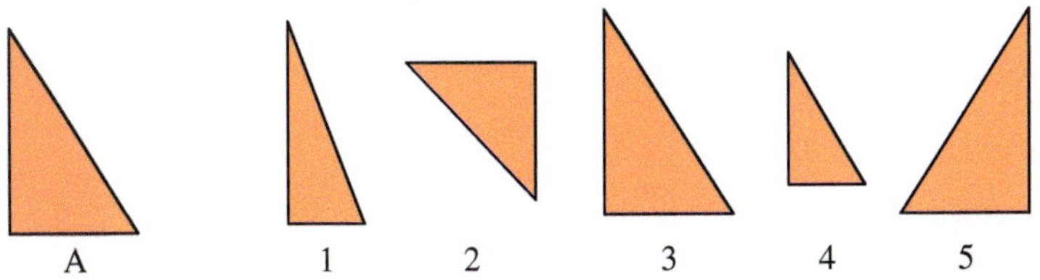

c

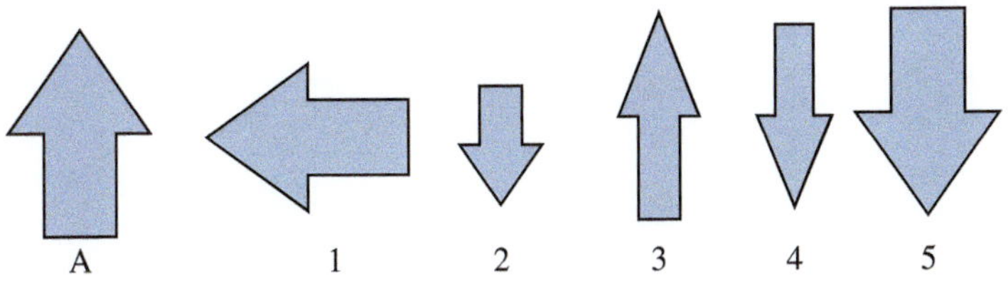

**2** The diagram shows two congruent shapes.

One of them has sides labelled *a*, *b*, *c*, *d*, *e* and *f*.

The other has sides labelled *m*, *n*, *o*, *p*, *q* and *r*.

Write down the pairs of sides that correspond.

For example, *a* corresponds to *n*.

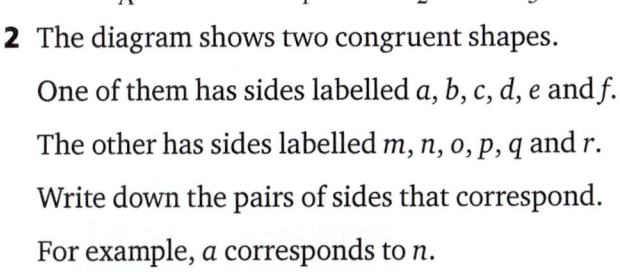

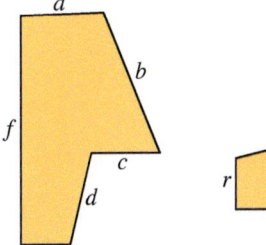

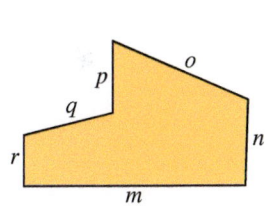

**3** Quadrilaterals *ABCD* and *STUV* are congruent.

Write **True** or **False** for each of these statements.

  **a** Angle *CDA* = angle *UVS*

  **b** *BC* = *TU*

  **c** Angle *ABC* = angle *TSV*

  **d** The shapes have the same area.

  **e** *AC* = *SU*

  **f** *AD* = *ST*

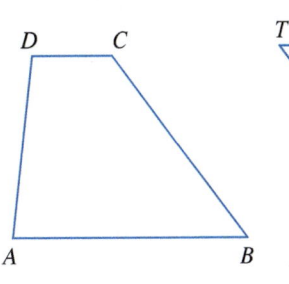

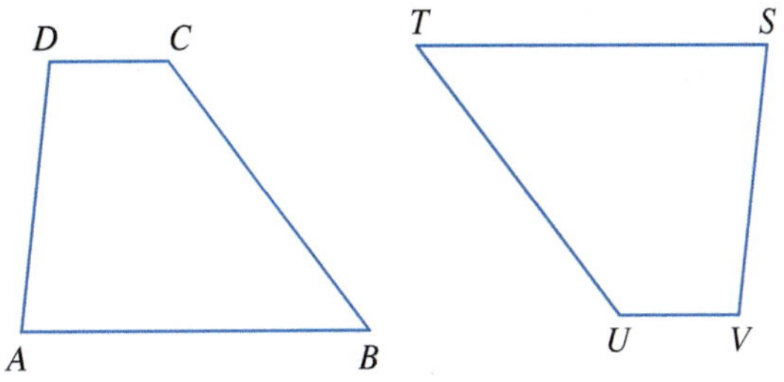

**4** *ABC* and *PQR* are congruent triangles.

Angle *ABC* = 67°

*AC* = 5 cm and *QR* = 3 cm

Find

  **a** Angle *PQR*

  **b** Length *BC*

  **c** Length *PR*

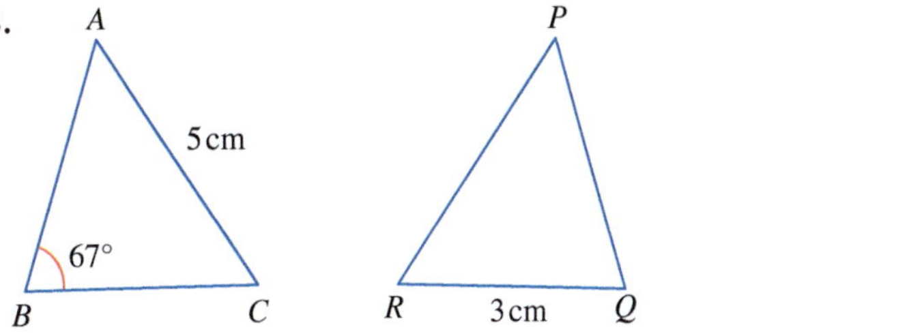

Not drawn accurately

41

# 3.4 Quadrilaterals

## Sum of the angles

A **quadrilateral** is a polygon with four straight sides.

A line that joins the opposite corners of a polygon is called a **diagonal**.

Here is a quadrilateral with one diagonal shown as a dotted line.

The diagonal splits the quadrilateral into two triangles.

The angles in each triangle add up to 180°.

The angles in the two triangles add up to 180 × 2 = 360°

This proves that the **angles in a quadrilateral add up to 360°**.

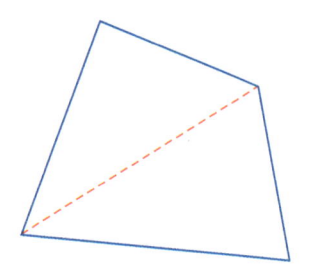

### Worked example

**a** Find the size of angle $y$.

**b** Find the size of angle $z$.

Give reasons for your answers.

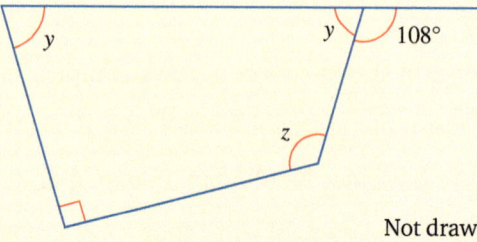

Not drawn accurately

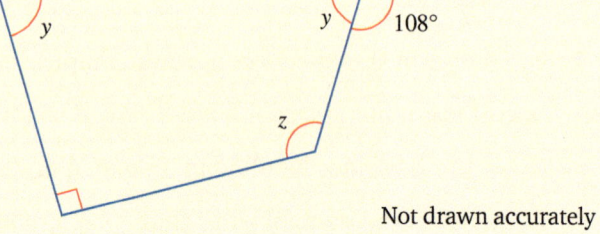

**a** $y + 108° = 180°$      Angles on a straight line add up to 180°.

   $y = 180° − 108° = 72°$

   Angle $y = 72°$

**b** $y + y + 90° + z = 360°$      Angles in a quadrilateral add up to 360°.

   $72° + 72° + 90° + z = 360°$      Angle $y = 72°$ from part **a**.

   $234° + z = 360°$

   $z = 360° − 234° = 126°$

   Angle $z = 126°$

## Exercise 3.4

The diagrams in this exercise are not drawn accurately.

For questions **1** to **5**, find the size of the angles marked with letters.

**1**  $a$, 100°, 110°, 55°

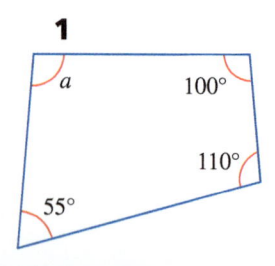

**2**  $b$, 145°, 100°

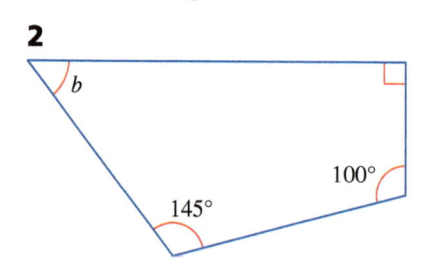

**3**  137°, $c$

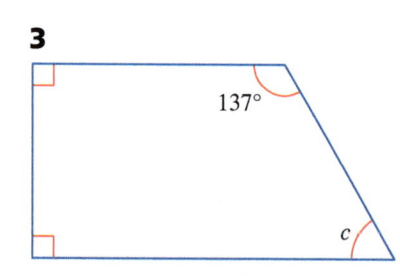

**4**

[parallelogram with angles 50°, 128°, and variables f, d, e]

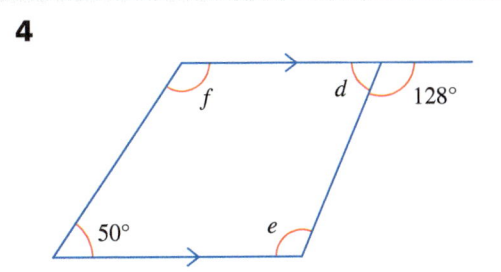

**5**

[quadrilateral with angles 84°, 42°, g, g]

**6** Find the value of x.

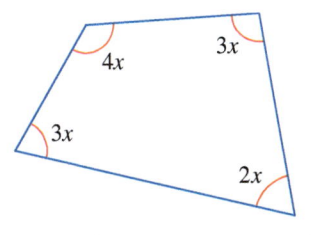

[quadrilateral with angles 4x, 3x, 3x, 2x]

> Use the sum of the angles to make an equation in x that you can solve.

## 3.5 Classification of quadrilaterals

In your Stage 7 Student Book, you saw a table showing the properties of some shapes, including different types of quadrilateral. Here is part of that table.

| Name | Shape | Sides | Angles | Line symmetry | Order of rotation symmetry |
|---|---|---|---|---|---|
| Square | | Four equal sides | All angles 90° | Four lines of symmetry | Rotation symmetry order 4 |
| Rectangle | | Two pairs of equal sides | All angles 90° | Two lines of symmetry | Rotation symmetry order 2 |
| Parallelogram | | Two pairs of equal sides | Opposite angles equal | No lines of symmetry | Rotation symmetry order 2 |

### Worked example

Four children are describing a quadrilateral.

Rahul says, 'The diagonals are the same length.'

Indira says, 'It has two pairs of parallel sides.'

Samed says, 'It has rotation symmetry of order 2.'

Devani says, 'It has two lines of symmetry.'

What type of quadrilateral is it?

If the diagonals are the same length it must be a square, rectangle or isosceles trapezium.

If it has two pairs of parallel sides it must be a square, rectangle, parallelogram or rhombus.

If it has rotation symmetry of order 2 it must be a rectangle, parallelogram or rhombus.

43

If it has two lines of symmetry it must be a rectangle or a rhombus.

The only shape in all four lists is a rectangle.

The shape is a rectangle.

## Exercise 3.5

Use this flowchart for questions **1**, **2** and **3**.

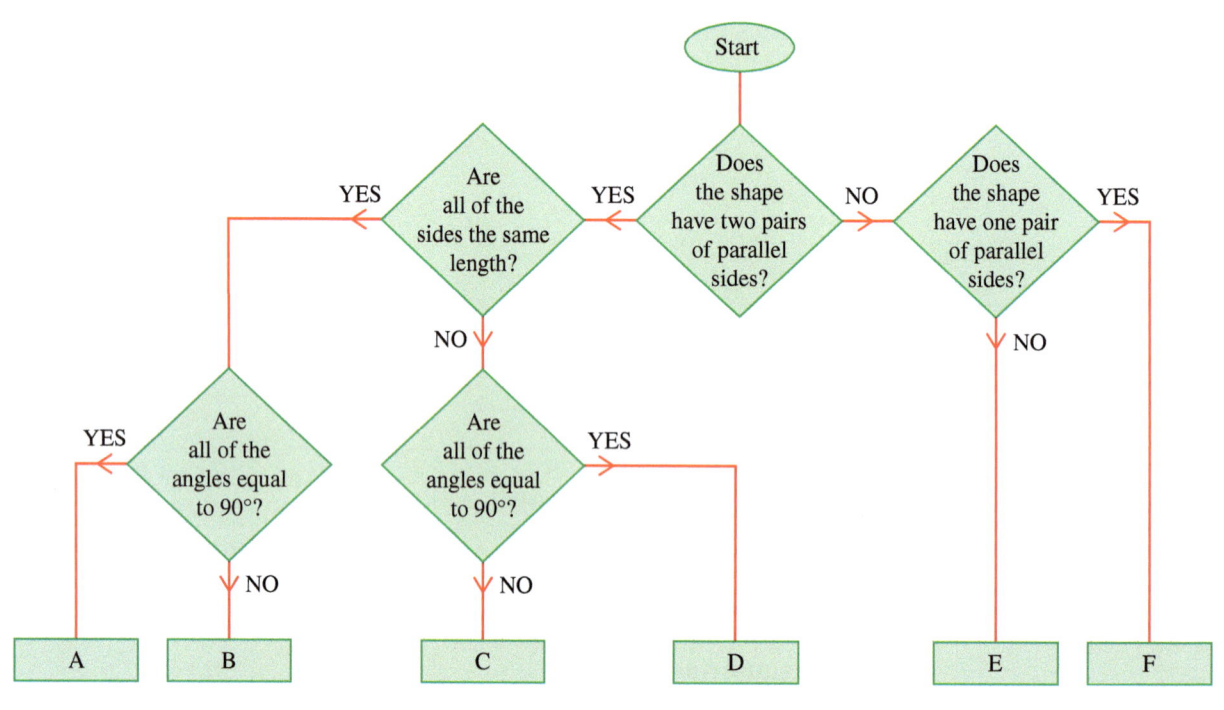

1. Work through the flowchart with these six quadrilaterals:

    Kite, parallelogram, rectangle, rhombus, square, trapezium

    Which type of quadrilateral should be in each box?

    For example, a kite, which has no parallel sides, is put into box E.

2. The quadrilateral shown here is a scalene quadrilateral.

    It has no parallel sides and no equal sides.

    a  Which box on the flowchart should this shape be put into?

    b  Copy the flowchart but add an extra question so that there is an extra box for scalene quadrilaterals.

3. What extra question would be needed for the flowchart to separate a trapezium from an isosceles trapezium?

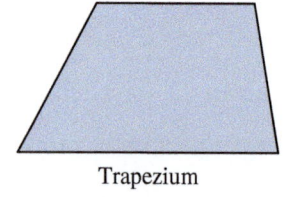

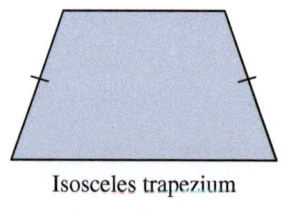

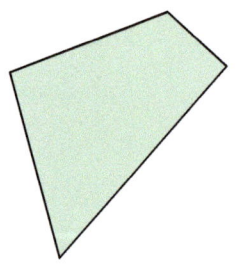

Trapezium

Isosceles trapezium

**3** Shapes and geometric reasoning 1

**4** Here is another sorting flowchart for quadrilaterals.

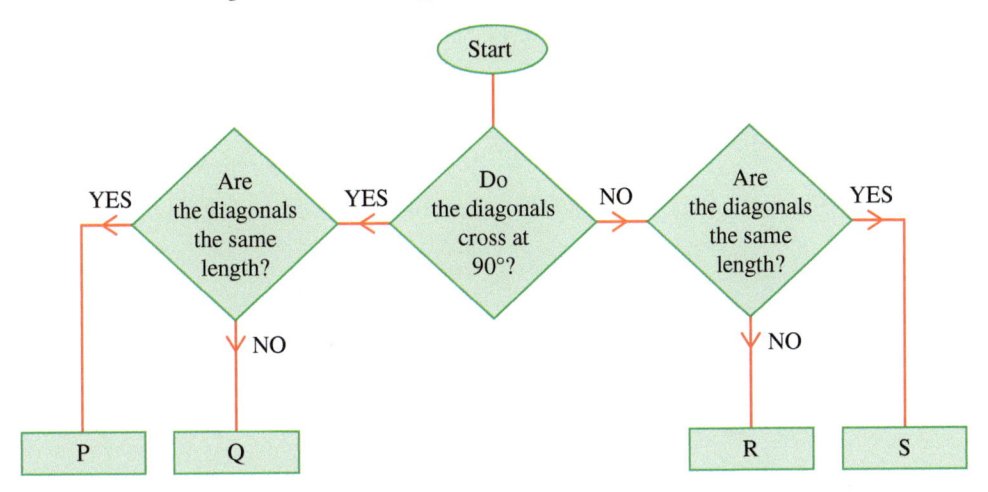

**a** Into which box does the flowchart sort a square?

**b** Into which box does the flowchart sort a rectangle?

**c** Which two shapes get sorted into box Q by the flowchart?

**d** What extra question could you ask to separate these two shapes?

**e** Which two shapes get sorted into box R by the flowchart?

**f** What extra question could you ask to separate these two shapes?

**5** Four children describe a shape.

James says, 'It is a quadrilateral.'

Logan says, 'It has one line of symmetry.'

Christina says, 'It has one pair of equal sides.'

Luisa says, 'It has rotation symmetry of order 1.'

What type of quadrilateral is it?

> Check which of the quadrilaterals in questions **1**, **2** and **3** fit these descriptions.

## 3.6 Nets of solids

The **net** of a solid is a flat, or two-dimensional, shape that can be used to make a model of the solid by folding it up.

For example, this net would fold to make a cube.

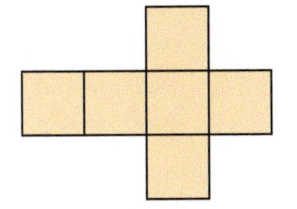

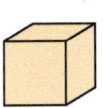

This is not the only possible net for a cube. Here are two more.

45

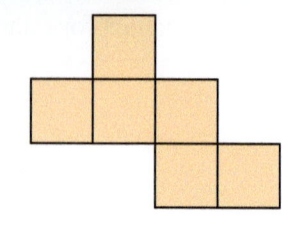

But not all arrangements of six squares form a net of a cube. Here is one that would not work.

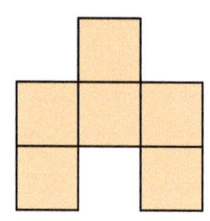

Here is a net for an equilateral triangular **prism**. It would fold up to make the prism shown on the right.

### Worked example

Draw a possible net for this square-based pyramid.

Mark all the lengths on the net.

The easiest net for a pyramid is to imagine unfolding each of the sloping sides outwards.

This is the net formed in that way.

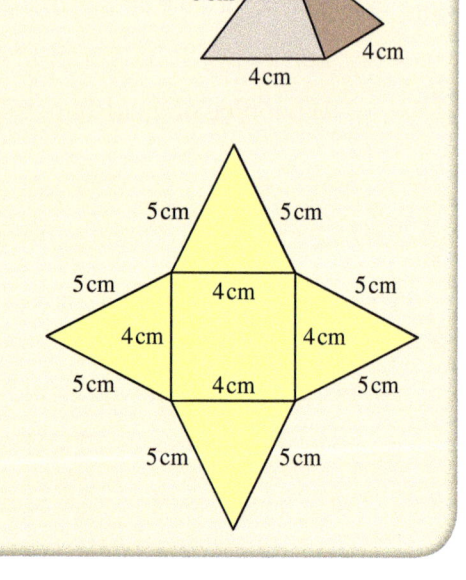

## Exercise 3.6

For questions **1** to **4**, draw a net for the solid shown.

**1** A cuboid

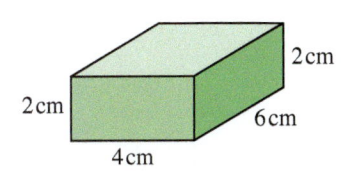

**2** A right-angled triangular prism

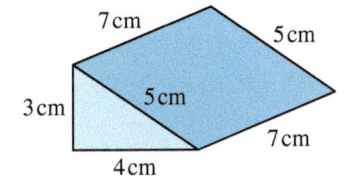

**3** A regular tetrahedron or equilateral triangular pyramid.

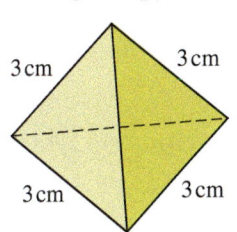

**4** An L-shaped prism

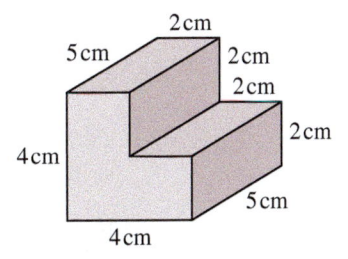

**5** When this net is folded to make a cube, the edges at B and C meet.

Pair up the edges that go together.

> It may help to cut the nets out of paper or card and fold them up to make the shapes.

**6** Pair up the edges that meet when this net is folded to make a triangular prism.

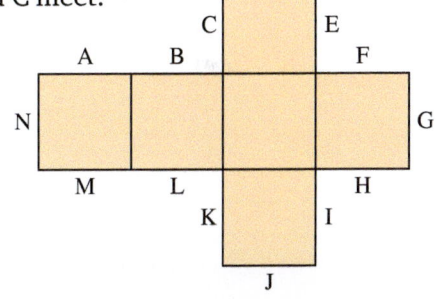

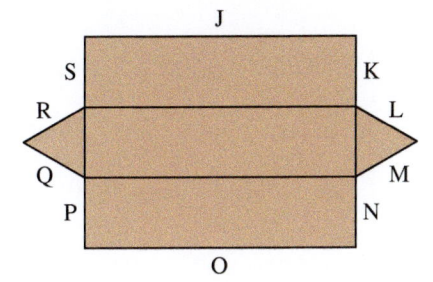

**7 a** Arrange six squares together in as many different ways as you can find.

**b** How many of your arrangements are nets for a cube?

> Use squared paper to draw the arrangements. It may help to cut the nets out and fold them up to see if they make a cube.

47

## 3.7 Symmetry

There are two types of symmetry that you met in your Stage 7 Student Book.

**Reflection symmetry** is when a shape is reflected in a line. If you place a mirror along the line the reflection looks the same as the original shape.

The example here shows a shape with one line of symmetry.

The line of symmetry, or **mirror line**, is shown as a blue dotted line.

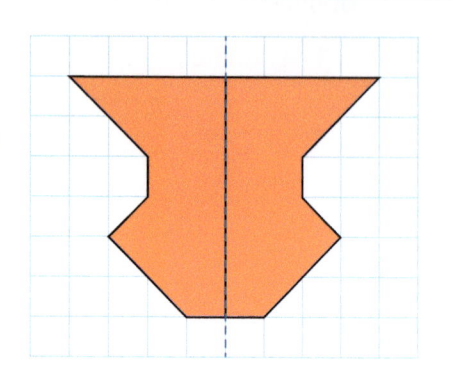

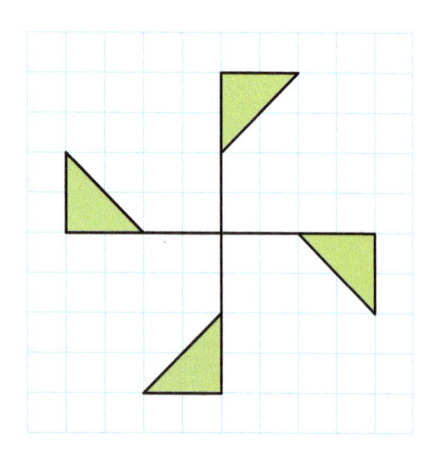

**Rotation symmetry** is when a shape looks the same if it is rotated through an angle.

The example here shows a shape with rotation symmetry of order 4.

If the shape is rotated 90°, 180°, 270° or 360° clockwise it would look the same.

This shape has no lines of symmetry.

The red shape above has rotation symmetry of order 1.

> Every shape looks the same when turned through 360° so every shape has rotation symmetry of order 1.

### Worked example

Identify all of the symmetries of these shapes.

**a** A regular pentagon

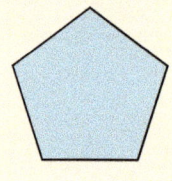

**b** A parallelogram

**a** There is an obvious line of symmetry down the middle of the shape.

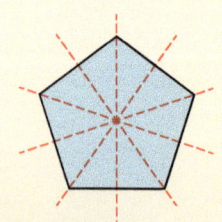

Always look for other lines at an angle.

There are in fact five lines of symmetry, shown as red lines here.

The shape has rotation symmetry of order 5.

**3** Shapes and geometric reasoning 1

This diagram shows how the shape can be rotated through 72° five times and will look the same each time.

The dot shows the centre of rotation.

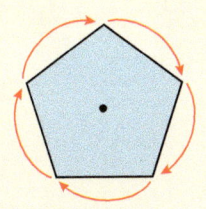

The regular pentagon has five lines of symmetry and rotation symmetry of order 5 around the centre.

**b** The parallelogram has rotation symmetry of order 2.

The dot in the middle of the shape shows the centre of rotation.

It has no lines of symmetry.

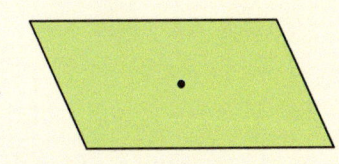

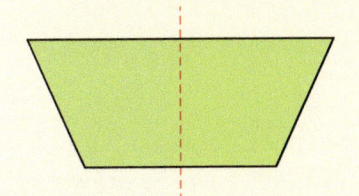

The diagram below shows what would happen if you put a mirror down the middle.

If you try a mirror in any other place a similar thing happens.

## Exercise 3.7

For each of the shapes in questions **1** to **12**, write down:

  **a**  the number of lines of symmetry
  **b**  the order of rotation symmetry.

**1**

**2**

**3** N

**4**

**5**

**6** F

49

Mathematics for Cambridge Secondary **1**

**7**      **8**       **9**

**10**       **11**      **12**

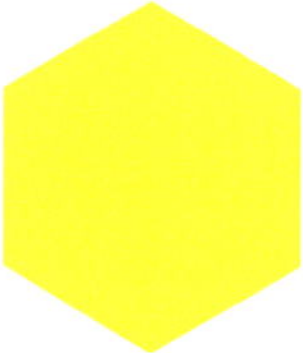

**13** Make four copies of this 4 by 4 grid.

Shade squares to make shapes that have the following symmetry.

  **a** One line of symmetry and rotation symmetry of order 1.
  **b** No lines of symmetry and rotation symmetry of order 4.
  **c** Four lines of symmetry and rotation symmetry of order 4.
  **d** Two lines of symmetry and rotation symmetry of order 2.
  **e** No lines of symmetry and rotation symmetry of order 2.

> Do not forget that lines of symmetry can be drawn diagonally across the square.

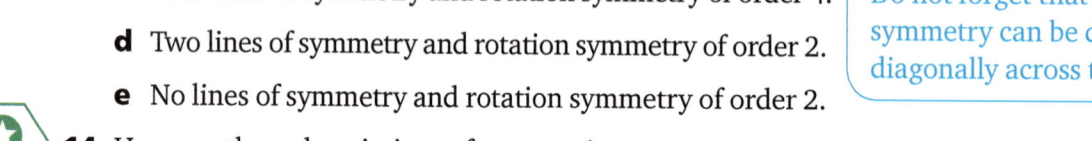

**14** Here are three descriptions of symmetries.

Two of these are not possible.

Draw the one that can be done.

  **a** Three lines of symmetry and rotation symmetry of order 1.
  **b** No lines of symmetry and rotation symmetry of order 3.
  **c** Two lines of symmetry and rotation symmetry of order 4.

> It may help to look back at the answers to questions **1** to **12** before answering this question.

## Review

For questions **1** to **5**, find the angles marked with letters.

**1** 37°, $a$, $b$

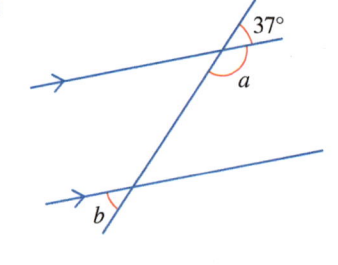

Not drawn accurately

**2** 120°, $d$, $c$

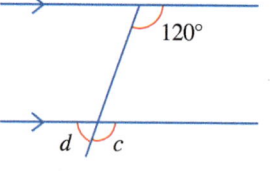

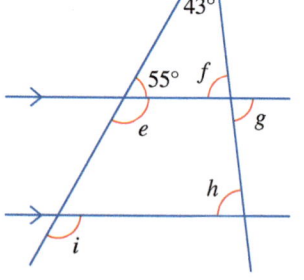

Not drawn accurately

**3** 43°, 55°, $f$, $e$, $g$, $h$, $i$

Not drawn accurately

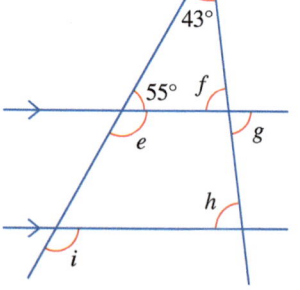

**3** Shapes and geometric reasoning 1

**4**

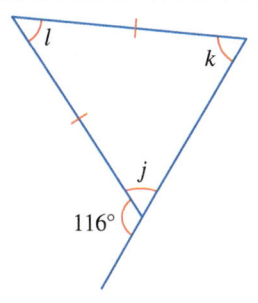

116°, j, k, l

Not drawn accurately

**5**

m, n, 75°

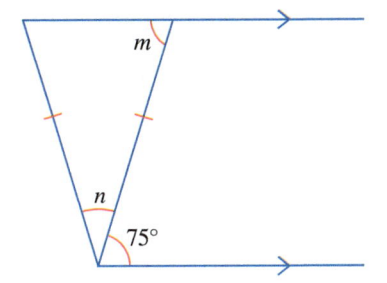

Not drawn accurately

**6 a** Which triangle is congruent to triangle A?

**b** Which triangle is congruent to triangle B?

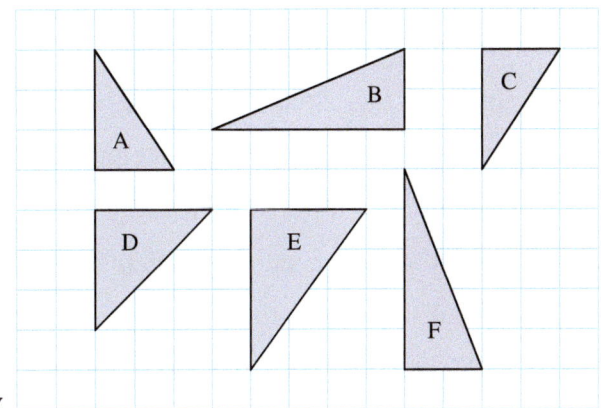

Not drawn accurately

**7** Triangles *ABC* and *PQR* are congruent.

Find the angles marked with letters.

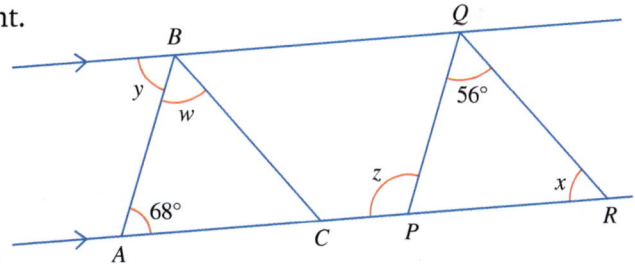

Not drawn accurately

(angles: y, w, 68°, z, 56°, x)

**8** Find angles *p* and *q*.

Give reasons for your answers.

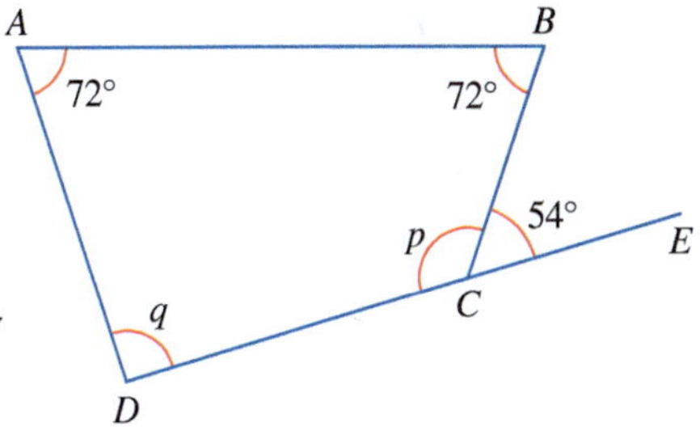

Not drawn accurately

(72° at A, 72° at B, 54° at C, p, q at D)

**9** *ABC* is a triangle. Side *AB* is extended to *E*.

*XY* is a line through *C*, parallel to *AB*.

*CBF* is a straight line.

Angle *EBF* = 63° and angle *XCA* = 71°.

Find these angles. Give reasons for your answers.

**a** *ACB*

**b** *CAB*

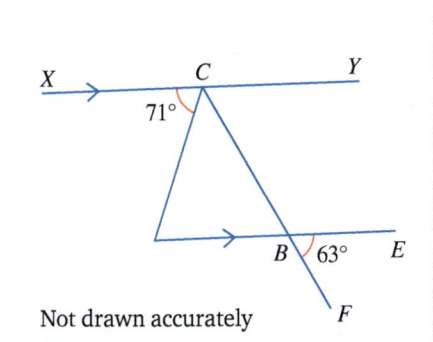

Not drawn accurately

51

**10** In this diagram EC = ED and AF is parallel to BC.

BEC and DEF are straight lines.

Angle BED = 72° and angle FAB = 84°.

Find these angles. Give reasons for your answers.

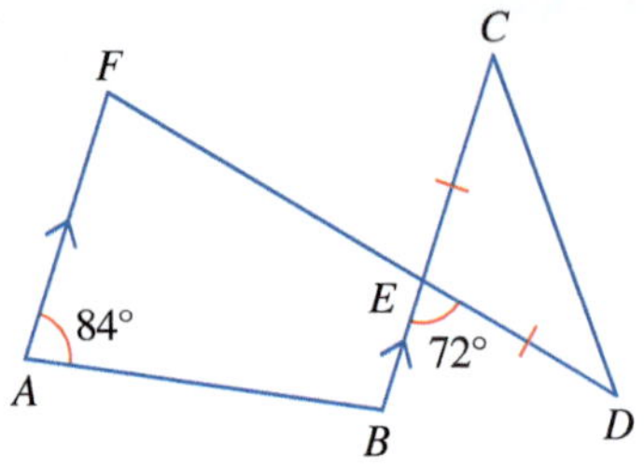

  **a** CED        **b** CDE

  **c** AFE        **d** ABE

**11** Four children describe a shape.

Wasim says, 'It is a quadrilateral.'

Shakeera says, 'It has one pair of parallel sides.'

Hamid says, 'It has one pair of equal sides.'

Sunitra says, 'It has one line of symmetry.'

Write down the name of the shape they are describing.

**12** Here is the net of a solid.

  **a** Write down the name of the solid the net would make.

  **b** How many faces are there on the solid?

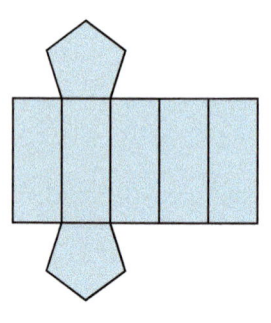

**13** Draw a net for each of these solids.

  **a**

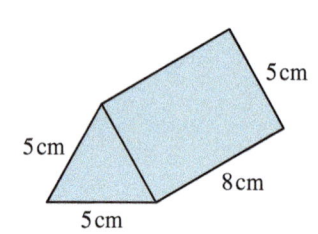

  **b**

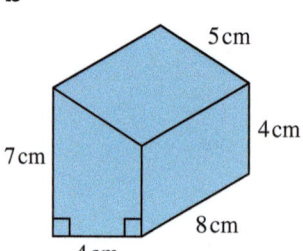

**14** Identify all the symmetries for these shapes.

  **a**    **b** 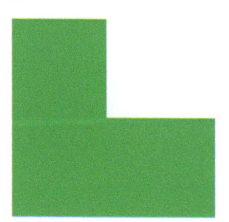    **c**

# 4 Fractions

### Learning outcomes

- Add and subtract fractions and mixed numbers.
- Calculate fractions of quantities.
- Multiply and divide an integer by a fraction.
- Order fractions by writing with common denominators.

## Unit fractions

Fractions have been used for a very long time.

The Ancient Egyptians wrote all fractions with 1 as the numerator. These are called unit fractions. They did not use fractions such as $\frac{5}{8}$

They used combinations of fractions such as $\frac{1}{2} + \frac{1}{4}$

Use the fraction button on your calculator to work out how Ancient Egyptians would write $\frac{11}{12}$, $\frac{7}{10}$ and $\frac{7}{12}$

After the work in this chapter you should not need a calculator to do this.

## 4.1 Comparing fractions

### Equivalent fractions

The fractions $\frac{1}{4}$, $\frac{2}{8}$, $\frac{3}{12}$, $\frac{4}{16}$ are equivalent to each other. They are called **equivalent fractions**.

You can multiply the **numerator** and **denominator** by the same number to obtain an equivalent fraction.

$$\frac{1}{4} \underset{\times 3}{\overset{\times 3}{=}} \frac{3}{12}$$

You can divide the numerator and denominator by the same number.

$$\frac{4}{16} \underset{\div 4}{\overset{\div 4}{=}} \frac{1}{4}$$

This is called simplifying.

When a fraction cannot be simplified further it is said to be in its **simplest form** or **lowest terms**.

## Comparing and ordering fractions

It is easy to see that $\frac{6}{8}$ is greater than $\frac{5}{8}$

They have the same denominator so you can just compare the numerators to see which is the larger fraction.

It is not so easy to see whether $\frac{6}{8}$ is greater or less than $\frac{2}{3}$

You need to change them to fractions that have the same denominator.

$$\frac{6}{8} = \frac{18}{24}$$

$$\frac{2}{3} = \frac{16}{24}$$

$\frac{6}{8}$ is greater than $\frac{2}{3}$, or $\frac{6}{8} > \frac{2}{3}$

Remember that > means 'is greater than' and < means 'is less than'.

### Worked example 1

Simplify $\frac{28}{32}$

Give your answer in its lowest terms.

$$\frac{28}{32} \xrightarrow{\div 2} \frac{14}{16} \xrightarrow{\div 2} \frac{7}{8}$$

This could be done in one step by dividing the numerator and denominator by 4.

$$\frac{28}{32} = \frac{7}{8}$$

This cannot be simplified further. It is in its lowest terms.

### Worked example 2

Write these fractions in order of size, smallest first.

$$\frac{5}{12}, \frac{3}{8}, \frac{1}{3}$$

Change these to fractions that have the same denominator.

This is the lowest common multiple of 3, 8 and 12.

This is 24.

$$\frac{5}{12} \xrightarrow{\times 2} \frac{10}{24} \qquad \frac{3}{8} \xrightarrow{\times 3} \frac{9}{24} \qquad \frac{1}{3} \xrightarrow{\times 8} \frac{8}{24}$$

It is now easy to write the fractions in order of size.

$$\frac{8}{24}, \frac{9}{24}, \frac{10}{24}$$

The answer to the question is $\frac{1}{3}, \frac{3}{8}, \frac{5}{12}$

## Exercise 4.1

**1** Copy and complete the following equivalent fractions.

  **a** $\frac{7}{8} = \frac{\square}{24}$  **b** $\frac{5}{6} = \frac{15}{\square}$  **c** $\frac{7}{10} = \frac{28}{\square}$  **d** $\frac{15}{18} = \frac{\square}{6}$  **e** $\frac{18}{24} = \frac{\square}{8}$  **f** $\frac{9}{24} = \frac{\square}{8}$

**2** There are three sets of equivalent fractions here.

They have been mixed up.

Sort them into the three sets.

$\frac{8}{24}, \frac{10}{25}, \frac{4}{12}, \frac{8}{20}, \frac{3}{12}, \frac{5}{20}, \frac{6}{24}, \frac{6}{15}, \frac{5}{15}$

**3** Write each of these fractions in their lowest terms.

  **a** $\frac{14}{20}$  **b** $\frac{16}{24}$  **c** $\frac{15}{45}$  **d** $\frac{24}{60}$  **e** $\frac{24}{84}$  **f** $\frac{18}{48}$

**4** Which fraction in each pair is greater?

  **a** $\frac{5}{7}, \frac{3}{5}$  **b** $\frac{4}{7}, \frac{2}{3}$  **c** $\frac{3}{10}, \frac{2}{7}$  **d** $\frac{2}{3}, \frac{5}{8}$  **e** $\frac{3}{5}, \frac{7}{11}$  **f** $\frac{3}{8}, \frac{2}{5}$

**5** Complete each statement with the correct sign <, = or >.

  **a** $\frac{3}{4} \square \frac{11}{12}$  **b** $\frac{5}{7} \square \frac{2}{3}$  **c** $\frac{11}{16} \square \frac{3}{4}$  **d** $\frac{9}{15} \square \frac{3}{5}$  **e** $\frac{7}{9} \square \frac{4}{5}$  **f** $\frac{2}{3} \square \frac{11}{16}$

**6** Adil, Elena and Billy share two identical bags of sweets between them.

Adil keeps $\frac{4}{5}$ of the sweets in the first bag and gives the rest to Elena.

Billy keeps $\frac{2}{3}$ of the sweets in the second bag and gives the rest to Elena.

  **a** Who has the greatest number of sweets?

  **b** Who has the least number of sweets?

Show how you work out your answers.

> The easiest way to start this is to choose a number for the sweets in each bag. Make sure the number is a multiple of both 5 and 3.

**7 a** I am equivalent to $\frac{1}{2}$

The sum of my numerator and denominator is 21.

What fraction am I?

> Find some fractions that are equivalent to ½. To find the sum of the numerator and denominator you need to add them together.

  **b** I am equivalent to $\frac{3}{5}$

The product of my numerator and denominator is 240.

What fraction am I?

> To find the product of two numbers you multiply them together.

  **c** I am equivalent to $\frac{3}{4}$

The difference between my numerator and denominator is 7.

What fraction am I?

> To find the difference between two numbers you subtract one from the other.

## 4.2 Addition and subtraction of fractions and mixed numbers

### Addition

Fractions need to have the same denominator in order to be added together.

The method is:

1. Find the lowest common multiple of the denominators.
2. Write each fraction with this denominator.
3. Add the two fractions.
4. Simplify the answer if possible.

When adding mixed numbers it is best to add the integer and fraction parts separately.

### Worked example 1

Work out $\frac{1}{3} + \frac{1}{4}$

The lowest common multiple of 3 and 4 is 12.

$$\frac{1}{3} \xrightarrow[\times 4]{\times 4} \frac{4}{12} \qquad \frac{1}{4} \xrightarrow[\times 3]{\times 3} \frac{3}{12}$$

$$\frac{1}{3} + \frac{1}{4} = \frac{4}{12} + \frac{3}{12} = \frac{4+3}{12} = \frac{7}{12}$$

### Worked example 2

Work out $\frac{5}{6} + \frac{7}{8}$

The lowest common multiple of 6 and 8 is 24.

$$\frac{5}{6} \xrightarrow[\times 4]{\times 4} \frac{20}{24} \qquad \frac{7}{8} \xrightarrow[\times 3]{\times 3} \frac{21}{24}$$

$$\frac{5}{6} + \frac{7}{8} = \frac{20}{24} + \frac{21}{24} = \frac{20+21}{24} = \frac{41}{24} = 1\frac{17}{24}$$

### Worked example 3

Work out $1\frac{1}{4} + 2\frac{1}{3}$

$$1\frac{1}{4} + 2\frac{1}{3} = 1 + 2 + \frac{1}{4} + \frac{1}{3}$$
$$= 3 + \frac{3}{12} + \frac{4}{12}$$
$$= 3 + \frac{7}{12}$$
$$= 3\frac{7}{12}$$

# 4 Fractions

## Subtraction

This is done in almost exactly the same way as for addition.

The method is:

1. Find the lowest common multiple of the denominators.
2. Write each fraction with this denominator.
3. Subtract the two fractions.
4. Simplify the answer if possible.

When subtracting mixed numbers it is best to write them as improper fractions first.

> Remember that a fraction is an improper fraction if the numerator is larger than the denominator.

### Worked example 4

Work out $\frac{3}{4} - \frac{2}{5}$

The lowest common multiple of 4 and 5 is 20.

$$\frac{3}{4} \xrightarrow{\times 5} \frac{15}{20} \qquad \frac{2}{5} \xrightarrow{\times 4} \frac{8}{20}$$

$$\frac{3}{4} - \frac{2}{5} = \frac{15}{20} - \frac{8}{20} = \frac{15 - 8}{20} = \frac{7}{20}$$

### Worked example 5

Work out $1\frac{1}{2} - \frac{4}{5}$

Write mixed numbers as improper fractions:

$$1\frac{1}{2} - \frac{4}{5} = \frac{3}{2} - \frac{4}{5}$$

The lowest common multiple of 2 and 5 is 10.

$$\frac{3}{2} \xrightarrow{\times 5} \frac{15}{10} \qquad \frac{4}{5} \xrightarrow{\times 2} \frac{8}{10}$$

$$\frac{3}{2} - \frac{4}{5} = \frac{15}{10} - \frac{8}{10} = \frac{15 - 8}{10} = \frac{7}{10}$$

### Worked example 6

Work out $3\frac{1}{4} - 1\frac{2}{5}$

Write mixed numbers as improper fractions:

$$3\frac{1}{4} - 1\frac{2}{5} = \frac{13}{4} - \frac{7}{5}$$

The lowest common multiple of 4 and 5 is 20.

$$\frac{13}{4} \xrightarrow{\times 5} \frac{65}{20} \qquad \frac{7}{5} \xrightarrow{\times 4} \frac{28}{20}$$

# Mathematics for Cambridge Secondary 1

$$\frac{13}{4} - \frac{7}{5} = \frac{65}{20} - \frac{28}{20} = \frac{65 - 28}{20} = \frac{37}{20} = 1\frac{17}{20}$$

## Worked example 7

When $\frac{2}{5}$ is added to a fraction the answer is $\frac{11}{15}$. What is the fraction?

The fraction is $\frac{11}{15} - \frac{2}{5}$     *The inverse of addition is subtraction.*

$= \frac{11}{15} - \frac{6}{15}$

$= \frac{5}{15} = \frac{1}{3}$

## Worked example 8

When $\frac{2}{7}$ is subtracted from a fraction the answer is $\frac{8}{21}$. What is the fraction?

The fraction is $\frac{8}{21} + \frac{2}{7}$     *The inverse of subtraction is addition.*

$= \frac{8}{21} + \frac{6}{21}$

$= \frac{14}{21} = \frac{2}{3}$

## Exercise 4.2

**1** Work these out.

Simplify your answer where possible.

- **a** $\frac{5}{8} + \frac{1}{8}$
- **b** $\frac{2}{7} + \frac{3}{7}$
- **c** $\frac{5}{6} + \frac{1}{6}$
- **d** $\frac{7}{10} - \frac{3}{10}$
- **e** $\frac{7}{9} - \frac{1}{9}$
- **f** $\frac{4}{7} - \frac{1}{7}$

**2** Work these out.

Simplify your answer where possible.

- **a** $\frac{1}{2} + \frac{1}{4}$
- **b** $\frac{1}{6} + \frac{5}{12}$
- **c** $\frac{5}{16} + \frac{3}{8}$
- **d** $\frac{7}{8} - \frac{1}{4}$
- **e** $\frac{2}{3} - \frac{1}{6}$
- **f** $\frac{3}{5} - \frac{3}{10}$

**3** Work these out.

Simplify your answer where possible.

- **a** $\frac{2}{3} + \frac{1}{4}$
- **b** $\frac{2}{5} + \frac{1}{3}$
- **c** $\frac{1}{4} + \frac{2}{5}$
- **d** $\frac{1}{3} - \frac{2}{7}$
- **e** $\frac{3}{8} - \frac{1}{5}$
- **f** $\frac{1}{6} - \frac{1}{8}$

**4** Work these out.

Simplify your answer where possible.

- **a** $\frac{4}{5} - \frac{1}{3}$
- **b** $\frac{3}{5} - \frac{1}{4}$
- **c** $\frac{7}{8} - \frac{2}{3}$
- **d** $\frac{5}{6} - \frac{1}{5}$
- **e** $\frac{7}{10} - \frac{1}{3}$
- **f** $\frac{7}{10} - \frac{2}{15}$

**5** Work these out.

Simplify your answer where possible.

a $\frac{3}{4} + \frac{2}{3}$
b $\frac{5}{6} + \frac{3}{8}$
c $\frac{5}{7} + \frac{4}{5}$
d $\frac{11}{12} - \frac{3}{8}$
e $\frac{9}{10} - \frac{5}{6}$
f $\frac{2}{3} - \frac{3}{16}$

**6** When $\frac{1}{3}$ is added to a fraction the answer is $1\frac{1}{12}$. What is the fraction?

**7** When $\frac{3}{5}$ is subtracted from a fraction the answer is $\frac{1}{15}$. What is the fraction?

**8 a** What do the fractions on the top row of the grid add up to?

  **b** Copy the grid.

  Fill in the gaps to make a magic square.

  Every row, every column and the two diagonals must have the same total.

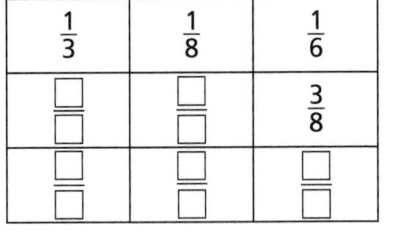

| $\frac{1}{3}$ | $\frac{1}{8}$ | $\frac{1}{6}$ |
|---|---|---|
| | | $\frac{3}{8}$ |
| | | |

**9** Work these out.

Simplify your answer where possible.

a $\frac{1}{3} + \frac{1}{4} + \frac{1}{5}$
b $\frac{1}{3} + \frac{1}{5} - \frac{1}{6}$

**10** Work out

a $1\frac{1}{4} + \frac{1}{3}$
b $\frac{1}{6} + 2\frac{1}{4}$
c $1\frac{1}{3} + 1\frac{1}{5}$
d $2\frac{2}{5} + 1\frac{1}{4}$

**11** Work out

a $2\frac{2}{3} - \frac{1}{6}$
b $1\frac{4}{5} - \frac{1}{3}$
c $3\frac{3}{8} - 1\frac{1}{4}$
d $2\frac{5}{8} - 1\frac{1}{3}$

**12** Work these out.

Give your answers in their lowest terms.

a $1\frac{1}{2} + 2\frac{1}{3}$
b $2\frac{3}{4} + 1\frac{7}{8}$
c $3\frac{2}{5} + 1\frac{3}{4}$
d $2\frac{1}{2} - \frac{3}{4}$
e $1\frac{1}{2} - \frac{2}{3}$
f $2\frac{1}{4} - 1\frac{4}{5}$

**13** This fraction sum is made from four different digits 1, 2, 4 and 8.

The fraction sum is 1.

$$\frac{1}{2} + \frac{4}{8}$$

> Start with two fractions that add up to 1, such as $\frac{1}{4}$ and $\frac{3}{4}$, and then find equivalent fractions so that all four digits are different.

Find other fraction sums. Use four different digits. Make sure the fraction sum is 1.

**14** On four days each week Penny cycles for $1\frac{1}{4}$ hours.

On the other three days she walks for $2\frac{1}{2}$ hours and runs for $\frac{3}{4}$ hour.

  **a** How many hours does Penny exercise for each week?

  **b** Penny decides to cycle for three days each week and walk and run on the other four days.

  Will the time she spends exercising increase or decrease?

  By how many hours will it change?

## 4.3 Multiplying and dividing an integer by a fraction

### Multiplying an integer by a fraction

Remember an integer is a whole number.

$3 \times \frac{4}{5}$ means the same as $\frac{4}{5} + \frac{4}{5} + \frac{4}{5}$, which is $\frac{4+4+4}{5} = \frac{3 \times 4}{5} = \frac{12}{5}$

To multiply an integer by a fraction you multiply the numerator by the integer.

This gives you the numerator of your answer.

The denominator does not change.

> **Worked example 1**
>
> Work out $7 \times \frac{1}{4}$
>
> $7 \times \frac{1}{4} = \frac{7 \times 1}{4} = \frac{7}{4} = 1\frac{3}{4}$

### Finding a fraction of a quantity

To find $\frac{1}{4}$ of 5, you can think of this as:

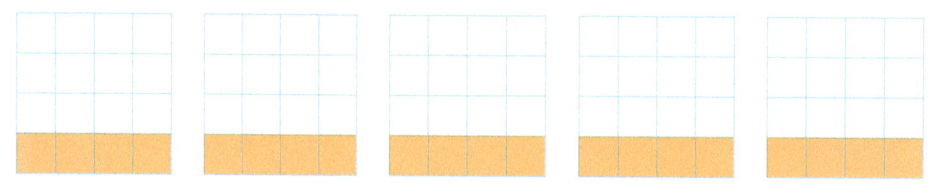

This is the same as $5 \times \frac{1}{4}$

$= \frac{5}{4}$

$= 1\frac{1}{4}$

When you see 'of' in maths it usually means '×'.

> **Worked example 2**
>
> Find $\frac{1}{3}$ of 7.
>
> $\frac{1}{3}$ of $7 = \frac{1}{3} \times 7$
>
> $= \frac{7}{3} = 2\frac{1}{3}$

# 4 Fractions

## Dividing an integer by a fraction

When you work out $12 \div 2$ you are finding how many 2s there are in 12.

The same applies to fractions.

$2 \div \frac{1}{4}$ means 'how many $\frac{1}{4}$'s are there in 2?'

Remember the denominator tells you the number of parts each whole is divided into.

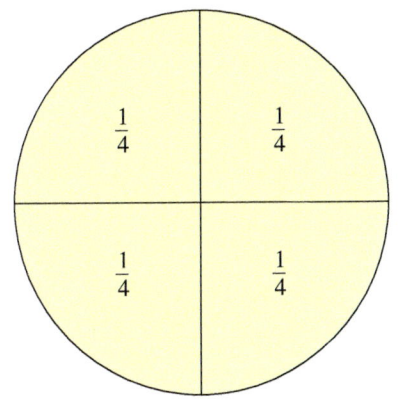

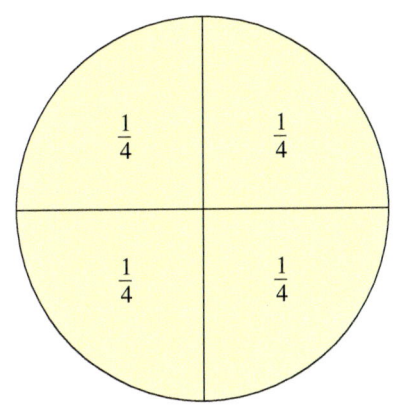

You can see from this diagram $2 \div \frac{1}{4} = 8$

There are four quarters in each 'whole'.

In two 'wholes' there are $2 \times 4 = 8$ quarters

You can work out $2 \div \frac{1}{5}$ in the same way.

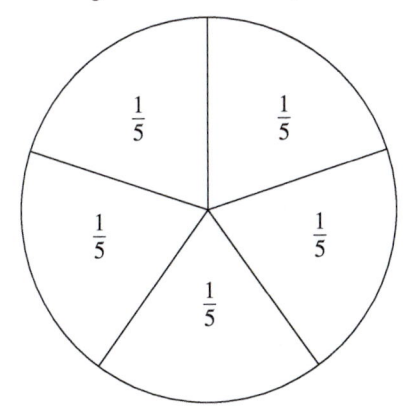

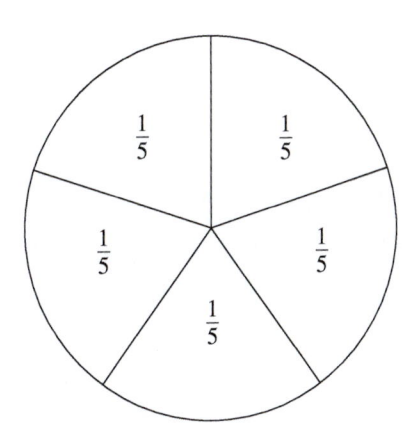

$2 \div \frac{1}{5} = 2 \times 5 = 10$

When you work out $2 \div \frac{2}{5}$ this fraction does not have 1 as the numerator.

As $\frac{2}{5}$ is twice $\frac{1}{5}$ there will be half as many.

$2 \div \frac{2}{5} = 5$ as shown in this diagram.

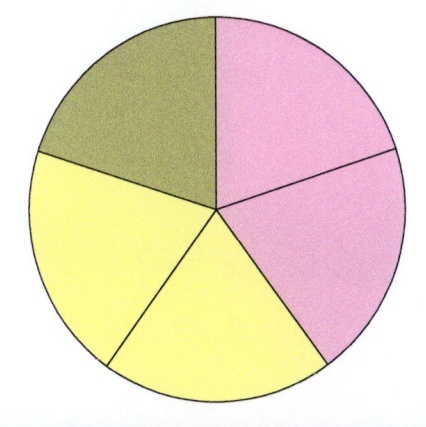

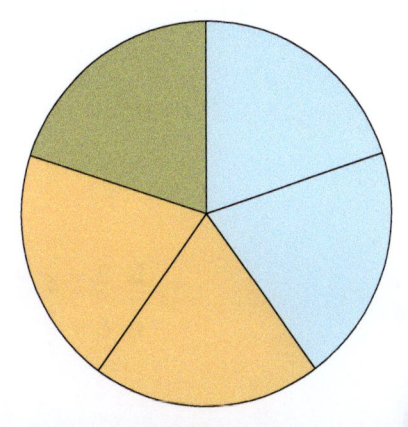

61

This is worked out as $2 \times \frac{5}{2} = \frac{10}{2} = 5$

To divide an integer by a fraction, you turn the fraction 'upside down' and multiply by it.

> **Worked example 3**
>
> Work out $4 \div \frac{2}{3}$
>
> $$4 \div \frac{2}{3} = 4 \times \frac{3}{2} = \frac{12}{2} = 6$$

## Exercise 4.3

**1** Work out

   **a** $2 \times \frac{3}{11}$     **b** $2 \times \frac{2}{5}$     **c** $4 \times \frac{2}{15}$

   **d** $7 \times \frac{2}{19}$     **e** $5 \times \frac{3}{16}$     **f** $3 \times \frac{2}{7}$

**2** Work these out.

Give your answers in their lowest terms.

Write any improper fractions as mixed numbers.

   **a** $4 \times \frac{3}{8}$     **b** $4 \times \frac{5}{7}$     **c** $5 \times \frac{2}{3}$

   **d** $15 \times \frac{5}{6}$     **e** $15 \times \frac{2}{5}$     **f** $20 \times \frac{3}{4}$

   **g** $12 \times \frac{3}{4}$     **h** $3 \times \frac{10}{27}$     **i** $40 \times \frac{3}{8}$

**3** Find

   **a** $\frac{1}{3}$ of 15     **b** $\frac{1}{4}$ of 20     **c** $\frac{2}{3}$ of 12

   **d** $\frac{3}{8}$ of 24     **e** $\frac{2}{5}$ of 15     **f** $\frac{3}{5}$ of 30

**4** Find

   **a** $\frac{2}{3}$ of 5     **b** $\frac{3}{4}$ of 7     **c** $\frac{3}{8}$ of 20

   **d** $\frac{2}{5}$ of 17     **e** $\frac{7}{8}$ of 12     **f** $\frac{5}{6}$ of 15

**5** Which of the following amounts is greater?

   **a** $\frac{3}{5}$ of 125 or $\frac{3}{8}$ of 240

   **b** $\frac{4}{5}$ of 130 or $\frac{2}{3}$ of 144

**6** Work out

   **a** $2 \div \frac{1}{3}$     **b** $3 \div \frac{1}{4}$     **c** $5 \div \frac{1}{7}$

   **d** $6 \div \frac{1}{5}$     **e** $4 \div \frac{1}{8}$     **f** $7 \div \frac{1}{6}$

**7** Work out

   **a** $2 \div \frac{2}{3}$     **b** $3 \div \frac{3}{4}$     **c** $5 \div \frac{5}{7}$

   **d** $4 \div \frac{2}{5}$     **e** $6 \div \frac{3}{5}$     **f** $14 \div \frac{7}{10}$

**8** Work these out.

Give your answers in their lowest terms.

Write any improper fractions as mixed numbers.

a $6 \div \frac{3}{4}$  b $5 \div \frac{3}{4}$  c $3 \div \frac{2}{3}$

d $5 \div \frac{3}{8}$  e $6 \div \frac{4}{5}$  f $7 \div \frac{2}{3}$

**9** Copy and complete these patterns.

a $60 \times \frac{1}{6} = 10$  b $10 \div \frac{1}{6} = 60$

$30 \times \frac{2}{6} = 10$  $10 \div \ldots$

$20 \times \frac{3}{6} = 10$  $\ldots$

$\ldots$  $\ldots$

$12 \times \frac{5}{6} = 10$  $\ldots$

## Review

**1** Write these fractions in their lowest terms.

a $\frac{8}{12}$  b $\frac{9}{15}$  c $\frac{7}{35}$

d $\frac{8}{18}$  e $\frac{18}{60}$  f $\frac{12}{30}$

**2** Which fraction in each pair is greater?

a $\frac{1}{4}, \frac{3}{20}$  b $\frac{2}{5}, \frac{3}{10}$  c $\frac{14}{25}, \frac{7}{15}$

**3** Work these out.

Simplify your answer where possible.

a $\frac{1}{4} + \frac{1}{3}$  b $\frac{3}{4} + \frac{2}{3}$  c $\frac{2}{3} - \frac{1}{8}$

d $\frac{5}{8} - \frac{1}{5}$  e $\frac{7}{8} + \frac{2}{3}$  f $\frac{5}{6} - \frac{3}{7}$

g $3\frac{4}{5} + 2\frac{5}{8}$  h $3\frac{2}{9} - \frac{5}{6}$  i $2\frac{3}{8} - 1\frac{2}{3}$

**4** Work these out.

Do not simplify your answers.

a $\frac{1}{2} + \frac{1}{4}$

b $\frac{1}{2} + \frac{1}{4} + \frac{1}{8}$

c $\frac{1}{2} + \frac{1}{4} + \frac{1}{8} + \frac{1}{16}$

d Your answers to **a**, **b**, and **c** are the start of a sequence.

What are the next two terms in the sequence?

**5** Work these out.

Simplify your answer where possible.

Write any improper fractions as mixed numbers.

a $4 \times \frac{1}{5}$  b $7 \times \frac{3}{5}$  c $\frac{3}{4} \times 36$  d $\frac{5}{7} \times 24$

**6** Work out

a $7 \div \frac{1}{5}$  b $5 \div \frac{1}{8}$  c $3 \div \frac{3}{5}$  d $4 \div \frac{5}{8}$

# 5 Decimals

## Learning outcomes

- Read and write positive integer powers of 10.
- Multiply and divide integers and decimals by 0.1 and 0.01
- Round whole numbers to a positive integer power of 10.
- Round decimals to the nearest whole number, or to 1 or 2 decimal places.
- Order decimals, including measurements, using the =, ≠, > and < signs.
- Convert a fraction to a decimal using division.
- Know that a recurring decimal is a fraction.
- Order fractions by converting to decimals.

## It's about …

Large numbers are often given approximately.

A country has 1 278 765 people out of work.

Both these people are correct.

However, one is making the number of people out of work look smaller, the other is making the number appear larger.

*There are almost 1.5 million people out of work.*

*There are just over 1 million people out of work.*

## 5.1 Integer powers of 10

### Reading and writing integer powers of 10

One hundred is $100 = 10 \times 10 = 10^2$.

$10^2$ is read as '10 squared' or '10 to the power of 2'.

One thousand is $1000 = 10 \times 10 \times 10 = 10^3$. This is read as '10 to the power of 3'.

Ten thousand is $10\,000 = 10 \times 10 \times 10 \times 10 = 10^4$.

One hundred thousand is $100\,000 = 10 \times 10 \times 10 \times 10 \times 10 = 10^5$.

One **million** (one thousand thousand) is $1\,000\,000 = 10 \times 10 \times 10 \times 10 \times 10 \times 10 = 10^6$.

64

# 5 Decimals

One **billion** (one thousand million) is
$1\,000\,000\,000 = 10 \times 10 \times 10 \times 10 \times 10 \times 10 \times 10 \times 10 \times 10 = 10^9$.

Notice the number of 0's in each number is the same as the digit in the power. For example, $1\,000\,000$ has six 0's so $1\,000\,000 = 10^6$.

> ### Worked example 1
>
> Elvio has his 14th birthday today.
>
> He says he is more than 1 million minutes old.
>
> Is he correct?
>
> There are 60 minutes in 1 hour.
>
> There are 24 hours in 1 day.
>
> There are 365 days in 1 year (ignoring leap years).
>
> 14 years = 14 × 365 days = 14 × 365 × 24 hours = 14 × 365 × 24 × 60 minutes = 7 358 400 minutes.
>
> Yes, he is correct because 7 358 400 is greater than 1 000 000.

## Multiplying by 0.1 and 0.01

0.1 is the same as $\frac{1}{10}$

Multiplying by 0.1 has the same effect as multiplying by $\frac{1}{10}$

To multiply by $\frac{1}{10}$ you divide by 10.

0.01 is the same as $\frac{1}{100}$

Multiplying by 0.01 has the same effect as multiplying by $\frac{1}{100}$

To multiply by $\frac{1}{100}$ you divide by 100.

> ### Worked example 2
>
> Work out
>
> **a** 234 × 0.1
>
> **b** 6.5 × 0.01
>
> **a** $234 \times 0.1 = 234 \times \frac{1}{10} = \frac{234}{10} = 234 \div 10 = 23.4$
>
> **b** $6.5 \times 0.01 = 6.5 \times \frac{1}{100} = \frac{6.5}{100} = 6.5 \div 100 = 0.065$

# Mathematics for Cambridge Secondary 1

## Dividing by 0.1 and 0.01

Dividing by 0.1 has the same effect as dividing by $\frac{1}{10}$

To divide by $\frac{1}{10}$ you multiply by 10.

Dividing by 0.01 has the same effect as dividing by $\frac{1}{100}$

To divide by $\frac{1}{100}$ you multiply by 100.

> **Worked example 3**
>
> Work out
>
> **a** $23 \div 0.1$
>
> **b** $4.5 \div 0.01$
>
> **a** $23 \div 0.1 = 23 \div \frac{1}{10} = 23 \times 10 = 230$
>
> **b** $4.5 \div 0.01 = 4.5 \div \frac{1}{100} = 4.5 \times 100 = 450$

## Exercise 5.1

**1** Write the following numbers in words.

  **a** 100 000    **b** 10 000 000    **c** 100 000 000 000

  **d** $10^5$    **e** $10^7$    **f** $10^{10}$

**2** Write these numbers using figures.

  **a** 1 million    **b** 4 million    **c** 30 billion

**3** Work out

  **a** $1.4 \times 10$    **b** $0.02 \times 100$    **c** $30.5 \times 100$    **d** $0.03 \times 1000$

  **e** $435 \div 100$    **f** $102 \div 10$    **g** $4035 \div 1000$    **h** $32 \div 100$

**4** Work out

  **a** $52 \times 0.1$    **b** $330 \times 0.1$    **c** $340 \times 0.01$    **d** $403 \times 0.01$

  **e** $5.3 \times 0.1$    **f** $405.1 \times 0.1$    **g** $6.2 \times 0.01$    **h** $0.56 \times 0.01$

**5** Work out

  **a** $38 \div 0.1$    **b** $30 \div 0.1$    **c** $670 \div 0.01$    **d** $134 \div 0.01$

  **e** $3.4 \div 0.1$    **f** $2.03 \div 0.1$    **g** $2.1 \div 0.01$    **h** $0.06 \div 0.01$

**6** Copy each of the following.

  Replace the ? with 0.1 or 0.01 to make the calculation correct.

  **a** $8.6 \times ? = 0.86$    **b** $5.06 \div ? = 506$    **c** $0.85 \div ? = 85$    **d** $5 \times ? = 0.05$

**5** Decimals

**7** Isaac has been given a calculation by his teacher.

He works out the answer as 0.4

What could the question have been?

Use ÷, ×, 0.1 and 0.01 to find some possible questions.

> To get the answer 0.4 using ÷, ×, 0.1, or 0.01, you must have the digit 4 somewhere in a number in your question.

**8** Copy each of the following.

Replace the ? with the number that makes the calculation correct.

**a** 0.5 × 0.1 = ?   **b** 0.8 × ? = 0.08   **c** 0.7 ÷ 0.1 = ?

**d** 0.6 ÷ ? = 6   **e** ? ÷ 0.1 = 12   **f** ? × 0.01 = 5

**g** ? × 0.1 = 0.2   **h** ? ÷ 0.01 = 0.01

> You can use inverse operations in some of these to help.
> ? ÷ 0.1 = 12
> so     ? = 12 × 0.1

## 5.2 Rounding

Sometimes you do not need to know an exact value.

You can round figures to give an approximate value.

For example, you may only need to know an approximate value for a book that has a height of 29.76324 cm.

You can round numbers to the nearest whole number, nearest 10, nearest 100, nearest 1000, and so on. Rounding to the nearest integer is the same as rounding to the nearest whole number.

You can also round numbers to a given number of **decimal places**.

Here you will round to 1 decimal place and 2 decimal places.

Rounding to 1 decimal place gives you 1 digit after the decimal point.

Rounding to 2 decimal places gives you 2 digits after the decimal point.

Instead of writing decimal places, you can write d.p. to save time.

### Worked example 1

Round 982 to:

**a** the nearest 100

**b** the nearest 10.

**a** 982 is between 900 and 1000

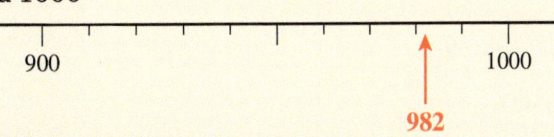

900 ———————————— 982 ——— 1000

It is closer to 1000 than 900.

982 is rounded up to 1000.

67

**b** 982 is between 980 and 990

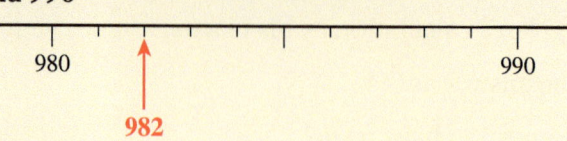

It is closer to 980 than 990.

982 is rounded down to 980.

## Worked example 2

Round 4.325 to:

**a** 1 decimal place

**b** 2 decimal places.

**a** 4.325 is between 4.3 and 4.4

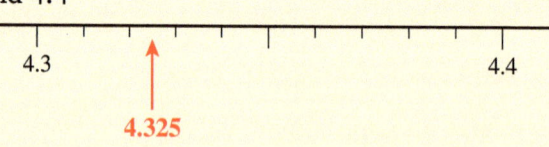

It is closer to 4.3 than 4.4

4.325 is rounded down to 4.3

**b** 4.325 is between 4.32 and 4.33

In fact, 4.325 is exactly halfway between 4.32 and 4.33 so there are two 'nearest' whole numbers. When this happens you usually round up, so 4.325 is rounded up to 4.33

## Worked example 3

Round 3.98 to 1 decimal place.

3.98 is between 3.9 and 4.0

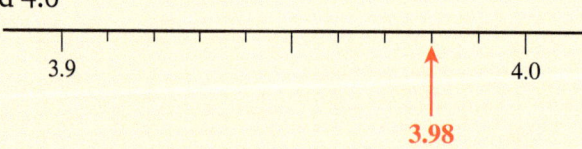

3.98 is closer to 4.0 than 3.9

3.98 rounds up to 4.0

You should always include the '.0' to show the number was rounded to 1 decimal place.

# Exercise 5.2

**1** Round each of these numbers.

   **a** 458 to the nearest 10         **b** 3564 to the nearest 100

   **c** 4805 to the nearest 10       **d** 36 455 to the nearest 1000

   **e** 52.39 to the nearest whole number

**2** Round these to 1 decimal place.

   **a** 4.67    **b** 17.09    **c** 28.428    **d** 7.028    **e** 7.892    **f** 8.45

**3** Round these to 2 decimal places.

   **a** 3.884    **b** 7.876    **c** 3.032    **d** 13.7952    **e** 24.004    **f** 27.095

**4** Andy works out the answer to a calculation.

   He writes the answer as 40.

   This is correct to the nearest 10.

   What is the smallest his answer could be before rounding?

> Think about the numbers that round to 40.

**5** Calum says 'I have $80 to the nearest $10. If I had any more money I would have $90 to the nearest $10'.

   Juanita says 'I have $50 to the nearest $10. If I had any less I would have $40 to the nearest $10'.

   How much more money does Calum have than Juanita?

> For Calum, think about all the numbers that round to $80 and $90 to the nearest $10. Do the same for Juanita with numbers that round to $40 and $50.

**6** Round each of these numbers.

   **a** 3.042 to 1 decimal place       **b** 0.3004 to 2 decimal places

   **c** 14.0991 to 2 decimal places    **d** 4.996 to 2 decimal places

**7** Matthew and Leysi count the money in their pockets.

   Matthew says 'I have $50 to the nearest dollar'.

   Leysi says 'I also have $50 to the nearest dollar. We must have the same amount of money'.

   Matthew says 'No, I have more than you'.

   **a** Explain how Leysi could be correct.    **b** Explain how Matthew could be correct.

## 5.3 Calculating with decimals

### Adding and subtracting decimals

To add and subtract decimals you must make sure that the decimal points are lined up. You can do this by using a place value table.

# Mathematics for Cambridge Secondary 1

> **Worked example 1**
>
> Work out
>
> **a** 4.9 + 2.15    **b** 4.7 − 2.46
>
> **a**
>
> | Units | . | Tenths | Hundredths |
> |---|---|---|---|
> | 4 | . | 9 | 0 |
> | + 2 | . | 1 | 5 |
> | 7 | . | 0 | 5 |
>
> It is a good idea to put 0 in the 'space' to make both numbers line up on the right.
>
> **b**
>
> | Units | . | Tenths | Hundredths |
> |---|---|---|---|
> | 4 | . | $^6\cancel{7}$ | $^10$ |
> | − 2 | . | 4 | 6 |
> | 2 | . | 2 | 4 |
>
> It is a good idea to put 0 in the 'space' to make both numbers line up on the right.
>
> You can check your answers by using inverse operations.
>
> | Units | . | Tenths | Hundredths |
> |---|---|---|---|
> | 2 | . | 4 | 6 |
> | + 2 | . | 2 | 4 |
> | 4 | . | 7 | 0 |

## Multiplying by a decimal

You can use facts you already know to help you multiply decimals.

You can use **equivalent calculations** to help you multiply decimals.

To multiply by 0.3 you multiply by 3 and then divide the result by 10.

To multiply by 0.03 you multiply by 3 and then divide the result by 100.

> **Worked example 2**
>
> Work out
>
> **a** 0.7 × 9    **b** 15 × 0.06    **c** 0.7 × 0.6
>
> **a** 0.7 × 9 = 9 × 0.7
>
> $\qquad\quad$ = 9 × 7 ÷ 10    ← This is an equivalent calculation, as it gives the same answer.
>
> $\qquad\quad$ = 63 ÷ 10
>
> $\qquad\quad$ = 6.3
>
> **b** 15 × 0.06 = 15 × 6 ÷ 100
>
> $\qquad\qquad$ = 90 ÷ 100
>
> $\qquad\qquad$ = 0.9

**c** $0.7 \times 0.6$

First remove the decimal points: $6 \times 7 = 42$

Then count up the number of digits after the decimal points in the question.

There are two digits after the decimal points in the question $0.7 \times 0.6$

You need two digits after the decimal point in the answer.

The answer is 0.42

You can use this method to work out the answer to part **a**. It will give the same answer.

## Dividing by a decimal

When you divide by a decimal you need to use an equivalent calculation.

You have divided numbers by 0.1 and 0.01 already.

You can use this to help you divide by numbers such as 0.2 or 0.03

### Worked example 3

Work out

**a** $63 \div 0.7$    **b** $2.1 \div 0.03$

**a** $63 \div 0.7 = (63 \div 0.1) \div 7$
$= (63 \times 10) \div 7$
$= 630 \div 7$
$= 90$

You can check your answers by using inverse operations.

Check $63 \div 0.7 = 90$ by working out $90 \times 0.7$

$90 \times 0.7 = 63$

> Use the method shown in example 2c above to work this out

**b** $2.1 \div 0.03 = (2.1 \div 0.01) \div 3$
$= (2.1 \times 100) \div 3$
$= 210 \div 3$
$= 70$

## Dividing a decimal by a whole number

Sometimes the answer will work out exactly.

Sometimes the answer has to be rounded. If this is the case, always work out the answer to one more decimal place than you need.

Be careful to keep the decimal points in line in your working.

> **Worked example 4**
>
> Work out
>
> **a** 3.8 ÷ 4          **b** 3.8 ÷ 7
>
> Give your answer to 2 decimal places.
>
> **a**
> ```
>     0. 9 5
> 4)3.³8 ²0
> ```
>
> Here the answer has come out exactly.
>
> **b**
> ```
>     0. 5 4 2...
> 7)3.³8 ³0 ²0
> ```
>
> Here the answer has to be rounded.
>
> You need to work out one more decimal place than you are asked. Then you can round.
>
> 0.542... rounds down to 0.54 to 2 decimal places.

## Exercise 5.3

**1** Work out
  - **a** 14.7 + 7.43
  - **b** 13.08 + 9.45
  - **c** 16.56 − 3.7
  - **d** 18.4 − 8.56

**2** Work out
  - **a** 2.346 + 3.565
  - **b** 3.47 + 0.352
  - **c** 4.582 − 3.254
  - **d** 4.276 − 1.3462

**3** Write down an equivalent calculation for each of the following.
  - **a** 12 × 0.8
  - **b** 8 × 0.06
  - **c** 15 × 0.4
  - **d** 11 × 0.7
  - **e** 21 × 0.7
  - **f** 0.02 × 35

**4** Work out the answers to question **3**.

**5** Work out
  - **a** 0.7 × 31
  - **b** 12 × 0.7
  - **c** 450 × 0.3
  - **d** 400 × 0.08
  - **e** 320 × 0.5
  - **f** 14 × 0.06

**6** Work out
  - **a** 0.3 × 0.4
  - **b** 1.2 × 0.4
  - **c** 14 × 0.3
  - **d** 16.2 × 0.2
  - **e** 4.53 × 0.3
  - **f** 3.65 × 0.5

**7** Work out
  - **a** 42 ÷ 0.7
  - **b** 23.4 ÷ 0.6
  - **c** 2.4 ÷ 0.3
  - **d** 92.4 ÷ 0.06
  - **e** 23.4 ÷ 0.09
  - **f** 16.1 ÷ 0.07

**8** **i** Write down a calculation that could be used to check each of your answers for question **7**.

   **ii** Work out the answer to each of your calculations.

9 Work out

    a  20.3 ÷ 7      b  8.6 ÷ 4      c  14.1 ÷ 3      d  3.6 ÷ 5

10 Work these out.

    Give your answers to 1 decimal place.

    a  8 ÷ 3      b  13 ÷ 7      c  15 ÷ 8      d  40.1 ÷ 7

    e  68 ÷ 7      f  45.6 ÷ 9

11 Work these out.

    Give your answers to 2 decimal places.

    a  2.9 ÷ 8      b  24.1 ÷ 7      c  0.82 ÷ 6

12 Cloth costs $3.50 for each metre.

    What is the cost of 0.6 metres?

13 Wire costs $1.30 for each metre.

    Work out the cost of 0.9 metres.

14 Cheese costs $5.90 for 1 kg.

    How much does 0.2 kg cost?

15 Farid needs to fill 36 glasses with apple juice.

    Each glass holds 0.2 litres.

    Apple juice is sold in 1 litre cartons.

    Each carton costs $1.30.

    How much does the apple juice cost Farid altogether?

> Start by finding the total number of litres of apple juice needed to fill the glasses.

16 Paint costs $4.30 per litre.

    Adrienne needs 7 litres.

    She has $30. Is this enough to buy the paint?

17 Ivete buys 0.4 kg of cheese from shop A. She pays $5.40

    Yanqun buys 0.3 kg of the same cheese from shop B. She pays $4.20

    Which shop is cheaper for the cheese? Explain your answer.

> A good way to start is to find the cost of 0.1 kg of cheese from each shop.

## 5.4 Fractions and decimals

### Inequality signs

You already know that '=' means 'equals' or 'has the same value as'.

There are other signs that you need to know how to use:

- '≠' means 'is not equal to'
- '<' means 'is less than'
- '>' means 'is greater than'.

## Worked example 1

Joseph is doing his maths homework.

He has to choose from the signs =, ≠, <, and > to make the statements correct.

Each sign must be used once.

His answers are

**a**  3 × 5 < 12

**b**  4 + 5 = 9

**c**  24 ÷ 12 > 3

**d**  5 × 6 ≠ 28

Check Joseph's answers. Which are correct and which are not correct?

**a**  3 × 5 is 15. Joseph is not correct as 15 > 12. The correct answer is 3 × 5 > 12.

**b**  4 + 5 is 9. Joseph is correct.

**c**  24 ÷ 12 is 2. Joseph is not correct as 2 < 3.

**d**  5 × 6 = 30. Joseph is correct as 30 ≠ 28.

## Worked example 2

Put these measurements in order of size, smallest first.

**a**  0.5 cm, 0.2 cm, 4 mm, 0.1 cm

**b**  0.25 kg, 0.18 kg, 0.3 kg, 125 g

**a**  Write the measurements using the same units.

  0.5 cm = 5 mm

  0.2 cm = 2 mm

  0.1 cm = 1 mm

> Remember: 10 mm = 1 cm. To convert from cm to mm you multiply by 10.

  In order of size these are: 1 mm, 2 mm, 4 mm, 5 mm

  The answer is 0.1 cm, 0.2 cm, 4 mm, 0.5 cm.

**b**  Write the measurements using the same units.

  0.25 kg = 250 g

  0.18 kg = 180 g

  0.3 kg = 300 g

> Remember: 1000 g = 1 kg. To convert from kg to g you multiply by 1000.

  In order of size these measurements are: 125 g, 180 g, 250 g, 300 g

  The answer is 125 g, 0.18 kg, 0.25 kg, 0.3 kg.

# 5 Decimals

## Changing from fractions to decimals

To compare and order fractions you can change them to decimals.

To change from a fraction to a decimal you divide the numerator (top number) by the denominator (bottom number) on your calculator.

$\frac{4}{5}$ means $4 \div 5$ so $\frac{4}{5}$ written as a decimal is 0.8

When you change fractions to decimals you get two types of answer.

Some decimals stop, such as 0.5 and 0.125

These are called **terminating decimals**.

Some decimals have a repeating pattern and do not stop, such as 0.333333… and 0.4545454545…

The three dots show that the digits go on forever.

These are called **recurring decimals**.

There is a special way to write recurring decimals.

Dots are used above the first and the last digit in the repeating pattern.

0.33333333… is written as $0.\dot{3}$

0.45454545… is written as $0.\dot{4}\dot{5}$

> ### Worked example 3
>
> Change these fractions to decimals.
>
> **a** $\frac{5}{8}$ **b** $\frac{2}{3}$ **c** $\frac{1}{6}$ **d** $\frac{23}{27}$ **e** $\frac{1}{15}$
>
> Give your answer to **e** correct to 2 decimal places.
>
> **a** $\frac{5}{8}$ means $5 \div 8$, so $\frac{5}{8} = 0.625$
>
> This is a terminating decimal, so write down all the digits.
>
> **b** $\frac{2}{3}$ means $2 \div 3$, so $\frac{2}{3} = 0.666666… = 0.\dot{6}$
>
> **c** $\frac{1}{6}$ means $1 \div 6$, so $\frac{1}{6} = 0.1666666… = 0.1\dot{6}$
>
> **d** $\frac{23}{27}$ means $23 \div 27$, so $\frac{23}{27} = 0.851851851… = 0.\dot{8}5\dot{1}$
>
> **e** $\frac{1}{15}$ means $1 \div 15$, so $\frac{1}{15} = 0.0666666… = 0.07$ (to 2 d.p.)
>
> Remember: only the first and last digits in the repeating pattern have dots above.

## Exercise 5.4

**1** Copy each of the following.

Replace the ? with one of =, <, or >.

  **a** $4 \times 5 \; ? \; 21$   **b** $96 \div 8 \; ? \; 100$   **c** $125 \div 25 \; ? \; 4$   **d** $7 \times 6 \; ? \; 42$

Mathematics for Cambridge Secondary 1

**2** Copy each of the following.

Replace the ? with one of = or ≠.

   **a** $2 \times 3 \; ? \; 3 \times 2$    **b** $36 \div 3 \; ? \; 6 \times 3$    **c** $4 \times 12 \; ? \; 16 \times 3$    **d** $15 \div 3 \; ? \; 24 \div 6$

**3** Write these in order of size, smallest first.

   **a** 0.3, 0.15, 0.28, 0.09          **b** 0.876, 0.786, 0.883, 0.0887

   **c** 0.586, 0.6581, 0.658, 0.661    **d** 1.205, 2.106, 1.036, 2.061

**4** Copy each of the following.

Replace the ? with either < or >.

   **a** 32.056 ? 32.065    **b** 5.06 ? 5.21    **c** 0.56 ? 0.18    **d** 0.035 ? 0.102

**5** Write these measurements in order of size, smallest first.

   **a** 400 g, 0.28 kg, 200 g, 0.35 kg

   **b** 1250 m, 250 m, 1.4 km, 800 m

> Remember 1000 g = 1 kg and 1000 m = 1 km

**6** Kia says '0.025 kg > 0.2 kg as 25 is greater than 2.'

Explain why Kia is wrong.

> Think about the place value of the digits.

**7** Change these fraction to decimals.

   **a** $\frac{3}{5}$   **b** $\frac{4}{25}$   **c** $\frac{5}{16}$   **d** $\frac{1}{20}$   **e** $\frac{3}{20}$   **f** $\frac{7}{40}$

**8** Change these fractions to decimals.

   **a** $\frac{1}{3}$   **b** $\frac{5}{9}$   **c** $\frac{7}{33}$   **d** $\frac{3}{11}$   **e** $\frac{4}{11}$   **f** $\frac{38}{99}$

**9** Change these fractions to decimals.

   **a** $\frac{11}{45}$   **b** $\frac{7}{15}$   **c** $\frac{11}{15}$   **d** $\frac{35}{111}$   **e** $\frac{16}{27}$   **f** $\frac{5}{24}$

**10** Change these to decimals.

Give your answers to 2 decimal places.

   **a** $\frac{5}{9}$   **b** $\frac{8}{15}$   **c** $\frac{13}{15}$   **d** $\frac{1}{12}$

**11** Which of the following is larger?

   **a** $\frac{9}{10}$ or $\frac{8}{9}$   **b** $\frac{3}{7}$ or $\frac{6}{13}$   **c** $\frac{7}{9}$ or $\frac{39}{50}$   **d** $\frac{3}{5}$ or $\frac{5}{9}$

**12** Write these fractions in ascending order.

   **a** $\frac{4}{9}, \frac{5}{13}, \frac{2}{5}, \frac{7}{15}$

   **b** $\frac{3}{10}, \frac{5}{24}, \frac{2}{9}, \frac{6}{31}$

**13** Write these fractions in ascending order.

Change them to decimals to help.

   $\frac{5}{8}, \frac{3}{5}, \frac{5}{9}, \frac{29}{49}$

**14** **a** Use your calculator to find $\frac{1}{7}$ as a decimal.

   **b** Pete says '$\frac{1}{7}$ gives a recurring decimal.'

      Is Pete correct?

> To write a fraction as a decimal you divide the numerator by the denominator. Look for any patterns in the digits. Some calculators automatically round the last digit on the display, check with your teacher to see if yours does this.

**c** Find $\frac{2}{7}$ and $\frac{3}{7}$ as decimals.

What do you notice?

**d** Can you write $\frac{4}{7}, \frac{5}{7}, \frac{6}{7}$ as decimals without using your calculator?

Check your answers with a calculator.

**15** Change $\frac{1}{11}$ to a decimal.

Use your answer to write down $\frac{2}{11}, \frac{3}{11}, \ldots$ up to $\frac{10}{11}$ as decimals without using your calculator.

Remember: $\frac{2}{11}$ is twice as much as $\frac{1}{11}$

## Review

**1** Write these numbers using figures.

   **a** 1 million    **b** 3 billion

**2** Write these numbers in words.

   **a** 10 000    **b** 1 000 000 000    **c** $10^8$

**3** Work out

   **a** 74 × 0.1    **b** 348 × 0.01    **c** 38 ÷ 0.1    **d** 23 ÷ 0.01

**4** Round 2345.054 correct to:

   **a** the nearest 10    **b** 1 decimal place    **c** 2 decimal places.

**5** Work out

   **a** 15 × 0.3    **b** 120 × 0.05    **c** 3.6 × 0.5    **d** 18.4 × 0.02

**6** Work out

   **a** 63 ÷ 0.9    **b** 4.8 ÷ 0.6    **c** 14.7 ÷ 0.07    **d** 2.4 ÷ 0.08

**7** Work these out.

Give your answers to 1 decimal place.

   **a** 35 ÷ 9    **b** 12.9 ÷ 7

**8** Copy each of the following.

Replace the ? with one of <, >, or =.

   **a** 2 × 9 ? 36 ÷ 2    **b** 15 × 3 ? 23 + 21    **c** 32 − 19 ? 48 ÷ 4    **d** 18 × 3 ? 2 × 28

**9** Change these fractions to decimals.

   **a** $\frac{1}{16}$    **b** $\frac{7}{18}$    **c** $\frac{31}{33}$    **d** $\frac{10}{27}$

**10** Put these fractions in ascending order of size.

Change them to decimals to help.

$\frac{3}{8}, \frac{18}{49}, \frac{8}{25}, \frac{5}{13}$

# 6 Processing, interpreting and discussing data

**Chapter 18 covers collecting data**
**Chapter 10 covers presenting data**

> **Learning outcomes**
> - Calculate statistics for sets of discrete and continuous data.
> - Recognise when to use the range, mean, median and mode and, for grouped data, the modal class.
> - Compare two distributions, using the range and one or more of the mode, median and mean.

## Statistics helps with decoding

People have passed coded messages to each other for centuries. One of the simplest ways to code a message is to replace one letter by another letter, or by a symbol.

No one knows who first discovered how to break codes based on how commonly used a letter is in a particular language. The first documents explaining how to break codes using this method were written by a 9th century Arab philosopher called Abu Yusuf Ya'qub ibn Is-haq ibn as-Sabbah ibn 'omran ibn Ismail al-Kindi.

The most common letters in English are 'e', then 't', then 'a'.

If the most common letter in an English coded message is 'x', then it probably represents the letter 'e'.

If the next most common letter is 'y' then it probably represents the letter 't'.

Al-Kindi wrote almost 300 books on medicine, music, mathematics and cooking. The photograph shows the first page of his book *A Manuscript on Deciphering Cryptographic Messages*. It is one of the first books with some reference to statistics.

## 6.1 Calculating statistics from data sets

### Calculating statistics from lists

A **distribution** is a set of data.

An **average** value is a single value that is used to represent a set of data.

This is then used to make comparisons.

**Mode**, **median** and **mean** are average values.

The mode is the value that is the most common.

The median is the middle value when all the values are listed in order of size.

The mean is found using the formula:

$$\text{Mean} = \frac{\text{the sum of all the values}}{\text{the number of values}}$$

The mode is often used for qualitative data. For example, clothing sizes, opinions and colours.

The median is used for data that can be written in order of size. For example, income or wealth.

The mean is used for numerical data. For example, pay, prices and heights.

A **measure of spread** tells us how much a set of data is spread out. It is helpful when comparing sets of data.

The **range** is a measure of spread. It is found using the formula:

Range = largest value − smallest value.

> ### Worked example 1
>
> Here are the test scores for a class of students.
>
> 23, 45, 36, 32, 36, 37, 42, 39, 28, 44
>
> Find
>
> **a** the mode
>
> **b** the median
>
> **c** the mean
>
> **d** the range.
>
> **a** The mode is 36.
>
> **b** Write the data in order of size first:
>
> 23, 28, 32, 36, 36, 37, 39, 42, 44, 45
>
> The median is 36.5     This is halfway between 36 and 37, the 'middle pair'.
>
> **c** The mean is $\frac{23 + 45 + 36 + 32 + 36 + 37 + 42 + 39 + 28 + 44}{10} = \frac{362}{10} = 36.2$
>
> **d** The range is 45 − 23 = 22

## Calculating statistics from frequency tables

When the data set becomes too large to list, a frequency table is used.

The frequency column tells you how many times each value occurs.

## Mathematics for Cambridge Secondary 1

### Worked example 2

The frequency table shows the numbers of people in cars passing a school one morning.

a  Find the mode.
b  How many cars were counted?
c  Find the median.
d  How many people were counted altogether?
e  Find the mean.
f  Find the range.

| People in car | Frequency |
|---|---|
| 1 | 6 |
| 2 | 13 |
| 3 | 18 |
| 4 | 10 |
| 5 | 3 |

a  The mode is 3.   This is the most common number as 18 cars have 3 people in them.

b  6 + 13 + 18 + 10 + 3 = 50   The frequency tells you how many of each number there is.

c  The median is 3.   The first 6 cars in the table have 1 person, the next 13 have 2 people, the next 18 have 3.

d

| People in car, $x$ | Frequency, $f$ | $x \times f$ |
|---|---|---|
| 1 | 6 | 6 |
| 2 | 13 | 26 |
| 3 | 18 | 54 |
| 4 | 10 | 40 |
| 5 | 3 | 15 |
| Total |  | 141 |

There were 141 people counted altogether.

e  Mean = $\frac{141}{50}$ = 2.82

f  Range = 5 − 1 = 4

### Exercise 6.1

1  Find the mode, mean, median and range for each of the following sets of data.

   a  3, 5, 6, 6, 8, 10, 13, 14, 14, 14
   b  1, 3, 5, 7, 9, 11, 13, 15, 17, 19

2  Mikael asks some of his class how many televisions they have in their homes.

   Here are his results.

   0, 0, 0, 1, 1, 1, 1, 1, 1, 1, 1, 1, 1, 1, 1, 2, 2, 2, 2, 2, 3, 3, 3, 3, 4

   a  Find the median.
   b  Find the mode.

**3** Jamal carries out the same survey with his class.

He records his results in this tally chart.

  **a** How many people did Jamal ask?

  **b** Find the median.

  **c** Find the mode.

| Number of televisions | Tally | Frequency |
|---|---|---|
| 0 | \|\|\|\| | 4 |
| 1 | ⊮ \| | 6 |
| 2 | ⊮ \|\|\| | 8 |
| 3 | \|\|\|\| | 4 |
| 4 | \| | 1 |

**4** Thomasina also does the same survey with her class.

  **a** Find the median.

  **b** Find the mode.

| Number of televisions | Frequency |
|---|---|
| 0 | 2 |
| 1 | 7 |
| 2 | 9 |
| 3 | 6 |
| 4 | 2 |

**5** This table gives the number of students in each class at a school.

Work out the mode, mean, median and range for these data.

| Students in class, $n$ | Number of classes, $f$ |
|---|---|
| 27 | 4 |
| 28 | 9 |
| 29 | 8 |
| 30 | 12 |
| 31 | 7 |

**6** Amelie counts the eggs in some birds' nests.

Her results are shown in the frequency table.

Work out the mean number of eggs in each nest.

| Number of eggs, $x$ | Frequency, $f$ |
|---|---|
| 0 | 3 |
| 1 | 2 |
| 2 | 7 |
| 3 | 8 |
| 4 | 3 |
| 5 | 2 |

Mathematics for Cambridge Secondary 1

**7** The heights of 10 people are measured.

The smallest height is 160 cm.

The mean height is 170 cm.

Read each of the following statements.

Say whether each statement **must be correct, may be correct** or **must be incorrect**.

Give a reason for each of your answers.

  **a** The median height is 170 cm.
  **b** The median height is 160 cm.
  **c** The total of all the heights is 1700 cm.
  **d** The range of the heights is 10 cm.
  **e** The range of the heights is 40 cm.

**8** Copy the table and fill in the frequencies so the mode of the data set is 2 and the median is 3.

| $n$ | Frequency, $f$ |
|---|---|
| 1 |  |
| 2 |  |
| 3 |  |
| 4 |  |

There are lots of possible answers to this. Remember: the frequencies tell you how many of each there are, and the median is the middle value when they are listed in order of size, so the middle value is 3.

**9** A set of five numbers has a range of 5, a mode of 9 and a median of 6.

Find the set of numbers.

The median is 6 and the mode is 9. As there are only five values what can you say about the other three values?

**10** The mean of a set of three numbers is twice the median.

Find a possible set of numbers that fits this statement.

Write down the mean and median to check your answer.

Start with a value as the median, double this gives the mean value. From here you can find the total of the three values.

**11** Valentina opens some boxes of straws.

She counts the straws in each box.

Her results are shown in this frequency table.

| Number of straws | 46 | 47 | 48 | 49 | 50 | 51 |
|---|---|---|---|---|---|---|
| Number of boxes | 5 | 6 | 18 | 17 | 13 | 11 |

  **a** How many boxes have more than the mode?
  **b** How many boxes have more than the median?
  **c** How many boxes have more than the mean?

Start by finding the mode, median and mean number of straws.

# 6.2 Calculating statistics from grouped data

## Discrete data

**Discrete data** usually come from counting. For example, the number of flowers on a plant can be 0, 1, 2, 3, 4, 5, ... but not numbers like 1.23 or 5.9

When there are a lot of values, this type of data is often put into groups, or classes, such as 0–9, 10–19, and so on.

Because the data are discrete there are gaps between each class.

You cannot find the mode, mean, median or range for grouped data. Instead, you can find the **class that contains the median**, the **modal class** and an **estimate of the mean**.

Use the frequencies to find the class containing the median.

The modal class has more values in it than the other classes. That is, it has the greatest frequency.

If data about the number of flowers on plants are grouped, the exact number of flowers in each class will not be known. Instead, the **mid-class value** is used as an estimate for the number of flowers in each class. An estimate of the mean value is found by using these mid-class values.

> ### Worked example 1
>
> The number of flowers on a group of plants is shown in the table.
>
> | Number of flowers, $n$ | Frequency, $f$ |
> | --- | --- |
> | 0–4 | 3 |
> | 5–9 | 5 |
> | 10–14 | 8 |
> | 15–19 | 12 |
> | 20–24 | 2 |
>
> **a** Find the class containing the median.
>
> **b** Which is the modal class?
>
> **c** Calculate an estimate of the mean number of flowers per plant.
>
> **a** Add the frequencies to find the total number of plants.
>
> 3 + 5 + 8 + 12 + 2 = 30  The median is halfway between the 15th and 16th values.
>
> The first 3 + 5 = 8 values are between 0 and 9.
>
> The first 16 values are between 0 and 14.
>
> Therefore, the median is in the class 10–14.
>
> **b** The modal class is 15–19.  This is the class with the greatest frequency.
>
> **c** The class 0–4 contains three values chosen from 0, 1, 2, 3, 4.
>
> The mid-class value is 2, as it is exactly in the middle of these values.
>
> The mid-class values for the other classes are 7, 12, 17, and 22.
>
>> It is always best to copy the table given and add columns to help with working. This is done in the same way as for finding the mean from discrete frequency distributions.

| Number of flowers, n | Frequency, f | Mid-class value, m | m × f |
|---|---|---|---|
| 0–4 | 3 | 2 | 6 |
| 5–9 | 5 | 7 | 35 |
| 10–14 | 8 | 12 | 96 |
| 15–19 | 12 | 17 | 204 |
| 20–24 | 2 | 22 | 44 |
| Total | 30 | | 385 |

The estimate of the total number of flowers on the plants is 385.

The number of plants is 30.

The estimate for the mean number of flowers per plant

$= \dfrac{\text{estimate of the total number of flowers}}{\text{total number of plants}}$

Mean $= \dfrac{385}{30} = 12.8\dot{3}$ flowers

## Continuous data

**Continuous data** usually come from measuring. For example, the length of a car could be 3 metres, 4 metres or anything between 3 metres and 4 metres (such as 3.5 metres or 3.216 metres). It depends on how precisely you can measure the length.

When there are a lot of values, this type of data is often put into groups or classes, such as $0 \leqslant n < 5$. In this case, $\leqslant$ means that $n$ is greater than or equal to 0 and less than (but not equal to) 5.

There are no gaps as the data are continuous.

An example of continuous data is the heights of students in a class. The heights can be grouped and shown in a grouped frequency table like the one below.

Heights of students (cm):   122, 125, 131, 133, 133, 139, 140, 143, 143, 145, 146, 151

| Height, h (cm) | Frequency |
|---|---|
| $120 \leqslant h < 130$ | 2 |
| $130 \leqslant h < 140$ | 4 |
| $140 \leqslant h < 150$ | 5 |
| $150 \leqslant h < 160$ | 1 |

# 6 Processing, interpreting and discussing data

## Worked example 2

The thickness of 20 books is measured in millimetres.

The results are shown in the grouped frequency table.

| Thickness, $t$ (mm) | $0 \leq t < 5$ | $5 \leq t < 10$ | $10 \leq t < 15$ | $15 \leq t < 20$ |
|---|---|---|---|---|
| Frequency | 3 | 5 | 8 | 4 |

**a** Find the modal class.

**b** Which class contains the median?

**c** Calculate an estimate of the mean thickness of the books.

**a** The modal class is $10 \leq t < 15$     *This is the class with the greatest frequency.*

**b** There are 20 books. Both the 10th and 11th book are in the class $10 \leq t < 15$, so the median is also in this class.

**c** The mid-class value for the class $0 \leq t < 5$ is 2.5

The mid-class values for the other classes are 7.5, 12.5, 17.5

| Thickness, $t$ (mm) | $0 \leq t < 5$ | $5 \leq t < 10$ | $10 \leq t < 15$ | $15 \leq t < 20$ | Total |
|---|---|---|---|---|---|
| Frequency, $f$ | 3 | 5 | 8 | 4 | 20 |
| Mid-class value, $m$ | 2.5 | 7.5 | 12.5 | 17.5 | |
| $m \times f$ | 7.5 | 37.5 | 100 | 70 | 215 |

The estimate of the total thickness of all the books together is 215 mm.

The number of books is 20.

The estimate for the mean thickness of the books = $\dfrac{\text{estimate of the total thickness}}{\text{total number of books}}$

Mean = $\dfrac{215}{20}$ = 10.75 mm

> When you are given tables that have rows rather than columns, as in example 2, you can always write them the other way around, as in example 1, if you prefer.

## Exercise 6.2

**1** Decide whether each of the following is a discrete quantity or a continuous quantity.

   **a** Time, in seconds, to solve a puzzle.

   **b** Number of pets in a family.

   **c** Average speed of some runners.

   **d** Shoe size.

**2** The table shows the number of days that each of 50 guests stayed in a hotel.

| Length of stay (days) | Frequency |
|---|---|
| 1–3 | 21 |
| 4–6 | 6 |
| 7–9 | 12 |
| 10–12 | 7 |
| 13–15 | 4 |

  **a** Does the table show discrete data or continuous data?

  **b** Write down the modal class.

  **c** Which class contains the median?

  **d** Use mid-class values to calculate an estimate of the mean.

**3** People living in village A are asked how many times they walk to village B each month.

The results are shown in the table.

| Number of walks | 0–4 | 5–9 | 10–14 | 15–19 | 20–24 |
|---|---|---|---|---|---|
| Frequency | 5 | 8 | 15 | 12 | 10 |

Calculate an estimate of the mean number of times people walk to village B each month.

**4** The times taken by some runners to do a charity run are shown in the table.

| Time, $t$ (minutes) | $10 \leq t < 20$ | $20 \leq t < 30$ | $30 \leq t < 40$ | $40 \leq t < 50$ | $50 \leq t < 60$ |
|---|---|---|---|---|---|
| Frequency | 3 | 15 | 9 | 2 | 1 |

  **a** Does the table show discrete data or continuous data?

  **b** Write down the modal class.

  **c** Which class contains the median?

  **d** Calculate an estimate of the mean.

**5** A group of 20 students record the distance, in km, they walk to school each day.

Calculate an estimate of the mean distance walked.

| Distance, $d$ (km) | Frequency |
|---|---|
| $0 \leq d < 1$ | 3 |
| $1 \leq d < 2$ | 6 |
| $2 \leq d < 3$ | 5 |
| $3 \leq d < 4$ | 3 |
| $4 \leq d < 5$ | 2 |
| $5 \leq d < 6$ | 1 |

**6** The test marks of 40 students are shown in the table.

| Mark | 1–10 | 11–20 | 21–30 | 31–40 | 41–50 |
|---|---|---|---|---|---|
| Frequency | 4 | 7 | 9 | 12 | 8 |

  **a** Explain why it is not possible to find the range for these marks.

  **b** Work out the smallest and largest possible values the range could take.

  **c** Find an estimate for the median value.

  **d** Stephen takes the test after the 40 students.

> Think about the possible values in the lowest and highest classes.

He scores a mark of 30.

Is Stephen's score better or worse than the mean for the 40 students? Show how you decide.

7  Graeme has some bags of sweets.

The mass, in grams, of each bag is recorded.

| Mass, $m$ (g) | Frequency |
|---|---|
| $80 \leq m < 90$ | 9 |
| $90 \leq m < 100$ | 8 |
| $100 \leq m < 110$ | 5 |
| $110 \leq m < 120$ | 3 |
| $120 \leq m < 130$ | 5 |

a  Write down the modal class.

b  Work out an estimate of the mean mass.

c  Maria says, 'The modal class represents the masses best because it shows the mass of most bags.'

Graeme says, 'The mean represents the masses best.'

Give a reason why Graeme is correct.

## 6.3 Making comparisons

It is often useful to summarise data. This makes it possible to compare two sets of data.

In order to summarise, you need some idea of the average and also an idea of how spread out the data are.

The mode, median and mean can be used as an average. Sometimes one of these may be better than the others.

The measure of spread you have found so far is the range. The larger the value of the range, the more spread out the data are.

### Worked example

The number of eggs laid by two hens, Peggy and Leggy, are recorded.

| Number of eggs | 1 | 2 | 3 | 4 | 5 | 6 | 7 |
|---|---|---|---|---|---|---|---|
| Frequency for Peggy | 4 | 7 | 4 | 3 | 2 | 0 | 0 |
| Frequency for Leggy | 5 | 6 | 3 | 2 | 2 | 1 | 1 |

Use suitable statistics to compare the number of eggs laid by Peggy and Leggy.

For Peggy:

Mode = 2

Median = 2

Mean = $\dfrac{1 \times 4 + 2 \times 7 + 3 \times 4 + 4 \times 3 + 5 \times 2}{4 + 7 + 4 + 3 + 2} = \dfrac{52}{20} = 2.6$

Range = 5 − 1 = 4

For Leggy:

　Mode = 2

　Median = 2

　Mean = $\dfrac{1 \times 5 + 2 \times 6 + 3 \times 3 + 4 \times 2 + 5 \times 2 + 6 \times 1 + 7 \times 1}{5 + 6 + 3 + 2 + 2 + 1 + 1} = \dfrac{57}{20} = 2.85$

　Range = 7 − 1 = 6

Peggy and Leggy both have the same mode and median.

The mean suggests that, on average, Leggy lays slightly more eggs than Peggy.

The range for Leggy is larger. This suggests that the number of eggs laid by Leggy is more spread out.

## Exercise 6.3

**1** Emeka grows plants called carnations.

　He grows two varieties: Kira and Heracles.

　He records the number of flowers he gets from each plant.

| Number of flowers | 1–3 | 4–6 | 7–9 | 10–12 | 13–15 |
|---|---|---|---|---|---|
| Frequency for Kira | 1 | 8 | 10 | 5 | 1 |
| Frequency for Heracles | 3 | 8 | 9 | 3 | 2 |

　Use estimates of the mean values to decide which variety has more flowers.

**2** Two classes, A and B, take a test.

　Their marks are recorded.

| Class A marks | Frequency |
|---|---|
| 1–10 | 3 |
| 11–20 | 7 |
| 21–30 | 10 |
| 31–40 | 4 |
| 41–50 | 1 |

| Class B marks | Frequency |
|---|---|
| 1–10 | 1 |
| 11–20 | 5 |
| 21–30 | 14 |
| 31–40 | 3 |
| 41–50 | 2 |

　Use estimates of the mean to compare the marks of the two classes.

**3** The tables show the mass, in kg, of some male and female babies.

| Mass, $m$ (kg) | $2 \leqslant m < 4$ | $4 \leqslant m < 6$ | $6 \leqslant m < 8$ | $8 \leqslant m < 10$ | $10 \leqslant m < 12$ | $12 \leqslant m < 14$ |
|---|---|---|---|---|---|---|
| Female frequency | 2 | 4 | 9 | 6 | 4 | 0 |
| Male frequency | 1 | 3 | 6 | 8 | 6 | 1 |

　For each group of babies, find:

　**a** the modal class

　**b** the class containing the median

**6** Processing, interpreting and discussing data

   c an estimate for the mean mass
   d the largest and smallest possible values for the range.
   e Use your answers to compare the masses of the female and male babies.

4 20 people join a diet club.

Each person's mass is measured when they join.
It is measured again after two weeks.

The results are shown in the table.

| Mass, $m$ (kg) | When joining | After two weeks |
|---|---|---|
| $70 \leqslant m < 80$ | 1 | 3 |
| $80 \leqslant m < 90$ | 5 | 6 |
| $90 \leqslant m < 100$ | 8 | 7 |
| $100 \leqslant m < 110$ | 2 | 3 |
| $110 \leqslant m < 120$ | 3 | 1 |
| $120 \leqslant m < 130$ | 1 | 0 |

> To compare two distributions you need an average and a measure of spread.

   a Compare the two distributions using suitable statistics.
   b Was everyone lighter after joining the club? Explain your answer.

5 A survey is carried out to find the time taken to get home from school.

Both teachers and students are interviewed.

| Time taken to get home, $t$ (minutes) | $10 \leqslant t < 20$ | $20 \leqslant t < 30$ | $30 \leqslant t < 40$ | $40 \leqslant t < 50$ | $50 \leqslant t < 60$ | $60 \leqslant t < 70$ |
|---|---|---|---|---|---|---|
| Student frequency | 12 | 20 | 10 | 7 | 1 | 0 |
| Teacher frequency | 1 | 2 | 8 | 5 | 3 | 1 |

Use suitable statistics to compare the times taken by the teachers and the students.

## Review

1 During the holidays, Kafi and Lien go fishing every day.

They keep a record of the number of fish they catch each day.

Kafi's catches are 2, 0, 1, 3, 2, 2, 5, 3, 4, 1.

Lien's catches are 2, 2, 1, 4, 3, 3, 0, 0, 0, 1.

   a Calculate the mode, median, mean and range for each person.
   b Use the mean and range to compare the number of fish caught by Kafi and Lien.
   c Give a reason why the mode is not helpful when comparing the number of fish Kafi and Lien caught.

89

**2** Find the mean of each distribution.

a

| $x$ | Frequency |
|---|---|
| 4 | 3 |
| 5 | 7 |
| 6 | 8 |
| 7 | 2 |

b

| $x$ | Frequency |
|---|---|
| 1–5 | 5 |
| 6–10 | 7 |
| 11–15 | 6 |
| 16–20 | 2 |

c

| $x$ | Frequency |
|---|---|
| $10 \leq x < 20$ | 7 |
| $20 \leq x < 30$ | 8 |
| $30 \leq x < 40$ | 6 |
| $40 \leq x < 50$ | 4 |

**3** Serge is reading two books.

He thinks one is more difficult to read than the other.

He counts the letters in the first 40 words of each book.

| Number of letters | 1 | 2 | 3 | 4 | 5 | 6 | 7 | 8 | 9 | 10 | 11 |
|---|---|---|---|---|---|---|---|---|---|---|---|
| Book A frequency | 3 | 4 | 3 | 6 | 4 | 7 | 4 | 3 | 2 | 1 | 3 |
| Book B frequency | 5 | 3 | 5 | 4 | 6 | 2 | 3 | 2 | 3 | 4 | 3 |

**a** Which book do you think Serge finds more difficult? Use the median values and estimated mean values to help you decide.

**b** Next, Serge counts the number of words in each sentence on the first page of each book.

| Number of words | 5–9 | 10–14 | 15–19 | 20–24 | 25–29 |
|---|---|---|---|---|---|
| Book A frequency | 2 | 4 | 8 | 6 | 5 |
| Book B frequency | 3 | 7 | 5 | 2 | 3 |

Which book do you think Serge finds more difficult now? Use the estimated mean values to help you decide.

**4** Katherine has two routes to get to and from school.

To help decide which route is better, she records the time taken for each route every day for a month.

| Time (nearest minute) | 10–12 | 13–15 | 16–18 | 19–21 | 22–24 |
|---|---|---|---|---|---|
| Route 1 | 0 | 3 | 5 | 8 | 4 |
| Route 2 | 2 | 4 | 7 | 4 | 3 |

**a** Use suitable statistics to compare the two routes.

**b** One day Katherine forgets her watch.

She realises that she has only 20 minutes to get home.

Which way would you suggest she takes? Explain how you decide.

# 7 Length, mass and capacity

> **Learning outcomes**
> - Choose suitable units of measurement to estimate, measure, calculate and solve problems in a range of contexts, including units of mass, length, area, volume or capacity.
> - Know that distances in the USA, the UK and some other countries are measured in miles, and that one kilometre is about $\frac{5}{8}$ of a mile.

## Mission to Mars

In December 1998, NASA (the space agency from the USA) sent a mission to Mars.

The Mars Climate Orbiter was intended to fly round Mars collecting data about the planet.

Unfortunately something went wrong when it was approaching Mars and the spacecraft was lost.

The problem was caused by a confusion between metric units of force (newtons) and the older non-metric units (pounds).

## 7.1 The metric system

### Metric units

The **metric system** uses different units for each type of measurement.

There are three units that you know from your Stage 7 Student Book:

| | | |
|---|---|---|
| Length | metres | (m) |
| Mass | grams | (g) |
| Capacity | litres | (l) |

### Metric prefixes

All metric units use the same prefixes for bigger or smaller measurements.

Mathematics for Cambridge Secondary 1

These are the ones you should know:

- **kilo-** (k)    1000    For example, 1 kilogram = 1000 grams
- **centi-** (c)   $\frac{1}{100}$   For example, 1 centimetre = $\frac{1}{100}$ metre (or 100 centimetres = 1 metre)
- **milli-** (m)   $\frac{1}{1000}$  For example, 1 millimetre = $\frac{1}{1000}$ metre (or 1000 millimetres = 1 metre)

> There are other prefixes for bigger or smaller measurements. If you use a computer you will know about gigabytes. Giga- is a prefix meaning $10^9$ so 1 gigabyte is 1 000 000 000 bytes.

## Worked example 1

What would be the appropriate unit for measuring the following?

a The mass of a suitcase

b The capacity of a cooking pot

c The height of a postage stamp

a The normal units of mass are g and kg.

   Grams are for very light objects.

   The mass of a suitcase would be measured in kg.

b The normal units of capacity are ml and l.

   Millilitres are for small quantities.

   The capacity of a cooking pot would be measured in litres.

c The normal units of length are mm, cm, m and km.

   Metres are for bigger distances such as walls or curtains.

   Kilometres are for very large distances.

   The height of a postage stamp would be measured in either centimetres or millimetres.

## Worked example 2

Convert these measurements into the stated units.

a 3.5 kg into g     b 230 cm into m     c 1.9 l into ml

a 1 kg = 1000 g so the conversion factor is 1000.

   3.5 kg = 3.5 × 1000 = 3500 g

> When changing **from a bigger unit to a smaller one**, you **multiply** by the conversion factor.

**7** Length, mass and capacity

**b** $1\text{ cm} = \frac{1}{100}\text{ m}$ so the conversion factor is 100.

$230\text{ cm} = 230 \div 100 = 2.3\text{ m}$

> When changing **from a smaller unit to a bigger one**, you **divide** by the conversion factor.

**c** $1\text{ ml} = \frac{1}{1000}\text{ l}$ so the conversion factor is 1000.

$1.9\text{ l} = 1.9 \times 1000 = 1900\text{ ml}$

> When changing **from a bigger unit to a smaller one**, you **multiply** by the conversion factor.

## Exercise 7.1

**1** Write down the units you would use for each of these measurements.

  **a** The mass of a train
  **b** The distance between two cities
  **c** The capacity of a medicine bottle
  **d** The length of a cricket pitch
  **e** The mass of a calculator
  **f** The amount of water in a pond

**2** Write down an estimate for:

  **a** the length of a car 
  **b** the capacity of a watering can 
  **c** the mass of an apple

  **d** the height of a house plant 
  **e** the capacity of a coffee cup 
  **f** the mass of a grown man.

**3** Change these measurements into the given units.

  **a** 3 m into cm
  **b** 5 l into ml
  **c** 2.5 km into m
  **d** 700 cm into m
  **e** 2500 mm into m
  **f** 9500 g into kg
  **g** 90 mm into cm
  **h** 750 ml into l
  **i** 1200 mm into m
  **j** 375 cm into m
  **k** 5.25 kg into g
  **l** 6.5 cm into mm
  **m** 4.8 tonnes into kg
  **n** 6.95 m into mm
  **o** 7580 kg into tonnes

93

**4** Silas has a piece of wood 2.4 metres long.

To make a toy he needs to cut the following lengths:
- One piece that is 0.75 metres long
- Three pieces that are 35 centimetres long
- Four pieces that are 45 millimetres long

   **a** Work out the total length Silas needs to cut. Give your answer in centimetres.

   **b** Does he have enough wood to cut all of these pieces?

**5** The recipe shows the ingredients needed to make cheese and walnut bread.

An egg weighs about 50 g.

100 ml of milk weighs about 100 g.

   **a** What is the total mass of all the ingredients in grams?

   **b** How many kilograms is that?

> $\frac{1}{2}$ kg plain flour
> 200 g butter
> 4 eggs
> 170 g cheese
> 100 g walnuts
> 200 ml warm milk

**6** A fertiliser is mixed by adding 250 ml of concentrate with 3 l of water.

   **a** Work out how much liquid there is altogether after they are mixed.

   **b** What is the ratio of fertiliser to water?

   **c** The mixture is to be put into bottles that hold 400 ml each.

   Work out how many bottles can be filled from the mixture.

**7** A bottle of vinegar contains 75 centilitres. How many millilitres is that?

**8** The prefix deci- means $\frac{1}{10}$

A decilitre is $\frac{1}{10}$ litre.

   **a** How many decilitres are there in 1 litre?

   **b** A bottle has 8 decilitres written on the label. What is this in litres?

   **c** How many millilitres does the bottle contain?

**9** The prefix mega- means $10^6$ or 1 million.

   **a** How many metres are there in a megametre?

   **b** How many kilometres are there in a megametre?

> Use your answer to part **a** and convert that into kilometres.

**10** Convert into the given unit:

   **a** 3 km into cm

   **b** 5.8 km into mm

> Convert the kilometres into metres first.

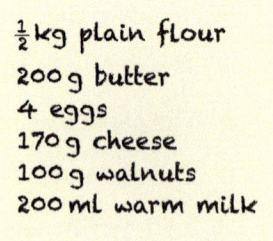

# 7 Length, mass and capacity

## 7.2 Area and volume

### Units of area

The units used for measuring area are based on the metric units of length.

**Square millimetres (mm²)** are used for **very small areas**.

For example, the area of a coin would be measured in mm².

**Square centimetres (cm²)** are used for **fairly small areas**.

For example, the area of the cover of a book would be measured in cm².

**Square metres (m²)** are used for **fairly large areas**.

For example, the area of a garden would be measured in m².

**Square kilometres (km²)** are used for **very large areas**.

For example, the area of a country would be measured in km².

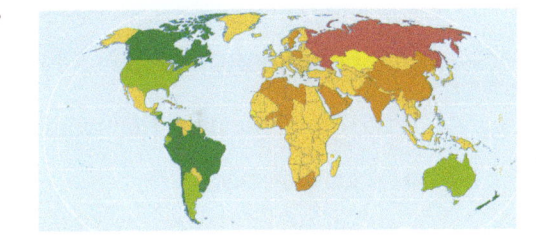

### Worked example 1

Isambard plans to tile a wall.

The wall is 4.2 m long and 2.4 m high.

The tiles are 30 cm wide and 40 cm high.

  a  How many tiles will fit along the wall?
  b  How many rows of tiles will fit up the wall?
  c  How many tiles does Isambard need altogether?
  d  What is the area of one tile in cm²?
  e  What is the area of the wall in cm²?
  f  Check your answer to part **c** by division.

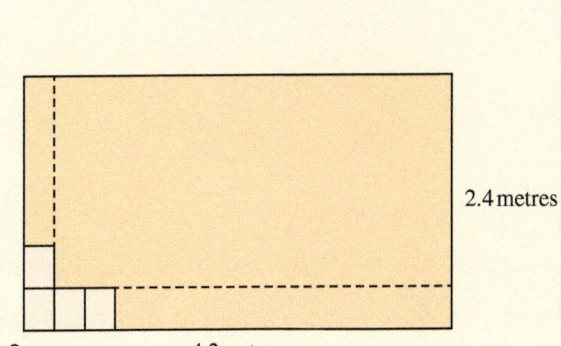

95

**a** $420 \div 30 = 14$                              Convert 4.2 m into 420 cm.

14 tiles will fit along the wall.

**b** $240 \div 40 = 6$                                Convert 2.4 m into 240 cm.

6 rows of tiles will fit up the wall.

**c** $14 \times 6 = 84$                                  6 rows of 14 tiles.

Isambard needs 84 tiles for the wall.

**d** Area of one tile = $40 \times 30 = 1200 \, cm^2$        Area of rectangle = length × width

**e** Area of the wall = $420 \times 240 = 100\,800 \, cm^2$

**f** $100\,800 \div 1200 = 84$

This agrees with the answer from part **c**.

> Note that this method of checking only works when no tiles have been cut to fit around the edge.

## Units of volume

The units used for measuring volume are also based on the metric units of length.

**Very small volumes** are measured in **cubic millimetres (mm³)**.

**Fairly small volumes** are measured in **cubic centimetres (cm³)**.

**Large volumes** are measured in **cubic metres (m³)**.

**Very large volumes** are measured in **cubic kilometres (km³)**.

### Worked example 2

Write down the units that would be used to measure these volumes.

**a** A garden shed          **b** A suitcase          **c** A dice

**a** The sides and height of a shed are measured in m so the volume is measured in m³.

**b** The suitcase would be measured in cm so the volume would be measured in cm³.

**c** The dice would be measured in mm so the volume would be measured in mm³.

# 7 Length, mass and capacity

## Worked example 3

a Which of these cuboids has the larger volume?

b Work out the difference in the volumes.

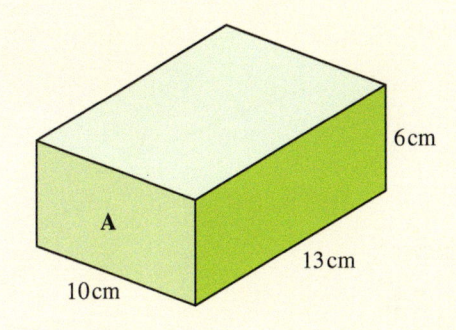

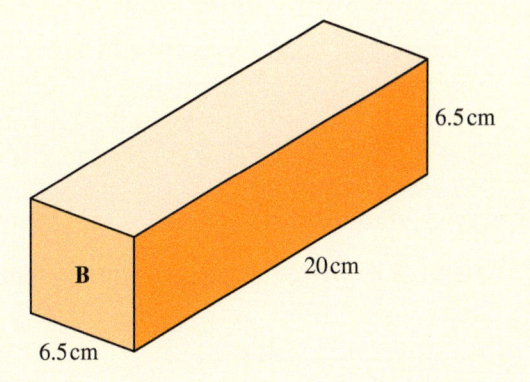

a Cuboid A has volume 10 × 13 × 6 = 780 cm³.

Cuboid B has volume 6.5 × 20 × 6.5 = 845 cm³.

Cuboid B has the larger volume.

b The difference is 845 − 780 = 65 cm³.

> In your Stage 7 Student Book you learnt that the volume of a cuboid = length × width × height

## Exercise 7.2

1 Write down the units you would use to measure the following areas.

  a The area of a football pitch

  b The area of a postcard

  c The area of the Atlantic Ocean

  d The area of a postage stamp

2 Write down the units you would use to measure the following volumes.

  a The volume of a box of breakfast cereal 

  b The volume of the Moon 

  c The volume of a storage container

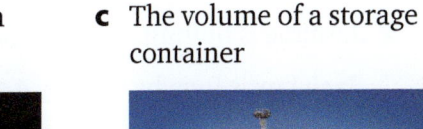

97

**3 a** Write down the units you would use to measure the volume of this prism.

**b** Write down the units you would use to measure the total length of the edges of the prism.

**c** Write down the units you would use to measure the surface area of the prism.

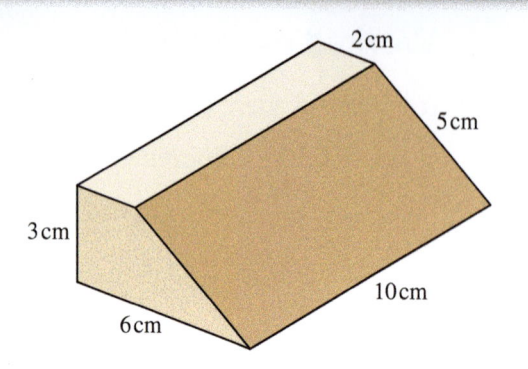

**4** For each of these shapes, find:   **i** the area   **ii** the perimeter.

Remember to write the correct units for each answer.

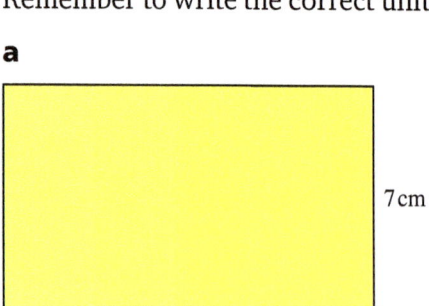

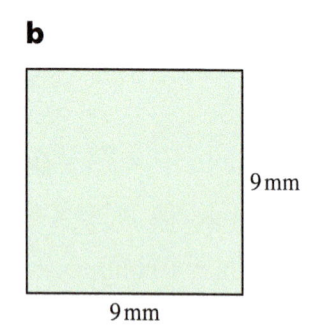

**a**

7 cm
12 cm

**b**

9 mm
9 mm

**5** A tin of paint will cover 12 m².

Hugo wants to paint a garden wall that measures 23.5 m by 1.8 m.

**a** Work out the area of the wall in m².

**b** How many tins of paint does Hugo need to buy?

**6** Suzette has a bag containing 1500 cm³ of bird seed.

She plans to put it into small boxes measuring 6 cm by 4 cm by 2 cm.

**a** Work out the volume of one box.

**b** How many boxes can Suzette fill from the bag of seed?

**c** How much seed will be left over?

**7** Jasmine is putting small boxes into a large container.

Each box is 9 cm by 6 cm by 4 cm.

The container is 45 cm by 30 cm by 36 cm.

**a** How many boxes will fit along the container?

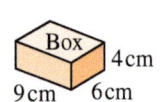

**b** How many boxes will fit across the container?

**c** How many layers of boxes will fit in the container?

**d** How many boxes will Jasmine fit in the container?

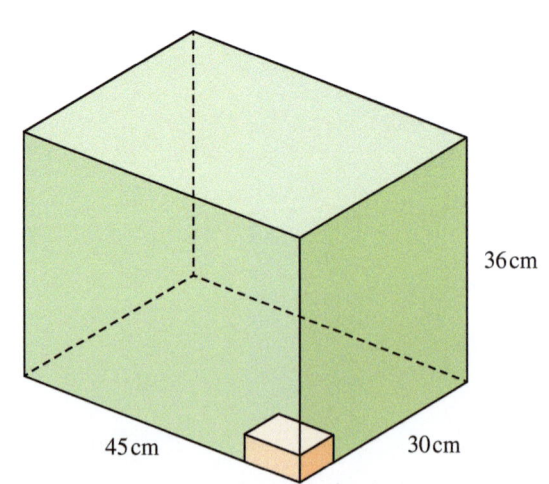

e What is the volume of one small box?

f What is the volume of the large container?

g Check your answer to part **d** by division.

8 This is a sketch plan of a forest.

It is made up of two large rectangular areas.

a Work out the total area of the forest in m².

b The hectare is a unit that is used for large areas.

1 hectare = 10 000 m²

Find the area of the forest in hectares.

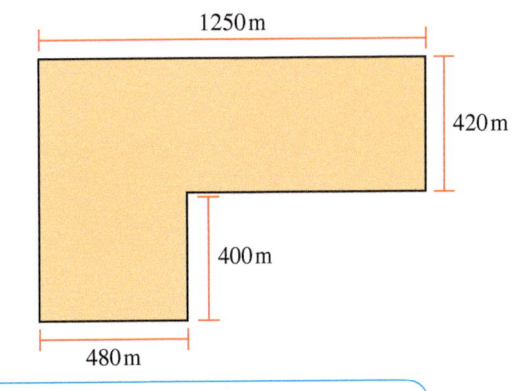

*You need to divide your answer to part **a** by 10 000 to find the number of hectares.*

## 7.3 Non-metric units

The metric system of measures is used in many countries.

Some countries still use older, non-metric units for some measurements.

In the UK, many people still use the older imperial units.

These include:

- pounds and ounces for measuring mass
- pints and gallons for measuring capacity
- inches, feet, yards and miles for measuring distances.

The measurements used in the USA, known as the United States customary units, are very similar to the British imperial units although there are a few differences.

### Miles and kilometres

You need to know the relationship between miles and kilometres.

The approximate equivalence is:    **5 miles = 8 kilometres**

The rule for converting miles into kilometres is $\div 5 \times 8$ or $\times \frac{8}{5}$

The rule for converting kilometres into miles is $\div 8 \times 5$ or $\times \frac{5}{8}$

### Worked example 1

a The distance between London and Birmingham is about 120 miles.

Convert this into kilometres.

b The distance between Paris and Rome is about 1100 km.

How many miles is this?

**a** The rule for converting miles into kilometres is ÷5 × 8 or × $\frac{8}{5}$

$120 ÷ 5 = 24$

$24 × 8 = 192$

The distance from London to Birmingham is about 190 km.

**b** The rule for converting kilometres into miles is ÷8 × 5 or × $\frac{5}{8}$

$1100 ÷ 8 = 137.5$

$137.5 × 5 = 687.5$

The distance from Paris to Rome is about 690 miles.

> You are using a rough conversion, so round the answer to 1 or 2 significant figures.

## Worked example 2

Marcus wants to buy a new petrol cap for his motorbike.

He is looking for one with a diameter of about 63 mm.

He finds one on the internet.

It has a diameter of $2\frac{1}{2}$ inches.

Marcus knows that 1 inch is approximately 2.54 cm.

Will the petrol cap fit his motorbike?

$1 \text{ inch} = 2.54 \text{ cm}$

$2.5 \text{ inches} = 2.5 × 2.54 \text{ cm}$

$= 6.35 \text{ cm}$

Use 2.5 instead of $2\frac{1}{2}$ on your calculator.

The diameter is 63.5 mm.

This is about 63 mm so it will fit his motorbike.

## Exercise 7.3

**1** Which is longer, a mile or a kilometre?

**2** Convert each of these distances into kilometres. If necessary, give your answer to the nearest whole number.

   **a** 5 miles    **b** 15 miles    **c** 40 miles    **d** 100 miles    **e** 25 miles

   **f** 250 miles    **g** 127 miles    **h** 437 miles    **i** 83 miles    **j** 236 miles.

**3** Convert each of these distances into miles. Give your answers to the nearest 10.

   **a** 48 km    **b** 144 km    **c** 200 km    **d** 135 km    **e** 59 km

   **f** 258 km    **g** 360 km    **h** 400 km    **i** 500 km    **j** 365 km

**4** The distance between Sydney and Melbourne is about 440 miles.

   How far is this in kilometres?

## 7 Length, mass and capacity

**5** The Taj Mahal is about 206 km from Delhi.

How far is this in miles?

**6** Shakara has enough fuel in her car to travel 350 km.

A road sign tells her that she has 200 miles still to go.

Work out whether she has enough fuel to get to her destination.

Show your working.

**7** Jon needs 174 cm of ribbon for a decoration he is making.

He finds a shop that sells ribbon in the lengths shown on the price list.

**a** 1 foot is approximately 30 cm.

Which length of ribbon does Jon need to buy?

**b** How many centimetres of ribbon will Jon have left over?

**Ribbon**
1 foot for 99 cents
2 feet for $1.80
4 feet for $3.50
6 feet for $5.00
8 feet for $6.40

**8** Angela is driving her car.

Her speedometer works in miles per hour.

The road signs are in kilometres per hour.

**a** Angela sees this sign on the road.

How fast can she go in miles per hour?

**50**

The rule for converting miles per hour to kilometres per hour is the same as converting miles to kilometres.

**b** Work out the equivalent speed in miles per hour for these signs.

**i** 70   **ii** 110   **iii** 130

**9** Amiira, Hassan, Shaliya and Faisal are on holiday in the USA.

They get into a hotel lift and see this sign.

Amiira weighs 55 kg, Hassan weighs 69 kg, Shaliya weighs 58 kg and Faisal weighs 72 kg.

They know that 1 kilogram is roughly equal to 2.2 pounds.

**a** Convert each of these figures into pounds.

**b** Find their total weight in pounds.

**c** Can they safely take the lift together?

**Maximum weight 600 pounds**

Round your answers to the nearest whole number before adding them together to find the total mass.

101

## Review

**1** The picture shows a grown man standing next to a double-decker bus.

  **a** Estimate the height of the man.

  **b** Estimate the height of the bus.

  **c** Estimate the length of the bus.

**2** Convert these measurements into the given units.

  **a** 5 m into cm     **b** 1.2 kg into g     **c** 3600 ml into l     **d** 4.5 cm into mm

  **e** 2 m into mm    **f** 65 mm into cm    **g** 8700 g into kg    **h** 10 000 mm into m

  **i** 3.6 l into ml    **j** 52 cm into m

**3** An athlete runs 12 times around a track.

  The track is 400 metres long.

  How many kilometres does he run?

**4** A large coffee jug holds 2.5 litres of coffee.

  It is to be poured into small cups that each hold 120 ml.

  How many cups can be filled from the jug?

**5** Here is a recipe for chocolate biscuits.

  Samarah wants to make 150 biscuits for a charity picnic.

  **a** Work out the quantities she will need of each item.

  **b** What is the total mass of her ingredients?
  Give your answer in kilograms.

  > 200 g plain flour
  > 85 g sugar
  > 175 g butter
  > 100 g chocolate chips
  > 30 g cocoa powder
  >
  > This makes 25 biscuits.

**6** Work out the area and the perimeter of this shape.

  Write the units of your answer.

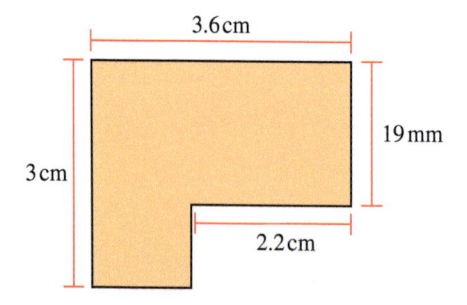

  3.6 cm, 19 mm, 3 cm, 2.2 cm

102

**7** A theatre group has 16 stage blocks that need to be painted.

Each block is 1.2 m square and 25 cm high.

Each block has four sides and a top, but the base is open.

  **a** Work out the surface area of one block **in m²**.

  **b** Find the total surface area of all 16 blocks.

  **c** Paint comes in 1 litre tins.

    1 litre of paint covers 12 m².

    Work out how many tins of paint the group needs to buy.

**8** Laura has a fish tank that she empties every week.

The tank is 15 cm by 36 cm by 20 cm.

  **a** Work out the volume of the tank in cm³.

  **b** 1 litre is equivalent to 1000 cm³.

    Write down how many litres Laura needs to completely fill the tank.

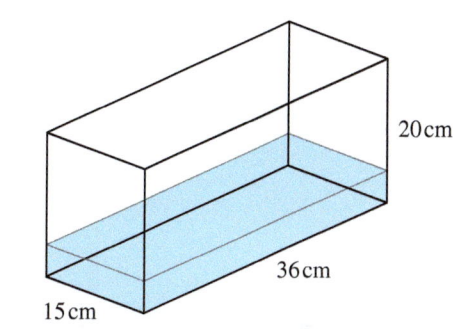

**9** Kurt wants to buy enough sand to fill this box.

The box is 125 cm by 150 cm by 30 cm.

  **a** Work out the volume of the box in cm³.

  **b** A sack of sand contains 12 500 cm³.

    How many sacks of sand does Andy need?

  **c** Each sack has a mass of 16 kg.

    Find the total mass of the sand in tonnes.

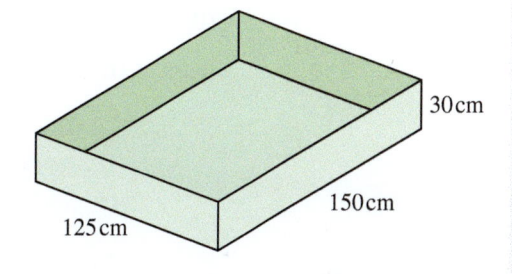

**10** The distance between Bideford and Barnstaple is about 10 miles. How far is it in kilometres?

**11** The chart shows the number of kilometres between each of five towns.

| Framston | | | | |
|---|---|---|---|---|
| 85 | Kelstall | | | |
| 47 | 72 | Alpston | | |
| 88 | 165 | 90 | Corston | |
| 56 | 106 | 28 | 64 | Bidstoke |

To find the distance between two towns find the number that is below one and across from the other.

For example, 165 is below Kelstall and to the left of Corston.

The distance from Kelstall to Corston is 165 kilometres.

**a** What is the distance, in kilometres, between Corston and Framston?

**b** Kelstall to Alpston is 72 kilometres. Convert this into miles.

**c** How many miles are there between Framston and Bidstoke?

**d** Copy this outline table.

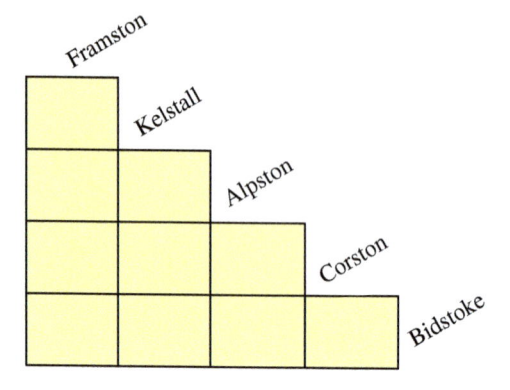

Convert each distance into miles and complete the new chart to show the number of miles between each town.

Round your distances to the nearest whole number.

# 8 Equations

> **Learning outcomes**
> 
> - Construct and solve linear equations with integer coefficients.

## Building bridges

Engineers and architects need to use equations when designing bridges.

If they do not get their equations correct, the bridge may collapse in strong winds or during an earthquake.

The Vasco da Gama Bridge in Portugal has been designed to stand up to wind speeds of 250 km/h and earthquakes 4.5 times stronger than the Great Lisbon Earthquake of 1755.

## 8.1 Solving equations using flow diagrams

An **equation** is a mathematical statement that says that two expressions (which involve just one unknown) are equal.

The equation $2x + 5 = 19$ means that if you start with the number $x$, **multiply by 2** and then **add 5** you obtain the number 19. This is shown on a flow diagram (or function machine – you will learn more about functions in chapter 16) as:

$$x \longrightarrow \boxed{\times 2} \longrightarrow \boxed{+5} \longrightarrow 19$$

To **solve** the equation you must undo these steps to find the value of $x$.

The opposite of **multiply by 2** is **divide by 2** and the opposite of **add 5** is **subtract 5**.

$$7 \longleftarrow \boxed{\div 2} \overset{14}{\longleftarrow} \boxed{-5} \longleftarrow 19$$

The steps must be done in reverse:

So the answer to the equation $2x + 5 = 19$ is $x = 7$

It is always sensible to check if your answer is correct by substituting your answer back into the original equation: $2 \times 7 + 5 = 14 + 5 = 19$ ✓

# Mathematics for Cambridge Secondary 1

## Worked example 1

Use a flow diagram to solve the equation $4x - 3 = 41$

Flow diagram for the equation:

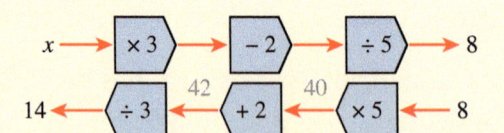

$x \to \boxed{\times 4} \to \boxed{-3} \to 41$

Reverse flow diagram:

$11 \leftarrow \boxed{\div 4} \leftarrow 44 \leftarrow \boxed{+3} \leftarrow 41$

The answer is $x = 11$

Check: $4 \times 11 - 3 = 44 - 3 = 41$ ✓

## Worked example 2

Use a flow diagram to solve the equation $\dfrac{3x - 2}{5} = 8$

Flow diagram for the equation:

$x \to \boxed{\times 3} \to \boxed{-2} \to \boxed{\div 5} \to 8$

Reverse flow diagram:

$14 \leftarrow \boxed{\div 3} \leftarrow 42 \leftarrow \boxed{+2} \leftarrow 40 \leftarrow \boxed{\times 5} \leftarrow 8$

The answer is $x = 14$

Check: $\dfrac{3 \times 14 - 2}{5} = \dfrac{42 - 2}{5} = \dfrac{40}{5} = 8$ ✓

## Exercise 8.1

**1** Copy and complete the flow diagrams to solve each of these equations.

  **a** $5x + 1 = 36$

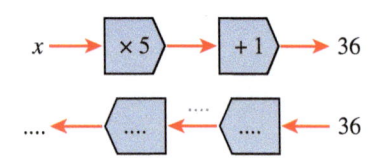

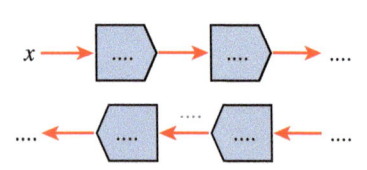

  **b** $3x - 8 = 28$

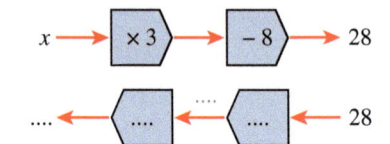

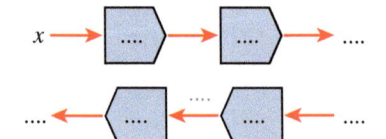

  **c** $4x + 12 = 72$

  **d** $\dfrac{x - 5}{3} = 18$

**2** Use flow diagrams to solve these equations.

  **a** $5x + 4 = 39$   **b** $7x - 3 = 39$   **c** $2x - 8 = 1$   **d** $4x + 6 = 42$

  **e** $3x - 2 = 7$   **f** $65 = 3x - 4$   **g** $4x + 23 = 7$   **h** $2x + 15 = 10$

  **i** $2x - 9 = -15$   **j** $5x + 3 = -7$   **k** $-8 = 7x + 13$   **l** $8 + 3x = -19$

**3** Use flow diagrams to solve these equations.

  **a** $\dfrac{x + 6}{4} = 15$   **b** $\dfrac{x - 5}{4} = 28$   **c** $\dfrac{x}{6} + 2 = 12$   **d** $\dfrac{x}{7} - 5 = 8$

  **e** $\dfrac{x - 8}{3} = -4$   **f** $\dfrac{32 + x}{3} = 2$   **g** $-8 = \dfrac{x}{3} + 5$   **h** $6 + \dfrac{x}{2} = 4$

# 8 Equations

**4** Copy and complete the flow diagram to solve the equation $\frac{5x + 3}{4} = 7$

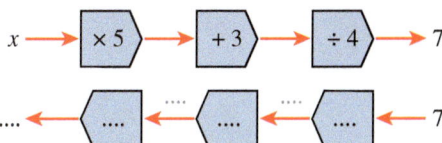

$x \rightarrow \boxed{\times 5} \rightarrow \boxed{+3} \rightarrow \boxed{\div 4} \rightarrow 7$

$\ldots \leftarrow \boxed{\ldots} \leftarrow \boxed{\ldots} \leftarrow \boxed{\ldots} \leftarrow 7$

**5** Use flow diagrams to solve these equations.

a $\frac{2x - 6}{4} = 3$  b $\frac{3x + 1}{2} = 11$  c $\frac{7x - 5}{3} = 24$  d $\frac{8x - 3}{5} = 9$

e $\frac{2x - 6}{3} = -4$  f $\frac{3x + 1}{4} = -5$  g $\frac{2x + 15}{3} = 4$  h $\frac{3x + 7}{2} = -8$

**6** Use flow diagrams to solve these equations.

a $\frac{5x - 4}{3} + 2 = 14$  b $\frac{5x + 8}{2} - 6 = 13$  c $8 + \frac{4 + 2x}{5} = 24$

## 8.2 Solving equations with the unknown on one side

Flow diagrams cannot be used to solve all equations, for example, equations where there is more than one term involving $x$.

Examples of these types of equations are:

$3(x + 5) - x = 49$    $2(x - 3) + 5(x + 4) = 28$    $3x = x + 26$    $4(2x + 1) = 6(x + 3)$

To solve equations such as these, you must use the balance method that you learnt in your Stage 7 Student Book.

When using the balance method you must remember the following rules:

- You can add the same number to both sides.
- You can subtract the same number from both sides.
- You can multiply both sides by the same number.
- You can divide both sides by the same number.

Remember: Do the same thing to both sides.

If an equation contains brackets, you must expand the brackets first.

To solve the equation     $2x + 8 = 17$        Subtract 8 from both sides.

$2x + 8 - 8 = 17 - 8$

$2x = 9$         Divide both sides by 2.

$x = \frac{9}{2}$         Change $\frac{9}{2}$ to a mixed number.

$x = 4\frac{1}{2}$

This can be set out more simply as follows:

$2x + 8 = 17$

$-8 \qquad\qquad -8$

$2x = 9$

$\div 2 \qquad\qquad \div 2$

$x = \frac{9}{2}$

$x = 4\frac{1}{2}$

107

## Worked example 1

Solve the equation $3x - 7 = 4$

$$3x - 7 = 4$$
$$3x = 11$$
$$x = \frac{11}{3}$$
$$x = 3\frac{2}{3}$$

(+7 to both sides; ÷3 to both sides)

Change $\frac{11}{3}$ to a mixed number.

Check: $3 \times 3\frac{2}{3} - 7 = 11 - 7 = 4$ ✓

## Worked example 2

Solve the equation $\frac{5x-2}{4} = 12$

$$\frac{5x-2}{4} = 12$$
$$5x - 2 = 48$$
$$5x = 50$$
$$x = 10$$

(×4 to both sides; +2 to both sides; ÷5 to both sides)

Check: $(5 \times 10 - 2) \div 4 = 48 \div 4 = 12$ ✓

## Exercise 8.2

In this exercise, you must use the balance method to solve the equations.

**1** Solve these equations.

- **a** $2x + 3 = 7$
- **b** $7x - 3 = 32$
- **c** $4x - 5 = 7$
- **d** $5x + 9 = 4$
- **e** $3x - 5 = -11$
- **f** $2x - 6 = 13$
- **g** $3x + 4 = 9$
- **h** $4x + 7 = 14$
- **i** $30 - 4x = 12$
- **j** $15 - 2x = 7$
- **k** $24 - 3x = 9$
- **l** $27 - 6x = 33$

**2** The diagram shows three rods.

Find the value of $x$.

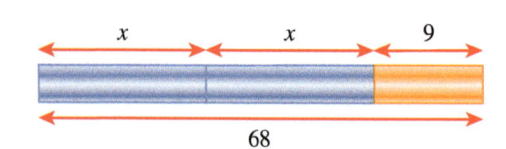

(Diagram: two rods of length $x$ and one of length 9, totalling 68)

**3** $5x - \blacksquare = 31$

The answer to the equation is $x = 7$

What is the number under the ink stain?

**4** Solve these equations.

   **a** $3(2x - 4) = 24$    **b** $2(5x + 3) = 96$    **c** $4(2x - 7) = 36$    **d** $2(2x + 9) = 10$

**5** Work out the value of $x$ for each of these squares.

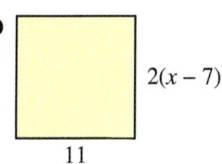

   **a** square with $3x + 8$ and $29$

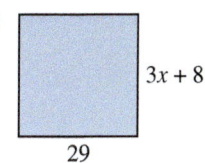

   **b** square with $2(x - 7)$ and $11$

   **c** square with $9 - 3x$ and $21$

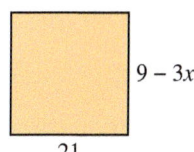

**6** Work out the values of $x$ and $y$ for each of these rectangles.

   **a** rectangle with sides $5x + 4$, $3y + 2$, $14$, $34$

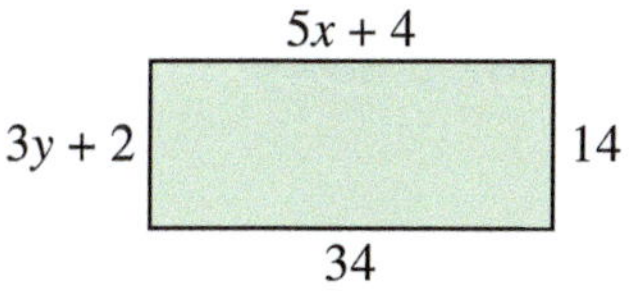

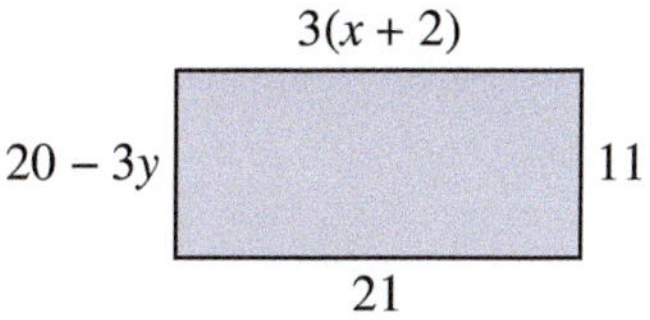

   **b** rectangle with sides $3(x + 2)$, $20 - 3y$, $11$, $21$

   **c** rectangle with sides $6 + 2x$, $9$, $2(y - 4)$, $15$

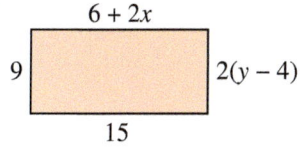

**7** Work out the value of $x$ for each of these shapes.

   **a** trapezium with $4x - 5$ and $13$

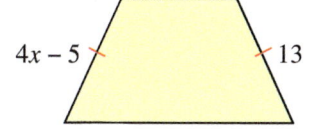

   **b** triangle with $2(x + 3)$ and $38$

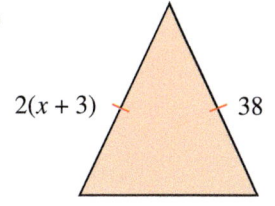

**8** Work out the values of $x$ and $y$ for this kite.

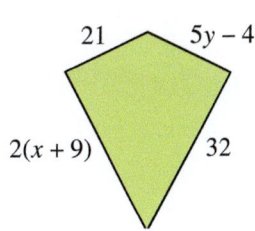

   kite with sides $21$, $5y - 4$, $2(x + 9)$, $32$

**9** Solve these equations.

   **a** $\dfrac{x}{4} + 3 = 6$    **b** $\dfrac{x}{2} - 8 = 2$    **c** $\dfrac{x}{6} - 1 = 3$    **d** $\dfrac{x}{3} + 2 = -4$

   **e** $\dfrac{x + 2}{5} = 2$    **f** $\dfrac{x - 4}{3} = 7$    **g** $\dfrac{2x - 1}{4} = 4$    **h** $\dfrac{3x + 5}{2} = 10$

**10** Solve these equations.

   **a** $2(x + 4) + 3(x + 2) = 34$    **b** $4(x + 5) + 2(x - 1) = 60$

   **c** $3(x - 2) + 4(x + 7) = 57$    **d** $2(3x - 2) + 2(2x + 7) = 30$

   **e** $3(x + 6) - 2(x + 1) = 22$    **f** $5(x - 2) - 4(x - 3) = 6$

   **g** $4(x + 3) - 2(x + 5) = 6$    **h** $3(2x + 5) - 2(x - 5) = 51$

   **i** $3(3x - 2) - 7(x - 2) = 20$    **j** $6(2x - 5) - 4(x - 2) = 14$

## 8.3 Solving equations with the unknown on both sides

Some equations have the unknown letter on both sides of the equation.

You must collect all the terms containing the letter on one side of the equation.

You must collect the numbers on the other side of the equation.

Remember if an equation contains brackets, you must expand the brackets first.

### Worked example 1

Solve the equation $3x + 1 = x + 9$

$$3x + 1 = x + 9$$
$-x \qquad\qquad -x$
$$2x + 1 = 9$$
$-1 \qquad\qquad -1$
$$2x = 8$$
$\div 2 \qquad\qquad \div 2$
$$x = 4$$

Remember to check your answer.

### Worked example 2

Solve the equation $3(3x - 1) = 7(x + 4)$

$$3(3x - 1) = 7(x + 4)$$  Expand the brackets.
$$9x - 3 = 7x + 28$$
$-7x \qquad\qquad -7x$
$$2x - 3 = 28$$
$+3 \qquad\qquad +3$
$$2x = 31$$
$\div 2 \qquad\qquad \div 2$
$$x = \frac{31}{2}$$
$$x = 15\tfrac{1}{2}$$

Remember to check your answer.

### Exercise 8.3

In this exercise, you must use the balance method to solve the equations.

**1** Solve these equations.

a  $5x = 4x + 12$
b  $7x = 5x + 2$
c  $3x = x + 8$
d  $4x = 2x - 10$
e  $6x + 2 = 5x + 8$
f  $7x - 3 = 6x + 4$
g  $5x - 8 = 4x + 3$
h  $9x + 6 = 8x - 2$
i  $4x - 3 = 2x + 5$
j  $9x + 7 = 7x + 13$
k  $5x - 6 = 2x + 9$
l  $6x - 1 = 4x - 13$

**2** $7x - 3 = 5x + \blacksquare$

The answer to the equation is $x = 6$

What is the number under the ink stain?

**3** Expression A is 12 more than expression B.

Find the value of $x$.

| A | $5x + 4$ |
|---|---|

| B | $3x - 4$ |
|---|---|

**4** Solve these equations.

**a** $4(x + 2) = 3x + 11$
**b** $3(x - 5) = x - 7$
**c** $5(2x + 3) = 3(3x + 8)$
**d** $10x + 2 = 6(x + 5)$
**e** $10 + x = 5(x - 2)$
**f** $2 + 3(x + 2) = 18 - 2x$
**g** $4(3x - 1) + 6 = 5(2x + 4)$

**5** Explain why there are no answers to the equation $3(4x + 3) = 6(2x + 5)$

**6** Explain why there are an infinite number of answers to the equation $4(5x + 3) = 2(10x + 6)$

**7** Solve these equations.

**a** $3 - 2x = 8 - x$
**b** $10 - 3x = 5 + 2x$
**c** $6 - 7x = 3 - 5x$
**d** $5 - 2x = 40 - 7x$
**e** $2 - 4x = 25 - 6x$
**f** $2(7 - 3x) = 19 - x$

## 8.4 Using equations to solve problems

You can use equations to solve many real life problems.

You must read the problem carefully and then **construct** (write) an equation to help you solve the problem.

### Worked example

**a** Find the value of $x$.

**b** Write down the size of each of the three angles.

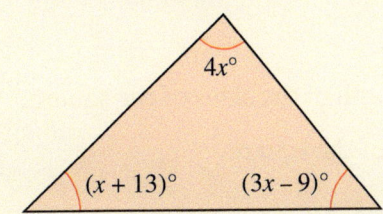

Triangle with angles $4x°$, $(x + 13)°$, $(3x - 9)°$.

111

**a** The three angles of a triangle add up to 180°.

$$x + 13 + 3x - 9 + 4x = 180 \qquad \text{Collect like terms.}$$
$$8x + 4 = 180$$
$$-4 \qquad\qquad -4$$
$$8x = 176$$
$$\div 8 \qquad\qquad \div 8$$
$$x = 22$$

**b** $x + 13 = 22 + 13 = 35 \qquad 3x - 9 = 3 \times 22 - 9 = 66 - 9 = 57 \qquad 4x = 4 \times 22 = 88$

The three angles are 35°, 57° and 88°.

## Exercise 8.4

In this exercise, you must first construct an equation to represent the problem.

You must then solve the equation using the balance method.

**1** Paul thinks of a number.

He multiplies the number by 2 and then adds 4.

His answer is 17.

What was the number that Paul thought of?

**2** A rectangle has perimeter 54 cm.

The length of the rectangle is 8.5 cm.

Find the width of the rectangle.

**3** Zara thinks of a number.

She subtracts 4 from the number and then multiplies by 5.

Her answer is the same as multiplying the number by 3 and then adding 2.

What was the number that Zara thought of?

**4** The sum of two consecutive odd numbers is 172.

What are the two numbers?

> Let the two consecutive odd number be $x$ and $x + 2$

**5** The sum of three consecutive even numbers is 774.

What are the three numbers?

**6** The diagram shows a square.

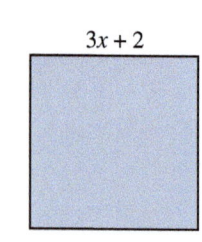

The perimeter of the square is 92 cm.

  **a** Find the value of $x$.

  **b** Write down the length of the sides of the square.

  **c** Work out the area of the square.

$3x + 2$

**7** *AB* is a straight line.

   **a** Find the value of *x*.

   **b** Write down the size of each of the three angles.

   > Angles on a straight line add up to 180°.

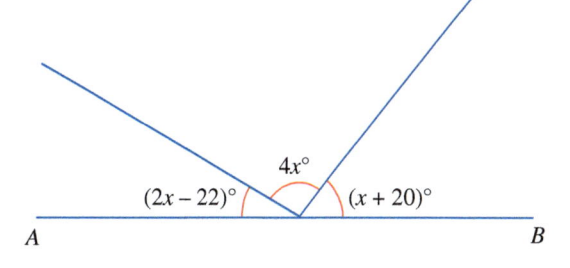

**8** The diagram shows a quadrilateral.

   **a** Find the value of *x*.

   **b** Write down the size of each of the four angles in the quadrilateral.

   > Angles in a quadrilateral add up to 360°.

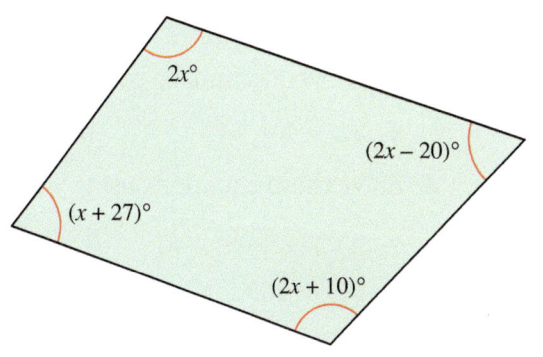

**9** The diagram shows a parallelogram.

   **a** Find the value of *x*.

   **b** Write down the size of each angle in the parallelogram.

   > Opposite angles in a parallelogram are equal.

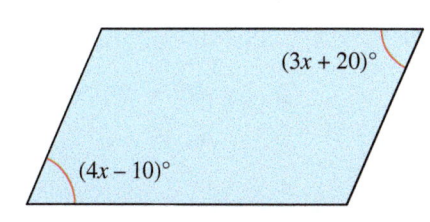

**10** A bag costs $23 more than a calculator.

   The total cost of a bag and a calculator is $54.

   Find the cost of a calculator.

**11** The two rectangles have the same area.

   Find the value of *x*.

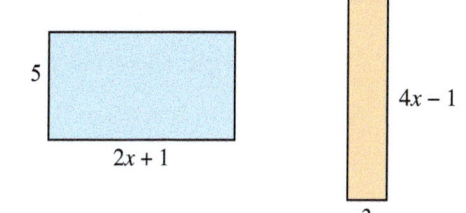

**12** A square has sides of length $(x + 2)$ cm.

   A rectangle has sides of length $(x + 3)$ cm and $(2x - 5)$ cm.

   The perimeter of the square is the same as the perimeter of the rectangle.

   Find the value of *x*.

**13** This is a number wall.

To find the numbers in each block you add the numbers in the two blocks below.

Find the value of $x$ in this wall.

Top: 46
Bottom row: $2x$, $x+4$, $x-7$

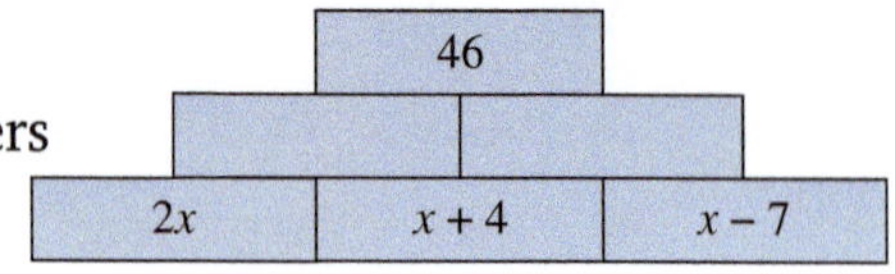

## Review

**1** Use flow diagrams to solve these equations.

   **a** $3x - 4 = 14$    **b** $\dfrac{x}{2} - 3 = 4$    **c** $\dfrac{x+4}{3} = 8$    **d** $\dfrac{2x-5}{7} = 4$

**2** Solve these equations using the balance method.

   **a** $6x - 3 = 9$    **b** $3(x + 5) = 36$    **c** $5(x - 2) - x = 26$

   **d** $\dfrac{x}{5} + 2 = 9$    **e** $\dfrac{x + 20}{3} = 4$    **f** $2 + 3(x + 5) = 11$

   **g** $2(x - 3) + 3(x - 2) = 13$    **h** $4(2x + 3) - 2(3x - 4) = 16$

**3** Solve these equations using the balance method.

   **a** $5x - 7 = 3x + 8$    **b** $4x - 6 = x + 9$    **c** $4(x - 3) = 2x + 2$

   **d** $3(x + 7) = 8x + 6$    **e** $5(x - 3) = 2(x + 6)$    **f** $25 - 4x = 3 - 2x$

**4** Sabeena thinks of a number.

   She adds 4 and then multiplies by 2.

   Her answer is the same as multiplying the number by 4 and then subtracting 10.

   What was the number Sabeena thought of?

**5** The perimeter of the rectangle is 58 cm.

   **a** Find the value of $x$.

   **b** Write down the length of the sides of the rectangle.

   **c** Work out the area of the rectangle.

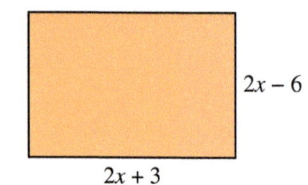

   Rectangle sides: $2x - 6$ and $2x + 3$

**6** Expression A is 40 more than expression B.

   Find the value of $x$.

   **A** $5x + 4$    **B** $3(x - 2)$

**7** This is a number wall.

   To find the numbers in each block you add the numbers in the two blocks below.

   Find the value of $x$ in this wall.

   Top: 62
   Bottom row: $x + 6$, $2x - 1$, $3x + 2$

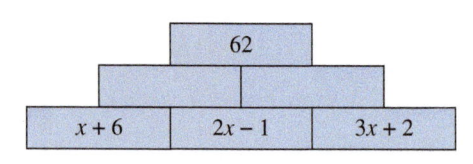

# 9 Shapes and geometric reasoning 2

> **Learning outcomes**
>
> - Use a straight edge and compasses to construct:
>   - the midpoint and perpendicular bisector of a line segment
>   - the bisector of an angle.
> - Use a ruler and compasses to construct:
>   - circles and arcs
>   - a triangle, given three sides (SSS)
>   - a triangle, given a right angle, hypotenuse and one side (RHS).
> - Interpret and make simple scale drawings.

## Making plans

Deniz wants to rearrange the furniture in his bedroom.

He decides that he needs a plan of the room.

A plan is a type of drawing that shows an area as if you are looking down on it from above.

Deniz asks a friend to help him measure the room.

He then makes a scale drawing to help him decide where to position his furniture.

He also has to measure all of the furniture to draw it on the plan.

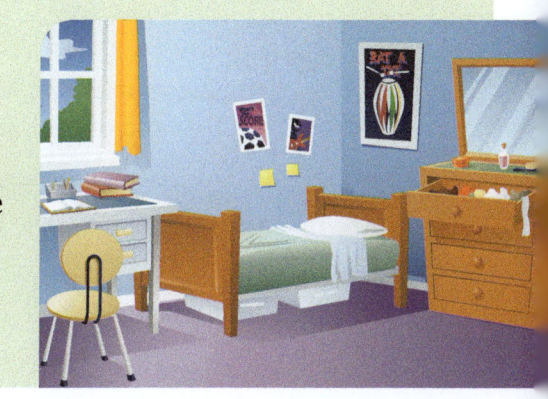

## 9.1 Constructions

### Perpendicular bisector of a line

Two lines that are at right angles are said to be **perpendicular**.

One line **bisects** another if it cuts it into two equal sections.

In the diagram, the line $AB$ is at right angles to $XY$.

It also passes through the midpoint of $XY$ so it cuts $XY$ in half.

$AB$ is the **perpendicular bisector** of $XY$.

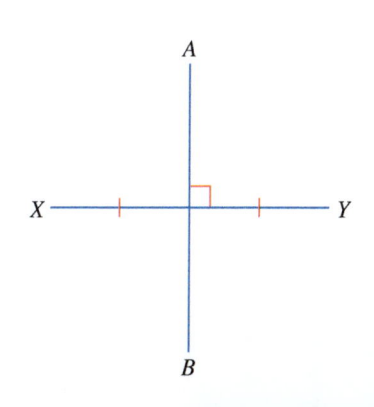

## Worked example 1

*PQ* is a line of length 9 cm.

Construct, using a straight edge and compasses only, the perpendicular bisector of *PQ*.

First draw a straight line 9 cm long and label it *PQ*.

Note that this is the only time you use your ruler to measure a length.

### Step 1

Use your compasses to draw two **arcs**, centred at one end of the line as shown here.

One arc should be above the line, the other below it.

The radius is not important as long as it is more than half the length of *PQ*.

These arcs are **construction lines**.

> When you are learning how to use compasses, you may find it easier to draw full circles or much longer arcs than those shown for your construction lines.

### Step 2

Without changing your compasses, draw two arcs with the centre at the other end of the line.

The arcs need to cross those you drew in Step 1.

If the first arc does not meet the second one, repeat the first arc making it slightly longer.

Your diagram should now look like this.

### Step 3

Use your straight edge to draw a line through the two points where the arcs **intersect** (cross).

This line is the perpendicular bisector of *PQ*.

Every point on the line is an equal distance from *P* and *Q*.

You can check with your ruler that it cuts at the midpoint of *PQ*.

You can check with your protractor that it is at right angles to *PQ*.

## Worked example 2

Using a straight edge and compasses, find the midpoint of the line *XY*. Label the point *M*.

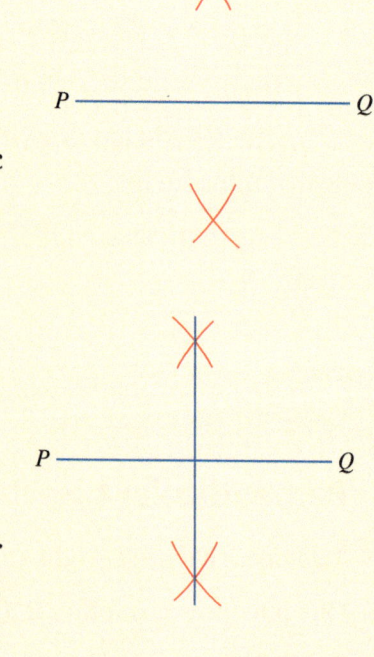

9 Shapes and geometric reasoning 2

Follow the first two steps as used in Worked example 1:

**Step 1** Draw arcs from one end of the line.

**Step 2** Draw arcs from the other end of the line.

This time, you do not need to draw the line between the arcs.

Instead, line up your straight edge with the two points where the arcs intersect and mark the point where it crosses the line *XY*.

Label the point *M*.

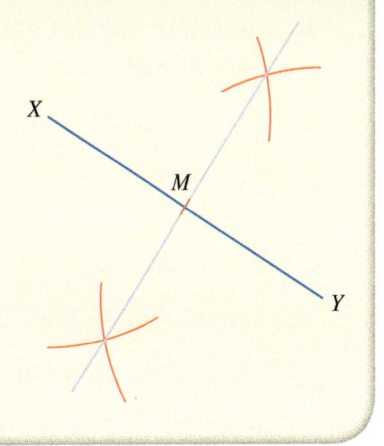

## Exercise 9.1a

For questions **1** to **5**, copy the lines on to plain paper. They do not have to be exactly the right length.

Construct the perpendicular bisector of each line.

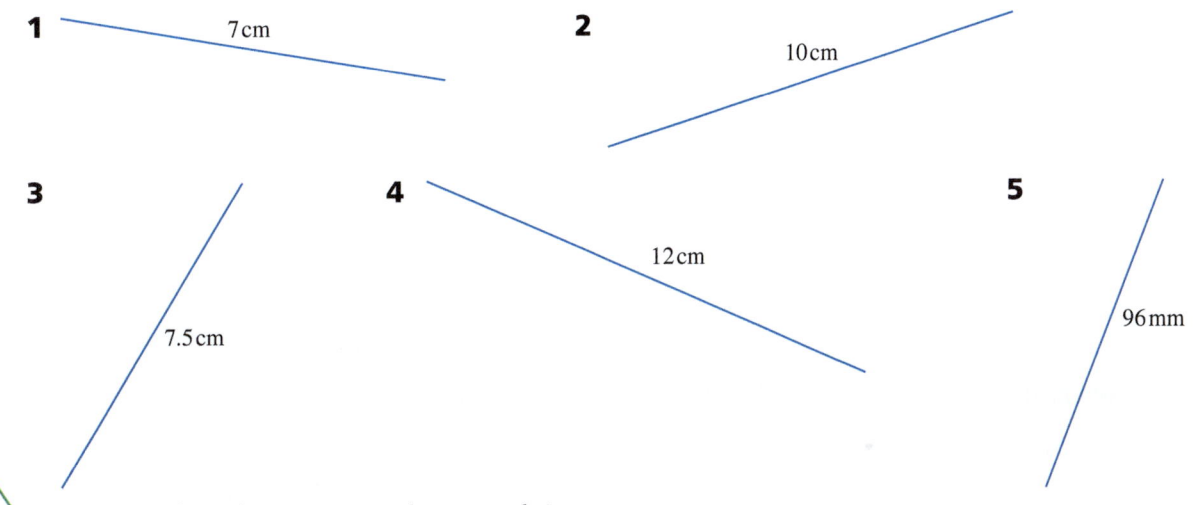

**1** 7 cm

**2** 10 cm

**3** 7.5 cm

**4** 12 cm

**5** 96 mm

**6 a** Copy these lines accurately on to plain paper.

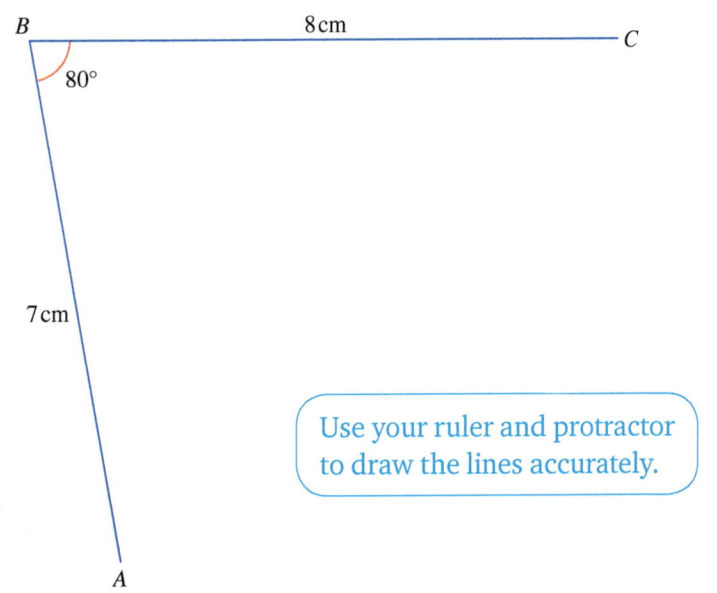

B — 8 cm — C
80°
7 cm
A

Use your ruler and protractor to draw the lines accurately.

**b** Carefully construct the perpendicular bisector of the line BC.

**c** Construct the perpendicular bisector of the line AB.

Mark the point where the perpendicular bisectors cross as X.

You should have a diagram that looks like this.

**d** Measure AX, BX and CX.

What do you notice about the answers?

**e** Use your compasses to draw a circle with centre at X passing through A, B and C.

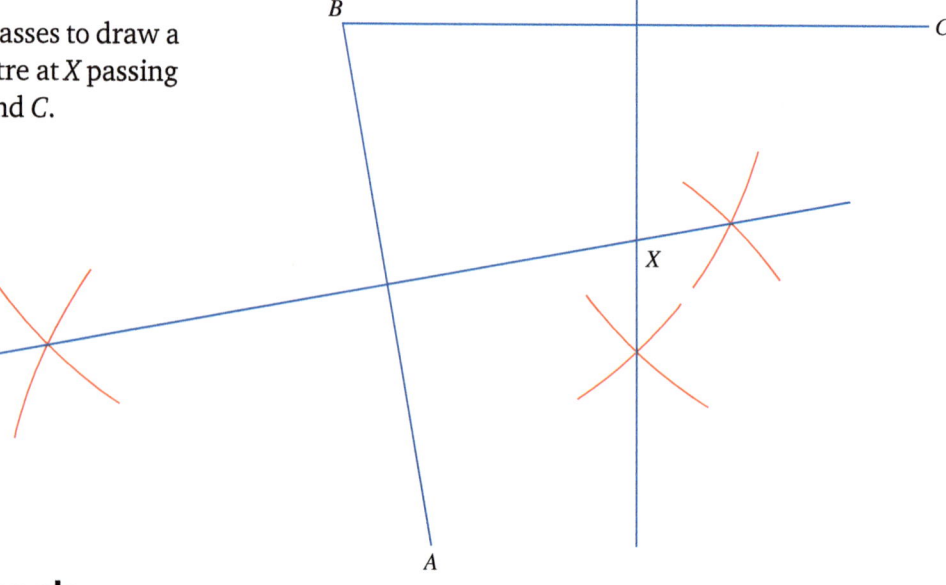

## Bisector of an angle

The bisector of an angle is the line that cuts the angle into two equal parts.

To draw an **angle bisector** you need a pair of compasses and a straight edge.

> Note that you do not use a protractor to draw an angle bisector.

### Worked example 3

Construct the bisector of the angle ABC.

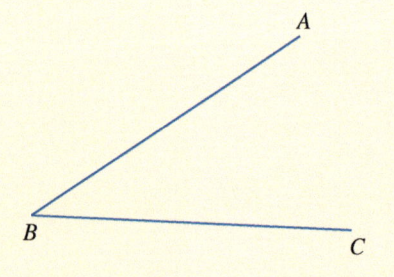

**Step 1**

Use your compasses, centred at the vertex B, to draw two small arcs equal distances along the lines BA and BC.

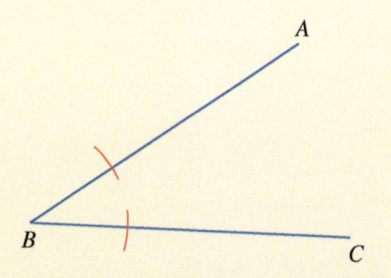

## 9 Shapes and geometric reasoning 2

### Step 2

Without changing the radius, put the point of your compasses on one of these intersections and draw an arc between *BA* and *BC*.

Repeat using the other intersection as the centre.

The two new arcs should cross as shown here.

### Step 3

Use your straight edge to draw a line from the vertex *B* through the point of intersection of the two arcs.

This line bisects the angle *ABC*.

You can check with your protractor that the two angles are equal.

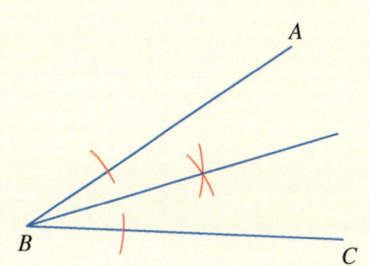

## Exercise 9.1b

For questions **1** to **6**, copy the angles on to plain paper. They do not have to be exactly the same size.

Construct the bisector of each angle.

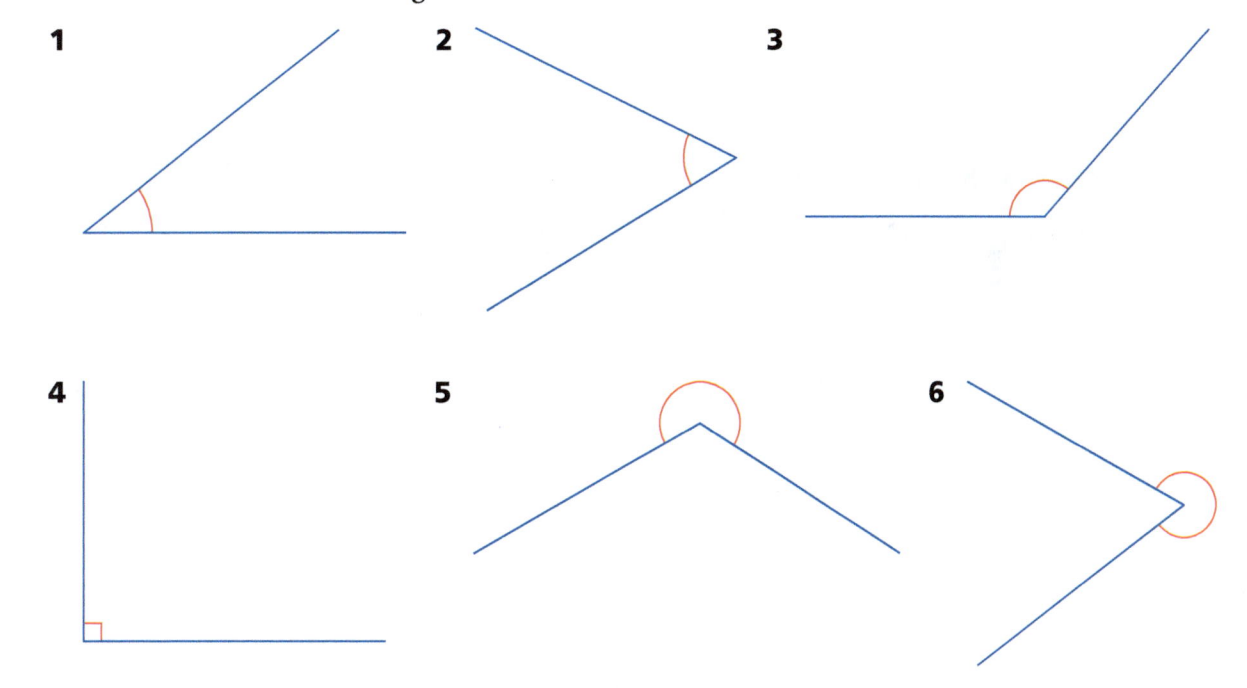

**1**

**2**

**3**

**4**

**5**

**6**

**7** Draw a triangle similar to the one on page 120. It does not need to be an exact copy.

   **a** Construct the bisector of angle *PQR*.

   **b** Construct the bisector of angle *QPR*.

   Mark the point where the bisectors intersect as *X*.

   > To bisect angle *PQR*, start by putting the point of your compasses on the point *Q*.

c Construct the bisector of angle QRP.

d What do you notice about the three angle bisectors?

e Draw a circle, centre X, that just touches side QR of the triangle.

What do you notice about this circle?

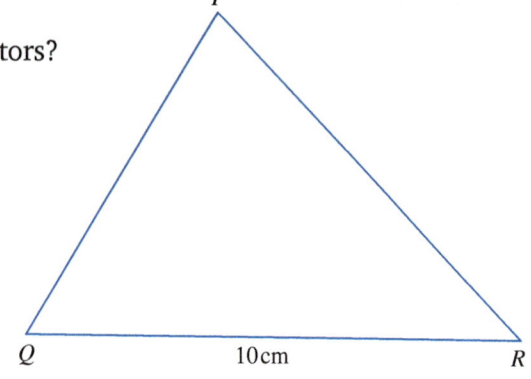

## 9.2 Triangles

### Constructing triangles

It is possible to construct a triangle if you know the length of the three sides.

To do this, you need to use a ruler and a pair of compasses.

This example shows the method to use.

> ### Worked example 1
>
> Construct a triangle with sides 8 cm, 7 cm and 6 cm.
>
> **Step 1**
>
> Draw a straight line 8 cm long.
>
> You need space above the line for the rest of the triangle.
>
> Note that you can start with any of the three sides, it does not need to be the longest side.
>
> **Step 2**
>
> Set your compasses at a radius of 7 cm.
>
> Using one end of the line as the centre, draw an arc as shown in this diagram.
>
> **Step 3**
>
> Set your compasses at a radius of 6 cm.
>
> Using the other end of the line as the centre, draw another arc to cross the first one.
>
> If they do not cross, you will need to go back and draw the arc with 7 cm radius longer.

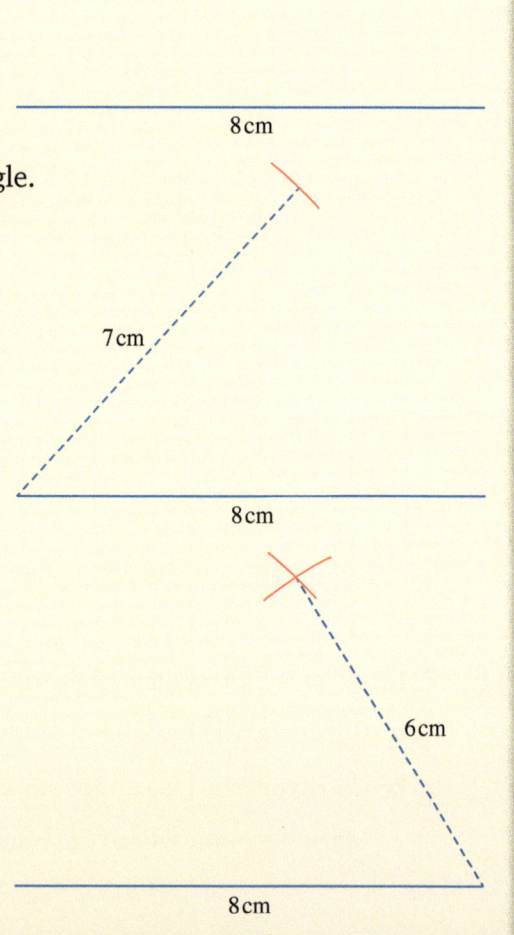

**9** Shapes and geometric reasoning 2

**Step 4**

The point where the arcs cross is 7 cm from one end of the line and 6 cm from the other end of the line.

Draw straight lines from the crossover point to each end of the line.

This is now the required triangle.

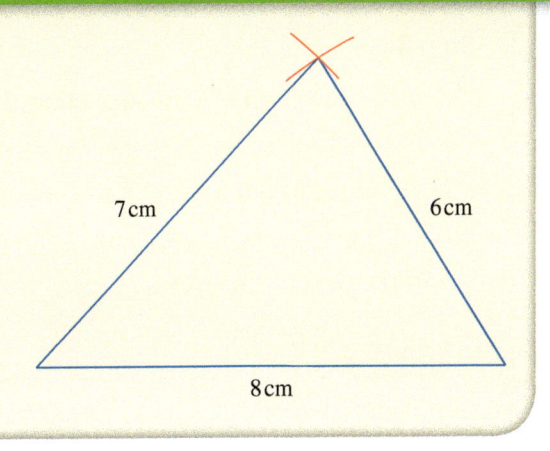

## Constructing right-angled triangles

When drawing a right-angled triangle, you need to construct a 90° angle.

You can do this by constructing the bisector of a 180° angle.

The next example shows the method.

### Worked example 2

Construct a triangle *ABC*, with a right angle at *A*, where side *AB* is 7 cm and side *BC* is 10 cm.

It is sometimes a good idea to draw a sketch of the triangle.

This can make it easier to lay it out on your paper.

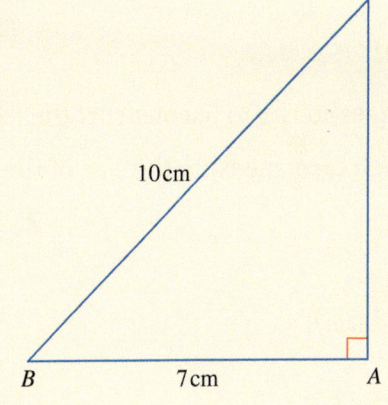

**Step 1**

Draw straight line *BA*, where *BA* = 7 cm.

Extend the line beyond the **vertex** *A*.

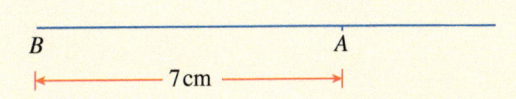

**Step 2**

With point *A* as the centre, mark two arcs equal distances either side of *A* on the line.

121

### Step 3

Using the points where the arcs cross the line as centres, mark two intersecting arcs above the line.

You will need to open the compasses a bit futher to do this.

Draw a line from the vertex A through the point of intersection of the arcs.

> As point A is fixed, only one pair of arcs (most usefully above the line) is needed.

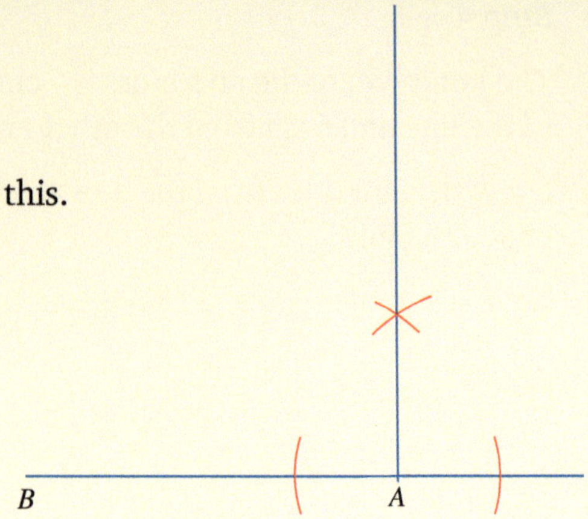

### Step 4

Set your compass at a radius of 10 cm.

Using vertex B as the centre, draw an arc intersecting the perpendicular line.

Mark vertex C at the intersection.

Join B to C.

The line BC is 10 cm long.

BC is the **hypotenuse** of the right-angled triangle.

The triangle is now complete.

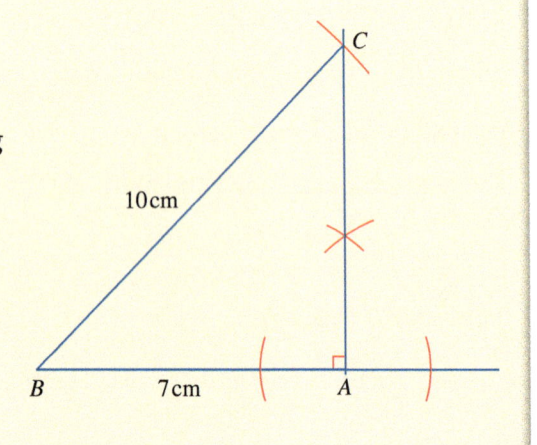

## Exercise 9.2

For questions **1** to **5**, construct the triangles accurately using ruler and compasses.

In each case, measure the size of the angles.

**1** 5 cm, 7 cm, 6 cm

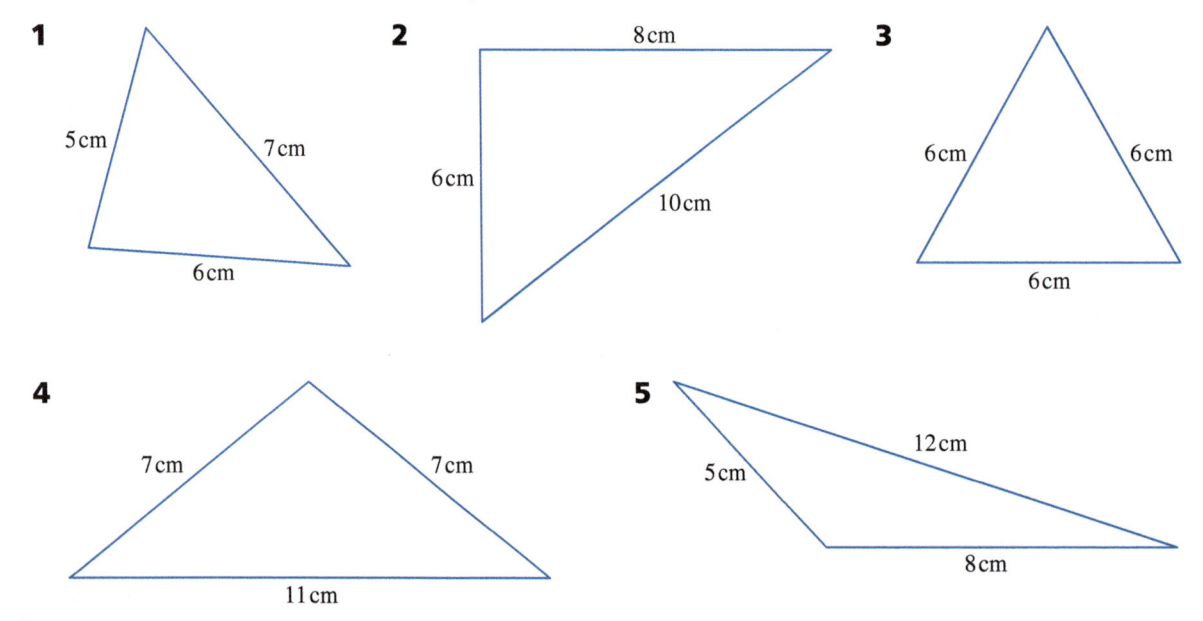

**2** 8 cm, 6 cm, 10 cm

**3** 6 cm, 6 cm, 6 cm

**4** 7 cm, 7 cm, 11 cm

**5** 5 cm, 12 cm, 8 cm

# 9 Shapes and geometric reasoning 2

For questions **6** to **8**, construct the right-angled triangles accurately.

In each case, measure the length of the third side.

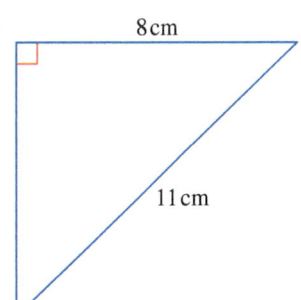

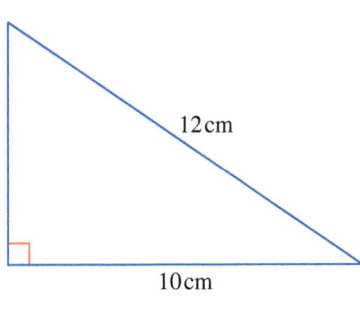

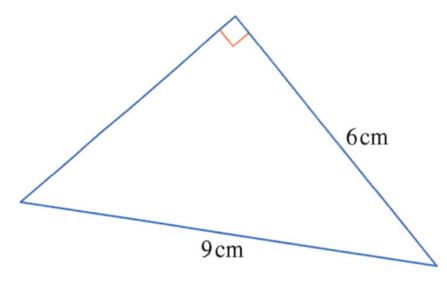

**6** 8 cm, 11 cm

**7** 12 cm, 10 cm

**8** 6 cm, 9 cm

**9** In triangle ABC, angle ABC = 90°.

Side AB = 5 cm and side BC = 8 cm.

   **a** Carefully construct triangle ABC using ruler and compasses.

   **b** Measure the length AC.

   **c** What name is given to the side AC?

**10** A and B are two points 10 cm apart on a straight line.

   **a** Construct the perpendicular bisector of AB.

   Label the midpoint of the line M.

   **b** Bisect the 90° angle at M to make two angles of 45°.

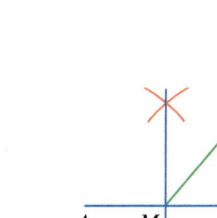

   **c** Construct triangle BMX in which angle BMX = 45°, side BM = 5 cm and side BX = 8 cm.

   The final diagram should look like this.

   **d** Measure the angle MBX.

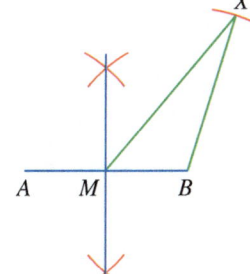

## 9.3 Circles

In mathematics, you will often need to use of a pair of compasses to draw circles or parts of circles.

You need to know how to draw a full circle, a semicircle and an arc of a circle.

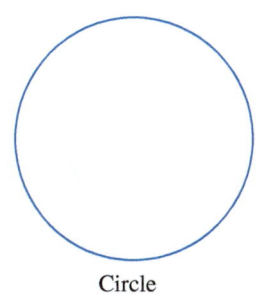

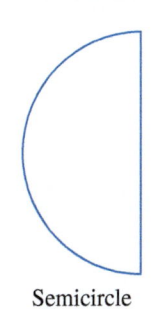

Circle    Semicircle    Arc of a circle

123

# Mathematics for Cambridge Secondary 1

In this section, you can practise using your compasses by drawing some patterns based on circles.

Remember, when using a pair of compasses you need to have a sharp pencil.

The compasses should not be loose or they will slip and change size.

## Worked example

Draw this design carefully on plain paper.

Use a radius of 6 cm.

Start by drawing a circle with radius 6 cm.

Keeping your compasses at the same radius, place the point anywhere on the circumference of the circle.

Draw an arc across the circle.

> For this design, the radius does not change.

Using one of the points where the arc touches the circle as centre, draw another arc across the circle.

Be careful not to let the compasses change radius.

Repeat this using the next intersection point on the circumference as the centre of the next arc.

Continue this process until the design is complete.

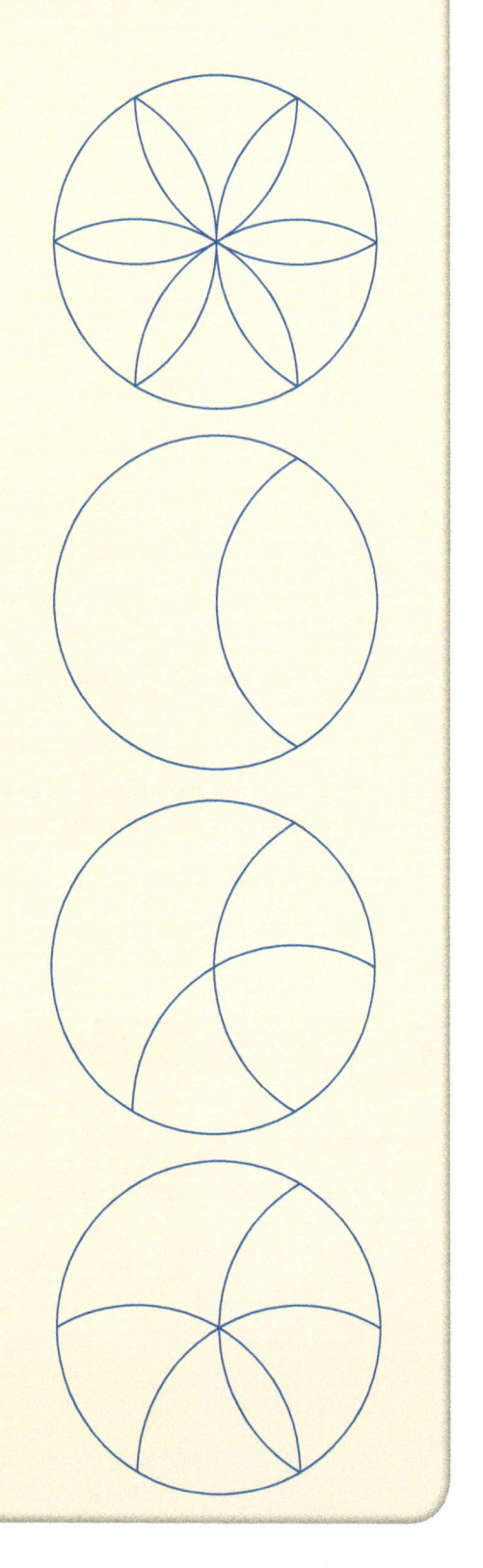

124

## Exercise 9.3

**1** For each part, accurately draw a circle with the given radius on squared paper.

**a** 4 cm

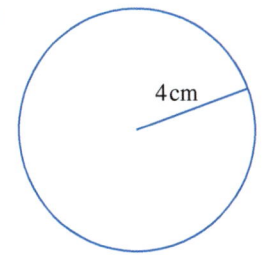

**b** 5.6 cm

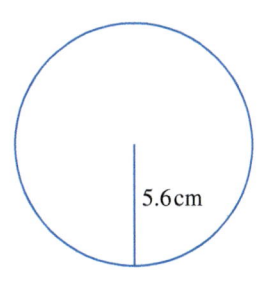

**c** 49 mm

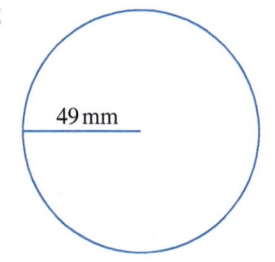

**2** For each part, accurately draw a circle with the given diameter on plain paper.

**a** 6 cm

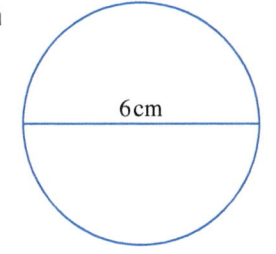

**b** 7.6 cm

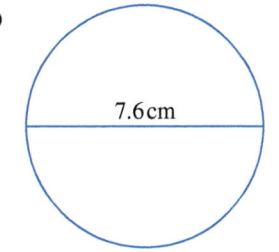

**c** 48 mm

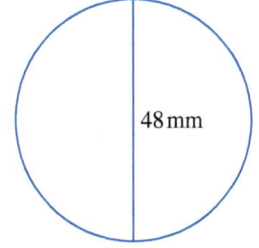

**3** Use your compasses to draw these designs.

**a**

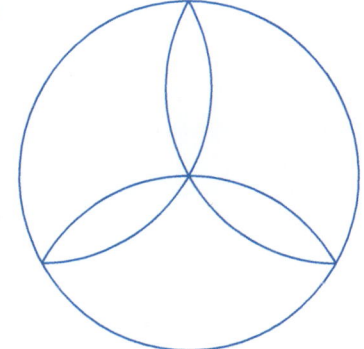

**b**

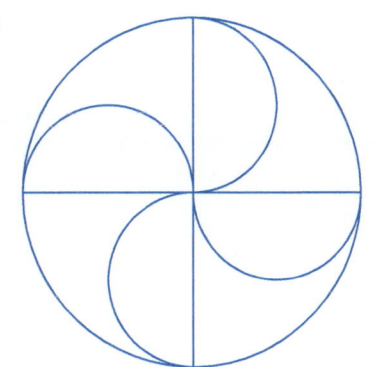

Use a pencil to draw more of the design and then rub out the bits you do not want to keep.

**c**

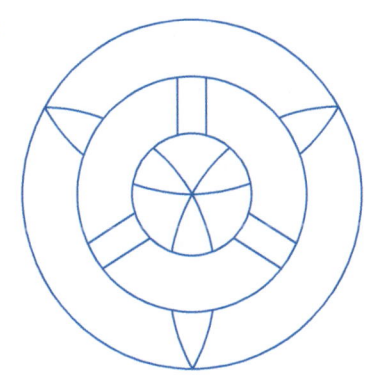

**d**

125

Mathematics for Cambridge Secondary 1

## 9.4 Scale drawings

It is sometimes not possible to draw a design full size as it is too big.

In these cases, you can use a **scale drawing** to reduce the size.

For example, an architect would use a scale drawing to design a building as it would not be possible to draw a house full size on a piece of paper.

Here is a plan of a garden showing a flower bed, a lawn and a pond.

The **scale** is 1 cm represents 2 m. This can also be written as 1 cm to 2 m.

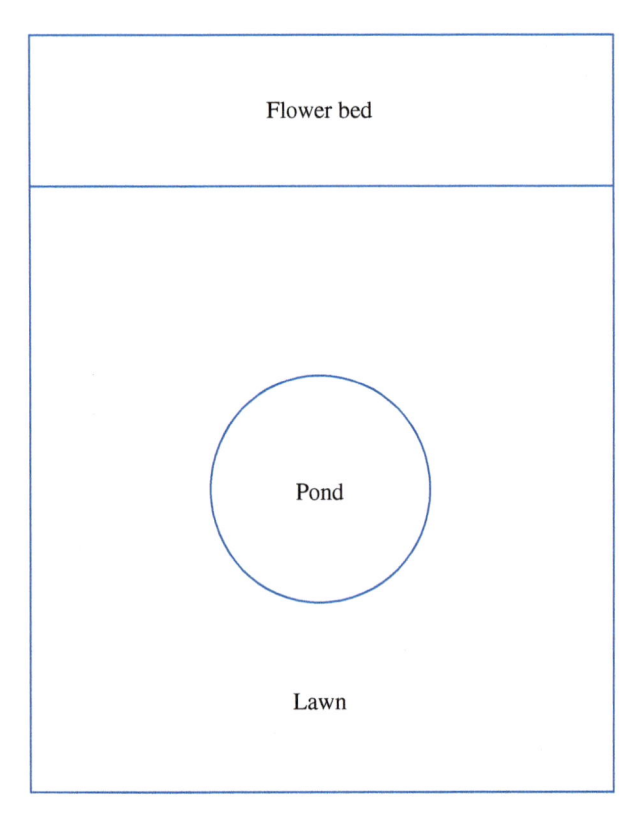

### Worked example

Use the garden plan above to answer these questions.

a  Measure the width of the flower bed on the plan. How wide is it in real life?

b  How long is the flower bed in real life?

c  What is the diameter of the pond in metres?

d  Write down the length and width of the garden in metres.

a  The flower bed is 2 cm wide.

   Each centimetre on the plan represents 2 metres in real life, so the width is 4 metres.

**9** Shapes and geometric reasoning 2

**b** The length of the flower bed is 8 cm.

8 × 2 = 16 so the flower bed is 16 metres long.

**c** The diameter of the pond is 3 cm.

3 × 2 = 6 so the diameter of the pond is 6 metres.

**d** The garden on the plan measures 8 cm by 10 cm.

8 × 2 = 16 and 10 × 2 = 20

The actual garden measures 16 metres by 20 metres.

## Exercise 9.4

**1** This is the plan of a room drawn to scale.

The scale is 1 cm represents 50 cm.

  **a** Measure the length of the window on the plan in centimetres.

  **b** What is the actual length of the window in metres?

  **c** Work out the length of the longest side of the room in metres.

  **d** Work out the perimeter of the room in metres.

**2** Work out the actual lengths of these lines drawn at the given scales.

  **a** 3 cm drawn at a scale of 1 cm to 4 m

  **b** 12 cm drawn at a scale of 1 cm to 50 cm

  **c** 45 mm drawn at a scale of 1 cm to 2 m

  **d** 15 cm drawn at a scale of 1 cm to 5 m

  **e** 3.8 cm drawn at a scale of 1 cm to 20 m

**3** This is a sketch plan of a garden design.

The garden is a large trapezium with a rectangular vegetable bed at one end.

There is also a flower bed, which is part of a circle of radius 20 m.

  **a** Draw an accurate scale drawing of the garden.

  Use a scale of 1 cm to 5 m.

  **b** *A* and *B* are marked at opposite corners of the garden.

  Use your plan to find the diagonal distance between points *A* and *B*.

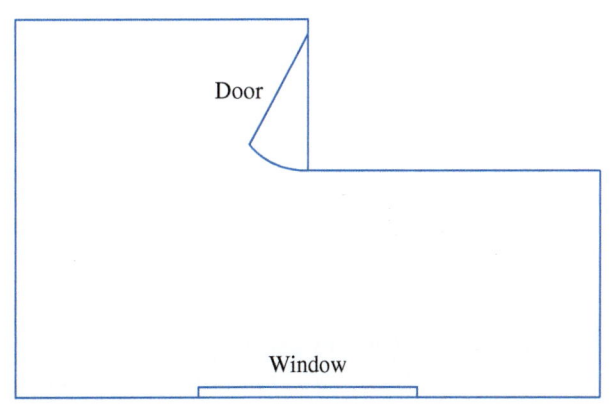

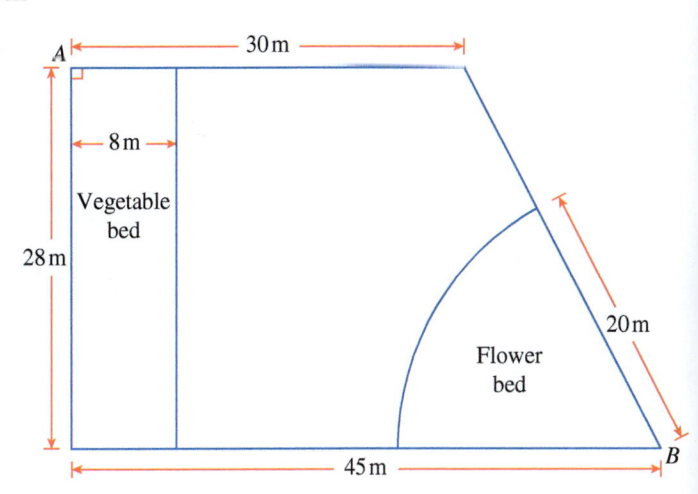

# Review

**1** Copy these lines on to plain paper. They do not need to be exactly the right length.

Construct the perpendicular bisector of each line.

**a** 7 cm

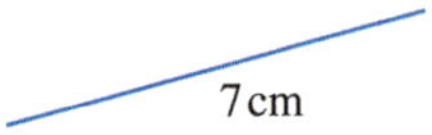

**b** 12 cm

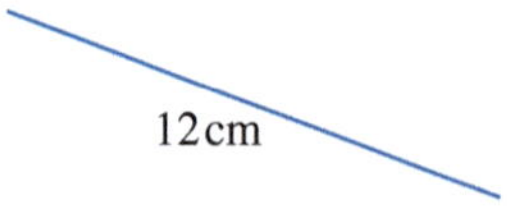

**c** 4.5 cm

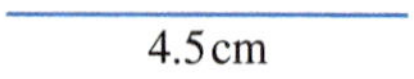

**2** Copy these angles on to plain paper. They do not need to be exact.

Construct the bisector of each angle.

**a** 48°

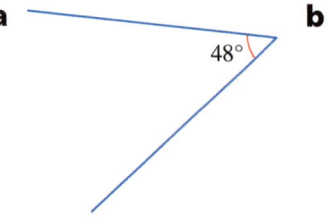

**b** 115°

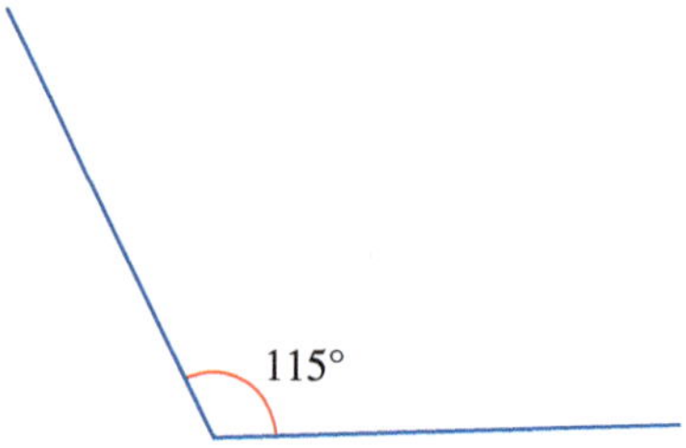

**c** 250°

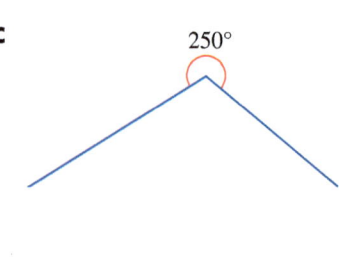

**3** Draw a straight line 12 cm long. Label the ends A and B.

Construct the perpendicular bisector of AB. Label the ends of the line X and Y.

Label the midpoint M.

Bisect the angle AMX to create two 45° angles.

Draw the triangle AMP where AM = PM = 6 cm.

The diagram shows a sketch of the final construction.

Using your own construction, measure and write down the length of AP.

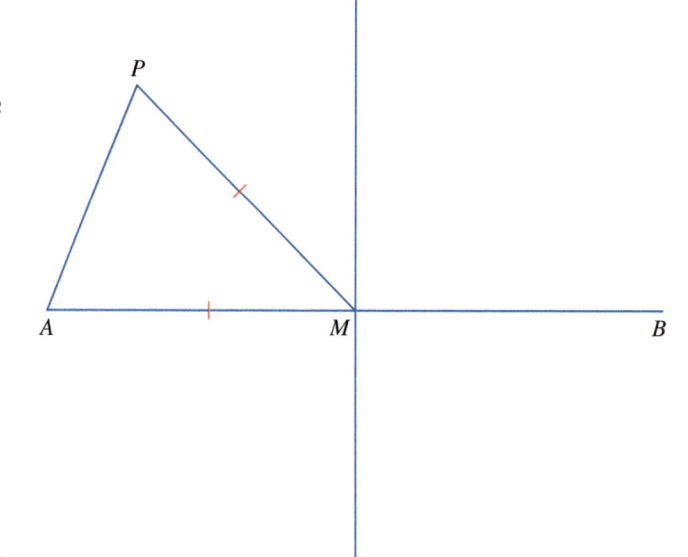

**4** Make accurate drawings of these triangles.

**a** 5.5 cm, 6 cm, 9 cm

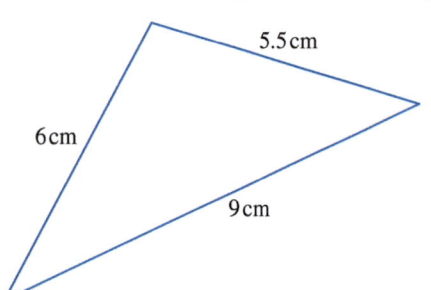

**b** 6 cm, 6 cm, 11 cm

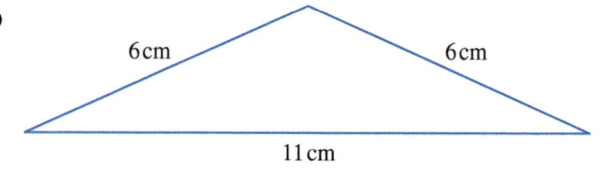

c

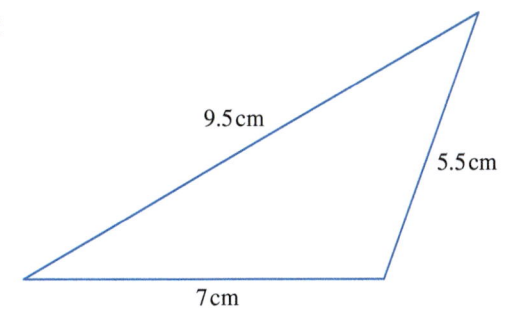

9.5 cm
5.5 cm
7 cm

d

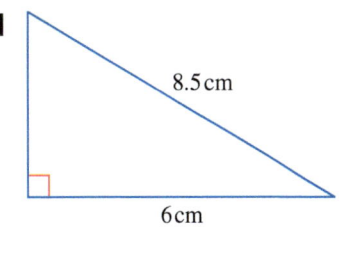

8.5 cm
6 cm

**5** Construct an equilateral triangle *ABC* with all sides 6 cm long.

Construct the bisector of angle *BAC*.

Label the point where the bisector meets the opposite side *X*.

Construct the bisector of angle *ACB*.

Label the point where the bisector meets the opposite side *Y*.

Label the point *M* where the two lines cross.

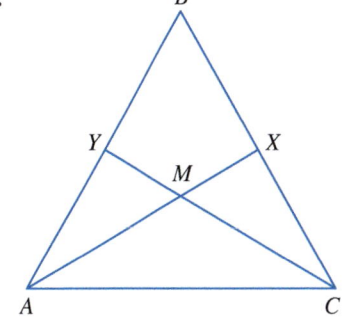

**a** Measure the length *AM*.

**b** What type of triangle is *AMY*?

**c** What type of triangle is *AMC*?

**d** What name is given to the shape *BYMX*?

**6** This garden design is made up of a right-angled triangle and a semicircle.

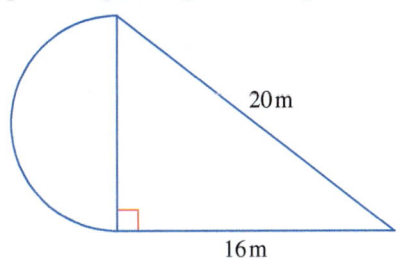

20 m
16 m

Draw an accurate scale drawing of the design on plain paper.

Use a scale of 1 cm to represent 2 m.

Start by constructing a right-angled triangle of the correct size.

Then use a straight edge and compasses to find the midpoint of the shortest side.

Finally, draw a semicircle to complete the design.

**7** This is a plan of Pablo's room. It shows his bed, bookcase and cupboard.

The scale is 1 cm represents 25 cm, or 1 to 25.

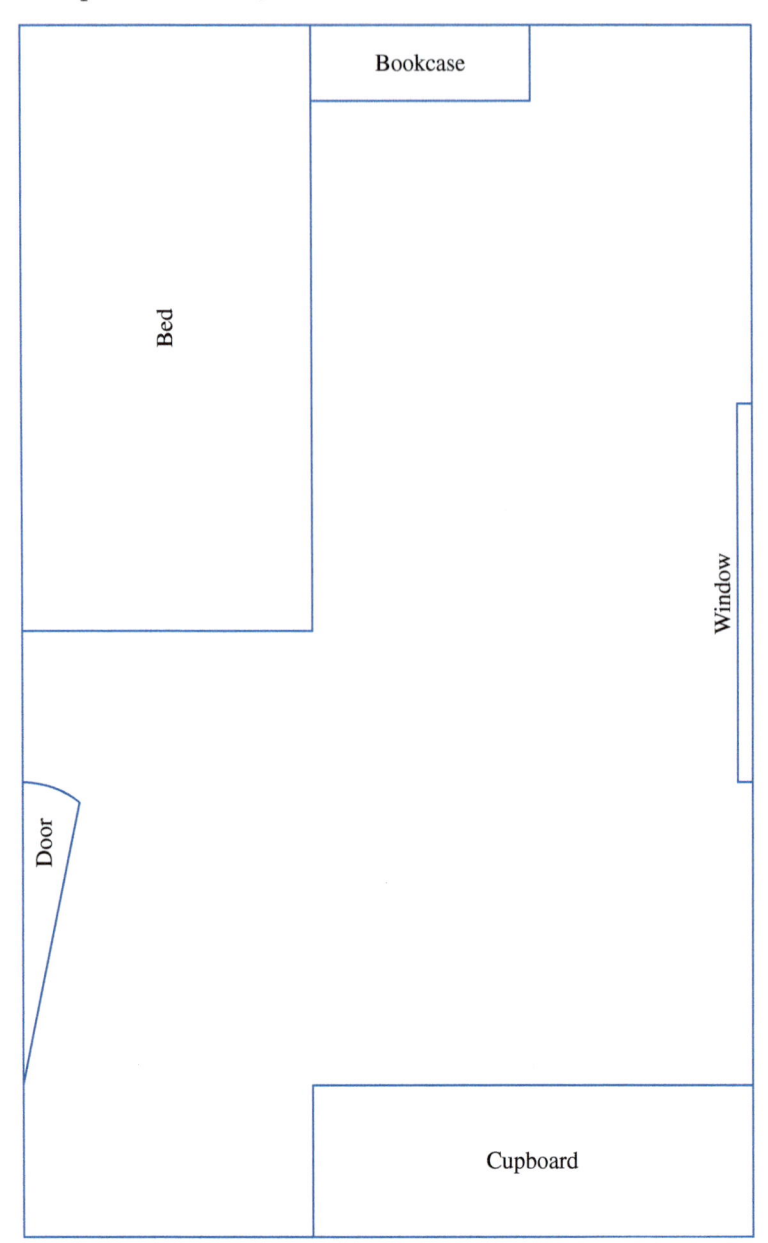

**a** How long is the drawing of Pablo's room in centimetres?

**b** Work out the actual length of the room in metres.

**c** Work out the actual length and width of the cupboard. Give your answer in metres.

**d** Find the actual length and width of Pablo's bookcase in centimetres.

**e** Pablo buys a desk that is 150 cm by 75 cm.

Copy the scale drawing and show where he could put the desk.

# 10 Presenting, interpreting and discussing data

Chapter 18 covers collecting data
Chapter 6 covers processing data

### Learning outcomes

- Draw and interpret:
  - frequency diagrams for discrete and continuous data
  - pie charts
  - simple line graphs for time series
  - stem-and-leaf diagrams.
- Interpret tables, graphs and diagrams for discrete and continuous data.
- Draw conclusions relating statistics and findings to the original question.
- Compare proportions in two pie charts that represent different totals.

## The best thing about statistics …

John Tukey was an American mathematician.

Born in New Bedford, Massachusetts in 1915, he invented a number of ways to analyse data that are still used in statistics today.

Tukey worked for lots of different organisations. He is known for this quote: 'The best thing about being a statistician is that you get to play in everyone's backyard.'

You will learn about some of the methods he invented later.

In this chapter, you will learn about stem-and-leaf diagrams.

## 10.1 Frequency diagrams for grouped data

**Frequency diagrams** show how often the values in a distribution occur.

For **discrete data**, frequency diagrams must have:
- a title
- a label on each axis
- values on the frequency axis, evenly spaced and starting at zero
- bars of equal width
- equal gaps between the bars
- a label under each bar.

131

Mathematics for Cambridge Secondary 1

For **continuous data**, frequency diagrams must have:
- a title
- a label on each axis
- values on the frequency axis, evenly spaced and starting at zero
- a sensible scale on the other axis
- bars of equal width
- no gaps between the bars.

## Worked example 1

The number of snacks sold by a café each day is shown in the grouped frequency table.

| Snacks | 0–19 | 20–39 | 40–59 | 60–79 | 80–99 |
|---|---|---|---|---|---|
| Frequency | 2 | 5 | 9 | 6 | 3 |

**a** Show this information on a frequency diagram.

**b** Write down the modal class.

**a**

Frequency diagram showing the number of snacks sold in a café each day

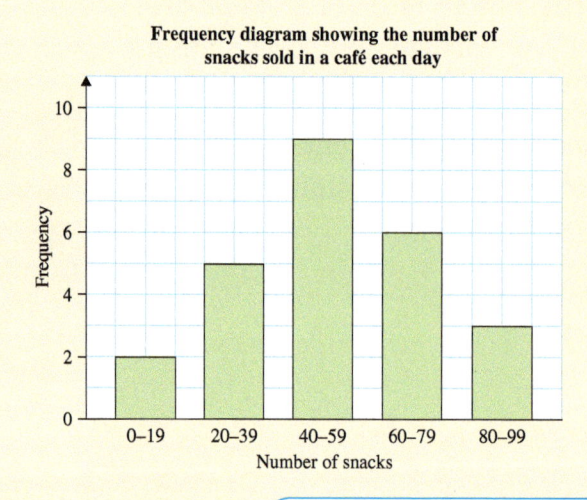

**b** The modal class is 40–59 snacks.

Remember: the modal class is the class with the highest frequency.

## Worked example 2

A group of students are asked how long it takes them to get home after school.

The results are shown in the frequency diagram.

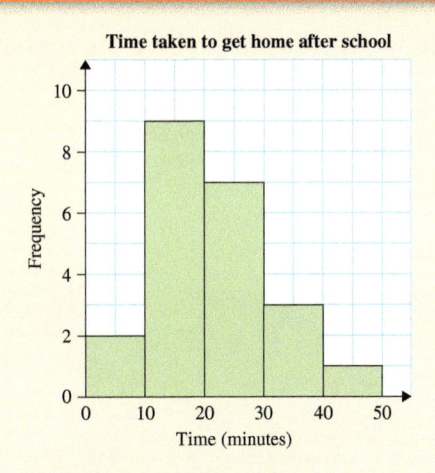

**Time taken to get home after school**

a How many students take between 20 and 30 minutes to get home?
b How many students take more than 30 minutes to get home?
c How many students take less than 20 minutes to get home?

a Seven students take between 20 and 30 minutes to get home.
b 3 + 1 = 4 students take more than 30 minutes to get home.
c 2 + 9 = 11 students take less than 20 minutes to get home.

## Exercise 10.1

1 A group of adults and a group of children are asked how many emails they send each day. The results are shown in the frequency diagrams.

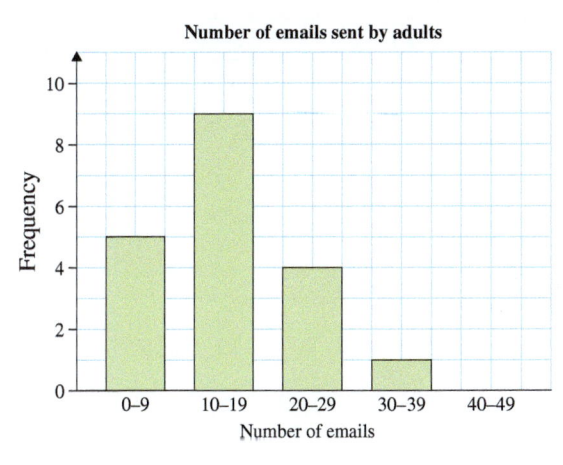

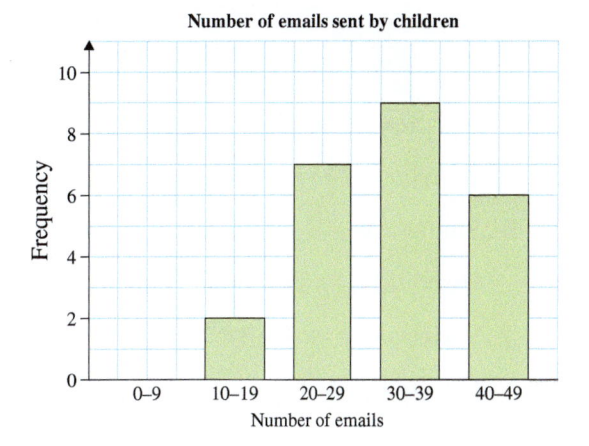

**Number of emails sent by adults**

**Number of emails sent by children**

a How many adults sent 20 or more emails?
b How many children sent 20 or more emails?
c What is the modal class for the adults?
d What is the modal class for the children?
e How many adults are there altogether?
f How many children are there altogether?

133

2 The frequency diagram shows the time taken by some students to complete a long distance run.

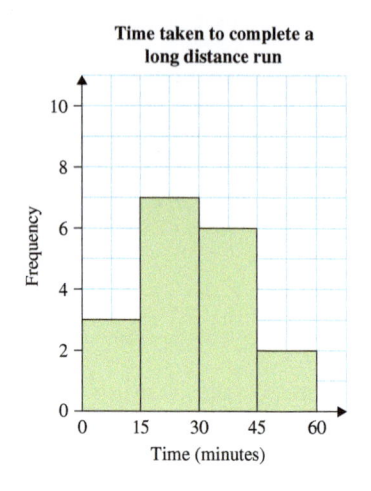

**Time taken to complete a long distance run**

(Frequency diagram: 0–15: 3, 15–30: 7, 30–45: 6, 45–60: 2)

a How many students take more than 45 minutes?

b How many students take less than 30 minutes?

c How many students complete the run?

3 The frequency table shows the length of time, in minutes, that 50 students took to solve a puzzle.

| Time, $t$ (minutes) | $5 \leq t < 10$ | $10 \leq t < 15$ | $15 \leq t < 20$ | $20 \leq t < 25$ | $25 \leq t < 30$ | $30 \leq t < 35$ | $35 \leq t < 40$ |
|---|---|---|---|---|---|---|---|
| Frequency | 1 | 4 | 12 | 15 | 8 | 7 | 3 |

Draw a frequency diagram to show this information.

4 The frequency table shows the marks scored in a test by a class of 30 students.

| Mark | 1–10 | 11–20 | 21–30 | 31–40 | 41–50 |
|---|---|---|---|---|---|
| Frequency | 1 | 5 | 8 | 11 | 5 |

a Draw a frequency diagram to show these marks.

b What is the modal class?

5 Shen grows two varieties of tomatoes in his garden.

He counts the number of tomatoes on each plant.

Variety A: 9, 8, 15, 14, 18, 21, 17, 24, 16, 13, 12, 18, 21, 20, 7, 12, 11, 7, 17, 14, 18, 19, 3, 8

Variety B: 16, 12, 8, 15, 6, 5, 8, 5, 12, 15, 5, 8, 9, 10, 7, 19, 21, 9, 4, 6, 2, 9, 12, 8

a Make a grouped frequency table for each variety.

Use the classes 0–4, 5–9 and so on.

b Draw a frequency diagram for each variety.

c Use your frequency diagram to decide which variety gives the larger number of tomatoes. Give a reason for your answer.

*Do not just look at the largest or smallest number of tomatoes.*

**10** Presenting, interpreting and discussing data

**6** Children from two villages all walk to the same school.

Sketch a frequency diagram to show the distances you would expect children to walk if:

   **a** the school is halfway between the villages

   **b** the school is in one of the villages.

> Use the horizontal axis of your diagram to represent distance walked. Think about the distance walked when children live close to the school and when they live further from the school.

**7** The frequency diagram shows the heights of a group of teachers at a school.

> You will find it helpful to find the frequency for each class.

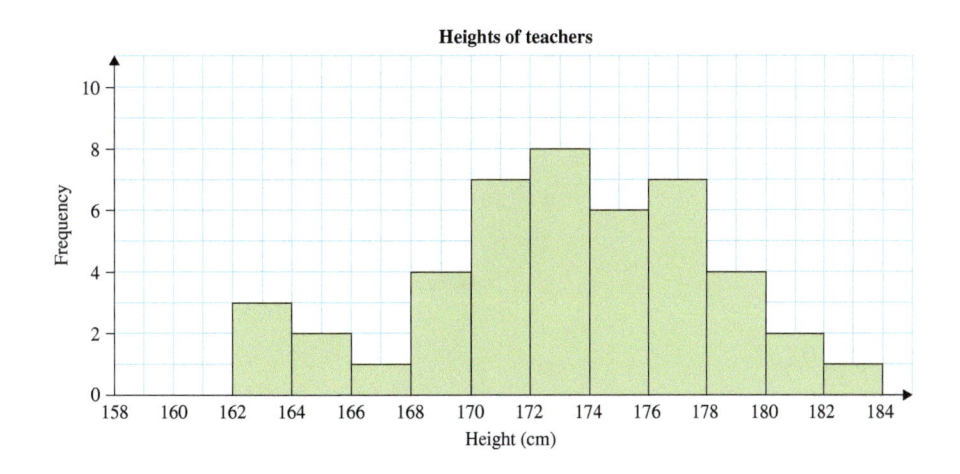

*Heights of teachers* (frequency diagram: heights 158–184 cm on horizontal axis; frequencies 3, 2, 1, 4, 7, 8, 6, 7, 4, 2, 1)

   **a** How many teachers are in this group?

   **b** How many of these teachers are 164 cm or shorter?

   **c** How many of these teachers are 178 cm or taller?

   **d** Neema says, 'Most of these teachers are taller than 174 cm.'

   Is Neema correct for this group of teachers?

   **e** Kate says, 'The shortest teacher is 162 cm.'

   Is Kate correct for this group of teachers?

## 10.2 Pie charts

A **pie chart** shows information on a circle.

The circle is divided into sectors.

The angle of each sector is in proportion to the amount of information it shows.

The angles in all of the sectors must add up to 360°.

You must label the sectors and draw the angles accurately.

Pie charts are useful to show how data are divided up.

## Worked example

A survey is done to find out which ice cream flavours people like.

The table shows the results for a group of 30 children.

| Ice cream flavour | Frequency |
|---|---|
| Vanilla | 6 |
| Strawberry | 10 |
| Raspberry | 8 |
| Cherry | 6 |

The pie chart shows the results for a group of 36 adults.

**Adults' favourite ice cream flavours**

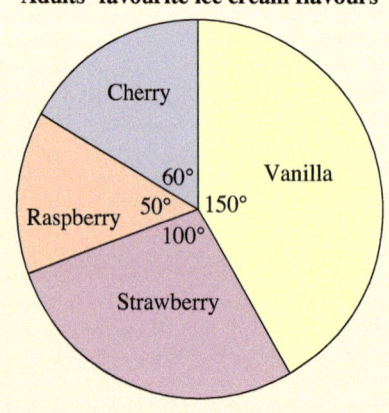

a  Draw a pie chart for the children.

b  How many adults like strawberry?

c  Compare the results for the children and the adults.

a  The total number of children is 30.

The 360° at the centre of the circle must be divided between the 30 children.

360° ÷ 30 = 12°

Each student will be represented by 12°.

You multiply each frequency by 12° to find the angle for each sector.

| Ice cream flavour | Frequency | Angle |
|---|---|---|
| Vanilla | 6 | 6 × 12° = 72° |
| Strawberry | 10 | 10 × 12° = 120° |
| Raspberry | 8 | 8 × 12° = 96° |
| Cherry | 6 | 6 × 12° = 72° |

> Before you draw the pie chart always check the angles add up to 360°:
> 72° + 120° + 96° + 72° = 360°

136

**10** Presenting, interpreting and discussing data

**Children's favourite ice cream flavours**

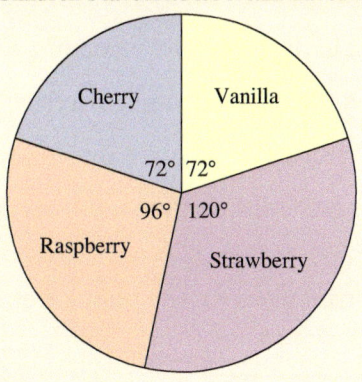

(Pie chart showing: Cherry 72°, Vanilla 72°, Strawberry 120°, Raspberry 96°)

**b** The adults' pie chart represents 36 adults.

Each adult is represented by 360° ÷ 36 = 10°

The angle for strawberry in the adults' pie chart is 100°.

　　100° ÷ 10° = 10 adults

**c** The pie charts represent different totals. You cannot compare the frequencies unless you work them all out. You can compare the more popular and less popular flavours.

Vanilla is more popular with the adults than with the children.

The most popular flavour with the children is strawberry.

The least popular flavour with adults is raspberry.

## Exercise 10.2

**1** The table shows the subjects chosen by a group of 90 students.

| Subject | Statistics | Geography | History | Music |
|---|---|---|---|---|
| Frequency | 23 | 41 | 17 | 9 |

Draw a pie chart to show this information.

**2** In a survey, a librarian asks people what type of book they prefer to read.

The pie charts show the results of the survey.

There are 90 adults in the survey.

There are 120 children in the survey.

**Adults' favourite books** (36°, 80°, 24°, 100°, 120°)

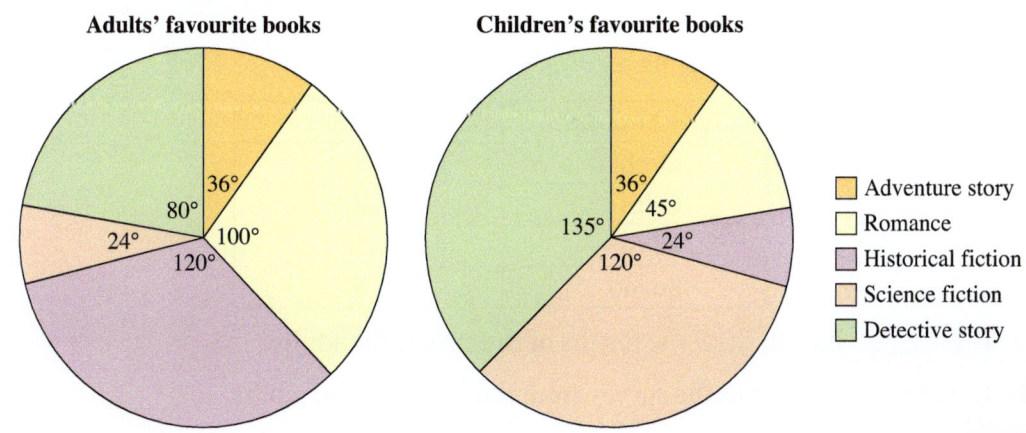

**Children's favourite books** (36°, 45°, 135°, 24°, 120°)

- Adventure story
- Romance
- Historical fiction
- Science fiction
- Detective story

137

a How many adults prefer historical fiction books?
b What percentage of the children prefer romance?
c How many more children than adults prefer science fiction?
d The sector for adventure stories is the same size for adults as for children.

Explain how you know more children than adults prefer adventure stories without doing any calculations.

3 The tables show the age distributions for the populations of South Africa and Austria.

| South Africa ||
|---|---|
| Age | Percentage |
| 0–14 | 28 |
| 15–24 | 21 |
| 25–54 | 38 |
| 55–64 | 7 |
| 65 and over | 6 |

| Austria ||
|---|---|
| Age | Percentage |
| 0–14 | 14 |
| 15–24 | 12 |
| 25–54 | 43 |
| 55–64 | 12 |
| 65 and over | 19 |

Source: adapted from the CIA World Factbook.

Draw a pie chart for each country.

Compare the age distributions for the two countries.

*To find the angle for 0–14 for South Africa, find 28% of 360°.*

4 A survey is done to find the favourite ways to eat potatoes.

The pie chart shows the results from a group of children.

**Children's favourite type of potato**

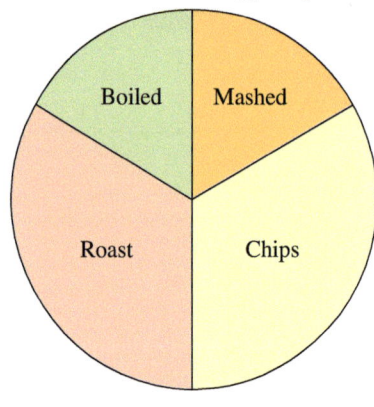

*Remember: you cannot compare frequencies, only proportions, from a pie chart. That is, you can only compare percentages or fractions.*

The table shows the results from a group of adults.

| Type of potato | Frequency |
|---|---|
| Mashed | 18 |
| Chips | 22 |
| Roast | 45 |
| Boiled | 5 |

a Draw a pie chart to show the results of the survey for adults.
b Compare the results of the survey from the children and adults.

# 10 Presenting, interpreting and discussing data

## 10.3 Line graphs

**Line graphs** are a series of points joined with straight lines.

You always have time on the horizontal axis.

Line graphs tell you how data change over a period of time.

The general increase or decrease in the data over time is called the **trend**.

Line graphs must have:

- a title
- a label on each axis
- evenly spaced values on the vertical axis
- time on the horizontal axis.

### Worked example

Masamba is growing a sunflower.

The table shows the height of the sunflower at the end of each week.

| Week | 1 | 2 | 3 | 4 | 5 | 6 |
|---|---|---|---|---|---|---|
| Height (cm) | 15 | 16 | 18 | 23 | 31 | 38 |

**a** Draw a line graph to show the data.
**b** During which week did the sunflower grow the most?
**c** Estimate the height of the sunflower after $5\frac{1}{2}$ weeks.
**d** Describe the trend shown in the graph.

**a**

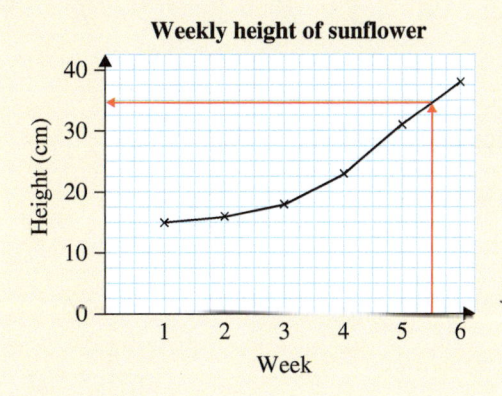

**Weekly height of sunflower**

**b** The sunflower grows most in week 5.

**c** About 34.5 cm   Read up from 5.5 on the horizontal axis, then across to the vertical axis as shown by the red arrows on the graph.

**d** The sunflower is increasing in height. Each week it is taller than the previous week.

139

## Exercise 10.3

1 The table shows the average temperature for each month in Israel.

| Month | Jan | Feb | Mar | Apr | May | Jun | Jul | Aug | Sep | Oct | Nov | Dec |
|---|---|---|---|---|---|---|---|---|---|---|---|---|
| Temperature (°C) | 11.4 | 12 | 14.4 | 18.1 | 21.6 | 24.4 | 26.3 | 26.8 | 25.3 | 22.4 | 17.7 | 13 |

Source: Weatherbase

   a Draw a line graph to show these data.

   b For how many months is the average temperature above 20°C?

2 The table shows the value of a car over a period of five years.

| Age of car (years) | 0 | 1 | 2 | 3 | 4 | 5 |
|---|---|---|---|---|---|---|
| Value ($) | 15 000 | 12 000 | 10 000 | 8500 | 7500 | 7000 |

   a Draw a line graph to show this information.

   b Estimate the value of the car when it was 6 months old.

   c Estimate the value of the car when it was $2\frac{1}{2}$ years old.

   d Describe the trend shown in the graph.

3 The line graph shows the cost, in dollars, of an item over a period of 12 months.

**Cost of an item over 12 months**

   a When is the price at its lowest?

   b What is the lowest price?

   c What is the highest price?

   d Describe the trend shown in the graph.

# 10 Presenting, interpreting and discussing data

**4** The line graph shows the rate of pay per hour to employees by a company.

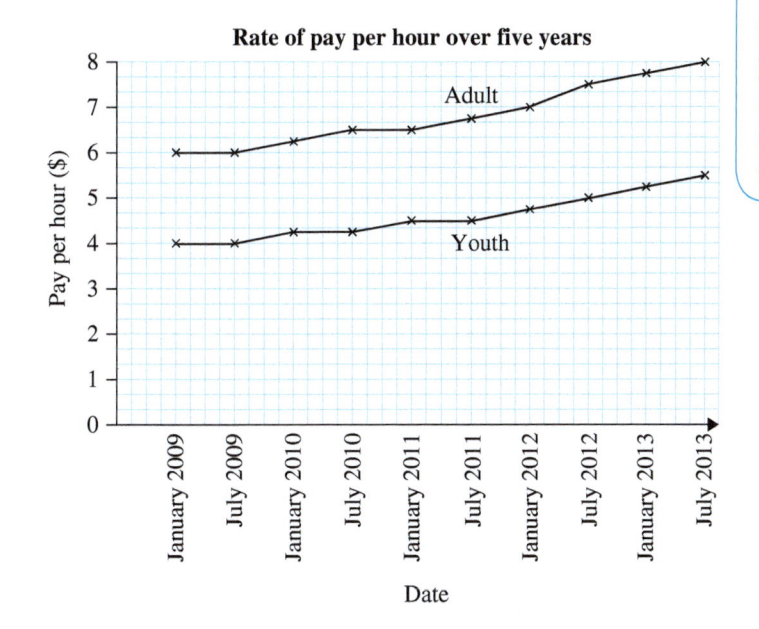

*Rate of pay per hour over five years*

> Does the graph show both adult and youth rates of pay as increasing, or decreasing? Are they changing at the same rate?

Compare the trends shown in the graph for adult and youth pay per hour.

**5** The line graph shows the sales, in $1000's, for a company that makes ice cream over a period of 12 months.

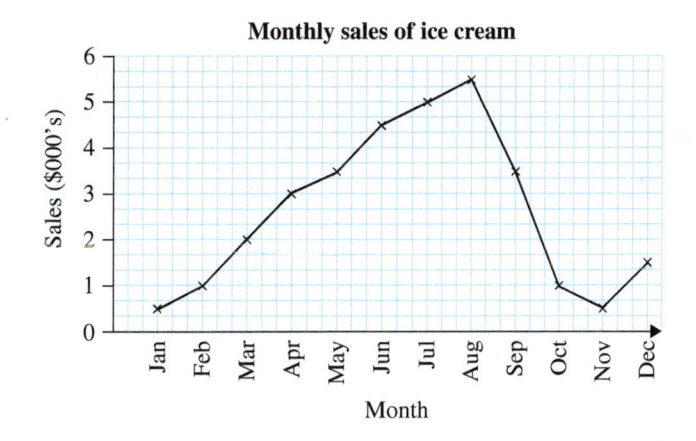

*Monthly sales of ice cream*

  **a** When were the sales at their highest?
  
  **b** When were the sales at their lowest?
  
  **c** The company makes a profit when the sales are over $2500.
  
  For how many months does the company make a profit?
  
  **d** Describe the trend shown in the graph.
  
  **e** Between which two months was the biggest change in sales?
  
  **f** Is the company likely to be based north of the equator or south of the equator? Give a reason for your answer.

141

## 10.4 Stem-and-leaf diagrams

**Stem-and-leaf diagrams** are used to organise data in order of size.

The **stem** is to the left of the vertical line.

The **leaves** are always just one digit. They are on the right of the vertical line.

The leaves must be organised in **order of size**.

Keep the leaves in vertical lines.

You must always include a **key**.

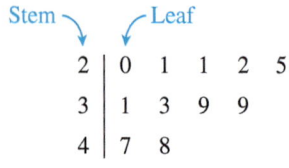

Stem → | ← Leaf
2 | 0  1  1  2  5
3 | 1  3  9  9
4 | 7  8

Key: 4|7 represents 47

### Worked example

The waiting times, to the nearest minute, for 20 people at a hospital are listed below.

23, 29, 31, 47, 32, 44, 37, 24, 29, 30, 38, 42, 58, 42, 40, 25, 51, 38, 20, 29

**a** Use a stem-and-leaf diagram to show the data.
**b** Find the range of the waiting times.
**c** Find the median of the waiting times.
**d** What percentage of people waited for 30 minutes or longer?

**a** The stem will be the 'tens' part of each number.

The data go from 20 to 58. This means there could be numbers in the 20's, 30's, 40's and 50's so the stem is 2, 3, 4 and 5, written in a vertical line.

The 'units' part of each number is a leaf. Go through the data putting the leaves on, one at a time.

2 | 3  9  4  9  5  0  9
3 | 1  2  7  0  8  8
4 | 7  4  2  2  0
5 | 8  1

Now the leaves need to be put into order of size.

2 | 0  3  4  5  9  9  9
3 | 0  1  2  7  8  8
4 | 0  2  2  4  7
5 | 1  8

Key: 5|1 represents 51 minutes ← Remember to include a key.

**10** Presenting, interpreting and discussing data

**b** Range = 38 minutes    Range = largest value − smallest value = 58 − 20 = 38

**c** The median is 34.5 minutes.    The 'middle pair' is 32 and 37, the median is halfway between these values.

**d** 13 people waited for 30 minutes or longer.

This is $\frac{13}{20} \times 100 = 65\%$

## Exercise 10.4

**1** The stem-and-leaf diagram shows the mass, to the nearest kilogram, of some parcels.

```
0 | 3
1 | 2 4 4 5 8
2 | 0 3 6 6 7
3 | 1 2 4 5 9 9
4 | 0 3 4 6 7
5 | 0
```
Key: 5|0 represents 5.0 kg

   **a** What is the mass of the lightest parcel?

   **b** Find the range of the masses.

   **c** How many parcels are shown in the stem-and-leaf diagram?

   **d** Find the median mass of the parcels.

**2** The stem-and-leaf diagram shows the number of people, to the nearest 100, at 31 football matches.

```
3 | 0 1 5 5 5 6 6 6
4 | 2 2 3 3
5 | 1 1 1 6 6 7 9
6 | 0 1
7 | 3
8 | 0 8 8
9 | 1 2 3 4 6 6
```
Key: 9|1 represents 9100

   **a** What is the smallest number of people shown?

   **b** What is the range of the numbers of people?

   **c** What is the median number of people?

   **d** How many matches had over 8000 people at them?

**3** The number of runs scored by players in a cricket match are:

   23, 12, 45, 36, 30, 21, 18, 13, 41, 21, 18, 14, 30, 20, 34, 28, 49, 50, 23, 28, 38, 7

   **a** Show this information in a stem-and-leaf diagram. Remember to include a key.

   **b** Find the range of the runs scored.

   **c** Find the median number of runs scored.

   **d** How many players scored more than 30 runs?

143

# Mathematics for Cambridge Secondary 1

**4** A class of students take a maths exam.

The marks are out of 80 for each paper.

The marks for the calculator paper are:

40, 61, 52, 35, 38, 41, 41, 76, 54, 68, 36, 37, 42, 59, 80, 73,

77, 38, 39, 62, 70, 43, 50, 44, 63, 48, 55, 64, 49, 59, 58, 51

The marks for the non-calculator paper are:

62, 44, 63, 78, 47, 50, 72, 56, 63, 77, 80, 36, 43, 64, 76, 49,

38, 74, 51, 69, 35, 58, 65, 75, 63, 44, 55, 69, 45, 51, 75, 58

**a** Draw a stem-and-leaf diagram for each paper.

**b** Which paper seems to have been harder? Give a reason for your answer.

> Do not just pick out the top or bottom mark in the exam papers. Use an average value.

**5** The stem-and-leaf diagram shows the 'all time best' times for the men's 400 m sprint.

```
431 | 8
432 | 9
433 | 9
434 | 4  5  9
435 | 0  0
436 | 2  5  6  6  8  8
437 | 1  4  5  5  6
438 | 1  2  3  4  6  6  6  7  8
439 | 0  1  1  2  2  3  3  3  4  4  5  6  6  6  7  7  8  8  9
```
Key: 439|0 represents 43.90 seconds

Source: Data used with the permission of the IAAF (International Association of Athletics Federations)

**a** What is the fastest time shown?

**b** What is the range of the times?

**c** What is the median time?

**d** In Beijing's National Stadium in August 2008, LaShawn Merritt ran 43.75 seconds.

How many of the times in the stem-and-leaf diagram are faster than this?

144

## Review

**1** The table shows the number of downloads per hour from a website.

| Downloads | 0–19 | 20–39 | 40–59 | 60–79 | 80–99 |
|---|---|---|---|---|---|
| Frequency | 4 | 10 | 24 | 18 | 6 |

Draw a frequency diagram to show this information.

**2** The frequency diagram shows the times taken to evacuate a school during fire practices.

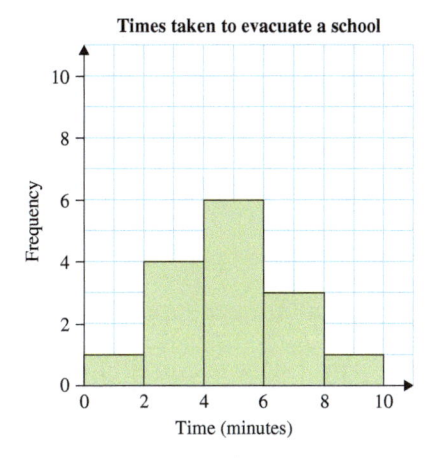

**a** How many times was the school evacuated in 4 minutes or less?

**b** The school's target is to evacuate everyone in less than 6 minutes 75% of the time.

Has the school met its target?

**3** The table shows the number of drinks sold in a café one lunchtime.

| Drink | Frequency |
|---|---|
| Tea | 23 |
| Coffee | 27 |
| Lemonade | 6 |
| Milkshake | 4 |
| Cola | 12 |

**a** Draw a pie chart to show this information.

**b** Was the data collected on a hot day or a cold day? Give a reason for your answer.

**4** The pie charts show the games won, drawn and lost for The Reds and The Blues.

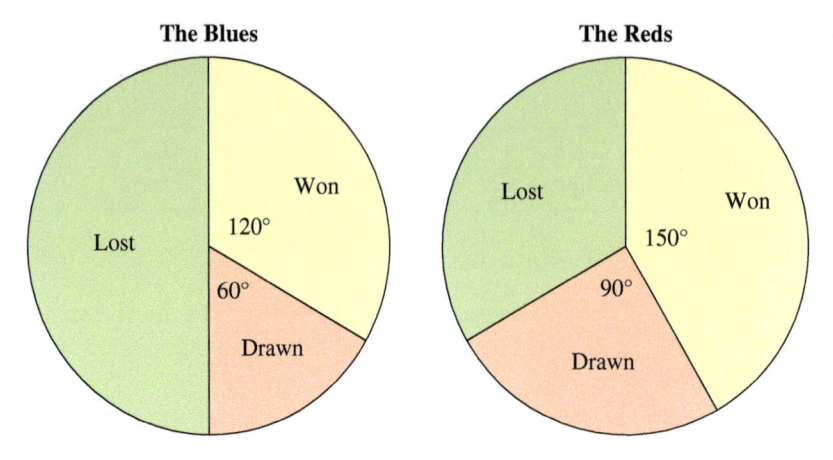

**The Blues**
- Won 120°
- Drawn 60°
- Lost

**The Reds**
- Won 150°
- Drawn 90°
- Lost

**a** Which team won a larger percentage of their games? How can you tell?

**b** Both teams drew three games.

How many more games did The Blues play than The Reds? Show how you decide.

**5** The table shows the average rainfall for each month in Greece.

| Month | Jan | Feb | Mar | Apr | May | Jun | Jul | Aug | Sep | Oct | Nov | Dec |
|---|---|---|---|---|---|---|---|---|---|---|---|---|
| Rainfall (mm) | 82.9 | 71.2 | 62 | 42 | 29.1 | 15.3 | 9.6 | 10.5 | 26.5 | 67.3 | 90.3 | 99.8 |

Source: Weatherbase

**a** Draw a line graph to show this information.

**b** For how many months is the average rainfall above 50 mm?

**6** These are the masses, in kg, of 20 babies.

2.5, 1.9, 3.4, 4.7, 3.8, 2.9, 3.2, 2.0, 4.2, 3.5, 3.0, 4.1, 2.7, 4.1, 3.6, 3.2, 2.4, 2.8, 2.1, 3.7

**a** Draw a stem-and-leaf diagram to show this information.

**b** Find the range of the masses.

**c** Find the median mass.

# 11 Area, perimeter and volume

> **Learning outcomes**
> - Know the definition of a circle and the names of its parts.
> - Know and use formulae for the circumference and area of a circle.
> - Derive and use formulae for the area of a parallelogram, triangle and trapezium.
> - Calculate areas of compound 2D shapes, and lengths, surface areas and volumes of cuboids.
> - Use simple nets of solids to work out their surface areas.

## Piems and pi

'May I have a small selection of cheese after tea?'

This is an example of a 'piem', a sentence, poem or story that is used to memorise the digits in pi ($\pi$). 'Piem' is a combination of the words 'pi' and 'poem'.

By counting the letters in the words of the piem, you get the digits 3.141592653, which are the first 10 digits of $\pi$.

In 2005, China's Chao Lu set a world record for memorising $\pi$. He memorised 67 890 digits and took over 24 hours to recite them.

## 11.1 Circles

### Parts of a circle

This diagram is labelled to show the names for the parts of a circle.

The **circumference** is the perimeter, or the distance all the way round a circle.

An **arc** is part of the circumference of a circle.

The **diameter** is the distance across a circle through the centre.

The **radius** is the distance from the centre of a circle to the circumference.

A **chord** is a straight line joining two points on the circumference of a circle.

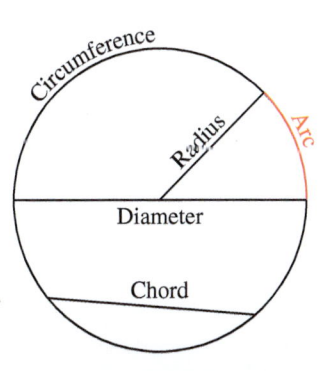

147

You can see from the diagram that the diameter (*d*) is twice as long as the radius (*r*).

As a formula, this is written:

$d = 2r$

## Circumference of a circle

This circle has a diameter of 5 centimetres.

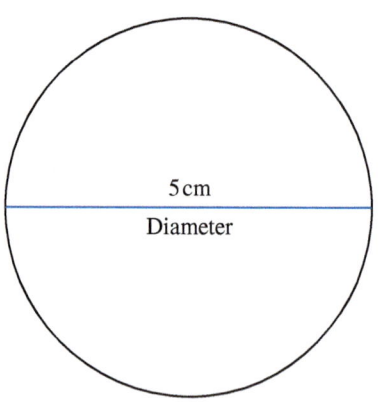

Using a piece of string, measure the circumference as accurately as you can.

You should find that the circumference is just over 15 centimetres.

Try drawing some circles with different diameters.

Measure their circumferences.

You should find that the circumference is always just over three times the diameter.

In fact, the circumference is approximately equal to 3.142 × diameter.

This number is known as **pi** and is written $\pi$.

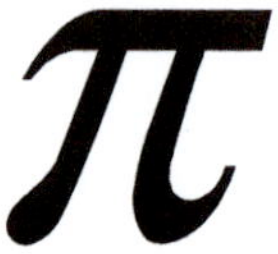

- $\pi$ is not exactly equal to 3.142
- It cannot be written exactly as it is a decimal that goes on forever.
- To 3 decimal places, $\pi$ is 3.142
- To 30 decimal places, it is 3.141592653589793238462643383279
- Your calculator will probably show the first 10 decimal places.

The formula connecting the circumference (C) and the diameter is:

$C = \pi \times d$ 　or　 $C = \pi d$

As $d = 2 \times r$, this can also be written as:

$C = 2 \times \pi \times r$ 　or　 $C = 2\pi r$

### Worked example 1

Find the circumference of each circle. Give your answers correct to 2 decimal places.

a　　6 cm

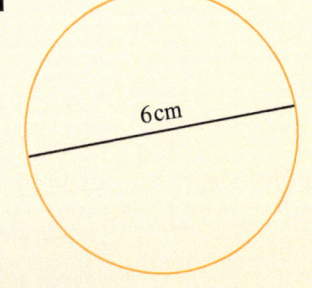

b　　5 cm

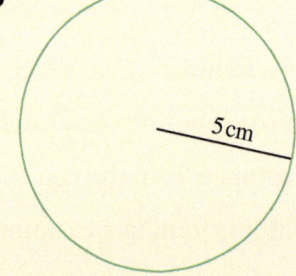

**a** The diameter, $d$, is 6 cm.

$C = \pi \times 6 = 18.84955592$   Using the $\pi$ button on a calculator.

$= 18.85$ cm   Rounded to 2 decimal places.

**b** The radius, $r$, is 5 cm.

$C = 2 \times \pi \times 5 = 31.41592654$   Using the $\pi$ button on a calculator.

$= 31.42$ cm   Rounded to 2 decimal places.

## Worked example 2

A circle has a circumference of 50 cm.

Work out the diameter to the nearest millimetre.

$50 = \pi \times d$   Because $C = \pi \times d$

$d = 50 \div \pi = 15.91549431$   Using the $\pi$ button on a calculator.

$= 15.9$ cm or 159 mm   Rounded to the nearest mm.

## Exercise 11.1

Unless told otherwise, give your answers correct to 1 decimal place.

**1 a** The radius of a circle is 4 cm. Work out the diameter.

  **b** The radius of a circle is 15 mm. Work out the diameter.

  **c** The radius of a circle is 2 m. Work out the diameter.

  **d** The diameter of a circle is 20 mm. Work out the radius.

  **e** The diameter of a circle is 1.8 m. Work out the radius.

  **f** The diameter of a circle is 56 cm. Work out the radius.

**2** Find the circumference of each circle.

  **a** 8 cm

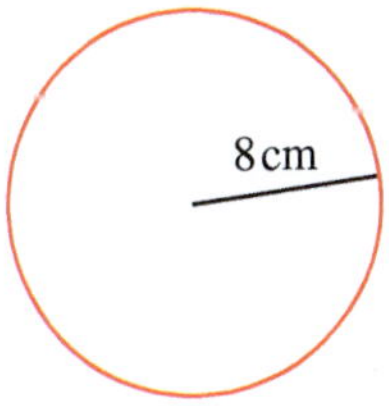

  **b** 4.5 cm

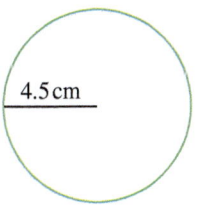

  **c** 16 mm

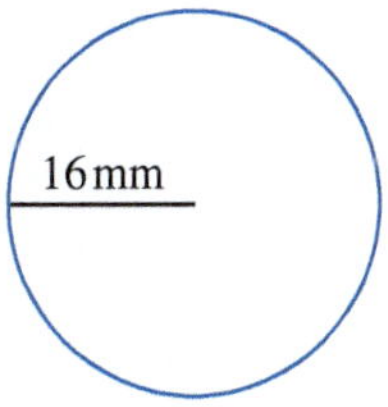

  **d** 9 cm

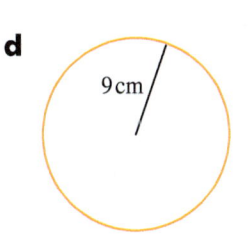

3 Find the circumference of each circle.

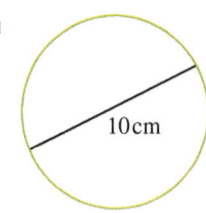

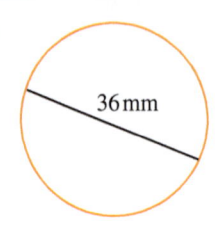

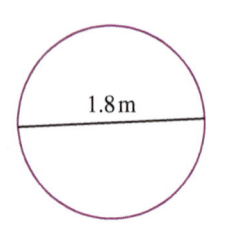

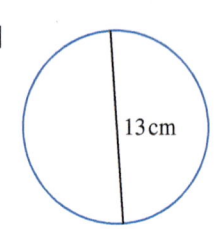

a 10 cm

b 36 mm

c 1.8 m

d 13 cm

4 Find the diameters of these circles. In each case, the circumference is given.

   a  C = 96 cm      b  C = 27 mm      c  C = 45 cm

5 Work out the radii of circles with the following circumferences.

   a  32 cm          b  18 mm          c  100 cm

6 Fill in the gaps in this table correct to 2 decimal places.

| Radius | Diameter | Circumference |
|---|---|---|
| 12 mm |  |  |
|  | 16 cm |  |
|  |  | 65 cm |
|  | 1.7 m |  |
| 0.6 m |  |  |

7 A circular table has a diameter of 1.4 m.

   What is the distance around the table?

8 What length of ribbon is needed to go round a cake with diameter 25 cm?

   Ignore any overlap needed.

9 Find the perimeter of each shape.

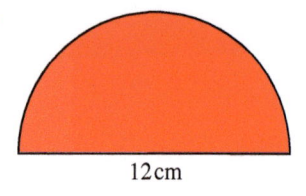

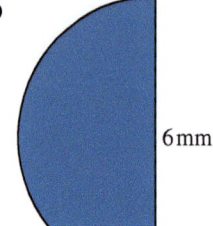

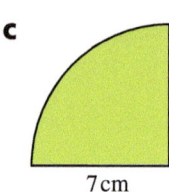

   a  12 cm (semicircle)
   
   b  6 mm (semicircle)
   
   c  7 cm (quarter circle)

> The curved edge of a semicircle is half the circumference of a full circle. Don't forget to add on the length of the straight lines.

10 a  A bicycle wheel has a radius of 30 cm.

   How far does the bicycle travel when the wheel makes one revolution?

   > The distance the bicycle travels in one revolution of the wheel is equal to the circumference.

   b  How many times does the wheel go round when the bicycle travels 250 metres?

11 Area, perimeter and volume

**11** This diagram shows an athletics track.

The two straight sections are each 80 m long.

The total distance around the track is 400 m.

Work out the radius of the curved sections of track at each end.

> Subtract the lengths of the straights to find the circumference of the circular end sections.

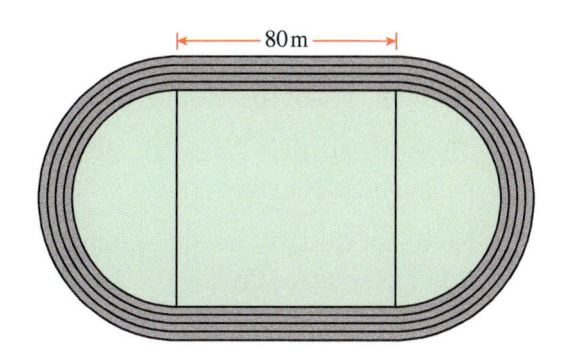

## 11.2 Area of a parallelogram

A parallelogram is a quadrilateral with two pairs of parallel sides.

One way of finding the area of a parallelogram is to turn it into a rectangle.

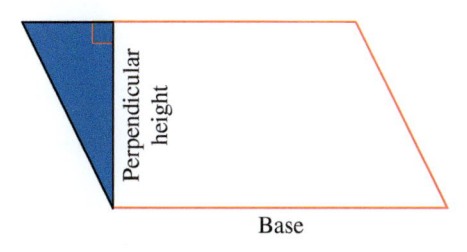

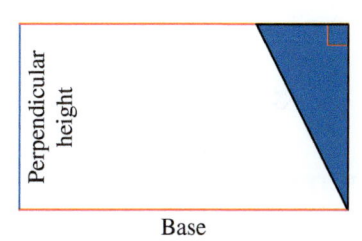

Draw a line perpendicular to the base of the parallelogram to create a triangle.

Move that triangle to the other end of the parallelogram to make a rectangle.

Area of the rectangle = base length × perpendicular height.

> Remember from Stage 7 that the area of a rectangle = length × width.

The area of the parallelogram is the same as the area of the rectangle:

Area of a parallelogram = base length × perpendicular height

This can be written as a formula:

$A = b \times h$    or    $A = bh$

It is important that the height used is perpendicular to the base, as shown in these diagrams.

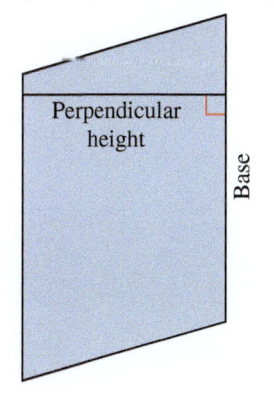

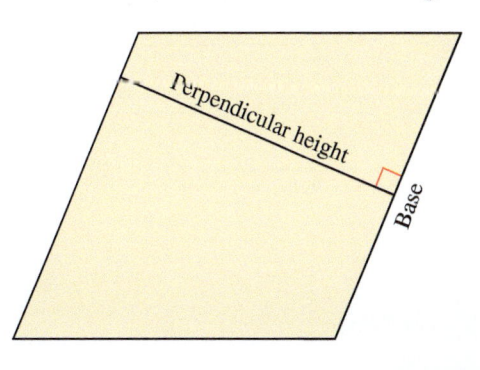

151

Mathematics for Cambridge Secondary 1

## Worked example 1

Find the area of this parallelogram.

The base length is 7.5 cm and the perpendicular height is 4 cm.

Note that the slant height, 4.8 cm, is not needed for finding the area.

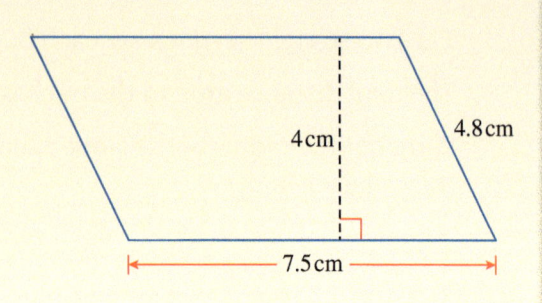

$$\text{Area} = 7.5 \times 4 = 30$$

The area is 30 cm².

*Remember to use the correct units for an area.*

## Worked example 2

The area of this parallelogram is 76 cm².

Find the perpendicular height.

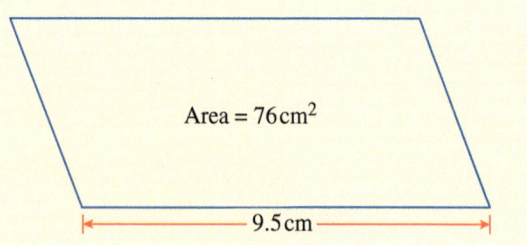

The area formula is $A = b \times h$

$$76 = 9.5 \times h$$
$$h = 76 \div 9.5 = 8$$

The perpendicular height is 8 cm.

*Substitute $A = 76$ and $b = 9.5$ in the formula.*

## Exercise 11.2

**1** Work out the area of each parallelogram.

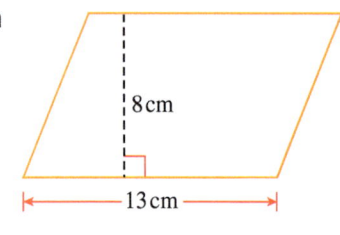

**a** 8 cm, 13 cm

**b** 11 mm, 6 mm

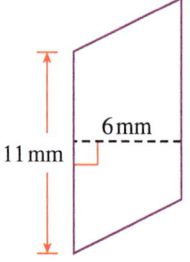

**c** 14 cm, 9 cm

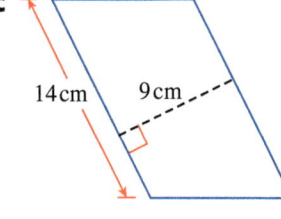

**2** Find the perpendicular height of each parallelogram.

**a** Area = 72 cm², 9 cm

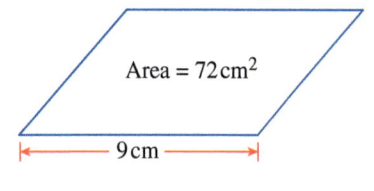

**b** Area = 72 mm², 6 mm

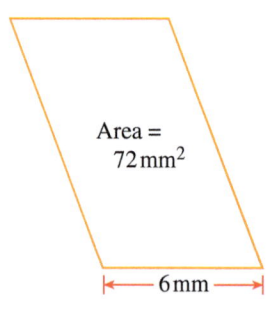

**c** Area = 40 cm², 7.5 cm

152

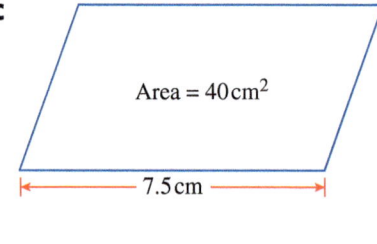

## 11 Area, perimeter and volume

**3** Copy and complete this table, which shows the base length, perpendicular height and area of some parallelograms.

| Base length | Perpendicular height | Area |
|---|---|---|
| 8.5 cm | 4 cm | |
| 12.5 mm | | 100 mm² |
| | 18 cm | 108 cm² |
| 1.2 cm | | 8.4 cm² |

**4** The base length of a parallelogram is 35 mm.

The perpendicular height is 1.8 cm.

  **a** Work out the area of the parallelogram in cm².

  **b** Work out the area of the parallelogram in mm².

**5** The diagrams show the same parallelogram.

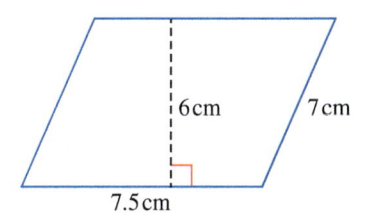

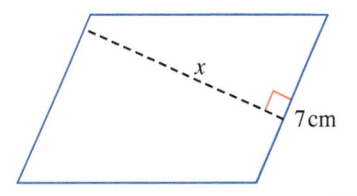

  **a** Use the diagram on the left to find the area of the parallelogram.

  **b** Use the diagram on the right to find the length marked $x$.
  Give your answer correct to 2 decimal places.

  *Use the area you found in part a to work out $x$, the perpendicular height, in part b.*

**6 a** These two parallelograms each have an area of 36 cm².

  Work out the length of the base of each one.

  **i** (4 cm)  **ii** (3 cm)

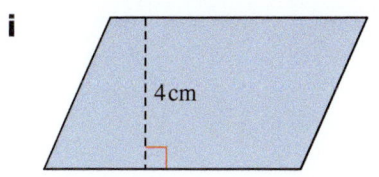

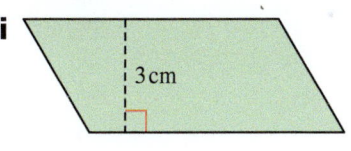

  *Think of all the factors of 36, but remember that the lengths do not need to be whole numbers.*

  **b** Find some more parallelograms with an area of 36 cm².
  How many can you find?

## 11.3 Area of a triangle

Now that you know how to find the area of a parallelogram, you can easily find the area of a triangle.

Two identical triangles can be put together to form a parallelogram by rotating one through 180°.

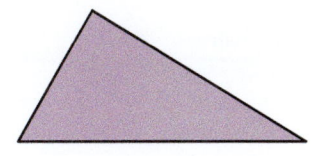

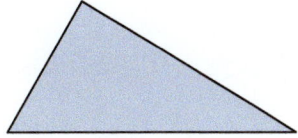

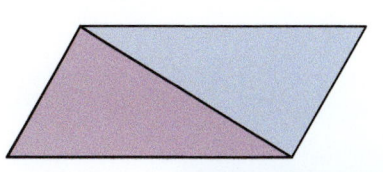

153

As the area of a parallelogram = base length × perpendicular height, the area of a triangle must be half of this:

Area of a triangle = $\frac{1}{2}$ × base length × perpendicular height

Written as a formula, this is:

$A = \frac{1}{2} \times b \times h$   or   $A = \frac{1}{2}bh$

It is important that the height used is perpendicular to the base, as shown in these diagrams.

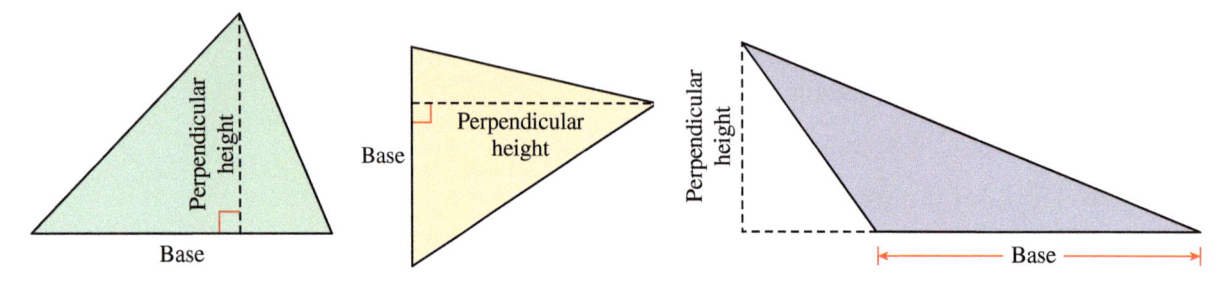

Notice that the perpendicular height must sometimes be measured outside the triangle.

## Worked example 1

Find the area of this triangle.

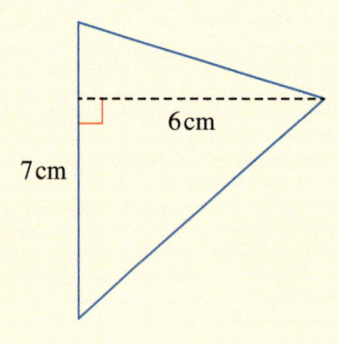

Substitute $b = 7$ and $h = 6$ into the formula $A = \frac{1}{2}bh$

$A = \frac{1}{2} \times 7 \times 6 = \frac{1}{2} \times 42 = 21$

The area of the triangle is 21 cm².

## Worked example 2

The area of this triangle is 76 cm².

Find the length of the base.

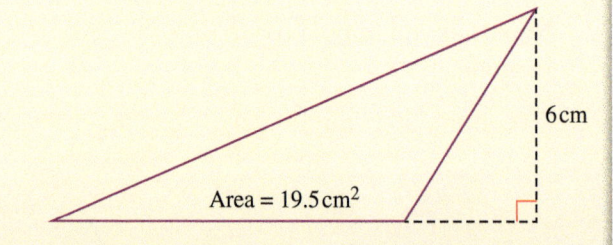

Substitute $A = 19.5$ and $h = 6$ into $A = \frac{1}{2}bh$

$19.5 = \frac{1}{2} \times b \times 6$

$39 = b \times 6$    The inverse of multiplying by $\frac{1}{2}$ is multiplying by 2.

$b = 39 \div 6 = 6.5$

The base of the triangle is 6.5 cm long.

## Exercise 11.3

**1** Work out the area of each triangle.

**a** 4 cm, 6 cm

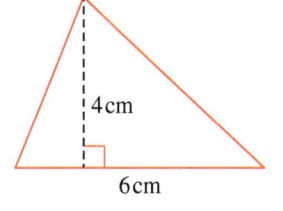

**b** 7 mm, 10 mm

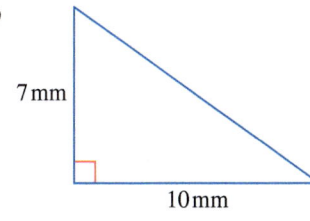

**c** 0.8 m, 1.7 m

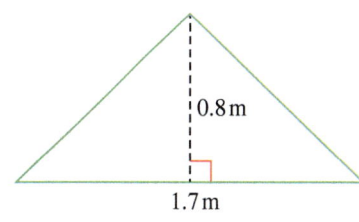

**d** 7 cm, 9 cm

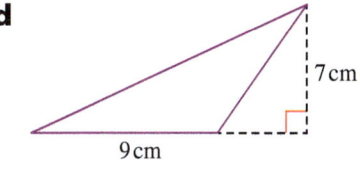

**e** 12 mm, 8 mm

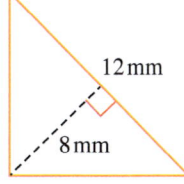

**f** 15 cm, 22 cm

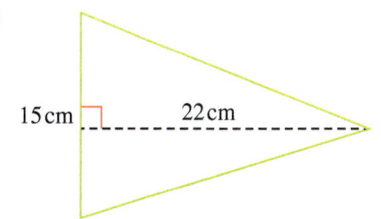

**2** Find the lengths marked with letters in these triangles.

**a** Height = $w$ cm, Base = 10 cm, Area = 45 cm²

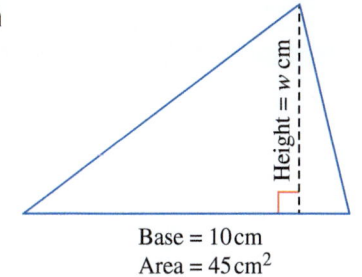

**b** Height = 10 mm, Base = $x$ mm, Area = 55 mm²

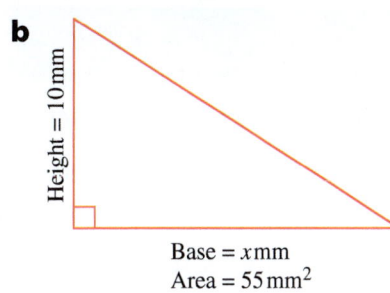

**c** Height = $y$ cm, Base = 7 cm, Area = 31.5 cm²

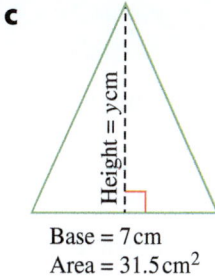

**3** Copy and complete this table, which shows the base length, perpendicular height and area of some triangles.

| Base length | Perpendicular height | Area |
| --- | --- | --- |
| 3 cm | 4 cm | |
| 7 mm | | 56 mm² |
| 2.5 m | 6 m | |
| | 12 mm | 120 mm² |
| | 15 cm | 90 cm² |
| 1.4 cm | | 8.4 cm² |

155

# Mathematics for Cambridge Secondary 1

**4** Triangle *ABC* has sides *AB* = 8 cm, *BC* = 7 cm and *AC* = 9 cm.

Draw triangle *ABC* accurately using ruler and compasses.

Measure the perpendicular height of the triangle from *C* to *AB*.

Work out the area in cm².

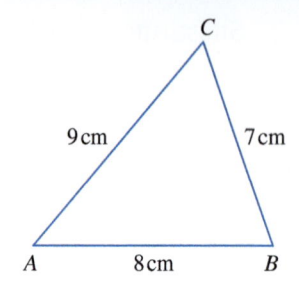

**5** The sail of Samuel's sailing boat is a triangular piece of canvas.

It is 15 metres high and the base is 8 metres long.

  **a** Work out the area of the sail in square metres.

  **b** Samuel needs to buy some canvas paint to cover the sail.

  1 litre of paint covers 18 m².

  Work out how many litres of paint he needs to buy.

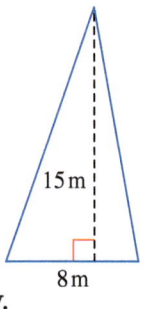

> You cannot buy part of a tin of paint so do not forget to round the answer up to a whole number.

**6** A farmer needed to find the area of one of his fields.

He measured it carefully and drew this sketch plan.

  **a** Draw an accurate scale drawing of the field.

  **b** Use your drawing to find the area of the field in m².

> Use ruler and compasses to draw an accurate diagram using the method shown in Chapter 9.

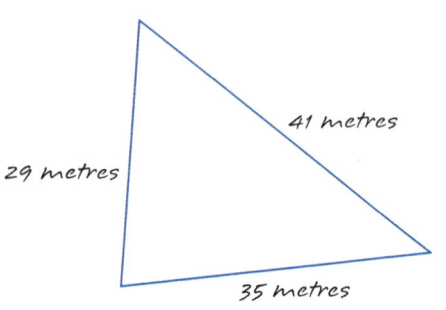

## 11.4 Area of a trapezium

A trapezium is a quadrilateral with one pair of parallel sides.

Here is a trapezium with parallel sides of length *a* and *b* with perpendicular height *h*.

Note that the two parallel sides are always different lengths so two letters are needed.

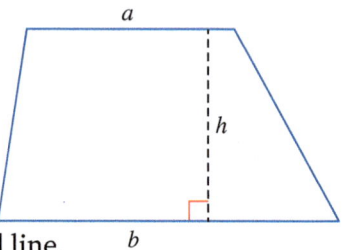

A trapezium can be made up of two triangles by drawing a diagonal line.

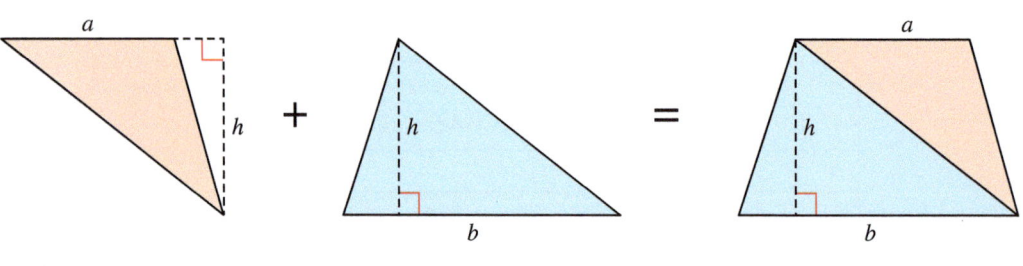

Area = $\frac{1}{2} \times a \times h$    +    $\frac{1}{2} \times b \times h$    =    $\frac{1}{2} \times a \times h + \frac{1}{2} \times b \times h$

Area of a trapezium is $\frac{1}{2} \times a \times h + \frac{1}{2} \times b \times h$, which is usually simplified to the following:

Area of a trapezium = $\frac{1}{2} \times (a + b) \times h$    or    $A = \frac{1}{2}(a + b)h$

## Worked example 1

Find the area of this trapezium.

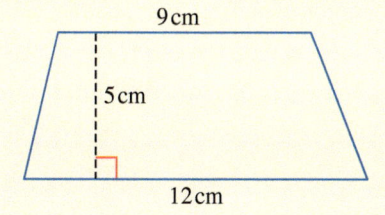

Substitute $a = 9$, $b = 12$ and $h = 5$ in the formula $A = \frac{1}{2}(a + b)h$

$A = \frac{1}{2} \times (9 + 12) \times 5$

$= \frac{1}{2} \times 21 \times 5$

$= \frac{1}{2} \times 105$

$= 52.5$

The area of the trapezium is $52.5\,\text{cm}^2$.

## Worked example 2

This is a diagram of the end of a shed.

The area of the end wall is $3.36\,\text{m}^2$.

Find the length of the side marked $x$.

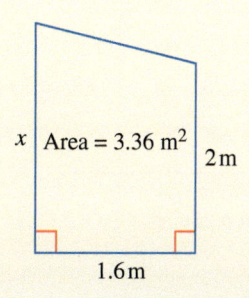

Substitute $A = 3.36$, $a = 2$ and $h = 1.6$ into the formula for the area of a trapezium.

> In this case, the height is equal to one side of the trapezium because the base is perpendicular to the uprights.
>
> You can substitute $a = 2$ or $b = 2$, it makes no difference to the solution.

$3.36 = \frac{1}{2} \times (2 + x) \times 1.6$

$6.72 = (2 + x) \times 1.6$     Multiply by 2 to remove the $\frac{1}{2}$

$6.72 \div 1.6 = 2 + x$     Divide both sides by 1.6

$4.2 = 2 + x$

$x = 2.2$     Subtract 2 from each side.

The side is 2.2 m tall.

## Exercise 11.4

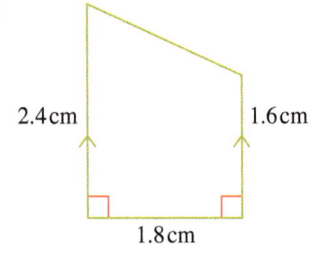

**1** Find the area of each trapezium.

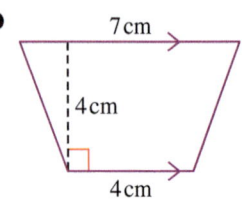

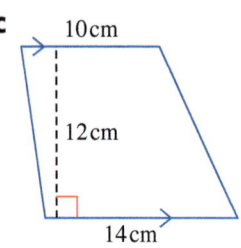

**a** 9 mm (top), 5 mm (height), 11 mm (bottom)

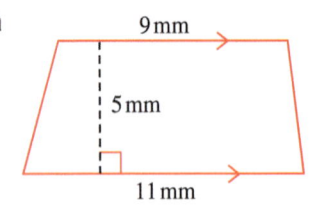

**b** 7 cm (top), 4 cm (height), 4 cm (bottom)

**c** 10 cm (top), 12 cm (height), 14 cm (bottom)

**d** 2.4 cm (left side), 1.6 cm (right side), 1.8 cm (bottom)

**e** 3 mm (top), 12 mm (height), 8 mm (bottom)

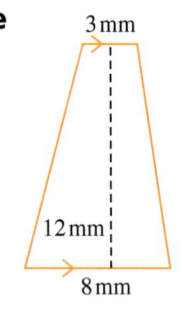

**2** Find the side marked with a letter in each of these diagrams.

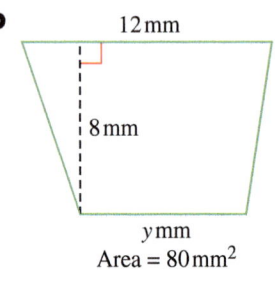

**a** 5 cm (top), $x$ cm (height), 8 cm (bottom), Area = 26 cm²

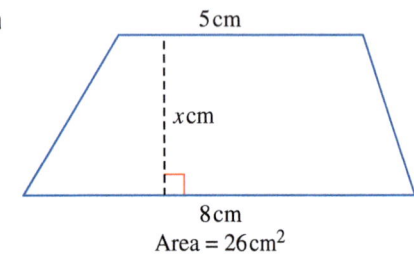

**b** 12 mm (top), 8 mm (height), $y$ mm (bottom), Area = 80 mm²

**c** 3 m, $z$ m, 1.5 m, Area = 4.125 m²

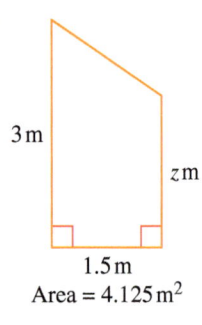

**3** The diagram shows the side wall of a swimming pool.

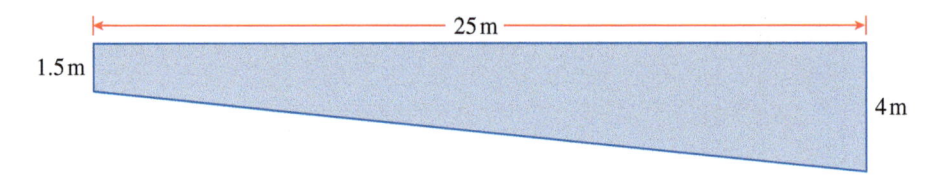

25 m, 1.5 m, 4 m

Work out the area of the wall in m².

**4** A pane of glass from a greenhouse is in the shape of a trapezium.

**a** Work out the area of the glass in m².

**b** Work out the area of the glass in cm².

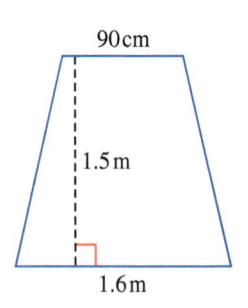

90 cm (top), 1.5 m (height), 1.6 m (bottom)

*Change the lengths to metres to do part **a** and change them all to centimetres for part **b**.*

# 11 Area, perimeter and volume

## 11.5 Area of a circle

In the diagram below, six equilateral triangles have been drawn inside a circle.

These triangles can be rearranged to make a parallelogram.

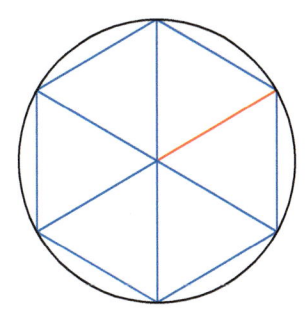

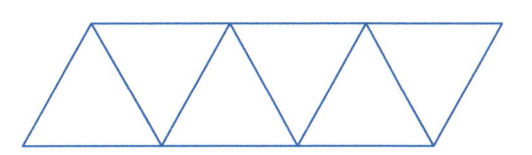

This parallelogram has a smaller area than the circle.

This circle is divided into 36 triangles. Because the triangles are so near to the circumference, it is not possible to draw the ends of the triangles clearly.

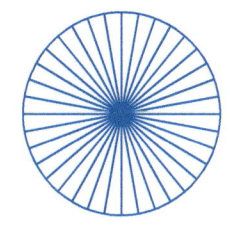

Here the 36 triangles are rearranged to make a parallelogram.

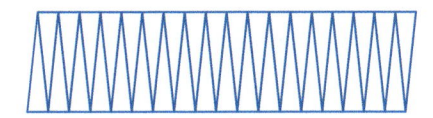

The sum of the top and bottom sides of the parallelogram is nearly equal to the circumference of the circle. The circumference is $2\pi r$ so half of that is $\pi r$.

The base of the parallelogram is approximately equal to $\pi r$.

The height is approximately equal to $r$.

Area of a parallelogram = base × perpendicular height = $\pi r \times r = \pi r^2$.

This is only approximate, but if the circle is divided into many more triangles it would be more accurate. This gives the correct formula for the area of a circle:

Area of a circle = $\pi \times r^2$   or   $A = \pi r^2$

### Worked example

Find the area of each circle. Give your answers correct to 1 decimal place.

a   3 cm

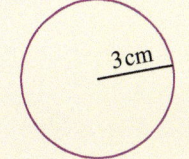

b   9 cm

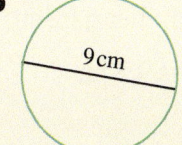

**a** In this case, $r$ (the radius) is given, so the formula can be used immediately.

$A = \pi \times 3^2$

$\phantom{A} = \pi \times 9$

$\phantom{A} = 28.27433388$     Using the $\pi$ button on a calculator.

$\phantom{A} = 28.3 \text{ cm}^2$     Rounded to 1 decimal place.

**b** Here the diameter is given.

The radius is half the diameter so $r = 4.5$

$A = \pi \times 4.5^2$

$\phantom{A} = \pi \times 20.25$

$\phantom{A} = 63.61725124$     Using the $\pi$ button on a calculator.

$\phantom{A} = 63.6 \text{ cm}^2$     Rounded to 1 decimal place.

## Exercise 11.5

1 Work out the area of each circle. Give your answers correct to 1 decimal place.

    **a** 4 cm     **b** 6 mm     **c** 7.5 cm     **d** 8 mm

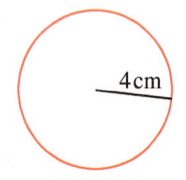

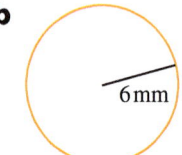

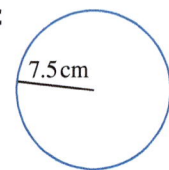

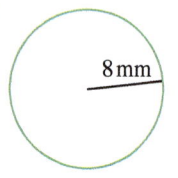

2 Find the area of each circle. Give your answers correct to 1 decimal place.

    **a** 5 cm     **b** 19 m     **c** 0.8 cm     **d** 3.8 mm

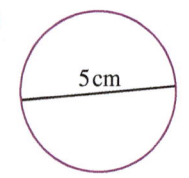

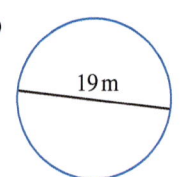

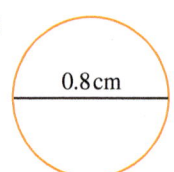

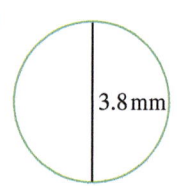

3 A circular garden pond has a diameter of 2.4 metres.

    **a** Work out the circumference of the pond correct to 2 decimal places.

    **b** Work out the area of the pond correct to 2 decimal places.

4 A window on a ship needs a new piece of glass.

The glass must be a circle of radius 28 cm.

What is the area of the glass? Give your answer correct to the nearest cm².

5 Olivia wants to sow a new lawn in her garden.

The lawn will be a circle of radius 9.5 m.

# 11 Area, perimeter and volume

A packet of grass seed covers 32 m².

   **a** Work out the area of the lawn. Give your answer correct to 1 decimal place.

   **b** Work out how many packets of seed Olivia needs to buy.

**6** Find the area of a circle with circumference 20 cm. Give your answer correct to 2 decimal places.

> Start by using the formula $C = 2\pi r$ to work out the radius. Then work out the area.

**7** Find the area of each shape. Give your answers correct to 1 decimal place.

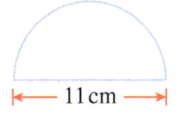

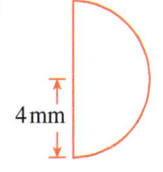

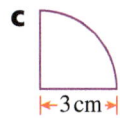

   **a** 11 cm

   **b** 4 mm

   **c** 3 cm

> The area of a semicircle is half the area of a full circle.

## 11.6 Compound areas

### Areas of compound shapes

A **compound shape** is a shape that is made of two or more shapes put together.

Here are some examples of compound shapes.

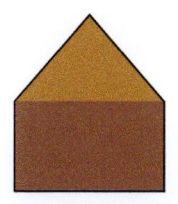

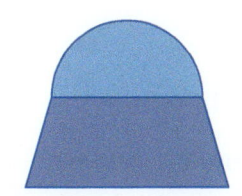

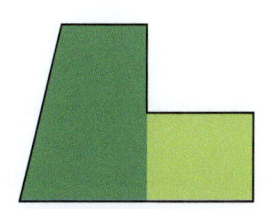

The first shape is made up of a rectangle and a triangle, the second is a semicircle and a trapezium and the third is a trapezium and a rectangle.

You can find the area of a compound shape by finding the area of each individual shape and adding them together.

### Worked example 1

Find the area of this shape.

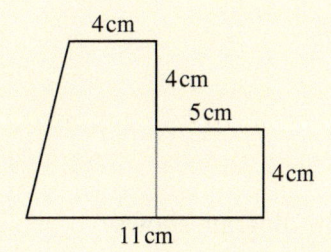

4 cm
4 cm
5 cm
4 cm
11 cm

The line on the shape shows how it is made from a trapezium and a rectangle.

161

**Step 1**

Work out the area of the rectangle.

The width is 5 cm and the height is 4 cm.

$$\text{Area of rectangle} = 5 \times 4$$
$$= 20 \text{ cm}^2 \quad [1]$$

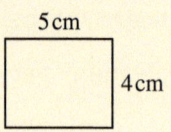

**Step 2**

Work out the area of the trapezium.

The base is $11 - 5 = 6$ cm and the height is $4 + 4 = 8$ cm.

Use $a = 4$, $b = 6$ and $h = 8$ in the formula $A = \frac{1}{2}(a + b)h$

$$\text{Area of trapezium} = \frac{1}{2} \times (4 + 6) \times 8$$
$$= \frac{1}{2} \times 10 \times 8$$
$$= 40 \text{ cm}^2 \quad [2]$$

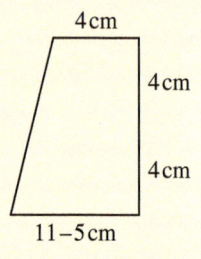

**Step 3**

Add [1] and [2] together.

$$\text{Total area} = 20 + 40$$
$$= 60 \text{ cm}^2$$

## Surface area using nets of solids

The net of a solid shape consists of several 2D shapes.

The solid shape can be created by folding the net.

To find the surface area of a solid, draw the net and find the total area of all of the faces.

### Worked example 2

Find the surface area of this triangular prism.

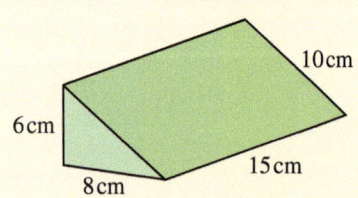

This prism has five faces. The diagram shows one possible version of its net.

To find the surface area, you can treat the three rectangles as one large rectangle 15 cm wide and 24 cm long.

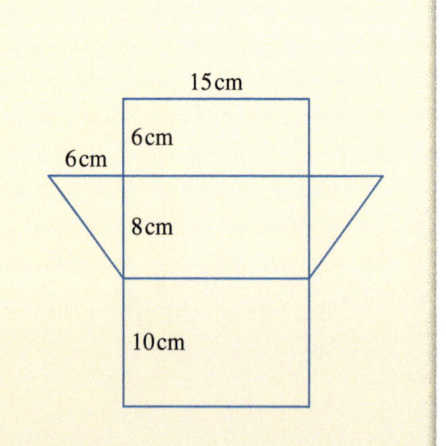

162

Area of rectangle = 15 × 24
= 360 cm²

Area of one triangle = $\frac{1}{2}$ × 6 × 8
= 24 cm²

Total surface area = 24 + 24 + 360 = 408 cm²

> You would get the same answer if you worked out the area of each rectangle separately.

## Worked example 3

This cuboid measures 7 cm by 5 cm by 2.5 cm.

**a** Work out the surface area of the cuboid.

**b** Find the volume of the cuboid.

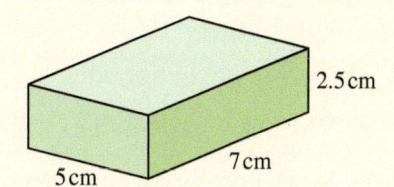

**a** A sketch of the net of the cuboid shows that it is made up of six rectangles.

Surface area = 2(7 × 5) + 2(2.5 × 5) + 2(7 × 2.5)
= 130 cm²

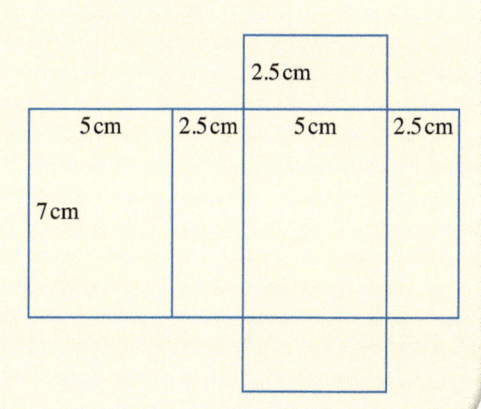

**b** In your Stage 7 Student Book, you learnt that the volume of a cuboid is length × width × height.

Volume = 7 × 5 × 2.5
= 87.5 cm³

## Exercise 11.6

**1** Work out the area of each compound shape. Give your answer to part **d** correct to 2 decimal places.

**a** 4 cm, 3.5 cm, 6 cm

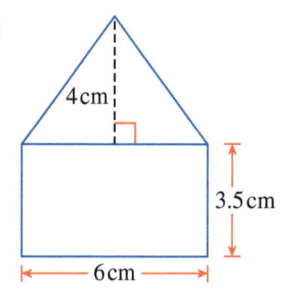

**b** 8 mm, 5 mm, 6 mm, 12 mm

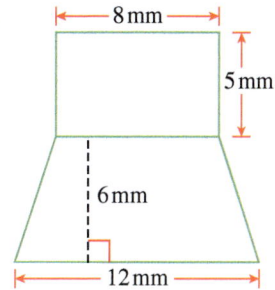

**c** 4.5 cm, 5 cm, 7.5 cm

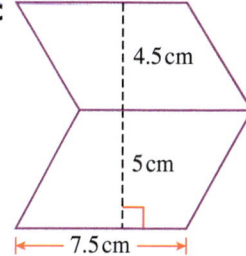

**d** 5.8 cm, 10 cm

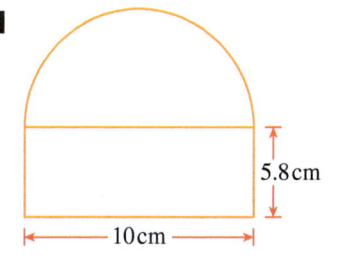

**e** 13 mm, 9 mm, 9 mm, 6 mm, 6 mm

163

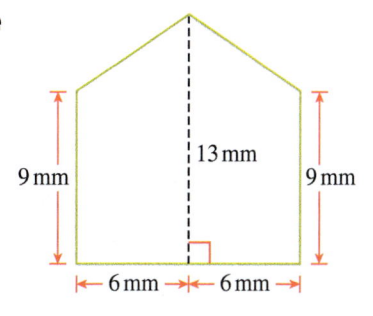

Mathematics for Cambridge Secondary **1**

**2** For each of these solids draw a net and then work out the surface area.

  **a**

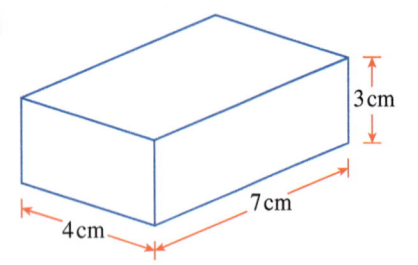

  **b**

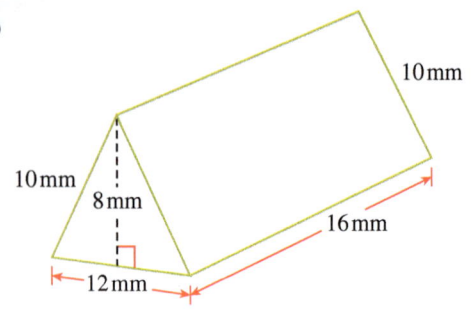

  3 cm, 7 cm, 4 cm

  10 mm, 8 mm, 12 mm, 16 mm, 10 mm

**3** This is the net of a solid.

  **a** Write down the name of the solid.

  **b** Work out the surface area of the solid.

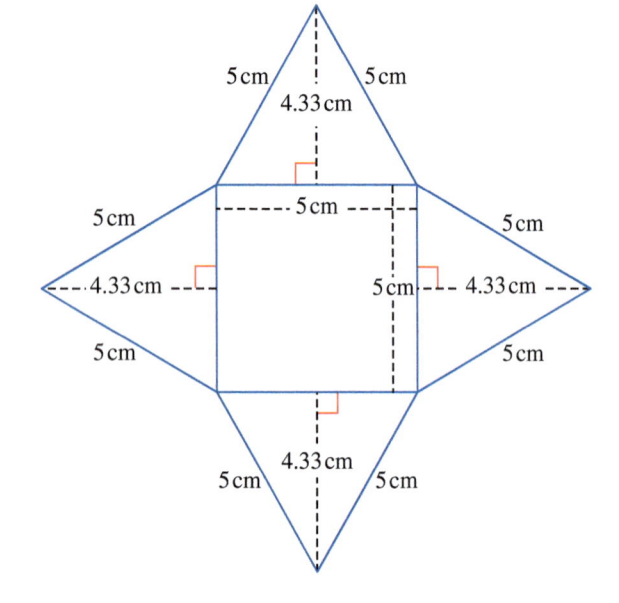

  5 cm, 4.33 cm, 5 cm, 5 cm, 5 cm, 4.33 cm, 5 cm, 5 cm, 4.33 cm, 5 cm, 5 cm, 4.33 cm, 5 cm

**4** This diagram shows the end of a greenhouse.

  Work out the area of the end of the greenhouse.

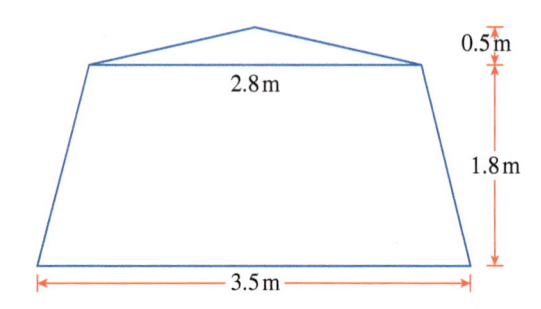

  0.5 m, 2.8 m, 1.8 m, 3.5 m

**5** This is the plan of a circular tin in a square box.

  The box is 8 cm by 8 cm.

  Work out the area that is shaded green.

  Give your answer correct to 2 decimal places.

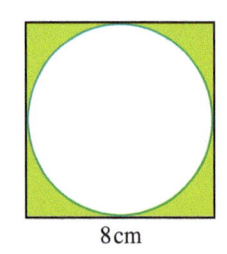

  8 cm

  > Subtract the area of the circle from the area of the whole square.

11 Area, perimeter and volume

6 For each of these 3D objects, work out:
  i the total surface area
  ii the volume.

> Treat this as two cuboids to work out the volume.

a  (cuboid: 7cm × 5cm × 4cm)

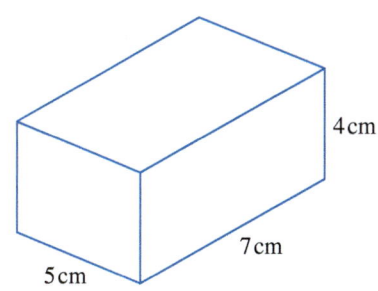

b  (stepped shape: 6cm, 6cm, 8cm, 6cm, 8cm, 18cm, 8cm)

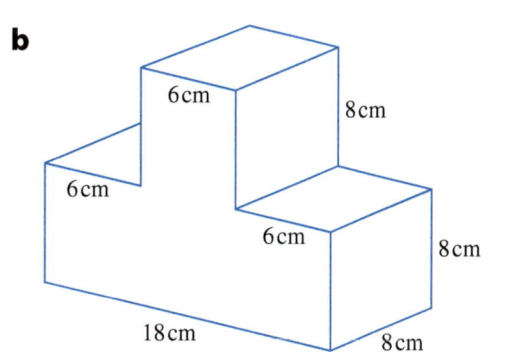

## Review

1 Find the circumference of each circle. Give your answers correct to 2 decimal places.
  a 12cm
  b 2.3mm
  c 1.9m
  d 16cm

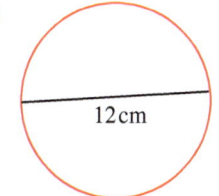

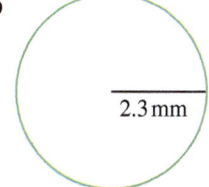

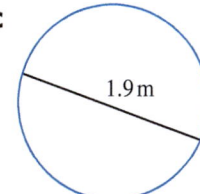

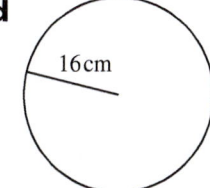

2 Find the area of each circle in question 1. Give your answers correct to 1 decimal place.

3 Find the area of each shape. Give your answer to part f correct to 1 decimal place.
  a triangle: 4cm, 7.5cm
  b parallelogram: 5mm, 13mm
  c trapezium: 5cm, 6cm, 8cm
  d triangle: 14cm, 9cm
  e triangle: 6m, 7m
  f semicircle: 16mm

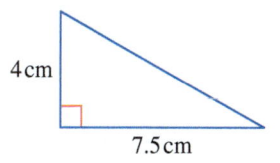

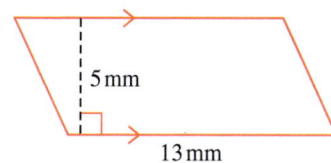

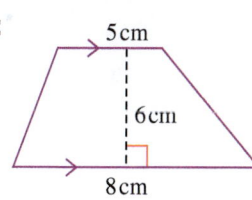

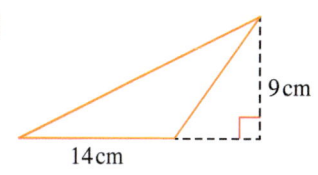

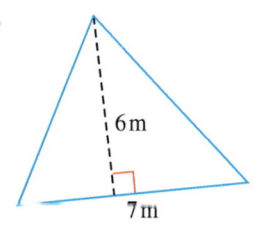

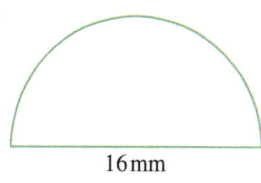

4 A circular pond in a park has a diameter of 50 m.
  a What is the distance all the way around the pond correct to the nearest metre?
  b Work out the area of the pond correct to the nearest whole number.

165

Mathematics for Cambridge Secondary **1**

**5** Find the area of each compound shape. Give your answer to part **c** correct to 1 decimal place.

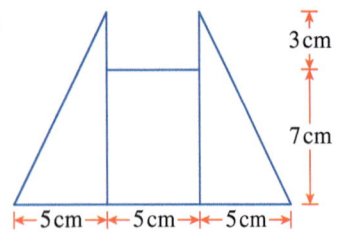

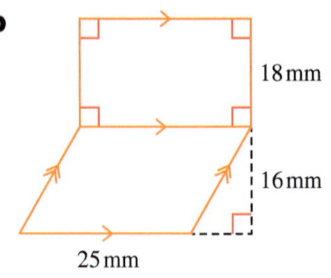

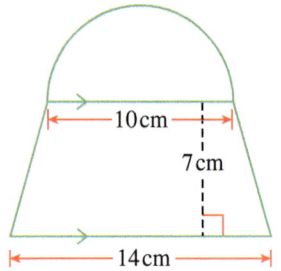

**a**  3 cm, 7 cm, 5 cm, 5 cm, 5 cm

**b**  18 mm, 16 mm, 25 mm

**c**  10 cm, 7 cm, 14 cm

**6** This is a prism with a trapezium-shaped cross section.

9 cm, 5 cm, 4 cm, 12 cm, 20 cm

  **a** Draw a net of the prism.

  **b** Work out the surface area of the prism.

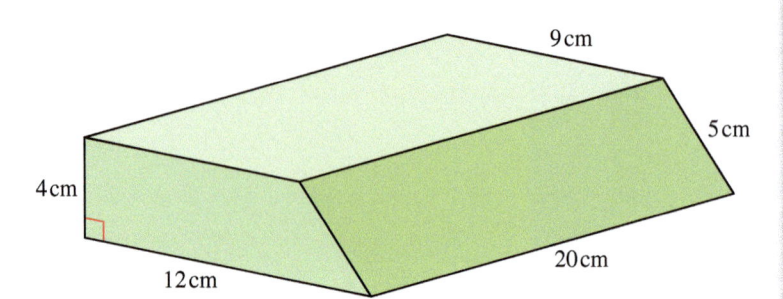

**7** This is a prism with an L-shaped cross section.

3 cm, 3 cm, 3 cm, 2 cm, 5 cm, 9 cm

  **a** Draw a net of the prism.

  **b** Work out the surface area of the prism.

  **c** By treating it as two cuboids, work out the volume of the prism.

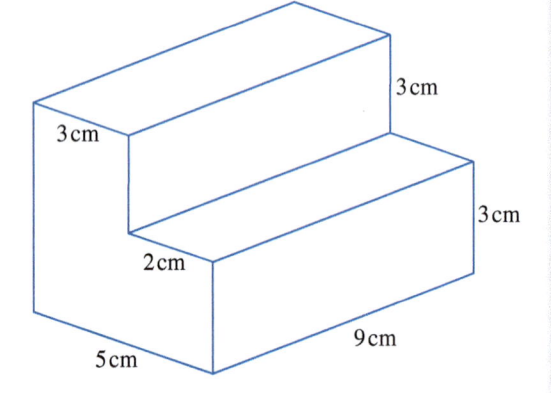

166

# 12 Formulae

> **Learning outcomes**
> - Know the meaning of formula.
> - Derive and use simple formulae.
> - Substitute positive and negative integers into formulae, including examples that lead to an equation to solve.

## Formulae in the kitchen

Chefs use formulae every day in their jobs.

Here are just a few situations where they use formulae:

- to convert temperatures from degrees Celsius to degrees Fahrenheit
- to calculate the mass of each ingredient that they need for a recipe
- to calculate the cooking time needed for a recipe
- to calculate the time when they should start preparing a meal
- to calculate the price that they should charge customers.

## 12.1 Deriving formulae

A **formula** is a rule that connects two or more variables.

For example, temperatures can be measured in degrees Celsius (°C) or degrees Fahrenheit (°F).

The table shows the freezing and boiling temperatures of water on both the Celsius and Fahrenheit scales.

|  | Freezing | Boiling |
| --- | --- | --- |
| Celsius | 0 °C | 100 °C |
| Fahrenheit | 32 °F | 212 °F |

On the Celsius scale, the freezing point and boiling point of water are 100 °C apart.

On the Fahrenheit scale, the freezing point and boiling point of water are 180 °F apart.

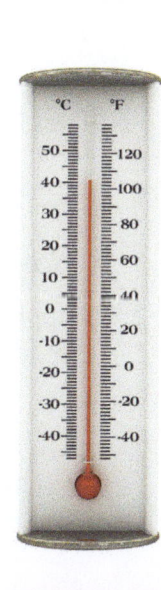

# Mathematics for Cambridge Secondary 1

So an increase of 1 °C is the same as an increase in 1.8 °F.

This leads to the rule for converting degrees Celsius (C) to degrees Fahrenheit (F):

> Multiply C by 1.8 and then add 32

This rule can then be written as a formula:

$$F = 1.8C + 32 \quad \text{or} \quad F = \frac{9}{5}C + 32$$

## Worked example 1

Derive a formula for the total number of days, $D$, in $w$ weeks.

*'Derive' means 'find and write'.*

There are seven days in a week.

To change weeks into days the rule is 'multiply the number of weeks by 7'.

The formula is: $\quad D = 7w$

## Worked example 2

Write a formula for the perimeter, $P$, of this parallelogram.

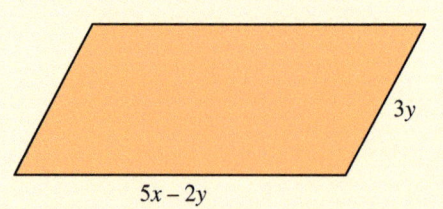

*(parallelogram with sides $3y$ and $5x - 2y$)*

Perimeter = the total length of the four sides of the parallelogram.

$P = 5x - 2y + 3y + 5x - 2y + 3y \qquad$ Simplify by collecting like terms.

$P = 10x + 2y$

## Exercise 12.1

**1 a** How many minutes are there in 2 hours?

   **b** Write a formula for the total number of minutes, $M$, in $x$ hours.

**2** An approximate method for changing a temperature, $C$, in degrees Celsius to a temperature, $F$, in degrees Fahrenheit is:

> Multiply by 2 and then add 30

Copy and complete the formula: $\quad F = \ldots$

**3** TAXI CHARGES:

Fixed fee: $5
AND THEN
$0.75 per kilometre

Write a formula for the total cost, C dollars, for a taxi ride of n kilometres.

**4** Write a formula for the perimeter, P, of each of these rectangles.

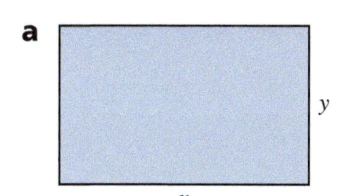

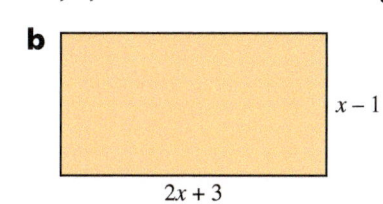

a  rectangle with sides x and y

b  rectangle with sides 2x + 3 and x − 1

c  rectangle with sides 2y − 5 and 3x

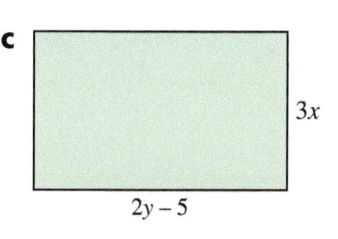

**5** Write a formula for the area, A, of each of these rectangles.

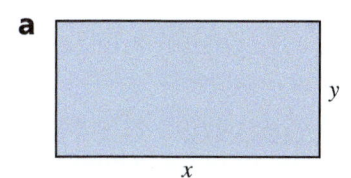

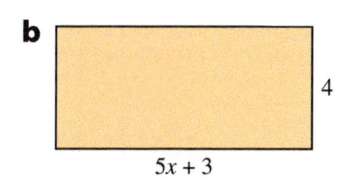

a  rectangle with sides x and y

b  rectangle with sides 5x + 3 and 4

c  rectangle with sides 2y + 7 and x

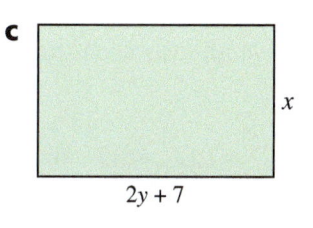

**6** A theatre sells 220 tickets at $15 each and n tickets at $18 each.

Write a formula for the total cost, C dollars, of the tickets.

**7** Light bulbs cost $b each and candles cost $c each.

Write a formula for the total cost, T dollars, of 5 light bulbs and 4 candles.

**8** Patrick buys x bags of rice.

Each bag costs $3.

He pays with a $20 note.

Write a formula for the amount of change, C dollars, that Patrick receives.

**9** Write a formula for the volume, V, of each of these cuboids.

a  cube with side x

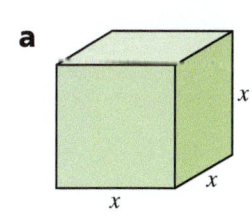

b  cuboid with sides y, y and 8

169

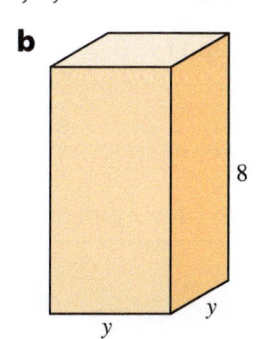

**Mathematics for Cambridge Secondary 1**

**10** Write a formula for the surface area, $A$, of each of these cuboids.

**a**

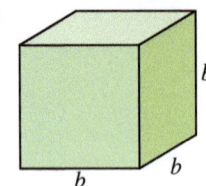

**b**

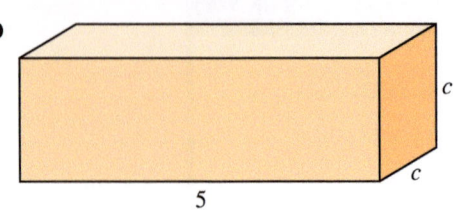

**11** Write a formula for the perimeter, $P$, of the shape.
Explain your answer.

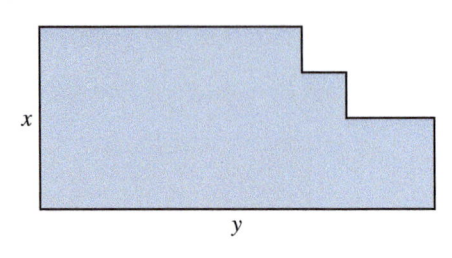

## 12.2 Substitution into formulae

**Substitution** into a formula means replacing the letters in the formula with given numbers.
You have already seen that the formula to convert degrees Celsius to degrees Fahrenheit is:

$$F = 1.8C + 32 \quad \text{or} \quad F = \tfrac{9}{5}C + 32$$

> The second version of the formula is usually easier to use if $C$ is a multiple of 5 and you do not have a calculator.

To convert a temperature of 20°C to degrees Fahrenheit, you substitute $C = 20$ into the formula:

$F = \tfrac{9}{5^1} \times 20^4 + 32$

$= 36 + 32$

$= 68$

So 20°C is the same as 68°F.

### Worked example 1

$s = \dfrac{(u + v)t}{2}$

Find the value of $s$ when $u = 7$, $v = 3$ and $t = 8$.

$s = \dfrac{(u + v)t}{2}$     Replace the letters with the given numbers.

$s = \dfrac{(7 + 3) \times 8}{2}$     Note: $(u + v)t$ means $(u + v) \times t$

$s = \dfrac{10 \times 8}{2}$

$s = 40$

170

## 12 Formulae

### Worked example 2

$s = ut + \frac{1}{2}at^2$

Find the value of $s$ when $u = -2$, $a = 6$ and $t = 15$.

$s = ut + \frac{1}{2}at^2$ — Replace the letters with the given numbers.

$s = -2 \times 15 + \frac{1}{2} \times 6 \times 15^2$ — Note: $\frac{1}{2}at^2$ means $\frac{1}{2} \times a \times t^2$

$s = -30 + \frac{1}{2} \times 6 \times 225$

$s = -30 + 675$

$s = 645$

### Exercise 12.2

**1** The formula for the perimeter, $P$, of the square is $P = 4x$

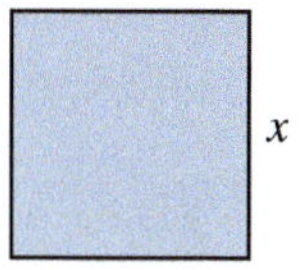

Find the value of $P$ when:

**a** $x = 5$ **b** $x = 17$
**c** $x = 6.5$ **d** $x = 12.3$

**2** The formula for the perimeter, $P$, of the rectangle is $P = 2b + 2h$

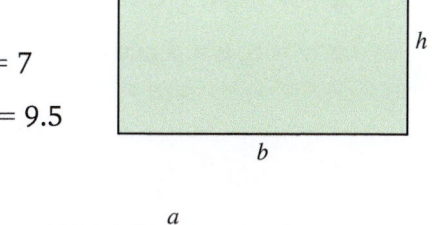

Find the value of $P$ when:

**a** $b = 4$ and $h = 8$ **b** $b = 13$ and $h = 7$
**c** $b = 6$ and $h = 4.5$ **d** $b = 6.5$ and $h = 9.5$

**3** The formula for the area, $A$, of the trapezium is $A = \frac{1}{2}(a + b)h$

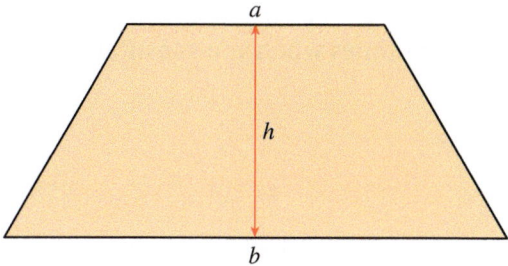

Find the value of $A$ when:

**a** $a = 4, b = 6$ and $h = 10$ **b** $a = 3, b = 9$ and $h = 5$
**c** $a = 5, b = 8$ and $h = 6$ **d** $a = 4, b = 7$ and $h = 3$

**4** The formula $F = \frac{9}{5}C + 32$ is used to change a temperature in degrees Celsius, $C$, to a temperature in degrees Fahrenheit, $F$.

Find the value of $F$ when:

**a** $C = 5$ **b** $C = 25$ **c** $C = 30$ **d** $C = 50$

**5** $F = ma$

Work out the value of $F$ when:

   **a** $m = 2$ and $a = 8$       **b** $m = 5$ and $a = -3$

**6** $v = u + at$

Work out the value of $v$ when:

   **a** $u = 15$, $a = 3$ and $t = 4$     **b** $u = 20$, $a = -2$ and $t = 8$

   **c** $u = -13$, $a = -5$ and $t = 3$   **d** $u = -8$, $a = -7$ and $t = 12$

**7** $s = ut + \frac{1}{2}at^2$

Hint: $\frac{1}{2}at^2$ means $\frac{1}{2} \times a \times t^2$

Work out the value of $s$ when:

   **a** $u = 10$, $a = 4$ and $t = 3$     **b** $u = 48$, $a = -2$ and $t = 6$

   **c** $u = 4$, $a = -1$ and $t = 5$     **d** $u = -15$, $a = -3$ and $t = 8$

**8** $f = \dfrac{uv}{u + v}$

Work out the value of $f$ when:

   **a** $u = 10$ and $v = 15$       **b** $u = 6$ and $v = 4$

**9** $s = \dfrac{v^2 - u^2}{2a}$

Work out the value of $s$ when:

   **a** $v = 10$, $u = 6$ and $a = 4$     **b** $v = 15$, $u = -12$ and $a = 1$

   **c** $v = 5$, $u = 7$ and $a = -2$     **d** $v = -6$, $u = -10$ and $a = -5$

## 12.3 Further substitution into formulae

Sometimes when you substitute into a formula you obtain an equation to solve.

### Worked example 1

$v = u + at$

Find the value of $t$ when $v = 14$, $u = 8$ and $a = 2$.

$v = u + at$     Replace the letters with the given numbers.

$14 = 8 + 2t$

$-8 \qquad\qquad -8$

$6 = 2t$

$\div 2 \qquad\qquad \div 2$

$3 = t$

## Worked example 2

$2f = 3g - 7h$

Find the value of $g$ when $f = 6.5$ and $h = 5$.

$2f = 3g - 7h$   Replace the letters with the given numbers.

$13 = 3g - 35$

$(+35)$   $(+35)$

$48 = 3g$

$(\div 3)$   $(\div 3)$

$16 = g$

## Exercise 12.3

**1** $y = 6x - 5$

Find the value of $x$ when:

  **a** $y = 7$      **b** $y = 43$      **c** $y = 16$      **d** $y = -17$

**2** $f = uv$

Find the value of $v$ when:

  **a** $f = 20$ and $u = 2$      **b** $f = 36$ and $u = 8$      **c** $f = -15$ and $u = 5$

**3** $f = 2g + 3h$

Find the value of $g$ when:

  **a** $f = 31$ and $h = 7$      **b** $f = 63$ and $h = 11$      **c** $f = 7$ and $h = -3$

**4** $A = xy + 4$

Find the value of $y$ when:

  **a** $A = 34$ and $x = 5$      **b** $A = 100$ and $x = 8$      **c** $A = 2$ and $x = 2$

**5** $I = mv - mu$

Find the value of $m$ when:

  **a** $I = 15, v = 9$ and $u = 4$      **b** $I = 46, v = 8$ and $u = -2$

**6** $xy = x^2 + 4y$

Find the value of $y$ when $x = 8$.

**7** $ax = bx + c$

Find the value of $x$ when $a = 7, b = 5$ and $c = 20$.

**8** $ax - b = cx + d$

Find the value of $x$ when $a = 7, b = 9, c = 3$ and $d = 19$.

# Mathematics for Cambridge Secondary 1

**9 a** Write a formula for the total surface area, $A$, of the cuboid.

**b** Find the value of $x$ when $A = 238\,\text{cm}^2$ and $y = 7\,\text{cm}$.

> A cuboid has six rectangular faces.

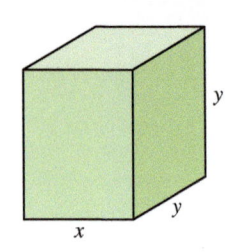

## Review

**1** Monique buys $m$ cans of cola.

Each can of cola costs $2.

She pays with a $50 note.

Write a formula for the amount of change, $C$ dollars, that Monique receives.

**2 a** Write a formula for the perimeter, $P$, of the rectangle.

**b** Write a formula for the area, $A$, of the rectangle.

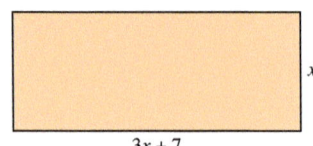

**3** Ice creams cost $4 each and ice lollies cost $3 each.

Write a formula for the total cost, $C$ dollars, of $x$ ice creams and $y$ ice lollies.

**4** Use the formula $V = IR$ to work out the value of $V$ when:

 **a** $I = 7$ and $R = 6$  **b** $I = 5$ and $R = 19$

**5** The formula for the area, $A$, of the triangle is $A = \frac{1}{2}bh$

Find the value of $A$ when:

 **a** $b = 6$ and $h = 4$  **b** $b = 14$ and $h = 7$
 **c** $b = 7$ and $h = 10$  **d** $b = 9$ and $h = 11$

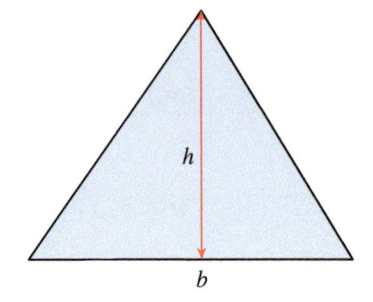

**6** The formula $C = \frac{5(F-32)}{9}$ is used to change temperatures from degrees Fahrenheit, $F$, to degrees Celsius, $C$.

Work out the value of $C$ when:

 **a** $F = 41$  **b** $F = 68$  **c** $F = 14$

**7** $y = 5x - 8$

Find the value of $x$ when:

 **a** $y = 7$  **b** $y = 27$  **c** $y = -18$  **d** $y = -29$

**8** $Ft = mv - mu$

Find the value of $v$ when:

 **a** $F = 8$, $t = 5$, $m = 10$ and $u = 3$  **b** $F = 18$, $t = 4$, $m = 8$ and $u = -4$

# 13 Position and movement

### Learning outcomes

- Transform 2D shapes by rotation, reflection and translation, and simple combinations of these transformations.
- Understand and use the language and notation associated with enlargement.
- Enlarge 2D shapes, given a centre of enlargement and a positive integer scale factor.
- Find the midpoint of the line segment AB, given the coordinates of points A and B.

## Pantograph

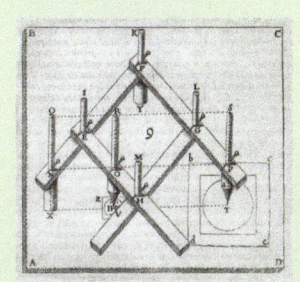

The diagram to the left shows a pantograph. This is a device that was invented in 1603 for copying diagrams.

By placing the pencil in different places on the structure it is possible to enlarge or reduce the original diagram.

The name 'pantograph' is also used for other extending arms that use a scissor action.

One example is the device collecting power on top of an electric train.

## 13.1 Transformations

### Review of transformations

In your Stage 7 Student Book, you learnt about three types of **transformation**.

**Reflection**

The object is reflected in a mirror line.

**Rotation**

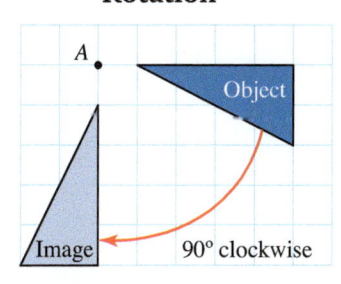

The object is rotated through a given angle in a given direction around a centre of rotation.

**Translation**

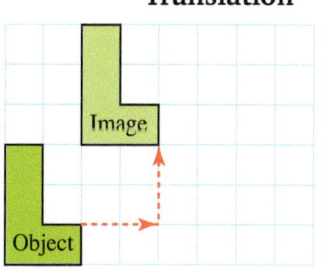

The object is moved with no reflection or rotation.

175

The original shape is called the **object**.

The final shape is called the **image**.

In each of these three transformations, the image is **congruent** to the object. This means that the image has identical size and shape to the object.

## Combining transformations

Sometimes two or more of these transformations are done one after another.

Any combination of the three transformations will always give an image that is congruent to the object.

It is a good idea to do all drawings in pencil.

Tracing paper is very helpful for finding the images.

Make sure that the final image is clearly shown.

### Worked example 1

Copy this diagram on to squared paper.

Translate the object shape 3 squares to the right and 1 square down.

Then rotate the image 90° anticlockwise around the point C.

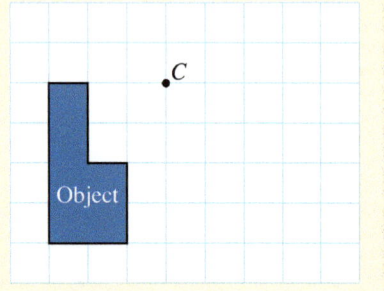

Firstly translate the object and draw in the required image.

This diagram shows the translated image.

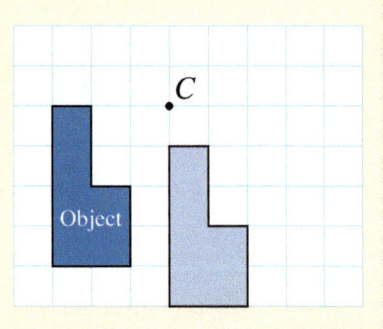

The next step is to rotate the new shape 90° anticlockwise around point C.

The final image is shown opposite.

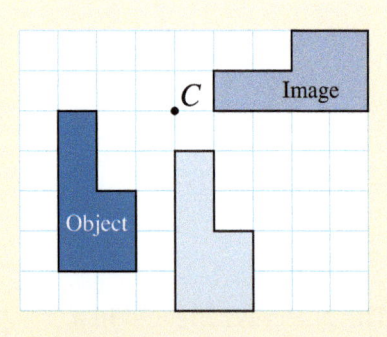

# 13 Position and movement

## Worked example 2

Copy these axes on to squared paper.

**a** Reflect shape A in the diagonal line. Label the new shape B.

**b** Reflect shape B in the y-axis. Label the new shape C.

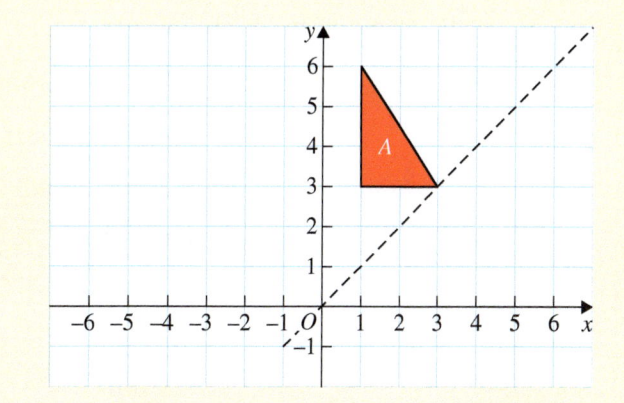

**a** Draw the axes and draw in the diagonal reflection of shape A. Label the shape B.

Remember when reflecting diagonally that each point must reflect at right angles to the mirror line.

The blue lines on the diagram show how two of the vertices on the object map to the new vertices on the image.

The vertex that is on the line of reflection does not move.

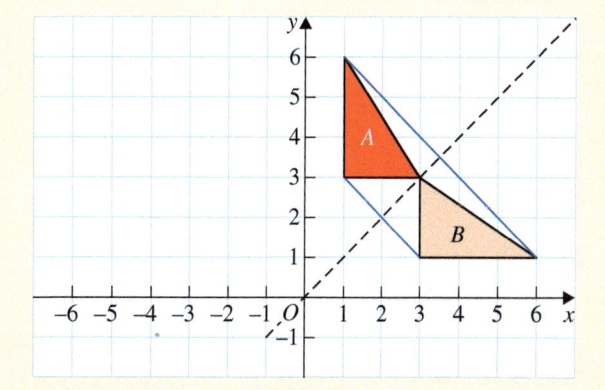

**b** Draw the reflection of triangle B in the y-axis as shown in the diagram.

Label the new shape C.

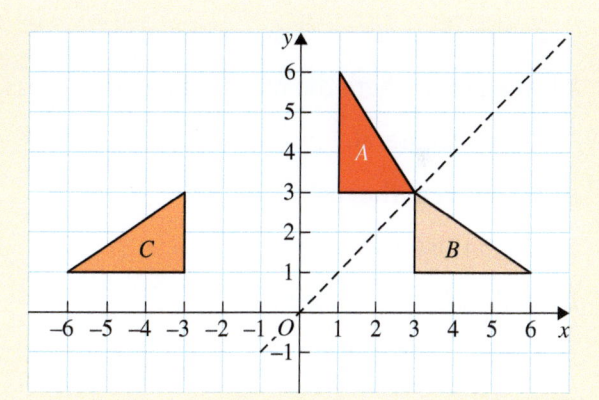

177

# Mathematics for Cambridge Secondary 1

## Exercise 13.1

**1** Copy these diagrams on to squared paper.

For each one, draw the image after the given transformation.

**a** Translation

4 squares right and 1 square down

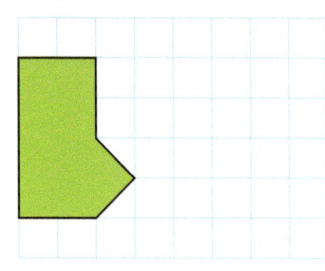

**b** Reflection

In the dotted mirror line

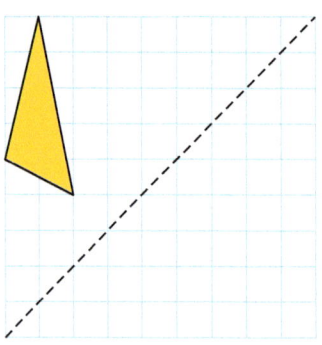

**c** Rotation

90° clockwise around point C

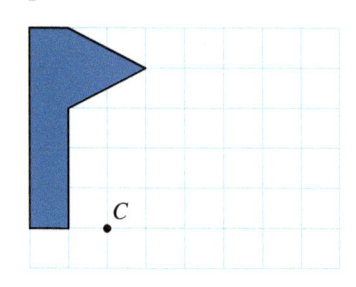

**2** Copy this diagram on to squared paper.

  **a** Reflect triangle A in the purple mirror line.
  
  Label the new triangle B.
  
  **b** Reflect triangle B in the green mirror line.
  
  Label the new triangle C.

**3** Copy this diagram on to squared paper.

X is the point where the red and blue lines cross.

A is a quadrilateral.

  **a** Reflect A in the red mirror line.
  
  Label the new shape B.
  
  **b** Reflect B in the blue mirror line.
  
  Label the new shape C.

**4** Copy these axes and shape P on to squared paper.

  **a** Translate the L-shape, P, 2 squares to the right and 6 squares down.
  
  Label the new shape Q.
  
  **b** Rotate Q through 180° around (0, 0).
  
  Label the new shape R.

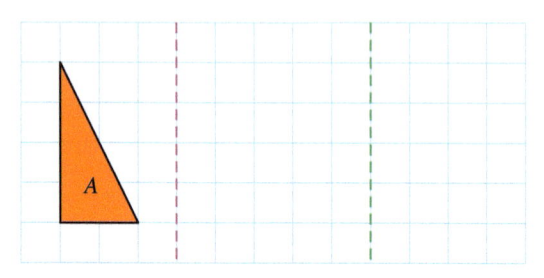

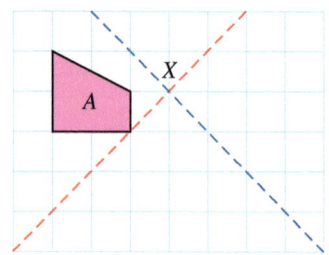

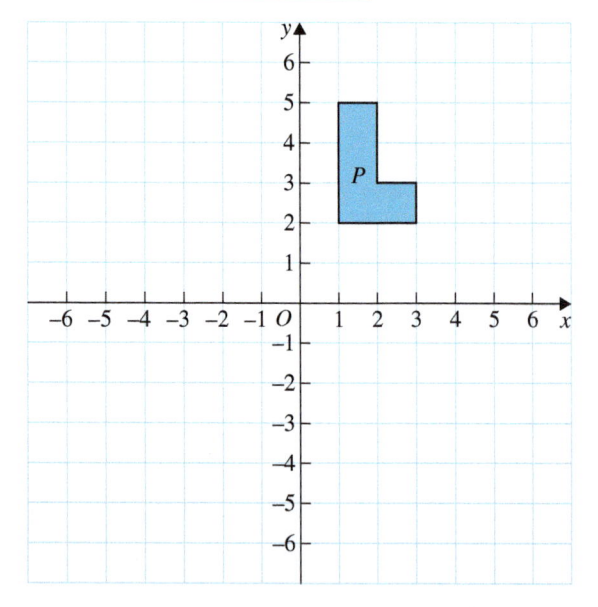

**5** Copy this diagram on to squared paper.

   *A* is a quadrilateral.

   **a** Rotate *A* 90° clockwise around the point (1, 2).

   Label the new shape *B*.

   **b** Reflect *B* in the *y*-axis.

   Label the new shape *C*.

   **c** Translate *C* 2 squares to the left and 3 squares up.

   Label the new shape *D*.

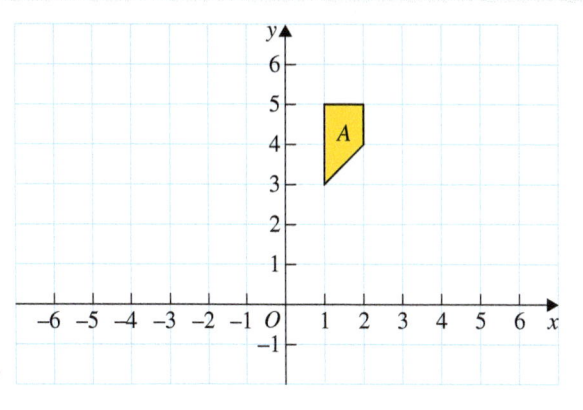

**6** Make another copy of the grid and L-shape from question **4**.

   **a** Reflect *P* in the line $x = -1$. Label the new shape *X*.

   **b** Rotate *X* through 90° anticlockwise around (0, 0). Label the new shape *Y*.

   **c** Translate *Y* 7 squares to the right and 9 squares up. Label the new shape *Z*.

   **d** Shape *P* can be transformed into shape *Z* by a reflection. Draw the mirror line on the diagram.

**7** In question **2**, you saw that two reflections were equivalent to a single translation.

   **a** Draw a diagram to show how two reflections can be equivalent to a single rotation.

   **b** Draw a diagram to show how two rotations can be equivalent to a single translation.

   > Use squared paper to try out some sets of reflections and rotations to investigate these.

   **c** Is it possible for two translations to be equivalent to a single rotation?

## 13.2 Enlargement

### Scale factors

An **enlargement** is a transformation that changes the size of the object.

Unlike the transformations you have already seen, the image is **not congruent** to the object.

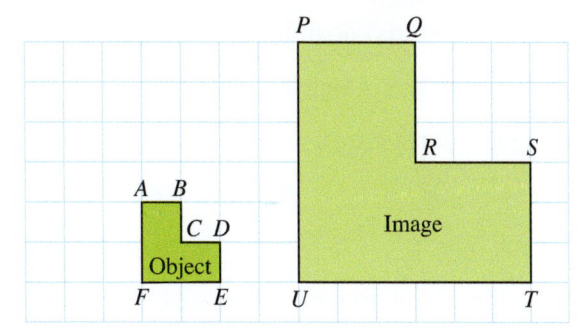

Here the object has been enlarged to form the image.

They are the same shape but different sizes. They are **similar** shapes.

The **scale factor** of the enlargement is 3. Each length in the image is 3 times as long as the corresponding length in the object.

For example, line AF is 2 squares long. The corresponding line, PU, is 6 (=2 × 3) squares long.

## Worked example 1

Write down the scale factors of these enlargements.

a

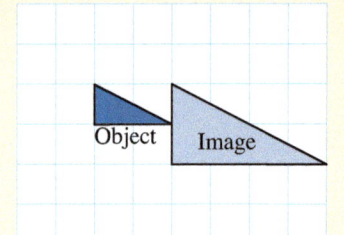

b

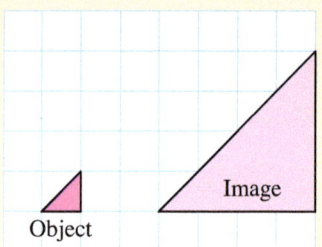

a  The length of the base is twice as long on the image.

The scale factor is 2.

b  The length of the base is four times as long on the image.

The scale factor is 4.

Sometimes the image can surround or overlap the object, as shown in the next example.

## Worked example 2

Write down the scale factors of these enlargements.

a

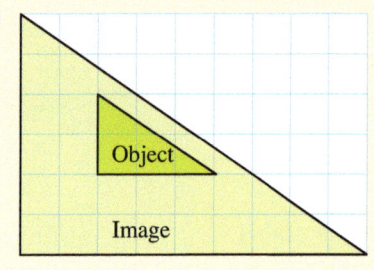

b

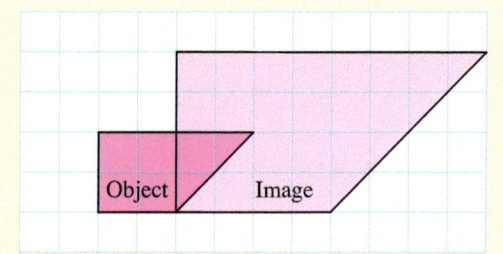

a  The image completely surrounds the object.

The perpendicular height of the image is 6 squares.

The perpendicular height of the object is 2 squares.

The scale factor is 6 ÷ 2 = 3

> You can always divide the lengths of corresponding sides to find the scale factor.

b  The image overlaps the object.

The length across the top of the image is 8 squares.

The length across the top of the object is 4 squares.

The scale factor is 8 ÷ 4 = 2

## Centre of enlargement

Look again at the example from the start of this topic.

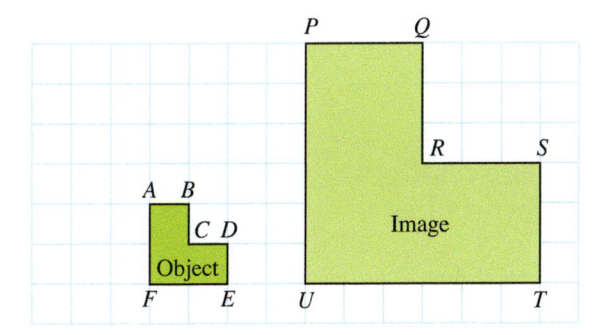

Draw lines through each pair of corresponding points as shown below.

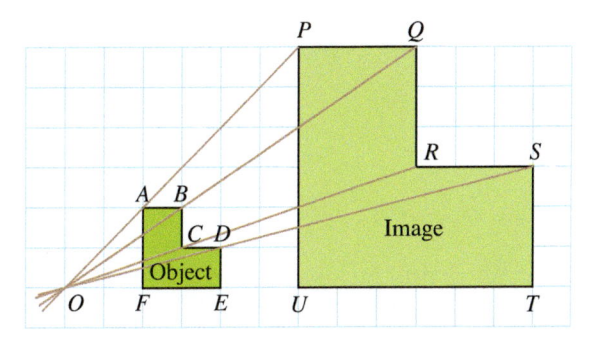

The lines all go through point *O* to the left of the object.

This point is called the **centre of enlargement**.

Every point on the image is 3 times as far from the centre of enlargement as the corresponding point on the object is.

Check by measuring that length $OP = 3 \times OA$

## Drawing enlargements

To draw an enlargement of a shape you use the scale factor and the centre of enlargement.

The distance of each point from the centre of enlargement is multiplied by the scale factor.

These examples show the method.

### Worked example 3

Enlarge this shape by a scale factor of 2 from the centre of enlargement *X*.

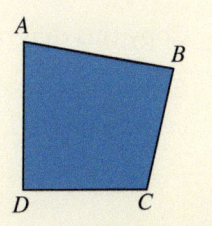

Draw a construction line from the centre of enlargement through vertex A.

Measure the length XA.

Mark A' so that XA' = 2 × XA

This is because 2 is the scale factor.

Repeat this process, drawing a construction line through each of the other vertices.

Note that the lines must be straight and accurate.

A sharp pencil is needed.

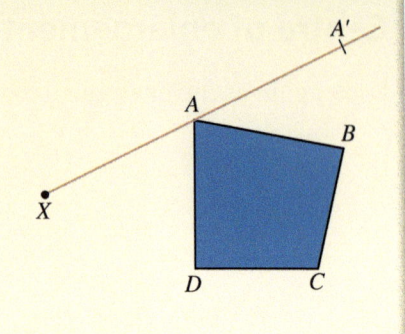

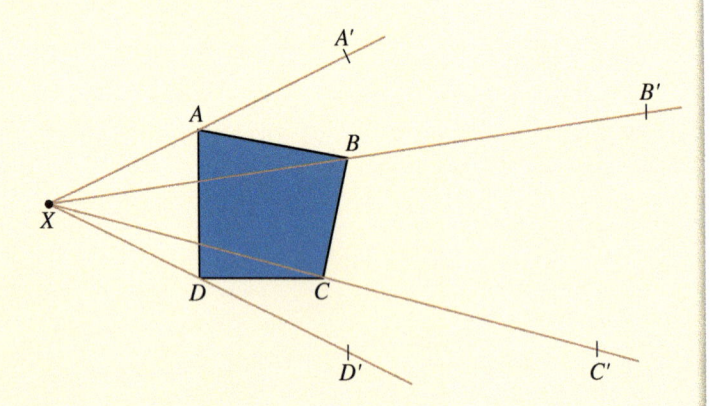

You now have four points A', B', C' and D'.

Join them up with straight lines.

The shape A'B'C'D' is an enlargement of ABCD.

Check that all the sides of A'B'C'D' are twice as long as the sides of ABCD.

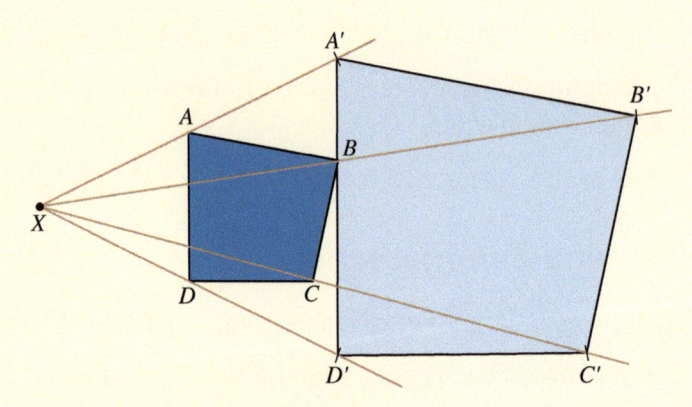

## Worked example 4

This example shows how you can use squared paper to help draw enlargements.

Copy this diagram on to squared paper.

Enlarge shape A by a scale factor of 3 from centre of enlargement C.

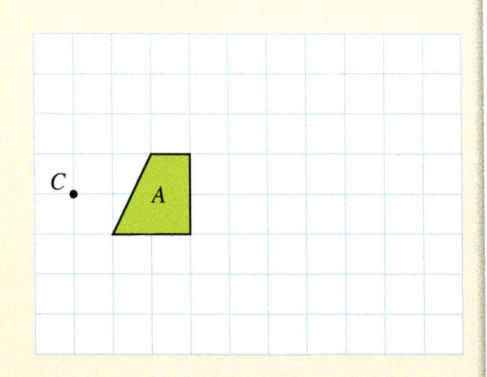

The top left corner of shape A is 2 squares to the right of C.

It is also 1 square up from C.

Multiplying by the scale factor 3 gives a point that is 6 squares to the right and 3 squares up from C.

Mark this point on the diagram.

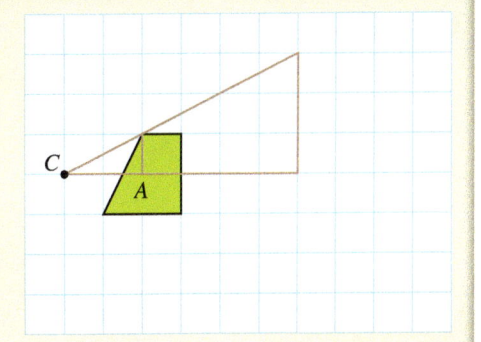

Repeat with the other three vertices.

Join up the four points to make the enlarged shape.

Label the enlarged shape A'.

Check that all of the sides of shape A' are 3 times the length of the original sides of shape A.

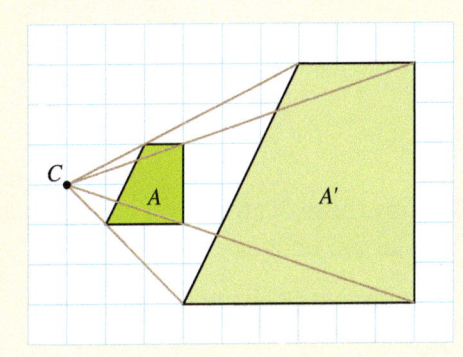

## Exercise 13.2

**1** Write down the scale factor for each of these enlargements.

**a**

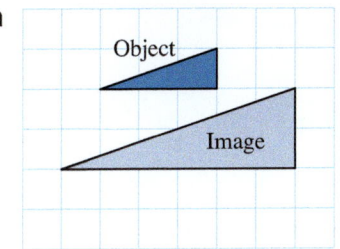

**b**

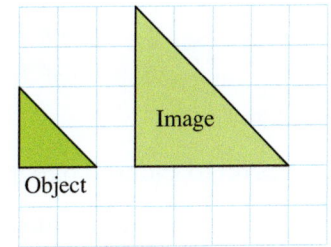

**c**

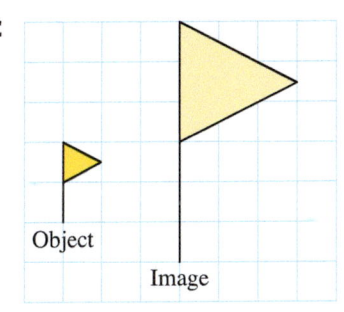

**d**

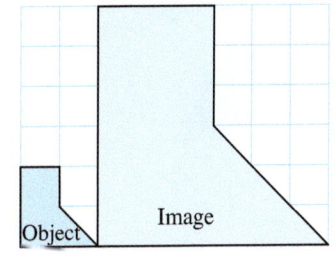

183

2 Measure carefully the sides of triangles *ABC* and *PQR*.

Work out the scale factor of the enlargement that moves *ABC* on to *PQR*.

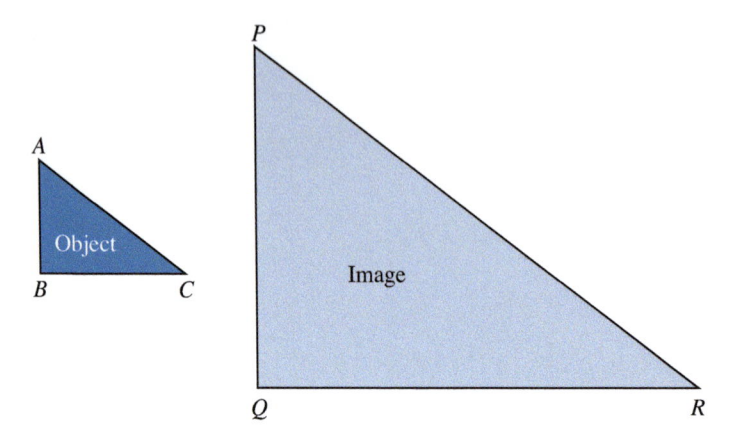

3 Copy these diagrams on to plain paper as accurately as possible. You need to leave space for the enlarged images.

Enlarge each shape by the given scale factor from the centre of enlargement *C*.

a

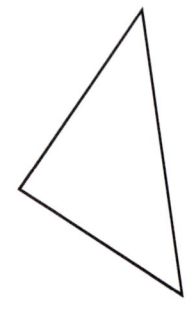

Scale factor 2

b

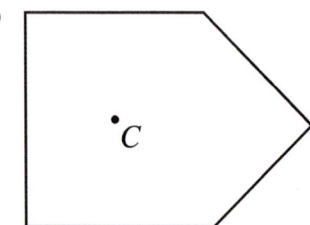

Scale factor 3

4 Copy these shapes on to squared paper.

Enlarge each shape by the given scale factor from the centre of enlargement *C*.

a

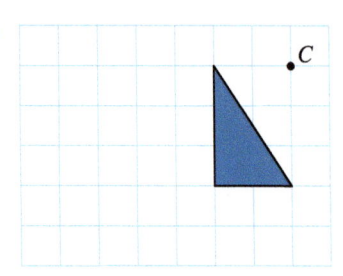

Scale factor 2

b

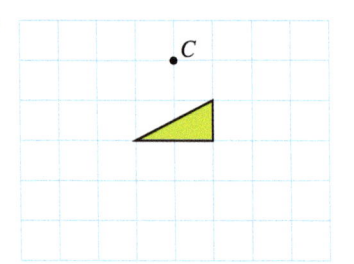

Scale factor 3

c

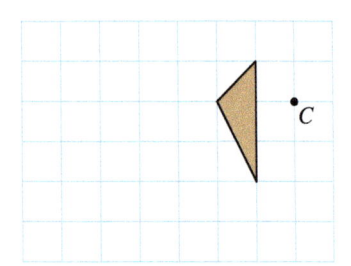

Scale factor 3

13 Position and movement

**d** Scale factor 2

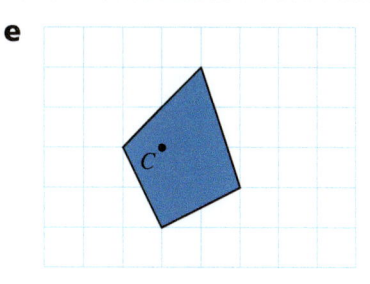

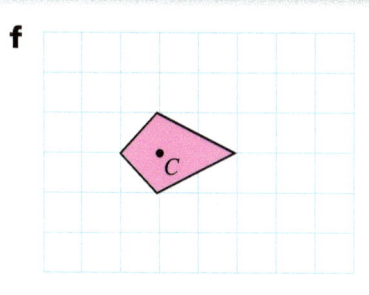

**e** Scale factor 2

**f** Scale factor 4

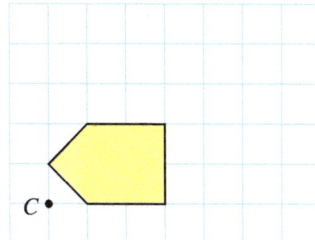

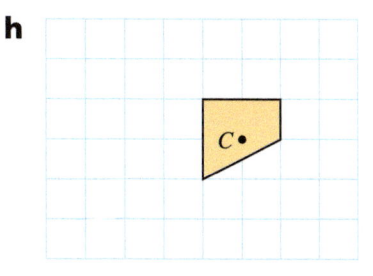

**g** Scale factor 3

**h** Scale factor 4

**5** Draw coordinate axes from 0 to 7.

  **a** Plot the points (2, 2), (4, 2) and (2, 3). Join the points up to make a triangle. Label the triangle P.

  **b** Enlarge triangle P using scale factor 2, centre of enlargement (2, 4). Label the image Q.

  **c** Enlarge triangle P using scale factor 2, centre of enlargement (3, 1). Label the image R.

  **d** Describe fully the single transformation that moves triangle Q on to triangle R.

> Label each triangle as you draw it so that you do not get the triangles confused.

**6** Draw coordinate axes from 0 to 13.

  **a** Plot the points (1, 1), (1, 3) and (3, 1). Join the points up to make a triangle. Label the triangle A.

  **b** Enlarge A using scale factor 2, centre of enlargement (0, 0). Label the image B.

  **c** Enlarge B using scale factor 2, centre of enlargement (0, 0). Label the image C.

  **d** Describe fully the single transformation that maps triangle A to triangle C.

> Don't forget to give a full description of the transformation.

## 13.3 Midpoints

The **midpoint** of a line (or **line segment**) can be found by drawing a graph or by calculation.

On a graph it is done by counting the squares between the end points.

To calculate the midpoint of a line you add the $x$-coordinates and divide by 2 then add the $y$-coordinates and divide by 2.

185

The midpoint of the line joining $(a, b)$ and $(c, d)$ is at $\left(\dfrac{a+c}{2}, \dfrac{b+d}{2}\right)$.

> This is finding the mean of the x-coordinates and the mean of the y-coordinates.

## Worked example

**a** Use the calculation method to find the midpoint of the line joining points (1, 2) and (6, 4).

**b** Check your answer by drawing a graph.

**a** The x-coordinates are 1 and 6. The y-coordinates are 2 and 4.

The mean of the x-coordinates is $\dfrac{1+6}{2} = \dfrac{7}{2} = 3\frac{1}{2}$

The mean of the y-coordinates is $\dfrac{2+4}{2} = \dfrac{6}{2} = 3$

The midpoint is at $(3\frac{1}{2}, 3)$.

**b** The graph on the right shows the points (1, 2) and (6, 4).

A line joining the two points has been drawn.

The red dot is at the midpoint of the line.

The coordinates of the red dot are $(3\frac{1}{2}, 3)$.

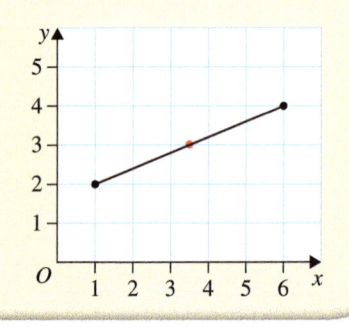

## Exercise 13.3

**1** Use the diagram on the right to write down the coordinates of the midpoints of these lines.

　**a** AB　　　　**b** CD
　**c** EF　　　　**d** GH
　**e** JK　　　　**f** LM

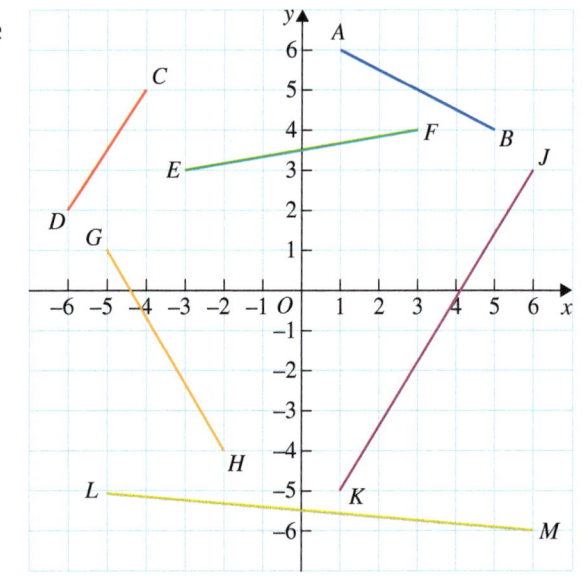

186

## 13 Position and movement

**2 a** Calculate the coordinates of the midpoint of the line joining (2, 1) and (6, 5).

  **b** Check your answer by drawing a graph.

**3** Calculate the midpoint of lines joining the following pairs of points.

  **a** (2, 4) and (6, 8)   **b** (5, 9) and (2, 1)   **c** (3, 8) and (6, 5)
  **d** (1, 1) and (−3, 7)   **e** (−9, 0) and (−3, 6)   **f** (0, 0) and (1, −6)
  **g** (2.5, 2) and (3.5, 7)   **h** (−12, 8) and (15, −13)   **i** (−5, −8) and (−3, −6)

**4** The midpoint of a line segment is at (3, 6). One end point is at (1, 1).

Find the coordinates of the other end of the line.

> You can do this by drawing a graph or by using the formula to make two separate equations.

**5** This table shows the coordinates of the end points and the midpoints of some lines.

Copy the table and fill in the missing values.

> It might help to draw graphs for some of these.

| End point | End point | Midpoint |
|---|---|---|
| (4, 7) | (−2, 1) | |
| (9, 1) | | (5, −4) |
| | (−5, 3) | (−1.5, 1.5) |
| (3.5, −5.5) | | (−3, −3) |

### Review

**1** Describe fully the single transformation that moves triangle:

  **a** A on to D   **b** A on to F
  **c** G on to E   **d** D on to E
  **e** B on to G   **f** F on to G
  **g** B on to H   **h** A on to B
  **i** E on to C   **j** B on to C.

187

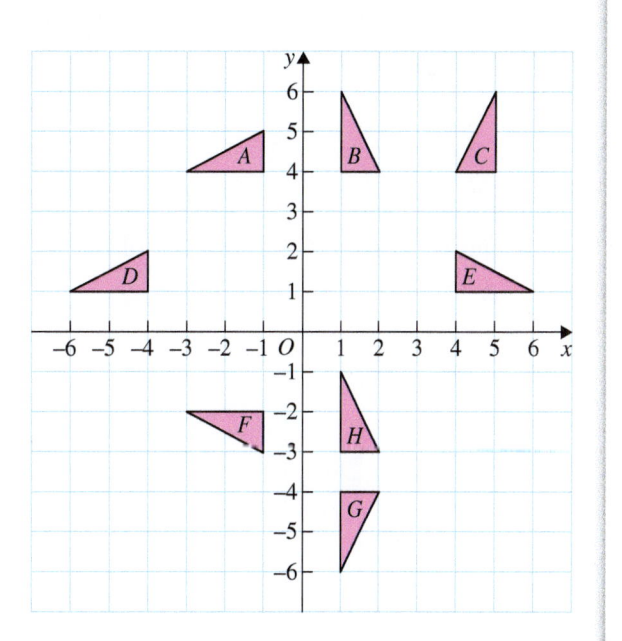

Mathematics for Cambridge Secondary 1

2 Copy this diagram on to squared paper.

  a Rotate shape X through 90° clockwise around point A.

    Label the new shape Y.

  b Rotate shape Y through 90° anticlockwise around point B.

    Label the new shape Z.

3 Copy these axes on to squared paper.

  a Plot points at (2, 1), (2, 4) and (4, 2).

    Join the points to form a triangle.

    Label the triangle T.

  b Reflect triangle T in the y-axis.

    Label the new triangle U.

  c Rotate triangle U through 180° around the point (0, 0).

    Label the new triangle V.

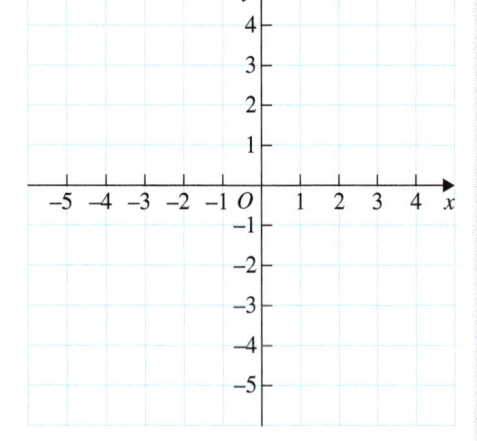

  d Write down the coordinates of the vertices of triangle V.

4 Write down which of these triangles are enlargements of triangle A.

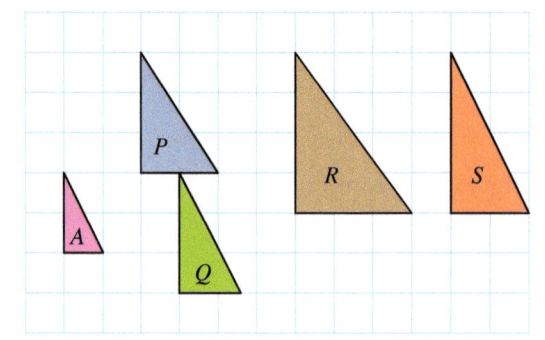

5 Find the scale factor for each of these enlargements.

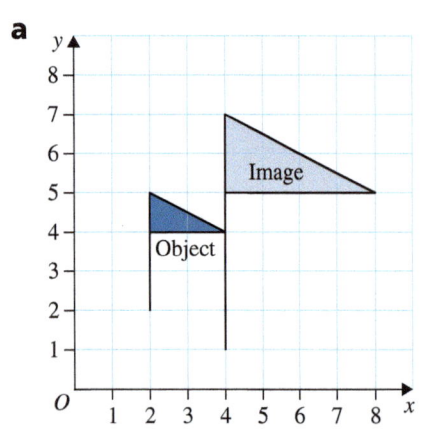

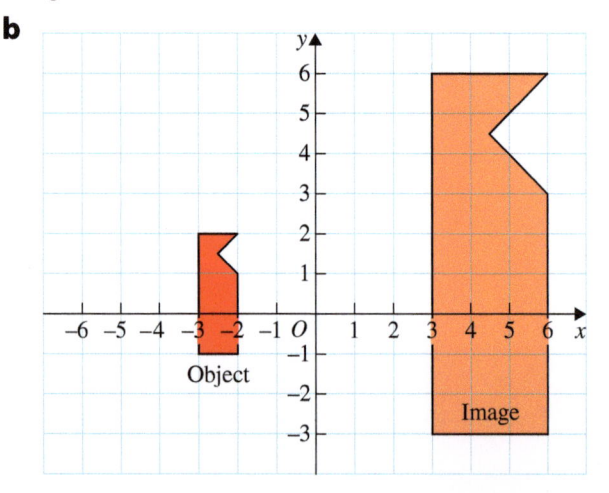

  a

  b

**c**

[Graph showing Object and Image triangles on coordinate axes from 0 to 8]

**6** Copy these shapes on to squared paper.

Enlarge each shape by the given scale factor from the centre of enlargement C.

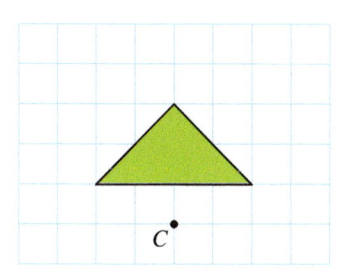

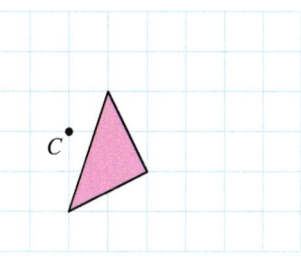

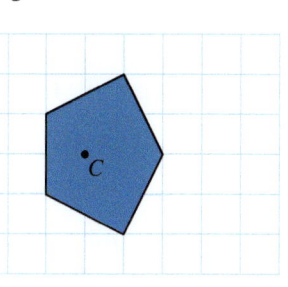

**a** Scale factor 2

**b** Scale factor 3

**c** Scale factor 2

**7** Draw coordinate axes from 0 to 8.

  **a** Plot the points (2, 2), (5, 2) and (3, 4). Join the points up to make a triangle. Label the triangle X.

  **b** Enlarge triangle X using scale factor 2, centre of enlargement (3, 3). Label the image Y.

  **c** Enlarge triangle X using scale factor 2, centre of enlargement (4, 1). Label the image Z.

**8** Calculate the midpoint of lines joining the following pairs of points.

  **a** (4, 4) and (7, 2)
  **b** (4, 0) and (3, −1)
  **c** (−2, 8) and (−6, 3)
  **d** (−5, −1) and (−8, 6)
  **e** (4, −4) and (−5, 7)
  **f** $(2\frac{1}{2}, 6\frac{1}{2})$ and $(-1\frac{1}{2}, -2)$

**9** AB is a line segment. The coordinates of A are (−7, 9).

The midpoint of AB is at $(-2, 3\frac{1}{2})$.

Find the coordinates of B.

# 14 Sequences

> **Learning outcomes**
> - Generate terms of a linear sequence using term-to-term and position-to-term rules, including special patterns.
> - Find term-to-term and position-to-term rules of sequences.
> - Use a linear expression to describe the $n$th term of a simple arithmetic sequence.

## Fibonacci sequence

The sequence 1, 1, 2, 3, 5, 8, 13, 21, … is a very famous sequence.

It is called a Fibonacci sequence and the numbers in the sequence are called Fibonacci numbers. Each number in the sequence is the sum of the two previous numbers.

Fibonacci numbers are often found in nature. They appear in the arrangement of leaves on the stem of a plant, the arrangement of seeds in a sunflower, the number of petals on a flower and the curve of waves.

The spiral on a nautilus shell can also be formed using a Fibonacci sequence. (You will be shown how to do this later.)

## 14.1 Linear sequences of numbers

A **sequence** is a list of numbers or diagrams that are connected by a rule.

4, 7, 10, 13, … is a linear sequence.

It is called a **linear sequence** (or **arithmetic sequence**) because the differences between the terms are all the same.

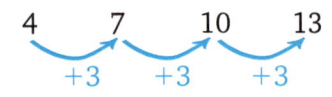

$$4 \xrightarrow{+3} 7 \xrightarrow{+3} 10 \xrightarrow{+3} 13$$

The rule to find the next term in the sequence (the **term-to-term rule**) is '+3' or 'add 3'.

You can also use a **position-to-term rule** to find the numbers in a sequence.

A position-to-term rule connects the terms in a sequence with their positions in the sequence.

14 Sequences

If the position-to-term rule is:   term = 7 × position number then add 4

This gives the sequence:
1st term = 7 × 1 + 4 = 7 + 4 = 11
2nd term = 7 × 2 + 4 = 14 + 4 = 18
3rd term = 7 × 3 + 4 = 21 + 4 = 25
4th term = 7 × 4 + 4 = 28 + 4 = 32

This information can be shown in a table:

| Position number | 1 | 2 | 3 | 4 |
|---|---|---|---|---|
| Term | 11 | 18 | 25 | 32 |

## Worked example 1

27, 23, 19, 15, …

Write down

**a** the term-to-term rule    **b** the ninth term of the sequence.

**a** The term-to-term rule is 'subtract 4'.

**b** One method for finding the ninth term is to continue to write down the terms in the sequence until you reach the ninth term:

| 1 | 2 | 3 | 4 | 5 | 6 | 7 | 8 | 9 |
|---|---|---|---|---|---|---|---|---|
| 27 | 23 | 19 | 15 | 11 | 7 | 3 | −1 | −5 |

−4  −4  −4  −4  −4  −4  −4  −4

A second method is:   ninth term = 27 + (9 − 1) × −4
                               = 27 + 8 × −4
                               = 27 − 32
                               = −5

## Worked example 2

The position-to-term rule for a sequence is:

term = 4 × position number then subtract 3

Find the first four terms of the sequence.

1st term = 4 × 1 − 3 = 4 − 3 = 1
2nd term = 4 × 2 − 3 = 8 − 3 = 5
3rd term = 4 × 3 − 3 = 12 − 3 = 9
4th term = 4 × 4 − 3 = 16 − 3 = 13

The sequence is:   1, 5, 9, 13, …

## Exercise 14.1

**1** For each sequence find:  **i** the term-to-term rule  **ii** the next three terms.
  **a** 3, 5, 7, 9, …
  **b** 0, 3, 6, 9, …
  **c** 2, 7, 12, 17, …
  **d** 7, 11, 15, 19, …
  **e** 4, 9, 14, 19, …
  **f** 21, 31, 41, 51, …

**2** For each sequence find:  **i** the term-to-term rule  **ii** the next three terms.
  **a** 25, 21, 17, 13, …
  **b** 17, 15, 13, 11, …
  **c** 63, 53, 43, 33, …
  **d** 53, 48, 43, 38, …
  **e** 80, 73, 66, 59, …
  **f** 124, 111, 98, 85, …

**3** For each sequence find:  **i** the term-to-term rule  **ii** the next three terms.
  **a** −5, −3, −1, 1, …
  **b** −26, −19, −12, −5, …
  **c** 12, 6, 0, −6, …
  **d** −5, −8, −11, −14, …
  **e** −35, −29, −23, −17, …
  **f** 26, 19, 12, 5, …

**4** Find the missing numbers in these linear sequences.
  **a** 17, 21, ☐, 29, ☐, 37, …
  **b** 6, ☐, ☐, ☐, 14, ☐, 18, 20, …
  **c** 8, ☐, ☐, −1, ☐, ☐, −10
  **d** −23, −17, ☐, ☐, ☐, 7, 13, …
  **e** 43, ☐, ☐, ☐, ☐, 18, …
  **f** 4, ☐, ☐, ☐, ☐, ☐, ☐, ☐, 52, …

**5** The first term in a sequence is 15.

The term-to-term rule is 'add 3'.

Saul and Haroon are asked to find the fifth term in the sequence.

Saul writes:
15  18  21  24  27
  +3  +3  +3  +3

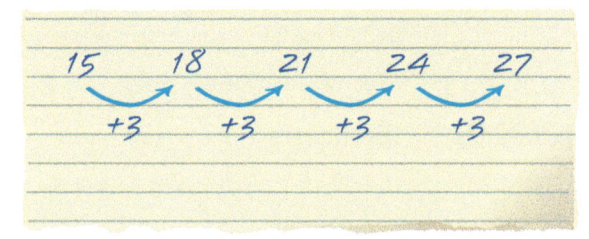

Haroon writes:
15 + (5 − 1) × 3
= 15 + 4 × 3
= 15 + 12
= 27

Saul says that his method is quicker.

  **a** Explain why Haroon's method is quicker for finding the 100th term.
  **b** Use Haroon's method to find:  **i** the 10th term  **ii** the 50th term  **iii** the 100th term.

**6** The first term in a sequence is 3.

The term-to-term rule is 'add 2'.

Find  **a** the 10th term  **b** the 50th term  **c** the 100th term.

**7** The sixth term in a sequence is 49.

The term-to-term rule is 'add 4'.

Find the first term of the sequence.

**8** The fifth term in a linear sequence is 43.

The seventh term in the sequence is 57.

  **a** Find the term-to-term rule.

  **b** Find the first term of the sequence.

**9** The position-to-term rule for a sequence is:

> term = 2 × position number then add 3

Copy and complete the table to find the sequence.

| Position number | 1 | 2 | 3 | 4 | 5 | 6 | 7 |
|---|---|---|---|---|---|---|---|
| Term |  |  | 9 |  |  |  | 17 |

**10** The position-to-term rule for a sequence is:

> term = 3 × position number then subtract 7

Copy and complete the table to find the sequence.

| Position number | 1 | 2 | 3 | 4 | 5 | 6 | 7 |
|---|---|---|---|---|---|---|---|
| Term |  |  |  | 5 |  | 11 |  |

**11** Use the position-to-term rule to find the first five terms of each sequence.

  **a** term = 4 × position number then add 5
  **b** term = 2 × position number then subtract 4
  **c** term = 6 × position number then subtract 2
  **d** term = 7 × position number then add 3
  **e** term = 3 × position number then subtract 11
  **f** term = 8 × position number then add 9
  **g** term = 5 × position number then subtract 20
  **h** term = 9 × position number then add 14
  **i** term = −2 × position number then add 4
  **j** term = −3 × position number then subtract 5

**12** The second term in a linear sequence is 7.

The sixth term in the sequence is 19.

Find the correct position-to-term card for the sequence.

**A** term = 2 × position number then add 3

**B** term = 5 × position number then subtract 3

**C** term = 4 × position number then subtract 1

**D** term = 3 × position number then add 1

**13** The fourth term of a linear sequence is 25.

A possible sequence is:   10, 15, 20, 25, 30, …

**a** Write down three other possible sequences.

**b** Write down the position-to-term rule for each of your sequences in part **a**.

**14** Helen and Ravi both write down a linear sequence.

6, 10, 14, 18, 22, …          5, 8, 11, 14, 17, …

The first term that is common to both sequences is 14.

Find the next three terms that are common to both sequences.

**15** 1, 1, 2, 3, 5, 8, …

This is a Fibonacci sequence. Each number in the sequence is the sum of the two previous terms.

The Fibonacci numbers can be used to form the spiral found in a nautilus shell.

The spiral can be drawn using quarter circles of radii 1, 1, 2, 3, 5 and 8 units.

Use a square grid and pair of compasses to make your own copy of the nautilus spiral.

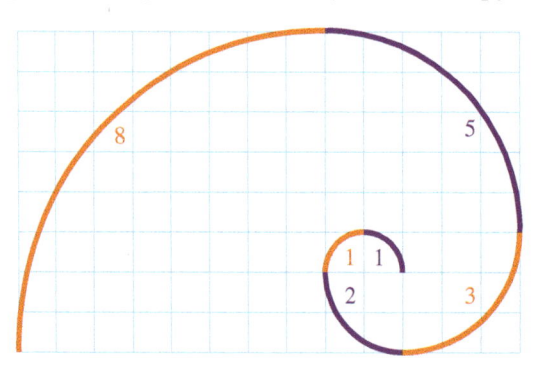

# 14 Sequences

## 14.2 Linear sequences from patterns of shapes

These patterns of shapes form a sequence.

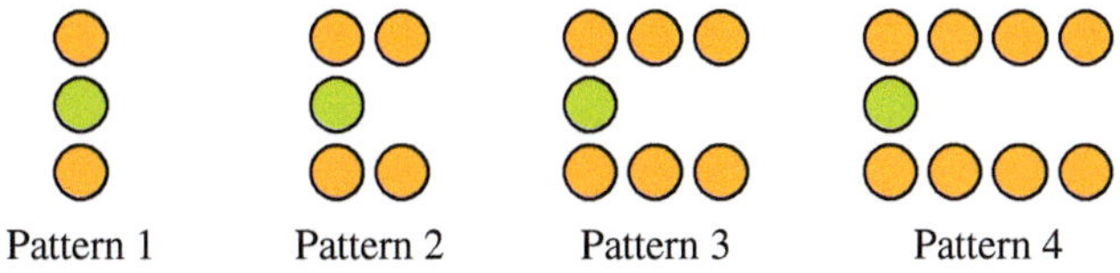

Pattern 1    Pattern 2    Pattern 3    Pattern 4

The number of circles in each pattern forms the sequence 3, 5, 7, 9, …

The term-to-term rule for the sequence is 'add 2'.

You can use the colours to help you find the rule for the total number of circles in a pattern.

The number of orange circles in each pattern is 2 × the pattern number.

There is also one green circle in each pattern.

So the rule for finding the total number of circles in each pattern is:

Number of circles = 2 × pattern number + 1

This can also be shown in a table.

| Pattern number ($n$) | 1 | 2 | 3 | 4 |
|---|---|---|---|---|
| Number of orange circles | 2 | 4 | 6 | 8 |
| Number of green circles | 1 | 1 | 1 | 1 |
| Total number of circles | 3 | 5 | 7 | 9 |

×2 then +1

The rule can be written using algebra as:

Number of circles = $2n + 1$

So the number of circles in pattern 100 = 2 × 100 + 1 = 201

### Worked example

These patterns of shapes form a sequence.

Find the rule connecting the number of hexagons with the pattern number $n$.

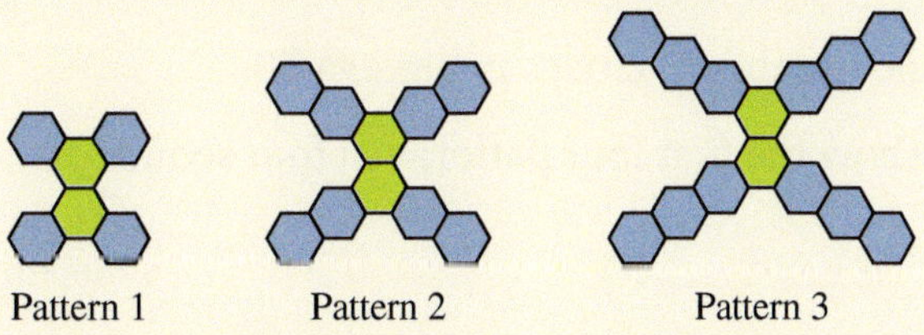

Pattern 1    Pattern 2    Pattern 3

The number of blue hexagons in each pattern is 4 × the pattern number.

There are also 2 green hexagons in each pattern.

So the rule for finding the total number of hexagons in each pattern is:

Number of hexagons = 4 × pattern number + 2    or    Number of hexagons = $4n + 2$

# Mathematics for Cambridge Secondary 1

## Exercise 14.2

**1** The diagrams show the first four patterns in three sequences.

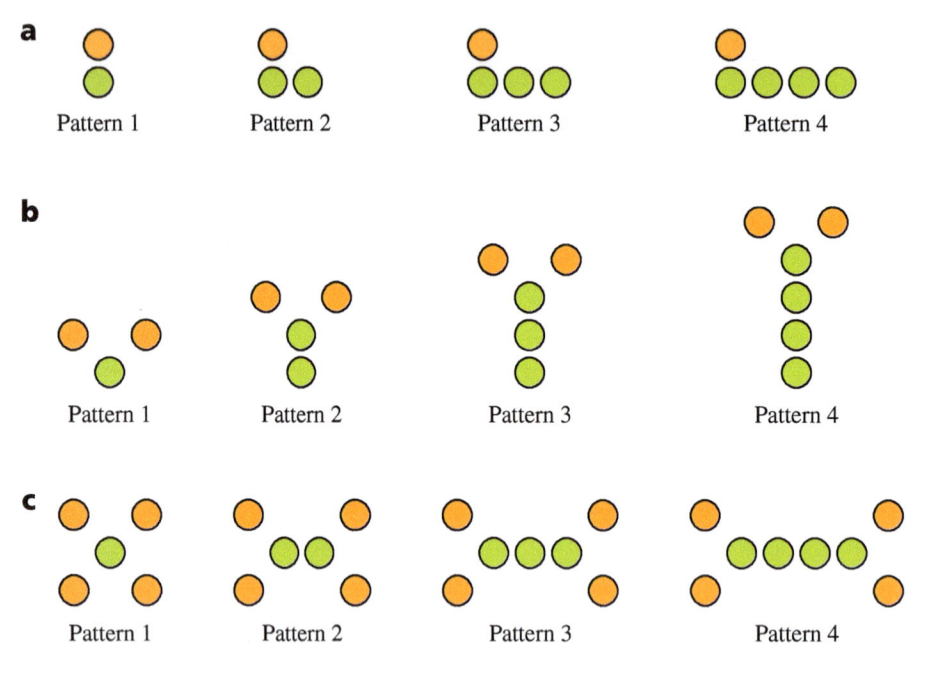

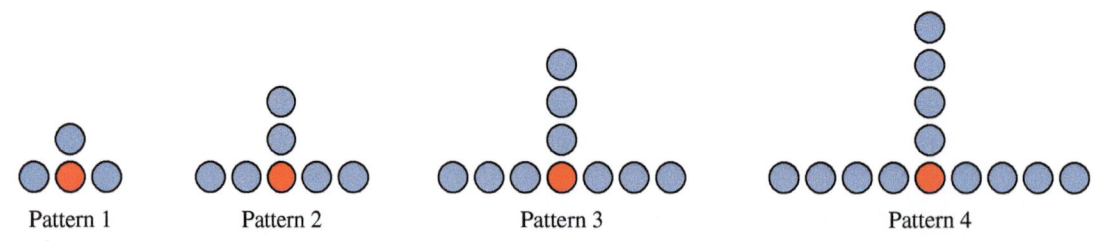

**a** Pattern 1, Pattern 2, Pattern 3, Pattern 4

**b** Pattern 1, Pattern 2, Pattern 3, Pattern 4

**c** Pattern 1, Pattern 2, Pattern 3, Pattern 4

For each pattern of shapes:

**i** write down the number sequence formed by the total number of circles in each pattern

**ii** write down the term-to-term rule for the number sequence

**iii** copy and complete the table

| Pattern number ($n$) | 1 | 2 | 3 | 4 |
|---|---|---|---|---|
| Number of green circles | | | | |
| Number of orange circles | | | | |
| Total number of circles | | | | |

**iv** write down the rule to find the total number of circles in pattern $n$

> Use the different coloured circles to help you.

**v** work out the number of circles in pattern 50.

**2** The diagrams show the first four patterns in four sequences.

**a** Pattern 1, Pattern 2, Pattern 3, Pattern 4

196

**b**

Pattern 1   Pattern 2   Pattern 3   Pattern 4

**c**

Pattern 1   Pattern 2   Pattern 3   Pattern 4

**d**

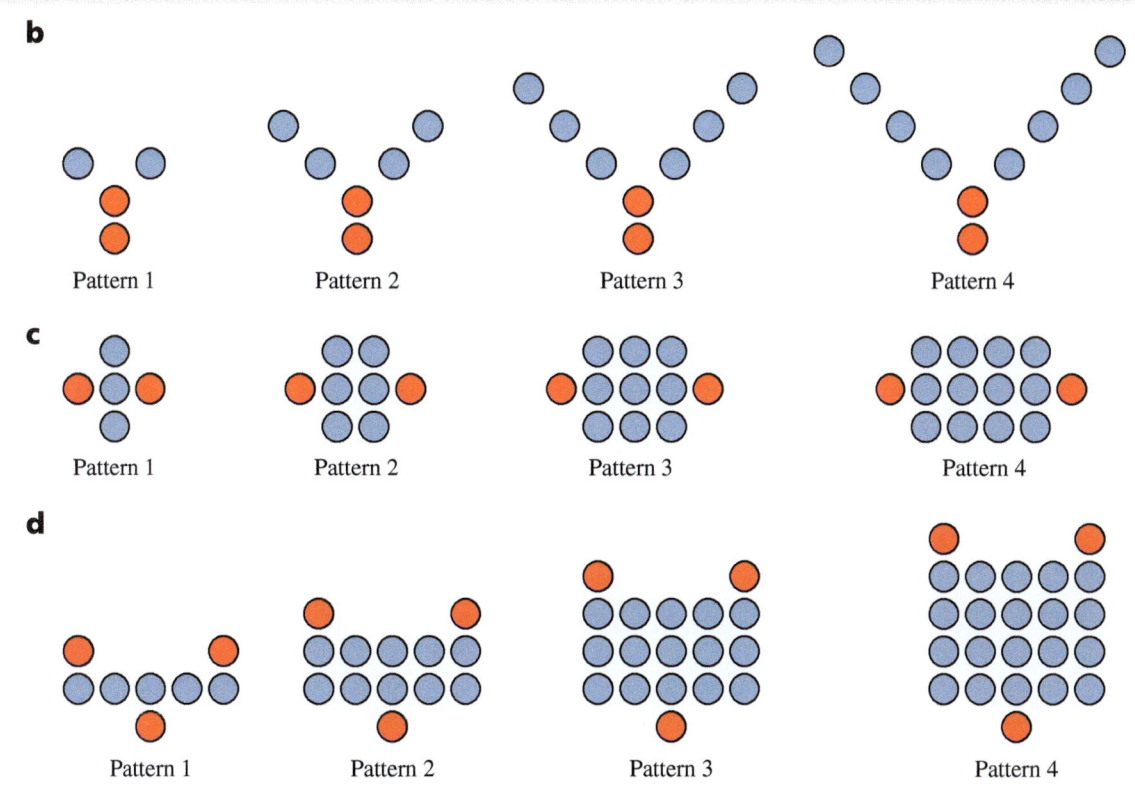

Pattern 1   Pattern 2   Pattern 3   Pattern 4

For each pattern of shapes:

**i** write down the number sequence formed by the total number of circles in each pattern

**ii** write down the term-to-term rule for the number sequence

**iii** copy and complete the table

| Pattern number ($n$) | 1 | 2 | 3 | 4 |
|---|---|---|---|---|
| Number of blue circles | | | | |
| Number of red circles | | | | |
| Total number of circles | | | | |

**iv** write down the rule to find the total number of circles in pattern $n$

**v** work out the total number of circles in pattern 40.

**3** The diagrams show the first three patterns in a sequence.

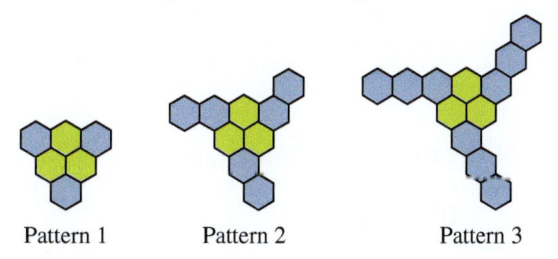

Pattern 1   Pattern 2   Pattern 3

**a** Write down the rule to find the total number of hexagons in pattern $n$.

**b** Work out the total number of hexagons in pattern 100.

# 14.3 The nth term of a linear sequence of numbers

When working with number sequences you may need to find the value of one of the terms in the sequence.

For example, you may be asked to find the 50th term in the sequence 5, 9, 13, 17, 21, ...

Writing down a long list of terms until you reach the term that you need is not an efficient method.

The most efficient method is to use the position-to-term rule.

The position-to-term rule is often written using algebra, as you have seen above. This is known as finding the **nth term**.

The nth term is a general term in a sequence.

To find the position-to-term rule you first look at the differences between the terms of the sequence.

| Position ($n$) | 1 | 2 | 3 | 4 | 5 |
|---|---|---|---|---|---|
| Term | 5 | 9 | 13 | 17 | 21 |

+4  +4  +4  +4

In this case, the terms increase by 4.

The numbers in the 4 × table also increase by 4.

To find the rest of the rule you must compare the terms with the 4 × table.

| Position ($n$) | 1 | 2 | 3 | 4 | 5 |
|---|---|---|---|---|---|
| 4 × table | 4 | 8 | 12 | 16 | 20 |
| Term | 5 | 9 | 13 | 17 | 21 |

×4
+1

The position-to-term rule is:        term = 4 × position number then add 1

This can be written using algebra as:        $n$th term = $4n + 1$

So the 50th term in this sequence is found using $n = 50$ in the formula:

$$50\text{th term} = 4 \times 50 + 1$$
$$= 200 + 1$$
$$= 201$$

## Worked example 1

Find the $n$th term and 50th term of the linear sequence 1, 4, 7, 10, 13, ...

1   4   7   10   13
 +3  +3  +3  +3

The terms increase by 3, so compare the terms with the 3 × table.

| Position ($n$) | 1 | 2 | 3 | 4 | 5 |
|---|---|---|---|---|---|
| 3 × table | 3 | 6 | 9 | 12 | 15 |
| Term | 1 | 4 | 7 | 10 | 13 |

×3
−2

The position-to-term rule is:   term = 3 × position number then subtract 2

So, $n$th term = $3n - 2$

And, 50th term = $3 \times 50 - 2$

$= 150 - 2$

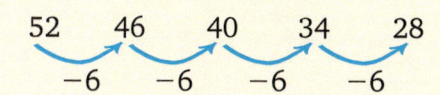

$= 148$

## Worked example 2

Find the $n$th term and 50th term of the linear sequence 52, 46, 40, 34, 28, …

52  46  40  34  28
 −6  −6  −6  −6

The terms decrease by 6, so compare the terms with the −6 × table.

| Position ($n$) | 1 | 2 | 3 | 4 | 5 |
|---|---|---|---|---|---|
| −6 × table | −6 | −12 | −18 | −24 | −30 |
| Term | 52 | 46 | 40 | 34 | 28 |

× −6
+58

The position-to-term rule is:   term = −6 × position number then add 58

So, $n$th term = $-6n + 58 = 58 - 6n$

And, 50th term = $58 - 6 \times 50$

$= 58 - 300$

$= -242$

## Exercise 14.3

**1** Write down the first four terms of the sequence whose $n$th term is:

   **a** $n + 3$     **b** $2n$     **c** $7n + 5$     **d** $4n - 2$

   **e** $8n + 1$     **f** $4n - 1$     **g** $2n - 9$     **h** $13 - 3n$

**2** For each sequence, find:   **i** the $n$th term   **ii** the 20th term.

   Show your working in a table.

   Part **a** has been done for you.

   **a** 7, 9, 11, 13, …

| Position ($n$) | 1 | 2 | 3 | 4 | 20 | $n$ |
|---|---|---|---|---|---|---|
| Term | 7 | 9 | 11 | 13 | 45 | $2n + 5$ |

×2 and add 5

+2  +2  +2

199

**b** 2, 5, 8, 11, …     **c** 7, 12, 17, 22, …     **d** 5, 11, 17, 23, …

**e** 7, 11, 15, 19, …     **f** 7, 10, 13, 16, …     **g** 1, 6, 11, 16, …

**3** Joanne is asked to find the $n$th term of the sequence 12, 17, 22, 27, …

Joanne writes:

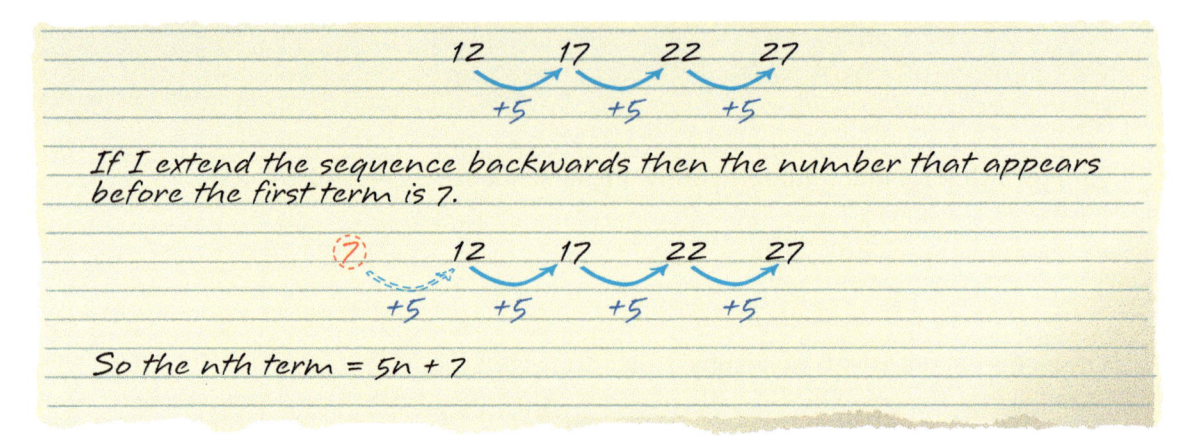

> 12    17    22    27
>     +5    +5    +5
>
> If I extend the sequence backwards then the number that appears before the first term is 7.
>
> (7)    12    17    22    27
>    +5    +5    +5    +5
>
> So the $n$th term = $5n + 7$

**a** Copy and complete these checks to show that the $n$th term of the sequence 12, 17, 22, 27, … is $5n + 7$

1st term = $5 \times 1 + 7 = 12$      2nd term = $5 \times 2 + 7 = \ldots$

3rd term = $5 \times 3 + 7 = \ldots$      4th term = $5 \times 4 + 7 = \ldots$

**b** Use Joanne's method to find the $n$th term of these linear sequences.

   **i** 9, 16, 23, 30, …     **ii** 4, 9, 14, 19, …     **iii** 2, 6, 10, 14, …

   **iv** −3, −1, 1, 3, …     **v** 10, 13, 16, 19, …     **vi** −2, 4, 10, 16, …

**4** For each linear sequence, find: **i** the $n$th term    **ii** the 50th term.

   **a** 23, 21, 19, 17, …     **b** 47, 44, 41, 38, …     **c** 32, 27, 22, 17, …

   **d** 56, 52, 48, 44, …     **e** 2, −4, −10, −16, …     **f** 1, −1, −3, −5, …

**5** The cards show four $n$th terms and five sequences.

| $n$th term = $2n + 3$ | $n$th term = $3n + 2$ | $n$th term = $4n − 3$ | $n$th term = $n + 4$ |

| 5, 13, 21, 29, … | 5, 6, 7, 8, … | 5, 8, 11, 14, … | 5, 7, 9, 11, … | 1, 5, 9, 13, … |

**a** Match each $n$th term with its sequence.

**b** Find the $n$th term for the remaining sequence.

**6** Write down an expression for the $n$th term of the linear sequence 0.41, 0.64, 0.87, 1.1, …

# 14 Sequences

## Review

**1** For each sequence, find:  **i** the term-to-term rule  **ii** the next three terms.

   **a** 14, 23, 32, 41, …     **b** 11, 8, 5, 2, …

**2** Find the missing numbers in these linear sequences.

   **a** ☐, ☐, 13, ☐, ☐, ☐, 29, …     **b** 7, ☐, ☐, −8, ☐, ☐, …

**3** The first term of a sequence is 6.

The term-to-term rule is 'add 7'.

Find the 100th term in the sequence.

**4** The position-to-term rule for a sequence is:

> term = 4 × position number then add 5

Copy and complete the table to find the sequence.

| Position number | 1 | 2 | 3 | 4 | 5 | 6 | 7 |
|---|---|---|---|---|---|---|---|
| Term | 9 | | | | 25 | | |

**5** The diagrams show the first four patterns in a sequence.

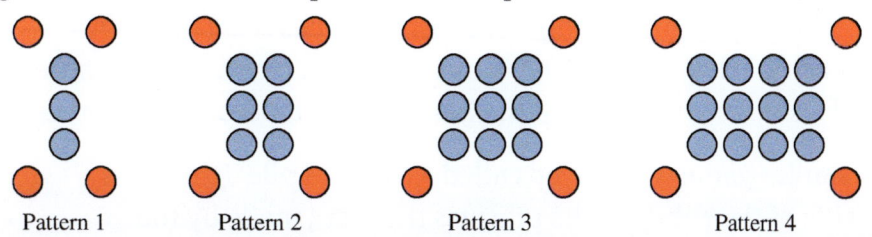

Pattern 1     Pattern 2     Pattern 3     Pattern 4

**a** Write down the number sequence formed by the total number of circles in each pattern.

**b** Write down the term-to-term rule for the number sequence.

**c** Copy and complete the table.

| Pattern number ($n$) | 1 | 2 | 3 | 4 |
|---|---|---|---|---|
| Number of blue circles | | | | |
| Number of red circles | | | | |
| Total number of circles | | | | |

**d** Write down the rule to find the total number of circles in pattern $n$.

**e** Work out the total number of circles in pattern 80.

**6** Write down the first five terms of the sequence whose $n$th term is:

   **a** $8n - 3$     **b** $11 - 4n$

**7** For each linear sequence, find:  **i** the $n$th term  **ii** the 60th term.

   **a** 11, 14, 17, 20, …     **b** 2, 9, 16, 23, …

   **c** 14, 19, 24, 29, …     **d** 9, 5, 1, −3, …

# 15 Probability

> **Learning outcomes**
>
> - Know that if the probability of an event occurring is $p$, then the probability of it not occurring is $1 - p$.
> - Find probabilities based on equally likely outcomes in practical contexts.
> - List systematically all the outcomes for a single event.
> - List systematically all the outcomes for two successive events.
> - Compare experimental probabilities with theoretical probabilities.
> - Recognise that when experiments are repeated different outcomes may result.
> - Recognise that increasing the number of times an experiment is repeated generally leads to better estimates of probability.

## Heads or tails?

Throwing a coin in the air and calling 'heads' or 'tails' has been used since at least Roman times. They called it *navia aut caput* ('ship or head') because some coins had a ship on one side and the head of the emperor on the other.

In England, a similar game was played called 'cross and pile' (the cross being on one side of the coin and the pile was the mark made by the hammer used to strike the coin on the other).

There are only two possible outcomes. Both outcomes are equally likely.

Today, flipping a coin is used in some sports to decide which way a team will play or who will start a game, such as a football or cricket match.

Before penalty shoot-outs were used to decide the outcome of a drawn football match, a coin flip was sometimes used. In 1968, Italy played the Soviet Union in a semi-final of the European Football Championship. After extra time, the score was 0–0. The result was decided by flipping a coin to see who reached the final. Italy won and went on to become European champions.

# 15 Probability

## 15.1 Calculating probabilities

### Equally likely outcomes

Probability is all about how likely a particular outcome is.

Equally likely outcomes are used to find **theoretical probabilities**. For example, when a fair dice is rolled, each of the numbers on the dice is equally likely.

Numbers are used to describe probability. They are always between 0 and 1.

An outcome with a probability of 0 is impossible and will not happen.

An outcome with a probability of 1 is certain to happen.

Outcomes that are very unlikely to happen have a probability close to 0.

Outcomes that are very likely to happen have a probability close to 1.

$$\text{Probability of a successful outcome} = \frac{\text{number of successful outcomes}}{\text{total number of outcomes}}$$

### Worked example 1

A letter is chosen at random from the word PROBABILITY.

What is the probability that the letter is:

**a** a letter B

**b** a vowel?

**a** $\text{Probability of a successful outcome} = \frac{\text{number of successful outcomes}}{\text{total number of outcomes}}$

Probability of a B $= \frac{2}{11}$ — There are 2 B's in the word 'PROBABILITY'.
— There are 11 letters in the word 'PROBABILITY'.

> You can use P(B) to mean 'the probability of a B'. This saves time in writing.

**b** $\text{Probability of a successful outcome} = \frac{\text{number of successful outcomes}}{\text{total number of outcomes}}$

Probability of a vowel $= \frac{4}{11}$ — There are 4 vowels in the word 'PROBABILITY'.
— There are 11 letters in the word 'PROBABILITY'.

### Worked example 2

A box of chocolates contains 8 hard-centred chocolates and 6 soft-centred chocolates.

Asel takes a chocolate from the box without looking.

What is the probability that the chocolate has:

**a** a hard centre

**b** a soft centre?

**a** Probability of a successful outcome = $\dfrac{\text{number of successful outcomes}}{\text{total number of outcomes}}$

Probability of a hard centre = $\dfrac{8}{14}$ —— There are 8 hard-centred chocolates in the box.
—— There are 14 chocolates in the box.

This fraction can be simplified: $\dfrac{8}{14} = \dfrac{4}{7}$

**b** Probability of a successful outcome = $\dfrac{\text{number of successful outcomes}}{\text{total number of outcomes}}$

Probability of a soft centre = $\dfrac{6}{14}$ —— There are 6 soft-centred chocolates in the box.
—— There are 14 chocolates in the box.

This fraction can be simplified: $\dfrac{6}{14} = \dfrac{3}{7}$

## Probability an outcome does not happen

In Worked example 2, above, a chocolate is taken from a box.

There are two possible outcomes.

It is either a soft-centred chocolate or a hard-centred chocolate.

A chocolate is taken from the box without looking.

P(soft centre) = $\dfrac{3}{7}$

P(not a soft centre) = $\dfrac{4}{7}$

If a chocolate is not a soft-centred chocolate then it must be a hard-centred chocolate.

Notice that $\dfrac{3}{7} + \dfrac{4}{7} = 1$.

Notice also that P(soft centre) = 1 − P(not soft centre), and
P(not soft centre) = 1 − P(soft centre)

For any event:

*Probability of the event not happening = 1 − probability of the event happening*

*Probability of the event happening = 1 − probability of the event not happening*

## Worked example 3

Baby Miguel has 3 teddy bears, 2 books, 1 ball and 10 blocks in his toy box.

His mum takes a toy out of the toy box.

She gives the toy to Miguel.

What is the probability the toy is:

**a** a teddy bear

**b** a book

**c** not a book

**d** either a block or a ball?

**a** Probability of a teddy bear = P(teddy bear) = $\frac{3}{16}$ ←— There are 3 teddy bears in the toy box.
←— There are 16 toys in the toy box.

**b** Probability of a book = P(book) = $\frac{2}{16}$ ←— There are 2 books in the toy box.
←— There are 16 toys in the toy box.

**c** Probability of not a book = P(not a book) = 1 − P(book)

$= 1 - \frac{2}{16} = \frac{16}{16} - \frac{2}{16} = \frac{14}{16}$

**d** Probability of either a block or a ball = P(block or ball)

$= \frac{11}{16}$ ←— 11 of the toys in the toy box are either a block or a ball.
←— There are 16 toys in the toy box.

## Exercise 15.1

1. This spinner is spun.
   
   **a** What is the probability the spinner will land on red?
   
   **b** What is the probability the spinner will not land on red?
   
   **c** What is the probability the spinner will land on black?
   
   **d** What is the probability the spinner will not land on black?

2. Junaid plays mini golf.
   
   The probability that he gets a hole-in-one is 0.2
   
   What is the probability that he does not get a hole-in-one?

3. The probability that Fran loses her house keys is $\frac{1}{30}$.
   
   What is the probability that she does not lose her house keys?

4. The probability that someone leaves a message on Todd's answering machine is 0.25
   
   What is the probability that the next caller does not leave a message?

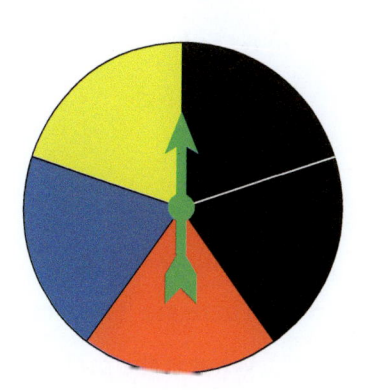

**5** Caroline has 12 socks in her sock drawer.

5 of the socks are blue.

She takes a sock from the drawer without looking.

What is the probability that the sock is:

**a** blue

**b** not blue?

**6** An ordinary fair dice is rolled.

  **a** What is the probability of getting a number less than 3?

  **b** What is the probability of getting a number not less than 3?

  **c** What is the probability of getting a number greater than 3?

  **d** Why are the answers to **b** and **c** not the same?

**7** 12 discs numbered from 1 to 12 are placed in a bag.

One of the discs is taken out without looking.

What is the probability of getting a disc with:

  **a** a number less than 3

  **b** a number that is divisible by 3

  **c** a square number

  **d** a number that is not a square number?

**8** A set of snooker balls consists of 15 red balls, and one ball each of white, black, pink, blue, brown, green and yellow.

One ball is chosen at random.

What is the probability that the ball is:

  **a** red

  **b** not red

  **c** black

  **d** not black

  **e** black or white?

**9** There are 3 blue cars, 5 red cars, 2 black cars and 1 white car parked in a school car park.

What is the probability that the first car to leave the car park is:

  **a** blue

  **b** red

  **c** black or white

  **d** not red?

**10** A bag contains only black and white counters.

The probability that the counter is white is $\frac{1}{6}$

A counter is taken from the bag at random.

The counter is white. It is not replaced in the bag.

> There are only black and white counters and the probability of a white counter is $\frac{1}{6}$. This tells you that for every white counter there are 5 black counters.

**a** What is the smallest number of black counters in the bag?

A second counter is taken from the bag.

This counter is placed next to the first counter.

It is also white.

**b** What is the smallest number of black counters that can now be in the bag?

**11** The members of a club live on three streets: Oak Street, Elm Street and Birch Street.

The table shows the number of members from each street.

|  | Oak Street | Elm Street | Birch Street |
|---|---|---|---|
| Male | 16 | 14 | 10 |
| Female | 9 | 7 | 18 |

One member of this club is chosen at random.

What is the probability that the member is:

**a** female

**b** male

**c** from Elm Street

**d** a male from Birch Street

**e** not from Oak Street

**f** from Birch Street, given that the member chosen is male?

## 15.2 Listing outcomes

Single events, such as throwing a coin or a dice, have a simple set of possible outcomes. These can be listed.

The outcomes for two events need to be listed carefully to make sure that none are missed out.

Once all outcomes have been listed, the probability of individual outcomes may be found using the usual formula.

$$\text{Probability of a successful outcome} = \frac{\text{number of successful outcomes}}{\text{total number of outcomes}}$$

## Worked example 1

Two coins are thrown.

List the possible outcomes.

What is the probability the coins will land the same way up?

The possible outcomes are below (where H = heads and T = tails).

| First coin | Second coin |
|---|---|
| H | H |
| H | T |
| T | H |
| T | T |

There are four possible equally likely outcomes: HH, HT, TH, TT.

P(same on both coins) = P(HH or TT) = $\frac{2}{4}$ = $\frac{1}{2}$

> Note that HT is not the same as TH. HT means 'heads' on the first coin and 'tails' on the second. TH means 'tails' on the first coin and 'heads' on the second.

## Worked example 2

A red bead, a blue bead and a black bead are in a bag.

A bead is taken from the bag without looking.

Its colour is recorded.

The bead is replaced in the bag.

A second bead is taken from the bag without looking.

Its colour is recorded.

List the possible outcomes.

The outcomes are:

| First bead | Second bead |
|---|---|
| Red | Red |
| Red | Blue |
| Red | Black |
| Blue | Red |
| Blue | Blue |
| Blue | Black |
| Black | Red |
| Black | Blue |
| Black | Black |

> Remember to be systematic when you list the possibilities.

## Exercise 15.2

1. A coin is thrown and a dice is rolled.
   
   a List all the possible outcomes.
   
   b What is the probability that heads and an even number are thrown?

2. These spinners are shown to be fair.
   
   They are both spun at the same time.
   
   a List all the pairs of numbers you can get.
   
   b What is the probability of getting a 2 and a 6 together?
   
   c What is the probability that the two numbers are both even?

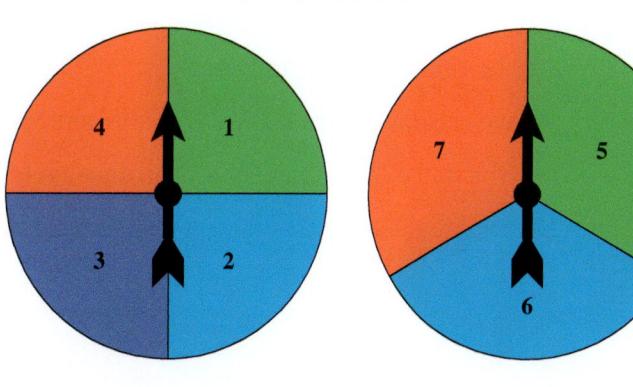

3. There are some red beads and some black beads in a bag.
   
   One bead is taken from the bag. Its colour is noted. The bead is then replaced in the bag.
   
   A second bead is taken from the bag. Its colour is noted and then it is replaced in the bag.
   
   List the possible outcomes.

4. In a restaurant, extra toppings for pizza can be chosen.
   
   You can choose from mushroom, onion or pepper.
   
   Jai chooses two toppings.
   
   List the possible outcomes.
   
   > The order of the toppings does not matter.

5. This spinner has the numbers from 1 to 5.
   
   Each number is equally likely.
   
   a List the possible outcomes when the spinner is spun twice.
   
   b What is the probability that the same number is spun both times?

6. All the names of all the teachers, students and other staff in a school are put in a box.
   
   One name is drawn out of the box.
   
   Phani says, 'There are only three possibilities. It is a teacher, a student, or another staff member. So, the probability it is a student is $\frac{1}{3}$.'
   
   Phani is wrong. Explain why.

7. A group of 8 girls are planning what to do on a day out.
   
   Their choices are swimming, going to the park or playing tennis.
   
   > Think about the probability of the choice of day out with each of the two ways the girls suggest.
   
   4 of the girls want to go swimming, 3 want to play tennis and 1 wants to go to the park.
   
   One of the girls suggests they write down the three activities on pieces of paper, put them in a box and take one without looking to decide.

One of the other girls suggests they each write what they want to do on a piece of paper, put all eight in a box and take one without looking to decide.

Which is the fairest way to decide what they should do?

Give reasons for your choice.

8  Martha has a box of chocolates.

The box contains 12 chocolates.

5 have caramel centres, 6 have cream centres and 1 has a nut in the centre.

Martha and a friend take one chocolate each from the box and eat them.

List the possible centres for the two chocolates that are eaten.

## 15.3 Estimating probabilities

Sometimes it is not possible to know whether all possible outcomes are equally likely.

For example, when a drawing pin is dropped there are two possible outcomes: it may land point up or point down. These two outcomes may, or may not, be equally likely.

You could do an **experiment** to estimate the probability.

You could drop a drawing pin lots of times and record the results.

Each time the drawing pin is dropped is called a **trial**.

You could then use the results to find **experimental probabilities**.

$$\text{Experimental probability} = \frac{\text{number of successful trials}}{\text{total number of trials}}$$

The larger the number of trials used to estimate the probability the better the estimate.

When an experiment is repeated you would not expect to get the same results.

### Worked example 1

Luke does an experiment to estimate the probability of a drawing pin landing point up.

He drops the drawing pin 10 times.

It lands point up 3 times.

Raffaele does the same experiment.

He drops the drawing pin 50 times.

It lands point up 20 times.

a  Work out the experimental probability of the drawing pin landing point up for both Luke and Raffaele.

b  Who is most likely to have the better estimate? Give a reason for your answer.

**a** The experimental probability for Luke is $\frac{3}{10}$

The experimental probability for Raffaele is $\frac{20}{50}$

**b** Raffaele is more likely to have the better estimate, as he has done the experiment more times.

## Worked example 2

Agnetta thinks a dice may be biased.

She rolls the dice 6 times and records her results.

| Number rolled | 1 | 2 | 3 | 4 | 5 | 6 |
|---|---|---|---|---|---|---|
| Frequency | 2 | 1 | 2 | 1 | 0 | 0 |

Agnetta says, 'My dice must be biased as I didn't get a 5 or 6.'

**a** What is the theoretical probability of getting a 1 with a fair dice?

**b** What is the experimental probability of getting a 1 with Agnetta's dice?

**c** What is the theoretical probability of getting a 5 with a fair dice?

**d** What is the experimental probability of getting a 5 with Agnetta's dice?

**e** Comment on Agnetta's statement.

**a** The theoretical probability of getting a 1 is $\frac{1}{6}$

**b** The experimental probability of getting a 1 is $\frac{2}{6}$

**c** The theoretical probability of getting a 5 is $\frac{1}{6}$

**d** The experimental probability of getting a 5 is $\frac{0}{6} = 0$

**e** Agnetta needs to roll the dice more times to have enough information to decide if the dice is biased or not.

When a fair dice is rolled, the theoretical probability of getting each number is $\frac{1}{6}$

Only one difference in the result of a roll will change an experimental probability from 0 to $\frac{1}{6}$, or from $\frac{2}{6}$ to $\frac{1}{6}$

## Exercise 15.3

**1** Two coins are flipped together 200 times.

The results are recorded.

| Outcome | Two heads | Two tails | One head, one tail |
|---|---|---|---|
| Frequency | 46 | 48 | 106 |

What is the experimental probability of getting:

**a** two heads

**b** two tails

**c** one head, one tail?

2  300 people are asked to choose a whole number between 1 and 10 at random.

The results are recorded.

| Outcome | 1 | 2 | 3 | 4 | 5 | 6 | 7 | 8 | 9 | 10 |
|---|---|---|---|---|---|---|---|---|---|---|
| Frequency | 8 | 20 | 30 | 36 | 54 | 52 | 36 | 34 | 21 | 9 |

   a  What is the theoretical probability of the number 1 being chosen?
   b  What is the experimental probability of the number 1 being chosen?
   c  What is the theoretical probability of the number 5 being chosen?
   d  What is the experimental probability of the number 5 being chosen?
   e  Sai wants some random numbers between 1 and 10.

   He thinks that he can ask some of his friends to choose them for him.

   Does the information in the table suggest this is a good way to obtain random numbers? Give a reason for your answer.

3  A large jar contains red and white marbles.

   An experiment consists of the following steps:

   i  A marble is taken out of the jar.
   ii  The colour of the marble is noted.
   iii  The marble is replaced in the jar.
   iv  The jar is shaken.

   Celestine and Girin repeat the experiment a number of times.

   They each record their results.

|  | Red | White |
|---|---|---|
| Celestine | 7 | 3 |
| Girin | 28 | 22 |

   a  Find the experimental probability of taking a red marble from the jar using Celestine's results.
   b  Find the experimental probability of taking a red marble from the jar using Girin's results.
   c  Whose results are more likely to give the better estimate of the probability of getting a red marble from the jar? Give a reason for your answer.
   d  Find the experimental probability of taking a red marble from the jar using Celestine's results and Girin's results added together.

4  Oscar records the number of people in 50 cars as they drive past his school.

| Number of people | 1 | 2 | 3 | 4 | 5 |
|---|---|---|---|---|---|
| Frequency | 13 | 16 | 10 | 9 | 2 |

   Use these results to estimate the probability that the next car has:

   a  one person in it
   b  at least three people in it.

**5** Mitchell makes this spinner.

He spins it 10 times and records the results.

| Colour | Red | Blue | Green | Yellow |
|---|---|---|---|---|
| Frequency | 2 | 4 | 3 | 1 |

**a** Estimate the probability of getting each colour.

**b** Do you think the spinner is fair? Give a reason for your answer.

**6** 12 cards are in a pile.

Each card has a number from 1 to 4.

A card is taken from the pile.

Its number is noted.

It is replaced in the pile.

The cards are then mixed up.

This is repeated 360 times.

The results are shown in the table.

| Number on card | Frequency |
|---|---|
| 1 | 58 |
| 2 | 148 |
| 3 | 94 |
| 4 | 60 |

*Use the frequencies to find experimental probabilities.*

Estimate the number of cards in the pile for each number.

**7** Tao throws two coins in the air.

He records the results.

| | One head, one tail | Two heads | Two tails |
|---|---|---|---|
| Frequency | 31 | 35 | 34 |

**a** How many times are the two coins thrown in the air altogether?

**b** Find the experimental probability of getting each result.

**c** Do you think that Tao recorded the results accurately? Give a reason for your answer.

## Review

**1** The probability that a student in a class is left-handed is 0.1

What is the probability that a student chosen from this class is not left-handed?

**2** The probability of getting a 6 when a dice is rolled is $\frac{1}{6}$

What is the probability of not getting a 6?

**3** A man is fitting windows.

He can fit red, blue or clear glass.

List all the possible outcomes when two windows are fitted.

4  The spinner shown is a fair spinner.

   It is spun and a coin is flipped at the same time.

   One possible outcome is (heads, 1).

   List all the possible outcomes.

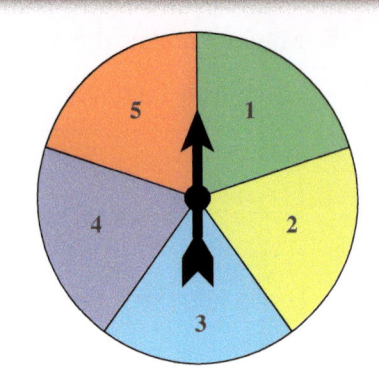

5  Ivan rolls a dice.

   He records the number of times a 6 is rolled.

   |           | 6   | Not a 6 |
   |-----------|-----|---------|
   | Frequency | 28  | 122     |

   a  How many times did Ivan roll the dice altogether?

   b  Find the experimental probability of getting a 6.

   c  Do you think Ivan recorded his results accurately? Give a reason for your answer.

6  Sonya collected information about 40 football matches.

   | Home win | 25 |
   |----------|----|
   | Away win | 10 |
   | Draw     | 5  |

   a  Use these results to estimate the probability that the next football match she sees will be:

      i   a home win

      ii  an away win

      iii a draw.

   b  Lucinda collected information about 40 different football matches.

   | Home win | 23 |
   |----------|----|
   | Away win | 10 |
   | Draw     | 7  |

   Use all 80 football matches to estimate the probability that the next football match seen will be:

      i   a home win

      ii  an away win

      iii a draw.

   c  Which set of probabilities do you think is better? Give a reason for your answer.

# 16 Functions and graphs

> **Learning outcomes**
> - Know the meaning of function.
> - Express simple functions algebraically and represent them in mappings.
> - Construct tables of values and use all four quadrants to plot the graphs of linear functions, where $y$ is given explicitly in terms of $x$.
> - Recognise that equations of the form $y = mx + c$ correspond to straight-line graphs.

## Cartesian coordinates

The famous mathematician René Descartes is known as the Father of Modern Mathematics.

One night when he was lying in bed trying to fall asleep, he noticed a fly on his ceiling. He thought about how he could describe the exact position of the fly.

Descartes decided that if he specified the shortest distance from two perpendicular walls, he could exactly describe the fly's position.

This was the birth of the coordinate grid system (known as Cartesian coordinates) that we use today.

The coordinate system has many practical uses, such as finding locations on a map and displaying trends in data.

## 16.1 Mapping diagrams

A **function** is a rule that connects two sets of numbers.

A **function machine** shows the steps in a function.

This function machine performs two operations.

It multiplies the input number by 2 and then adds 3.

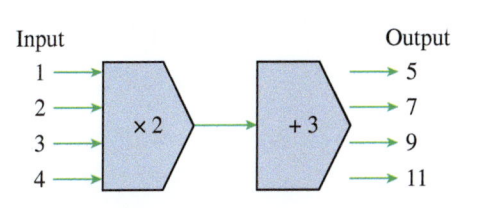

| Input | | | Output |
|---|---|---|---|
| 1 | ×2 | +3 | 5 |
| 2 | | | 7 |
| 3 | | | 9 |
| 4 | | | 11 |

215

The function can also be drawn as a **mapping diagram**.

This shows which **output** numbers the **input** numbers map on to.

The rule connecting the input and output is written algebraically as: $x \rightarrow 2x + 3$

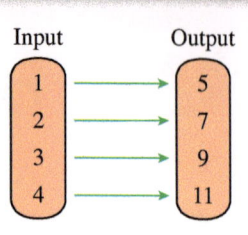

| Input | Output |
|-------|--------|
| 1 | 5 |
| 2 | 7 |
| 3 | 9 |
| 4 | 11 |

It is important to note that for the function $x \rightarrow 2x + 3$ if the inputs increase by 1, then the outputs increase by 2.

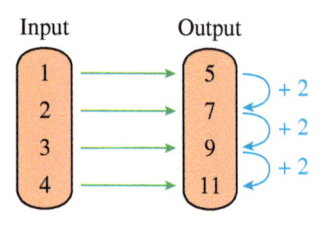

| Input | Output |
|-------|--------|
| 1 | 5 |
| 2 | 7 |
| 3 | 9 |
| 4 | 11 |

(+2, +2, +2)

Similarly, for the function $x \rightarrow 5x - 4$

when the inputs increase by 1, the outputs increase by 5.

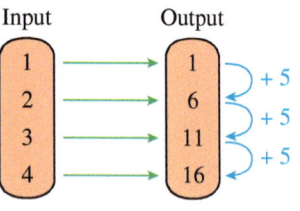

| Input | Output |
|-------|--------|
| 1 | 1 |
| 2 | 6 |
| 3 | 11 |
| 4 | 16 |

(+5, +5, +5)

## Worked example 1

Find the rule for this mapping diagram.

| Input | Output |
|-------|--------|
| 5 | 31 |
| 6 | 35 |
| 7 | 39 |
| 8 | 43 |

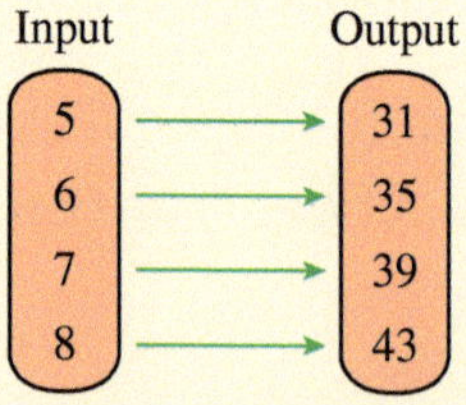

The input numbers increase by 1 and the output numbers increase by 4.

So the rule is of the form: $x \rightarrow 4x + ...$

Multiply each of the input numbers by 4 and then see what needs to be added (or subtracted) to obtain the output numbers.

| Input |  | Output |
|-------|--------|--------|
| 5 | 20 + 11 | 31 |
| 6 | 24 + 11 | 35 |
| 7 | 28 + 11 | 39 |
| 8 | 32 + 11 | 43 |

The rule is: $x \rightarrow 4x + 11$

## Worked example 2

Find the missing input for this mapping diagram by:

a using a reverse function machine

b writing down and solving an equation.

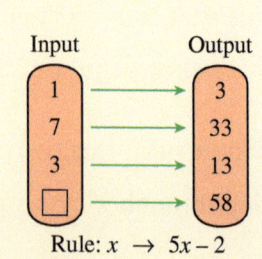

| Input | Output |
|-------|--------|
| 1 | 3 |
| 7 | 33 |
| 3 | 13 |
| ☐ | 58 |

Rule: $x \rightarrow 5x - 2$

**a** The function machine is:

Input → ×5 → −2 → 58

The reverse function machine is:

12 ← ÷5 ← 60 ← +2 ← 58

So the missing input is 12.

**b**  $5x - 2 = 58$

(+2)   $5x = 60$   (+2)

(÷5)   $x = 12$   (÷5)

So the missing input is 12.

## Exercise 16.1

**1 a** Copy and complete these mapping diagrams.

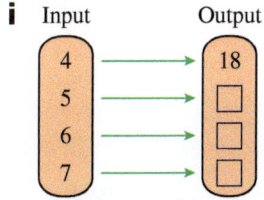

**i**
| Input | Output |
|---|---|
| 4 | 18 |
| 5 | ☐ |
| 6 | ☐ |
| 7 | ☐ |

Rule: $x \to 4x + 2$

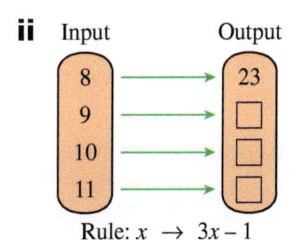

**ii**
| Input | Output |
|---|---|
| 8 | 23 |
| 9 | ☐ |
| 10 | ☐ |
| 11 | ☐ |

Rule: $x \to 3x - 1$

**iii**
| Input | Output |
|---|---|
| 5 | 28 |
| 6 | ☐ |
| 7 | ☐ |
| 8 | ☐ |

Rule: $x \to 5x + 3$

**b** Look at your mapping diagrams for part **a**.

What is the connection between the rule for the mapping diagram and the sequence of outputs?

**2** Priya, Raju and Aashif are asked to find the rule for this mapping diagram.

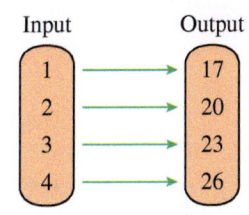

| Input | Output |
|---|---|
| 1 | 17 |
| 2 | 20 |
| 3 | 23 |
| 4 | 26 |

Priya says, 'The outputs increase by 3 so the rule is $x \to x + 3$'

Raju says, 'The outputs increase by 3 so the rule is $x \to 3x$'

Aashif says, 'The outputs increase by 3 so the rule is $x \to 3x + 14$'

Who is correct? Explain your answer.

# Mathematics for Cambridge Secondary 1

**3** Find the rule for each of these mapping diagrams.

Write your answers in the form $x \rightarrow ...$

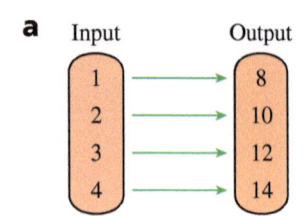

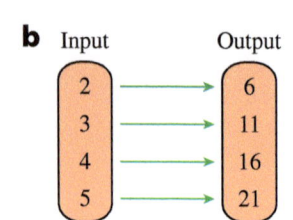

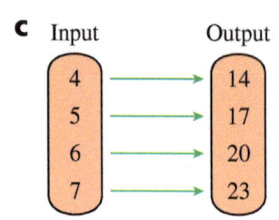

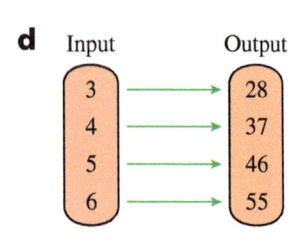

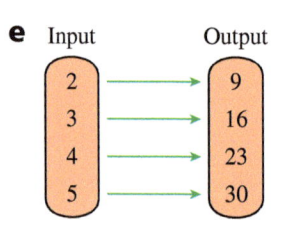

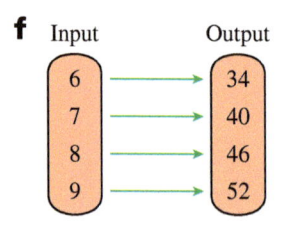

**a**
| Input | Output |
|---|---|
| 1 | 8 |
| 2 | 10 |
| 3 | 12 |
| 4 | 14 |

**b**
| Input | Output |
|---|---|
| 2 | 6 |
| 3 | 11 |
| 4 | 16 |
| 5 | 21 |

**c**
| Input | Output |
|---|---|
| 4 | 14 |
| 5 | 17 |
| 6 | 20 |
| 7 | 23 |

**d**
| Input | Output |
|---|---|
| 3 | 28 |
| 4 | 37 |
| 5 | 46 |
| 6 | 55 |

**e**
| Input | Output |
|---|---|
| 2 | 9 |
| 3 | 16 |
| 4 | 23 |
| 5 | 30 |

**f**
| Input | Output |
|---|---|
| 6 | 34 |
| 7 | 40 |
| 8 | 46 |
| 9 | 52 |

**4** Use reverse function machines to find the missing inputs for each of these mapping diagrams.

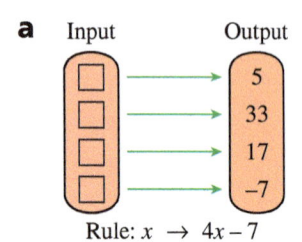

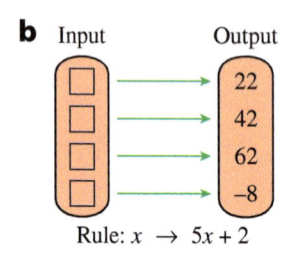

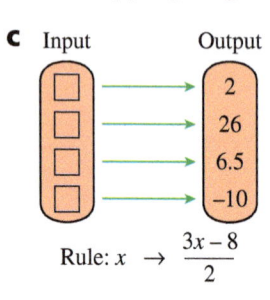

**a**
| Input | Output |
|---|---|
| □ | 5 |
| □ | 33 |
| □ | 17 |
| □ | −7 |

Rule: $x \rightarrow 4x - 7$

**b**
| Input | Output |
|---|---|
| □ | 22 |
| □ | 42 |
| □ | 62 |
| □ | −8 |

Rule: $x \rightarrow 5x + 2$

**c**
| Input | Output |
|---|---|
| □ | 2 |
| □ | 26 |
| □ | 6.5 |
| □ | −10 |

Rule: $x \rightarrow \dfrac{3x - 8}{2}$

**5** Copy and complete these mapping diagrams.

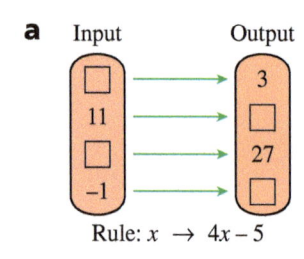

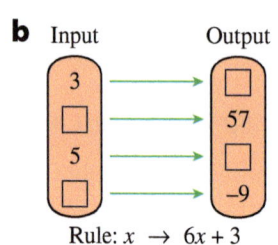

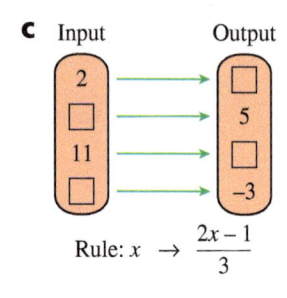

**a**
| Input | Output |
|---|---|
| □ | 3 |
| 11 | □ |
| □ | 27 |
| −1 | □ |

Rule: $x \rightarrow 4x - 5$

**b**
| Input | Output |
|---|---|
| 3 | □ |
| □ | 57 |
| 5 | □ |
| □ | −9 |

Rule: $x \rightarrow 6x + 3$

**c**
| Input | Output |
|---|---|
| 2 | □ |
| □ | 5 |
| 11 | □ |
| □ | −3 |

Rule: $x \rightarrow \dfrac{2x - 1}{3}$

## 16.2 Functions

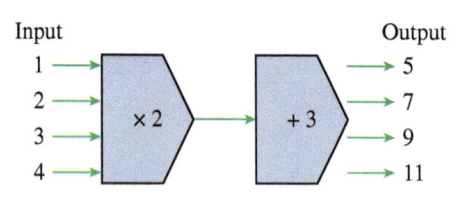

| Input | | | Output |
|---|---|---|---|
| 1 | ×2 | +3 | 5 |
| 2 | | | 7 |
| 3 | | | 9 |
| 4 | | | 11 |

If you use the letter $x$ to represent the input numbers and the letter $y$ to represent the output numbers, then the above function machine can be shown as:

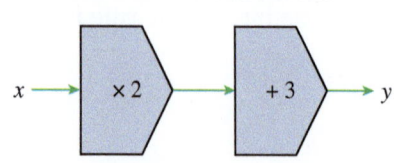

$x \rightarrow$ ×2 $\rightarrow$ +3 $\rightarrow y$

## 16 Functions and graphs

This means that if you start with the number $x$, multiply by 2 and then add 3, you obtain the number $y$.

The rule connecting $x$ and $y$ is written as $2x + 3 = y$

It is more common, however, to write the equation of the function as $y = 2x + 3$

The input numbers ($x$) and the output numbers ($y$) can be shown in a table of values:

| $x$ | 1 | 2 | 3 | 4 |
|---|---|---|---|---|
| $y$ | 5 | 7 | 9 | 11 |

This method of displaying the input and output numbers for a function is most commonly used in graph work.

### Worked example

Find the missing values in the table for the equation $y = 2x - 5$

| $x$ | −4 | 0 | 3 | |
|---|---|---|---|---|
| $y$ | | −5 | 1 | 9 |

The function machine is:

$x \rightarrow \boxed{\times 2} \rightarrow \boxed{-5} \rightarrow y$

$-4 \rightarrow \boxed{\times 2} \xrightarrow{-8} \boxed{-5} \rightarrow -13$

So when $x = -4, y = -13$

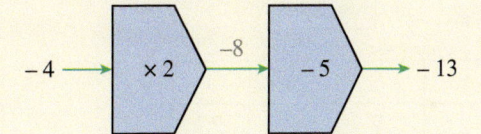

The reverse function machine is:

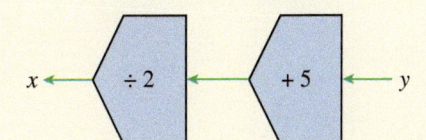

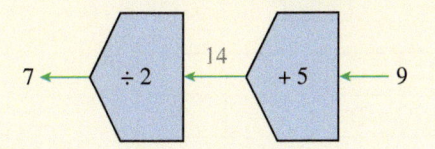

$x \leftarrow \boxed{\div 2} \leftarrow \boxed{+5} \leftarrow y$

$7 \leftarrow \boxed{\div 2} \xleftarrow{14} \boxed{+5} \leftarrow 9$

So when $y = 9, x = 7$

## Exercise 16.2

**1** Write each of these function machines as an equation in the form $y = \ldots$

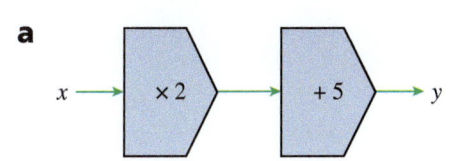

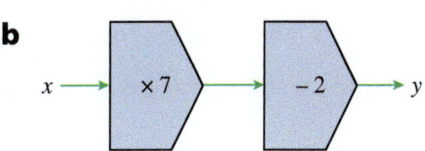

**a** $x \rightarrow \boxed{\times 2} \rightarrow \boxed{+5} \rightarrow y$

**b** $x \rightarrow \boxed{\times 7} \rightarrow \boxed{-2} \rightarrow y$

Mathematics for Cambridge Secondary 1

**c** $x \to [+5] \to [\times 4] \to y$

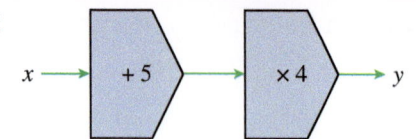

**d** $x \to [-3] \to [\div 2] \to y$

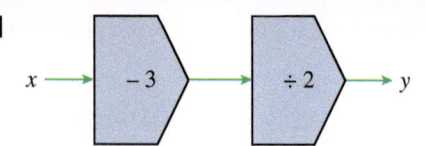

**e** $x \to [\times 3] \to [-2] \to [\div 5] \to y$

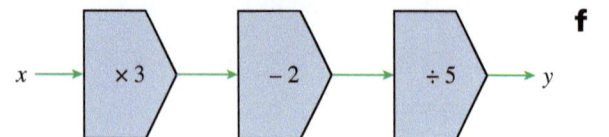

**f** $x \to [\times 8] \to [-1] \to [\div 3] \to y$

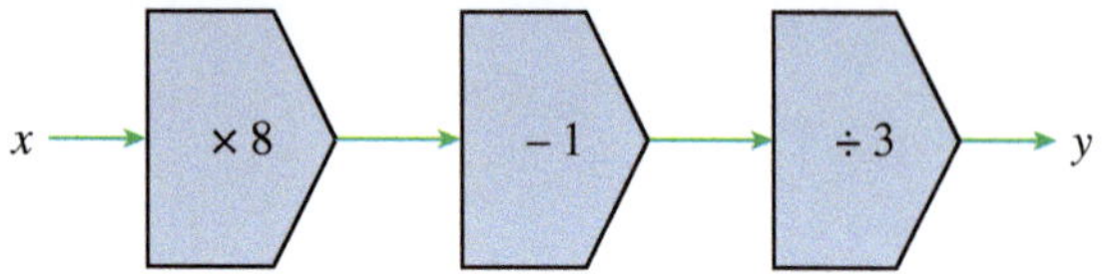

**2** Draw function machines for each of these equations.

   **a** $y = 5x + 7$     **b** $y = 2x - 8$     **c** $y = \dfrac{x+5}{8}$     **d** $y = \dfrac{3x-7}{2}$

**3** Copy and complete the function machine and table of values for each of these equations.

   **a** $y = 3x + 4$

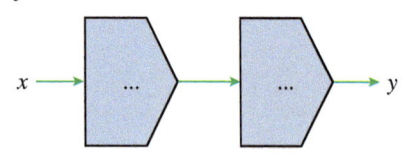

$x \to [\ldots] \to [\ldots] \to y$

| $x$ | −5 | −1 | 2 | 8 |
|---|---|---|---|---|
| $y$ | | | | |

   **b** $y = 7x - 6$

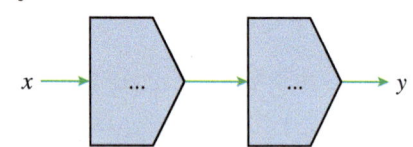

$x \to [\ldots] \to [\ldots] \to y$

| $x$ | −2 | 0 | 3 | 5 |
|---|---|---|---|---|
| $y$ | | | | |

   **c** $y = 2x + 9$

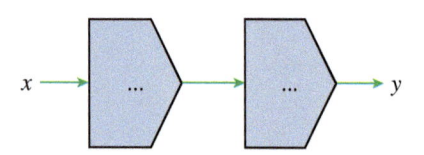

$x \to [\ldots] \to [\ldots] \to y$

| $x$ | −4 | | 2 | |
|---|---|---|---|---|
| $y$ | | 7 | | 21 |

   **d** $y = \dfrac{x}{2} - 3$

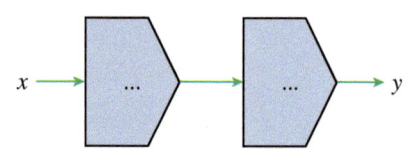

$x \to [\ldots] \to [\ldots] \to y$

| $x$ | −4 | | 4 | |
|---|---|---|---|---|
| $y$ | | −3 | | 1 |

   **e** $y = \dfrac{x+5}{2}$

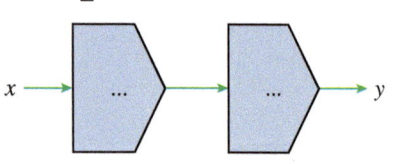

$x \to [\ldots] \to [\ldots] \to y$

| $x$ | −1 | | 3 | |
|---|---|---|---|---|
| $y$ | | 3 | | 7 |

   **f** $y = \dfrac{3x-5}{2}$

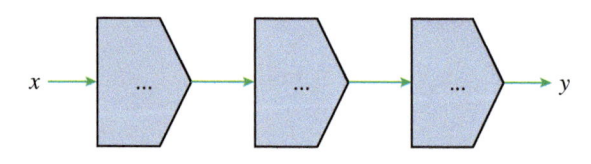

$x \to [\ldots] \to [\ldots] \to [\ldots] \to y$

| $x$ | −5 | | 3 | |
|---|---|---|---|---|
| $y$ | | −1 | | 11 |

**4**

| $x$ | 1 | 2 | 3 | 4 |
|---|---|---|---|---|
| $y$ | 4 | 13 | 22 | 31 |

Work out the equation of the function for this table of $x$ and $y$ values.

Write your answer in the form $y = \ldots$

Explain how you worked out your answer.

220

# 16 Functions and graphs

## 16.3 Linear graphs

In your Stage 7 Student Book you learnt that:

- $x = 2$ is a vertical line that crosses the x-axis at 2
- $y = 4$ is a horizontal line that crosses the y-axis at 4.

> The x-axis is the line $y = 0$.
> The y-axis is the line $x = 0$.

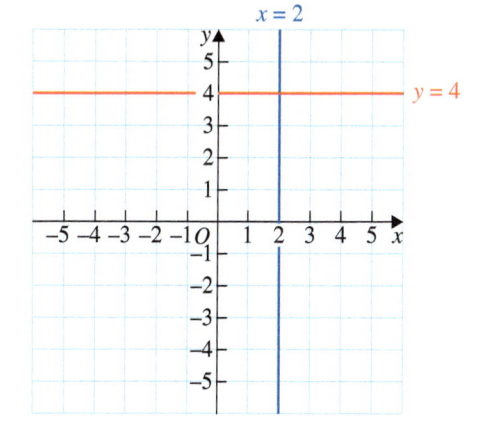

If an equation is more complicated, you should first make a table of values.

You then plot the points from your table and join them with a straight line.

It is possible to draw a straight line using only two points, but it is sensible to have at least three points to help check for mistakes.

(All the graphs in this section are straight lines.)

### Worked example

**a** Complete the table of values for $y = 2x + 1$

**b** On a grid, draw the graph of $y = 2x + 1$

| x | −3 | −2 | −1 | 0 | 1 | 2 |
|---|---|---|---|---|---|---|
| y | −5 |  | −1 |  | 3 |  |

**a** The function machine for $y = 2x + 1$ is:

$x \rightarrow \boxed{\times 2} \rightarrow \boxed{+ 1} \rightarrow y$

If $x = -2, y = 2 \times -2 + 1 = -3$
If $x = 0, y = 2 \times 0 + 1 = 1$
If $x = 2, y = 2 \times 2 + 1 = 5$

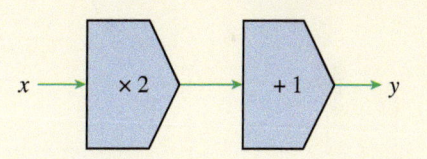

| x | −3 | −2 | −1 | 0 | 1 | 2 |
|---|---|---|---|---|---|---|
| y | −5 | −3 | −1 | 1 | 3 | 5 |

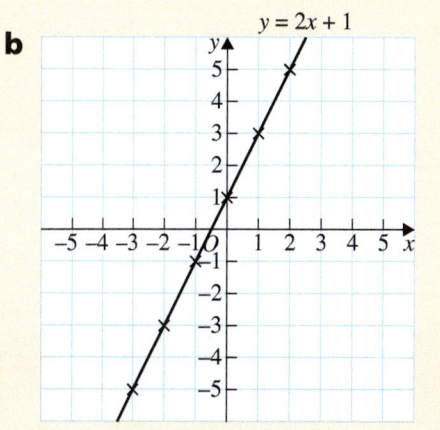

**b**

> Plot each point clearly with a cross.
>
> Use a ruler and pencil to draw the straight line.
>
> Extend the line to the edges of the grid.

# Mathematics for Cambridge Secondary 1

## Exercise 16.3

**1** In each part, you are given the equation of a function.

For each equation, copy and complete the function machine and table of values, and then draw its graph.

Use coordinate axes from $-5$ to $5$.

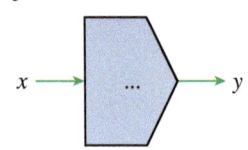

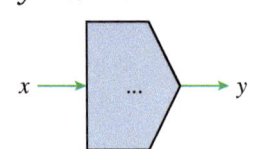

**a** $y = 2x$

| x | −2 | 0 | 2 |
|---|---|---|---|
| y | | | |

**b** $y = x + 3$

| x | −4 | 0 | 2 |
|---|---|---|---|
| y | | | |

**c** $y = x - 1$

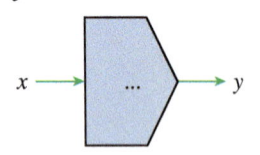

| x | −3 | 2 | 5 |
|---|---|---|---|
| y | | | |

**d** $y = 2x + 3$

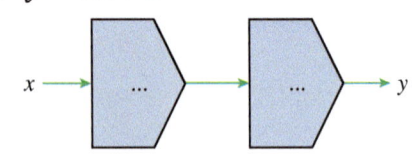

| x | −4 | 0 | 1 |
|---|---|---|---|
| y | | | |

**e** $y = \frac{1}{2}x + 1$

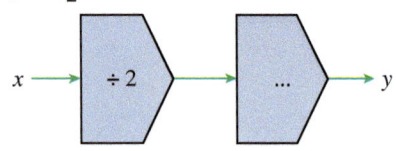

| x | −4 | 0 | 4 |
|---|---|---|---|
| y | | | |

**f** $y = 3x - 2$

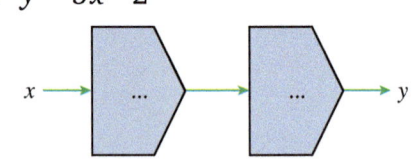

| x | −1 | 0 | 2 |
|---|---|---|---|
| y | | | |

**2** Make a table of values for each of these functions and then draw their graphs.

- **a** $y = x$
- **b** $y = 3x$
- **c** $y = x + 4$
- **d** $y = x - 2$
- **e** $y = 2x - 3$
- **f** $y = 2x + 2$
- **g** $y = 3x + 1$
- **h** $y = 3x - 3$
- **i** $y = \frac{1}{2}x + 2$
- **j** $y = \frac{1}{2}x - 5$

**3 a** The function machine for $y = -2x$ is: $x \rightarrow \boxed{\times -2} \rightarrow y$

Use the function machine to help you complete this table for $y = -2x$

| x | −2 | −1 | 0 | 1 | 2 |
|---|---|---|---|---|---|
| y | 4 | | | −2 | |

**b** Draw the graph of $y = -2x$

**c** Comment on the slope of this graph compared to the slope of the graphs in question **2**.

222

**4 a** The function machine for $y = -2x + 1$ is: $x \rightarrow \boxed{\times -2} \rightarrow \boxed{+1} \rightarrow y$

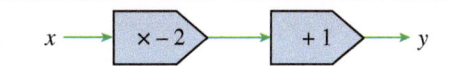

Use the function machine to help you complete this table for $y = -2x + 1$

| x | −1 | 0 | 1 | 2 | 3 |
|---|---|---|---|---|---|
| y |   | 1 |   |   | −5 |

**b** Draw the graph of $y = -2x + 1$

**5** For each of these functions, make a table of values and then draw its graph.

**a** $y = -3x$  **b** $y = -x + 5$  **c** $y = -x - 1$

**d** $y = -2x + 3$  **e** $y = -2x - 1$  **f** $y = -3x + 2$

**6** Which of these points lie on the line $y = 2x - 7$?

(2, −3)  (5, 3)  (−1, −9)  (0, −7)  (−3, 13)

**7** Which of these points lie on the line $y = \frac{1}{2}x + 8$?

(10, 13)  (6, 10)  (−4, 6)  (−18, −1)  (−10, 4)

**8** Which of these points lie on the line $2x + 3y = 12$?

(4, 1)  (7, −3)  (0, 6)  (3, 2)  (−9, 10)

## 16.4 Finding the equation of a line from its graph

You can use what you learnt in the sequences chapter to find the equation of a line from its graph. (You will learn an alternative method of doing this in the Stage 9 Student Book.)

### Worked example

Find the equation of the line drawn on the grid.

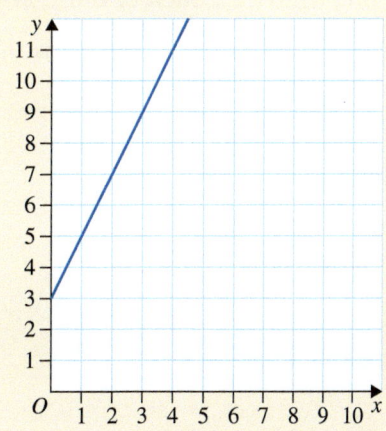

223

Mathematics for Cambridge Secondary 1

First use the graph to make a table of values for four consecutive integer $x$ numbers.

| $x$ | 1 | 2 | 3 | 4 |
|---|---|---|---|---|
| $y$ | 5 | 7 | 9 | 11 |

+2  +2  +2

The term-to-term rule for the $y$ numbers is 'add 2'.

So compare the $y$ numbers with 2 times the $x$ number.

| $x$ | 1 | 2 | 3 | 4 |
|---|---|---|---|---|
| $\times 2$ | 2 | 4 | 6 | 8 |
| $y$ | 5 | 7 | 9 | 11 |

$\times 2$
$+3$

So the equation of the line is $y = 2x + 3$

## Exercise 16.4

**1** Work out the equation of the function shown by each table of $x$ and $y$ values.

Write your answers in the form $y = \ldots$

a
| $x$ | 2 | 3 | 4 | 5 |
|---|---|---|---|---|
| $y$ | 10 | 15 | 20 | 25 |

b
| $x$ | 1 | 2 | 3 | 4 |
|---|---|---|---|---|
| $y$ | 2 | 5 | 8 | 11 |

c
| $x$ | 1 | 2 | 3 | 4 |
|---|---|---|---|---|
| $y$ | 7 | 11 | 15 | 19 |

d
| $x$ | −1 | 0 | 1 | 2 |
|---|---|---|---|---|
| $y$ | −1 | 2 | 5 | 8 |

e
| $x$ | −2 | −1 | 0 | 1 |
|---|---|---|---|---|
| $y$ | −3 | 1 | 5 | 9 |

f
| $x$ | −1 | 0 | 1 | 2 |
|---|---|---|---|---|
| $y$ | 8 | 6 | 4 | 2 |

g
| $x$ | 0 | 1 | 2 | 3 |
|---|---|---|---|---|
| $y$ | 7 | 3 | −1 | −5 |

h
| $x$ | 1 | 2 | 3 | 4 |
|---|---|---|---|---|
| $y$ | 10 | 4 | −2 | −8 |

**2** Find the equation of the line drawn on each of these grids.

a

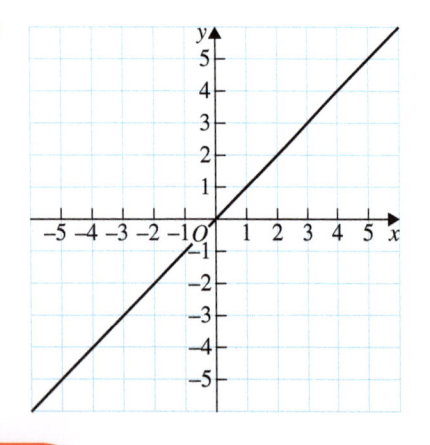

b

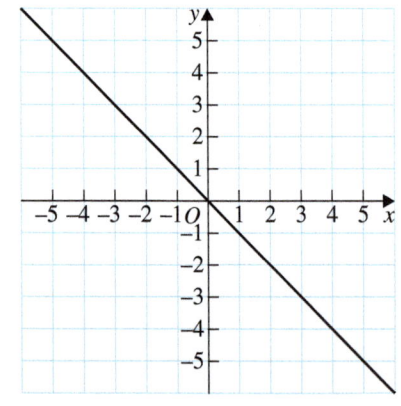

224

c
d
e
f
g
h
i

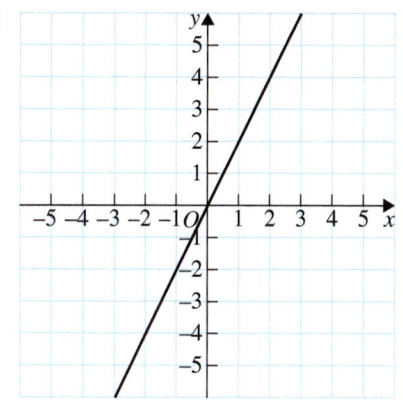

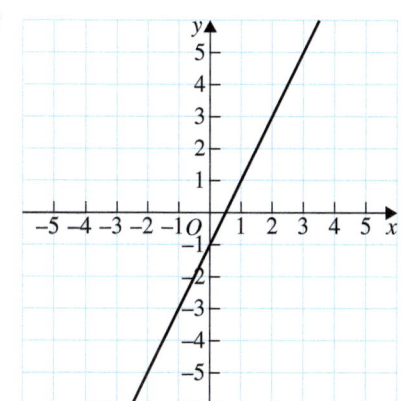

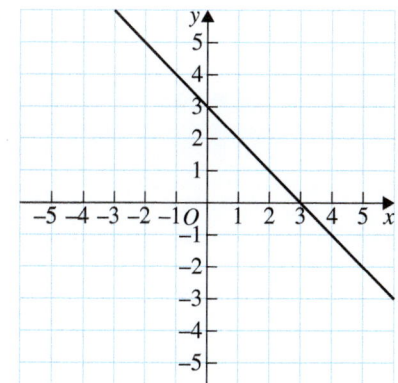

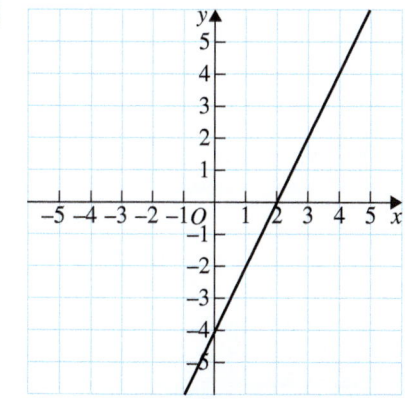

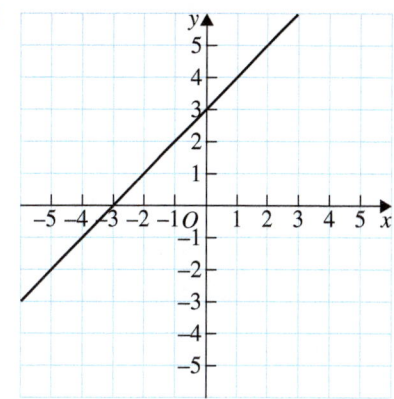

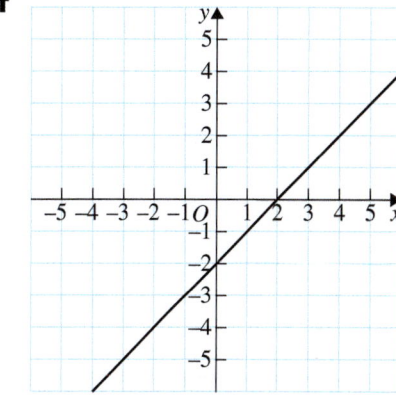

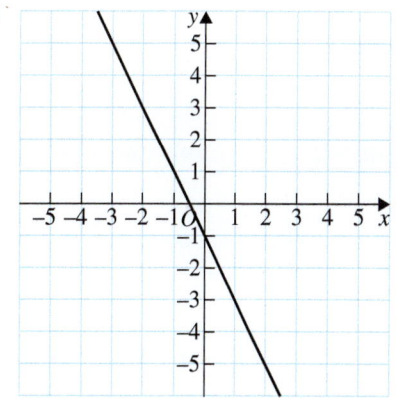

## 16.5 Equations of the form $y = mx + c$

$y = x + 3$    $y = 2x - 1$    $y = -3x + 2$    $y = \frac{1}{2}x + 5$    $y = 3x$    $y = 4$

These equations are all of the form $y = mx + c$

$m$ is the number of $x$'s and $c$ is the constant number.

Graphs of equations of this form are always straight lines.

$y = 7 - 3x$ is also of this form because it can be written as $y = -3x + 7$

You should have discovered that these lines can have:

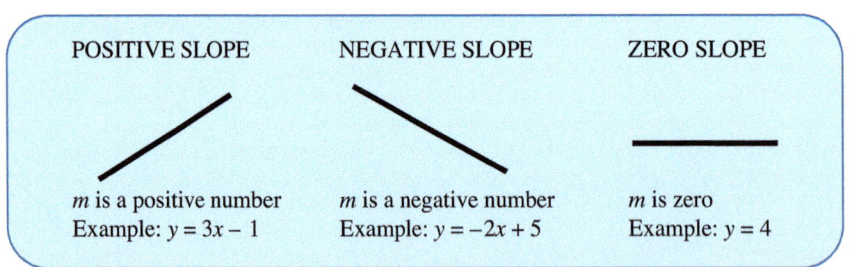

| POSITIVE SLOPE | NEGATIVE SLOPE | ZERO SLOPE |
|---|---|---|
| $m$ is a positive number | $m$ is a negative number | $m$ is zero |
| Example: $y = 3x - 1$ | Example: $y = -2x + 5$ | Example: $y = 4$ |

### Worked example

$y = x + 3$    $y = 2x - 1$    $y = -3x + 2$    $y = \frac{1}{2}x + 5$    $y = 3x$    $y = 4$

Find the $m$ and $c$ values for the six equations given above.

$y = 1x + 3$    $y = 2x - 1$    $y = -3x + 2$    $y = \frac{1}{2}x + 5$    $y = 3x + 0$    $y = 0x + 4$
$m = 1$        $m = 2$         $m = -3$         $m = \frac{1}{2}$         $m = 3$         $m = 0$
$c = 3$        $c = -1$        $c = 2$          $c = 5$                   $c = 0$         $c = 4$

## Exercise 16.5

**1** Compare each of these equations with the equation $y = mx + c$

For each equation, write down the values of $m$ and $c$.

**a** $y = 4x + 6$    **b** $y = 3x + 8$    **c** $y = 2x$    **d** $y = -3x + 7$

**e** $y = -2x + 1$    **f** $y = x - 5$    **g** $y = -x + 2$    **h** $y = -5x$

**i** $y = 3 + 2x$    **j** $y = 5 - 3x$    **k** $y = 6 + x$    **l** $y = 7$

**2** The cards show the equations of eight different lines.

| A $y = 2x + 7$ | B $y = -3x + 1$ | C $y = 5$ | D $y = 8x - 1$ |
| E $y = 5 - x$ | F $y = -2x - 7$ | G $y = x - 4$ | H $y = 3x$ |

Which of the lines have:

**a** positive slope    **b** negative slope    **c** zero slope?

# 16 Functions and graphs

**3** The blue line is the line $y = x + 2$

The red line is the reflection of the line $y = x + 2$ in the $y$-axis.

Find the equation of the red line.

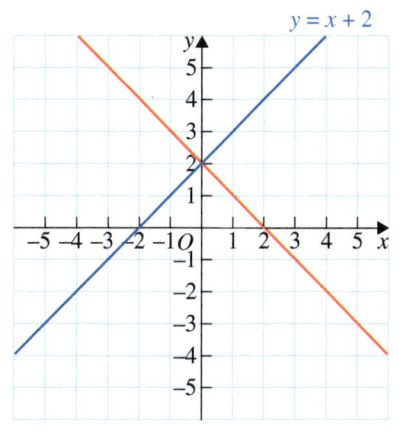

**4** The line $y = 2x + 3$ is reflected in the $y$-axis.

Find the equation of the reflected line.

## Review

**1** Copy and complete these mapping diagrams.

**a** Input → Output: □ → 19, 7 → □, □ → 49, −3 → □
Rule: $x \rightarrow 5x - 1$

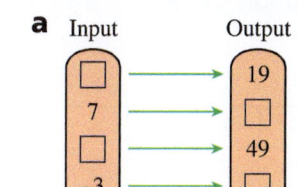

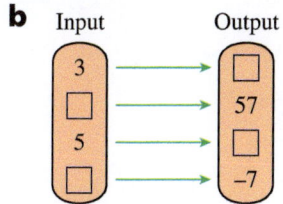

**b** Input → Output: 3 → □, □ → 57, 5 → □, □ → −7
Rule: $x \rightarrow 4x + 5$

**c** Input → Output: 2 → □, □ → 6, 15 → □, □ → −2
Rule: $x \rightarrow \dfrac{x + 4}{2}$

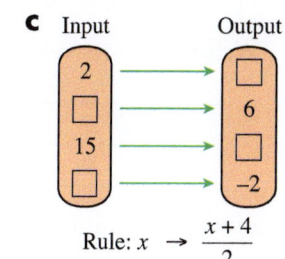

**2** Find the rule for each of these mapping diagrams.

Write your answers in the form $x \rightarrow \ldots$

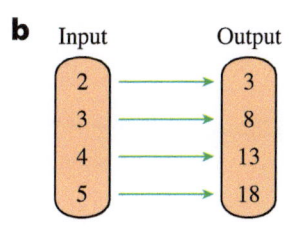

**a** Input → Output: 1 → 9, 2 → 11, 3 → 13, 4 → 15

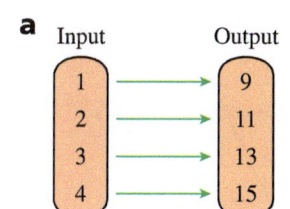

**b** Input → Output: 2 → 3, 3 → 8, 4 → 13, 5 → 18

**c** Input → Output: 4 → 6, 5 → 8, 6 → 10, 7 → 12

227

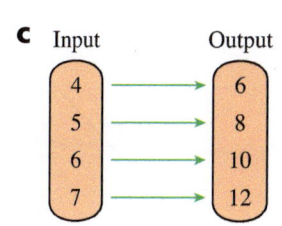

3 For each equation, copy and complete the function machine and table of values, and then draw its graph.

**a** $y = 3x + 2$

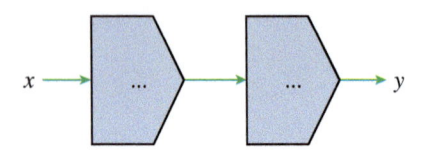

| x | −2 | 0 | 1 |
|---|---|---|---|
| y | | | |

**b** $y = \frac{1}{2}x - 4$

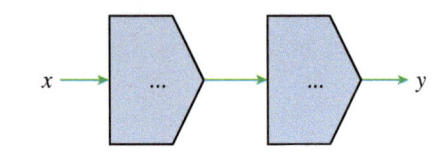

| x | −2 | 0 | 2 |
|---|---|---|---|
| y | | | |

**c** $y = -x + 2$

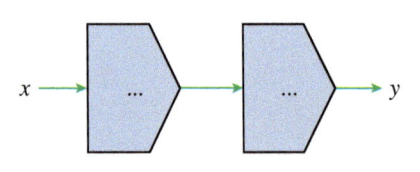

| x | −3 | 0 | 4 |
|---|---|---|---|
| y | | | |

**d** $y = -2x + 2$

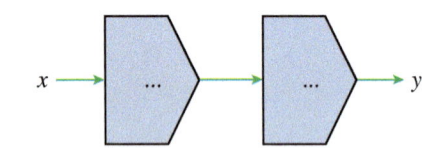

| x | −1 | 0 | 3 |
|---|---|---|---|
| y | | | |

4 Which of these points lie on the line $y = 3x - 5$?

(1, −3)   (5, 12)   (−1, −8)   (0, −5)   (−4, −12)

5 Work out the equation of the function shown by each table of $x$ and $y$ values.

Write your answers in the form $y = \ldots$

**a**

| x | 1 | 2 | 3 | 4 |
|---|---|---|---|---|
| y | 9 | 13 | 17 | 21 |

**b**

| x | 1 | 2 | 3 | 4 |
|---|---|---|---|---|
| y | 9 | 7 | 5 | 3 |

6 Find the equation of the line drawn on each of these grids.

**a**

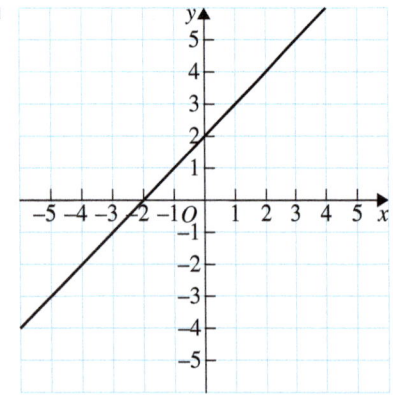

**b**

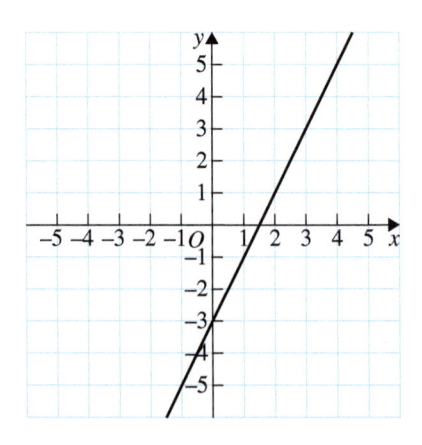

c

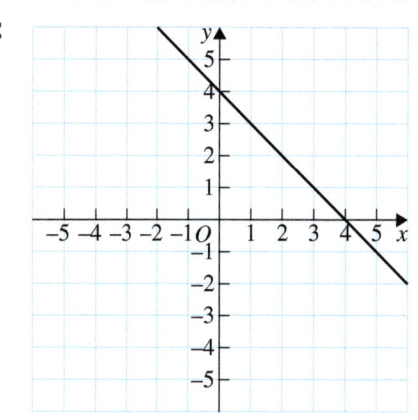

d

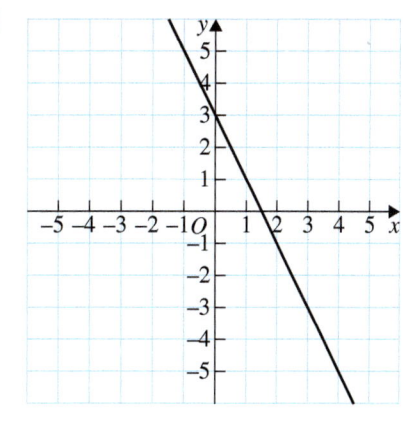

**7** The cards show the equations of eight different lines.

| A  $y = -3x - 5$ | B  $y = 2x + 1$ | C  $y = 6x - 3$ | D  $y = 8x$ |
| E  $y = -5$ | F  $y = 9 - 8x$ | G  $y = 2 + 7x$ | H  $y = x - 9$ |

Which of the lines have:

**a** positive gradient  **b** negative gradient  **c** zero gradient?

229

# 17 Fractions, decimals and percentages

### Learning outcomes

- Find equivalent fractions, decimals and percentages by converting between them.
- Use equivalent fractions, decimals and percentages to compare different quantities.
- Order fractions by writing with common denominators or dividing and converting to decimals.
- Calculate and solve problems involving percentages of quantities.
- Calculate and solve problems involving percentage increases or decreases.
- Express one given number as a fraction or percentage of another.

## Percentages all over

Percentages are used around the world for many different purposes. They are used to describe proportions and changes.

Percentages are used in the news, in shops, on the internet and in facts such as:

- about 70% of the earth's surface is covered in water
- during 2011, the earth's population grew by about 1.1%
- there is 78% nitrogen and 21% oxygen in the air that we breathe.

## 17.1 Finding equivalent fractions, decimals and percentages

**Percentage** means 'out of 100'. It is the same as a fraction with 100 as the denominator.

This petrol gauge shows the petrol tank is half full.

This is the same as 0.5 or 50% full.

# 17 Fractions, decimals and percentages

You should already know some equivalents.

| Fraction | Decimal | Percentage |
|---|---|---|
| $\frac{1}{10}$ | 0.1 | 10% |
| $\frac{1}{5}$ | 0.2 | 20% |
| $\frac{1}{4}$ | 0.25 | 25% |
| $\frac{3}{10}$ | 0.3 | 30% |
| $\frac{2}{5}$ | 0.4 | 40% |
| $\frac{1}{2}$ | 0.5 | 50% |
| $\frac{3}{5}$ | 0.6 | 60% |
| $\frac{7}{10}$ | 0.7 | 70% |
| $\frac{3}{4}$ | 0.75 | 75% |
| $\frac{4}{5}$ | 0.8 | 80% |
| $\frac{9}{10}$ | 0.9 | 90% |

## Converting to a decimal

You can already change a fraction to a decimal.

You do this by dividing the numerator (number on the top) by the denominator (number on the bottom).

To convert a percentage to a decimal you divide by 100.

### Worked example 1

Convert $\frac{13}{20}$ to a decimal.

$\frac{13}{20} = 13 \div 20 = 0.65$

### Worked example 2

Convert these percentages to decimals.

a  38%      b  30%      c  5%

a  38 ÷ 100 = 0.38
b  30 ÷ 100 = 0.3
c  5 ÷ 100 = 0.05

## Converting to a percentage

To convert a decimal to a percentage you multiply by 100.

To convert from a fraction to a percentage first change the fraction to a decimal, then multiply by 100.

> ### Worked example 3
>
> Convert the following decimals to percentages.
>
> a  0.8   b  0.23   c  0.125
>
> a  $0.8 \times 100 = 80\%$
>
> b  $0.23 \times 100 = 23\%$
>
> c  $0.125 \times 100 = 12.5\%$
>
> ### Worked example 4
>
> Convert the following fractions to percentages.
>
> a  $\frac{2}{5}$   b  $\frac{7}{8}$
>
> a  $\frac{2}{5} = 2 \div 5 = 0.4$
>
> $0.4 \times 100 = 40\%$
>
> b  $\frac{7}{8} = 7 \div 8 = 0.875$
>
> $0.875 \times 100 = 87.5\%$

## Converting to a fraction

To convert a percentage to a fraction you write the percentage as the numerator of the fraction and write 100 as the denominator.

To convert a decimal to a fraction first multiply by 100 to convert it to a percentage. Then write it as the numerator of the fraction and write 100 as the denominator.

The fraction can then be reduced to its simplest form.

> Remember that percentages are always 'out of 100'.

> ### Worked example 5
>
> Convert these percentages to fractions.
>
> a  45%   b  5%   c  12.5%   d  49.5%
>
> a  $45\% = \frac{45}{100} = \frac{9}{20}$
>
> b  $5\% = \frac{5}{100} = \frac{1}{20}$

**c** $12.5\% = \frac{12.5}{100} = \frac{1}{8}$

**d** $49.5\% = \frac{49.5}{100} = \frac{495}{1000} = \frac{99}{200}$

## Worked example 6

Convert these decimals to fractions.

**a** 0.85          **b** 0.07

**a** $0.85 = 0.85 \times 100\% = 85\% = \frac{85}{100} = \frac{17}{20}$

**b** $0.07 = 0.07 \times 100\% = 7\% = \frac{7}{100}$

## Exercise 17.1

**1** Match these decimals with their equivalents in the box.

   **a** 0.15

   **b** 0.95

   **c** 0.4

   **d** 0.75

   **e** 0.8

   **f** 0.35

| 95% |
| 80% |
| 35% |
| $\frac{3}{20}$ |
| $\frac{3}{4}$ |
| $\frac{2}{5}$ |

**2** Convert these to decimals.

   **a** 14%          **b** 36%          **c** 17%          **d** 6%

   **e** $\frac{11}{20}$          **f** $\frac{1}{8}$          **g** $\frac{12}{25}$          **h** $\frac{7}{16}$

**3** Convert these to percentages.

   **a** 0.76          **b** 0.98          **c** 0.85          **d** 0.09

   **e** $\frac{3}{4}$          **f** $\frac{4}{25}$          **g** $\frac{17}{20}$          **h** $\frac{5}{8}$

**4** Convert these to fractions. Write each answer in its simplest form.

   **a** 17%          **b** 38%          **c** 35%          **d** 5%

   **e** 0.36          **f** 0.18          **g** 0.375          **h** 0.185

**5** Write these in order of size, smallest first.

   23%     $\frac{1}{5}$     0.22     0.18

> You need to convert 23% and $\frac{1}{5}$ to decimals.

**6** Write each of these lists in order of size, smallest first.

   **a** 0.41   38%   $\frac{2}{5}$   0.43

   **b** $\frac{4}{5}$   83%   $\frac{3}{4}$   0.79

233

**7** Which of these gives the bigger discount?

  **a** 35% off   **b** $\frac{1}{3}$ off

  Show how you have made your decision.

**8** Bismuth bronze is $\frac{13}{25}$ copper, $\frac{3}{10}$ nickel, $\frac{3}{25}$ zinc, 1% bismuth and some lead.

  Find the percentage of lead that is in bismuth bronze.

## 17.2 Increasing and decreasing by a percentage

To **increase** an amount by a percentage, you find the percentage then **add** it to the original amount.

To **decrease** an amount by a percentage, you find the percentage then **subtract** it from the original amount.

Sometimes decreasing by a percentage is called a **percentage reduction**.

### Worked example 1

Klaus gets paid $4 per hour for his work.

He gets a pay increase of 3%

What is his new pay?

Work out the increase:      3% of $4 = $\frac{3}{100}$ × 4 = 0.12

Add this to his original pay:   $4 + $0.12 = $4.12 per hour

### Worked example 2

The price of a television is $420.

It is reduced in a sale by 20%

What is the sale price?

Work out the reduction:      $\frac{20}{100}$ × 420 = 84

Subtract this from the original price:   $420 − $84 = $336

## Exercise 17.2

**1** Work these out.

   **a** 10% of 30        **b** 20% of 45        **c** 35% of 80        **d** 75% of 120

**2** Work these out.

   **a** 15% of $80        **b** 85% of 200 kg        **c** 55% of 140 m        **d** 5% of 40 ml

**3**  **a** Increase $90 by 10%        **b** Increase $50 by 30%

   **c** Increase $25 by 20%        **d** Increase $160 by 5%

   **e** Decrease $80 by 20%        **f** Decrease $40 by 15%

   **g** Decrease $80 by 25%        **h** Decrease $60 by 12%

**4** A camera costs $80.

   It is reduced in a sale by 20%

   **a** By how much is the camera reduced?

   **b** What is the sale price of the camera?

**5** A bag of seeds costs $8.

   The price increases by 5%

   What is the new price of the bag of seeds?

**6** Mei-Yin has 380 magazines.

   She sells 45% of them.

   How many magazines does she have left?

**7** Bus fares increase by 20%

   Find the new bus fare when the old fare was:

   **a** $1.20        **b** $1.80        **c** $2.40        **d** $3

**8** A shop has this sign in the window.

> **SALE**
> **All prices reduced by**
> **15%**

   Find the sale prices of items costing:

   **a** $300        **b** $120        **c** $80        **d** $110

**9** A shop sells a radio for $30.

   One week, the price goes up by 10%

   **a** Work out the new price of the radio.

   **b** The week after, the radio is reduced by 10% in a sale.

       Show that the sale price is not $30.

**Mathematics for Cambridge Secondary 1**

10. A shop reduces everything in a sale by 20%

    On Friday, they reduce the sale prices by 10%

    Thom says, 'There is 30% off the original prices on Friday.'

    Craig says, 'There is less than 30% off the original prices on Friday.'

    Explain why Craig is correct.

    > You can use a particular price to show this, for example $100.

11. Afia has a different way to work out percentage change.

    > To increase by 25%, you change 25% to a decimal to get 0.25 Add this to 1 to get 1.25, and then multiply the amount you want to increase by 1.25

    **a** Use Afia's method to increase the following by 25%

        **i** $360    **ii** 480 metres    **iii** 280 kg

    **b** What do you multiply by to increase by 30% using Afia's method?

12. Moesha is training for a marathon and runs 10 km every day.

    She then increases the distance she runs by 10% each week for 4 weeks.

    How far does she run each day after the 4 weeks?

## 17.3 Finding percentages

### Finding a fraction or percentage

There are times when you need to write one number as a fraction or a percentage of another.

To do this you write the number as a fraction, then convert this fraction to a percentage.

When you find a percentage increase or decrease you compare the change with the original value.

> **Worked example 1**
>
> 80 people are in a room.
>
> 30 of the people are men.
>
> What percentage of the people in the room are men?
>
> $\frac{30}{80}$                             This is the fraction of the people in the room that are men.
>
> $\frac{30}{80} = 30 \div 80 = 0.375$       This is the decimal equivalent.
>
> $0.375 \times 100 = 37.5\%$         This is the percentage of the people in the room that are men.

## 17 Fractions, decimals and percentages

### Worked example 2

A shirt is priced at $32.

It is reduced in a sale to $28.

What is the percentage decrease?

| $32 − $28 = $4 | First find the actual decrease. |
| $\frac{4}{32} = 0.125$ | Actual decrease ÷ original price. |
| $0.125 \times 100 = 12.5\%$ | This is the percentage decrease. |

## Using percentages

Percentages are used to make comparisons.

They can be more useful than comparing actual changes when:

- comparing price or wage increases
- comparing test scores when the totals are not the same
- comparing proportions.

### Worked example 3

A survey is done to find out what people think about two cafés.

The results are shown in the table.

|  | Poor | Satisfactory | Good | Total asked |
|---|---|---|---|---|
| Café Amis | 12 | 30 | 28 | 70 |
| Café Bergamot | 8 | 20 | 22 | 50 |

Which café do people think is better?

Percentages are a good way to compare because different numbers of people are asked in each of the two cafés.

**Good rating**

Café Amis: $\frac{28}{70} = 0.4 = 40\%$

Café Bergamot: $\frac{22}{50} = 0.44 = 44\%$

A greater proportion of people think Café Bergamot is good.

**Poor rating**

Café Amis: $\frac{12}{70} = 0.17$ (to 2 decimal places) = 17%

Café Bergamot: $\frac{8}{50} = 0.16 = 16\%$

A smaller proportion of people think that Café Bergamot is poor.

There are only small differences in the percentages, but people think that Café Bergamot is better.

## Exercise 17.3

1. There are 120 students in a year group and 75 of them are male.

   a  What percentage of the students are male?

   b  What percentage of the students are female?

2. In a batch of 80 items, 30 of them have faults.

   a  What percentage have faults?

   b  What percentage do not have faults?

3. Tarun sleeps for 6 hours every day.

   For what percentage of the day does Tarun sleep?

4. The cost of a car is $8000.

   It is reduced in a sale by $500.

   What percentage decrease is this?

5. The cost of a holiday increases from $320 to $360.

   a  What is the increase in price?

   b  What is the percentage increase?

6. Roisin plays cricket.

   Last season, her scoring rate was 20 runs.

   This season, her scoring rate is 24 runs.

   What is the percentage increase in her scoring rate?

7. Last week, a telephone receptionist took 24 calls each hour.

   This week, he takes 30 calls each hour.

   He says, 'The percentage increase in phone calls is 20%'

   a  What mistake has the receptionist made in his calculation?

   b  What is the correct percentage increase?

8. A phone costs $160.

   Sally buys the phone. She gets $25 off for paying in cash.

   What percentage decrease is this?

9. The prices of three houses are shown in the table.

   |         | 2003 ($) | 2013 ($) |
   |---------|----------|----------|
   | House A | 90 000   | 108 000  |
   | House B | 75 500   | 94 375   |
   | House C | 120 000  | 147 600  |

   Which house has seen the greatest percentage increase?

**10** A survey is done to find out what people think of two films.

The results are shown in the table.

|  | Poor | Satisfactory | Good | Total asked |
|---|---|---|---|---|
| **Comedy film** | 72 | 108 | 60 | 240 |
| **Disaster movie** | 40 | 64 | 56 | 160 |

Which film do people like more?

Show how you have made your decision.

> Use percentages to help you decide.

**11** The table shows information about people living in three villages.

|  | Under 50 | Over 50 |
|---|---|---|
| **Village A** | 180 | 20 |
| **Village B** | 440 | 60 |
| **Village C** | 276 | 24 |

Which village has the greatest percentage of older people?

## Review

**1** Convert $\frac{7}{16}$ to:

   **a** a decimal       **b** a percentage.

**2** Convert 0.28 to:

   **a** a percentage       **b** a fraction.

**3** Convert 85% to:

   **a** a fraction       **b** a decimal.

**4** Write these in order of size, smallest first.

   65%    0.7    $\frac{16}{25}$

**5** Last year Farook paid $250 for a season ticket.

This year the price has increased by 2%

How much does he pay this year?

**6** A phone is priced at $175.

It is reduced by 15% in a sale.

What is the sale price?

**7** A painting is bought for $400.

It increases in value by 35%

What is its new value?

8  There are 12 boys and 13 girls in a class of students.
   a  What percentage of the students are boys?
   b  What percentage of the students are girls?

9  Simon buys a bike for $850.

   Later he sells it for $510.

   What is the percentage decrease in the bike's value?

10 A school starts the year with 650 students.

   Later in the year it has 702 students.

   What is the percentage increase in the number of students?

11 A car is on sale for $7500.

   The price then increases by 10%
   a  What is the new price of the car?
   b  One week after the price was increased, it is reduced by 10% in a sale.

      Explain why the price of the car does not return to $7500.

# 18 Planning and collecting data

Chapter 6 covers processing data
Chapter 10 covers presenting data

### Learning outcomes

- Identify and collect data to answer a question.
- Select the method of collection, sample size and degree of accuracy needed for measurements.
- Know the difference between discrete and continuous data.
- Construct and use frequency tables with given equal class intervals to gather continuous data.
- Construct and use two-way tables to record discrete data.

## Very useful tables

Much of the work in this chapter is about using tables.

Tables can be used to store information, but can also be used to store answers to calculations. Sometimes these have been called 'look up' tables and sometimes 'ready reckoners'.

Tables have been used for many years to help with calculating.

They are still in common usage.

This is an example of an early ready reckoner, the table is actually inside.

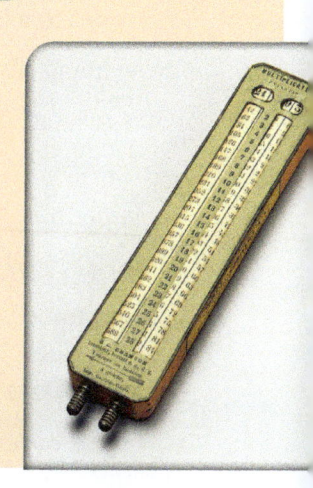

## 18.1 Identifying and collecting data

### Deciding on which data are needed

Starting with a given question, you need to be able to identify the data needed.

Sometimes related information is needed as well as the obvious information.

### Worked example 1

Abdullah wants to investigate the most likely time for the first goal to be scored in a football match.

Describe a suitable data collection method that Abdullah can use.

Data may be collected by attending lots of football matches and recording the time in the match that the first goal is scored. Unfortunately, this will take a lot of time. It can also cost a lot of money to pay for tickets. So, this is not a good way to collect the data.

Data may be collected from the internet. The number of goals and number of minutes into the match that each goal is scored can easily be found. This will give a lot of data quite quickly.

## Sample size

The **population** is everyone or everything being considered in a question. Using the whole population is called a **census**. When part of the population is used it is called 'taking a **sample**'.

The amount of data needed will vary depending on the question being asked.

When taking a sample from a population you need to make sure the sample is **representative** of the population. A very small sample will not give good results as it cannot be representative. A very large sample will be expensive in resources and time. The place where data are collected can affect how representative the sample is of the whole population.

There are no real rules about sample size, but generally a sample size of about 30 to 50 will be sufficient.

### Worked example 2

Teresa wants to know whether boys in her college play more hockey than girls in her college. She goes to a large college.

How many students should Teresa use in a survey to answer this question?

Give reasons for your answer.

As the college is large, Teresa should not use a census. It would take too long to obtain the data. It would also take too long to work with the data.

Teresa could use boys and girls from each year group. If there are three year groups at the college, then 10 boys and 10 girls from each year group would be the minimum needed to compare boys and girls across the college.

If Teresa wants to investigate to see whether boys play more sport than girls in different year groups, then 30 boys and 30 girls from each year group will allow this comparison to be made.

### Worked example 3

The manager of a railway station wants to do a survey to find out what people like and dislike about the service provided.

He decides to ask the first 10 people arriving at his railway station on a Monday morning.

Is this likely to provide a good sample?

Suggest how the manager can improve his data collection method.

This is unlikely to provide a good sample. There are a number of reasons for this:

1. **He asks people at the railway station**

   The manager is very likely to only ask people who use the railway station. He will not find out why people do not use the railway station.

2. **He only asks the first people to arrive on a Monday morning**

   This will not be likely to represent the people who travel during the rest of the week. For example, they may all be on their way to work.

> **3 The sample size is too small**
>
> Asking 10 people is only a small fraction of the number of people who use the railway station.
>
> The manager can improve his data collection method by doing the following:
>
> **1 Using a neutral location**
>
> The centre of town, for example, because a more representative group of people is likely to be there. In a neutral location, the manager is more likely to ask people who do not use the railway station as well as those who do.
>
> **2 Varying the timing of the survey**
>
> Asking people at different times of the day and on different days through the week.
>
> **3 Using a bigger sample**
>
> Asking more people will make the sample more representative.

## Exercise 18.1

1. Malila wants to find out whether people buy music in shops or online.

   She asks the first 10 people who enter a music shop on a Monday morning.

   **a** Give a reason why this is unlikely to give good results.

   **b** Suggest how Malila could obtain a better sample.

2. Rafad wants to find out whether people like school dinners at his school.

   He considers the following options:

   **a** Ask the first 10 people to arrive at the school canteen one Monday lunchtime.

   **b** Ask all of his friends what they think.

   **c** Ask all of the form tutors to ask five people in each form.

   **d** Give a questionnaire to everyone in the school and leave a collection box in the library.

   **e** Stop 30 people randomly in the corridor one morning.

   **f** Leave a pile of questionnaires by the front door of the school next to a collection box.

   Comment on each of these options. Would they provide a good sample?

3. Revina wants to find out whether the newspaper her mother reads is easier to read than the one her father reads.

   **a** Identify the data Revina needs.

   **b** Why should Revina use a sample and not a census?

   **c** How can Revina make sure her sample is representative?

4. A newspaper article has the following headline:

   > Local bus service not as good as it was 10 years ago

   How can you find out whether this is true?

   *Things to think about: what is meant by 'good'? Frequency of bus, quality of seat/ride and cost of journey are possibilities.*

   *Include the following in your answer: who you would ask, where you would ask and how large a sample you would need.*

## 18.2 Frequency tables for continuous data

### Discrete and continuous data

Numerical data are either **discrete data** or **continuous data**.

Discrete data take separate values. Shoe size is an example of a discrete variable. In US and British shoe sizes you can have sizes 4, $4\frac{1}{2}$, 5, and so on, but there is nothing between 4 and $4\frac{1}{2}$. They are separate values with a gap between.

Any variable that is **counted** is discrete. For example, the number of people in a car is a discrete variable. You can have 1 person, 2 people, 3 people, and so on, in a car, these are all separate values. You cannot have values between 1 and 2 people in a car.

Continuous data can take any value on a **continuous scale**. The length of pencils in a pencil case is a continuous variable as each pencil can take any value in a range. You can measure the length of a pencil as 8 cm and another one as 8.5 cm. There is no limit to the number of values between 8 and 8.5 cm as measurement is on a continuous scale.

> **Worked example 1**
>
> Scott is classifying oranges. He collects the following information from a sample of oranges:
>
> Mass, number of dimples, thickness of skin, number of pips, number of segments.
>
> Sort this information into two lists, one for discrete data and one for continuous data.
>
> **Continuous data:** Mass, thickness of skin
>
> **Discrete data:** Number of dimples, number of pips, number of segments

### Frequency tables

As measurement is always on a continuous scale it is impossible to be 100% exact. So, when you measure, you need to decide how precise you want your measurement to be. Usually you measure to the nearest unit. This could be the nearest kilometre, metre, centimetre, millimetre, and so on, depending on what is being measured and why.

When you record continuous data it is often useful to record it in **groups**. It is important that there are **no gaps** between the groups. The signs $<$ and $\leqslant$ are used to make sure there are no gaps between classes.

> Remember: $<$ means 'less than' and $\leqslant$ means 'less than or equal to'.

## Worked example 2

The times, $t$ seconds, taken by 10 students to solve a puzzle were:

35   46   33   51   63   48   38   42   59   40

Complete the frequency table to show this information.

| Time, $t$ (seconds) | Tally | Frequency |
|---|---|---|
| $30 < t \leq 40$ |  |  |
| $40 < t \leq 50$ |  |  |
| $50 < t \leq 60$ |  |  |
| $60 < t \leq 70$ |  |  |

| Time, $t$ (seconds) | Tally | Frequency |
|---|---|---|
| $30 < t \leq 40$ | \|\|\| | 3 |
| $40 < t \leq 50$ | \|\|\|\| | 4 |
| $50 < t \leq 60$ | \|\| | 2 |
| $60 < t \leq 70$ | \| | 1 |

Note that the value '40' is recorded in the $30 < t \leq 40$ class and not in the $40 < t \leq 50$ class.

## Exercise 18.2

1  A swimming club keeps records of the attendance of its members.

   Decide whether each of the following is an example of discrete or continuous data.

   **a**  The number of members swimming in a session
   **b**  The length of time they swim each session
   **c**  The number of lengths each member swims

2  Sabitha walks by the sea front with her dog.

   Decide whether the following data are discrete or continuous.

   **a**  The number of other dogs they see
   **b**  The number of minutes for which they are walking
   **c**  The number of steps Sabitha takes
   **d**  The length of the walk in metres
   **e**  The number of people they see
   **f**  The size of Sabitha's shoes
   **g**  The air temperature
   **h**  The height of the high tide that day

**Mathematics for Cambridge Secondary 1**

**3** Yi Ling measures the times, *t* minutes, some of her friends take to travel to school.

33   45   21   32   7   37   19   18   25   30
24   41   6   31   46   20   15   17   23   29

  **a** Are the times continuous data or discrete data?

  **b** Record the times in a frequency table. Use these classes.

| Time, *t* (minutes) | Tally | Frequency |
|---|---|---|
| $0 < t \leq 10$ | | |
| $10 < t \leq 20$ | | |
| $20 < t \leq 30$ | | |
| $30 < t \leq 40$ | | |
| $40 < t \leq 50$ | | |

**4** Felix records the lengths of time, *t* minutes, that some customers wait before getting served at the checkout in a supermarket. He uses the following table.

| Time, *t* (minutes) | Frequency |
|---|---|
| 0 to 3 | |
| 3 to 6 | |
| 9 to 12 | |
| 12 to 15 | |

  **a** Write down two different mistakes that Felix has made in this table.

  **b** Correct the mistakes you have found by completing the left-hand column in this table.

  Make sure that the classes are equal widths and cover the range from 0 to 15.

| Time, *t* (minutes) | Frequency |
|---|---|
| | |
| | |
| | |
| | |
| | |

**5** The members of the Diet-Fast club recorded the weight they lost in the last month.

| Weight lost, *w* (kg) | Frequency |
|---|---|
| $0 \leq w < 2$ | 6 |
| $2 \leq w < 4$ | 4 |
| $4 \leq w < 6$ | 3 |
| $6 \leq w < 8$ | 1 |
| $8 \leq w < 10$ | 1 |

  **a** How many members lost less than 2 kg?

  **b** How many members lost 4 kg or more?

**c** Can you tell, from this table, if anyone lost no weight?

**d** How many members are in the Diet-Fast club?

**6** The weights, *w* grams, of books in one section of a library are listed below.

| 376 | 425 | 610 | 550 | 370 | 410 | 390 | 387 | 540 | 350 |
| 400 | 276 | 510 | 372 | 452 | 539 | 449 | 551 | 375 | 289 |
| 280 | 351 | 286 | 540 | 623 | 513 | 309 | 340 | 321 | 539 |
| 450 | 432 | 360 | 550 | 431 | 410 | 380 | 390 | 310 | 486 |

Use the frequency table to sort these data.

| Weight, *w* (g) | Tally | Frequency |
| --- | --- | --- |
| $250 < w \leqslant 300$ | | |
| $300 < w \leqslant 350$ | | |
| $350 < w \leqslant 400$ | | |
| $400 < w \leqslant 450$ | | |
| $450 < w \leqslant 500$ | | |
| $500 < w \leqslant 550$ | | |
| $550 < w \leqslant 600$ | | |
| $600 < w \leqslant 650$ | | |

## 18.3 Two-way tables

Two-way tables are often used to show data in one table rather than two. You read them across as well as down.

### Worked example 1

The tables show the number of left-handed and right-handed boys and girls in a class.

| Boys | Frequency |
| --- | --- |
| Left-handed | 5 |
| Right-handed | 12 |

| Girls | Frequency |
| --- | --- |
| Left-handed | 6 |
| Right-handed | 11 |

Show this information in a two-way table.

| | Left-handed | Right-handed | Total |
| --- | --- | --- | --- |
| Boys | 5 | 12 | 17 |
| Girls | 6 | 11 | 17 |
| Total | 11 | 23 | 34 |

Showing the information this way rather than in two separate tables makes it much easier to make comparisons.

## Worked example 2

Three surveys recorded the method of transport shoppers use to travel to three shopping centres.

The results are shown in the two-way table.

|  | Car | Bus | Walk | Other |
|---|---|---|---|---|
| Out of town shopping centre | 45 | 11 | 3 | 6 |
| Town centre shopping | 12 | 34 | 5 | 7 |
| Local village shopping | 7 | 9 | 28 | 13 |

a  How many people use a car to get to the town centre for shopping?

b  Which shopping centre do most people catch a bus to travel to?

c  Which is the most popular method of transport used by shoppers?

a  12 people use a car to go shopping in the town centre.

b  Most people catch a bus to the town centre.

c  The totals are:

  Car  45 + 12 + 7 = 64

  Bus  11 + 34 + 9 = 54

  Walk  3 + 5 + 28 = 36

  Other  6 + 7 + 13 = 26

  Car is the most popular method of transport.

## Worked example 3

Karthik carries out a survey of the students in his year group to find out how people travel to school.

Some of the results are shown in the two-way table.

|  | Car | Bus | Walk | Bike | Total |
|---|---|---|---|---|---|
| Boys | 30 | 48 |  |  | 90 |
| Girls | 25 |  |  | 1 | 80 |
| Total | 55 |  | 16 | 6 | 170 |

Complete the two-way table.

The first number to enter is the total number of students who catch the bus to school using the totals from the bottom row:

  55 + total bus + 16 + 6 = 170, so 77 + total bus = 170

  Total bus = 170 − 77 = 93

  Add this information to the two-way table.

Now find the number of girls who catch the bus to school from the column with the heading 'Bus':

    48 + girls bus = 93

    Girls bus = 93 − 48 = 45

    Add this information to the table.

Now find the number of girls who walk to school using the 'Girls' row:

    25 + 45 + girls walk + 1 = 80

    71 + girls walk = 80, so girls walk = 80 − 71 = 9

    Add this information to the table.

Now use the column headed 'Walk' to find the number of boys who walk to school:

    Number of boys who walk = 16 − 9 = 7

Finally, find the number of boys who bike to school. Either use the row labelled 'Boys' or the column labelled 'Bike'. The column labelled 'Bike' is easier:

    6 − 1 = 5, so 5 boys bike to school.

The completed two-way table is:

|  | Car | Bus | Walk | Bike | Total |
|---|---|---|---|---|---|
| **Boys** | 30 | 48 | 7 | 5 | 90 |
| **Girls** | 25 | 45 | 9 | 1 | 80 |
| **Total** | 55 | 93 | 16 | 6 | 170 |

## Exercise 18.3

**1** The two-way table shows the numbers of students in three classes in a school.

|  | Boys | Girls | Total |
|---|---|---|---|
| **Class 8A** | 18 | 12 | 30 |
| **Class 8B** | 16 | 15 | 31 |
| **Class 8C** | 14 | 14 | 28 |
| **Total** | 48 | 41 | 89 |

    **a** How many girls are in Class 8B?

    **b** How many boys are in Class 8C?

    **c** Which class is largest?

    **d** Which class has the same number of boys as girls?

**2** These tables show information about the students in a class.

Show the information in a two-way table.

| Boys | Frequency |
|---|---|
| Have a computer | 12 |
| Do not have a computer | 2 |

| Girls | Frequency |
|---|---|
| Have a computer | 11 |
| Do not have a computer | 1 |

3  The two-way table shows some information about the students in a class.

|  | Wear glasses | Do not wear glasses | Total |
|---|---|---|---|
| Boys | 5 |  | 12 |
| Girls |  | 6 |  |
| Total |  |  | 30 |

Copy and complete the two-way table.

4  The two-way table shows information about the houses for sale in a town.

|  | \multicolumn{5}{c}{Number of bedrooms} |
|---|---|---|---|---|---|
|  | 1 | 2 | 3 | 4 | 5 |
| Detached | 0 | 8 | 23 | 14 | 6 |
| Semi-detached | 0 | 5 | 41 | 6 | 2 |
| Terraced | 1 | 7 | 15 | 3 | 0 |

a  Copy the table. Add row and column totals.

b  How many detached houses have four bedrooms?

c  One of these houses is chosen at random. It has three bedrooms.

   Which type of house is it most likely to be?

d  How many houses have two bedrooms or fewer?

e  Alicia wants to buy a house in this town.

   She wants a house with at least three bedrooms.

   She does not want to buy a terraced house.

   How many houses are for sale that she could choose?

5  The numbers of cats and goldfish owned by a group of pet owners are shown in the two-way table.

|  |  | \multicolumn{4}{c}{Number of cats} |
|---|---|---|---|---|---|
|  |  | 0 | 1 | 2 | 3 |
| Number of goldfish | 0 | 0 | 8 | 6 | 2 |
|  | 1 | 6 | 3 | 4 | 3 |
|  | 2 | 5 | 3 | 2 | 1 |
|  | 3 | 2 | 1 | 1 | 0 |

a  How many of these people have only goldfish?

b  How many of these people have only cats?

c  How many of these people have two cats and two goldfish?

d  How many of these people have two cats?

e  How many of these people have exactly three pets?

6 The fat content in 25 g of yogurt is shown in the two-way table.

| Yogurt (25 g) | Saturated fat (g) | Total fat (g) |
|---|---|---|
| Yogurt, plain, low fat | trace | 0.2 |
| Yogurt, plain, regular | 0.2 | 1 |
| Greek yogurt | 1.2 | 2.2 |
| Yogurt, fruit, low fat | 0.1 | 0.3 |
| Yogurt, fruit, regular | 0.2 | 1 |

a How much fat is there in 25 g of plain, regular yogurt?

b Which yogurt has least saturated fat per 25 g?

c Dale buys yogurt in pots of 50 g. He wants to eat less than 2 g of fat.
Which yogurts can Dale buy?

7 Use these clues to complete the two-way table.

There are 12 paperback thrillers.

There are 8 hardback biography books

A third of the thrillers are hardback.

There are 10 biography books altogether.

For every hardback comedy book there are 12 paperback comedy books.

There are 39 comedy books in total.

There are 25 romance books altogether.

There are 74 paperback books altogether.

> Read through the information carefully before you start. Draw up a two-way table with four columns and two rows and an extra row and column for any totals. Fill it in rough first, then copy it out neatly.

|  | Thriller | Biography | Romance | Comedy | Total |
|---|---|---|---|---|---|
| Paperback |  |  |  |  |  |
| Hardback |  |  |  |  |  |
| Total |  |  |  |  |  |

## Review

1 Jerry wants to find out how much television students in his school watch.

He asks five of his best friends.

a Is this sample likely to be representative? Give reasons for your answer.

b Briefly, explain how a better sample can be obtained.

2 Siti is comparing the tomatoes she grows in her greenhouse.

Name something about a tomato that is:

a continuous

b discrete.

3  Kane works in a nursery. He measures the height, $h$ cm, of each tree before it is sent out for delivery.

The heights of one batch of trees are listed below.

| 105 | 115 | 126 | 96 | 120 | 122 | 116 | 93 | 89 | 88 |
| 87 | 97 | 101 | 100 | 109 | 110 | 129 | 131 | 123 | 107 |

Complete the frequency table to show these heights.

| Height, $h$ (cm) | Tally | Frequency |
|---|---|---|
| $80 < h \leq 90$ | | |
| $90 < h \leq 100$ | | |
| $100 < h \leq 110$ | | |
| $110 < h \leq 120$ | | |
| $120 < h \leq 130$ | | |
| $130 < h \leq 140$ | | |

4  In a survey of cars in a car park, the following data were recorded.

| | | Colour | | | | |
|---|---|---|---|---|---|---|
| | | Red | Blue | White | Black | Other |
| Number of doors | 2 | 5 | 3 | 7 | 5 | 6 |
| | 3 | 2 | 5 | 6 | 2 | 9 |
| | 4 | 6 | 6 | 3 | 8 | 6 |
| | 5 | 1 | 7 | 2 | 10 | 4 |

a  How many cars were red with three doors?

b  How many cars were blue with two doors?

c  Copy the table. Add row and column totals.

5  100 students each study one of three languages.

Complete the two-way table.

| | French | German | Dutch | Total |
|---|---|---|---|---|
| Male | 20 | | | 40 |
| Female | | | 18 | 60 |
| Total | 34 | | 30 | 100 |

# 19 Ratio and proportion

> **Learning outcomes**
> - Simplify ratios, including those expressed in different units.
> - Divide a quantity into more than two parts in a given ratio.
> - Use the unitary method to solve simple problems involving ratio and direct proportion.

## In the frame

Rory's parents have taken a photograph of him playing with an old camera.

They want to put the picture in a frame to display it.

They find an attractive wooden frame that they want to use.

Unfortunately, the ratio of the sides is not the same for the frame as it is for the picture so it will not fit without being trimmed.

## 19.1 More ratio

### Ratios with more than two parts

Here is a set of flags.

There are 9 red flags, 6 green flags and 3 blue flags.

The ratio of red to green to blue flags is $9 : 6 : 3$

This simplifies to $3 : 2 : 1$

> Divide by the highest common factor. The highest common factor of 3, 6 and 9 is 3.

What is the ratio of blue to red to green? Remember that the order is very important.

Mathematics for Cambridge Secondary 1

> ### Worked example 1
>
> A bag contains 50 bars of chocolate.
>
> 25 of them are milk chocolate, 15 are dark chocolate and 10 are white chocolate.
>
> Work out the ratio of white chocolate to milk chocolate to dark chocolate.
>
> The ratio is 10 : 25 : 15     Make sure they are in the right order.
>
> This simplifies to 2 : 5 : 3     Divide each number by 5.

## Ratios containing units

Sometimes a ratio involves measurements.

To simplify these you must make sure that the units are the same.

You do not include the units in the final ratio.

These examples show you how to do this.

> ### Worked example 2
>
> Nelson measures two pieces of wood.
>
> One of them is 75 cm long and the other is 2 m long.
>
> What is the ratio of their lengths?
>
> One length is in centimetres and the other is in metres.
>
> Convert 2 metres to 200 centimetres.     Remember 1 metre = 100 centimetres.
>
> The ratio is 75 : 200     Do not include the units in the ratio.
>
> This simplifies to 3 : 8     Divide by the highest common factor, which is 25.

## Exercise 19.1

**1** Here are some sets of flags. In each case, write down the ratio of red flags to white flags to black flags.

Give each answer in its simplest form.

a

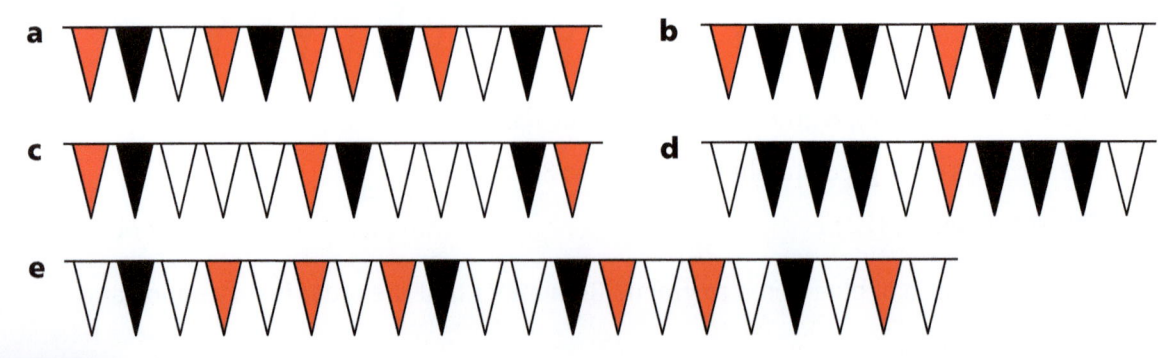

b

c

d

e

**2** Write each of these ratios in its simplest form.

  **a** 5 : 10 : 5     **b** 3 : 9 : 3     **c** 12 : 15 : 6     **d** 70 : 50 : 20

  **e** 49 : 63 : 14    **f** 32 : 16 : 8    **g** 125 : 65 : 75    **h** 26 : 65 : 91

**3** In a classroom there are 32 coloured balls.

16 of them are yellow, 10 of them are green and the rest are red.

What is the ratio of yellow balls to green balls to red balls? Give your answer in its simplest form.

**4** On a school trip there are 24 boys, 20 girls and 8 adults.

Write down the ratio of boys to girls to adults in its simplest form.

**5** Write down the ratio of white to blue to black to red flags here.

**6** Write each of these ratios in its simplest form.

  **a** 12 : 6 : 24 : 12    **b** 15 : 5 : 15 : 20    **c** 6 : 6 : 6 : 30    **d** 96 : 36 : 120 : 60

**7** Simplify these ratios.

  **a** 2 days : 1 week     **b** 75 cm : 2 m     **c** 1.5 l : 450 ml    **d** 1200 g : 3 kg

  **e** 2 kg : 4.5 kg : 1250 g    **f** 350 mm : 75 cm : 1 m    **g** 3 weeks : 9 days

**8** Jane took $2\frac{1}{2}$ hours to walk between two villages.

Philippa took 75 minutes to do the same walk.

Write down the ratio of their times. Give your answer in its simplest form.

**9** Three children guessed the length of a piece of ribbon.

Albee said it was 90 mm.

Moira said it was 7.5 cm.

Davide said it was 0.1 m.

Work out the ratio of their guesses. Simplify your answer.

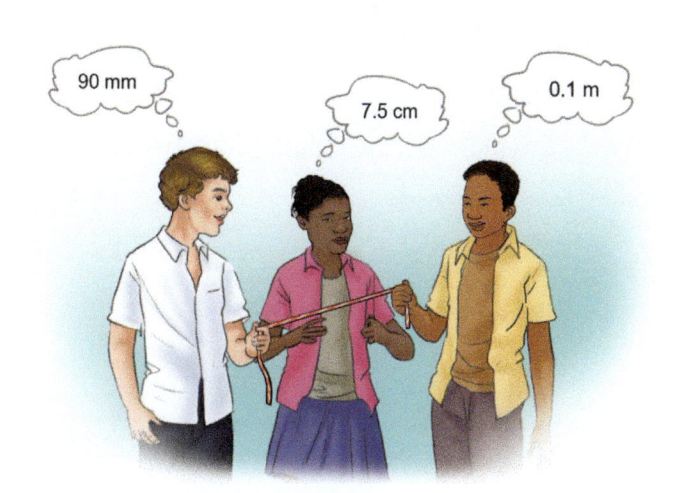

**10** Ariana, Sunisa and Bervi shared a sum of money in the ratio 5 : 3 : 2

What fraction did they each receive?

255

# Mathematics for Cambridge Secondary 1

**11** A large jar of beads contains red, blue, green and yellow beads.

There are twice as many red beads as blue beads.

There are five times as many green beads as red beads.

There are half as many yellow beads as green beads.

What is the ratio of blue to red to green to yellow beads?

> Let the number of blue beads be $x$ and write the number of each colour in terms of $x$.

**12** Errol, Wayne and Maureen shared a packet of sweets.

Errol took $\frac{1}{2}$ of the sweets and Maureen took $\frac{1}{3}$ of the sweets.

Wayne took the rest.

**a** What fraction of the sweets did Wayne take?

**b** Work out the ratio of Errol's sweets to Wayne's sweets to Maureen's sweets. Simplify your answer.

> Add $\frac{1}{2}$ and $\frac{1}{3}$ to find what fraction of the sweets Errol and Maureen have between them.

## 19.2 Dividing in a given ratio

In your Stage 7 Student Book, you learnt how to divide a quantity in a given ratio.

The three steps were:

**1** Add to find the total number of portions

**2** Divide to find the size of each portion

**3** Multiply to find the size of each share

If a ratio has more than two parts, you do it in the same way.

### Worked example

Divide $360 in the ratio $4:3:2$

$4 + 3 + 2 = 9$   Add to find the total number of portions.

$360 \div 9 = 40$   Divide to find the size of each portion.

$40 \times 4 = 160$   Multiply to find the size of each share.

$40 \times 3 = 120$

$40 \times 2 = 80$

The three amounts are $160, $120 and $80.

> Check that $160 + 120 + 80 = 360$

**19** Ratio and proportion

## Exercise 19.2

1. Divide each of these quantities in the given ratio.
   a  $300 in the ratio 3 : 5 : 2
   b  $36 in the ratio 1 : 1 : 4
   c  $100 in the ratio 2 : 7 : 1
   d  48 sweets in the ratio 3 : 2 : 1
   e  84 plants in the ratio 4 : 1 : 2
   f  $1000 in the ratio 11 : 5 : 4
   g  $789.60 in the ratio 7 : 4 : 3
   h  32 000 kg in the ratio 9 : 5 : 2

2. Divide 5 litres in the ratio 11 : 5 : 9 giving your answer in millilitres.

3. Alberta, Erica and Susanna share a flat.
   They divide the rent in the ratio 2 : 2 : 1
   The total rent is $520 per month.
   How much does each of them pay?

4. A cinema sold 120 tickets for a film.
   The ratio of adult tickets to children's tickets to senior tickets was 5 : 2 : 1
   Work out how many adult tickets were sold.

5. A piece of wood 3 metres long is to be cut into three pieces.
   The ratio of the lengths of the pieces must be 4 : 6 : 1
   Work out how long each piece should be. Give your answers to the nearest millimetre.

6. The angles of a triangle are in the ratio 3 : 2 : 5
   Work out the size of the largest angle in degrees.

   > Remember: the angles of a triangle add up to 180°.

7. The angles of a quadrilateral are in the ratio 4 : 3 : 4 : 1
   Work out the size of the two equal angles.

   > Remember: the angles of a quadrilateral add up to 360°.

8. A bag contains orange beads, red beads and blue beads.
   The ratio of orange beads to red beads to blue beads is 3 : 6 : 5
   There are 45 more red beads than orange beads.
   Work out how many blue beads there are.

   > 6 portions are red and 3 portions are orange. The difference, which is 45 beads, is 3 portions.

## 19.3 Direct proportion – the unitary method

Two quantities are in **direct proportion** if they increase or decrease at the same rate.

For example, if one quantity doubles the other quantity doubles as well.

If you work, the number of hours worked is directly proportional to the pay received.

These examples show you how to answer questions using the **unitary method**.

## Worked example 1

Georgina is paid $37.80 for working 6 hours.

How much would she be paid for working 11 hours?

Pay for 6 hours is 37.80

Pay for 1 hour is 37.80 ÷ 6 = 6.30     Divide by 6 to find the pay for 1 hour.

Pay for 11 hours is 6.30 × 11 = 69.30     Multiply by 11 to find the pay for 11 hours.

Georgina would be paid $69.30 for working 11 hours.

> This is called the **unitary method** because you find the value of **one** item before finding the answer.

## Worked example 2

Alistair, Rachel and Felicity share a sum of money in the ratio 4 : 5 : 3

Rachel receives $140.

**a** How much does Alistair receive?

**b** What is the total amount of money?

**a** Rachel has received 5 portions.

   5 portions = 140

   1 portion = 140 ÷ 5 = 28     Divide by 5 to find what 1 portion is.

   4 portions are worth 28 × 4 = 112     Multiply by 4 to find what Alistair gets.

   Alistair receives $112.

**b** Altogether there are 12 portions.

   28 × 12 = 336

   The total amount is $336.

## Exercise 19.3

**1** Annie bought 7 metres of ribbon for $16.80.

   Work out how much she would pay for 12 metres of the same ribbon.

**2** Pipe costs $7.35 for 3 metres.

   Work out how much 13 metres of the same pipe would cost.

**3** When Aziz worked for 6.5 hours he was paid $49.40.

How much would he be paid if he worked for 20 hours?

**4** Janice needs to buy 5.5 metres of ribbon.

She can buy it from two shops.

**Huxley Haberdashers**
*Ribbon - Special Offer*
Only $1.00 for 3 metres

**Min's Materials**
Buy 2.5 metres of ribbon for only 80 cents

Work out how much it will cost her from each shop.

Which is the cheaper shop for Janice to use?

**5** A car uses 25 litres of fuel when travelling 355 kilometres.

How far can it travel with 42 litres of fuel?

**6** Here is an advertisement for grass seed.

It says that 500 grams of seed will cover 15 square metres.

Cyd has an area of 55 $m^2$ to sow with grass seed.

**a** How much seed does Cyd need?

**b** If it comes in 500 g packs, how many packs does he need to buy?

**Grass seed**
500 g packs
Only $2.30 per pack
Enough for 15 $m^2$

**7** A note on a box of breakfast cereal says: 'Sufficient for 24 servings.'

There are 325 people at a scout camp.

The camp is due to last for three days.

Work out how many boxes of cereal are needed to give everyone at the camp one serving per day.

**8** At a football match only $\frac{1}{20}$ of the people there are female.

**a** Write down the ratio of males to females at the match.

**b** There are 21 926 males at the match.

How many people attended the football match altogether?

*Work out what fraction of the people are males.*

**9** Three friends Arturo, Salvo and Kiyoko share a sum of money in the ratio 5 : 3 : 7

Kiyoko receives $748 more than Salvo.

**a** How much does Salvo receive?

**b** Work out the total amount of money that they shared.

*Kiyoko receives 4 more portions than Salvo.*

**10** Here is a recipe for vanilla shortbread.

It shows the quantities needed to make 16 biscuits.

**a** How much sugar would you need to make 40 biscuits?

**b** Write out the ingredients needed to make 48 biscuits.

**c** What problem do you have if you increase the recipe to make 36 biscuits?

> **Vanilla shortbread**
>
> 100g sugar
> 225g plain flour
> 75g cornflour
> 200g butter
> 1 vanilla pod
>
> Makes enough for 16 biscuits

**11** A company has three identical machines that produce electrical components.

When all three machines are working they can produce 1620 components in two hours.

One of the machines has stopped working.

Work out how long it will take two machines to produce 675 components.

> Work out how many components one machine can produce in one hour.

## Review

**1** Look at this string of flags.

**a** Write down the ratio of red flags to yellow flags to black flags. Give your answer in its simplest form.

**b** Two of the red flags blow away in a high wind.

Write down the new ratio of red flags to yellow flags to black flags.

**2** Simplify these ratios.

   **a** $45:60:15$     **b** $24:12:90$     **c** $18:108:54$     **d** $77:21:91$

**3** Simplify these ratios.

   **a** $1.5\,\text{kg}:500\,\text{g}$     **b** $600\,\text{ml}:2.7\,\text{l}$

   **c** 2 weeks : 12 days     **d** $900\,\text{cm}:2.4\,\text{m}$

   **e** $3\,\text{kg}:900\,\text{g}:1.5\,\text{kg}$     **f** $2\tfrac{1}{2}$ minutes : 50 seconds

   **g** $200\,\text{mm}:1.2\,\text{m}:40\,\text{cm}$

**4** Divide these quantities in the given ratios.

   **a** $270 in the ratio $2:5:2$    **b** $480 in the ratio $2:2:6$    **c** $1250\,\text{cm}$ in the ratio $5:4:1$

**5** Divide $750 in the ratio $2:5:4$

Give your answers to the nearest cent.

**6** Three gardeners buy a bag containing 250 onion bulbs.

They decide to share them in the ratio 2 : 2 : 5

Work out how many bulbs they should each receive.

> You cannot split onion bulbs so the answers must be whole numbers.

**7** Four students share a flat together.

The bedrooms are not all the same size so they share the rent in the ratio 1 : 1 : 2 : 3

The total rent is $574 per month.

Work out how much they each pay.

**8** George has a part-time job filling envelopes for an advertising company.

He prepared 72 envelopes, which took him 1 hour and 30 minutes.

How long would it take him to prepare 350 envelopes?

**9** Sarmed has just been paid $38 for three weeks of work.

He wants to buy a new telephone for $100.

He thinks that if he works for eight weeks at the same rate he will have enough money.

Is he right?

**10** This is a recipe for a fish pie. It makes enough for four people.

   **a** How many eggs do you need to make a pie for 11 people?

   **b** How much fish do you need for 11 people?

   **c** Helga wants to make a fish pie for 13 people.

      Write out the ingredients that she needs.

> **FISH PIE**
> Serves 4
>
> 800g fish
> 600ml milk
> 1 onion
> 4 eggs
> 100g butter
> 50g plain flour
> 1kg potatoes
> 50g cheese

**11** A family has three children: Anya, Karol and Martin.

Anya is nine years old, Karol is seven years old and Martin is four years old.

They inherit a large sum of money and divide it in the ratio of their ages.

Anya noticed that she received exactly $1250 more than Martin.

Work out how much they inherited altogether.

261

# 20 Time and rates of change

> **Learning outcomes**
>
> - Draw and interpret graphs in real life contexts involving more than one component.

## A matter of time

Travel graphs are used to show distances travelled over time.

However, graphs can be used to show many different quantities.

Examples of these include temperatures, water levels or populations.

The one thing they have in common is that they are all plotted over a period of time.

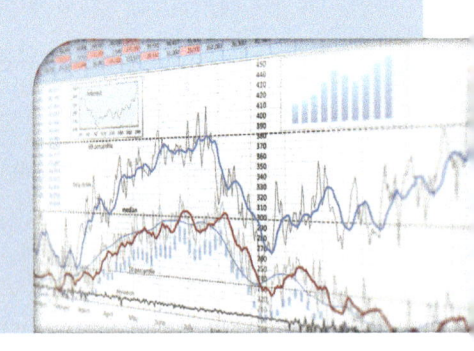

## 20.1 Travel graphs

In your Stage 7 Student Book, you looked at how travel graphs show distance travelled over a period of time.

Travel graphs can show more than one set of data.

One day, Wendy cycled 50 kilometres from her home to a friend's house.

Her brother, Andrew, went part of the way with her before turning back.

This graph shows details of their movements.

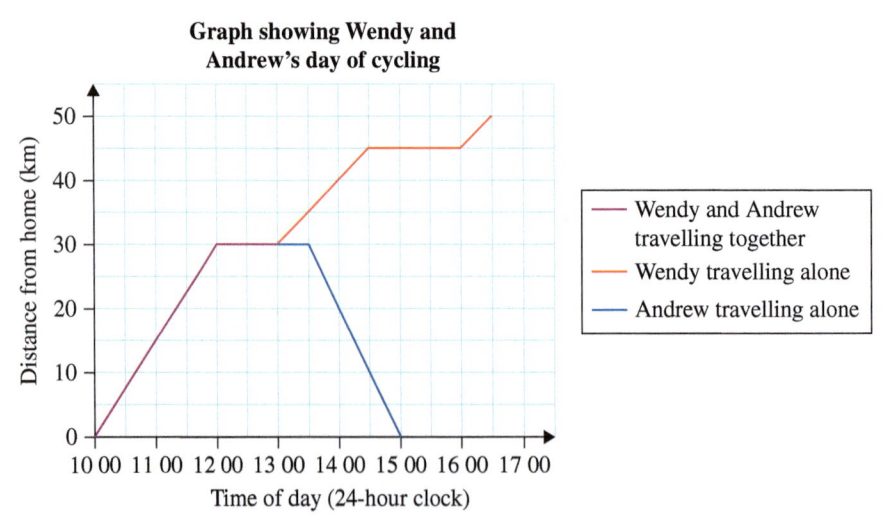

**Graph showing Wendy and Andrew's day of cycling**

— Wendy and Andrew travelling together
— Wendy travelling alone
— Andrew travelling alone

The purple line shows that they left home together at 10 00 and cycled 30 km in two hours.

262

**20** Time and rates of change

### Worked example

Use the graph of Wendy and Andrew's day to answer these questions.

**a** How far did Wendy and Andrew go in the first hour of the cycle ride? How fast are they cycling in that hour?

**b** After Wendy carried on to her friend's house, how much longer did Andrew rest for?

**c** How long did Andrew take to cycle home?

**d** At what time did Wendy arrive at her friend's house?

**e** Who cycled further on the day, Wendy or Andrew?

**f** During which part of the trip was Wendy cycling fastest?

**a** Wendy and Andrew cycled 15 km in the first hour.

They are cycling at 15 km per hour.

**b** Wendy carried on to her friend's house at 13 00.

Andrew set off home at 13 30.

He waited an extra 30 minutes before setting off.

**c** Andrew set off home at 13 30 and arrived home at 15 00.

He cycled for $1\frac{1}{2}$ hours.

**d** Wendy arrived at her friend's house at 16 30.

**e** Wendy cycled 50 km during the day.

Andrew cycled 30 km to where they stopped and then 30 km back home.

He cycled 60 km altogether.

Andrew cycled 10 km further than Wendy.

**f** The first part of Wendy's trip was the fastest. It is the steepest part of her graph.

## Exercise 20.1

**1** A bus left the bus station at 12 00 to travel to another town.

At 13 30 a car left the bus station to make the same journey.

They arrived at the destination at the same time.

This graph shows their journeys during the day.

**a** At what time did the bus and the car both reach their destination?

**b** Write down the distance between the two towns.

**c** Work out how long the car took to travel between the two towns.

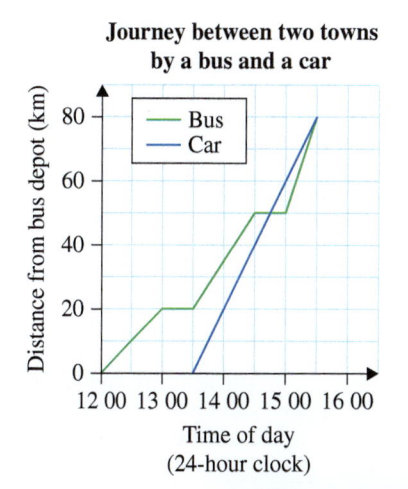

263

**d** The bus journey was in three parts. Work out the speed of the bus during the first hour.

**e** During which part of the journey was the bus travelling fastest?

**f** Explain how you can tell which the fastest part of the journey is without doing any calculations.

**2** Hashim and Faisal live 12 km apart.

Hashim starts to walk from his house to see Faisal.

Faisal later walks to meet Hashim before they go to Faisal's house together.

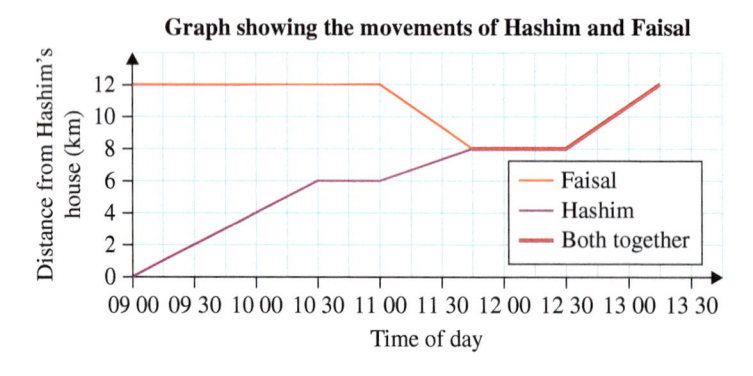

**Graph showing the movements of Hashim and Faisal**

**a** At what time did Faisal leave home?

**b** Write down the time at which Hashim and Faisal both reached Faisal's house.

**c** Write down the time at which they met.

**d** How far was each of them from home when they met?

**e** How long did Hashim take altogether from leaving home until he reached Faisal's house?

**3** This graph shows the movements of two trains between 9am and 4pm.

**a** Work out how far train A travelled altogether during the day.

**b** The two trains passed each other twice during the day. Write down the times at which this happened.

**c** Work out the speed of train B during the first hour of its journey.

**d** What time did train B arrive back at the station?

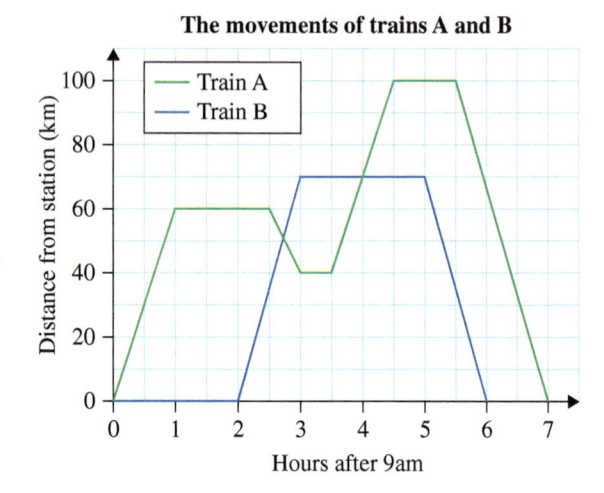

**The movements of trains A and B**

**4** Peter went for a walk from his home to see his grandmother who lives 15 km away.

He left home at 10am and walked 5 km in the first hour.

He then stopped for a rest at a friend's house, staying there for 90 minutes.

After leaving his friend's house, Peter walked to his grandmother's house without stopping.

He arrived at her house at 2pm and stayed there for two hours.

# 20 Time and rates of change

Peter's father left home in the car at 3pm and drove to the grandmother's house to meet him.

His father took 15 minutes to reach the grandmother's house.

At 4pm, they both left the grandmother's house in the car and drove home.

They arrived home at half past four.

**a** Copy these axes on to squared paper.

**b** Draw a line on the axes to show Peter's movements during the day.

**c** Use a different colour to show his father's movements on the same axes.

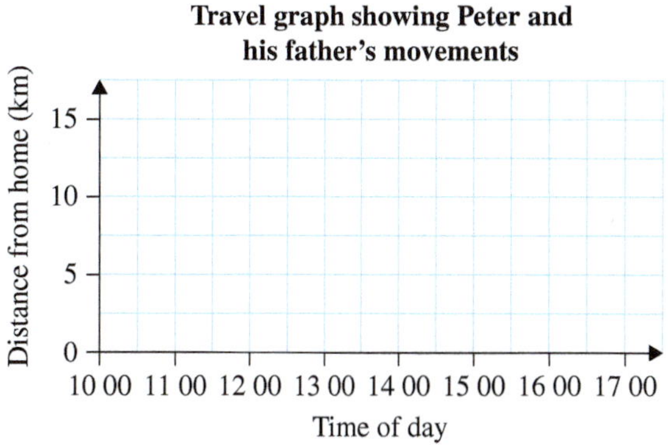

Travel graph showing Peter and his father's movements

**5** Four students were asked to draw a travel graph showing a bus journey.

The journey started and finished at the same place.

Only one of the students produced a correct graph.

Which one of them must be the right answer?

Explain why the other graphs must be wrong.

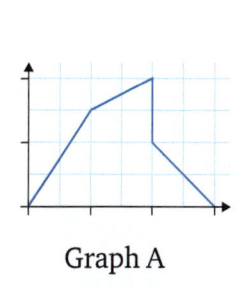

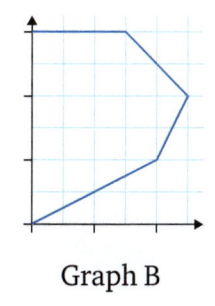

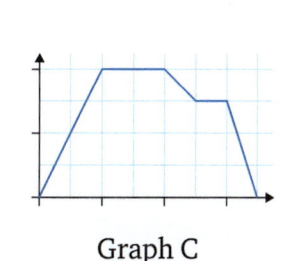

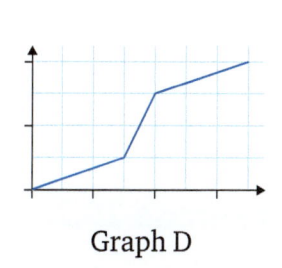

Graph A    Graph B    Graph C    Graph D

> Look again at the graphs from questions **1** to **4** to see what correct graphs look like.

## 20.2 Other graphs

Graphs can be used to show many other types of information apart from distance.

Sarah and Roger are two charity workers who spend a day collecting money for their charity.

They both start at 8am with some money in their tin and they collect until 3pm.

During the day they keep a tally of how much money is in each tin and they plot it on a graph.

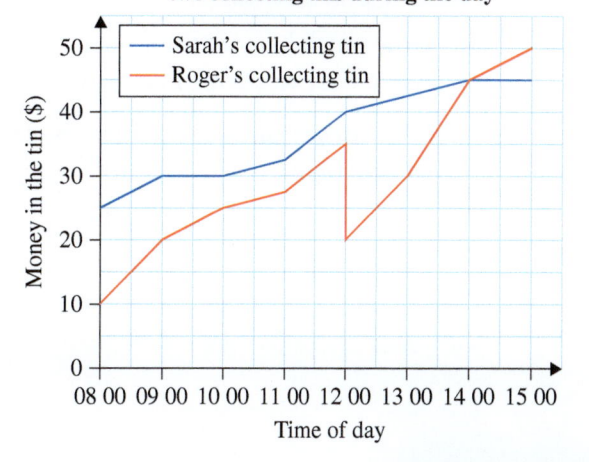

Graph showing the amount in two collecting tins during the day

265

Mathematics for Cambridge Secondary 1

> **Worked example**
>
> Use the graph on page 265 to answer these questions.
>
> a  Write down how much was in Sarah's tin at the start of the day.
>
> b  How much did Sarah collect during the day?
>
> c  At one point some money was taken out of Roger's tin.
>
>    How much was taken out?
>
> d  At what time of day did both tins hold the same amount of money?
>
>    How much did each hold at that time?
>
> a  The blue line starts at 25. Sarah started the day with $25.
>
> b  Sarah ended the day with $45. She collected $20.
>
> c  At 12 00 Roger's line drops from $35 to $20.
>
>    $15 was taken out of the tin.
>
> d  The lines cross at 14 00.
>
>    They had the same amount at 2pm.
>
>    At that time they each held $45

## Exercise 20.2

1  A growth chart shows how children develop after birth.

   This growth chart shows the growth of Fiona and Gareth, who were born on the same day.

   a  What was Fiona's weight when she was born?

   b  How much weight did Gareth gain in the first month?

   c  How much heavier than Gareth was Fiona when they were one month old?

   d  Write down the age at which they were the same weight.

   e  Work out how long it took Fiona to double her birth weight.

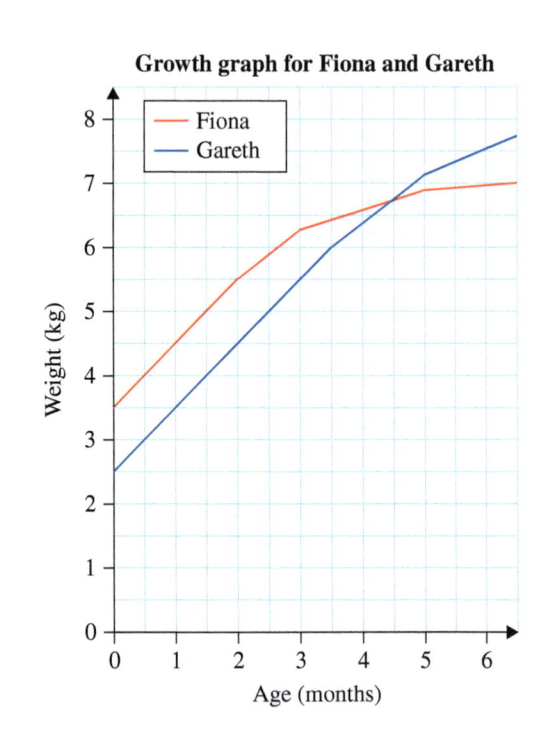

**2** Two neighbouring villages, Littleham and Parkham, grew in size during the 20th century.

This graph shows the populations between the years 1900 and 2000.

**a** Which was the smaller village in 1900?

**b** Which was the smaller village in 2000?

**c** Write down the approximate year in which the populations were the same size.

**d** Which village grew at a faster rate between 1900 and 1920?

**e** A new housing development was built in Littleham during the century.

Over which two decades do you think it was built?

**f** Work out the percentage increase in the population of Parkham between 1900 and 2000.

**3** A veterinary surgeon operated on two cats, known as cat X and cat Y.

She recorded their body temperatures for six hours after the operations.

This graph shows the temperatures recorded for cat X.

**a** What was the highest temperature that the cat's body reached during these six hours?

**b** In which hour did the temperature go up at the fastest rate?

**c** This table shows the temperature of cat Y during the same period.

Copy the graph for cat X on to squared paper.

Add the information about cat Y to the graph using a different coloured line.

Draw the graph as accurately as you can using a ruler and a sharp pencil.

**d** The cats had the same body temperature immediately after the operation.

At what other time were they at the same temperature?

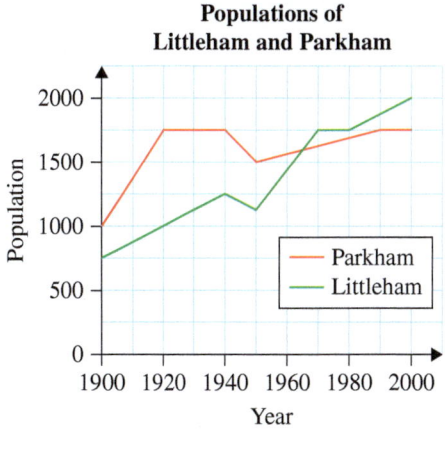

| Time | Temperature (°C) |
|---|---|
| 0 | 36.0 |
| 1 | 35.5 |
| 2 | 38.5 |
| 3 | 40.0 |
| 4 | 40.0 |
| 5 | 39.0 |
| 6 | 38.5 |

## Review

1. Train A left Mumbai station at 9.30am to travel to Kasara, 120 kilometres away.

   An hour later, train B left Kasara to travel to Mumbai.

   This graph shows the movements of the two trains.

   **a** Write down the time that train A arrived in Kasara.

   **b** Work out how long it took for train A to travel from Mumbai and Kasara.

   **c** Work out how long it took for train A to make the return journey.

   **d** How far from Mumbai were the trains when they first passed one another?

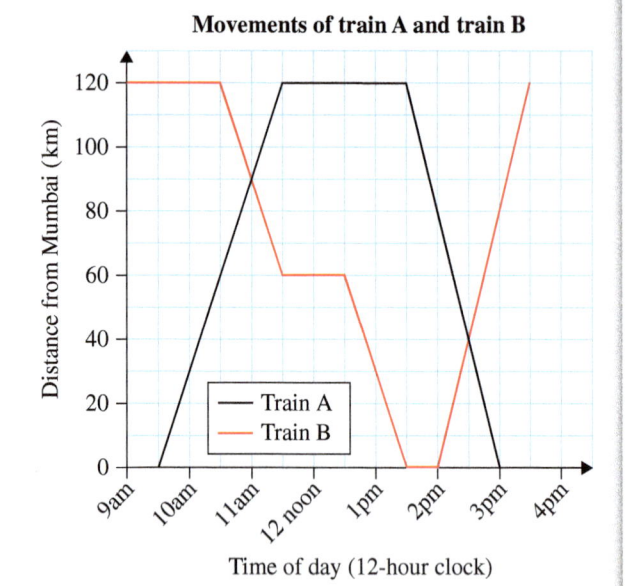

   **e** At what time did the trains pass one another for the second time?

   **f** How long did train B stay in Mumbai before returning to Kasara?

2. A scientist wanted to know the effect of a chemical experiment on temperature.

   He recorded the temperature at two sensors for 10 hours after the experiment.

   The temperatures are shown in this table.

   | Time (hours) | Sensor A temperature (°C) | Sensor B temperature (°C) |
   |---|---|---|
   | 0 | 100 | 100 |
   | 1 | 400 | 200 |
   | 2 | 375 | 350 |
   | 3 | 350 | 400 |
   | 4 | 300 | 400 |
   | 5 | 300 | 375 |
   | 6 | 250 | 375 |
   | 7 | 225 | 300 |
   | 8 | 200 | 200 |
   | 9 | 150 | 125 |
   | 10 | 125 | 75 |

**a** Copy these axes on to squared paper.

Temperatures shown by two sensors after a chemical experiment

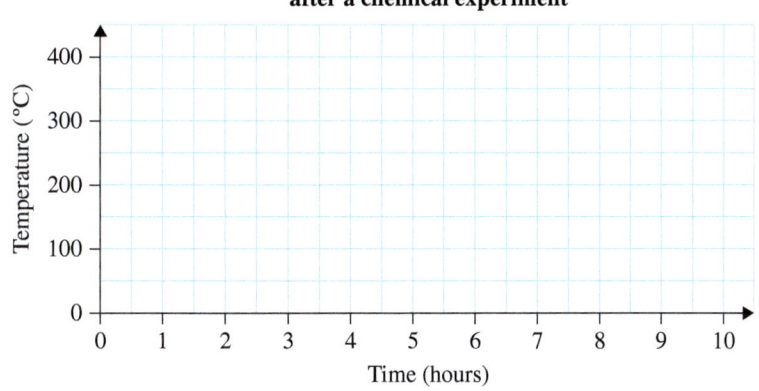

**b** Draw a graph to show the change in temperature at each sensor over the 10-hour period.

Use a different colour for each sensor.

**c  i** Write down the three times at which both sensors were showing the same temperature.

**ii** Write down the temperatures recorded at each of these three times.

**3** Jeremy handed in this travel graph for his homework.

His teacher found five things wrong with the graph.

Write down what Jeremy has done wrong.

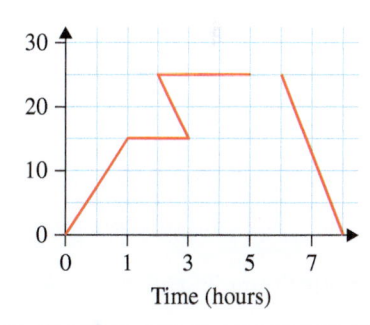

# 21 Sets

> **Learning outcomes**
> - Use set language and notation.

## Venn diagrams

Venn diagrams consist of overlapping circles. They are used to show relationships between sets and logical relationships.

Venn diagrams were invented by British logician and philosopher, John Venn.

John Venn was a student at the University of Cambridge. His work on set theory is so important that there is a stained-glass window to honour it at the university. The design shows the only way that three sets can triply intersect.

Although Venn diagrams were invented around 1880, the set theory and logic theory linked to them have many important uses in computer science today.

## 21.1 Set notation

In your Stage 7 Student Book, you learnt about the following symbols.

$$\in \quad \notin \quad \varnothing \quad \cap \quad \cup \quad \subset$$

It is important that you remember what each symbol means.

$\in$ means 'is a **member** of' or 'is an **element** of'. For example, $6 \in \{1, 2, 6, 7, 9\}$

$\notin$ means 'is not a member of'. For example, $8 \notin \{1, 2, 6, 7, 9\}$

$\varnothing$ or { } means 'the **empty set**'. For example, {triangles with two obtuse angles} = $\varnothing$

### Intersection and union

$A \cap B$ is the **intersection** of A and B. It contains the members that are in both A and B.

$A \cup B$ is the **union** of A and B. It contains the members that are in A or B or both.

Intersection and union can be seen on a **Venn diagram** in which sets and their relationships are shown as overlapping circles.

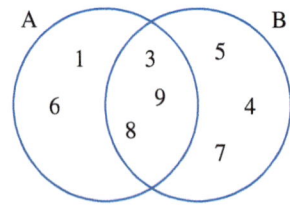

For this diagram, $A \cap B = \{3, 8, 9\}$ and $A \cup B = \{1, 3, 4, 5, 6, 7, 8, 9\}$

A ∩ B can be shaded on a diagram as:

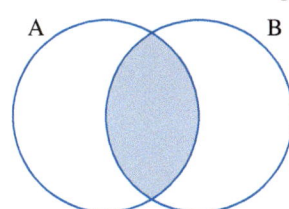

A ∪ B can be shaded on a diagram as:

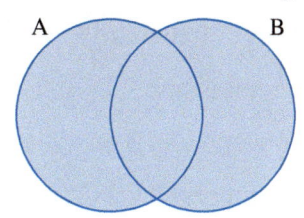

## Subsets

A is called a **proper subset** of B if all the elements of A are contained in the larger set B.

The symbol for a proper subset is ⊂.

For example, if A = {2, 5} and B = {1, 2, 4, 5, 7} then A ⊂ B.

A ⊂ B can be shown on a diagram as:

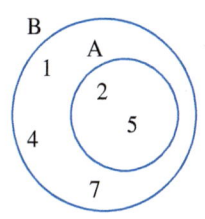

### Worked example

X = {3, 6, 9, 12, 15, 18} and Y = {2, 4, 6, 8, 10, 12, 14, 16, 18}

**a** List the members of:  **i** X ∩ Y  **ii** X ∪ Y

**b** Show the sets X and Y on a diagram.

**a i** X ∩ Y = {6, 12, 18}  **ii** X ∪ Y = {2, 3, 4, 6, 8, 9, 10, 12, 14, 15, 16, 18}

**b**

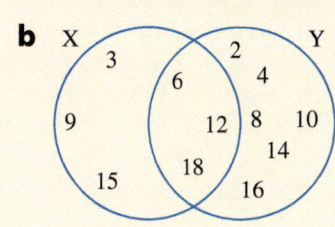

## Exercise 21.1

**1** List the elements of:

   **a** A         **b** B

   **c** A ∩ B   **d** A ∪ B

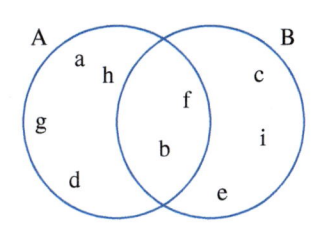

**2** A = {4, 8, 12, 16, 20, 24, 28}  B = {3, 6, 9, 12, 15, 18, 21, 24, 27, 30}

List the members of:

   **a** A ∩ B   **b** A ∪ B

271

3  A = {multiples of 6 that are less than 50}
   B = {multiples of 8 that are less than 50}
   
   **a** List the members of:  **i** A  **ii** B
   
   **b** Show the sets A and B on a diagram.
   
   **c** List the members of:  **i** A ∩ B  **ii** A ∪ B
   
   **d** Describe the set A ∩ B.

4  On copies of this diagram, shade the sets: 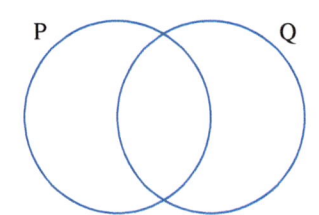
   
   **a** P  **b** Q
   
   **c** P ∩ Q  **d** P ∪ Q

5  A = {2, 4, 6, 8}  B = {1, 3, 5, 7, 9}  C = ∅
   
   **a** Find
   
   **i** n(A)  **ii** n(B)  **iii** n(C)
   
   > Remember: n(A) means the number of elements in the set A.
   
   **b** Which of these statements are true and which are false?
   
   **i** 8 ∈ A  **ii** 6 ∈ B  **iii** 9 ∈ C
   
   **iv** 0 ∈ C  **v** 3 ∈ A ∩ B  **vi** 3 ∈ A ∪ B

6  Which of these statements are true and which are false?
   
   **a** {3, 7} ⊂ {3, 6, 9, 12}
   
   **b** 51 ∈ {prime numbers}
   
   **c** {prime numbers} ⊂ {odd numbers}
   
   **d** 625 ∈ {square numbers}

7  List the members of: 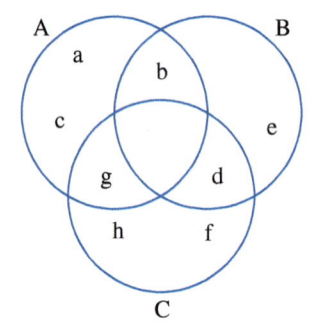
   
   **a** A ∩ B  **b** A ∩ C
   
   **c** B ∩ C  **d** A ∩ B ∩ C
   
   **e** A ∪ B  **f** A ∪ C
   
   **g** B ∪ C  **h** A ∪ B ∪ C

## 21.2 Further set notation

### The universal set

The **universal set** is denoted by the symbol ξ.

The universal set contains all the elements being considered in a particular problem.

The sets ξ = {days of the week} and A = {Tuesday, Thursday} can be shown on a Venn diagram.

The shaded region shows the set A.

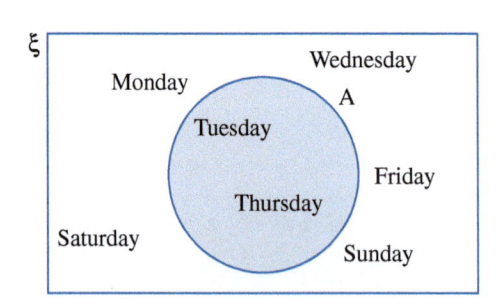

## Complement

The **complement** of set A is the set of all the elements not in A.

The complement of set A is denoted by A′.

The shaded region on the Venn diagram shows the set A′.

So A′ = {Monday, Wednesday, Friday, Saturday, Sunday}

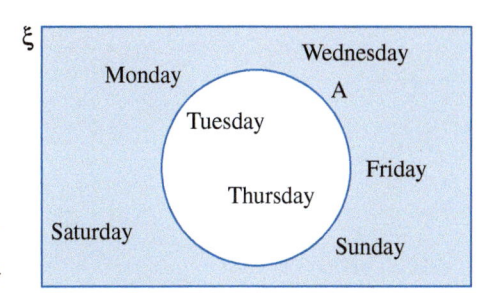

### Worked example

List the elements of:

**a** A **b** A′ **c** A ∩ B
**d** (A ∩ B)′ **e** A ∪ B **f** (A ∪ B)′
**g** ξ

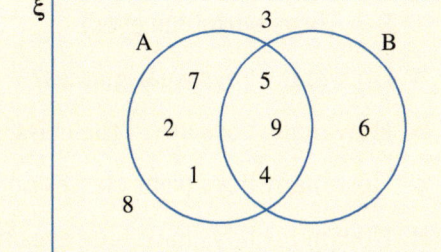

**a** A = {1, 2, 4, 5, 7, 9}
**b** A′ = {3, 6, 8}
**c** A ∩ B = {4, 5, 9}
**d** (A ∩ B)′ = {1, 2, 3, 6, 7, 8}
**e** A ∪ B = {1, 2, 4, 5, 6, 7, 9}
**f** (A ∪ B)′ = {3, 8}
**g** ξ = {1, 2, 3, 4, 5, 6, 7, 8, 9}

## Exercise 21.2

**1** List the elements of these sets.

    **a** ξ     **b** Q     **c** Q′

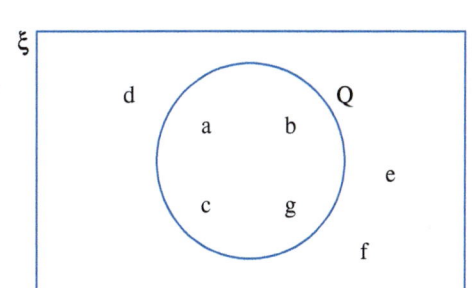

**2** ξ = {1, 2, 3, 4, 5, 6, 7, 8}

    A = {2, 3, 5, 7}

    **a** Draw a Venn diagram to show this information.

    **b** List the members of A′.

**3** A group of students were asked if they have any brothers (B) or sisters (S).

    The table shows the responses.

| Name | Xiu | Ben | Jin | Dan | Ivy | Fay | Tak | Hal | Ian |
|---|---|---|---|---|---|---|---|---|---|
| Brothers (B) | ✗ | ✓ | ✗ | ✓ | ✓ | ✓ | ✗ | ✗ | ✓ |
| Sisters (S) | ✓ | ✓ | ✗ | ✗ | ✓ | ✗ | ✓ | ✗ | ✓ |

273

Copy and complete the Venn diagram to show this information.

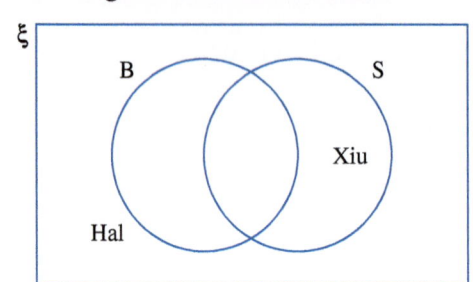

**4** In the Venn diagram:

ξ = {boys in a class}

G = {boys who wear glasses}

B = {boys with blue eyes}

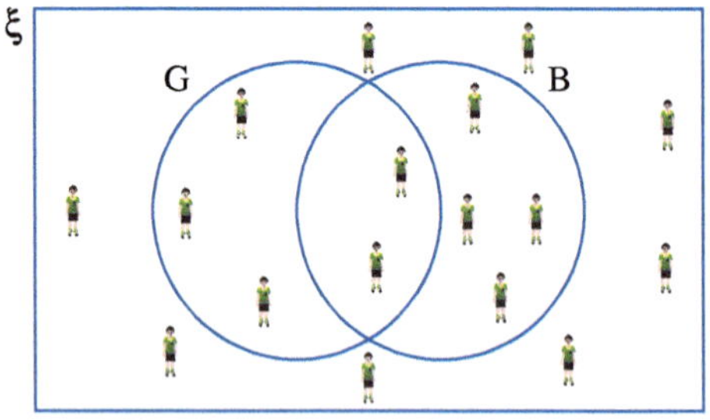

  **a** How many boys wear glasses?

  **b** How many boys are in the class?

  **c** How many boys wear glasses and have blue eyes?

  **d** How many boys have blue eyes but do not wear glasses?

**5** On copies of this diagram, shade the sets:

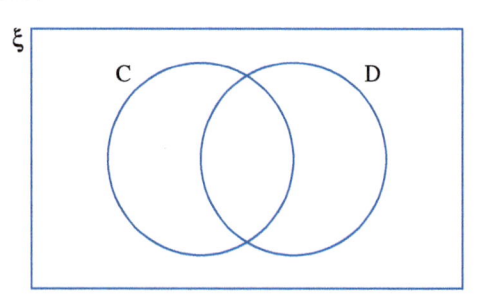

  **a** C          **b** D'          **c** C ∩ D

  **d** C ∪ D     **e** (C ∩ D)'    **f** (C ∪ D)'

**6** List the elements of:

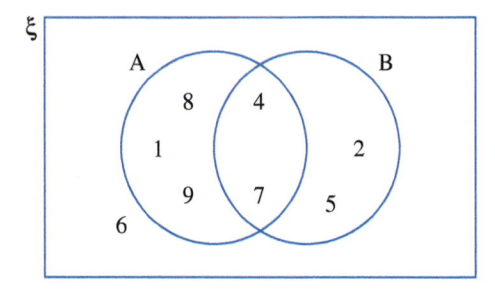

  **a** A          **b** B          **c** A'          **d** B'

  **e** A ∩ B     **f** A ∪ B     **g** (A ∪ B)'    **h** ξ

**7** ξ = {a, b, c, d, e, f, g, h}

C = {a, c, d, e, h}

D = {b, c, e, f}

Copy the Venn diagram and put the elements in the correct places.

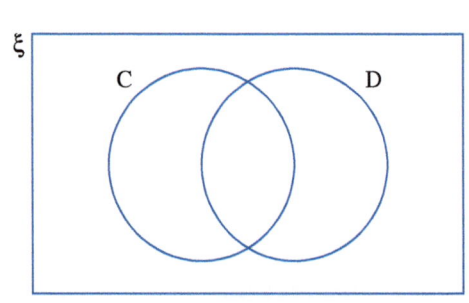

21 Sets

8 A group of students were asked which of the three sciences biology (B), chemistry (C) and physics (P) they study.

The table shows the results.

| Name | Anu | Leo | Coe | Ren | Eva | Una | Gia | Araf | Suni |
|---|---|---|---|---|---|---|---|---|---|
| Biology (B) | ✗ | ✓ | ✗ | ✓ | ✗ | ✓ | ✗ | ✗ | ✓ |
| Chemistry (C) | ✗ | ✓ | ✗ | ✓ | ✓ | ✗ | ✗ | ✓ | ✓ |
| Physics (P) | ✓ | ✓ | ✗ | ✗ | ✓ | ✓ | ✓ | ✗ | ✓ |

a Copy and complete the Venn diagram to show this information.

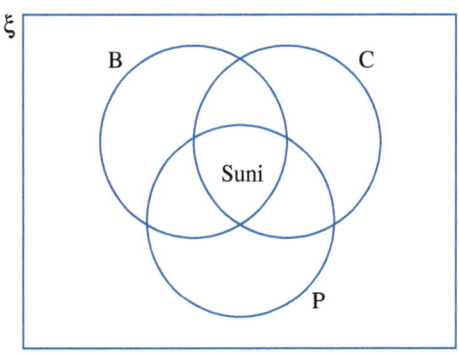

b How many students studied:

  i biology  ii all three sciences  iii physics, but not chemistry?

9 In the Venn diagram:

ξ = {cars in a car park}

R = {red cars}

F = {cars with four doors}

B = {cars with baby seats}

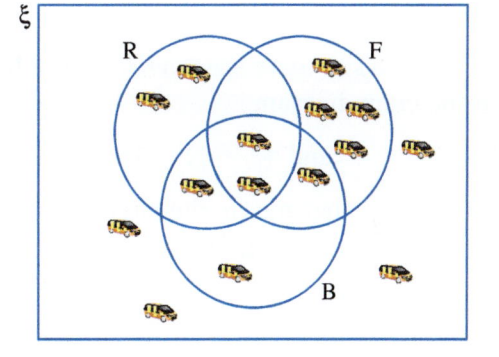

a How many cars are red?

b How many red cars have baby seats?

c How many cars are in the car park?

d How many cars do not have baby seats?

10 List the elements of:

a A
b B
c C′
d A ∩ B
e A ∪ C
f A ∩ B ∩ C
g (B ∪ C)′
h ξ

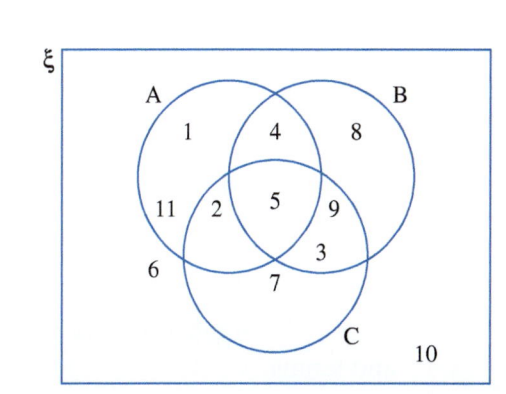

275

Mathematics for Cambridge Secondary 1

## 21.3 Using sets to solve problems

You can use Venn diagrams to show the number of elements in each set.

This is useful when solving problems.

### Worked example

There are 35 girls in a sports club.

22 play badminton (B), 25 play tennis (T) and 4 play neither badminton nor tennis.

How many play both badminton and tennis?

**Method 1**

4 girls play neither badminton nor tennis, so the number 4 goes outside the sets B and T.

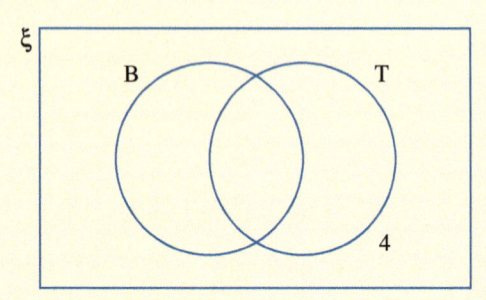

$35 - 4 = 31$ so there are now 31 girls left to put on the Venn diagram.

$22 + 25 = 47$ and $47 - 31 = 16$

The number that goes in the intersection is 16 and the remaining numbers can now be filled in.

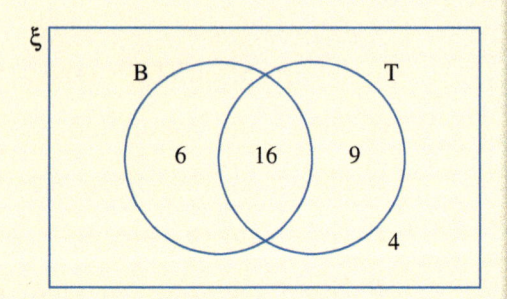

The number of girls who play both badminton and tennis is 16.

**Method 2** (using algebra)

The number 4 goes outside the sets B and T on the Venn diagram.

Let $x$ = the number of girls who play badminton and tennis.

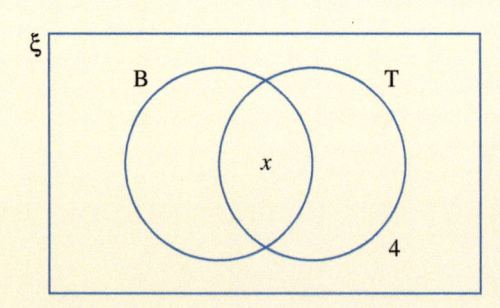

The number of girls who play badminton and not tennis = $22 - x$

The number of girls who play tennis and not badminton = $25 - x$

Put this information on the Venn diagram.

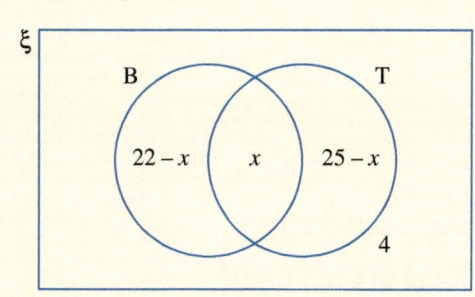

ξ
B        T
$22 - x$   $x$   $25 - x$
4

The total number of girls is 35.

So $(22 - x) + x + (25 - x) + 4 = 35$

$51 - x = 35$

$x = 16$

The number of girls who play both badminton and tennis is 16.

## Exercise 21.3

**1** The Venn diagram shows information about the number of elements in the sets.

For example, n(A) = 3 + 7 = 10

Find

**a** n(B)　　**b** n(A′)

**c** n(B′)　　**d** n(A ∩ B)

**e** n(A ∪ B)

ξ
A        B
3   7   4
5

**2** n(A) = 14, n(B) = 12 and n(A ∩ B) = 5

**a** Copy and complete the Venn diagram.

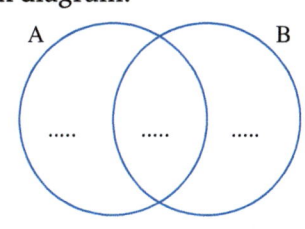

A        B
.....  .....  .....

**b** Write down the value of n(A ∪ B).

**3** n(C) = 23, n(D) = 15 and n(C ∩ D) = 12

**a** Show this information on a Venn diagram.

**b** Write down the value of n(C ∪ D).

# Mathematics for Cambridge Secondary 1

**4** $n(P) = 30$, $n(Q) = 23$ and $n(P \cup Q) = 41$

  **a** Copy and complete the Venn diagram.

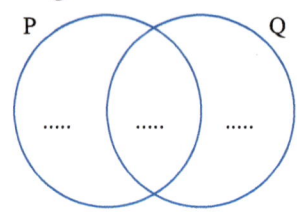

  **b** Write down the value of $n(P \cap Q)$.

**5** $n(X) = 56$, $n(Y) = 47$ and $n(X \cup Y) = 90$

  **a** Show this information on a Venn diagram.

  **b** Write down the value of $n(X \cap Y)$.

**6** There are 26 students in a class.

  15 study physics (P), 17 study chemistry (C) and 2 study neither physics nor chemistry.

  **a** Copy and complete the Venn diagram.

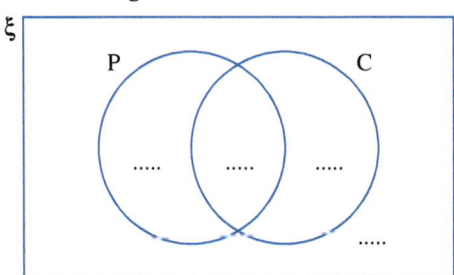

  **b** How many students study both physics and chemistry?

**7** There are 32 students in a class.

  21 like cola (C), 15 like lemonade (L) and 3 students don't like either drink.

  **a** Copy and complete the Venn diagram.

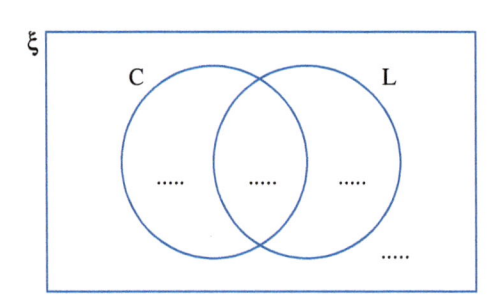

  **b** How many students like both cola and lemonade?

**8** There are 36 students in a class.

  30 have a mobile phone (M), 28 have a calculator (C) and 2 students have neither.

  **a** Show this information on a Venn diagram.

  **b** How many students have a mobile phone and a calculator?

**9** There are 38 members in a sports club.

3 members play football, hockey and tennis.

4 members do not play football or hockey or tennis.

19 play football. 16 play hockey. 12 play tennis.

7 play football and hockey. 4 play hockey and tennis.

**a** Copy and complete the Venn diagram to show this information.

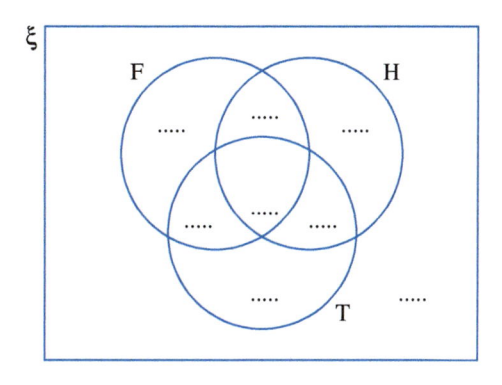

**b** How many members play football and tennis?

## Review

**1** A = {multiples of 7 that are less than 40}

B = {multiples of 5 that are less than 40}

**a** List the members of: **i** A **ii** B

**b** Show the sets A and B on a diagram.

**c** List the members of: **i** A ∩ B **ii** A ∪ B

**d** Describe the set A ∩ B.

**2** Which of these statements are true and which are false?

**a** {even numbers} ∩ {odd numbers} = ∅ **b** 47 ∈ {prime numbers}

**c** {2, 3, 4, 5} ⊂ {2, 5} **d** {1, 3, 5} ∩ {2, 4, 6} = {1, 2, 3, 4, 5, 6}

**3** ξ = {1, 2, 3, 4, 5, 6, 7, 8, 9}

A = {3, 5, 7, 9}

**a** Draw a Venn diagram to show this information.

**b** List the members of A′.

**4** List the elements of:

  **a** A  **b** B  **c** A′
  **d** B′  **e** A ∩ B  **f** A ∪ B
  **g** (A ∪ B)′  **h** ξ

**5** $n(A) = 52$, $n(B) = 41$ and $n(A \cap B) = 14$

  **a** Copy and complete the Venn diagram.
  **b** Write down the value of $n(A \cup B)$.

**6** $n(P) = 25$, $n(Q) = 32$ and $n(P \cup Q) = 50$

  **a** Copy and complete the Venn diagram.
  **b** Write down the value of $n(P \cap Q)$.

**7** There are 30 students in a class.

  18 students like music (M), 22 like art (A) and 6 don't like music or art.

  **a** Copy and complete the Venn diagram.
  **b** How many students like both music and art?

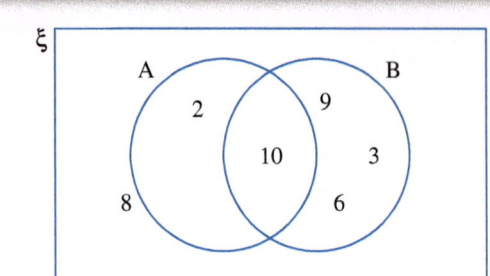

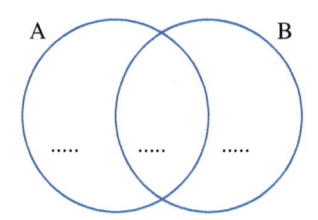

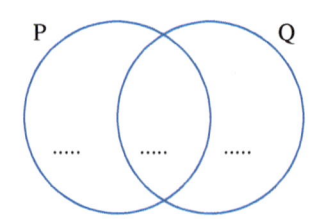

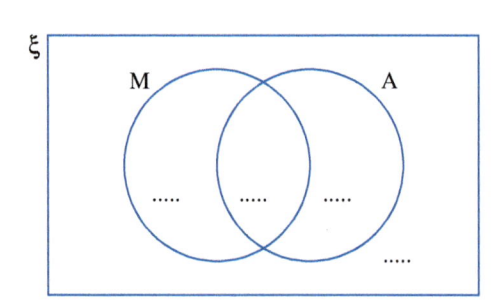

# 22 Matrices

> **Learning outcomes**
> - Add, subtract and multiply matrices.

## Using matrices to protect information

Matrices are used in cryptology.

Cryptology is about using codes to keep information private.

Large rectangular matrices are used to encode messages and these encoded messages are very difficult to break.

The use of coding has become very important in recent years because of the increase in the use of the internet.

When you have completed this chapter, you may wish to find out more about how matrices are used for coding on the internet.

### 22.1 Multiplying a row matrix by a column matrix

|  | TV | Radio |
|---|---|---|
| Monday | 6 | 2 |
| Tuesday | 5 | 7 |
| Wednesday | 8 | 6 |

The table shows the sales of TVs and radios in a shop on Monday, Tuesday and Wednesday.

If a TV cost $400 and a radio cost $50, you can work out the amount of money taken on Monday as follows:

$$6 \times 400 + 2 \times 50 = 2400 + 100 = 2500$$

In your Stage 7 Student Book, you learnt that a **matrix** is a rectangular array of numbers.

281

# Mathematics for Cambridge Secondary 1

You can write the money taken on Monday in matrix form as:

$$(6 \quad 2)\begin{pmatrix}400\\50\end{pmatrix} = (2500)$$

For Tuesday, you can write: $(5 \quad 7)\begin{pmatrix}400\\50\end{pmatrix} = (2350)$

For Wednesday, you can write: $(8 \quad 6)\begin{pmatrix}400\\50\end{pmatrix} = (3500)$

$(6 \quad 2)$ is called a **row matrix**.

$\begin{pmatrix}400\\50\end{pmatrix}$ is called a **column matrix**.

## Worked example 1

Work out **a** $(3 \quad 2)\begin{pmatrix}8\\4\end{pmatrix}$   **b** $(1 \quad -5 \quad 2)\begin{pmatrix}8\\0\\3\end{pmatrix}$

**a** $(3 \quad 2)\begin{pmatrix}8\\4\end{pmatrix} = (3 \times 8 + 2 \times 4) = (32)$

**b** $(1 \quad -5 \quad 2)\begin{pmatrix}8\\0\\3\end{pmatrix} = (1 \times 8 + -5 \times 0 + 2 \times 3) = (14)$

## Worked example 2

$(x \quad 2)\begin{pmatrix}3\\1\end{pmatrix} = (23)$

Find the value of $x$.

Multiplying the matrices gives an equation to solve:

$3x + 2 = 23$      −2
$3x = 21$       ÷3
$x = 7$

## Exercise 22.1

**1** Work out

**a** $(2 \quad 7)\begin{pmatrix}5\\9\end{pmatrix}$

**b** $(0 \quad 4)\begin{pmatrix}7\\11\end{pmatrix}$

**c** $(-3 \quad 8)\begin{pmatrix}-2\\3\end{pmatrix}$

**d** $(2 \quad 9 \quad 1)\begin{pmatrix}4\\6\\3\end{pmatrix}$

**e** $(7 \quad 0 \quad 5)\begin{pmatrix}2\\6\\8\end{pmatrix}$

**f** $(4 \quad -3 \quad 8)\begin{pmatrix}-1\\-5\\3\end{pmatrix}$

**g** $(3 \quad 0 \quad 4 \quad 7)\begin{pmatrix}5\\6\\8\\0\end{pmatrix}$

**h** $(5 \quad 3 \quad 2 \quad 6)\begin{pmatrix}1\\2\\7\\3\end{pmatrix}$

**i** $(3 \quad 2 \quad -9 \quad 0)\begin{pmatrix}0\\-8\\-5\\4\end{pmatrix}$

## 22 Matrices

**2** Find the value of $x$ for each of these matrix multiplications.

**a** $(x \quad 5)\begin{pmatrix} 2 \\ 1 \end{pmatrix} = (17)$

**b** $(x \quad -2)\begin{pmatrix} 1 \\ 6 \end{pmatrix} = (8)$

**c** $(x \quad 7 \quad 2)\begin{pmatrix} 2 \\ 5 \\ -3 \end{pmatrix} = (21)$

**d** $(x \quad 4 \quad x)\begin{pmatrix} 1 \\ -3 \\ 2 \end{pmatrix} = (9)$

> Hint: Form an equation in $x$ and then solve to find the value of $x$.

**e** $(x \quad 1 \quad 5 \quad 2)\begin{pmatrix} 2 \\ 3 \\ 0 \\ 1 \end{pmatrix} = (7)$

**f** $(x \quad 0 \quad 3 \quad 1)\begin{pmatrix} 4 \\ 2 \\ -1 \\ 0 \end{pmatrix} = (37)$

**3** $(2x \quad -1 \quad x \quad 2)\begin{pmatrix} 2 \\ 4 \\ -1 \\ -5 \end{pmatrix} = (5x)$

Find the value of $x$ for this matrix multiplication.

## 22.2 Multiplying matrices

In the last section, you saw that when a TV cost $400 and a radio cost $50, the money taken in a shop on each day was:

Monday: $(6 \quad 2)\begin{pmatrix} 400 \\ 50 \end{pmatrix} = (2500)$

Tuesday: $(5 \quad 7)\begin{pmatrix} 400 \\ 50 \end{pmatrix} = (2350)$

Wednesday: $(8 \quad 6)\begin{pmatrix} 400 \\ 50 \end{pmatrix} = (3500)$

|  | TV | Radio |
|---|---|---|
| Monday | 6 | 2 |
| Tuesday | 5 | 7 |
| Wednesday | 8 | 6 |

These can be combined into one matrix equation:

$$\begin{pmatrix} 6 & 2 \\ 5 & 7 \\ 8 & 6 \end{pmatrix} \begin{pmatrix} 400 \\ 50 \end{pmatrix} = \begin{pmatrix} 2500 \\ 2350 \\ 3500 \end{pmatrix}$$

Order: $3 \times 2 \quad 2 \times 1 \quad 3 \times 1$

> Write the number of rows first, followed by the number of columns.

Remember that the **order** of a matrix is the number of rows and columns that the matrix has.

You can only multiply two matrices when the number of columns in the first matrix is the same as the number of rows in the second matrix.

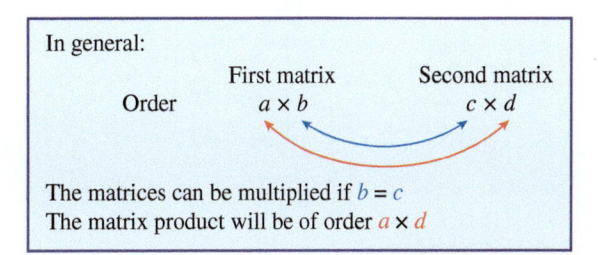

> In general:
> 
> Order    First matrix    Second matrix
>          $a \times b$    $c \times d$
> 
> The matrices can be multiplied if $b = c$
> The matrix product will be of order $a \times d$

283

Mathematics for Cambridge Secondary 1

## Worked example 1

Work out $\begin{pmatrix} 3 & 2 \\ 4 & 1 \end{pmatrix} \begin{pmatrix} 7 \\ 5 \end{pmatrix}$

First write down the order of the matrices:   $2 \times 2 \quad 2 \times 1$

It is possible to multiply the two matrices because the numbers in the middle are the same.

The answer will be a $2 \times 1$ matrix.

$\begin{pmatrix} 3 & 2 \\ 4 & 1 \end{pmatrix} \begin{pmatrix} 7 \\ 5 \end{pmatrix} = \begin{pmatrix} * \\ * \end{pmatrix}$

> Multiply each row in the first matrix with the column in the second matrix to find the unknown numbers.

$3 \times 7 + 2 \times 5 = 31$

$4 \times 7 + 1 \times 5 = 33$

$\begin{pmatrix} 3 & 2 \\ 4 & 1 \end{pmatrix} \begin{pmatrix} 7 \\ 5 \end{pmatrix} = \begin{pmatrix} 31 \\ 33 \end{pmatrix}$

## Worked example 2

$A = \begin{pmatrix} 1 & 5 \\ 8 & 2 \\ 0 & 6 \end{pmatrix} \quad B = \begin{pmatrix} 9 & 4 \\ 3 & 7 \end{pmatrix}$

Find AB.

First write down the order of the matrices:   $3 \times 2 \quad 2 \times 2$

It is possible to multiply the two matrices because the numbers in the middle are the same.

The answer will be a $3 \times 2$ matrix.

$\begin{pmatrix} 1 & 5 \\ 8 & 2 \\ 0 & 6 \end{pmatrix} \begin{pmatrix} 9 & 4 \\ 3 & 7 \end{pmatrix} = \begin{pmatrix} * & * \\ * & * \\ * & * \end{pmatrix}$

> Multiply each row in the first matrix with each column in the second matrix to find the unknown numbers.

$1 \times 9 + 5 \times 3 = 24 \qquad 1 \times 4 + 5 \times 7 = 39$

$8 \times 9 + 2 \times 3 = 78 \qquad 8 \times 4 + 2 \times 7 = 46$

$0 \times 9 + 6 \times 3 = 18 \qquad 0 \times 4 + 6 \times 7 = 42$

$\begin{pmatrix} 1 & 5 \\ 8 & 2 \\ 0 & 6 \end{pmatrix} \begin{pmatrix} 9 & 4 \\ 3 & 7 \end{pmatrix} = \begin{pmatrix} 24 & 39 \\ 78 & 46 \\ 18 & 42 \end{pmatrix}$

## Exercise 22.2

**1 a** If A is a 2 × 4 matrix and B is a 4 × 3 matrix, write down the order of the matrix AB.

**b** If P is a 5 × 3 matrix and Q is a 3 × 2 matrix:

   **i** write down the order of the matrix PQ

   **ii** explain why it is not possible to calculate the matrix QP.

**2** $C = \begin{pmatrix} 0 & 1 \\ 5 & 2 \\ 1 & 1 \end{pmatrix}$      $D = \begin{pmatrix} 4 & 2 & 0 & 0 & 8 \\ 1 & 4 & 3 & 7 & 0 \end{pmatrix}$

**a** The order of the matrix CD is $x \times y$.

Write down the values of $x$ and $y$.

**b** Is it possible to work out the matrix DC? Explain your answer.

**3** Find the value of $x$ for each of these matrix multiplications.

**a** $\begin{pmatrix} 1 & 3 \\ 2 & 5 \end{pmatrix}\begin{pmatrix} 2 & 0 \\ 4 & 3 \end{pmatrix} = \begin{pmatrix} 14 & x \\ 24 & 15 \end{pmatrix}$      **b** $\begin{pmatrix} 7 & 2 & 5 \\ 1 & 1 & 8 \end{pmatrix}\begin{pmatrix} 2 \\ 3 \\ 1 \end{pmatrix} = \begin{pmatrix} 25 \\ x \end{pmatrix}$

**4** Multiply these matrices.

**a** $\begin{pmatrix} 5 & 1 \\ 0 & 2 \end{pmatrix}\begin{pmatrix} 1 & 3 \\ 2 & 4 \end{pmatrix}$    **b** $\begin{pmatrix} 4 & 0 \\ 1 & 1 \end{pmatrix}\begin{pmatrix} 1 & 0 & 2 \\ 3 & 2 & 5 \end{pmatrix}$    **c** $\begin{pmatrix} 7 & 1 \\ 4 & 2 \end{pmatrix}\begin{pmatrix} 0 \\ 3 \end{pmatrix}$

**d** $\begin{pmatrix} 2 & 5 \end{pmatrix}\begin{pmatrix} 4 \\ 1 \end{pmatrix}$    **e** $\begin{pmatrix} 4 & 0 & 1 \\ 1 & 2 & 0 \end{pmatrix}\begin{pmatrix} 3 & 1 \\ 1 & 2 \\ 6 & 0 \end{pmatrix}$    **f** $\begin{pmatrix} 3 \\ 0 \end{pmatrix}\begin{pmatrix} 1 & 4 \end{pmatrix}$

**g** $\begin{pmatrix} 3 & 2 & 0 \\ 1 & 5 & 2 \\ 0 & 2 & 1 \end{pmatrix}\begin{pmatrix} 6 \\ 1 \\ 0 \end{pmatrix}$    **h** $\begin{pmatrix} 2 & 0 & 2 & 0 \\ 0 & 1 & 0 & 1 \end{pmatrix}\begin{pmatrix} 7 & 1 \\ 1 & 6 \\ 5 & 1 \\ 1 & 4 \end{pmatrix}$

**5 a** If $A = \begin{pmatrix} 2 & 1 \\ 4 & 3 \end{pmatrix}$, find $A^2$.

> Hint: $A^2$ means $A \times A$.

**b** If $B = \begin{pmatrix} 1 & 0 & 3 \\ 5 & 7 & 1 \\ 2 & 1 & 4 \end{pmatrix}$, find $B^2$.

## 22.3 2 × 2 matrices

All the matrices in this section are 2 × 2 matrices.

You will need to remember the work that you did in your Stage 7 Student Book on how to:

- add and subtract matrices
- multiply a matrix by a number.

# Mathematics for Cambridge Secondary 1

## Worked example

$A = \begin{pmatrix} 5 & 1 \\ 4 & 3 \end{pmatrix} \qquad B = \begin{pmatrix} 1 & 2 \\ 6 & 0 \end{pmatrix}$

Find **a** 2A **b** A + B **c** AB **d** BA

**a** $2A = \begin{pmatrix} 2\times 5 & 2\times 1 \\ 2\times 4 & 2\times 3 \end{pmatrix} = \begin{pmatrix} 10 & 2 \\ 8 & 6 \end{pmatrix}$

> Remember: 2A means multiply each number in the matrix A by 2.

**b** $A + B = \begin{pmatrix} 5 & 1 \\ 4 & 3 \end{pmatrix} + \begin{pmatrix} 1 & 2 \\ 6 & 0 \end{pmatrix} = \begin{pmatrix} 5+1 & 1+2 \\ 4+6 & 3+0 \end{pmatrix} = \begin{pmatrix} 6 & 3 \\ 10 & 3 \end{pmatrix}$

> Remember: To calculate A + B you must add corresponding numbers.

**c** $AB = \begin{pmatrix} 5 & 1 \\ 4 & 3 \end{pmatrix}\begin{pmatrix} 1 & 2 \\ 6 & 0 \end{pmatrix} = \begin{pmatrix} 11 & 10 \\ 22 & 8 \end{pmatrix}$

> Remember: The order of matrix multiplication is important. AB is not the same as BA.

**d** $BA = \begin{pmatrix} 1 & 2 \\ 6 & 0 \end{pmatrix}\begin{pmatrix} 5 & 1 \\ 4 & 3 \end{pmatrix} = \begin{pmatrix} 13 & 7 \\ 30 & 6 \end{pmatrix}$

## Exercise 22.3

**1** $A = \begin{pmatrix} 1 & 2 \\ 2 & 5 \end{pmatrix} \qquad B = \begin{pmatrix} 3 & 4 \\ 0 & 1 \end{pmatrix}$

Find

**a** 2A **b** 3B **c** A + B **d** A − B
**e** AB **f** BA **g** $A^2$ **h** $B^2$

**2** $A = \begin{pmatrix} 6 & 0 \\ 1 & 3 \end{pmatrix} \qquad B = \begin{pmatrix} 7 & 2 \\ 4 & 0 \end{pmatrix}$

Find

**a** 5A **b** 2B **c** AB **d** BA **e** $A^2$ **f** $B^2$

**3** $A = \begin{pmatrix} -1 & 0 \\ 1 & 2 \end{pmatrix} \qquad B = \begin{pmatrix} 5 & -2 \\ 2 & -1 \end{pmatrix}$

Find

**a** 4A **b** 3B **c** AB **d** BA **e** $A^2$ **f** $B^2$

**4** $A = \begin{pmatrix} 1 & 0 \\ 0 & 1 \end{pmatrix} \qquad B = \begin{pmatrix} 3 & 5 \\ 4 & 2 \end{pmatrix} \qquad C = \begin{pmatrix} 4 & 1 \\ 9 & 2 \end{pmatrix}$

**a** Find **i** AB **ii** BA **iii** AC **iv** CA

**b** Comment on your answers to part **a**.

**5** $A = \begin{pmatrix} 7 & -2 \\ -1 & 3 \end{pmatrix}$. Find the 2 × 2 matrix B such that $A + B = \begin{pmatrix} 0 & 0 \\ 0 & 0 \end{pmatrix}$

**6** $A = \begin{pmatrix} 5 & 1 \\ 0 & 3 \end{pmatrix}$    $B = \begin{pmatrix} 0 & 3 \\ 3 & 7 \end{pmatrix}$    $C = \begin{pmatrix} -2 & 0 \\ 4 & 2 \end{pmatrix}$    $D = \begin{pmatrix} 4 & -5 \\ 1 & -2 \end{pmatrix}$

Find

**a** $5A + 2B$    **b** $5A - 2B$    **c** $4C + 3D$    **d** $4C - 3D$

## Review

**1** Write down the order of these matrices.

**a** $\begin{pmatrix} 3 \\ 5 \end{pmatrix}$    **b** $\begin{pmatrix} 1 & 4 & 0 & 4 & 6 \\ 2 & 8 & 1 & 2 & 1 \\ 0 & 3 & 8 & 4 & 2 \end{pmatrix}$    **c** $(4 \ 2 \ 0 \ 5)$    **d** $\begin{pmatrix} 1 & 0 & 1 \\ 1 & 1 & 1 \end{pmatrix}$

**2** Work out

**a** $(1 \ 4)\begin{pmatrix} 3 \\ 6 \end{pmatrix}$    **b** $(5 \ 0 \ -2)\begin{pmatrix} 3 \\ 1 \\ -5 \end{pmatrix}$    **c** $(8 \ 2 \ -3 \ -1)\begin{pmatrix} 4 \\ 0 \\ 6 \\ -5 \end{pmatrix}$

**3** $(3 \ 4)\begin{pmatrix} x \\ -5 \end{pmatrix} = (4)$

Find the value of $x$.

**4** $A = \begin{pmatrix} 1 & 8 & 6 \\ 0 & 2 & 1 \end{pmatrix}$    $B = \begin{pmatrix} 3 & -5 & 2 & 0 & 1 & 0 \\ 1 & 1 & 2 & 0 & 3 & 0 \\ 5 & 7 & 2 & -1 & 3 & -2 \end{pmatrix}$

**a** The order of the matrix AB is $x \times y$.

Write down the values of $x$ and $y$.

**b** Is it possible to work out the matrix BA? Explain your answer.

**5** Multiply these matrices.

**a** $\begin{pmatrix} 2 & 3 & 1 & 0 \\ 0 & 2 & 2 & 1 \end{pmatrix}\begin{pmatrix} 5 \\ 6 \\ 0 \\ 4 \end{pmatrix}$    **b** $\begin{pmatrix} 3 & 1 \\ 0 & 2 \end{pmatrix}\begin{pmatrix} 5 & 7 & 0 & 5 \\ 1 & 2 & -3 & 2 \end{pmatrix}$

**6** $A = \begin{pmatrix} 1 & -3 \\ 2 & 5 \end{pmatrix}$    $B = \begin{pmatrix} 0 & 4 \\ -1 & 8 \end{pmatrix}$

Find

**a** $5A$    **b** $2B$    **c** $AB$    **d** $BA$    **e** $A^2$    **f** $B^2$

**7** $A = \begin{pmatrix} 2 & 4 \\ -3 & 1 \end{pmatrix}$    $B = \begin{pmatrix} -4 & 0 \\ 3 & 7 \end{pmatrix}$

Find

**a** $5A + 2B$    **b** $5A - 2B$

# Glossary

## A

**alternate angles** Equal angles formed in opposite positions when a straight line crosses two parallel lines.

**angle bisector** A line that divides an angle into two equal parts.

**arc** Part of the circumference of a circle.

**average** A single value that is used to represent a set of data.

## B

**billion** One thousand million = 1 000 000 000 = $10^9$.

**bisect** To divide a line or an angle into two equal parts.

**bisector** A line that cuts another line or an angle into two equal parts.

## C

**census** A survey that includes all of the population.

**centi-** The metric prefix for $\frac{1}{100}$.

**centre of enlargement** A fixed point from which an enlargement is measured.

**chord** A straight line joining two points on the circumference of a circle.

**circumference** The perimeter of a circle.

**complement** The complement of set A is the set of all the elements not in A.

**composite number** A number that is the product of two or more factors other than 1 and itself.

**compound shape** A shape that is made of two or more shapes.

**congruent** Identical shape and size. Congruent shapes have identical lengths and angles.

**construct** Use the given information to write down an equation.

**construction line** A line used during a geometric construction.

**continuous data** Data that are usually found by measuring. For example, the length of a car could be 3 metres, 4 metres or anything between 3 metres and 4 metres (such as 3.5 metres or 3.216 metres).

**corresponding angles** Equal angles formed in corresponding positions when a straight line crosses two parallel lines.

**cube number** A number formed by multiplying an integer by itself and then by itself again. The third power of the integer.

**cube root** The cube root of a number is the number that, when cubed, equals the first number.

## D

**decimal place** This follows the decimal point. For example, 1 decimal place (1 d.p.) means one digit after the decimal point.

**denominator** The name given to the number on the 'bottom' of a fraction.

**diagonal** A line within a polygon joining two vertices.

**diameter** The distance across a circle through the centre.

**direct proportion** If two quantities are in direct proportion then the ratio of one to the other stays the same as they increase or decrease.

**discrete data** Data that take separate values; usually data that have been found by counting. For example, the number of flowers on a plant can be 0, 1, 2, 3, 4, 5, ... but not numbers like 1.23 or 5.9

**distribution** A set of data.

## E

**element (member)** An item that belongs to a set.

**empty set** A set that contains no elements.

**enlargement** A transformation that changes the size of the object.

**equation** A mathematical statement that says that two expressions (which involve just one unknown) are equal.

**equivalent calculations** Calculations that give the same answer. For example, $13 \times 0.03$ has an equivalent calculation $13 \times 3 \div 100$.

**equivalent fractions** Two fractions that have the same value.

**expand brackets** Multiply each term inside the brackets by the term outside the brackets.

**experiment** A series of trials.

**experimental probability** A probability found by carrying out an experiment. It is calculated using the formula: Experimental probability
$$= \frac{number\ of\ successful\ outcomes}{total\ number\ of\ trials}$$

**expression** A collection of terms that does not include an equals sign.

**exterior angle** An angle formed outside a shape when one side of the shape is extended.

## F

**formula** A rule that connects two or more variables.

**frequency diagram** Any type of diagram that shows frequencies, for example, a bar chart.

**function** A rule that connects two sets of numbers.

**function machine** A diagram that shows the steps in a function.

## H

**hypotenuse** The longest side of a right-angled triangle. The side opposite the right angle.

## I

**image** The final shape after a transformation.

**index number** A small number used to show power (how many times to multiply a number by itself). For example, the 2 in $5^2$.

**input** A number that goes into a function machine.

**intersection** The intersection of sets A and B is the set that contains the elements that are in both A and B.

## K

**kilo-** The metric prefix for 1000.

## L

**like terms** Terms containing the same variables.

**line graph** A series of points joined with straight lines. A line graph shows how data change over a period of time.

**line segment** Part of a line between two points.

**linear expression** An algebraic expression in which each term is either a constant or the product of a constant and (the first power of) a single variable. Linear expressions can have one or more variables. For example, $\frac{x}{4}$, $2x$, $2x + 3$ and $3(x + 8)$

289

**linear sequence** A sequence in which the differences between the terms are all the same.

**lowest terms (also called simplest form)** A fraction that cannot be simplified any further.

# M

**mapping diagram** A diagram that shows which output numbers the inputs of a function map on to.

**matrix** A rectangular array of numbers.

**mean** An average value that is found by adding all the values together and dividing the total by the number of values.

**measure of spread** A way of showing how much a set of data is spread out. It is helpful when comparing sets of data.

**median** The middle value when all the values are listed in order of size. It is used as an average value.

**member (element)** An item that belongs to a set.

**metric system** A system of measurement based on the decimal system.

**mid-class value** This is used to find an estimate of the mean when data are grouped. It is the value in the middle of a class.

**midpoint** The point exactly halfway along a line segment.

**milli-** The metric prefix for $\frac{1}{1000}$.

**million** One thousand thousand = 1 000 000 = $10^6$

**modal class** The modal class has more values in it than the other classes. It has the greatest frequency.

**mode** The value that occurs most. It is used as an average value.

# N

**negative** A negative number is less than zero.

**net** A two-dimensional shape that can be folded to create a three-dimensional object.

**nth term** A general term in a sequence.

**numerator** The name given to the number on the 'top' of a fraction.

# O

**object** The original shape before a transformation.

**order** The order of a matrix is the number of rows and columns that a matrix has. For example, 2 × 3 means 2 rows and 3 columns.

**output** A number that comes out of a function machine.

# P

**parallel** Two or more lines that never meet or intersect are said to be parallel.

**percentage** Means 'out of 100'.

**percentage reduction** The percentage by which something is reduced. It is the same as the percentage decrease.

**perpendicular** If two lines are perpendicular they are at right angles.

**perpendicular bisector** A line that is perpendicular to another line that it cuts into two equal parts.

**pi** The ratio of the circumference to the diameter of a circle.

**pie chart** A method of showing information on a circle that is divided into sectors. The angle of each sector is in proportion to the amount of information it shows.

# Glossary

**population** Every member that is in the group being considered.

**position-to-term rule** A rule connecting a term in a sequence with its position in the sequence.

**positive** A positive number is greater than zero.

**prime factor** A factor of a number that is itself prime.

**prime number** A number with exactly two factors: 1 and itself.

**prism** A solid with a constant cross-sectional shape.

**proof** A step-by-step argument to show the truth of a statement.

**proper subset** A is a proper subset of B if all the elements of A are contained in the larger set B.

## Q

**quadrilateral** A polygon with four straight sides.

## R

**radius** The distance from the centre of a circle to the circumference.

**range** The difference between the largest and smallest values, it is used as a measure of spread.

**recurring decimal** A decimal that recurs (repeats). For example, 0.454545…, which can be written $0.\dot{4}\dot{5}$

## S

**sample** Part of a population.

**scale** The ratio used in a scale drawing.

**scale drawing** A diagram showing a large object in which all the lengths are reduced by the same scale factor.

**scale factor** The ratio of the lengths of an object and an enlarged image.

**sequence** A list of numbers or diagrams that are connected by a rule.

**similar** Similar shapes are the same shape but different sizes.

**simplest form (also called lowest terms)** A fraction that cannot be simplified any further.

**solve** Work out the correct answer, for example, the value of an unknown letter in an equation.

**square number** A number formed by multiplying any integer by itself. The second power of the integer.

**square root** The square root of a number is the number that, when squared, equals the first number.

**stem-and-leaf diagram** A frequency diagram that organises the data in order of size, using the actual data values split into a stem and leaves.

**substitution** Replacing the letters in an expression or a formula with given numbers.

## T

**term** A single number or a variable, or the product of several numbers or variables. 5, 3x and 7xy are all terms.

**terminating decimal** A decimal that stops. For example, 0.5 or 0.625

**term-to-term rule** A rule that connects a term in a sequence with the previous term in the sequence.

**theoretical probability** A probability based on equally likely outcomes.

**transformation** A movement of one shape to another position.

291

**trend** The general pattern shown in data plotted on a line graph. For example, a set of data may be generally increasing or decreasing over time.

**trial** A single experiment, such as the roll of a dice.

# U

**union** The union of sets A and B is the set that contains the elements that are in A or B or both.

**universal set** The set of all elements being considered in a particular problem.

# V

**Venn diagram** A diagram showing sets as overlapping circles, used to show relationships between sets and logical relationships.

# Index

Key terms that appear in the glossary are in **bold**.

2 × 2 matrices — 285–6

## A
addition — 1
   and BIDMAS — 6–7, 29
   of decimals — 69–70
   of fractions — 56
   of matrices — 285–6
al Kindi — 78
algebra — 18
algebraic **expressions** — 18–29
   collecting like terms — 24, 27
   **expanding brackets** — 26–7
   multiplying algebraic terms — 22
   **substitution** into — 29
   using letters for unknown numbers — 18–19
**alternate angles** — 34, 35
Ancient Egyptians — 53
**angle bisectors** — 118–19
angles — 33–8
   **alternate** — 34, 35
   **bisectors** of — 118–19
   **corresponding** — 34
   **exterior** — 37–8
   and parallel lines — 33–5
   in quadrilaterals — 42
   in triangles — 36–7
      exterior angles — 37–8
   vertically opposite — 33–4, 35
**arcs** — 147
   constructing — 116–17, 123–4
area — 151–63
   of circles — 159–60
   of compound shapes — 161–2
   of parallelograms — 151–2
   of semicircles — 161
   surface area — 162–3
   of trapeziums — 156–7
   of triangles — 153–5
   units of — 94–6
arithmetic sequences — 190
   *see also* **linear sequences**
average — 78–9
   *see also* **mean**; **median**; **modal class**; **mode**

## B
balance method — 107–8
BIDMAS (order of operations) — 6–7
   and substitution — 29
**billion** — 65
**bisectors, angle** — 118–19
**bisectors, perpendicular** — 115–17

brackets
   and BIDMAS — 6–7
      **substitution** into expressions — 29
   expanding — 26–7
bridges, building — 105
British imperial units — 99–100
building bridges — 105

## C
capacity
   metric units for — 91–3
   non-metric units for — 99
   *see also* volume
Cartesian coordinates — 215
**census** — 242
**centi-** (c) — 92
centimetres, cubic ($cm^3$) — 96
centimetres, square ($cm^2$) — 95
**centre of enlargement** — 181
   drawing enlargements — 181–3
centre of rotation — 175
change, percentage — 234, 236–7
**chords** — 147
circles — 147–9
   area of — 159–60
   constructing — 123–4
**circumference** — 147, 148–9, 150
co-prime numbers — 16
coded messages — 78
coding in cryptology — 281
coins, flipping — 202, 208
collecting data — 241–3
collecting like terms — 24, 27
column matrices — 281–2
common multiples, lowest (LCM) — 14–15
   in fraction addition — 56
   in fraction subtraction — 57–8
compasses in constructions
   angle bisectors — 118–19
   circles — 123–4
   perpendicular bisectors — 116–17
   triangles — 120–2
**complement** — 273
composite numbers — 13
compound shapes — 161–2
**congruent** — 40
congruent shapes — 39–40, 176
**construct** — 111
**construction lines** — 116
constructions — 115–24
   angle bisectors — 118–19
   circles — 123–4
   perpendicular bisectors — 115–17
   triangles — 120–2
   *see also* drawing graphs

293

| | |
|---|---|
| continuous data | 84–5, 244 |
|   frequency diagrams for | 132–3 |
|   frequency tables for | 244–5 |
| continuous scales | |
| conversion factors | 92–3 |
| coordinate grid system | 215 |
| coordinates | |
|   Cartesian | 215 |
|   midpoints | 185–6 |
| corresponding angles | 34 |
| cryptology | 281 |
| cube numbers | 8–9 |
| cube roots | 11 |
| cubes | 8–9 |
|   nets of | 45–6 |
| cubic centimetres (cm$^3$) | 96 |
| cubic kilometres (km$^3$) | 96 |
| cubic metres (m$^3$) | 96 |
| cubic millimetres (mm$^3$) | 96 |
| cuboids | 97, 163 |
| customary units, United States | 99–100 |

## D

| | |
|---|---|
| data | 78–88 |
|   collecting | 241–3 |
|   continuous | 84–5, 244 |
|     frequency diagrams for | 132–3 |
|     frequency tables for | 244–5 |
|   discrete | 83–4, 244 |
|     frequency diagrams for | 131, 132 |
|     two-way tables for | 247–9 |
|   grouped | 83–5 |
|     frequency diagrams for | 131–3 |
|     frequency tables for | 244–5 |
|   presenting see presenting data | |
| data sets | 78–80 |
|   comparing | 87–8, 136–7 |
|   frequency tables for | 79–80 |
|   grouped data | 83–5 |
|   see also presenting data | |
| deci- | 94 |
| decimal places (d.p.) | 67, 68 |
| decimals | 64–75 |
|   adding | 69–70 |
|   converting to percentages | 232 |
|   division with | 71–2 |
|     by 0.1 and 0.01 | 66 |
|   equivalent fractions | 230–1 |
|   equivalent percentages | 230–1 |
|   from fractions | 75, 231 |
|   multiplying | 70–1 |
|     by 0.1 and 0.01 | 65 |
|   from percentages | 231 |
|   recurring | 75 |
|   subtracting with | 69–70 |
|   terminating | 75 |
| decoding coded messages | 78 |
| decrease, percentage | 234, 236–7 |
| decreasing by percentages | 234 |

| | |
|---|---|
| denominators | 53, 54, 56 |
|   in fraction addition | 56 |
|   in fraction subtraction | 57–8 |
| Descartes, René | 215 |
| diagonals | 42 |
|   of quadrilaterals | 42, 43, 45 |
| diameters | 147, 148–9 |
| dice rolling | 203, 211 |
| direct proportion | 257–8 |
| discrete data | 83–4, 244 |
|   frequency diagrams for | 131, 132 |
|   two-way tables for | 247–9 |
| distance | |
|   on travel graphs | 262–3 |
|   units for | 99–100 |
| distributions | 78 |
| division | |
|   and BIDMAS | 6–7, 29 |
|   with decimals | 71–2 |
|     by 0.1 and 0.01 | 66 |
|   of integers | 4–5 |
|     by fractions | 60–1 |
|   in ratios with more than two parts | 256 |
| drawing enlargements | 181–3 |
| drawing graphs | 221 |
| drawings, scale | 126–7 |

## E

| | |
|---|---|
| Egyptians, Ancient | 53 |
| element of sets | 270 |
| *Elements*, Euclid's | 33 |
| empty sets | 270 |
| enlargements | 179–81 |
|   drawing | 181–3 |
| equally likely outcomes | 203–4 |
| equations | 105–12 |
|   of functions | 218–9 |
|   of lines | 223–4, 226 |
|   solving | 105–6 |
|     balance method | 107–8 |
|     from substituted formulae | 172–3 |
|     problem-solving with | 111–12 |
|     unknown on both sides | 110 |
| equivalent calculations | 70, 71 |
| equivalent decimals | 230–3 |
| equivalent fractions | 53, 230–3 |
| equivalent percentages | 230–3 |
| Euclid | 33 |
| expanding brackets | 26–7 |
| experimental probability | 210–11 |
| experiments | 210–11 |
| expressions | 18–29 |
|   collecting like terms | 24, 27 |
|   expanding brackets | 26–7 |
|   multiplying algebraic terms | 22 |
|   substitution into | 29 |
|   using letters for unknown numbers | 18–19 |
| exterior angles of triangles | 37–8 |

# Index

## F

| | |
|---|---|
| factor trees | 13–14 |
| factors, **prime** | **12–14** |
| to find LCM and HCF | 14–15 |
| fair dice | 203, 211 |
| Fibonacci numbers | 190, 194 |
| Fibonacci sequence | 190, 194 |
| flipping coins | 202, 208 |
| flow charts | 44–5 |
| flow diagrams | 105–6 |
| **formulae** | **167–73** |
| deriving | 167–8 |
| **substitution** into | **170**–1, 172–3 |
| fractions | 53–61 |
| addition of | 56 |
| changing to decimals | 75, 231 |
| comparing | 53–4, 75 |
| converting percentages to | 232–3 |
| dividing integers by | 60–1 |
| equivalent decimals | 230–1 |
| **equivalent fractions** | **53**, 230–3 |
| equivalent percentages | 230–1 |
| finding | 236–7 |
| improper fractions | 57 |
| multiplying by integers | 59–60 |
| subtraction of | 57–8 |
| unit fractions | 53 |
| **frequency diagrams** | **131–3** |
| frequency tables | 79–80 |
| for continuous data | 244–5 |
| two-way | 247–9 |
| **function machines** | 105, **215**, 216–7, 219 |
| functions | **215**–17, 218–19 |

## G

| | |
|---|---|
| geometry | 33 |
| giga- | 92 |
| grams (g) | 91 |
| graphs | |
| drawing | 221 |
| equations from | 223–4 |
| **line graphs** | **139** |
| linear graphs | 221 |
| **midpoints** on | 185 |
| in real life contexts | 262, 265–6 |
| of straight lines | 221, 223–4, 226 |
| time on | 262, 265–6 |
| travel graphs | 262–3 |
| grouped data | 83–5 |
| **frequency diagrams** for | **131–3** |
| on frequency tables | 244–5 |

## H

| | |
|---|---|
| HCF *see* highest common factor | |
| heads or tails? | 202 |
| highest common factor (HCF) | 14–15 |
| **hypotenuse** | **39**, **122** |

## I

| | |
|---|---|
| identifying data | 244 |
| **image** | 39, **176** |
| in enlargement | 179–80 |
| imperial units | 99–100 |
| improper fractions | 57 |
| increase, percentage | 234, 236–7 |
| index notation | 9 |
| **index numbers** | **9** |
| indices/powers | 8–9 |
| and BIDMAS | 6–7, 29 |
| integer powers of ten | 64–6 |
| inequality signs | 73–4 |
| **input** | **216–17** |
| integer powers of ten | 64–6 |
| integers | 1–3 |
| dividing | 4–5 |
| by fractions | 60–1 |
| multiplication | 2 |
| by fractions | 59–60 |
| squares and cubes of | 8–9 |
| internet and coding in cryptology | 284 |
| **intersection** of sets | **270**–1 |
| inverse operations | 4, 5 |
| isosceles trapeziums | 44 |
| isosceles triangles | 38 |

## K

| | |
|---|---|
| keys on stem-and-leaf diagrams | 142–3 |
| **kilo-** (k) | **92** |
| kilometres (km) | 99–100 |
| kilometres, cubic (km$^3$) | 96 |
| kilometres, square (km$^2$) | 95 |
| kitchens, formulae in | 167 |
| kites | 44 |

## L

| | |
|---|---|
| large numbers | 64 |
| integer powers of ten | 64–5 |
| LCM *see* lowest common multiples | |
| length, units for | 91–3 |
| non-metric | 99–100 |
| letters in expressions | 18–19 |
| **like terms** | **24**, 27 |
| **line graphs** | **139** |
| *see also* lines | |
| **line segments** | **185** |
| **linear expressions** | **19** |
| linear graphs | 221 |
| *see also* lines | |
| **linear sequences** | **190** |
| of numbers | 190–1 |
| *n*th **term** of | **198–9** |
| patterns of shapes | 195 |
| lines | |
| equations of | 223–4, 226 |
| graphs of | 221, 223–4 |
| **line graphs** | **139** |
| parallel lines | 33–5 |
| **perpendicular bisectors** of | **115–17** |

295

| | |
|---|---|
| lines of symmetry | 43–4, 48–9 |
| listing outcomes | 207–8 |
| litres (l) | 91 |
| look up tables | 241 |
| lowest common multiples (LCM) | 14–15 |
| in fraction addition | 56 |
| in fraction subtraction | 57–8 |
| **lowest terms** | **53** |
| Lu, Chao | 147 |

# M

| | |
|---|---|
| **mapping diagrams** | **216–17** |
| Mars Climate Orbiter | 91 |
| mass, units for | 91–3 |
| non-metric | 99 |
| **matrices** | **281–6** |
| $2 \times 2$ matrices | 285–6 |
| addition of | 285–6 |
| column matrices | 281–2 |
| multiplication | 283–4, 285–6 |
| of rows by columns | 281–2 |
| row matrices | 281–2 |
| **mean** | **79** |
| comparing data sets | 87–8 |
| frequency tables for | 80 |
| grouped data | 83–4, 85 |
| **measures of spread** | **79** |
| comparing data sets with | 87–8 |
| **median** | **79** |
| comparing data sets | 87–8 |
| frequency tables for | 80 |
| grouped data | 83, 85 |
| on **stem-and-leaf diagrams** | 142–3 |
| mega- | 94 |
| **members of sets** | **270** |
| Mersenne, Marin | 1 |
| Mersenne prime numbers | 1 |
| metres (m) | 91 |
| metres, cubic (m³) | 96 |
| metres, square (m²) | 95 |
| **metric system** | **91–3** |
| metric units | 91–3 |
| of area | 94–6 |
| of volume | 96–7 |
| **mid-class value** | **83** |
| **midpoints** | **185** |
| of a line segment | 185 |
| and perpendicular bisectors | 115–117 |
| miles | 99–100 |
| **milli- (m)** | **92** |
| millimetres, cubic (mm³) | 96 |
| millimetres, square (mm²) | 94 |
| **million** | **64** |
| mirror lines | 48, 175, 177 |
| mixed numbers | 56, 57–8 |
| **modal class** | **83**, 85, 132 |
| **mode** | **79** |
| comparing data sets | 87–8 |
| frequency tables for | 80 |
| grouped data | 83 |

| | |
|---|---|
| multiples, lowest common (LCM) | 14–15 |
| in fraction addition | 56 |
| in fraction subtraction | 57–8 |
| multiplication | 2–3 |
| of algebraic terms | 22, 26–7 |
| and BIDMAS | 6–7, 29 |
| by decimals | 70–1 |
| by 0.1 and 0.01 | 65 |
| of integers | 2–3 |
| by fractions | 59–60 |
| of matrices | 283–4, 285–6 |
| of rows by columns | 281–2 |
| of negative numbers | 2–3 |
| of positive numbers | 2, 3 |

# N

| | |
|---|---|
| nautilus shell spirals | 190, 194 |
| **negative** numbers | 1 |
| addition | 1 |
| division | 4–5 |
| multiplication | 2–3 |
| and brackets | 26–7 |
| as square roots | 10 |
| subtraction | 1 |
| negative slope | 226 |
| **nets** | 45–6, 162–3 |
| non-linear expressions | 19 |
| non-metric units | 99–100 |
| *n*th **term** of sequences | **198–9** |
| numbers | |
| **composite** | **13** |
| **cube** | **8–9** |
| Fibonacci | 190, 194 |
| large, integer powers of ten | 64–5 |
| **linear sequences** | **190–1** |
| *n*th **term** of | **198–9** |
| mixed | 56, 57–8 |
| negative *see* negative numbers | |
| positive *see* positive numbers | |
| **prime** | 1, **12** |
| co-prime | 16 |
| square | 8–9 |
| **numerators** | **53**, 54 |

# O

| | |
|---|---|
| object | 39, **176** |
| in enlargement | 179–80 |
| **order** of matrices | **283–4** |
| order of operations (BIDMAS) | 6–7, 29 |
| outcomes | 202 |
| equally likely | 203–4 |
| listing outcomes | 207–8 |
| probability of events not happening | 204–5 |
| **output** | **216–17** |

# P

| | |
|---|---|
| pantographs | 175 |
| **parallel** | **34** |
| parallel lines | 33–5 |
| parallel sides | 43, 44 |

# Index

| | |
|---|---|
| parallelograms | 43 |
|   area of | 151–2 |
|   symmetry of | 48–9 |
| patterns of shapes in sequences | 198 |
| pentagons, symmetry of | 48–9 |
| percentage change | 234, 236–7 |
| percentage decrease | 234, 236–7 |
| percentage increase | 234, 236–7 |
| **percentage reduction** | **234** |
| **percentages** | **230–7** |
|   comparing figures with | 237 |
|   converting decimals to | 232 |
|   converting to decimals | 231 |
|   converting to fractions | 232–3 |
|   equivalent decimals | 230–1 |
|   equivalent fractions | 230–1 |
|   finding | 236–9 |
|   increasing and decreasing by | 234 |
|   using | 237 |
| perimeter of circles | 147, 148–9 |
|   semicircles | 150 |
| **perpendicular** | **115** |
| **perpendicular bisectors** | **115–17** |
| pi | 147, **148**–9 |
| **pie charts** | **135–7** |
| piems | 147 |
| place value tables | 69–70 |
| plans | 115 |
| polygons | 42 |
|   symmetry of | 48–9 |
|   *see also* shapes | |
| **population** | **242** |
| **position number** | **191** |
| **position-to-term rule** | **190–1** |
|   algebra for | 198–9 |
| **positive** numbers | **1** |
|   addition | 1 |
|   division | 4–5 |
|   multiplication | 2, 3 |
|     with brackets | 26–7 |
|   subtraction | 1 |
| positive slope | 226 |
| powers/indices | 8–9 |
|   and BIDMAS | 6–7, 29 |
|   integer powers of ten | 64–6 |
| precision in measurements | 84, 244 |
| prefixes, metric | 91–2, 94 |
| presenting data | 131–43 |
|   frequency diagrams | 131–3 |
|   line graphs | 139 |
|   pie charts | 135–7 |
|   stem-and-leaf diagrams | 142–3 |
|   *see also* graphs | |
| prime factors | 12–14 |
|   to find LCM and HCF | 14–15 |
| prime numbers | 1, **12** |
|   co-prime numbers | 16 |
| prisms | 46, 47 |
|   cuboids | 97, 163 |
|   triangular | 46, 47, 162–3 |
| probabilities | 202–11 |
|   calculating | 203–5 |
|   estimating | 210–11 |
|   listing outcomes | 207–8 |
| problem-solving with sets | 276–7 |
| **proof** | **36** |
| **proper subsets** | **271** |
| **proportion**, **direct** | **257–8** |
| pyramids | 46, 47 |

## Q

| | |
|---|---|
| **quadrilaterals** | **42–5** |
|   angles in | 42 |
|   area of | 151–2, 156–7 |
|   classification of | 43–5 |
|   **congruent** | **40** |
|   symmetry of | 43–4, 48–9 |

## R

| | |
|---|---|
| **radius** | **147**, 148 |
| **range** | **79**, 87–8 |
|   frequency tables for | 80 |
|   on **stem-and-leaf diagrams** | 142–3 |
| ratios | 253–6 |
|   containing units | 254 |
|   more than two parts | 253–4, 256 |
| ready reckoners | 241 |
| rectangles | 43, 151 |
| **recurring decimals** | **75** |
| **reduction**, **percentage** | **234** |
| reflection | 39, 40, 175–6 |
| reflection symmetry | 48–9 |
| representative samples | 242 |
| rhombuses | 43–4 |
| right-angled triangles | 39 |
|   constructing | 121–2 |
| robotics | 18 |
| rolling dice | 203, 211 |
| roots | 10–11 |
| rotation | 39, 40, 175–6 |
|   combining with other transformations | 176 |
| rotation symmetry | 43, 48–9 |
| rounding | 67–8 |
| row matrices | 281–2 |

## S

| | |
|---|---|
| **sample** | **242** |
| sample size | 242–3 |
| **scale** | **126** |
| **scale drawings** | **126–7** |
| **scale factors** | **179–80** |
|   centre of enlargement | 181–3 |
|   and drawing enlargements | 181–3 |
| scalene quadrilaterals | 44 |
| semicircles | 150 |
|   area of | 161 |
|   constructing | 123–4 |
| **sequences** | **190–9** |
|   Fibonacci sequence | 190, 194 |
|   of numbers | **190–1** |
|     *n*th term of | **198–9** |
|   and patterns of shapes | 198 |

297

# Mathematics for Cambridge Secondary 1

sets                                       270–7
   **complement** of                  273
   **intersection** of                270–1
   solving problems with             276–7
   subsets                           271
   **union** of                      270–1
   **universal set**                 272
shapes                                     39–40
   area of                           94–6, 151–63
   circles *see* circles
   **compound shapes**               161–2
   **congruent** shapes              39–40, 176
   quadrilaterals *see* **quadrilaterals**
   sequences of                     195
   **similar shapes**                179
   triangles *see* triangles
   *see also* polygons; solids
similar shapes                             179
**simplest form**                          53
simplifying expressions                    18–19
   collecting like terms             24, 27
   **expanding brackets**            26–7
simplifying fractions                      53
slope of lines                             226
solids
   cuboids                           97, 163
   **nets** of                       45–6, 162–3
   *see also* prisms; shapes
solving equations                          105–6
   balance method                    107–8
   from substituted formulae        172–3
   problem-solving with              111–12
   unknown on both sides             110
solving problems with sets                 276–7
speed
   on travel graphs                  263
   units of                          101
spirals on nautilus shells                 190, 194
**spread, measures of**                    79
   comparing data sets with          87–8
square centimetres ($cm^2$)                95
square kilometres ($km^2$)                 95
square metres ($m^2$)                      95
square millimetres ($mm^2$)                94
**square numbers**                         8–9
**square roots**                           10–11
square-based pyramids, net of              46
squares                                    8–9, 43
statistics                                 131
   from data sets                    78–80
   grouped data                      83–5
**stem-and-leaf diagrams**                 142–3
straight lines
   equations of                      223–4, 226
   graphs of                         221, 223–4
   *see also* lines
subsets                                    271
**substitution**                           29, 170
   into expressions                  29
   into formulae                     170–1, 172–3

subtraction                                1
   and BIDMAS                        6–7, 29
   of decimals                       69–70
   of fractions                      57–8
surface area                               162–3
   *see also* area
symmetry                                   43–4, 48–9

# T

tables                                     241
   frequency tables                  79–80
      for continuous data     244–5
      two-way                  247–9
   place value tables                69–70
   of values                         219, 221, 224
temperature scales                         167–8
**term-to-term rule**                      190, 191
   for equations from graphs        224
   patterns of shapes                195
**terminating decimals**                   75
terms                                      24
   like terms                        24
   in sequences                      190–1
      $n$th term              198–9
   *see also* **term-to-term rule**
tetrahedrons                               47
**theoretical probabilities**              203–4
   and experimental compared        211
time on graphs                             262, 265–6
   travel graphs                     262–3
**transformations**                        39, 175–83
   combining                         176–7
   **enlargements**                  179–81
      drawing                  181–3
   reflection                        39, 40, 175–6
      combining                176
   rotation                          39, 40, 175–6
      combining                176
   translation                       39, 175–6
translation                                39, 175–6
trapeziums                                 44
   area of                           156–7
travel graphs                              262–3
**trends**                                 139
trials                                     210–11
triangles
   angles in                         36–7
   area of                           153–5
   congruent                         39–40
   constructing                      120–2
   **exterior angles**               37–8
   isosceles                         38
   right-angled                      39, 121–2
triangular **prisms**                      **46**, 47
   net of                            46, 162–3
triangular pyramids                        47
Tukey, John                                131
two-way tables                             247–9

298

# Index

## U
| | |
|---|---|
| UK, units used in | 99 |
| **union** of sets | **270–1** |
| unit fractions | 53 |
| unitary method for direct proportion | 257–8 |
| United States customary units | 99–100 |
| units | |
|     imperial units | 99–100 |
|     metric | 91–3, 94–7 |
|     non-metric | 99–100 |
|     in ratios | 254 |
|     of speed | 101 |
|     temperature scales | 167–8 |
|     United States customary | 99–100 |
| **universal set** | **272** |
| USA, units used in | 99 |

## V
| | |
|---|---|
| variables | 167 |
| Vasco da Gama Bridge | 105 |
| **Venn diagrams** | **270** |
|     and sets | 270–1, 272–3 |
|         problem-solving with | 276–7 |
| Venn, John | 270 |
| vertically opposite angles | 33–4, 35 |
| volume | |
|     of cuboids | 97, 163 |
|     units of | 96–7 |
|     *see also* capacity | |

## X
| | |
|---|---|
| $x$-axis | 221 |

## Y
| | |
|---|---|
| $y = mx + c$ equation | 226–7 |
| $y$-axis | 221 |

## Z
| | |
|---|---|
| zero slope | 226 |